Carmel Impresarios

a cultural biography of
Dene Denny & Hazel Watrous
the visionary California women
who brought music and harmony
to their community and the world

David Gordon

Lucky Valley Press
Carmel-by-the-Sea, California
2014

Lucky Valley Press
Carmel-by-the-Sea, California

ISBN 978-0-9856655-4-8

Cover design by David and Ginna Gordon
Book design, layout, and typography by David Gordon
Cover illustration © 2014 David Gordon
Printed in the United States of America

Monterey Cypress woodblock illustration on the title page by Mallette Dean,
from the Northern California Art Project of the of the WPA.

For Nancy, Nana, Melissa, and Lucy,
three generations and more than six decades
of loving dedication to Music and Art in Carmel,

and for Ginna,
who believed in this book from the very beginning
and helped to make it a reality.

"What has music done for Main Street? ...it has put a new song into the hearts of Main Streeters, and cemented with acquaintanceship the different social strata, nationalities, occupations, ages, and opinions. It has helped to shelve old prejudices, jealousies, and feuds...

The new song in the hearts of Main Streeters and the new rhythm in their movements has made their health better, their work more efficient, has turned them into truer comrades and more valuable citizens.

Music has provided a medium by which the people of Main Street can better understand each other."

Robert Haven Schauffler, *Music as a Social Force* (1927)

Contents

Looking south on Scenic Drive, Carmel-by-the-Sea. Early 1920s.

Detail from a postcard, photographer unknown. Courtesy of the author.

Foreword

by Barbara Rose Shuler

You hold in your hands a precious chapter in the history of Carmel-by-the-sea.

This lovingly researched and engrossing biography of Dene Denny and Hazel Watrous is a long-overdue account of a partnership that inspired an artistic Renaissance in Carmel's early days. These two entrepreneurial women served their community with vision, heart and skill, bequeathing to future generations an extraordinary and lasting cultural inheritance. Yet, until now, for all their accomplishments, surprisingly little could be found about Hazel and Dene.

From the vantage point of this buzzing, techno-dynamic early 21st century, it may be easy to overlook their significance to the area. In this splendid book, David Gordon brings the Denny-Watrous alliance and legacy center stage where it belongs, inextricably linked with the region's celebrated artistic identity.

Exploring the life journeys of these brilliant and creative souls, David shows how their leading-edge ideas in visual and performing arts, architecture, design, and in community collaboration not only transformed the local cultural scene but spread their influence far beyond the Monterey Peninsula. The two women embodied "the Carmel spirit"—a quality of infectious joy and generous love of the arts that thrives to this day, notably at the Carmel Bach Festival, the glory crown of Dene and Hazel's legacy.

But who were these intrepid cultural heroines?

Until now, the teasingly brief statements in brochures, program books and newspaper articles have left many of us yearning for more information about Dene and Hazel. These mentions typically recount how they founded several Carmel-based music organizations that still attract world-renowned soloists and ensembles and that they owned a trendy Carmel art gallery. Sometimes there would be allusions that they had cultivated impressive national and international connections in the art world by the time they settled in Carmel.

As someone immersed each summer in the music and events of the Carmel Bach Festival, I confess to sometimes giving myself over to Doctor-Who-like time travel fantasies where I would be dropped into mid-1920's Carmel, meeting and mingling with Dene and Hazel and the artists of the day.

This book is the real time-travel experience.

Where did Hazel and Dene come from? What education did they have? How and where did they meet? Why did they choose Carmel? How did they achieve so much as women in a male-dominated society? What challenges did they face during their most productive years?

Now, at last, we have in-depth answers to these questions and many more.

The ideal biographer for the Denny-Watrous partnership has taken on the task. A knowledgeable and talented musician with a zeal for scholarly historical research, David is also endowed with an abiding gift for words together with a love for the arts and for Carmel. He is also a personification of the Carmel spirit himself. Revered Dramaturge of the Carmel Bach Festival, acclaimed tenor, lecturer, educator, scholar and writer, he is without doubt a virtuoso lineage holder in the Carmel way of the arts as passed down from the Denny-Watrous era.

In the process of illuminating the lives and visions of his beloved impresarios, David provides abundant fresh material about early Carmel and its distinctive history. Moreover, he reveals how its astonishing artistic ferment interwove with the larger, changing world and established in the region an enduring passion for joyful creative excellence.

On to the adventure!

Barbara Rose Shuler
Pacific Grove, California
May 2014

Preface

The Denny-Watrous Project

In June 1982 I left San Francisco in a rental car on a cold foggy morning and headed south on Route 101. The San Francisco Opera brought me to California for the first time in my life the previous year, and I was back again this summer. In the car with me were a map with written directions and phone numbers (no cell phones then), a bottle of water, and a 3-ring binder of sheet music—tenor arias by Bach, Handel, Haydn, and Mozart, and probably some Schubert songs.

Highway 101 follows the general route of El Camino Real, the 600-mile "Royal Road," conceived by Spain in the late 1700s to connect the missions and towns along the Pacific coast from San Diego to San Francisco.

The eight–lane highway heads south along San Francisco Bay and past the airport where I had arrived three weeks before. Beyond that point I was in unfamiliar territory. The highway skirts the city of San José and heads south past the towns of Morgan Hill and Gilroy. It then leaves the urban environment behind, and winds through 20 miles of rolling hills, all golden in June of 1982 and dotted with a kind of California oak tree I had never seen before.

In a place called Prunedale, I exited Route 101 (and El Camino Real) and drove west on Route 156 toward the Pacific Ocean. The road leaves the coastal hills and passes through broad, flat agricultural land in the Salinas River delta. When it nears Monterey Bay, the highway joins Route 1 and heads south along the Monterey Bay dunes. This is the Cabrillo Highway, one of the most scenic roads in America, reaching from Oregon to Mexico along the California coast.

Almost 2 1/2 hours after leaving San Francisco, I turned right at the "Carmel" sign and drove down a hill into a small town I knew almost nothing about. There was a Bach Festival there and my agent in NYC had set up an audition.

I found my way to the side door of Church of the Wayfarer and awaiting me there was one of the most charming, persuasive and inspiring persons I have ever met. The inflections of his Hungarian accent and the pitch and modulation of his voice gave his speech the character of a vintage cello. It was mesmerizing. I also experienced what I later learned was a well-known part of his charm: during the time that we were together that day, he made it seem that nothing else in the world interested him except talking with me. His name was Sandor Salgo ("Shahndor Shahlgo"), he had been Music Director of the Carmel Bach Festival since 1956, and in my personal experience he was one of the surprisingly few conductors who actually deserve to be called "maestro" while in conversation with them. He introduced me to his American-born wife Priscilla, and to Ken Ahrens, the keyboardist on the Festival staff, and I handed Ken my 3-ring binder.

With Ken's accompaniment, I sang several selections—no doubt Bach and Handel, although I don't recall specifically. I do know for sure that I sang the tenor aria "Un aura amorosa" from Mozart's Così fan tutte, because Maestro Salgo reminded me of it more than 20 years later, several years after his retirement from conducting.

The 1983 Carmel Bach Festival presented the St. John Passion, and Maestro Salgo invited me to sing the Evangelist (the narrator). I spent the month of July at the Cypress Inn, in a room with a tiny balcony overlooking Lincoln Street and Church of the Wayfarer. That summer I fell in love with Carmel. Since then I have participated in 26 Carmel Bach Festivals, first as tenor soloist, and later as Dramaturge, master class teacher, lecturer, and researcher. That first meeting with Sandor Salgo in 1982 was an important link in the chain of connections and events that resulted in this book.

In 2012, the Carmel Bach Festival celebrated its 75th anniversary, and I was looking for interesting material to use in scripting a narrated concert about the Festival's history. I began by studying early Festival programs and other ephemera. When work took me away from home for a few months, my friend Richard Flower searched the microfilms of the weekly Carmel Pine Cone and gathered a trove of valuable and inspiring press clippings. I drew on all this material to create a 2,300-word script for the anniversary concert.

It is common knowledge in Carmel that two women—Dene Denny and Hazel Watrous—"founded" the Carmel Bach Festival in 1935 and managed it until their deaths in the 1950s. (Dene is pronounced "Deen.")

Decades of published articles in the Carmel Bach Festival program books and the local press have drawn from a basic inventory of commonly known events, facts, dates, and supporting characters; only rarely over the years did a writer add a new detail to the established but sketchy chronicle. Moreover, the photos that appeared year after year seemed to be drawn from a dozen or so images of Dene and Hazel taken during the final decade of their lives, at a time when the community was honoring them for what they had created many years before.

It became clear to me that a fuller, richer story was waiting to be told. I found myself wanting to know more about Dene and Hazel in their early creative years: what made them who they were, and what led them to Carmel? How did they actually accomplish things in Carmel, and why did their organizations endure?

In August 2012, I paid my first visit to the Henry Meade Williams Local History Room of the Harrison Memorial Library in Carmel, California. The Local History Room's holdings, managed by the superb History Librarian Ashlee Wright, were essential to the writing of this book. In the space of about a year, I viewed every page of every issue of every newspaper published in Carmel-by-the-Sea from 1922 to 1960. In the Local History Room I also found wonderful photographs, concert programs, and other historical records. Through all this material I caught a glimpse of the village coming into existence, and I followed Dene and Hazel as they entered the community and became a part of it.

My research went far beyond Carmel, and by the middle of 2013 I had collected more than a thousand pages of primary source material including a century of newspaper clippings, vintage photographs and postcards, oral histories, extensive and detailed family trees, and countless other documents and records.

Research sources included the archives of the organizations that Dene and Hazel founded on the Monterey Peninsula, as well as other archives across the country: libraries and museums, universities, historical societies, theaters, private collectors, and friends, students, and descendants of individuals discussed in this book. I obtained a staggering amount of (literally) vital information on the internet via genealogical research websites. Information about all these sources is organized in the Appendix and End Notes. The Acknowledgements pages list the names of the many wonderful people and organizations who generously helped me along the way.

Dene Denny and Hazel Watrous had enormous, generous hearts, great strength of character, and very high standards. In their work together, they recognized and collaborated with artists in every discipline who shared their mission: to connect with others, to help others to connect with each other, and to create artistic excellence and shared joy. I am grateful to be able to tell their story.

D.G.

Pen and ink drawing of Carmel Bay by Charlotte Morton.
Carmel Spectator, July 14, 1949. Courtesy of the author.

Names

Issues #1–3 below arise at the beginning of the book and #4 & 5 are basic, and it seemed like a good idea to put this page where it could be read first.

1. "Dene"

Dene Denny's name was Ethel Adele Denny. In her 40s, she dropped "Ethel Adele" and began using the first name "Dene" [pronounced "Deen"]. For the rest of her life she went by "Dene Denny," and that name appears on her headstone in the Monterey cemetery. Throughout the narrative of this book she is almost always referred to as "Dene" unless there is a particular reason to call her Ethel.

2. The use of first names

The author usually refers to Dene and Hazel by their first names. It would seem dry and impersonal to call them "Denny" and "Watrous" and it would be cloying and cumbersome to adopt the 1920s usage of "Miss Denny and Miss Watrous" or even "the Misses Denny and Watrous." The author took his cue from a 1938 interview in the Carmel Pine Cone, the town's weekly newspaper. After the first few paragraphs, the writer takes a stand:

> Why the formality of Miss-Denny-and-Miss-Watrousing them? To Carmel they are as they have always been, Dene and Hazel ... (Pine Cone, July 1, 1938)

3. Names of US territories and states

Until 1848, the large territory of "Alta California" was part of the Viceroyalty of New Spain, a Spanish colony with its capital in Mexico City. Alta California included most of the modern states of California, Nevada, Arizona, Utah, western Colorado and southwestern Wyoming. At the end of the War between the US and Mexico, the treaty of Guadalupe-Hidalgo in February 1848 ceded Alta California to the United States.

In the same year, the Oregon Territory was declared, making that region—the present-day states of Oregon, Washington, Idaho, and parts of Western Montana—a US Territory.

Spurred by the 1849 Gold Rush, California became the 31st state in 1850, but the other states listed above did not actually achieve statehood for a decade or more. When the author refers to a US state by name, he means the area within the present-day borders of that state, whether or not that state or those borders officially existed at the time of the events being described.

4. "Bach"

There were many musicians named Bach in the central German region of Thuringia in the 17th and 18th centuries, dozens and dozens of them. Some were composers who might be better known to us now were it not for Johann Sebastian, born in 1685. Nonetheless, music by other Bachs is performed today, some of it relatively often, and to avoid confusion it has become customary to give either the full name or the initials and last name: J.S. Bach, C.P.E. Bach, W.F., J.C., J.C.F., P.D.Q., and so on.

It is generally considered especially important to use initials or full name for J. S. Bach himself, to distinguish him from all his relatives. Nonetheless, in the narrative of this book, unless context demands otherwise, Johann Sebastian Bach often will be referred to as "Bach." The sons, cousins, and uncles play virtually no role in this story, and referring to Johann Sebastian Bach by only his last name will simply make things easier.

5. The titles of J. S. Bach's compositions

There is a more or less established way of referring in print to a composition by Johann Sebastian Bach, including the obligatory "BWV" number. Musicologist Wolfgang Schmieder created and published an index of J. S. Bach's compositions: the "Bach-Werke-Verzeichnis" (Bach Works Catalogue) in which each composition has its own unique BWV number.

Many works by Bach are mentioned in this book, most only in passing. The question for the author was how to refer to these works in a narrative text. For example, in the printed program of the 1937 Carmel Bach Festival, the final work on the second concert is listed as:

"Concerto in C major for two pianos and orchestra"

This concerto actually was written for harpsichords, but someone unfamiliar with Bach's music might view the 1937 title above and assume that Bach wrote it for two grand pianos, which is untrue. Bach also didn't use the word "orchestra" in the original title, but for the uninitiated it might be useful to confirm that an orchestra was involved. A modern printed program would probably list this concerto as:

"Concerto in C Major for Two Harpsichords, BWV 1061"

A more descriptive but less formal style might be:

"Concerto for 2 harpsichords, strings & continuo in C major, BWV 1061"

The author deeply respects the need for the precise naming of compositions, but wanted to avoid placing long titles such as these within a paragraph of text. Yet why mention these works at all if they are identified in a vague or confusing way?

There is only one Bach concerto for two harpsichords in the key of C Major, so this is how it is referenced in the chapter about the 1937 Bach Festival:

"...the concert ended with the Concerto in C Major for Two Harpsichords and Orchestra, performed on Baldwin grand pianos by Ann Greene and Winifred Howe."

Population of the California Towns and Cities Mentioned in this Narrative

City/Town	Estimate 1847	June 1 1850	June 1 1860	June 1 1870	June 1 1880	June 2 1890	June 1 1900	April 15 1910	January 1 1920	April 1 1930	April 1 1940	April 1 1950	April 1 1960
Alameda			460	1,557	5,708	11,165	16,464	23,383	28,806	35,033	36,256	64,430	63,855
Carmel-by-the-Sea									638	2,260	2,837	4,351	4,580
Berkeley						5,101	13,214	40,434	56,036	82,109	85,547	113,805	111,268
Etna					361	271	500	518	425	379	456	649	596
Monterey	400	1,092	n/a	1,112	1,396	1,662	1,748	4,923	5,479	9,141	10,084	16,205	22,618
Oakland			1,543	10,500	34,555	48,682	66,960	150,174	216,261	284,063	302,163	384,575	367,548
Pacific Grove						1,336	1,411	2,384	2,974	5,558	6,249	9,623	12,121
Sacramento		6,820	13,785	16,283	21,420	26,386	29,282	44,696	65,908	93,750	105,958	137,572	191,667
Salinas				599	1,854	2,339	3,304	3,736	4,308	10,263	11,586	13,917	28,957
San Francisco	300	21,000	56,802	149,473	233,959	298,997	342,782	416,912	506,676	634,394	634,536	775,357	740,316
San Jose				9,089	12,567	18,060	21,500	28,946	39,642	57,651	68,457	95,280	204,196
Santa Clara					2,416	2,891	3,650	4,348	5,220	6,302	6,650	11,702	58,880
Santa Cruz			950	2,561	3,898	5,596	5,659	11,146	10,917	14,395	16,896	21,970	25,596
Sausalito					476	1,334	1,628	2,383	2,790	3,667	3,540	4,828	5,331
Visalia			548	913	1,412	2,885	3,085	4,550	5,753	7,263	8,904	11,749	15,791
Watsonville			398	1,151	1,799	2,149	3,528	4,446	5,013	8,344	8,937	11,572	13,293
Yreka		500	2,028	1,063	1,059	1,100	1,254	1,134	1,277	2,126	2,485	3,227	4,759

Primary Source: California State Data Center, Demographic Research Unit. www.dof.ca.gov/research/demographic/state_census_data_center/historical_census_1850-2010/
Dates indicate the actual date of the federal census. Table © 2014 David Gordon

The cost of things

The following chart is based on the Consumer Price Index and other sources listed below. For a rough modern equivalent of a price in US dollars mentioned in the narrative, find the approximate year below and multiply the historical price by the inflation factor for that year. For example: In 1856, the price of a train ride across the Isthmus of Panama was $25. It sounds sounds cheap now, but it wasn't back then. Multiply the 1856 ticket price by that year's inflation factor ($25 x 28) to calculate the equivalent cost in 2014 dollars: $700.

year	factor	year	factor
1840	28	1900	29
1850	31	1907	26
1852	31	1910	25
1853	28	1915	23
1855	28	1917	18
1856	28	1920	12
1860	29	1922	14
1865	15	1923	14
1870	18	1925	13
1875	22	1926	14
1880	24	1927	14
1885	25	1930	14
1888	26	1932	17
1890	26	1935	17
1895	29	1938	16

This chart is for informal *price* comparisons and is intended to give only a somewhat general idea. In reality, there is no single way to compare the relative "value" of the dollar then vs. now. There are several other methods, each serving a different purpose and producing differently scaled results.

Sources:

Bureau of Labor Statistics, United States Department of Labor.
Consumer Price Index Online Databases. Accessed January 2014.
www.bls.gov/data/ and www.bls.gov/cpi/

San Francisco Wholesale Prices and California Wages 1870-1928 (spreadsheets)
Economics Department of the University of California, Davis.

Historical Statistics of the United States.
US Bureau of the Census, Washington, DC: Government Printing Office, 1975.

Measuring Worth www.measuringworth.com
An informational website created by Lawrence H. Officer and Samuel H. Williamson. Accessed Feb 2014.

The State of California

Oregon

Nevada

Yreka
Siskiyou County
Etna
Gold discovered in 1851

Yuba County
Timbuctoo &
Smartsville

El Dorado
County

Sacramento

Gold discovered at
Sutter's Mill in 1848

San Francisco

San José

Santa Cruz

Monterey Bay

Monterey Peninsula

Visalia

Tulare County

Nevada

N
NW NE
W E
SW SE
S

Los Angeles

Pacific Ocean

Arizona

San Diego

Mexico

The line in the US map indicates the route
taken by Albert and Edgar Denny in 1852,
from Milwaukee to Yreka

0   50   100   150   200 miles
0 50 100 150 200 250 300 kilometers

Part One
Family and Roots
1829–1903

This 1847 engraving depicts "a faithful and accurate representation of San Francisco as it really appeared in March 1847." That statement is signed by John D. Stevenson, Commander of the NY Volunteers in the War with Mexico; General M. G. Vallejo; and George Hyde, the First Alcade (Mayor) of San Francisco in 1846. Note that Montgomery Street in those days formed the shoreline of the Bay. *Library of Congress.*

Down from the heights
by Clinton Scollard

Down from the heights of Carmel, pine boughs

And cypress arms in blended beauty reach;

Below them in an undulating line,

The beryl billows break upon the beach.

Beyond, the sea kelp sways on the long surge,

And toward the horizon, miles on golden miles,

The fathomless Pacific sweeps away

To beckoning palms on dream envisaged isles.

Clinton Scollard (1860–1932) was a New England poet, and wrote
this impression of Carmel in 1924, just after marrying the Carmel
poet Jessie Belle Rittenhouse. The poem appeared in 1925 in Daisy
Bostick's book, *Carmel at Work and Play*.

Introduction: Río del Carmelo

In 1542, Juan Rodríguez Cabrillo and the crew of his three Spanish ships became the first Europeans to see what is now known as Monterey Bay. As he was hurrying southward along the coast, chased by storms and bad weather, Cabrillo noticed a wide, open bay with a peninsula at the southern end covered with pine trees. As he passed by, he named it Bahía de los Pinos, the "Bay of the Pines," and hastened on to Acapulco.

In 1595, the Portuguese sea captain Sebastião Rodrigues Soromenho (better known today by his Spanish name Sebastián Rodríguez Cermeño) sighted the same bay from afar as he cruised the coast, and in his log he called it "San Pedro Bay."

Sebastián Vizcaíno (1548-1624) was on that 1595 voyage. Vizcaíno was a Basque conquistador of many talents, and in his lifetime he commanded successful Spanish voyages of maritime exploration to Central and South America, Japan, and the Philippines (which the Spaniards had named in honor of King Philip II of Spain). In 1602 the Spanish Viceroy in Mexico City (the Count of Monte Rey), appointed Vizcaíno general-in-charge of an expedition to locate safe harbors on the California coast for Spanish galleons, and also to create a more detailed chart of the entire coastline. Vizcaíno departed Acapulco with three ships on May 5, 1602.

Sebastian Vizcaíno

As Vizcaíno sailed north along the California coast, he gave enduring Spanish names to prominent places along the way, including San Diego, Santa Barbara, the Santa Catalina and San Clemente Islands, San Simeon, Point Conception, Point Lobos, San Francisco, and Point Reyes. Vizcaíno also named Point Pinos—the tip of the Monterey Peninsula and part of present-day Pacific Grove.

On December 16 the ships rounded Point Pinos and entered what Cabrillo sixty years before had called the "Bay of the Pines." It was bitterly cold, and the Santa Cruz Mountains to the north across the bay were covered in snow, a rare sight on the Central Coast of California.

Vizcaíno was the first European to approach the shore closely enough to note the details of the local vegetation, especially the distinctive coniferous evergreen tree growing on the peninsula: the Cupressus macrocarpa, or Monterey cypress. (See the Appendix for brief description of this tree and other Monterey Peninsula flora.)

On December 17, 1602, Vizcaíno and his crew went ashore to celebrate a thanksgiving Mass. They had arrived at one of their primary destinations, and they formally named the peninsula and the bay "Monterey" in honor of the Viceroy of New Spain.

On January 3, 1603, Vizcaíno, accompanied by ten soldiers and a padre of the Carmelite order, headed southeast on foot intending to explore inland. After a trek of four or five miles over pine-forested hills they came to a white sandy beach, and found beyond it a small cove at the mouth of a strongly flowing river descending from the snowy hills to the east. To honor the three Carmelite monks who were traveling with the expedition, Vizcaíno named this river Río del Carmelo.

Vizcaíno's naming of the Carmel River in 1603 took place four years before the founding of the Jamestown Colony in Virginia, and seventeen years before the pilgrims and their ship The Mayflower reached Plymouth Rock, Massachusetts.

Hoping to encourage settlement of the area, Vizcaíno exaggerated the size of the river, the shape of the bay, the arability of the land, and even the climate (he said it was as warm as Sevilla), causing subsequent 17th century European explorers to overlook Monterey Bay altogether. Vizcaíno's maps and written account of his entire journey were filled with errors and distortions, but no further maps of the coast were made for more than a century. Meanwhile, disputes and intrigue in the governments of Spain and New Spain delayed and then cancelled further plans for exploration and settlement along the California coast. No European ship entered Monterey Bay for more than a century and a half, and during that time Alta California was temporarily forgotten by the Spanish.

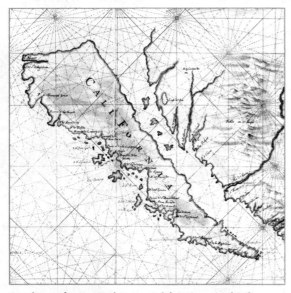

Dutch map from 1650 showing California as an island.
Courtesy of the author.

In 1769, Carlos Francisco de Croix, the Flanders-born Viceroy of New Spain, issued an order from Mexico City to "Occupy and fortify San Diego and Monterey for God and the King of Spain." The glory of the Spanish Empire was fading, Russian fur traders were starting to show an interest in the coastal areas of Alaska and the Pacific Northwest, and British ships were exploring the region as well. In response to these (still tentative) threats of foreign encroachment, Spain was finally taking steps to establish more than just a legal claim of ownership of Alta California. A Spanish colonization project was to begin with the building of a series of Catholic missions between San Diego and Monterey, two of the bays Vizcaíno had described and named in his writings 160 years before. The missions were intended to form the nucleus of new Spanish settlements along 500 miles of the California coast.

The 1769 expedition was led by the Governor of California, Don Gaspar De Portolà and by Fray (Brother) Junípero Serra, a Franciscan monk. Serra was born in 1730 in Majorca, a Spanish island in the Mediterranean Sea, where he received his education. In 1749 he had come to Mexico to do missionary work co-sponsored by the Catholic church and the government of New Spain. After his successes in Baja California, he had been selected to lead the missionaries traveling with Portolà's soldiers.

In July 1769, Portolà and Serra established the first Mission and Presidio on the Alta California coast. (The presidios were military bases and barracks for the Spanish troops.) Using the name shown on Vizcaíno's 1602 map, they called the place San Diego.

Vizcaíno's inaccurate charts caused the expedition a year of difficulties and missed connections, all made worse by illnesses. Finally, a party of four dozen soldiers and Franciscan missionaries reached the southern shore of Monterey Bay on foot in 1770 and established El Presidio Reál de San Carlos de Monterey (The Royal San Carlos Presidio of Monterey), thus establishing the location of the modern city of Monterey.

Serra established the Mission San Carlos Borroméo near the Presidio, about a half mile from the bay. (Carlo Borromeo was Cardinal Archbishop of Milan in the 1500s, and had been canonized in 1610.)

New Spain was engaged in colonization, and its intention for the missions was not only to minister to the Spanish soldiers and future Spanish settlers, but also to attract the native peoples to European ways—to convert them to Christianity, teach them Spanish, and put them to work for their own good, for the good of the communities-to-be, and for the Glory of God and the King of Spain. But the hardened and weathered Spanish soldiers mistreated and abused the Native Americans who came to the chapel, and the military commander viewed the outpost as a military installation first and a House of God second, despite Serra's protestations. Because the mission was close to the presidio, the Indians began avoiding Serra and the Spaniards altogether.

In 1771, the Spanish Viceroy in Mexico City granted Serra's request to relocate the mission to a beautiful, peaceful, and more practical site a few miles south of Monterey, well known to the Esselen and Ohlone Indians. There was land for livestock, it was far away from the Spanish soldiers and sailors, and (unlike Monterey) it had a source of fresh water for at least part of the year. There, within sight of the Pacific Ocean and the mouth of the Carmel River, Junípero Serra established his mission and gave it a new and longer name: Mission San Carlos Borroméo del río Carmelo, a historic place most widely known today as the "Carmel Mission." Serra died there in 1784 and his grave is beneath the floor near the altar of the present building, which was completed after his death.

Carmel Mission about 1800. *Library of Congress.*

On July 25, 1937, a century and a half after the death of Junípero Serra, Dene Denny and Hazel Watrous produced a live nationwide NBC radio broadcast by the Carmel Bach Festival from Serra's Carmel Mission.

That summer evening, when a thirty-minute Bach cantata was performed for more than 300 people crowded into the old Carmel Mission—and for radio listeners all across the country— was the culmination of more than a decade of visionary creativity and endless, selfless work by two remarkable women. Dene Denny and Hazel Watrous brought music and artistic joy to Carmel-by-the-Sea and far beyond, and this is the story of their partnership.

Dene Denny and Hazel Watrous born in California in the 1880s, the daughters and granddaughters of true pioneer families. They taught high school in San Francisco and environs for more than ten years before their paths finally crossed, but once they met, they were inseparable. As one journalist once wrote, "...it is when they say 'we' that they are happiest."

Partners in life and art, Dene and Hazel began to put down roots in the quirky town of Carmel in 1924, and by 1937 they were among the leaders in the cultural life of the Monterey Peninsula.

Their accomplishments in that time span are astounding: They designed and built three dozen houses in Carmel, and also designed Carmel's first art gallery in 1926. Their own Denny-Watrous Gallery was a cultural hub of 1930s Carmel. They guided the creation of the Carmel Music Society, a concert booking organization that continues to bring world-class performing artists to the Monterey Peninsula. During the darkest years of the Great Depression, Dene and Hazel created an orchestra of local townspeople, and after three years of grooming, that orchestra became the nucleus of the first Carmel Bach Festival in 1935.

Only weeks before the Bach Festival's 1937 radio broadcast from the Carmel Mission, Dene and Hazel celebrated the opening night of their new theater company: the Troupers of the Gold Coast. This band of thespians performed weekly at California's First Theater, a historic landmark built in Monterey in 1844 and newly renovated by Dene and Hazel. And only a few months after the radio broadcast, these same two women assumed management of a major concert and performing arts series in the 3,300–seat San José Civic Auditorium.

Dene Denny and Hazel Watrous were intelligent, resourceful, and imaginative; by 1937 they had become beloved figures in their region, and renowned far beyond its borders. In order to fully characterize their remarkable partnership, this book begins with the story of their families, the uniquely colorful individuals whose role in this story is to set the scene, bring Dene and Hazel into the world, raise them, and help to form their resilient spirits.

* Dene Denny's actual name was Ethel Adele Denny. In her early forties, she
   began using the first name "Dene" (pronounced "Deen").

Geography plays a central role, as well: this is a quintessentially "California" story, and a significant part of what is described in this narrative could not have happened anywhere else.

Therefore, Part One begins in the 19th century, with the ancestors who made their various ways west in the 1850s from New York, Vermont or Maine to the brand new state of California. They, and thousands of others, were all coming for the same reason: gold.

El Dorado

In 1847, the area now known as California had a non-Indian population of fewer than 10,000, most of whom spoke Spanish. For decades, California had been part of the huge Spanish/Mexican territory of Alta California, all of which was ceded to the US with the signing of a treaty with Mexico on February 2, 1848.

Just nine days before that treaty was signed, carpenter James Marshall made history. He and John Sutter were operating their new, water-wheel-driven sawmill on the South Fork of the American River, 140 miles northeast of San Francisco. In order to increase the water flow and the speed and power of the wheel, Marshall had been re-directing the mill stream water at night to excavate portions of the channel. As he wrote later, on the morning of January 24,

> "...I went down as usual, and after shutting off the water from the race I stepped into it, near the lower end, and there, upon the rock, about six inches beneath the surface of the water, I DISCOVERED THE GOLD." [the upper case emphasis is in the original.]

The moment when Marshall reached his hand into the cold Sierra Nevada water and came up with a few tiny flakes of gold marks the beginning of California's rapid transformation from a remote western outpost to a major center of intense and international activity.

News traveled slowly at first, but within a few months, rumors were confirmed in the North American press that gold had been discovered in California, and by early 1849 all the world knew. By 1850, the non-Indian population of the state had soared to at least 120,000. Spurred on by current events, a state constitution was drafted in Monterey, statehood was fast tracked by the territorial and federal governments, and California officially became a US state in September 1850.

Between 1849 and 1855 the Gold Rush brought more than 300,000 new residents to California (not all of whom stayed), and San Francisco grew from a small settlement of a few hundred to a boomtown of about 45,000. More than half of these newcomers traveled by ship from the East Coast to San Francisco, and the rest journeyed from the eastern states via the overland trails. Some came to look for gold, and others came to sell goods and supplies to the miners. (See the Appendix for a chart of California city and town populations.)

The California Gold Rush actually took place in two separate regions. The area of the 1848 discovery, better-known today and more productive then, is northeast of San Francisco in the foothills of the Sierra Nevada.

In 1851, gold was discovered 300 miles north of San Francisco near the town of Yreka, in remote Siskiyou County.

One year later, at the age of 17, Dene Denny's father arrived in Yreka—penniless and more or less by chance—after spending seven months on the Oregon Trail with his older brother. This narrative begins with the story of Albert and Edgar Denny.

Breaking up Camp at Sunrise, 1858-1860. Watercolor on paper. Alfred Jacob Miller (American, 1810-1874)
In reality, wagon trains were often a confused, dusty mess, and not neat and tidy as depicted here.
Walters Art Museum: Commissioned by William T. Walters, 1858-1860. Public domain.

Denny

"My father was a born pioneer," Dene Denny recalled in a 1938 interview. Albert Hendrickson Denny was in fact a very resourceful and successful pioneer. An intelligent and industrious man, he was a loving presence in the lives of his many children. Since Dene's father was an important figure in her youth, in order to understand Dene we need to meet her father first.

Dene's paternal grandfather, Amasa Denny, was born in 1798 in Northfield, Vermont, deep in the Green Mountains south of Montpelier. Amasa was a school teacher, and from all existing accounts he was a charming, intelligent, and artistic fellow. Around 1720, he left Vermont and made his way to Long Island, NY, where he met Sally Ann Hendrickson.

Amasa and Sally Ann Denny

Sally Ann was born on Long Island in 1805 to a highbrow family of Dutch immigrants, and while she may have loved Amasa Denny, the rest of her upper crust family definitely did not. They were aghast at the thought of their daughter marrying a lowly schoolteacher with no head for business, and the family pressures apparently became so unpleasant that the young couple eloped. Before that happened, Sally Ann's parents had begrudgingly but dutifully given her a set of silver as a wedding present. She treasured it, and it plays a role in this story, but she never restored her relationship with her parents.

The newly married couple lived on Long Island and then in Manhattan, where their first two children were born: Edgar (1831) and Jane (1833). Then, in what seems to be only one of several odd and unsuccessful choices that Amasa made in his life, he moved with his young family to New Jersey and attempted to eke out an existence while living in a log cabin near the town of Summit, about 13 miles west of Newark.

In that log cabin in the cold and moonless pre-dawn hours of February 27, 1835, their third child was born, and he is central to our story: his name was Albert Hendrickson Denny.

After seven years of subsistence farming, Amasa and his family migrated to Wisconsin in 1842 at the encouragement of Amasa's uncle, who was homesteading west of Milwaukee. They went to New York to bid Sally Ann's family an awkward farewell, and then traveled north to Vermont to say goodbye to Amasa's family. From Vermont they made the trip to Wisconsin by boat: up the Hudson River, westward on the Erie Canal from Albany to Buffalo, and by ship through the Great Lakes to Milwaukee. Albert was seven, and would recall this journey for the rest of his life.

Times were hard for the Denny family, and on arrival in Milwaukee Amasa had barely enough money left to hire an ox-cart to take his family and belongings to their new home a few miles west of town: a log cabin in the midst of a small clearing, abandoned by its former owner. It had been hard to scrape out a living in rural New Jersey, but it was brutal in Wisconsin because of the colder winters and shorter growing season.

The following spring they moved to the farm of Amasa's uncle 20 miles away, and the family worked the farm as sharecroppers while Amasa taught school. In 1844 Amasa moved his family to a homestead of their own, and soon afterward he built a small inn with money that Sally Ann inherited from her uncle in New York. This venture constantly floundered, and by the beginning of 1852 Amasa again found himself in dire financial straits and facing foreclosure.

For ten years Albert Denny and his older brother Edgar had worked either on the family farm or for neighboring farmers, and had spent little time in schools. It was a tough life of poverty and privation, and especially hard in the cold Wisconsin winters.

Word of the 1848 Sierra Nevada Gold Rush had surely reached the Denny family by 1849. Gold and California had quickly become the national topic of conversation, but if Edgar and Albert were thinking about emigrating to California they had no way to do so: it was not an option for the poor. Basic supplies for the two of them would have cost a minimum of $250-$300, and this figure would double or triple if they needed to purchase a wagon and draft animals.

It was the love of a mother that made the trip possible for the two boys: Sally Ann Hendrickson Denny sold the silver she had received as a (pre-elopement) wedding present from her parents in New York. She had been estranged from her family since before she married Amasa, and she had left the comforts of life in New York City to struggle on a desolate homestead. The silver was among the few cherished belongings she had brought with her to Wisconsin, and it was a powerful reminder of the civilized world she had left behind. Nonetheless she sold the precious silver in order to give her boys a chance for a better life. The money would get them started on a 2,000 mile journey to California.

Supplies could be replenished along the way, but that was an expensive prospect, so most of the weight in their wagon would be food: flour, hardtack, sugar, bacon, dried beef and fish, tea, coffee beans, lard, spices, dried fruit, dried beans, and rice. A Dutch oven and skillet were indispensable, and a water barrel was kept in the wagon and refilled at every opportunity as a supply for humans and livestock.

To carry it all they bought four oxen and a lumber wagon. To deal with wagon repairs on the trail, they probably carried tools and materials such as extra axles, wheels, wagon tongues, ax, hatchet, augurs of various diameters, chisels, drawing knife, handsaw, wrought nails, spade, and heavy rope. A well equipped "medicine" kit would include patent medicine pills, castor oil, spirits such as rum or whiskey, quinine for malaria, oil of peppermint, hartshorn for snakebite, citric acid for scurvy, opium, laudanum, morphine, calomel, and tincture of camphor.

Although the precise inventory of the Denny brothers' supplies is not known, when all had been paid for they had $1.50 in cash left in their pockets.

They left Waukesha County, Wisconsin, on March 29, 1852, as part of a larger group that included several women, something Albert's mother told him was a good precaution in case of illness. Albert was 17 and Edgar was 21.

Travelers on the overland trails west were known as "emigrants." Most emigrants walked the entire distance, and the Denny brothers started the journey that way, too. Their ox wagon would have been filled with all it could carry, and every pound counted. Besides, the ox wagon had no springs, and it was a brutally uncomfortable ride.

Although emigrants were traveling by the thousands, there was no single trail to the West Coast. What is today generically referred to as "The Oregon Trail" had started as a route to Oregon in 1843, but by the end of the decade it had become several routes from the Midwest to destinations on the Pacific coast. By the early 1850s, all these trails were heavily traveled. The average wagon train journey from one of the Missouri or Iowa trailheads to the West Coast was 2,000 miles, and at least one in ten died along the way, (an estimated total of 20,000 deaths occurred during 1843–1869), making the Oregon Trail the longest graveyard in the United States.

The brothers traveled southwest from Milwaukee to Nauvoo, Illinois, where a trail to the West had been opened in 1847 by Brigham Young and his Pioneer Company of 148 Latter-Day Saints. By 1852 the trail had become well-established and heavily traveled. From Nauvoo they headed northwest out of Missouri and across Iowa, to Council Bluffs, where they crossed the wide Missouri River and entered Nebraska.

There are two detailed accounts of Albert Denny's months on the trail, filled with anecdotes. For example, printed books were precious items in a wagon train, and were traded from reader to reader along the way. When traveling with the slow-moving wagon train, Albert—tall and long-legged—would walk on far ahead, find a comfortable spot, sit and read a book until the wagon train passed him, read a bit more, and then walk to catch up with the wagons.

In the early 1850s the greatest danger from Indians along the trail in Nebraska was robbery. A few days after the Council Bluffs crossing, Albert walked ahead of the train and sat down under a tree to read. After the wagon train had passed by, an Indian on horseback approached him and made threatening signs indicating that he wanted money.

Albert jumped up to walk to the wagons ahead, and as he did so he reached behind his back to tuck his shirt tail into his overalls. The Indian thought Albert was threatening to draw a pistol from his back pocket and he backed off a bit but did not leave. Albert realized what was going on and he repeated the bluffing movements every time the Indian came closer, maintaining a standoff until the wagon train was within earshot and the Indian departed.

By the time they reached south central Nebraska, the Denny brothers were growing frustrated by the slow speed of the wagon train. Oxen were the most commonly used wagon train draft animal, but they travel at about 2 miles per hour, and a wagon train might cover 15 miles on good day. The reality of a wagon in Nebraska and Wyoming was not the neat, orderly line of wagons depicted in the painting at the beginning of the chapter. The trail was crowded with large, confused groups traveling slowly, each wagon swimming in the clouds of dust created by the wagons ahead.

With the restless energy of two young men age 17 and 21, the Denny brothers decided to leave the group and continue on ahead by themselves. Those in charge of the wagon train tried to dissuade them, but the brothers insisted, and finally they all struck a deal: Albert and Edgar gave their four oxen and their heavy wagon to the wagon train, and in return the brothers were given two saddle horses, some supplies, and a spring wagon (lighter-built than an ox wagon, with a box body hung on platform springs, and most commonly pulled by horses). Now, with 500 miles already behind them, they could finally move at their own pace, hooking up with wagon trains for security only when passing through dangerous territory.

Traveling alone the brothers would stop for supper in the late afternoon, build a fire and eat (typically beans or rice with bacon or dried meat, and coffee or tea). Then they put the fire out, rode on until nightfall, and made camp for the night without a fire to avoid attracting the attention of Indians. As a further precaution, they slept with the reins of their horses tied to their arms or legs to prevent the Indians from stampeding the horses in the night. Their trail continued west through Nebraska, following the Platte River, passing Ft. Kearney and Scott's Bluff, and into Wyoming, past Fort Laramie. The route was a busy one in July, but with their lighter rig they could overtake the lumbering ox wagons and get ahead of them.

The Sweetwater River is a 200-mile tributary of the Platte flowing across southwest Wyoming; the Oregon Trail follows it and climbs to South Pass, a 12-mile wide valley at 7,500 feet that was the easiest place north of Arizona for wagons to cross the formidable Rocky Mountains. This stretch of the trail was shared by every overland route to California, Utah, or the Pacific Northwest. In 1852, Albert and Edgar were among the nearly 70,000 emigrants who followed the Platte-Sweetwater Trail over South Pass.

The main trail continued on to Fort Bridger in southwest Wyoming, where supplies could be obtained, and that is where the Denny brothers headed.

Standing in the tracks of the actual Oregon Trail today brings history to life, and helps the onlooker imagine the experience of the emigrants. The author has seen the Oregon Trail in several high plains states, and the one of the most memorable locations is on South Pass at 7,500 feet, above the headwaters of the Sweetwater River, not far from Wyoming State Highway 28. One walks a few dozen yards from the modern automobile and into another century. The land heals slowly here, and the deep scars made by tens of thousands of wagon wheels before the Civil War are still clearly visible today.

The Hastings Cutoff

> I look back upon the long, dangerous and precarious emigrant road with a degree of romance and pleasure; but to others it is the graveyard of their friends. (Lansford Hastings, 1853)

The Denny brothers followed the trail from South Pass to Fort Bridger. From there most emigrants turned north to Soda Springs, Idaho, and joined trails to Oregon and California. This detour north was not the most direct route, but there was water along the way and it was more suitable for wagons and livestock.

That route was not for Albert and Edgar. They chose a shortcut to the Sierra Nevada gold country that had first been described by Lansford Hastings in his 1845 guidebook. The "Hastings Cutoff" saved around 300 miles of travel (two or three weeks of wagon travel time), but the emigrants, with their wagons and animals, had to cross the 8,000 foot Wasatch Mountains into Utah and then survive 100 miles of the Great Salt Desert.

Hastings wrote the book in 1845 after charting the route on horseback, but he had never actually traveled that route with wagons. Among the first followers of the Hastings Cutoff was the Donner wagon train in 1846. Based on Hastings' description of the route, they vastly underestimated the time needed to clear a trail and get their ox wagons over the Wasatch Mountains and make it across the Great Salt Desert. Delayed by months, they were tragically caught in snow in the high Sierra in November.

The fate of the Donner Party did not deter others from following the same route over the Wasatch. The following year, Mormons further established the first portion of the Hastings Cutoff route—from Fort Bridger over the Wasatch and down Emigration Canyon into the Salt Lake Valley. There they had founded Great Salt Lake City in 1847. By 1852 it had grown to a city of 10,000 residents and countless emigrants and prospectors heading for California.

The Hastings Cutoff route was a challenge, but Albert and Edgar were fit, resourceful and eager, and traveling light with two horses and a spring wagon; this quicker but difficult trail was an obvious choice.

The Denny brothers crossed the Wasatch Range and arrived in Salt Lake City hungry and broke in mid August 1852, with only their spring wagon, two saddle horses, worn out tack, and their ragged clothes. Since leaving Wisconsin on March 29, they had traveled 1300 miles, averaging about 9 miles per day.

They had no cash at all, and at first they went door to door looking for work for pay or food. Albert chopped wood for a housewife who made him breakfast. Fortunately it was haying season, and the boys got work in the fields for $1.50 per day while they considered their next steps. Finally, with their labor earnings and the cash from the sale of their spring wagon, they bought new saddles and boots, supplies, and two ponies to be used as pack animals.

To the west of Salt Lake City lies the Great Salt Lake, and beyond the lake is the Great Salt Desert, an infamous trek across 100 miles of flat, waterless terrain. Because of this, most emigrants heading west from Salt Lake City traveled north into Idaho to meet the trails coming from South Pass and Fort Bridger.

The Denny brothers took the quicker route, and followed the Hastings Cutoff west from Salt Lake City. Passing just to the south of the Great Salt Lake, they trekked for 4 to 6 days straight across the desolate salt flats, and crossed into Nevada south of present-day Wendover. Near Elko they met the Humboldt River and followed its course west through the dry and alkaline basin of northern Nevada. The acrid river must have seemed like an oasis after the miles of salt desert. West of Elko, the Hastings Cutoff Route joined with the California Trail coming down from Idaho.

> The Humboldt is not good for man nor beast…and there is not timber enough in three hundred miles of its desolate valley to make a snuff-box, or sufficient vegetation along its banks to shade a rabbit, while its waters contain enough alkali to make soap for a nation. (Across the Plains in 49, by Reuben Cole Shaw, 1849)

After following the Humboldt River for 250 miles through Nevada, they reached a gravelly watering hole known as Lassen's Meadow (at the north end of present-day Rye Patch Reservoir, 30 miles west of Winnemucca). There they spotted a gravel island in the middle of the shallow river, staked out by a group of cowboys who were gathering up abandoned livestock, resting them up, and herding them on to California.

Hot and parched, Albert and Edgar asked if they could spend the night on the island and the trail boss agreed. The next morning when the brothers awoke they found that a hungry old mare had eaten or ruined all their bacon, sugar, flour, salt—everything they had bought in Salt Lake City. The trail boss offered to feed the boys on the trip if they agreed to help with the livestock and take their turn standing guard at night. They were headed for a town called Yreka.

The Denny brothers had originally planned to continue westward, up the Truckee River Valley, over the Sierra Nevada at Donner Summit and down into the very center of the Sierra Nevada Gold Country. But now they were headed for Siskiyou County, a remote region of northern California bordering the former Oregon Territory.

After a few more days of rest in Lassen's Meadow, the boys helped drive the livestock northwest on the infamous Applegate Trail. Established in 1846 and notoriously tough, it led first through the Black Rock Desert, named for the massive triangular formation used as a navigation landmark by travelers (and also the site of the modern-day Burning Man festival). After the flatness of the Black Rock Playa, the trail entered a rocky and perilous segment, a place well-known for breaking the axles of the wagons and the legs of the livestock.

"I shall never forget that march on the Applegate Trail. The road was lined on both sides with the carcasses of animals, which had perished on the way." (J. Goldsbourough Bruff in his diary, 1849)

The trail continued northwest near Goose Lake and passed through the northeast corner of California, an area known to be dangerous for wagon trains and live stock. In 1850 and 1851, the Modocs had been bitterly persecuted and the Shasta tribe deliberately and almost completely wiped out by settlers and miners. The surviving Modocs were bitter and desperate, and by 1852 professional scouts and former army cavalry were serving as paid wagon train escorts through Modoc country to protect the emigrants from attacks.

The route then entered Oregon, but rather than heading onward to Klamath Falls and beyond, the Denny brothers and their companions took the Yreka Trail cutoff to the left, leading south and back into California.

On October 29, 1852, Albert and Edgar Denny arrived in Yreka, the Siskiyou County Seat. From Wisconsin they had journeyed seven months and more than 2,000 miles, an overall average of 10 miles per day.

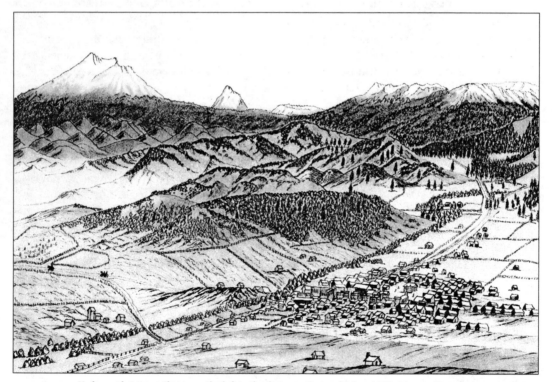

Yreka, with Mount Shasta on the left in the distance. Pen and ink, c.1860. *Library of Congress.*

Placer mining at Scott's Bar, on the Scott River, in 1857. Stone lithograph by Britton and Rey. *Courtesy of the author.*

Siskiyou County

Present day Siskiyou County is the central of the three northernmost counties of California, bounded on the East by Modoc County; on the South by Humboldt, Trinity, and Shasta counties; on the West by Humboldt and Del Norte Counties; and on the North by its 143 mile border with the state of Oregon. Siskiyou contains within its boundaries 6,300 square miles of territory (an area larger than the state of Connecticut).

Siskiyou County has no counterpart on the entire Pacific slope. Within its borders are high valleys and plains surrounded by forest covered mountains, precipitous cliffs, serrated ridges, rocky mountain peaks, canyons, gorges, and (in the East) lava beds. The lowest spot in Siskiyou County is only about 500 feet above sea level and the highest point is the summit of Mt. Shasta, at 14,179 feet the fifth highest mountain in the state.

The first Europeans to enter Siskiyou County were trappers coming south from Oregon in the 1830s and 1840s. The discovery of gold in 1848 in the Sierra foothills served to intensify mineral exploration throughout the rest of the state, and the discovery of gold near Yreka in 1851 led to a second California gold rush in Siskiyou County.

But the layout of the mountain ranges in Siskiyou County meant that until the late 1850s the only routes into the central valleys that were passible by wagons and livestock came from the North out of Oregon (the route the Denny Brothers had traveled on the final leg of their journey). The only route to the south connecting Siskiyou with the rest of California was the old Hudson Bay Trail heading south over Scott Mountain and down the Sacramento River Valley. Established by the earliest trappers and prospectors, the trail was rugged enough for pack mules, and was so far impassable for wagons and livestock

It was to this remote and beautiful frontier that Albert and Edgar Denny had come.

The Dennys of Scott Valley

Arrival

The first problem facing the two brothers in early November 1852, was surviving the long winter ahead. They owned two saddle horses, had less than two dollars in their pockets, and supplies were expensive in Yreka. (Flour was $1/pound and meat 40¢/pound.) They worked a few days cutting hay for George Herd, one of the trailbosses they had ridden with from Nevada. They earned $5 each before the haying was rained out.

It was less than a year since gold was first discovered in Siskiyou, and the entire region was in a gold rush frenzy. George Herd advised the nearly destitute brothers to try their hand at placer mining along Deadwood Creek, a few miles west of Yreka.

Deadwood was a typical western mining town: in its day it was a small, busy, active place with a butcher, saloon, houses, shacks, barns, sheds, and livestock. 150 years later nothing is left but the stream.

They arrived at Deadwood Creek in November with no tools and no idea of what to do, but they traded one of their horses for a small cabin in a neighboring canyon and began to learn about placer mining. Albert began by bailing water for another miner for 50¢ a day, and when he saw how things worked he and Edgar acquired pans, tools, lumber, and began extracting the precious gold bits and flakes from the endless buckets of sand and gravel. Whether using a hand-held-pan or a large, lumber-built sluice, the process is the same: the movement of water is used to separate the lighter sand, fine gravel and dirt from the heavier flakes and nuggets of gold.

Placer Mining

The methods of gold mining used by Albert Hendrickson Denny and (in a later chapter) Forrest Gooch Jefferds did not involve digging a tunnel underground to find a vein of gold. Hard rock mines were not uncommon, especially in the Sierra Nevada Mountains, but most of the early California prospectors were placer or hydraulic miners.

The English word "placer" (pronounced "plasser" in American English) comes from the Spanish placer, meaning shoal or sand bar. The word derives from the Medieval Latin placea (place), which is also the origin of the English words "place" and "plaza."

A placer is a deposit of sand and/or gravel in or along the bed of a modern or ancient stream, or occasionally in an ancient glacial deposit. Particles of gold were eroded from veins by ancient (or modern) streams, and as the particles washed downstream in the swirling water they mixed with fine gravel or sand. Over time this "ore" gathered in an eddy, or built up on the embankment at a certain place, or formed a sandbar.

Prospectors might find gold in a sand bar in an existing stream, or in an exposed vein of sand in a dry area where an ancient stream once flowed. To the unpracticed eye it might look like any other sand, the only difference is that it contains gold. Because gold is heavier than sand the gold particles tend not to be found on the surface of a placer, but a talented prospector could read the clues and knew just where to look. Since you cannot dig a tunnel into sand and gravel, you must laboriously dig it all up and somehow separate the tiny bits of gold from the huge amount of sand and detritus.

The simplest technique for extracting gold from placer ore is hand panning. A handful or two of ore is placed in a large shallow pan with sloping sides, a generous amount of water is added, and the pan is agitated so that the (heavier) gold particles settle to the bottom and the impurities are suspended in the swirling water. The water is quickly poured over the side of the pan, taking with it some of the sand, gravel, and dirt, leaving behind whatever gold is present. The process is repeated until only the gold remains in the pan.

Once a good placer deposit is located by panning, the miner usually shifted to the use of larger equipment (with colorful names like Rocker, Sluice Box, Trommel, and Long Tom) that worked on the same principle as panning but could process larger volumes of sand and gravel more quickly and efficiently.

Placer Mining in a mountain stream at 3,500 feet at any time of the year is cold, wet, exhausting and grim work, and the Denny brothers were novices; all through the winter they made barely enough to buy food. William Davidson had a store and butcher shop in Deadwood Creek, and he sold them beef on credit. All winter they ate nothing but meat, with no flour, vegetables or even salt. By early spring their teeth had started to become loose.

Prospectors working at a Long Tom sluice box.
The Century magazine, January 1883. Courtesy of the author.

In the spring of 1853 the boys came down from Deadwood to William Davidson's ranch, where they paid their winter meat bill by splitting fence rails while still keeping their mining claim active. By summer they began to get the hang of placer mining, and by October Albert and Edgar had mined enough gold to buy supplies for the winter. They worked their claim on Deadwood Creek for two more years with increasing success, each netting about $800.

Early in 1855 Albert Denny began to encounter bouts of lung trouble, and he attributed the ailments to his three wet years of placer mining in and around the water of Deadwood Creek. At the age of 20 he decided to quit the mining business and Edgar followed him soon after. From Deadwood they headed south into Scott Valley, where Albert would make his home for the rest of his life.

The valley of the northward-flowing Scott River is 40 miles long by 6 miles wide, surrounded by lofty ranges of forest-covered mountains, and with good pasture and arable land at an average altitude of 3,000 feet.

In 1856 the brothers purchased 160 acres at the mouth of Wildcat Creek near the southern end of the valley, where the North, East, and South Forks flow down from the mountains to form the Scott River flowing north to meet the Klamath.

Albert was becoming a good businessman, and he realized that selling food and goods to the miners might be easier, safer, and more reliably profitable than actual mining. He bought cows at $60 a head and began selling milk to the miners at 75¢ a gallon. It was a lucrative business and he worked it for two years, increasing his herd and his income.

Parents

As Edgar and Albert were establishing themselves in California they learned that the situation had become grim for their parents and siblings back in Wisconsin. The little hotel Amasa had built and tried to manage had burned down, and although Amasa's wife Sally Ann had financed the construction with her own inheritance, she had wisely purchased insurance for the structure. Now, with most of her funds back in her hand, she and Amasa resolved to buy their way to California. Their sons Albert and Edgar were prospering there, and perhaps they could do the same.

Eleven family members left Wisconsin and traveled through the Great Lakes and down the Hudson River to New York City: Amasa and Sally Ann Denny; their sons Thomas (18) and Joseph (14); their daughter Jenny and her husband and three young children; and their oldest son Edgar, who had returned from California to marry his Wisconsin sweetheart and take her back to Siskiyou.

The overland trail was not the only way to get to California; if you had a bit of money, there was an easier and quicker route. In the spring of 1857, the Denny retinue sailed from New York, possibly stopping in Charleston, Savannah, or Havana, and arriving in Chagres, Panama on the seventh day. From the Atlantic side of the isthmus to the City of Panama on the Pacific side had been a journey of about sixty miles using canoes and mules, but a railroad had been opened in 1855 and the group reached the Pacific shore in just a few hours. A train ticket cost a hefty $25, but it could cost much more to travel the same route with canoes and mules.

SS Brother Jonathan. *Library of Congress.*

After arriving in Panama City they "laid up" (waited) a few days to rest before taking a steamer to San Francisco (the Brother Jonathan, a 230-foot side-wheeler). They then transferred to a smaller side or stern paddle riverboat that took them up the Sacramento River all the way to Red Bluff. From there the eight adults and three children continued on horseback up the Sacramento Valley through Trinity County, over the mountains, and down the rugged six-mile mule trail into Scott Valley, their new home.

In gratitude for their mother's generosity and financial sacrifice in Wisconsin back in 1852, when she sold the family silver to pay for their trip to California, Albert and Edgar had purchased a ranch on Wildcat Creek as a home for their parents and siblings. When Amasa and Sally Ann reached Scott Valley in June 1857, the house was ready for them to move into.

In 1858 Albert sold his successful dairy business on Wildcat Creek and he and his brothers bought 310 acres of ranch property in Noyes Valley about 10 miles to the north—flat, productive bottomland. Within a year they had four horses, 10 mules, numerous wagons, mowing and reaping machines, 100 head of cattle, and two new houses, one for Edgar and his new bride from Wisconsin, and one for Albert and the wife he hoped to find. They sold all the hay, grain, meat, hams, bacon, milk, and butter they could produce, and they prospered.

During the next few years, Albert managed the farm and became involved in the operations of the mule train route over Scott Mountain pass, impassible to wagons but the most direct supply route between Scott Valley and the south. (The original "Hudson Bay" trail established by trappers.) He began by selling hay from the ranch to feed the oxen used to keep the pass open for the mule trains in the winter months. He would load up a four mule wagon with hay at the ranch before daylight, travel 6 miles to the foot of Scott Mountain, and then head up the rough Scott Mountain trail 6 miles to the north end of the pass. There he would unload the hay, turn the wagon, and head back down the mountain, a round trip of 24 miles in one day. In the coming years Albert would invest in his own mules and establish the profitable Denny Train.

By 1862 Albert felt that he was financially secure enough to seek a wife; but to his disappointment, as he later wrote, any girl over 15 in Scott Valley was "either married, a prostitute, or a hurdy-gurdy."

("Hurdy gurdys" or "gurdy girls" were saloon entertainers (not prostitutes) who sang, danced and interacted with the customers. An agency in Yreka supplied gurdy girls to mining town saloons by the day or week, especially during the slow winter months, simply to drum up business.)

And so at age 28, just eleven years after departing from Wisconsin with $1.50 in his pocket, Albert was headed back east to Vermont where his father had been born and where he had family he hardly knew. This time his transcontinental journey would be much easier. He traveled by horseback on the trail over Scott Mountain to Red Bluff, and then took a riverboat to San Francisco. From there he took a side-wheel steam ship to Panama, rode the new railroad to the Atlantic side, and took another steamer to New York. If the weather cooperated, he could be in Vermont in a few weeks.

Albert departed California with $1000 cash, an invitation from relatives in Northfield Vermont to visit them, and a letter of recommendation from his father to his father's younger brother, Uncle Joseph Denny. It included this paragraph:

> "Our second son Albert starts for the States tomorrow morning...he goes to Vermont to seek a wife in the land of his father and if not among his kindred as least among his kindreds friends and acquaintances. I hope and trust that he will find a wife among the green Mountain girls, and although she may not possess jewels of silver or jewels of gold, yet if she possesses a sound discretion and a good heart she has a far greater treasure."

In a postscript to this letter, written in the middle of the Civil War, Amasa Denny makes his views clear: "We hope this most wicked rebellion will soon be crushed out, and the leaders and instigators of it be shown such mercy as is usually shown murderers and thieves."

Eliza Roxanna Webber

Meanwhile in Vermont, a "sweet pretty schoolteacher," Eliza Roxanna Webber, accepted an invitation to visit her friend Mrs. Robinson in Northfield. There she looked out the window and saw Albert chopping wood. When he saw her looking out the window at him, he said to himself "Albert there's the girl for me."

Eliza was born in Vermont in 1842, attended the Spalding Academy in Barrie, Vermont, and was a schoolteacher. Her parents lived on a small rocky farm near Glover Vermont and were educated but dirt poor. Albert was smitten with Eliza and without delay he proposed.

Eliza Webber photo courtesy of her great-grandson, Tomas Eller.

She of course was faced with a poignant choice: should she go to California with a man she had met only a few weeks before, and leave her home, her family, and everything she has ever known? In those days a decision such as this often meant that you would never see your family again. After deliberation and prayer, and loving encouragement from her brother, she said yes.

Documents from that time tell us that Albert was 6 feet tall, weighed 169 pounds, had a ruddy complexion, blue eyes, brown hair, a few whiskers and a mustache.

Eliza herself described him in a letter to her brother:

Albert Hendrickson Denny, 1870s.
Courtesy of Thomas Eller.

"He has firm integrity, a good moral character, and a strong will and perseverance. He is large, strong and athletically built, with no outside polish, he is a good mathematician but poor in grammar, he used to study when they were mining. He is a great reader especially the poets, he will quote page after page of Shakespeare, Byron, Scott, and Burns, and can repeat a great portion of Milton's Paradise Lost. He is well posted on the war, has excellent general information, he is set in his own way, has a mind of his own and thinks it a good one."

(Letter to her brother Alpha Webber. Alpha later moved to Oakland, and Dene Denny boarded with him during her three years of high school.)

Albert and Eliza were married in Vermont on April 17, 1864. On May 4 they left Northfield by train for a visit to Niagara Falls, and from there they went on to New York City where they visited Barnum's Museum and "many picture galleries," walked through Frederick Law Olmstead's new Central Park, strolled up and down Broadway, and saw a production of Hamlet featuring Edwin Booth. Twice on one Sunday they heard the great Henry Ward Beecher speak at his Congregational Church in Brooklyn. (Albert later sponsored the building of the Congregational Church in Scott Valley.)

They departed from New York on the steamer Ocean Queen, crossed the Isthmus of Panama by railroad, and sailed on the steamer Constitution from Panama City to San Francisco. After a few days in San Francisco, they traveled by riverboat to Sacramento, train to Lincoln, stagecoach through Marysville, Chico, Shasta, Trinity Center, then over Scott Mountain and down into Scott Valley.

The entire journey to California—Vermont, Niagara Falls, Manhattan, Panama, San Francisco, Siskiyou—took 37 days. Only 12 years before, Albert and Edgar had spent 7 months on the trail from Wisconsin to California.

Callahan's Ranch and South Fork

The Siskiyou Gold Rush began in 1851 when gold was discovered on the South Fork of the Scott River. That fall Mr. M. B. Callahan bought some property at the junction of the East Fork and the South Fork, at the foot of a peak known as Mt. Bolivar. There he built a cabin and sold "slender meals" (plain food) to the miners and travelers. The following summer he opened a hotel and expanded the business to a store, and before long a town began to grow up around Callahan's original cabin. Miners and ranchers came to Callahan's for food and goods, and

Callahan's was the trailhead for mule trains taking freight (and sometimes passengers) over Scott Mountain to Red Bluff or over the more rugged route southwest into the Salmon River watershed. The "Callahan's Ranch" Post Office opened in 1858 but the town changed its name officially to Callahan in 1892.

Upon his return to Scott Valley with Eliza in 1864 Albert found that his younger brothers Thomas and Joseph had bought the Callahan Store. Mr. Callahan was long gone and the original store and hotel from 1852 had been expanded by previous owners before Tom and Joe Denny bought it and changed its name to the Denny Brothers Store. The town was becoming an important commercial location in Scott Valley, and the Denny Brothers business served the ranchers, travelers, and miners.

While his brothers minded the store, Albert managed the lucrative Denny Ranch while he continued to expand his teaming business: he now owned and managed mule trains transporting goods back and forth across the mountain routes into the Sacramento Valley as far as Red Bluff.

Eliza Denny gave birth to their first child, Emma Jane, in 1865, and a second daughter, Mary Alma, followed in 1866. Eliza, now 25, wrote to her mother back in Vermont on July 27, 1866,

> "California possesses everything but society but we did enjoy some on the evening of the fourth when we all were over to White Hall to a dance. Now, mother, you a New England woman of high principles, please understand it did me no harm, for I did not dance but only looked on."

In 1867 Albert and Eliza sold their half of the Denny ranch to Edgar and his wife for $3,000 and moved to the now-flourishing town of Callahan, where they purchased a home for $350. (Albert lived in Scott Valley within a dozen miles of Callahan until his death in 1907.)

The newly-built Denny Brothers Store in Callahan was doing well; Albert invested $3,000 and became a silent partner with his brothers, while he continued his mule team business.

1881 illustration of the Denny home in Callahan, Dene Denny's birthplace in 1885.
Source: Wells, History of Siskiyou County. Courtesy of the author.

In 1870 Tom and Joe Denny bought a second store for $1500 in the still-busy mining camp of South Fork, the site of the original gold discovery in Northern California. By that time the Scott Mountain road was becoming more passable by wheeled vehicles, and the mule teams were becoming less important. Mules were being sold and teams were consolidating. Albert cashed in the Denny Train altogether and involved himself fully in running the South Fork store; he, Eliza, and the two girls spent most of their time living in South Fork, and not in their new home in Callahan.

The town of Callahan, with a few hundred inhabitants, might have been far from genteel (see the photo from the 1880s below), but it was a real town with a Main Street, two stores, a hotel, a school house, a Catholic church, a meeting hall and a few houses with nice fences.

South Fork, by contrast, was a miners' town like Deadwood, only bigger, more established and probably more unsavory. It was rough, loud, and very dirty—a place for hurdy girls and not for a mother and her two young daughters, age 4 and 5. Eliza Denny was not happy, and wrote to her mother in Vermont:

1874 advertisement in the Yreka Journal. French was one of several partners who were involved in the Denny stores. *Courtesy of the author.*

"Although I have the best of husbands and a comfortable home, I do not like it here [in South Fork]. It is very difficult to think of making New England women of my little girls in this mining town. I hope they do not have to go to school here or get to know the heathenish surroundings, but that soon we can move to another home and be placed under better influences."

While in South Fork, Albert re-entered the mining business as co-investor in the Montezuma Placer Mine, one of the best mines in Siskiyou County. About a mile from Callahan, it produced nearly one hundred ounces of gold per day for a decade and netted profits between $10,000 and $15,000 a year. The partners sold the mine in the 1880s for $50,000, after which it continued to produce for decades.

Among the Denny brothers, Albert was the most savvy businessman, and by 1872 he had become the managing partner of the Denny Brothers business. Albert and Eliza returned to their house in Callahan, and added several more rooms to make the place more comfortable. Albert was active in local affairs, and was appointed justice of the peace in 1873. Several more children were born, and during the 1870s the Denny house in Callahan was a social center: Eliza had a charming home, an ample budget, a large and happy family, and a devoted husband. They entertained visitors locally and for overnight stays of days at a time. Their parties were famous for card games and other entertainment.

In 1869 the first rail link was opened between East Coast cities and San Francisco. In 1874, to celebrate their tenth wedding anniversary, Albert and Eliza made a trip to the East Coast, but Panama was no longer in their itinerary. They first traveled to Oakland by coach and riverboat, and stayed briefly in the home of Eliza's older brother Alpha and his family. Albert, Eliza, and Alpha departed Oakland in early July on what was colloquially known as the "overland train," a multi-connection trip from San Francisco to the East Coast. (The name "Overland" would not be officially used by the railroad for

1881 illustration of the Denny Store in Callahan.
From: Wells, History of Siskiyou County. Courtesy of the author.

another decade.) They spent the summer in Vermont, the first time Eliza had been with her family since the death of her father three years before. In early September, Albert, Eliza, her brother Alpha, and their widowed mother, Maria Webber, traveled the route of the overland train back to Oakland. Maria lived there with Alpha and his family until her death in 1887.

Two accounts state that in 1879 Albert spent $700 on a piano, although the record does not specify if that amount included the cost of shipping the piano to Etna by train and mule wagon, plus the expense of the repairs the instrument no doubt would have needed after it arrived. It must have survived the trip unscathed; several late-19th century sources mention the piano in the Denny home, and that it became a center of attention among friends and neighbors in Scott Valley. Around that time, Albert also brought back a brand-new carriage from San Francisco in which he and Eliza would take overnight trips together.

The Denny store in Callahan was flourishing; it served as the Wells Fargo express office, the telegraph office, and the US Post Office (Albert was Postmaster). Freight wagons pulled up to the front of the store so the bags of flour and grain and other staples could be unloaded into the specially built hydraulic elevator that took the supplies to the basement. Miners cashed in their precious raw gold for food and other goods. During the height of the mining days it is said that the Denny company turned in over $1 million worth of raw gold each year.

Gardner Landon was the husband of Sylvia Denny Landon, Albert Denny's youngest daughter. He did not know Eliza, but from family records he relates:

> Eliza Webber Denny was no ordinary woman and all the family records show that Albert realized this fact. Eliza was an excellent mother, cook, nurse, housekeeper, teacher of the children, and general manager of the family affairs. These were not the qualities, however, that made her such a valuable business asset. It was her outgoing warm personality, her ability to meet and make friends with everyone, and to be able to cope, no matter who or how may people Albert brought home. (Gardner Landon, unpublished biography of Albert Denny)

But now in 1879 Eliza Roxanna Denny was neither happy nor well. Ever since leaving Vermont she held the hope that after Albert had made his fortune they would all return to the East Coast. As each of the past sixteen years had passed, the grim reality had become more inescapable: she was now Eliza Denny of Scott Valley, California. She was 37 years old, and she would live in this remote frontier community for the rest of her life.

Eliza had a history of asthma, and had developed a chronic cough during their time living in primitive conditions in South Fork. In addition, like so many women of her time, she was overwhelmed with so many babies: she had given birth eight times in fourteen years: Emma, 1865; Mary Alma, 1866; Albert Alpha, 1867; Joseph Amasa, 1869; Phoebe, 1871; Eliza, 1873; Karl, 1876; and Robert, 1878. As the birth of her ninth child approached she became anxious and apprehensive, and several times mentioned or wrote to her family of her feeling of impending death.

Edmund, the ninth child of Eliza and Albert Denny, was born on November 23, 1880, but Eliza's postpartum recovery proceeded slowly. Her breathing became more difficult, and she could not sleep lying down but had to sit up in bed or in a chair at all times. In December she seemed to rally, and she made several local visits over the Christmas and New Year holidays, but her shortness of breath never left her, and the cold winter air did her no good. In early January 1881, she suddenly developed a fever; the local doctor diagnosed her illness as pleuropneumonia, and several other physicians were consulted, but Eliza continued to grow weaker. Finally on January 15, Eliza Roxanna Webber Denny left this world, just ten weeks after her 38th birthday, leaving behind a 46-year-old husband and nine children including a 7-week-old baby.

Albert wrote a lengthy and emotional letter to his mother-in-law in Vermont, describing in exacting detail the final weeks and days of Eliza's life. He was clearly stricken.

> "Oh, what shall I do without her? In all the wide world I could not have found so good, so loving, so sweet, so pure a wife as she. And it seems so hard to have her taken in the prime of life leaving me with our nine children to take care of alone."

Albert's father Amasa had died more than a decade before, but Albert's mother was still living with them and she could help take care of the children. However in April, just four months after Eliza's death, Sally Ann Hendrickson Denny also died. The final blow came on July 28, when baby Edmund, the last child of Albert and Eliza, died at the age of eight months.

Death was a frequent visitor to 19th century families, especially in remote spots like Scott Valley, but these three deaths in such a short timespan must have been a vicious shock to Albert. He had lost his wife, his newborn son, and his mother, and was now left alone with eight children ranging in age from 2 to 16.

Gertrude Althea Cadwell

It was unlike Albert to allow sorrow and loss to claim him forever. It was in his nature to stay active and he was the sole owner of a very busy business. He also needed a wife, and a mother for his children.

In September 1881, he made a trip south to Petaluma in Sonoma County, where he courted and attended church with a young woman, but nothing developed from that encounter. Sometime in the late winter or early spring of 1882 he met Gertrude Althea Cadwell, a schoolteacher born in Shasta in 1857. She was the daughter of an American father and a Welsh mother who had emigrated overland from New York to Shasta in the 1850s. Gertrude's father had died when she was only nine, and she understood the pain felt by children who have lost a parent.

On September 14, 1882, Albert and Gertrude were married in Callahan. He was 47 and she was 26. On their honeymoon they went to San Francisco and Yosemite for two weeks, and upon returning home they decided that they wanted to be alone in the Callahan house for the first year of their marriage. Albert's two oldest girls Emma (17) and Mary (16) went to Petaluma where they boarded with an aunt. The older boys went to the Denny ranch, which was continuing to be a profitable venture. In 1882 it produced more than 5,000 bushels of grain and more than 300 tons of hay.

On the day she and Albert were married, Gertrude became the stepmother of eight children, age 17, 16, 15, 13, 11, 9, 6, and 3. Without delay, she and Albert continued to add to the Denny family, beginning in 1883 with their first child, Mildred. On February 11, 1885, another daughter was born, Albert's 11th child and his 2nd with Gertrude. They named her Ethel Adele Denny. (When she grew up she called herself Dene, and she is one of the two reasons for this book.)

Gertrude Althea Cadwell, second wife of Albert Denny and mother of Dene Denny. *Courtesy of Thomas Eller.*

The 1885 Siskiyou County Directory describes the prospering town of Callahan the year Dene was born:

"A post, express and telegraph town, forty-two miles south of Yreka. It is surrounded by quite a favorable mining district, as well as some good farming land. It has two good hotels, two general stores, a church, blacksmith shop, etc. It has a population of one hundred and fifty, and lies a little west of the future route of the California and Oregon Railroad."

Albert Denny had a total of eighteen children—nine by each of his two wives—and at least two of those offspring died in infancy. This list represents only actual documented live births or baptisms, and does not include undocumented stillbirths or miscarriages.

It is worth noting that even after giving birth to nine more of Albert's children, and continuing to raise several of them after his death, Gertrude Denny outlived her husband by forty-two years, and died in Siskiyou in 1949 at the age of 92.

The children of Eliza Roxanna Webber *b. Oct 29 1842, Glover, VT; m. Apr 17, 1864* *d. 15 Jan 1881, Callahan, CA*	The children of Gertrude Althea Cadwell *b. Jun 12 1857, Shasta, CA; m. Sept 14, 1882* *d. Jun 3 1949, Stanislaus, CA*
Emma J. Denny, 1865–?	Mildred Denny, 1883–1974
Mary Alma Denny, 1866–1966	**Ethel Adele "Dene" Denny, 1885–1959**
Albert Alpha Denny, 1867–1942	Harvey Denny, 1887–1887
Joseph Amasa Denny, 1869–1930	Gertrude A. Denny, 1888–1916
Phoebe A. Denny, 1871–1949	Margaret M. Denny, 1890–?
Eliza Webber "Lila" Denny, 1873–1950	Edward P. Denny, 1892–?
Karl Van de Water Denny, 1876–1961	Genevieve Marie Denny, 1895–1949
Robert Roy Denny, 1878–1954	Homer Denny, 1897–1984
Edmund W. Denny, 1880–1881	Sylvia Denny, 1902–1992

Oak Farm, on the Denny ranch in Scott Valley, 1890. This was Dene's home until she was 15. The family photo opposite page was taken on the front porch of this house. *Courtesy of Thomas Eller.*

Albert, Gertrude, and the children lived at the house in Callahan until 1888, when Albert paid $12,000 for the 800-acre McConoughy Ranch and renamed it Oak Farm. Unlike Callahan, which was located in the cul-de-sac at the south end of Scott Valley, Oak Farm was farther north, in a wide pastured vale today called McConoughy Gulch. On that property Albert built a beautiful large home in which the Denny family lived for many years.

The Denny children attended school about six miles north of Oak Farm in Etna, Scott Valley's largest town. In inclement weather, especially in the winter, travel was difficult, and so that his children could attend school with regularity, Albert bought a house in Etna where the entire family lived during the winter months.

The Dennys loved to entertain guests, and the Etna house was enlarged in the 1890s. A guest room was kept ready for the frequent overnight visitors, and the children named it "the strangers' room." Albert and Gertrude were active in town life: Albert was a founding sponsor of the Etna library, and he helped underwrite the construction of the Congregational Church, the first church in Etna. They were among the first in the region to champion the cause of women's suffrage, and Gertrude was a strong supporter of prohibition.

In the summers they returned to Oak Farm where the children participated in ranching activities and learned to ride. (Horseback was often the most efficient means of travel locally in an area that was still mostly roadless.) Like her father, Dene was strikingly tall and lanky, and was totally involved in the lifestyle and activities on the ranch.

> There were lots of brothers and sisters and we were all ardent ranchers, rode miles and miles every day, and even we girls were taught how to handle cattle.
> (Dene Denny, 1939 interview.)

Among the laborers and ranch hands there were many local Shasta Indians and immigrants from Mexico and Europe. As an adult Dene mentioned to musicologist Alan Lomax that she had loved to hear the variety of languages, music and songs. Lomax believed that this early multicultural experience opened Dene to a wider musical appreciation throughout her life.

Albert became more of a country gentleman, ran his numerous business ventures, and amassed considerable capital, which he put to good use. He traveled regularly to San Francisco to order goods for the stores, but grew tired of taking huge amounts of cash with him. Convinced

Denny family on the porch at Oak Farm, summer, 1893. In order of descending age: Albert (58), Gertrude (36), Karl (17), Phoebe (22), Mildred (10), Ethel/Dene (8), Gertrude, (5) Margaret (3), and Edward (1). Albert and Gertrude would have three more children, in 1895, 1897, and 1902. *Courtesy of Thomas Eller.*

that Scott Valley commerce could support it, he raised capital and founded the Denny Bank in Etna, which later became the Scott Valley Bank.

The Scott Valley Creamery was also founded by Albert, who served as the first president. That is a long way from selling milk to the miners for 75¢ per gallon.

Jacob Bar, one of Albert's business partners, bought a share of Albert's retail business, and together the two men developed and managed what were in effect the first chain stores in California. During Albert's lifetime there were as many as nine "Denny-Bar Stores," and at their peak there were sixteen branches, the last of which closed in 1944.

Albert took great interest in the upbringing of his children and he was committed to their intellectual and cultural education. The beautiful piano he had bought in 1879 was a centerpiece of social activity in the house, especially under the fingers of his 11th child, little Ethel Adele.

"My love of music started so early that I don't remember when." (Dene Denny, 1938 Interview)

The Denny houses in Siskiyou were large and the family was social; the piano was in the house before Dene was born, and her older sisters took piano lessons, so music was a part of Dene's life from birth. As an adult, although Dene could not remember when she actually began playing, she did mention to an interviewer the thrill she felt when she first could stretch the thumb and little finger of one hand to reach an octave on the piano keyboard.

This detail of the photo on the porch shows Dene and her father when she was 8 years old. (Although he looks like her grandfather, Albert was only 58, a testament to the rigors of pioneer life.)

The small hand on Albert's shoulder was already well acquainted with the piano keyboard. Six years after this photo was taken, the 14-year-old Dene was piano accompanist for a selection heard in the May 1899 concert of the Etna Brass Band. It was a new and popular song by Gussie Davis—*In the Baggage Coach Ahead*—in an arrangement for singer, trumpet, and piano. Three decades later, in her early 40s, Dene had a brief, fascinating, and intense career as a concert pianist, but this was her first documented public performance.

Detail of photo on previous page. Oak Farm, Etna, 1893. Albert Hendrickson Denny (58) and his 11th child, Ethel Adele Denny (8 1/2). Albert is holding baby Edward.

By the time she reached her early teens it was clear that Dene needed a quality of schooling and piano training that Siskiyou County could not provide. Several of her older siblings had been schooled in other places while boarding with relatives or friends, and in the spring of 1900 Albert and Gertrude made plans to send Dene to San Francisco where she could finish high school and study privately with one of the city's fine piano teachers.

1890s photo of the original A. H. Denny Store in Callahan. Dene Denny was born in Callahan in 1885.
Courtesy of the Siskiyou Historical Society.

Two views of Etna, California, the home town of Dene Denny, born here in 1885. Above: late 1890s. Right: c.1900, the year Dene moved to Oakland. *Library of Congress.*

In July 1900, Dene (now 15) moved with her older sister Mildred (16) from Siskiyou to Oakland, where they lived with their "Uncle Alpha," an older brother of Albert Denny's first wife, Eliza.

Alpha Augustus Webber (1835-1920) and his wife, Amelia, moved to San Francisco in 1866, after after he graduated from the University of Vermont. In California he became a successful agent for the Continental Life Insurance Company, and made enough money to become an investor and eventually president of a gold mining company and a water utility company. By 1900 the Webbers had three older children (31, 24, 21) living elsewhere, and only their fourth child (Alpha Augustus, Jr., age 10) was living with them in their comfortable house at 1924 Myrtle Street in Oakland. Dene lived with Alpha and Amelia during her three years at Oakland High School and for at least the first year of her studies at UC Berkeley.

While attending high school in Oakland, Dene became a piano pupil of the 29-year-old Gyula Ormay. Born in Russia in 1871, Ormay was active in San Francisco musical circles as a chamber musician and first rate accompanist until his death in 1947. During the 1920s he was the Music Director of Graumann's Imperial Theater on Market Street in San Francisco, and later Music Director of the San Francisco NBC Studio.

In May 1903, Dene and Mildred graduated from Oakland High School, and in September, Dene began her freshman year at the University of California in Berkeley. She had gone from riding horseback through the valleys of Siskiyou County to a prestigious and rigorous university located in a thriving metropolitan area that was becoming more exciting every year.

Just 45 miles south of Berkeley in that same month, Hazel Watrous graduated from the 3-year teacher training program at the California Normal School in San José. Hazel was 19 and Dene was 18. They would spend the next 18 years living and working in San Francisco and the East Bay before actually meeting each other.

Jefferds & Watrous

Hazel Watrous' grandfather possessed a perfect name for a prospector panning for gold in the Sierra Nevada foothills. Forrest Gooch Jefferds plays an early but important role in the story in this book. He was born in 1829 in Brownsville, Maine, to Alpheus and Rebecca Gerrish Jefferds, and he lived on the family farm until the age of 15, when:

> "...in the fall of 1844 I bought my time* of father. I paid him about $125. I went to Lowell Massachusetts, where I got work at a printing press for 75¢ a day. I paid $1.25 a week for room and board." (F.G.J. Autobiography, transcribed by Minnie Jefferds Watrous.)
>
> [* An apprentice—or, in this case, the son of a poor farmer—was said to "buy his time" from the master for the unexpired remainder of his time of service, in order to be released from his obligation.]

Forrest worked various odd jobs in the Boston area until January, 1847, when he enlisted in the Massachusetts Volunteer Regiment and found himself in Mexico for the final year of the Mexican-American War. After mustering out of the Army at the age of 19, he signed a three-year contract in a manufacturing plant in Boston at 75¢ a day, and by the time his contract was up he was 22 and had made up his mind to go to California.

After saying goodbye to his father and family in Watertown, Maine, he traveled to New York City and on August 31, 1851, Forrest departed on a seven-day steamer trip to Panama. This was six years before Amasa and Sally Ann Denny made their trip from New York to Siskiyou, and Forrest Jefferds' experience was quite different: the trans-isthmus railroad had not yet been built, and so instead of paying $25 for a few hours on the train as the Denny family would do in 1857, Forrest paid upwards of $100 for a guided trek across the isthmus.

"The Isthmus of Panama on the height of the Chagres River, 1850." Oil painting by Charles Christian Nahl. Travelers sit in a broad canoe being poled upstream by Indians.

He and a dozen others hired a boat and Indian guides to take them up the Chagres River for five days, sometimes making only two or three miles a day. It was fiercely hot and the mosquitoes were notoriously vicious in the Panamanian summer. Finally they hired mules to carry their baggage and walked the final 18 miles.

In Panama City they laid up about a week and then took passage to San Francisco on the twin-side-wheel steamer Republic. 21 miles below San Francisco during a heavy early morning fog, the steamer ran on to the rocks and tore a hole in the hull. The boat broke free, and an anchor was dropped to keep it off the rocks, but the boiler fires had been extinguished so the boat was dead in the water. A crew member went ashore in a rowboat, acquired a horse, and rode to San Francisco for help. The passengers were divided into four crews and took turns bailing for 24 hours until the old steamer California came for them a few hours after dawn. After their all–night ordeal, the passengers expected to be taken onto the rescuing boat, but were instead ordered to remain on the Republic and bail all day while the California towed the boat 20 miles to San Francisco Bay. By the time they arrived, the boat was half underwater. Amazingly, the wooden-hulled Republic was salvaged and remained in service another decade.

Forrest left New York on August 31, 1851; crossed the Isthmus of Panama by canoe and on foot; survived a shipwreck in the Pacific Ocean; and arrived in San Francisco on October 5, 1851. His entire journey took 35 days. This was only one year before Albert and Edgar Denny spent seven months on the overland trail from Wisconsin to California.

After remaining in San Francisco for two days the 22-year-old Forrest started for Nevada County, in the northern part of the Sierra Nevada gold rush area. He traveled up to Sacramento by steamer, and from there by stagecoach to Nevada City, where his brother Phineas was already working a claim and bringing in $200–$300 every week. Jefferds worked various claims in the Grass Valley/Nevada City area all winter and never cleared less than $100/week.

Before leaving Boston, Forrest became engaged to a young lady, Miss Zanetta Whitney, a native of Waltham, Massachusetts. Forrest learned that a Federal judge from Massachusetts was living in Marysville and was sending for his family to join him there, and Forrest arranged for Zanetta to accompany them.

Again they came by ship, but did not cross the Isthmus of Panama. A propeller driven steamship called the City of Pittsburgh advertised boldly that it could sail from New York to San Francisco in 60 days around the tip of South America. Disaster plagued much of the journey: the steamer broke down near Rio de Janeiro, and then in the harbor of Valparaiso the boat caught fire and burned, but the passengers and baggage were saved.

Zanetta Whitney and her traveling companions finally arrived in San Francisco and traveled by riverboat to Marysville where Forrest met them on New Year's Day 1853. It was a winter of heavy rains, and the flood waters were so high that the river boat sailed up the main street of Marysville. Because Zanetta's travel had been so perilous and the engaged couple had encountered so many difficulties in getting together, Judge May insisted on officiating at their wedding that very night.

The newlyweds settled down in the aptly named town of Rough and Ready, west of Grass Valley. Their first home was a rude affair made of shakes and partitioned off inside with calico, and in that cabin on July 25, 1854, their first child Edward M. Jefferds was born.

Forrest continued to work on his nearby claims until 1855, when, he, Zanetta, and their baby boy left their house in Rough and Ready and moved 15 miles west to Timbuctoo in Yuba County. Timbuctoo is situated on a dramatic U-shaped bend in the Yuba River—an area of productive sand bars in and around the river. At its height, Timbuctoo and nearby Smartsville were busy mining towns, with churches, stores, businesses, hotels, saloons, and (in Timbuctoo) a Wells Fargo office and a theater. The wealth flowing from the placer ore of the Timbuctoo Bend enabled the construction of permanent buildings of brick and wood, a few of which still survive.

Forrest bought an interest in a large claim in the Timbuctoo Ravine, and there for a total of six years he engaged in hydraulic mining.

In California, from 1853 to 1884, the most aggressive and infamous method of placer mining was "hydraulicking," a productive but brutally destructive method of excavating huge amounts of ore. Powerful jets of water were used to wash massive amounts of soil, sand, and gravel into sluices where the ore was screened and processed to extract the gold particles. Hydraulic mining took place over broad areas of Gold Rush country, and left the landscape horribly scarred. The Timbuctoo Bend in the Yuba River is located between Grass Valley and Yuba City and the map coordinates are 39°13'39.6"N, 121°19'13.1"W. The ravages of the hydraulic mining in that area are clearly visible in satellite images today.

Hydraulic mining in Yuba County, 1870s. *Engraving from a German geology textbookcourtesy of the author.*

Hydraulicking also became a serious economic and environmental problem. After the screening and sluicing had removed the gold particles, the tons of unwanted soil and sand were carried far downstream, decreasing the depth of the navigable rivers and forming sand bars in parts of San Francisco Bay. During floods in the 1860s and 1870s, the sediment also spread over the flat Central Valley farmland and in some areas it raised the level of the ground by several feet. An "Anti-Debris Association" was formed to stop the process, and in 1884 the flushing of debris into streams was banned, gradually bringing the hydraulic mining frenzy in California's gold country to an end.

Forrest Jefferds practiced hydraulic mining from 1855 until 1861, but began to lose his taste for it when a gravel embankment collapsed and completely buried him. It took his frantic co-workers several minutes to excavate him, and he almost died of suffocation. His left leg was broken, but he said later that they got several dollars worth of gold from the gravel in his mouth. Several other close calls motivated him to begin the slow process of cashing out and moving down to the lowlands.

In 1858, while still mining in Timbuctoo, Forrest paid $800 for 80 acres near Visalia in Tulare County, southwest of San Francisco. Tulare's borders encompass a richly productive area of Central Valley farm and orchard land as well as most of present-day Sequoia National Park. Forrest went to San Francisco to complete the paperwork for the real estate purchase, and then traveled to Visalia to see his new property for the first time. The route Forrest took from downtown San Francisco to Visalia is about 240 miles, and can easily be driven today in under four hours. Forrest's own description gives a sense of what it was like to travel in 1858.

The trip from San Francisco to Visalia was made in a stagecoach, the Overland Stage, which ran at that time from San Francisco all the way to Texas. We took the stage [departed] at noon near the old City Hall on Portsmouth Square in San Francisco. We went south through San Mateo and arrived in San José about sundown. We passed Gilroy in the night and went over Pacheco Pass and into the San Joaquin Valley before daylight. We rode all the next day and into the next morning when we arrived in Visalia, being 48 hours on the trip. (ibid.)

After acquiring and securing the Visalia ranch, Forrest hired someone to plant out trees and vines and improve the property while he went back north to continue working on his claims on the Yuba River.

He built a small house in the ravine south of the river bend, between Timbuctoo and Smartsville, and there on September 27, 1858, Forrest and Zanetta's second child was born, a daughter named Minnie. Her birth certificate colorfully lists her birthplace as "up the ravine between Timbuctoo and Smartsville." Minnie Jefferds was the mother of Hazel Watrous and she will be part of this story until her death in 1941 in Carmel.

Main Street, Timbuctoo, 1860s. *Courtesy of the author.*

Forrest worked the Timbuctoo claim until September 1861 when he gave up mining completely and moved with his family to the Visalia ranch. Two full growing seasons had passed since the planting of his trees and vines, and his orchard was starting to produce.

In 1862 Forrest filed a homestead on 80 adjoining acres, and in 1860 he bought 160 more. He now had 320 acres, on which he raised grain, corn, fruits of all kinds, and livestock including hogs, horses and cattle.

Zannetta Jefferds had long suffered from poor health, and in 1877 she was diagnosed with cancer. Forrest rented a house in Visalia where she could be under more constant care, but by early fall there was nothing more to be done for her. They moved back out to their ranch, and there Zanetta lingered, becoming ever more ill, until she passed away on October 20, 1868.

Forrest was stricken at the loss of the wife Minnie later referred to as "his dear beloved." He sold all his remaining mining interests for $5,000 by the end of the year, and, just as Albert Denny had done, Forrest began looking for a wife, and for a mother for his three children, aged 14, 10, and 8.

In 1869, Forrest met and married Elinor Frakes. Born in Ohio in 1831, she came to California with her parents on the Oregon Trail in 1850. After arriving in California she married Tilden Reed, with whom she had five children. He went on to become Tulare County sheriff and tax collector, and had died two years before.

The only child of Elinor Frakes and Forrest Jefferds was a daughter—Nellie Forrest Jefferds, born in 1872. That same year Forrest was elected Tulare County Assessor. They prospered in Visalia, and in the early 1880s Forrest and Elinor made a trip to the East Coast: Michigan, Illinois, Ohio, Washington DC, Philadelphia, New York, Boston, and finally as Forrest himself said, "down to Maine, my native state."

The Watrous Family

...we children grew up in an atmosphere of pioneering in the arts. (Hazel Watrous)

We know little about Minnie Jefferds, the daughter of Forrest and Zanetta Jefferds who was born "up the ravine" near Timbuctoo in 1858. However we do know that in 1878, in Visalia, Minnie married a photographer named Stephen West Watrous.

Stephen Watrous was born in Massachusetts in 1844 (according to a 2-paragraph obituary) and came with his family to California in 1852 (according to his daughter a century later). There is not much else in the public records regarding him, his family or his origins. By 1865 he was living in San Bernardino, California, about 50 miles east of Los Angeles, and by 1866 he had established a "photographing business" there.

In San Bernardino in 1868, Stephen married a young woman named Lucy, a teenager from Michigan, to whom the public records give no last name, only the initial "L". Lucy bore Stephen two sons, both of whom died in infancy in 1871 and 1872. At that point Stephen left San Bernardino, not to return for 18 years. History loses track of Lucy L. altogether, as it does so many people in stories like this about pioneers in the 19th century, especially the long-suffering wives and mothers.

By 1874, two years after the death of his second son, the San Francisco City Directory lists Stephen Watrous as single and employed as a "photograph printer" for the Jacob Shew photography studio in San Francisco, which also was listed as his residence.

Jacob Shew and his three brothers were born in the 1820s in Watertown, New York. In 1838 the Frenchman Louis Daguerre invented the first practicable photographic process, which bore his name. Samuel Morse, the eminent painter and co-inventor of the telegraph, studied this new Daguerreotype process in France and introduced it to the US in 1839 with great fanfare; the Shew brothers read an article by Morse and all four of them moved to New York to be among Morse's first pupils.

By the 1850s, Jacob and William were doing business in San Francisco and were known for their landscape and portrait Daguerreotypes. Their separate studio galleries were near Montgomery and Sacramento Streets, a block from the location of the modern-day Transamerica Building. In 1874 when Stephen Watrous joined them, the Shew brothers had  moved beyond the outmoded Daguerre method and were using the new wet plate technique. A glass plate coated with wet emulsion was inserted in the camera to capture the image, and then was developed quickly before the emulsion had a chance to dry. The chemistry and timing were tricky enough in the studio, but even more so in the field, where a portable darkroom was used. Using this method, the Shew studios did a good business in portrait and architectural photography.

Stephen Watrous worked for Shew for more than four years, and during that time he lived on the premises, which was Jacob Shew's residence as well. According to the City Directories, Watrous was a "phot. developer" and probably worked in the darkroom developing glass negatives and printing photographs.

Forty years before, the Shew brothers had been among the first to create images with the new Daguerrotype method, and now they and Stephen were experimenting with the recently developed technology of gelatin emulsion, still in its infancy, which enabled photographers to work with dry glass plates that needn't be rushed to the darkroom immediately after the shot was taken. The 1870s and 1880s were decades of fast change and progress in the technology of photography and Stephen was attuned to these developments.

In early 1878 fire destroyed the Shew gallery. Apparently a volatile man, Jacob could not take the stress of the loss and took his own life with a revolver. The coroner's report ruled that his cause of death was "Pecuniary embarrassment." (See Appendix for a timeline of 19th century photography.)

Meeting Minnie

By the late 1870s, California's central valley was becoming an important agricultural region, and it was on the edge of some of the world's most beautiful mountains. Visalia was Tulare County's most important center for agricultural shipping and commerce, and the citizens hoped that the new railroad being planned would be routed near the town. Stephen Watrous had spent five years working for someone else in San Francisco, and in now the spring of 1878 he headed for Visalia to be an independent photographer.

In his studio in Visalia Stephen took the portraits and the smaller photographic "visiting cards," and he also captured photographs of mines, mountains, and local agriculture with his view camera and wooden tripod.

At that time, Forrest Gooch Jefferds was happy and successful. He was Tulare County Assessor, and lived on his farm near Visalia with his second wife Elinor and their two children, Tilden (14, son of Elinor's first husband) and Nellie Forrest (6). Also with them was Forrest's daughter by his first wife—Minnie (20). Sometime that year, Minnie and Stephen met, and by the end of 1878 they were married.

In 1884 Stephen and Minnie Watrous had their first child, a daughter named Hazel, who is one of the two reasons for this book. Two years later, Hazel's younger sister Zanetta was born, named for Forrest Jefferds' "dear beloved" first wife.

Also in 1884, Forrest Jefferds sold the farm and orchard in Visalia for a "fine profit" and he, Elinor, and their 12-year-old daughter Nellie moved to Oakland, where Forrest dabbled in the real estate and furniture businesses for a few years.

Stephen, Minnie and the two little girls were visiting Forrest in Oakland when the Watrous home in Visalia burned to the ground.

> **Incendiarism at Visalia.**
> At 11 o'clock last night the residence of S. W. Watrous took fire by some means and became a total loss, the fire gaining too much headway before the fire company arrived. The family is absent for the summer, and no one was in the house. It is thought by some to be the work of an incendiary. (Sacramento Daily Union, July 5, 1887)

A fire in which personal belongings are lost forever is heartbreaking. But because his home had also served as his photo studio, the fire also destroyed all of Stephen's negatives and much of his professional equipment. Fortunately that summer he had brought a camera and tripod with him in order to visit the seaside town of Capitola, a pleasant village just south of Santa Cruz. The hotel and summer beach resort there were growing busier each year and Stephen hoped to drum up some business.

Upon returning to Visalia in the fall of 1887, the Watrous family moved into a new home, and Stephen established a photography studio in the Holt Block, a large building on the northwest corner of Main and Court Streets in downtown Visalia. Remarkably, the building still exists in 2014, although the exterior is nearly unrecognizable.

The side trip to Capitola in 1887 had paid off, and in 1888, Stephen, Minnie, and their little girls (age two and four) escaped the Central Valley summer heat by spending four months in Capitola, where Stephen leased the exclusive photo franchise for the hotel and camp from owner Frederick Hihn. The lease ordered him "not to sell, give away or deliver any liquors, candy, fruit or any merchandise, other than articles usually manufactured and sold by a Photograph Gallery."

The Capitola photo studio had a three-room apartment upstairs where the family spent the next few summers. By 1893 the hotel and resort were flourishing, and Stephen held the photo franchise year-round. For several years they rented a home in the nearby village of Soquel. Five decades later Hazel recalled those times:

> I was born into a family where pictures and their creation were of prime importance… because my New England born father, Stephen Watrous, who crossed the country to California in 1852… was one of the original group who successfully used dry plates in photography, and we children grew up in an atmosphere of pioneering in the arts. I do not remember ever "studying" design as a child. Knowing the form and balance of a picture was as much a family routine as reading books and listening to music.
> (Hazel Watrous, 1949 interview in the Carmel Spectator)

The Hihn Resort in Capitola in the 1890s. *Postcard courtesy of the author.*

1895 was a momentous year for the Watrous and Jefferds families. Stephen Watrous was 51, and was living in Soquel with Minnie, 37, Hazel, 11, and Zanetta, 9. Minnie's father, Forrest Jefferds, was only 65 but his beloved second wife Elinor had died four years before and he was in declining health. (After four decades he still felt the effects of the injuries he had suffered during his hydraulic mining in Timbuctoo.) In 1888, Forrest had traded his Oakland property for a house and five acres of fruit and nut trees near the little community of Campbell, halfway between San José and Los Gatos. Forrest's youngest daughter, Nellie, had been living with him there, but she was to be married in August, leaving Forrest ailing and alone. In September 1895, Minnie, Hazel and Zanetta Watrous moved to Campbell to live with grandfather Forrest in the beautiful Santa Clara Valley. Stephen maintained his photography studio in Capitola until at least 1897, an it is unclear how much time, if any, he spent in Santa Clara.

The Santa Clara Valley was named by Junípero Serra in 1777 when he founded the Mission Santa Clara de Asis. (St. Clare of Assisi was one of the first followers of St. Francis.) The valley cradles the southern end of San Francisco Bay, and reaches far enough south to include Morgan Hill and Gilroy. Today the northwest region of the Santa Clara Valley is the most densely populated area, and includes San José, Palo Alto, Mountain View, Campbell, Los Gatos, Saratoga, Cupertino, Los Altos, Sunnyvale, and Stanford University (founded in 1885). This relatively urbanized area is known today as Silicon Valley, but in the 1890s it was a sunny area of rich, fertile soil and productive ranches, farms and orchards promoted by developers as the "Valley of the Heart's Delight." It already had an agricultural tradition going back half a century, and would continue to prosper well into the 20th century. Until the early 1960s the Santa Clara Valley was the largest fruit production and packing region in the world with more than three dozen canneries. But in 1895 there were no canneries, just fertile soil and miles of orchards. In this beautiful place Forrest Gooch Jefferds had chosen to spend his final years.

In Campbell, while Minnie looked after her father and took care of the housekeeping, Hazel and Zanetta became students in city schools for the first time in their lives, Zanetta in the fifth grade and Hazel in the Horace Mann Middle School.

Forrest's vitality continued to fail, and on April 9, 1897, he died. He is interred in the Visalia Public Cemetery next to his two beloved wives Zanetta and Elinor.

One year later, on June 24, 1898, Stephen Watrous died of stomach cancer at the age of 53.

Minnie and her daughters continued to live in Forrest's house near San José; Hazel graduated from the Horace Mann School (8th grade) in 1899 and finished 9th grade at Santa Clara High School in 1900. By that time she had turned sixteen and was eligible to enroll in the California State Normal School in San José.

Normal School

The term "normal school" derives from the French "École Normale." In 19th century America it referred to a teacher training college that sought to maintain standards or "norms" of teaching and curriculum in the public schools. The California Normal School was founded in 1862 in San Francisco, and by 1900 it stood on a 27-acre tract in San José bordered by San Fernando, San Carlos, Fourth and Seventh Streets. (The Normal School was later renamed San José State University, and was the first campus in the California State University system.) Countless boarding houses surrounding the campus were used by the new school as dormitories, and during her studies 1900-1903 Hazel boarded at several of those addresses.

The Sappho Society

During the last two decades of the 19th century, a half-dozen faculty-sponsored clubs on the Normal School campus were formed to promote the study of speech, literature, and drama. For the members of these societies and clubs their theater projects often took precedence over the formal curricular training, and by the 1890s some students entered the Normal School primarily to be involved in drama and theater activities. By September 1900, when Hazel arrived at the Normal School, more extracurricular time and energy was devoted to theater activities on campus than to any other extracurricular activity, including the athletics programs.

The Sappho Society at San José Normal School. May 1901. *SJNS Pennant. Courtesy of the author.*

Chief among these clubs was the Sappho Society, founded on the campus in 1898 and sponsored by Dr. Morris E. Dailey, president of the School. The Sappho Society later became a chapter of the distinguished national sorority Kappa Alpha Theta. The photograph above shows the Society in May 1901. Hazel, age 17, is in the front row, third from the right.

The name of this club deserves an explanation for 21st century readers. In 1900 the term "sapphic" had not yet assumed its 20th-century sexual connotations. Sappho herself was a great lyric poet born on the Greek isle of Lesbos around 620 B.C.E, and her erotic and romantic verse actually embraced men as well as women. Nonetheless, in the 19th century, increased emphasis was placed on Sappho's poetry about erotic love between women; this general connotation first appears in print in 1825, although the specific words deriving from it appear much later. The word "lesbian" came into use, derived from the name Lesbos, the island of Sappho's birth. "Lesbianism" as a noun is first documented in the 1870s. "Lesbian" as an adjective meaning "relating to homosexual relations between women" dates from the 1890s. The first written use of "lesbian" as a noun appeared in the 1920s.

Meanwhile, all of this seems to have been of no consequence to ladies' clubs in America, who were ignoring, or perhaps unaware of, the evolving sexual connotations around Sappho's name. They apparently focused on Sappho instead as a great and admirable female literary figure who actually predated Aristotle and Plato by several centuries. As a result, there were quite a few Sappho Societies and Clubs throughout America by 1900, in large and small communities. All were women's clubs, and all focused in some way on literature, public speaking and music. A "ladies' musical society" was organized in Ypsilanti, Michigan in 1888 by the wife of the Director of the Normal Conservatory there: they had a 24-voice chorus called the Sappho Club that presented concerts throughout Michigan for several decades. As late as 1921, the Sappho Club of Tuskegee, Alabama was an affiliate of the Alabama Federation of Women's Clubs.

May 1903

By the end of the 19th century, the other San José Normal School drama societies—female, male, and co-ed—were producing dramatic readings, variety shows, farces, and theatrical pageants, but the newly-formed Sappho Society established a Normal School milestone. In June 1899, one year after its founding, the Society presented the first documented on-campus production of an entire play: a shortened (and all-female) version of Shakespeare's *A Midsummer Night's Dream*. This event marks the beginning of live drama at what is now San José State University.

One year later, during this golden age of drama clubs at San José Normal School, Hazel began her three-year course of studies there. She joined the Sappho Society, and it continued to produce dramas and variety shows, but there is no record of Hazel's specific activities in that club or elsewhere at the school.

In June 1903 Hazel Watrous was in the largest class (115) ever to graduate from the San José Normal School. She was qualified to teach in the California public schools, and her area of concentration was art. Now, at the age of 19 and armed with a teaching certificate, she began looking for a job.

Hazel in May 1901, at the end of her first year of teacher training. She is 17.

Hazel Watrous in 1901 and 1903, from The Pennant, *a student publication of San Jose Normal School. Courtesy of the author.*

Looking north across the Golden Gate, c.1910, with Fort Point in the foreground and the Marin Headlands in the distance. Today, the approach to the southern end of the Golden Gate Bridge passes almost directly over Fort Point. Postcard, hand-colored photograph, postmarked 1911. *Courtesy of the author.*

Looking west through the Golden Gate toward the sun setting over the Pacific Ocean, c.1900. Fort Point is the tiny flat shape on the left by the water, and the Marin Headlands are on the right. Postcard, hand-colored photograph, postmarked 1904. *Courtesy of the author.*

Part Two
Coming of Age in San Francisco
1903–1923

"Evening Hour, Ferry Building." Postcard, postmarked 1912.
The "1915" on the tower is in anticipation of the Panama–Pacific International Exposition,
which took place in 1915, and the Panama–California Exposition, which began that year.
Printed by R. J. Waters & Co. *Courtesy of the author.*

The artistic spirit endures, even in San Francisco in April, 1906. San Franciscans coped with the aftermath of the Great Earthquake in many ways. Painter and Photographer unknown. *From the digital collection of the Library of Congress.*

Dene 1900–1918

> My love of music started so early that I don't remember when. My parents encouraged me with piano lessons locally and as soon as I was old enough I was sent to San Francisco where I studied under Gyula Ormay and the great and much lamented Frederick Zech. Going on to New York I worked with Leo Ornstein.
>
> Dene Denny quoted in the Monterey Herald, 1949

After graduating from Oakland High School in 1903, Dene Denny entered the freshman class at the University of California at Berkeley in September, and continued to live in Oakland with her uncle Alpha and aunt Amelia Webber. At about this time she left her piano teacher, Gyula Ormay, with whom she had studied since arriving in Oakland in 1900, and began private piano lessons with Frederick Zech.

Frederick Zech, pianist and composer, was born in Philadelphia, Pennsylvania, in 1858 and came to San Francisco with his family in 1860. His father, Frederick Sr., was a piano maker with a studio on Market Street. Frederick Jr. began his musical studies early in life, and by the age of 20 he was performing, composing, conducting and teaching. From 1882 to 1887 he lived in Berlin and studied composition and piano with Theodore Kullack, a friend of Czerny and Liszt and one of the most active European piano teachers of the nineteenth century. Upon returning to San Francisco, Zech became a popular piano teacher and was a very prolific composer: his output included a long list of symphonies, concerti, orchestral tone poems, choral works, and operas. A decade later, in 1920, the young Ansel Adams studied piano in San Francisco with Zech.

During the spring semester of Dene's third year on the Berkeley campus, life throughout the Bay Area was convulsed by the great San Francisco earthquake of April 18, 1906, followed by the three days of raging fire. The devastation for a large part of the city was utter and complete, and the effects extended as far north as Santa Rosa (10,000 homeless) and as far south as Santa Barbara, where buildings sustained damage. One Berkeley student later recalled the quake:

> I was awake in bed in my sorority when the shock came. Preceding the shock there was a low, rumbling noise, which first sounded like distant thunder. The noise rapidly increased in volume until it grew to be a muffled roar. The shock came about 30 seconds after the sound had begun. The house began rocking like a cradle and the timbers and rafters creaked and cracked. It did not seem possible that the building could withstand the shock. Outside I could hear the sound of falling bricks and the rattle of glass and dishes. I looked out of the window and saw the trees swaying as if shaken by a great wind. A second but lighter shock came at 8:30 in the morning. In the meantime I went to the ferries and saw boatloads of people coming across the bay. Men women and children were utterly crazed with terror. (*The San Francisco Earthquake.* Henry Neal, Chicago, 1906.)

Although structures in Berkeley and the East Bay communities sustained relatively little serious physical damage, the economic and social upheaval throughout the region was beyond comprehension. Much of San Francisco had been totally leveled, modes of transportation and communication were disrupted, records and documents were destroyed, and refugees flooded Oakland, Berkeley, and other East Bay communities. In all, at least 300,000 San Francisco residents were left homeless following the earthquake and fire, and more than half of those people were evacuated by boat or railroad to Oakland and Berkeley within the first few days. For months, an outpouring of aid from the Bay Area and from around the world helped San Francisco begin to recover.

Despite the earthquake and its aftermath in 1906, Dene finished her degree on schedule, and in June 1907 UC Berkeley awarded Ethel Adele Denny a Bachelor of Letters degree in English and philosophy. Of her graduating class of 286, she was one of only 18 to receive the Phi Beta Kappa key.

Ethel Adele Denny's senior photo in the 1907 UC Berkeley Senior Record. *(There was no Blue and Gold yearbook in 1907.) Courtesy of the author.*

Dene's father, Albert Hendrickson Denny, who would have been proud of his daughter's achievement, did not live to see the event. The man Dene later described as "a born pioneer" passed away in his home in Etna in January of 1907 at the age of 71, just six months before Dene's graduation. Albert Denny in his will bequeathed the sum of $5,000 to each of his living children and left the Etna house to his wife, Gertrude. The rest of his considerable estate, including Oak Farm and ranch land, mining stock, and business investments, was divided among Gertrude and the children.

Dene continued to live in the Chi Omega sorority on Piedmont Avenue near the campus until June 1909, when she received the Master of Letters degree and became a college graduate seeking employment. She moved to Oakland, shared an apartment with one of her sisters, and looked for a teaching position.

One of the most unique performance spaces in the San Francisco Bay Area is Berkeley's Hearst Theater. Constructed

The official dedication ceremony of the Hearst Theater, Berkeley. All-school convocation, September 24, 1903. This was the first official event in the new Hearst Theater, and the entire student body was in attendance. *Postcard, postmarked 1911, courtesy of the author.*

in the spring of 1903, the opening ceremonies took place in September of Dene's freshman year at UC Berkeley. Financed by William Randoph Hearst (for whom it is named), its design was based on the ancient Greek theater of Epidaurus. When Berkeley's "Greek Theater" was opened, it was the only campus venue big enough to seat the entire student body and faculty, and it immediately became the location for convocations, graduation ceremonies, plays and concerts.

J. Fred Wolle was the founder of the Bach Choir of Bethlehem, Pennsylvania, in 1898 and the Bethlehem Bach Festival in 1903, and in 1905 he had been invited to establish a music department at the University of California at Berkeley. (Although classes in music theory and history were offered during the last three of Dene's six years on campus, she enrolled in no music classes at Berkeley.)

In 1909, Wolle led the first Bach Festival in California: a single performance of the *Mass in B Minor* at the Greek Theater for an audience some estimated to be 10,000. Another Bach Festival followed in May 1910, with performances of the *Mass in B Minor* and the *St Matthew Passion*. For more information on Wolle, his brief presence in Berkeley, and his California Bach Festival, please see "Bach in Berkeley, 1906" in the Appendix.

Dene continued her private piano study with Frederick Zech, and in October 1909 she played a few selections to open the final session of the annual convention of the Northern California Teachers Association in Red Bluff.

In 1910, Dene began teaching high school English in San Francisco. The Lick, Wilmerding, and Lux High Schools were innovative schools that had been founded separately but shared faculty, facilities, and mission in a progressive and cooperative arrangement; by the mid-20th century the three had become a single institution, which continues to thrive today, Lick-Wilmerding High School.

Her subject area was English, but the trio of schools had no faculty-led musical ensembles, and Dene tried to remedy that; she created a Glee Club, a "Choral" that sang at pep rallies, and a music appreciation club where students could discuss, listen to, and play music.

In a December 1914 L-W school bulletin this item appears:

The new Lux School, built in 1912.
Library of Congress.

The Noon-Time Recitals.

With the purchase of a Victrola by the school, a new activity has been originated by Miss Denny, in the form of recitals to be held during the noon hour. The first recital, held on Wednesday, October 20th, was opened by a solo, entitled "Fiddle and I," sung by Miss Hopkinson, accompanied by Mr. E. Johnson, violin, and Miss Fredericks, piano. Delius, who was acting as chairman, then gave a brief outline of the opera, "Il Trovatore." Following this, "The Tempest of the Heart" and "Miserere" were given on the Victrola. Since the whistle cut the hour short, the records entitled "Tremble, ye Tyrants," "Oh, Joy! He's Saved," and "Naught on Earth is Left Me" were postponed until the next day. The large attendance at the recital proved that the idea was a practical and successful one, so more of the same will be arranged for during the rest of the year.

The student publications during her time at L-W-L indicate that Dene was held in high esteem by the students.

Dene Denny at Lick-Wilmerding High School, San Francisco

To our friend, to our advisor, to the one so interested in the Class of 1915, to Miss Ethel Adele Denny, in grateful appreciation of her earnest work, her deep concern, and her everlasting loyalty, is dedicated this volume—our last supreme effort.

Dene in May, 1912, after her first year of teaching.

The senior class dedicated the yearbook each June to a teacher or staff member, and in 1915, after her fourth year of teaching, Dene received the honor. The framed photo to the left and the inscription above were given their own page in the yearbook. The Class of 1915 were freshmen when Dene began teaching at L-W in 1911.

In this grainy photo from the 1917 Lick-Wilmerding yearbook, Dene is standing in the middle of the front row of her Glee Club, with an old-fashioned conductor's "wand" in her right hand. Dene was an English teacher at L-W, but she created the first organized musical activities at the school. *(The Glee Club photo used in the printing of the yearbook had been damaged or soiled.)*

From the 1912, 1915, and 1917 Lick-Wilmerding and Cal. School of Mechanical Arts June yearbooks. *Courtesy of the author.*

Commuting in San Francisco before the bridges

The Lick-Wilmerding-Lux schools were located at 17th and Potrero Streets, just southwest of downtown San Francisco. During her first three years of teaching, Dene lived across the Bay in Oakland, and her school days began with Glee Club at 8:20am. How did she get to work? Wallace Stegner wrote that for history to be truly remembered "it must be vividly imagined." To vividly imagine the daily lives of people in the San Francisco Bay Area in the first decades of the 20th century, it helps to understand what modes of daily transportation were available to them. In 1910, automobiles were flimsy and still rare, and horse-drawn vehicles were the norm. A very busy network of cable cars and electric trolleys crisscrossed San Francisco in much greater numbers than

Ferry boats arriving and departing from the Ferry Terminal. Looking east across the bay to Berkeley, Oakland, and Alameda. *Detail of 1908 postcard. Courtesy of the author.*

we can imagine today. But a large and sometimes treacherous expanse of water separated San Francisco from dozens of nearby cities and towns. The situation was unique, and so were the solutions.

The city of San Francisco is on the seven-mile-wide northern tip of a peninsula extending 45 miles south to San José. It is bordered on the west by the Pacific Ocean, on the north by the 1.75-mile-wide Golden Gate on the north, and on the east by the enormous San Francisco Bay stretching south to San José. When Dene began teaching high school in 1910, there were no bridges across the Bay or the Golden Gate, and the only route from San Francisco to Oakland was a 90 mile trip by coach or train via San José. But a boat could make the trip from San Francisco to Oakland in 20 minutes, and with the influx of thousands of gold seekers, passenger ferry boats had begun operating in 1850. By the 1870s, San Francisco Bay ferries had entered their Golden Age and ferry boats served more than two dozen destinations. The boats were double ended and could dock in either direction, so they never needed to turn around. Their covered side paddle wheels were powered by a huge one-cylinder walking beam steam engine, and by 1900 most were fueled by coal instead of wood.

When Dene and Hazel lived and worked in San Francisco and Oakland, the most heavily traveled ferry routes were between the East Bay cities of Oakland and Alameda and the Union Ferry Terminal at the

The Southern Pacific Ferry Steamer "Alameda served the San Francisco–Oakland route. *1911 postcard. Courtesy of the author.*

foot of Market Street in San Francisco. During most of the years between 1910 and 1920, Hazel and Dene commuted these routes on the same days, but usually in opposite directions: for a while Dene lived in Oakland while working in San Francisco, and Hazel had several San Francisco addresses during the time she worked in Alameda. They had not yet met, but they were among the forty to sixty thousand passengers who passed through the Ferry Terminal each day.

By 1920, ferry boats traveled the East Bay routes in each direction at fifteen or twenty minute intervals and connected at each terminal with electric trolley cars and commuter trains. (The larger illustration on the title page of Part Two shows the Ferry Terminal at the time Dene was commuting to her teaching job.) Streetcars left the San Francisco Ferry Terminal every 20 seconds for destinations around the city, and a similar network of trains and trolleys connected with the East Bay terminals. In 1920 the San Francisco-Oakland-Alameda route was the most extensive ferry and electric train system in the United States, and the boats on those two routes connected daily with 826 trains and trolleys.

View of the trolley loop from the roof of the Ferry Terminal about 1910. This loop was only part of the Terminal's interface with the trolley system. Although it is impossible to discern in this small black and white image, there are eleven horse-drawn vehicles shown, and only three automobiles. *Detail from postcard, hand colored, postmark 1912. Courtesy of the artist.*

This complex and busy system of local travel was as deeply rooted in the daily lives of Bay Area residents then as cars, busses, Muni and BART are now. San Franciscans depended utterly on the ferry system until the 1930s, when the Oakland Bay Bridge and the Golden Gate Bridge were built by the Works Progress Administration, part of President Roosevelt's New Deal.

In 1913, after three years of commuting, Dene moved to San Francisco and lived first on 16th Street, then on Noe, and then on Fillmore Street. By 1918 she was sharing an apartment with her sister Mildred at 1301 Leavenworth, a shorter commute to school by cable car and trolley. She must have had time for the piano again: in April she performed some offbeat repertoire at the Greek Theater.

In 1907 or 1908, J. Fred Wolle, the founding director of the UC Berkeley Music Department, established a series of brief Sunday afternoon concerts at the Greek Theater. On Sunday, April 21, 1918, Dene accompanied soprano Nellie Walker in a program titled "Zuni Ceremonial Chants." According to the UC Berkeley annual report: "The Zuni ceremonial songs included a sunrise call, the Apache medicine chant, hunting songs, lullabies, and a lover's wooing song, transcribed and harmonized for voice and piano by Charles Troyer." (Troyer was a German-born San Franciscan by then well-known for his settings of Native America music.)

In addition to the Zuni songs, Miss Walker sang four classical selections and Dene played music by Chopin: the *Waltz in C Sharp Major*, the *Berceuse*, and the *Polonaise, op 25.*

"Her work was clean cut, characterized by fine technique, great drama, and excellent finish. She also received the warm applause of the audience. She is a pianist of musicality and strong individuality." (Berkeley daily Call, April 22, 1918)

Given the nature of the musical world then and now, and the eagerness of young musicians to perform, it's likely that Dene took part in other concerts that were never written about or documented. We know that she taught English at Lick-Wilmerding-Lux for one more academic year while she engineered a major change in her professional life.

Postscript:

Perhaps Dene was in the Colonial Ballroom of the St. Francis Hotel on Thursday evening January 20, 1916, when her former piano teacher, Gyula Ormay, played the harpsichord in the first San Francisco performance of Bach's Brandenburg Concerto No. 5. This "ensemble concerto" is written for violin, flute and harpsichord, accompanied by a small group of string instruments. The harpsichord part is prominent and famously showy, and musicologists believe that Bach wrote the concerto as a performance vehicle for himself, to demonstrate his well-known virtuosity. Scholars consider this to be the first example of a concerto featuring a keyboard soloist.

What makes this 1916 concert worth mentioning is that in the early 20th century the harpsichord was a rarity, especially on the West Coast of North America. New instruments, such as those from the Pleyel company, were heavy and expensive, so performers of Baroque music in the early 20th century usually used piano instead. The great pioneers of the 20th century harpsichord revival—including Wanda Landowska and her pupil Alice Ehlers—were just beginning their work in Europe but the result would not be felt in the US for several decades. (Ehlers appeared as soloist at the Carmel Bach Festival in the 1930s.)

Pacific Coast Music Review
San Francisco, Saturday, January 22, 1916
   ...The concert was given at the colonial ballroom of the St. Francis Hotel on Thursday evening, January 20. The program began with an old Bach classic, namely the Concerto Number Five (Brandenburg). It was the first presentation of this work in San Francisco.
The concerto was written for harpsichord, violin, and flute and was given a dainty and technically gratifying interpretation. There is an accompaniment of 2 violins, cello and double bass, which also received artistic attention at the hands of the musicians in charge of these instruments.
Mr. Ormay played the harpsichord part and, while he attended to the same with his usual fine musicianly instinct, he could not alter the fact that <u>a long composition on this old instrument is bound to become monotonous sooner or later no matter how well it was played.</u> The modern piano has spoiled us. A short dainty little work now and then on the harpsichord is to be accepted, but a concerto running through the usual number of movements is too lengthy to sound well nowadays on the harpsichord. We really believe that Bach, and some of his contemporaries and successors, heard in their imagination the possibilities of the modern piano when writing their compositions. [Emphasis added.]

Hazel 1903–1922

After graduation from the three-year teacher training curriculum at the California Normal School in San José in 1903, Hazel remained in San José during 1904 and 1905 and continued her studies as an artist while looking for employment as a teacher.

Hazel Watrous. Date and photographer unknown. *Courtesy of the H. M. Williams Local History Room, Harrison Memorial Library.*

The San Francisco Art Association (SFAA) was founded in 1871 by artists, writers, and community leaders who shared a cultural vision for the West, and in 1874 the SFAA established The California School of Design (CSD). Despite its name, it was a school of the fine arts, and by the 1890s every serious Northern California artist either had studied at the CSD or was going to. In 1916 the CSD was renamed The California School of Fine Arts, and in 1961 it became The San Francisco Art Institute. It is one of the oldest art schools in the United States and the oldest west of the Mississippi River.

In 1893 the school moved its classes into a spectacular mansion built high atop Nob Hill in the late 1870s by Mark Hopkins, one of the founders of the Central Pacific Railroad. He was one of the original owner/builders of the Hotel Del Monte in Monterey (discussed in Part Three), and the hotel and Hopkins' San Francisco mansion were designed by the same architect. The house was enormous, with a giant three story central hall and dozens of rooms. The equally splendid house next door belonged to Hopkins' fellow railroad mogul, Leland Stanford.

Hopkins didn't live to see his house completed, but his widow lived in it until her death, after which it was bequeathed to the SFAA. The school occupied the building from 1893 until 1906, and during those years it also was known as the Mark Hopkins Institute of Art. The State Normal School had prepared Hazel for teaching art in public schools, but at the "Hopkins Institute" she studied as an artist.

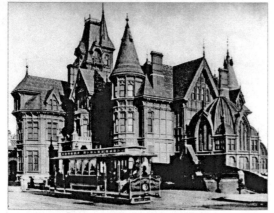

The former Mark Hopkins Mansion, during its time as the California School of Design. *Library of Congress.*

It is not clear where Hazel was on April 18, 1906; the Hopkins mansion and the adjacent Stanford mansion actually survived the earthquake itself, however Nob Hill was part of the five square miles of the city completely destroyed by the ensuing three days of fire. The school rebuilt on the site and remained there until 1925, when the property was sold and the school moved to its current location at 800 Chestnut Street. On December 4, 1926, on the spectacular hilltop site where the palatial Mark Hopkins mansion once stood, one of San Francisco's most famous landmarks opened its doors: the Mark Hopkins Hotel.

Before and after the 1906 earthquake, Hazel also studied privately with the Swiss-born California oil painter, muralist and sculptor Gottardo Piazzoni. Born in Switzerland in 1872, Piazzoni grew up on a farm in Carmel Valley, trained at the California School of Design in the 1890s, studied in Paris, and then returned to live and work in Northern California. Piazzoni's work was inspired and influenced by his Transcendentalist beliefs, by passages from the Bible, from the poetry of Dante, or the poems of his friend (and early Carmel resident) George Sterling (1869-1926).

The ruins of the Stanford (left) and Hopkins (right) mansions. All that remains are the buildings' two chimneys. *Library of Congress.*

Piazzoni shared a studio with sculptors Earl Cummings (1876–1936) and Arthur Putnam (1873–1930), in the "Monkey Block," the neighborhood surrounding the Montgomery Block, San Francisco's first fireproof and earthquake resistant building (the site of the Transamerica Building today). In the 19th and early 20th centuries, this was San Francisco's "Barbary Coast," a center for intellectuals, artists, and renegades from Ambrose Bierce to Mark Twain. The Piazzoni studio was frequented by writers Jack London and George Sterling; painters Maynard Dixon and Xavier Martínez; photographer Arnold Genthe, and other San Francisco "Bohemians."

Minnie

Hazel's mother Minnie Jefferds Watrous continues to thread her way through the background of this story. Minnie and her first husband, Stephen Watrous (Hazel's father), apparently separated in 1895 or 1896, and he died in 1898. In 1900, just before Hazel entered Normal School in San José, Minnie married Elias Holden, a successful San Francisco cigar store owner and merchant. Elias immigrated from Canada in 1887 with his wife Harriet and their nine-year-old son, Edgar. After the birth of their second son, James, in San Francisco, Harriet died in the early 1890s. At the time of their marriage in 1900, Minnie was 43, and Elias 50. Minnie went by the last name Holden for the rest of her life.

That summer, Hazel moved into a student boarding house near the campus of the Normal School. The rest of her family moved to a house in San Francisco at 1054 Geary, between Polk Street and Van Ness Avenue. Living there with Minnie and Elias were Minnie's daughter Zanetta Watrous (14), and Elias's sons Edgar (22) and James (17) Holden. It's possible that Hazel also lived there at some point after her graduation from Normal School in 1903, while she attended art classes at the Hopkins Institute and before she began teaching school.

The devastating fire that followed the 1906 earthquake was stopped in part by a valiant firebreak created along Van Ness Avenue. Sadly, the Holden home was just 1/2 block to the east of Van Ness and was leveled by the fire and/or by the dynamiting used to create the firebreak. For more than a mile along Van Ness Avenue, photos taken just after the fire show utter devastation on the east side of the street and buildings relatively untouched on the west side. It's not known where Minnie and Elias went immediately after the fire or how they survived, but they were in fact among the 300,000 people left homeless after the earthquake. By now Zanetta, Edgar, and James were out on their own and their whereabouts at the time of the quake are not known. Hazel, who was studying art in San Francisco, may well have been living with Minnie and Elias.

Minnie and Elias moved to a temporary home in San Francisco near Golden Gate Park. In 1908 they moved into a newly rebuilt Vallejo Street neighborhood on the summit of Russian Hill, where they lived until Elias' death in 1932. Minnie's marriage to a successful businessman, plus her inheritance from her father, made it possible for her to help her two daughters financially when necessary. From Hazel's student lodging in San José in 1900 to the apartment in the building where Hazel met Dene in 1922, it is Minnie's name that appears on the rental leases, not Hazel's.

Teacher

The Great Earthquake traumatized the San Francisco region, but the country was still enjoying an economic and artistic boom and life went on. The exodus from the city in 1906 caused surrounding communities to grow, and teachers were in demand. A few months after the earthquake, Hazel moved to the waterside village of Sausalito, her home for four years while she taught art in the Marin County schools. The golden hills of the Marin Headlands form the northern shore of the Golden Gate.

In the summer of 1910 Hazel was hired as a grammar school art teacher in the City of Alameda, an East Bay community adjacent to Oakland and across the Bay from San Francisco.

Almost immediately, she was drafted to fill a sudden vacancy as Drawing Supervisor for the entire Alameda School District, a position she held from October 1910 until 1918. The Alameda school system at that time had about 4,000 students from grades one through twelve. Hazel also served for several years as Drawing Instructor for the Summer Session of the School of Arts and Crafts. (See the Appendix for information about the School of Arts and Crafts.)

From 1910 to 1915 Hazel lived at 1732 Central Ave. in Oakland and commuted by trolley to the schools in Alameda. Then in 1916 while still

Alameda High School, 1912. *Courtesy of the author.*

employed by the Alameda schools, she moved to San Francisco and lived for the next three years near the intersection of Jones and Union Streets, southeast of Russian Hill. Now her morning commute was a cable car to the Ferry Terminal, a ferry boat across the Bay to Alameda, and a cable car down Central Avenue to the high school.

Hazel served as Drawing Supervisor for the Alameda School System until early 1918, when she left her job suddenly, apparently because of illness. Although it is not clear when she stopped working, the Alameda school rosters show the school system hiring a new "art and drawing" instructor in the middle of the school year.

There is no mention in the records of Hazel's religious upbringing, but her own words tell us that she was profoundly influenced by a book that had been published only ten years before she was born. It was originally titled "Science and Health" and the author was Mary Baker Eddy, the founder of a religious movement in New England in the late 19th century widely known today as Christian Science. Eddy established the Church of Christ, Scientist in Boston in 1879, and in 1883 the Church began publishing its official monthly, The Christian Science Journal, to describe practical applications of the Christian Science healing practice and attest to its effectiveness. In the issue of March 1921, this testimonial appears:

> That the Christian Science is the truth and is demonstrable has been proved to me over and over again. It was for the healing of tuberculosis of the lungs that I turned to Christian Science. The healing was immediate and complete, and with it came a desire earnestly to study the Christian Science textbook, Science and Health with Key to the Scriptures by Mary Baker Eddy. It has been my privilege to become a member of the Mother Church and of a branch church. This has been a great help to me, and an opportunity for closer communion with Principle.
>
> Through some knowledge of the oneness of Mind and its idea, I have seen my daily work in a very different light. Where there seem to be many minds in supervisory work, I can now see and prove that there is one mind, infinitely expressed. Christian Science is a wonderful revelation, and I feel that I can never cease being grateful to our Leader, who has given it to the world through her writings, the church, and the periodicals.
>
> — (Miss) Hazel Watrous, San Francisco, California.

A religion side note: Dene Denny and her family attended the Congregational Church in Etna, a church her father had helped to sponsor and build in the late 1870s, and both of Dene's parents listed their religions as Congregational. Several of Dene's sisters became members of the Church of Christ, Scientist, and at some point in her life Dene joined the Church as well. There was an active Christian Science community in Carmel when Dene and Hazel arrived there in the mid-1920s, and the weekly Carmel Pine Cone at that time often carried half- or full-page essays about Christian Science.

In 1919, Hazel moved into a new apartment at 1907 Leavenworth Street in San Francisco, just two blocks from the Russian Hill home of her mother, Minnie. Minnie's name is shown on the apartment lease as "head of household."

Known as the Summerton Apartments, the building was owned by the Misses Amelia and Elizabeth Summerton, whose family had come to San Francisco when the girls were young. Their father made a fortune over six or eight years, decided he did not like California, and wanted to return home to the midwest, but his two daughters did not want to leave San Francisco. Before he departed, Mr. Summerton built a beautiful little apartment house and gave it to his two girls. They lived in one of the eleven apartments and the rental income from the other ten units supported them for the rest of their lives.

1907 Leavenworth. Mid-20th century sketch. *Courtesy of the author.*

The apartments were spacious, sunny, three or four rooms, with high ceilings, fireplaces and spectacular views of the hills and water of the Golden Gate. Although the exterior has been modernized over the years, the building still stands on the northwest corner of Leavenworth and Green Streets.

Judging from her activities, Hazel's health had returned by mid-1919, and during the next two years she spent a significant amount of time in Los Angeles. In an interview thirty years later, Hazel said: "My primary interest was applied design," and in her professional career, Hazel Watrous was first and foremost a designer: of houses, home and business interiors, furniture, book covers, advertisements, printed matter, and stage sets. In LA she worked for Fisher Studios as a preview critic of their vaudeville and roadshow acts, and there also are third-hand reports that Hazel designed sets or costumes for Los Angeles theater productions. The author has found no actual documentation of Hazel's presence or activities in Los Angeles or the surrounding communities.

Although she may have spent time in LA, the San Francisco City Directories indicate that she maintained her legal residence at 1907 Leavenworth Street on Russian Hill.

In 1921, Hazel was appointed head of the Art Department of Alameda High School, a position she held for two academic years before leaving her teaching job altogether. Ironically, her new job as Head of the Art Department in a school of 600 students actually left her with less time for her own artistic pursuits. It was during this time that her ambitions began to change. "I felt that I wanted to produce again, rather than teach," she said later.

Dene Denny 1919–1921

By 1919, Dene had been a high school English teacher for nine years, and such a job makes serious piano performing impossible—there is never enough time or energy for the artistic concentration needed for daily practice—and in the fall Dene took steps toward a music-centered life filled with playing and teaching.

She moved out of her San Francisco apartment, and returned to the East Bay, where she lived for six months in a rented house in Oakland with her mother and several younger siblings. At the same time she leased a teaching studio on the 9th floor of the new Kohler and Chase Building at 26 O'Farrell Street.

A contemporary advertisement described it as "A Ten Story Music Trade Palace Containing Piano Parlors, Talking Machine Rooms, Player Demonstration Halls, Concert Auditorium, and Three Floors of Well-equipped Teaching Studios." It was a very busy and trendy location just a few steps from Market Street, and Dene maintained her piano studio there from October 1919 until early 1922 when she moved to a larger studio on Sutter Street.

In June 1920, Dene left the faculty of Lick-Wilmerding High School, and her days as an English teacher were over. She would be a dedicated teacher all her life, but never again in a classroom.

[*The "Talking Machine Room" displayed 78rpm wind-up "record players" called "Talking Machines." (RCA Victor was originally the Victor Talking Machine Company.) The "Player Demonstration Hall" was filled with player pianos.*]

Wager Swayne

That spring, Dene began taking private lessons with the American teacher Wager Swayne, with whom she studied until late 1923. Born in Toledo, Ohio in 1873, Swayne had been a pupil of the great Theodore Leschetizky in Vienna and remained in Europe, living as a piano teacher first in Vienna, then in Paris. Just before the outbreak of the first World War Swayne returned to the United States and lived in New York briefly before coming to San Francisco in 1919.

The list of Swayne's pupils includes French pianist Genia Nemenoff, who toured the world as duo pianist with her husband Pierre Luboschutz (they performed in Carmel in the 1930s); French pianist Emile Baume; Russian pianist Anatole Kitain; Nebraska native Marie Mikova, who studied with Swayne in Paris 1910-15 and toured Europe and the US as a concert pianist; San Franciscan Elizabeth Simpson, who went on to become an eminent west coast piano teacher; and Ethel Denny.

Like many teachers, Swayne presented regularly-scheduled "studio recitals" of his students; there was a rotating schedule, and each pupil played a few times per year. The recitals took place either in Swayne's studio at 2404 Broadway, or in the home of one of the participating pianists in San Francisco or Berkeley. The Pacific Coast Music Review and the San Francisco Call actually covered many studio recitals of the city's distinguished music teachers, and we can document Miss Ethel Denny's participation in five Wager Swayne recitals from May 1920 to May 1923. Swayne publicized these recitals of his most elite students as the "Wager Swayne Club," and the events were open to the public.

Alfred Metzger, Editor of the Pacific Coast Music Review, attended a recital in the Swayne studio on May 28, 1920, and in his review he emphasizes that the "students" are in fact all "genuine artist-pupils" and the affair is a very serious one.

> Miss Ethel Denny revealed a poetic nature and an easy pianistic adaptability by rendering Rubinstein's Barcarolle, Schnittke's Sur les steppes and Raff's Rigaudon, much to the gratification of those in attendance, emphasizing the romantic and rhythmic characteristics of the works. (PCMR, June 1920.)

Each of the five "Swayne Club" recitals in which Dene is known to have played (she may have played in others) featured six to nine pianists, almost all female. Each performer played two or three substantial short pieces (3–7minutes). The 71 compositions heard in these five recitals included one piece each by the 18th century composers Rameau, Scarlatti and Mozart, and 68 other works from the 19th and early 20th century composers Schubert, Chopin, Schumann, Liszt, Moszkowski, Rubinstein, Rachmaninoff, Debussy, Ravel, and Grainger. (Please see the Appendix for a complete list of Dene's repertoire in these and other recitals.)

Dene as Piano Teacher

From 1919 through 1929, Dene taught private piano lessons in her downtown San Francisco studio, and she, too, presented her pupils in studio recitals. In contrast to Wager Swayne's more advanced "artist-pupils," however, many of the pupils in Dene's studio recitals were younger and not as far along.

The Patterson Music Education Newsletter described a Dene Denny studio recital in San Francisco on Sunday, May 29th, 1921:

> Ethel Adele Denny presented a recital for her younger pupils last Sunday afternoon. The students played with a clever precision and an intelligent rhythm that showed a strong foundation. The sureness of the playing of even the youngest proved the value of the training received in Miss Denny's studio.

The article then goes on to list the students' names and their repertoire, and although much of the program includes titles like "The Merry Bobolink," "Goblins' Frolic," "Pixies Good-night Song," and "The Woodchopper and the Linnet," Dene's pupils also played "grown up" music by MacDowell, Chopin, Scarlatti and Chaminade. Dene did in fact have more advanced pupils, and at least one of her students, Adele Vollmer, became a popular Bay Area private piano teacher. Dene continued to teach private students in San Francisco even after moving to Carmel in 1924, and she maintained a large teaching studio on Sutter Street where she gave piano lessons and presented intimate musical gatherings until 1929.

Meanwhile, as Dene continued studying with Wager Swayne and developing her own career as a piano teacher, another new and totally unexpected change was coming into Dene's life. By October 1920, her private teaching income enabled her to move from the shared house in Oakland back to San Francisco. Dene's apartment was at 1907 Leavenworth, where Hazel Watrous had been living for two years. But Hazel was in Los Angeles at least part time through the spring of 1921, and the two women did not actually meet for nearly 12 more months.

There, in her own apartment, away from her mother and siblings, Dene would now be in the midst of the bubbling cultural life of San Francisco as it came into its own again and entered the Roaring Twenties. She was 36, free of her day job, she was supporting herself with her piano studio on O'Farrell Street, and was part of the cultural life of the city. She had become a professional musician.

The Partnership is Created 1921–1923

In late summer 1921, Hazel returned from her final freelance sojourn in Los Angeles to accept a full-time position as head of the art department at Alameda High School. She commuted daily from her apartment at 1907 Leavenworth to her teaching job across the Bay in Alameda, a total time of well over an hour in each direction. Meanwhile, Dene was giving piano lessons in her studio in downtown San Francisco. Finally, some time late that fall or very early in the new year, the two women finally met. As Hazel herself recalled a decade later, "…at the studio of a mutual friend, I met Dene Denny, and that is when and where the Denny-Watrous story began." It was apparently partnership at first sight. By late March 1922, they had purchased a lot on Dolores Street in Carmel as "Ethel A. Denny and Hazel Watrous." On April 5, Dene played works by Chopin in a recital of Wager Swayne students in San Francisco, after which she and Hazel returned to Carmel to file a building permit for their new house.

After Hazel's school year was finished in May, she and Dene left San Francisco and returned to Carmel where they lived over a friend's garage all summer during the construction of their Carmel cottage. By their own accounts and the recollections of others, the two women did a great deal of the work themselves.

> It was a case of live or die, sink or swim. Dene's hands had never laid down boards nor swung a hammer. And Hazel could not be called a master carpenter… They do not go so far as to say that they laid all those floors and placed the ridge poles in person, but

they did enough so that nailing shingles and applying coats of paint presented no more horrors. All this time, except for an occasional interim made necessary by a smashed thumb, Dene spent her free time at the piano. (Pine Cone, June 23, 1936)

This cottage would be known in the late 1920s as the "Denny-Watrous Studio," and it was their first performance venue in Carmel. The cottage—known today as Harmony House—is discussed more fully in Part III.

When the Carmel cottage was completed in September 1922, Hazel and Dene returned to San Francisco and Hazel began her second year as head of the Alameda High School Art Department. Not only were they not yet ready to leave the Bay Area arts community, they actually expanded their activities there. By December 1922 Hazel and Dene had secured their own unique live/work space in San Francisco, a venue where they could take their first professional steps as impresarios and performance artists.

The Fisk House 1922–1924

Asa Fisk was born on the family farm in Holliston, Massachussetts, on Christmas Day 1818. At the age of 14 he went to Boston, and found work at $2/week for a tailors' supply company. In a stunning example of the 19th century rags-to-riches archetype, by his mid 30s Fisk had become the owner of the supply company and the co-founder of the East Boston & Suffolk Railroad. He went on to establish the first trolley cars in the City of Boston, and he served a term in the Massachusetts State Senate. In 1863 after the death of his first wife, he took a trip to California, loved it, returned to Boston, sold everything, and with $75,000 cash and his two sons he returned to San Francisco in 1869. (One of those two sons, Arthur Fisk, later served as Postmaster General under Presidents Teddy Roosevelt and Robert Taft.) In San Francisco, Fisk became an investor and money lender, and allegedly made more than $500,000 through loans and investments.

In 1875 Asa Fisk married his second wife, Lydia, a Vermont native, and in 1884 their magnificent new house was completed near the northwest corner of Hayes and Buchanan Streets (the house was later moved to the corner lot). In his book Victorian Glory, interior designer, historian and author Paul Duchscherer describes the Fisk House as "Italianate/Second Empire/Classical Revival/Queen Anne style…" It has three stories and more than 5,000 square feet of floor space, and cost $20,000 to build. The eminent San Francisco architect Edward Heatherton was tasked with designing a dwelling big and grand enough to suit Asa Fisk, and he succeeded. The house has 15 rooms, 14-foot ceilings on the first two floors, and eight magnificent fireplaces; Cuban mahogany was used for all woodwork, doors, and detailing throughout the house. One of many striking design features both inside and outside the house is the three-story "tower" of alcoves on the SE corner.

The Fisk house was spared by the earthquake and fire of 1906. At one point the flames were spreading west after destroying City Hall and had broken through the Van Ness Avenue firebreak, only to be stopped along a short stretch of Octavia Street, just two blocks east of Hayes and Buchanan.

When Dene and Hazel lived there in 1923, the house was owned by members of the Duhem family. Victor Marie Duhem was born in France in 1843 and had immigrated with his parents to California in 1852. He and his sons Charles and Raymond were active in the fast-growing California film industry, and they did business in San Francisco and Los Angeles as the Duhem Motion Picture Manufacturing Co. The Duhems owned the Fisk house from about 1915 until the late 1930s, and they sometimes rented rooms to lodgers. (According to the 1920 Federal Census a male piano teacher had been living in the house at that time.) The neighborhood was filled with a mix of interesting people who wanted to live in an area untouched by earthquake or fire, and close to the newly rebuilt City Hall and Civic Center. (Moshe Menuhin, a teacher at the nearby Hebrew school, lived two doors up the street. His 7-year-old son Yehudi Menuhin appeared as violin soloist with the San Francisco Symphony in 1923.)

The third floor of the Fisk house consists of a large rectangular ballroom to the south, an open roof deck in the middle, and to the north a conservatory with windows on all four sides.

The conservatory was Hazel's art and design studio, with beautiful light and a splendid panoramic view. The ballroom was Dene's music studio and the venue where she and Hazel apparently produced small concerts, puppet shows, drama, lectures, and artistic salons. ("Apparently," because there is no actual record of these events, only comments made in passing over the years by Dene and Hazel themselves, plus a few vague recollections by others.)

The ballroom measures 33 x 45 feet and has an 11-foot ceiling. Dormer windows look out

in three directions, but the grandest view is from the alcove in the southeast corner—13 feet in diameter, with a domed ceiling and five windows giving a nearly 270-degree panoramic view. The architect designed the space to project the sound of voices and music out into the room; the author has personally experienced the acoustic effects in that splendid alcove.

Between the ballroom and the conservatory is the open-air roof garden. In 1923 the view of City Hall was unobstructed, and from three stories below one would have heard the ceaseless clatter and bells of the cable cars and trolleys on Hayes Street. It was here, in this unique penthouse studio, that Hazel and Dene actually began their careers as impresarios. In Hazel's own words, their partnership...

> "...had its real beginning...on the sun deck of the old Fisk residence in San Francisco. This roof garden, three stories high above the rumble of the Hayes Street cars, connected the studios of Hazel Watrous designer and Dene Denny pianist. Up the narrow, winding stairs came audiences of 75 and 100 to hear and see. Here Henry Cowell gave one of his first San Francisco recitals, puppet shows were experimented with and modern designers, artists, and musicians discussed the contemporary field." (Hazel Watrous writing in the Carmel Pine Cone, July 12, 1934)

Dene and Hazel lived and worked at 700 Hayes Street from the end of 1922 until early 1924. There was no running water on the third floor, and so it seems likely that they lived on the second floor, perhaps in one or more of the beautiful and spacious bedrooms, with their 14-foot ceilings and magnificent fireplaces. In any case, Fisk House was indeed their residence, and not merely a professional venue. During this time Dene continued to rent a piano studio downtown for private lessons. Minnie Watrous' name appears as "Head of Household" on the Fisk House lease, most likely as a rental guarantor for her daughter, but she was in fact residing with her husband Elias Holden on Russian Hill.

> Up the three flights of winding, red-carpeted stairs had climbed many of the great, the near great, and the gently appreciative, for the studio was opened evenings to artists and to musicians, and to all friends of artists and musicians. They put on puppet shows, too.
> It was a huge room. Many windows overlooked the bay. Thee were two grand pianos. There was a roof-garden and a glassed-in conservatory. And here, all unaware, was the very beginning of their impresario work. (Carmel Cymbal, July 14, 1939)

In 1923, Hazel was 39 and Dene was 38, and they were at the beginning of their three decades together. They were creators and connectors, and their power was in their partnership. As an interviewer wrote in the 1940s: "...it is when they say 'we' that they are happiest."

Photos: preceeding page, Gail Baugh; this two-page spread, David Gordon.

For background information on the Fisk House, the author is grateful to Gail Baugh and Jim Warshell, and to Joseph Pecora, author of The Storied Houses of Alamo Square, *published in 2014.*

"Follow your bliss and don't be afraid, and doors will open where you didn't know they were going to be."

— Joseph Campbell
who found his inspiration in the 1920s
in the library of Carmel-by-the-Sea

The third floor ballroom and alcove of the Asa Fisk House in San Francisco. *Photo by the author.*

Part Three

Impresarios in Carmel

1924–1930

This image was captured in 1926, looking southwest across Ocean Avenue at the entrance to Edward Kuster's Theatre of the Golden Bough. In the center-right of the photo is the former weaver's cottage brought to the site by Kuster in 1923 for use as a ticket office. The tiny cottage has been a popular Carmel candy store for generations. *(Postcard, photographer unknown. Courtesy of the author.)*

MONTEREY, CALIFORNIA
AMERICA'S FAMOUS WINTER AND SUMMER RESORT

BIRDS-EYE VIEW OF HOTEL DEL MONTE. MONTEREY, CAL.

" Where the leaf never dies in the still blooming bowers
And the bee banquets on thro' a whole year of flowers."

This advertisement from a Southern Pacific promotional book, circa 1889, shows the Hotel Del Monte rebuilt after the 1887 fire. In the distance on the shore, the little town of Pacific Grove. The Del Monte Express is arriving from San Francisco, and is visible beyond the far right corner of the hotel. *Courtesy of the author.*

The main facade of the Hotel Del Monte as it looked at the beginning of the 20th century.
Postcard detail. Courtesy of the author.

The Monterey Peninsula 1874–1920s

In 1874, nearly a century after Brother Junípero Serra's death, his Mission San Carlos Borroméo del río Carmelo was an abandoned, neglected ruin, and its surrounding buildings had crumbled back to dust. The population Monterey had been holding steady at only 1,000, but the quiet town was about to discover the two keys to its prosperity: tourists and fish.

That year, a narrow-gauge railroad spur was opened between Monterey and the main line of the Southern Pacific at Castroville, a busy agricultural hub north of Salinas. The rail connection greatly increased the number of visitors to Monterey, and was useful for freight and commerce as well. In 1875 the Pacific Retreat Association established its "Christian Seaside Resort" (now the City of Pacific Grove) west of Monterey, toward Point Pinos and the tip of the Peninsula.

Topiary Maze entrance, Hotel Del Monte.
Postcard courtesy of the author.

The Southern Pacific Railroad was owned by a quartet of moguls who had made their fortunes during the construction of the trans-continental railroad in the 1860s—Leland Stanford, Mark Hopkins, Charles Crockett, and Collis P. Huntington—and they had big plans for the Monterey Peninsula. In 1880 they widened the narrow-gauge spur from Castroville to Monterey, enabling a direct rail connection to and from San Francisco. Their new and upscale "Del Monte Express" made the trip several times daily in each direction.

To generate passenger traffic on the new line they opened the magnificent and upscale Hotel Del Monte in Monterey, located not far from the spot where Vizcaíno landed in 1602. The hotel had extensive facilities including a huge swimming pool called the Roman Plunge and acres of manicured gardens with an enormous topiary maze.

The 17–Mile–Drive, circa 1900. *Postcard courtesy of the author.*

Not content with the grounds immediately surrounding the hotel, the owners purchased an additional 7,000 acres of wooded land for guests to enjoy (known today as the Del Monte Forest). They also blazed a dirt and gravel 17-mile roadway around the perimeter of the Peninsula and offered guided tours in horse-drawn carriages through the otherwise largely roadless area. The hotel was destroyed by fire in 1887, but the (immediate) replacement was even larger and grander (shown opposite).

The other key to Monterey's prosperity was fish: when the Booth Cannery was built on the Monterey waterfront in 1902, an industry began that would in time lead Monterey to call itself "The Sardine Capital of the World."

Carmel: The Seacoast of Bohemia

The city of Monterey lies midway along the northern side of the hilly peninsula, which in the late 1800s was still almost completely covered with several varieties of pines. Just a few miles southwest of Monterey, where the southern shore of the Peninsula meets the mainland, was a beautiful forested area sloping gently down to a broad white sandy beach. The beach was protected on the north by the wooded hills of the Monterey Peninsula, and to the south it was separated from the mouth of the Carmel River by a large rocky outcropping known today as Carmel Point.

The location was visited and admired in the 1870s by David Starr Jordan, who became Stanford University's first President in 1891, and by the French-English painter Jules Tavernier (1844–1889). Tavernier came to the US in the early 1870s and was employed as an illustrator for Harper's Magazine in New York. In 1874, he traveled across the country on assignment from Harper's, making sketches and woodcut illustrations. He settled in San Francisco and became a member of the San Francisco Art Association and the Bohemian Club. By 1876 he had established a studio in Monterey that became a mecca for visiting artists and first brought the Monterey Peninsula to the attention of the San Francisco art world. Tavernier's time on the Peninsula was not long: he was constantly in debt, and his local disputes forced him to return to San Francisco in 1879, and ultimately to flee to Hawaii in 1884, where he spent the rest of his life.

Much of the area now known Carmel-by-the-Sea had been acquired in the 1850s by French businessman Honore Escolle, a prosperous Monterey resident who owned the first commercial bakery, pottery kiln, and brickworks in Central California. In the early 1880s work had begun on the slow restoration of the Carmel Mission, and in 1888, Escolle and a young Monterey developer named Santiago Duckworth filed a subdivision map with the County and began selling lots in a proposed "Catholic Resort" near the Mission.

In 1889, in a promotional mailing from Abbie Jane Hunter and her San Francisco-based Women's Real Estate Investment Company, we see the first use of the place name "Carmel-by-the-Sea". East-southeast of Carmel, 13 miles up the Carmel River Valley, is a community known since the 1940s as "Carmel Valley Village." In the 1880s and early 1890s it was called "Carmel" and there was a Post Office in the village with that name. It is thought that in 1889 Hunter added "-by-the-Sea" to her brochure to distinguish the seaside resort from the village in the valley.

George Sterling, Mary Austin, Jack London, and Jimmy Hopper on Carmel beach, at the foot of Ocean Avenue. Photograph by Arnold Genthe, 1906–1907. *Library of Congress.*

A loosely knit group of artists, writers, and artistic rebels already had been gathering beneath the Carmel pines, far away from the (to them, at least) gaudy and commercial Hotel Del Monte. Among the creatives who lived in or frequented Carmel between 1900 and 1915 were writers Mary Hunter Austin, Sinclair Lewis, Alice MacGowan, Jimmy Hopper and Grace MacGowan Cook; painters Percy Gray, William Keith, William Frederic Ritschel, Armin Hansen, Sydney Yard, and Ferdinand Burgdorff; poets Robinson Jeffers, Nora May French, George Sterling and Clark Ashton Smith; and photographer Arnold Genthe.

American author Jack London was in Carmel at that time as well, and he offers a vivid description of Carmel's early years in his novel, The *Valley of the Moon*.

Recalling Carmel in the first decade of the 20th century, American writer Mary Hunter Austin wrote:

> When I first came to this land, a virgin thicket of buckthorn sage and sea-blue lilac spread between the well-spaced long-leaved pines. The dunes glistened white with violet shadows, and in warm hollows, between live oaks, the wine of light had mellowed undisturbed a thousand years... We achieved, all of us who flocked there within the ensuing two or three years, especially after the fire of 1906 had made San Francisco uninhabitable to the creative worker, a settled habit of morning work... But by the early afternoon one and another of the painter and writer folk could be seen sauntering by piney trails... there would be tea beside driftwood fires, or mussel roasts by moonlight— or the lot of us would pound abalone for chowder. And to talk—Ambrosial unquotable talk. Strangeness of bearded men from Tassajara with bear meat and wild honey to sell. Great [mule] teams from the Sur, going by on the high road with the sound of bells... I think that the memorable and now vanished charm of Carmel lay, perhaps, most in the reality of the simplicity attained, a simplicity... as it can never be in any quarter of city life. (Mary Austin, *Earth Horizon*, 1932)

Powers and Devendorf

Frank Powers, a lawyer from San Francisco, had been deeply impressed by the beauty of Carmel's location, and the economic downturn in the late 1890s had worked to his advantage: by 1901 Powers had acquired by barter or trade more than 1,600 Carmel lots. His intention was to sell them carefully while preserving the natural beauty of the wooded setting. Powers still needed to maintain his busy legal practice in San Francisco, and in Frank Devendorf he found a partner who shared his real-estate savvy and his love of nature. Devendorf, like Powers, had acquired hundreds of Carmel lots, and together they formalized a street plan and established a commitment to maintaining the beauty of the natural surroundings, especially the trees. Over the next two decades Powers, Devendorf and the Carmel Development Company had an enormous and positive influence on the evolution of the town. In marketing the sale of lots, Devendorf wanted to attract what he called "brain workers"—artistic spirits, academics, professionals, painters, writers, musicians, teachers, people of learning and a love of the arts— who would create an interesting community and appreciate the natural beauty Devendorf was committed to preserving. At first the lots were sold for $10 down, with little or no interest, and pay whatever you could afford each month.

Mary Austin refers just above to the "fire of 1906" and indeed the San Francisco earthquake and fire displaced several hundred thousand people including countless "creative workers" who lost not only their homes and possessions but also their entire artistic community and infrastructure. The academic world was reeling as well: UC Berkeley was spared serious damage, but much of the Stanford University campus and surrounding buildings were destroyed.

In late 1906, the San Francisco Call ran a full page article about the "artists, poets and writers of Carmel-by-the-Sea". In 1910 the Call estimated that 60 percent of Carmel's houses were built by occupants who were "devoting their lives to work connected to the aesthetic arts." In those days Carmel was made up of three categories of people: those with great and often innovative artistic vision; others with and without talent who aspired to artistic significance; and others who appreciated art and artists and loved being around them.

In the years immediately following the great 1906 earthquake, Carmel was a haven for new residents escaping the Bay Area devastation, all of them carefully vetted by Frank Devendorf.

The remodeled barn of Jane Gallatin Powers, an accomplished painter and wife of Frank

A "milk shrine," with a spot for each house in the neighborhood. Lewis Slevin took this photo in 1923, but the milk shrines were in use for several decades after that. *Courtesy of the H.M. Williams Local History Department, Harrison Memorial Library.*

Powers, was probably the first artist's studio in Carmel. Mrs. Powers persuaded many San Francisco artists to relocate their studios to Carmel, after the 1906 earthquake. Other studios were soon established, including those of Mary DeNeale Morgan, Arthur Vachell, Laura Maxwell, Jessie Frances Short and William Silva.

One of Carmel's first formally established community organizations was the Arts and Crafts Club, founded in 1905 by Elsie Allen, former editor of Harper's magazine and a faculty member of Wellesley College. Other founders included Jane Gallatin Powers, photographer Louis Slevin, and a number of other like-minded artists. The Arts and Crafts Movement was an influential part of the international art scene at that time (See Appendix), but the Carmel group defined "Arts and Crafts" broadly to include not only the visual, decorative, and domestic arts, but also literature, music, and drama.

For the first year the club met in borrowed space on Ocean Avenue. Then, in 1906 they purchased a lot on Casanova Street between 8th and 9th Avenues (the location of the present-day Circle Theater). There they built the Arts and Crafts Hall at a cost of $2,500. It formally opened on August 1, 1907, with an exhibit of Club members' art. The Arts and Crafts Hall was the first cultural center and theater in Carmel, and was used for gatherings of all sorts including exhibits, meetings, instruction, dance, and plays. Mary Austin and George Sterling performed their "private theatricals" there, presentations performed for the amusement of the participants. The club also sponsored fund-raising events and promoted civic improvements.

In 1910, the Arts and Crafts Club organized its first summer school, called Cedar Croft. The program offered classes in botany, drawing and painting, pottery, china painting, art needlework,

Until the first issue of the Carmel Pine Cone in 1915, news and announcements were posted on a bulletin board in the middle of the village. *Courtesy of the H.M. Williams Local History Department, Harrison Memorial Library.*

dramatic reading, music, and metal art. The school operated for more than a decade, giving students from around the country the opportunity to work with nationally recognized artists and noted local artists.

By 1915 the Club had begun presenting leading artists in classes and workshops for aspiring painters, craftsmen, and even actors. Prominent painters including William Merritt Chase, Mary DeNeale Morgan, C. Chapel Judson, and Xavier Martinez offered instruction at reasonable prices.

A 1911 Forest Theater production of Shakespeare's *As You Like It. Library of Congress.*

Meanwhile the outdoor Forest Theater was established by the community in 1910. The site, donated by Frank Devendorf, was a natural amphitheater in a wooded setting just southeast of Ocean Avenue and Junípero Street. It was secluded by the pine trees, but in reality it was only a few blocks from the center of Carmel. A stage was constructed and a fire pit was built on either side of the stage.

Although many improvements have been made to the theater stage and audience seating area over the years, the Forest Theater with its two fire pits is still in use and has become a Carmel landmark. Two of the leading figures in the Forest Theater and early Carmel theater in general were Perry Newberry and Herbert Heron. Each played a major role in early Carmel history, and each served as mayor.

Embodying all the elements espoused by the Little Theater Movement sweeping the country at the time, community theater in Carmel was becoming a central operating force. The majority of the earliest Carmel residents participated in community-based theatrical events. The productions were "amateur" in every sense of sense word: the people involved loved doing it, most of them had no training or professional experience, and emphasis was placed on the overall effect of a production, and not on finesse or detail.

The presentations had achieved national attention by 1914, when an article in the San José Mercury Herald commented

> "...a fever of activity seems to have seized the community and each newcomer is immediately inoculated and begins with great enthusiasm to do something... with plays, studios and studies...."

On the stage of the outdoor Forest Theater, and in the Arts and Crafts hall, a community of theater enthusiasts produced plays and shows year-round and theater continued to be a central operating force as the village grew. The Carmel theater story continues in a later chapter.

Music in Carmel before 1924

Background

While theater flourished in Carmel's earliest days, music took root in the community much later. When Devendorf and Powers sold lots in the early 1900s, they marketed their real estate very well: the people they attracted to Carmel brought with them an appreciation for all the arts, including music, but that art form did not yet have a formal outlet in the village.

Theater was the central activity of the Carmel community until the early 1920s, and nearly all the public or semi-public musical events in Carmel took place either in private homes or within the framework of staged theatrical productions in the Arts and Crafts Theater or the outdoor Forest Theater. Very occasionally an out of town or local musician might be presented "in concert" in a large Carmel or Monterey home. (Discussed more fully in the "Carmel Music Society 1927–1928" chapter.)

This paragraph from *Carmel at Work and Play* (1925) describes musical life in Carmel as it was until the early 1920s.

> Music, like the deep undertone of the sea which bounds Carmel's shore, plays a running accompaniment to the song of village life. From the beginning, little informal groups of music lovers have gathered at one of their houses to hear resident or visiting artists play or sing. After the music, there comes usually a frank discussion of the player's interpretation—but always with that subtle sympathy and helpful interchange of ideas which is possible only when people have mutual interest in a common ground. (Bostick/Castelhun, 1925)

The same desire for community creative expression that had fueled the Little Theater movement also inspired a few early attempts at community music making. In 1922 the Peninsula Daily Herald underwrote the creation of a local amateur orchestra, the Peninsula Philharmonic Society under the leadership of David Alberto. The orchestra (no more than 15 players) did give a few small-scale concerts but there is no press coverage of them. Alberto's own public statements make it clear that the orchestra was more of a casual club than an enduring organization. In fact it had no future as an orchestra, and gave up that pretense but kept the name. The Society's primary activity became raising the money to present two or three out-of-town classical music artists each season in the Monterey Theatre at 21 Alvarado Street, a damp and unheated auditorium (it was demolished in 1967). Pianist Arthur Schnabel and dancer Isadora Duncan were among the artists presented by the Philharmonic Society in Monterey in 1923 and 1924. There was great enthusiasm for the Society series for a few years, but the organization had lost momentum by 1927 and was unable to sell enough subscriptions to keep going.

In 1923, the Arts and Crafts Club of Carmel formed its own Choral Society under the direction of Thomas Vincent Cator, a composer, piano teacher, and writer. The Carmel Pine Cone covered the preliminary meeting, where Mr. Cator said that the choral society was "to be a means of developing musical talent and was preliminary to a public appearance in a cantata, oratorio, or comic opera. Mr. Cator spoke of the great demand that has been made for a long time by the people of this community for some musical organization." The assembled group then joined in singing several songs including Annie Laurie, Swanee River, and Auld Lang Syne, and the Carmel Pine Cone reports that... "a number of good voices were discovered." The article goes on to say:

This Choral Society of the arts and crafts bids fair to become the most democratic organization in Carmel. Rich and poor, young and old, big and little, "highbrow" or "lowbrow," can all meet on a common basis, the love of good music, and there is no reason why this common interest should not be a link between what has been done in the past and the larger things possible in the future.

The sort of same enthusiasm led amateur players in Carmel to attempt to form their own community orchestra. San Francisco art and music critic Redfern Mason had lived in Carmel for a few years and maintained an interest in the town. In the fall of 1923 he wrote an article in the San Francisco Call in which he expressed optimism for Carmel's musical community.

There are signs that Carmel is outgrowing its dilettantism. The artisans have an orchestra and make music for their own pleasure. That orchestra interests me much. F. E. Coleman, who build houses as solid as the everlasting hills, is the leader. He is a cellist as well as a mason. William Garreskey, the carpenter, plays the fiddle; Ralph Hillis, plumber, beats the drum; the contra-base player is Fenton Foster, head of Peninsula, Incorporated. Others who take part of the ensemble are Charles Barkey, bank clerk; J. D. Johnston, who works in a grocery store; Mr. Titmouse, postal employee; Thomas de Neil Morgan, owner of the post office building; Mrs. Samuelson, teacher in the Carmel school; Mrs. A. J. Comstock, music teacher; Mrs. Mackenstock, Eugene Roehling, Albert Comstock, Robert Riegg, Teaby Nichols, and so on. Here are professional men and women, clerks, handy craftsman, teachers, school boys, all engaged in making music for their own delight. It is one of the most helpful things I have heard of in Carmel for years.

In February 1924, the orchestra gave its first concert, for an audience of friends and family at the new Arts and Crafts Theater on Monte Verde Street.

"New Carmel Orchestra"

An interesting feature of the weekend events at the Arts and Crafts Theater is the first appearance of the recently organized local orchestra. For some time the musicians have been practicing together several evenings a week, and are now capable of rendering very acceptable music.

F. E. Coleman is the conductor. The players are as follows: piano, Mrs. A.J. Comstock; violins, Mrs. Mecklinstock, William Grasske, Albert Comstock, Wesley Dickinson, Eugene (unknown); flute, T.W. Morgan, Jr.; saxophone, Teaby Nichols; coronets Robert Reigg and John Johnston; trombone, Charles Berkey; and drums, Ralph W. Hicks. (Pine Cone, February 23, 1924)

Putting on a concert with an orchestra of amateurs is no small task. The participants in an orchestra must already have a certain level of training not (necessarily) needed by an actor in a community theater or a singer in an amateur chorus. To succeed, an orchestra also must rehearse regularly—weekly if possible—over a period of months before it can achieve the ensemble cohesion, player skill, and artistic confidence needed for a performance that could satisfy both the participants and the audience.

In order to generate this sort of commitment, two factors need to be present. The leader needs to be consistently challenging and inspiring, and there needs to be a reason for it all, some overarching motivation or long-term goal that transcends merely the current rehearsal schedule, or the plans for the next concert. Without a deep and long-term commitment from its members, no orchestra can survive, and neither can a chorus of voices.

Apparently the Arts and Crafts Choral Society did indeed perform the oratorio "The Crucifixion" in April 1924. The work was written in 1887 by the English composer John Stainer for four-part chorus accompanied by organ, with tenor and baritone soloists. In the next few years, several more local attempts were made to establish a chorus and/or orchestra in Carmel, but the organizers did not sustain any of the projects beyond a single concert. The half dozen performances given by local ensembles between 1924 and 1928 each received a small notice in the Pine Cone in which all participants were thanked and the ensemble was given encouragement (rather than praise) for its "doubtless potential," "promise for the future," etc.

Theater was still the most active communal art form in Carmel: in 1924, three Carmel theater stages produced 25 plays, including several premieres. Meanwhile, the Carmel Pine Cone reported these public concerts in Carmel during the same year:

Arts and Crafts Theater (formerly "Hall") on Casanova Street
March 10	William Edward Johnson, baritone
March 14	Pacific Grove musical society (chorus)
April 18	Arts & Crafts Choral Society, Stainer's The Crucifixion

Theatre of the Golden Bough, Ocean Avenue
July 15	Henry Cowell, pianist
July 19	Lawrence Strauss tenor
July 31	Constance Pruhl, pianist; Spencer Yates, violinist; John Edward Hellman, baritone
August 3	Ellen Edwards, pianist
August 31	Edoard Deru, violinist
October 26	Radiana Pazmor, contralto
November 2	Annie Louise David, harpist; Roberta Leitch, soprano; Edward Kuster, cello

The Henry Cowell concert on the list was presented by "Denny and Watrous." Dene was his champion and she was committed to introducing Cowell and his ideas to the world. The connection between Dene and Cowell had started in 1923 in San Francisco, but he enters the story more fully in a later chapter.

Denny and Watrous 1924
Flashback to 1922

As described in Part Two, while still living in the apartment building at 1907 Leavenworth where they first met, Dene and Hazel purchased a lot in Carmel on Dolores Street between 2nd and 1st Avenues, and spent that summer constructing a cottage of Hazel's design. In September 1922, they returned to San Francisco, Hazel began her final year of teaching at Alameda High School, and Dene taught piano lessons in her Sutter Street studio.

By December they had moved into their rented space on the third floor of the Fisk House in San Francisco, where they spent 1923 presenting music and arts events. Dene continued to study piano with Wager Swayne, and took part in several more studio recitals. She was a busy piano teacher and had moved her downtown piano studio to a larger space at 376 Sutter Street.

June 1923 marked the end of Hazel's 17 years of high school teaching and the two women began to make plans to leave go to New York in 1924 to study. When they decided to return to California, their Carmel home would be waiting for them.

Now that Hazel had left her high school teaching job, both women were freelancers, and were able to spend time in Carmel in their cottage. Hazel's sister Zanetta moved to Carmel and purchased a lot almost directly across the street from Hazel and Dene, and she commissioned Hazel to design a small house for her and her young son. Work began in October 1923, and the construction was completed after a second round of work in April 1924. Although the cottage was not large (it still stands on Dolores Street) the total cost of Zanetta's house in 1923 and 1924 was nearly $1,000, a fairly large sum at the time.

Zanetta Watrous Catlett

Zanetta Watrous (b. Visalia 1886) was married in 1907 to Walter Catlett (1889-1960), a busy character actor on stage and later in film and on TV. They lived in New York and Los Angeles, and traveled together throughout the United States, to France, and to England where their son Richard was born in 1914.

By 1920 Zanetta and Walter had separated and Zanetta and Richard were on their own. They lived in Carmel until the early 1930s, when Zanetta remarried and moved to San Francisco. After the death of her second husband, she spent the last years of her life in Santa Cruz and died there in 1978. During the 1930s, the cottage Hazel designed for Zanetta became the home of their mother, Minnie, in her final years.

Walter Catlett

Change of plans

In April 1924, Dene and Hazel were planning to leave California and go to New York, but they went first to Carmel to oversee the second stage of work on Zanetta's house. In Carmel, their minds may have been changed by the people, the setting, and the enormous possibilities. Situated in a place of stunning and expansive natural beauty, populated by an array of fascinating artists and free-spirited intellectuals, Carmel-by-the-Sea was becoming one of the centers of artistic thought on the West Coast. It was a community the two of them could be part of, one that would welcome them in a way that crowded and bustling New York City never could. They were free from their public school teaching jobs and noisy city life, and in Carmel they could create any future they wanted for themselves.

Their planned New York trip was put on hold for what turned out to be 18 months, and they stepped enthusiastically into the Carmel community. The Carmel lots sold by Devendorf and Powers seemed too narrow for some new residents, and it was not uncommon for owners to buy the adjacent lot for elbow room and possible future expansion. By the first week of April, Dene and Hazel had done just that, and had begun their move from the San Francisco penthouse to the Carmel cottage they had built themselves two years before. Both women appear in the Carmel Voter Registry in 1924. (Dene is listed as "musician," and Hazel as "artist." Both are identified as Republicans.)

From this point on they were Carmel residents for the rest of their lives (although for the next five years Dene rented a San Francisco studio at 545 Sutter Street where she gave piano lessons one day every week or two).

Carmel has a mild, Mediterranean climate almost year-round, and the most serious weather problems are usually the cool, foggy nights and the frequent heavy rains during the winter months. For the artists escaping the commercialization of the city, housing in Carmel in the early decades was a highly individual affair, and until the early 1920s many homes were owner-built. Daisy Bostick was a Carmel resident in the early 1920s and she published this description in 1925.

> A walk in Carmel generally turns into a voyage of discovery. Even the natives find surprises when they set out for a ramble. Somebody has put up a little studio in the corner of the garden—somebody else has calmly picked up his house and migrated to another lot....that winding road through the pines disappeared completely since the last time you came this way! In its place is a little steep roofed, redwood board-and-bat house which must've sprung up like a mushroom overnight. Today it fits snugly into the embrace of the oaks and pines as if it had been there since time began. ...
>
> There is a certain air of mystery and romance about these glimpses of little redwood houses, with their gaily-painted windows and doors, which fascinates the passerby. Not the forbidding, standoffish reserve of the character whose dignity you must not forget, but a sort of quietly-mischievous, chuckling spirit of hide-and-go-seekness.
>
> There is moreover something subtly friendly and hospitable about them. Looking at these houses among the pines and dancing oaks, you realize that the people who dwell in them must live in comfortable freedom from the heavy hand of formality. Who cares about the famous book of etiquette when you cook your steak over a grill in the garden, and have your meals squeezed into a chummy breakfast nook, with birds picking crumbs from the windowsill. (Bostick/Castelhun, 1925)

Hazel and Dene are honored today for their contributions to the performing arts, but it was not through music or theater that they first established themselves in Carmel. By the mid 1920s, Carmel was moving beyond the era of the self-built house, and was experiencing a major real estate boom, and Dene and Hazel took part in it. The two cottages Hazel created on Dolores Street had startled the Carmel community: her designs were surprising and her choices and uses of color were innovative and whimsical. By late 1923 friends and colleagues had begun asking Hazel to be their design consultant, and Dene and Hazel seized that opportunity. Leveraging the attention that Hazel had attracted with her first two houses, their partnership entered its next chapter and they became "Denny and Watrous." An ad like the one shown on the opposite page appeared regularly in the Carmel Pine Cone from April 1924 through the end of 1926.

Over a period of nearly four years, Hazel Watrous and Dene Denny created three dozen houses in Carmel. Hazel's architectural ideas were influenced by the Arts and Crafts Movement, and her design concepts were colorful and eclectic—the houses are mostly small cottages with lots of natural redwood and exposed beams inside, arched windows and doors, large picture windows, and typically Carmel board-and-batten exteriors, but with extremely un-typical pastel colors on the exterior, and occasionally even on the cedar roof shingles.

The excerpt below is from a 32-page collection of essays and musings published in May 1925, by Stephen Allen Reynolds.

Carmel is marching on—marching toward the inevitable blending of the arts into Art, the fusing of the elements of painting and literature, of sculpture, music and drama, into one. And near the head of this march, we of Carmel find two women: an artist and a musician, each of whom has received marked recognition in her work. They are builders, and at the present writing they are on their 14th house. They build, not mere shelters against wind and rain, but fine imaginative creations, large, small, which speak the same language—through a different medium—spoken by the painted picture, whispered by the carved marble, breathed by fine opera or noble book.

Denny and Watrous
Designers, Builders, Decorators
of Homes
Box 282, Carmel, California

The artist in this board-and-batten medium is Hazel Watrous. The musician is Ethel Adele Denny. They aimed for New York, and hit Carmel. In the creative background of Hazel Watrous may be seen achievement in design, in batik, in interior decoration and stagecraft. Ethel Adele Denny is a highly

Courtesy of the H. M. Williams Local History Department, Harrison Memorial Library; and the Carmel Pine Cone.

cultivated musician. Together they are creative workers who are accomplishing big things in a fine way. Their San Francisco studio in the ballroom of an old residence was well-known to earnest toilers in the field of art. There, overlooking a thousand housetops, they loved to gather.

What these two women stand for, the manner in which they have worked out their inspirations, may be seen on numerous choice properties in Carmel from Dune to city limit. From the scooping of foundation to the hanging of the last curtain, they do it all; and we rejoice to witness their individual sense of art expressed in terms of line, form, balance and color, breathing in every detail the spirit of Carmel.

(From *Carmel–its poets and peasants* by Stephen Allen Reynolds, 1925)

The Theatre of the Golden Bough 1924
Background: The Little Theater Movement, or "constructive leisure"

As more and more people attended live theatrical performances throughout the US in the nineteenth century, a genre of sensational and large-scale melodramas had developed, drawing larger and larger audiences. With the expansion of the North American railroad network in the late 1800s, these formulaic works could be performed by touring companies over and over again in productions tailored for auditoriums of all sizes across the country.

In a confidential meeting in 1895, the owners and producers of most of America's theaters organized a Theatrical Syndicate to maximize their profits by controlling both competition and ticket prices. This Syndicate effectively stifled theatrical innovation and experimentation for several decades, but what they had not foreseen in 1895 was the development of the moving picture. By the second decade of the twentieth century, cinema was becoming the chief purveyor of spectacle and melodrama, with stereotypical characters and exaggerated plots and acting. It was much more profitable than live theater: with a few (mostly unskilled) employees, movie houses could play to several audiences each day and entertain them more cheaply and with even more spectacle and fantasy than a live show. Meanwhile, serious American live theater had been artistically shanghaied by the New York syndicate, and it needed a new start.

In 1887, Andre Antoine had established an experimental workshop theater company in Paris, the Théatre Libre (The Free Theater), and his work had a great influence on theater throughout Europe as the world approached the twentieth century. In his work Antoine had planted the seeds of the Little Theater Movement, which had its beginning in the US with three events in 1912.

Playwright and producer Percy MacKaye published his book, *The Civic Theater*, in which he argued for theater activity as a means of "constructive leisure" through which Americans could find meaning and fulfillment, forge relationships, and improve their communities.

The other events were the creation of two new theater companies: the Toy Theater in Boston and the Little Theater in Chicago. (Playwright and stage director Maurice Browne, a founder of the Chicago Little Theater and one of the pioneers of the Little Theater Movement, was influential in Carmel in the early 1920s.) Theater companies appeared in Seattle, Detroit, and a dozen other cities, all attempting to produce more intimate, noncommercial, and imaginative plays.

The Little Theater Movement first arose as a semi-professional response to the centralization and commercialization of theater in America. The central motivating force was a shift away from the New York theater syndicate's shallow, commercial, profit-centered approach. There was a desire to move beyond melodramas and "amusements" and toward greater artistic creativity, depth, and experimentation. Most Little Theater companies shared the same basic goals and intentions: there was a preference for short plays; European plays were performed in English translation; there was a real interest in staging new works, often written by members of the ensemble; and there was an openness to experimental, avant-garde staging and stagecraft techniques being used in Europe or written about in sources like the influential *Theater Arts Magazine* (founded in 1916).

Once the Little Theater Movement caught on in major centers like Boston and Chicago, its popularity soared in communities across the country, partly due to another wonderful element of the Little Theater experience: people of all backgrounds could connect and work together in a vivid, challenging, exciting, and satisfying creative pursuit. In his 1912 book, Percy McKaye was correct: "constructive leisure" was fulfilling and community–building on a local level and beyond.

The Pasadena Community Playhouse, east of Los Angeles, became the flagship of the Little Theater Movement in the United States. It began as a basic community theater and at its peak it operated six stages, each featuring a new production every two weeks. This theatrical palace was the largest theater complex west of Chicago at the time of its construction in 1925, and it continues to thrive today.

The residents of Carmel were a part of the society of arts lovers—and not only artists—who wanted to re-establish a living tradition of live theater in America. The opening of the Arts and Crafts Hall in Carmel in 1907 and the outdoor Forest Theater in 1910 marked the beginning of theater history in Carmel, just as the first Little Theaters were appearing in Boston, Detroit, and Chicago, and Percy McKaye was writing about it in his 1912 book.

As of 1910, the tiny village of Carmel with its few hundred residents had two stages—the outdoor Forest Theater and the Arts and Crafts Hall on Casanova Street. In the following decade it was as though the community was a year-round theater camp, and it is impossible to overestimate the influence these brief decades of theater activity had in determining how the world saw the town and how the town saw itself. This recollection was written in 1925:

> Then, as now, there was no dividing line between the artist and business people. Many of the latter played important parts of the performances and much talent was thus discovered and developed. Each did the thing he could do best. The grocer, the carpenter, the artist, with equal zest, dressed up as wild Indians and lent an atmosphere to the background of the pageants by skulking through the trees. Their wives made costumes by day and skulked along with their Indian husbands by night. Unsuspecting fellow artists arriving for a visit were pounced upon at the Monterey station, brought over the hill and made to carry a spear or to play the part of an assassin in that night's performance. It frequently happened that all Carmel was in the cast, and the audience for the play had to be recruited entirely from the outside. (Bostick/Castelhun, 1925)

Edward Kuster builds his theater

Into this environment of enthusiastic and quirky artistic adventure came Edward Gerhard Kuster. Born in Indiana in 1878, Kuster was a seriously devoted "amateur" ("lover") of the arts: he and his family had lived in Berlin when he was a boy (his father was a German-born physician), and he spoke fluent German. He performed small roles in productions at the Majestic Theater in Los Angeles; he played the cello well enough to perform in public concerts; and danced with the Ruth St. Denis Company.

Meanwhile, Kuster had a day job: he had made his considerable fortune as a lawyer with a Los Angeles law firm that worked on (and won) a huge case involving the trans-continental railroad. He took his earnings, left the law firm, and devoted the rest of his life to his one true passion: the theater. The Pasadena Playhouse had inspired Edward Kuster to leverage the theatrical energy of Carmel in order to use the community as a laboratory for his artistic vision. Kuster later wrote that he had chosen Carmel in 1921 because,

> "...the little village was simply boiling over with theater mindedness. I don't think that such a preoccupation with theater was ever encountered anywhere else in the country before or since. Everybody had got into the act. Everybody was a director or an actor or a backstage worker or stage carpenter or electrician—and if none of these, the remainder were a dependable and enthusiastic audience." (Quoted in Morgan Stock thesis.)

There is an odd sidebar to Kuster's story: When he was a young lawyer living in Los Angeles, his wife, Una, took graduate courses at Occidental College. There she met an intense young man named Robinson Jeffers, and they had an affair on and off for eight years. Finally she and Kuster were divorced and she married Jeffers the next day. They moved to Carmel, where Jeffers began hand-building his famous Tor House, a stone castle home overlooking the Pacific. Several years later, after Edward Kuster had made his fortune in LA and remarried, he and his wife also moved to Carmel. Their new Carmel home: an equally impressive stone house built to Kuster's design on the lot adjacent to Jeffers' Tor House.

During his first two years in Carmel, Kuster acted at the Forest Theater, arranged and led music for its performances, and got to know the locals, until finally in 1923 he was asked to direct a large production of George Bernard Shaw's "Caesar and Cleopatra." While the production received modest praise, there was frustration and resentment among the participants at Kuster's professional and disciplined style of direction. It was different from the relaxed, comfortable and easy-going tradition at the Forest Theater for the previous two decades.

Another sore spot was the trees. Trees have played a special role in Carmel-by-the-Sea for more than a century, and the Carmelites take their trees very seriously. The "Forest Theater," after all, was so named because it is surrounded by trees. Regardless of the particular drama being performed, the sight of those trees was part of the Forest Theater experience for the audience. Kuster, however, designed massive Egyptian scenery—including a huge sphinx—for his production of the Shaw play, and the scenery obscured the trees. For those who already found Kuster off-putting as a stage director, this was just another insult.

Albert Denny's first wife said of him "He has a mind of his own and thinks it a good one," and the same applied to Teddy Kuster. He was a brilliant and persuasive polymath who was quite sure of himself and was equally sure that everyone would quickly see his brilliant ideas as a gift to all theater lovers in Carmel. Unfortunately the brilliance of his ideas seems to have blinded him to the mood in Carmel, and to the fact that some in the village were beginning to resent his unasked-for intrusion.

Kuster was so committed to his dream—in a community he did not fully understand—that he was willing to invest more than $75,000 of his own money in the construction of a new theater in Carmel. He would build it on the southeast corner of Ocean Avenue and Monte Verde Street, and he planned to call it The Theatre of the Golden Bough.

Kuster came to Carmel in 1921 because he was interested in working with community-based theater and Carmel was becoming famous for it. He believed that amateur theater could be refined to a higher artistic level through the engagement of professionals to manage the amateur participants. Kuster's believed that the Carmel theatrical community's enthusiasm exceeded its ability and skill. He further believed that professional guidance for the Carmel actors, professional training for the stage crew, and professional quality theatrical equipment and sets could enable the amateur performers to rise to the fullest level of their ability. Everyone would certainly agree—or so he thought—that the joy of artistic fulfillment was a goal worth working toward. As he said at the time, his goal was to build an indoor theater in Carmel that would be the best-equipped in the country, and one "so beautiful that the town could not help trying to measure up to it with its plays."

Doing his neighborly duty, Kuster explained his project to a meeting of the Arts and Crafts Club of Carmel in May 1923. Kuster had known for several months that the club had been planning to build its own new theater behind their original Hall on Casanova Street, but although the construction plans had been approved, work had not yet started. Kuster described his new theater to the club members, and explained that the club's resident theater troupe, the Carmel Players, could use his Theatre of the Golden Bough free of charge for their productions. Not only could they save themselves the trouble and expense of building and operating their own theater, Kuster's theater would be a much more sophisticated venue. Perhaps Kuster was hoping for, if not collaboration, at least cooperation. He got less than nothing.

In his enthusiasm, and despite—or perhaps because of—his genius, Kuster made the common mistake of the dynamic and creative visionary who arrives in a small (read: unrefined) town and attempts to impose his vision upon people who see him as an outsider and do not want his unasked-for help. In all communities, especially small ones, there is a certain inertia at the center: most people tend to like the familiar and don't want things to change. Some like the status quo and feel they have worked hard to achieve it. Others believe that what is already in place is good enough, so don't mess with it. Others feel insulted by the very fact that someone even suggests they need to change. The bottom line was that the members of the Arts and Crafts Club did not want Kuster—or any other newcomer—telling them how to do theater in their town.

And so, even though Kuster was moving ahead on his enormous project, the Arts and Crafts Club pushed ahead with the construction of their new theater as well. On the lot to the east of the original Arts and Crafts Hall, they built a new theater fronting on Monte Verde Street, larger and a bit more upscale. (This is the location of the modern Golden Bough Theatre, owned by the Pacific Repertory Theatre.) During the fall months, the Carmel newspapers reported on the construction progress of the two theaters, sometimes featuring two articles next to each other on the same page. The Little Theater of the Arts and Crafts Club opened on December 31, 1923, and the Club continued to make improvements over the next year.

> It is marked by extreme simplicity in its furnishings and decorations, but the auditorium is roomy, comfortable and well-heated. The stage is exceptionally large, and the stage equipment probably more complete than that of most theaters in towns the size of Carmel. (Bostick/Castelhun, 1925)

But there was no theater "in towns the size of Carmel," and few anywhere else in the US, as technically sophisticated as the theater Edward Kuster was building on Ocean Avenue.

"...the most advanced step in theater design in this country."

Kuster's intention was not only to build a theater but to create a place of visual charm and style that would be one of the anchors of downtown Carmel. On his lot at the southeast corner of Ocean Avenue and Monte Verde Street, he began by building a group of shops and rental spaces intended as studios for artists and artisans. The design conceived by Kuster and his wife was deliberately whimsical. The cottages and structures had curving graceful roofs, walls with mottled colors, hooded doorways, overhanging eaves, nooks in the walls, floors at irregular heights, and unexpected glimpses of little turrets and other architectural details.

For his ticket office, Kuster bought an old weaver's cottage outside of town and had it moved to the Theatre property. In the twenty-first century, Kuster's ticket office serves as a beloved Carmel candy shop. The Theatre itself is no longer there, but most of the rest of the Court of the Golden Bough still stands, and although remodeling has been done, the architecture still maintains the original flavor.

Once this first group of small buildings was in place, Kuster constructed his truly remarkable theater behind them, away from Ocean Avenue. To reach the Theatre's main entrance one had to walk through the Court of shops and studios. Kuster designed the exterior of the Theatre with the churches and ecclesiastical buildings of northern Italy in mind, with tall slim buttresses, gaunt simple lines, exterior stucco of rich earth colors, and very few exterior window openings. The Theatre was built by local artisans and workmen under Kuster's supervision, with the assistance of a local contractor who had no experience in theater construction.

The audience entered the Theatre through a foyer where coffee was served during intermissions. The auditorium, accessed through doors on the sides, was softly lit and had mellow plaster walls with no decoration. The room was designed to focus attention on the unique stage.

At the time of its opening the Theatre of the Golden Bough may have had the most modern stagecraft facilities of any theater in the West, and was said to contain several features not to be found in any theater in the country. The proscenium opening of the main stage was 28 feet wide by 21 feet high, and the stage had a depth of 34 feet from the curtain line to the rear wall. Above the entire main stage was an enormous metal "sky dome" which took the place of a backdrop, and curved completely around and over the stage. It was constructed of metal lath on a steel framework, surfaced with plaster, and weighed 14 tons. The dome was filled with holes for an array of flood lamps and spotlights. A light bridge was built high above the front of the stage, hidden from the audience by the proscenium, and from there the lighting of the sky dome was managed.

The entire lighting system was controlled from a control board in the projection booth behind the audience (rather than the traditional location in the wings, where the operator often cannot see the stage action). The Monterey Herald described the setup:

"The idea of having the lighting controlled from the projection room is a radical departure from the usual. The advantages are easily seen. The operator has his keyboard of lights—there are 120 keys lettered and numbered in Kuster's switchboard—before him, much as a painter has his pigments on his palette, and he literally can paint his scene to suit the sentiment, emotion or passion of the moment, flooding the stage with varicolored lights and changing them at will, having the whole stage before him all the time, and noting the effect of the lights on the players and scenery, and their agreement with the tone of the play at that particular moment.

"Kuster has dispensed with footlights, borders, and sidelights, depending altogether on upper and oblique lighting for his effects. There are 42 floodlights above the stage and set in two crossbeams in the ceiling of the auditorium, and he has 21 large and 24 baby spotlights, supplied with current from 167 circuits of electricity." (Monterey Herald, June 12, 1924.

Kuster's original plan was for an auditorium capable of seating up to 800, but the dimensions of the actual lot led to a reduction in the size of the building, which reduced the audience size to 500. Kuster, still marching to his own drummer, reduced the numbers even more by doing away with the cramped, wooden, and often unupholstered seats found in the average theater of that day. He ordered 400 custom-made willow armchairs from the San Francisco Wicker Company, and on those chairs his audiences sat. One can only imagine watching a play while sitting in a room with 400 other people in softly creaking wicker chairs.

Across the entire front edge of the main stage were four wide steps leading down to a forestage—one of the most dramatic features of the auditorium. The forestage was 40 feet wide where it met the main stage, and it projected 20 feet out into the auditorium in the shape of a very rounded wedge. Two more shallow steps to the floor of the auditorium extended entirely around the forestage's curving perimeter.

There was no visible orchestra pit in The Theatre of the Golden Bough. Kuster had seen the opera house Richard Wagner designed in Bayreuth, Germany, in which the orchestra

and conductor are in a kind of orchestra pit but completely hidden from the audience. Kuster liked that idea but went even further with it: the orchestra pit of the Golden Bough was big enough to accommodate 12 or 14 musicians, but it was located directly under the 20x40 foot forestage. The musicians were not only out of sight of the audience at all times, they were effectively in a different room. A hidden periscope was used to project the image of the actors on the stage onto a screen in the hidden orchestra pit. A back wall of seasoned maple helped project the music into the auditorium through an array of concealed openings in the risers of the steps around the curved edge of the forestage, and these sound

Previous page, top and middle image courtesy of the author. Photographs of the facade and interior of the Theatre of the Golden Bough on these two and the next two pages are from Edward Kuster's scrapbooks. *Courtesy of the H. M. Williams Local History Department, Harrison Memorial Library.*

In mid October the Golden Bough presented a double bill. Shown here, *The Nursery Maid of Heaven*, by Thomas Wood Stevens. On the opposite page, the stage is set for the other play on the bill, *The Princess Who Wouldn't Say Die*, by Bertram Block. The actors on the extreme left and right are kneeling at the foot of the steps going from the forestage up to the main stage.

portals could be opened and closed with curtains and louvers to adjust the sound to the desired loudness or effect.

A few of the 10 dressing rooms were directly offstage, and a hallway with a padded floor led to the others in the basement. Also in the lower level were storage rooms and a scenery shop. There was hot and cold running water not only in the dressing rooms but also in the men's and women's showers, something that the Carmel Pine Cone suggested would *"bring joy to the too long-suffering victims of the Nubian, Hindu, and Arab makeup."*

Kuster had very high ideals, and his financial commitment was total. In his words:

There is no reason why artistry and common sense should not go hand-in-hand. We are not going to engage in "show business". This theater will not be an amusement hall designed to attract the money spending public. We expected to pay its own cost of operation and taxes; beyond that it need never return another dollar. It is not a business investment. (Kuster open letter to the Pine Cone, June 1, 1924)

Those in the community not connected with the Arts and Crafts Club supported Kuster's work and praised his plans for a new theater of professional capabilities. These colorfully laudatory words appeared in the Pine Cone:

Carmel's new Theatre of the Golden Bough is significant of many things in the present day development of the drama and other of the creative arts. It is more than the building; it is an embodiment of the highest type of mass-thought in the correlation of the arts, and it makes of Edward Gerhard Kuster, its founder, builder, architect, an outstanding figure in the dramatic history of the West, if not in all of America. Kuster is erecting a building beautiful in treatment and consecrated to the intelligent production of significant plays adapted for a mature-minded adult audience. (Pine Cone, June 8, 1924)

The Theatre of the Golden Bough opened to great fanfare on June 6, 1924. The play performed on opening night was the 3–hour drama The Mother of Gregory written and directed by Maurice Browne. Even before the construction of the Theatre had been completed, Kuster engaged Browne, one of the original founders of the Little Theater Movement in Chicago.

Kuster also saw his theater as an academy, not only for the local residents but also for university students. The University of California at Berkeley held its summer session in scenario writing, short story writing, and related subjects, at the Golden Bough in the summer of 1924. American actor and director Irving Pichel reviewed the play for the San Francisco Daily News. Pichel praised the performance, but saved his most effusive words for the Golden Bough:

America's Most Beautiful Theater

... There can be no question that the Theatre of the Golden Bough, which was dedicated Friday and Saturday evenings in Carmel, is the loveliest theater in America. It has been widely declared the most beautiful small theater, but I know of none larger to compare with it in beauty.

It is more than beautiful however; it represents today <u>the most advanced step in theater design in this country</u>. The auditorium and stage are radically different from those we are accustomed to, and both are notably more commodious of than those of the conventional playhouse. There are no longitudinal aisles but the space between each two rows of seats is wide enough to permit passage without disturbing those already seated.

Edward Kuster's theater, administered with the same vision that brought it into being and opened its career so significantly, should play an important part in molding the future of the noncommercial theater throughout the country. The building itself is an inspiration. The man who owns and manages it has the courage and foresight to do something creative and impulsive, reaching far into the future. (San Francisco Daily News, June 9, 1924) (emphasis added)

The stage is set for *The Princess Who Wouldn't Say Die*, by Bertram Block, half of a double bill featured at the Golden Bough in October 1924. Note the custom-made wicker chairs.

By early 1926—with the Theatre of the Golden Bough, the Arts and Crafts Theater, and the Forest Theater all in operation—there was so much community theater going on in Carmel that it seemed like every resident was involved. In fact, so many townspeople were active in the production of theatrical events in the summer of 1926 that a humorous column in the Carmel Pine Cone called "The Fool" included this item:

> It is rumored that there is to be a mass meeting of the local theatrical producers with a view to appointing someone to act as audience. (Pine Cone, June 22, 1926)

From June 1924 through August 1928, three Carmel stages were in use, and the messy theatrical rivalry that developed during those four years deeply affected not only Edward Kuster and the Denny-Watrous partnership but the entire Carmel community. It will be discussed in a later chapter.

Henry Cowell and the Ultra-Moderns 1924–1925

Dene met American composer and pianist Henry Cowell while she and Hazel were living in the Fisk House in San Francisco in 1923, and he began to acquaint her with the music that he and his fellow "Ultra-Moderns" were creating. Cowell was to be a major influence on Dene's piano career: he introduced her to new repertoire, new ideas about the aesthetics of music, and even new ways of playing the piano— Cowell's startling techniques included strumming the strings inside the piano and playing "clusters" by striking the keyboard with his elbows, forearms, and the sides of his hands.

Henry Cowell in 1923.
Photo by Margrethe Mather. Library of Congress.

> Cowell has developed the playing of a new kind of chord that transforms the piano into an orchestra, so far as tonal effect is concerned. He calls the chord a "tone cluster," as all the keys are played together by means of the entire forearm. The effect is like that of a percussion instrument, capable of both definite pitch and sustained tone. He employs these tone clusters in a marvelous way. (Pine Cone, July 12, 1924)

The London Musical Times reviewed a concert given by Cowell in Vienna early in 1923:

> Most unique of all perhaps was a recital given by and devoted exclusively to works of Henry Cowell, an American composer and pianist. His pianoforte pieces, doubtless the most radically modern ever heard in a Vienna hall, are apparently aimed at extending the scope of the keyboard as a medium for tonal expression. He asks for direct contact of the hand (even the fist) with the strings; the alternate application to the strings of the nails or flesh of the fingers and a manifold treatment of the pedals. Melodically, his compositions are comparatively simple, even conventional; yet some of them reveal supreme contrapuntal craftsmanship and decided rhythmic fancy. (Quoted in the Pine Cone, July 12, 1924)

Something about Cowell's ultra modernist views seems to have lit Dene on fire and she and Hazel presented Cowell in 1923 in their rooftop ballroom in the Fisk House. Cowell was a skilled pianist and an engaging and deeply thought-provoking speaker, and his lectures included examples and discussion of his own compositions as well as the latest music by other composers. In Cowell's subsequent lecture/demonstrations in San Francisco, Berkeley, and Carmel, Dene often played the musical examples on the piano, thereby freeing Cowell to focus on his lecture.

In May 1923, Dene performed in a recital of Wager Swayne pupils. She played works by 19th century masters Frédéric Chopin and Franz Liszt, precisely the genre of piano music with which people in 1923 were most familiar. This recital was Dene's last documented performance of that sort of music. From that time on she performed exclusively a new genre of piano repertoire that her audiences—and most of the music world—had never heard before.

Dene presented Cowell again in the spring of 1924 in a more public event at her large downtown San Francisco studio, and a few days later in Carmel.

> The [Cowell] concert took place on Friday evening, May 15 [1924], in the Ethel Denny studio, 376 Sutter Street. The spacious studio was packed with eager, interested listeners. There has been so little opportunity in the West to hear such as Schönberg, Stravinsky, Bela Bartok, or Cowell, the present leaders of the modern movement in music.
>
> It was inspiring to see Cowell, working like a scientist in his laboratory, in disregard to all tradition or organization of position, theory, law, reaching out over the strings for sounds unknown before, capturing the unheard overtones. (Pine Cone, July 19, 1924)

In July 1924 Dene and Hazel presented Cowell in a concert in Carmel, and threw an after-concert party for him at their house. The two dozen guests included German actress Hedwiga Reicher, American photographer Johan Hagemeyer, and architects Roger Sturtevant and Carol Aronovici.

> An enthusiastic group of friends of Henry Cowell were entertained by Ethel Adele Denny and Hazel Watrous at their home on North Dolores after the Cowell concert Tuesday night. (Pine Cone, July 19, 1924)

For the rest of 1924 and into early 1925, Dene and Hazel were occupied with designing, building, and decorating houses in Carmel. During this time there is no evidence of public performances by Dene, although she continued to rent a teaching studio in San Francisco through October 1929. An item in the Berkeley Gazette in March 1925 mentions that she took part in a mid-day concert at the Berkeley Art Association, but no other details are provided.

Leo Ornstein

In late September 1925, Dene and Hazel finally took their long–postponed trip to the East Coast, where they spent several months in and around New York City. Hazel took design classes at Columbia University and the Pratt Institute, although no paper trail of her activities there has come to light.

Dene studied with Leo Ornstein, a brilliant pianist, and a teacher known for his rigorous technical instruction. Her choice of Ornstein as a coach in New York is significant, and his place in the musical scene of the early 1920s should be explained.

Ornstein was born in 1893 in the Ukrainian province of Poltava. In 1906 his family emigrated to America, where he studied at what would later become the Juilliard School.

A virtuoso pianist and the enfant terrible of the music world, he dazzled the New York concert scene in 1915 at the age of 22 with four evenings of startlingly unfamiliar music by Schoenberg, Bartok, Scriabin, Ravel, Cyril Scott and other modernists, not to mention his own "futurist" compositions. Ornstein became wildly popular and his concerts were always sold out. In 1919 in Aeolian Hall in New York the audience "mobbed the lobbies, marched at intervals to the stage, and long clung there to walls, to organ pipes, pedal base, stairs, or any niche offering a view."

An article in the Baltimore Evening Sun referred to him as "the intransigent pianist, who has set the entire musical world by the ears and who is probably the most discussed figure on the concert stage."

Frederick H. Martens wrote a highly positive biography of Ornstein in 1918, when Ornstein was still in his twenties. Martens begins the preface to his book with hilarious over-the-top sarcasm intended derisively to exaggerate the negative opinions of Ornstein held by conservative "mainstream" musicians:

Leo Ornstein, 1926 press photo. *Courtesy of the author.*

> Leo Ornstein, to many, represents an evil musical genius wandering without the utmost pale of tonal orthodoxy, in a weird No-Man's Land haunted with tortuous sound, with wails of futuristic despair, with cubist shrieks and post-impressionistic cries and crashes. He is the great anarch, the iconoclast, the destructive genius who would root out what little remains of the law and the prophets since Scriabin, Stravinsky and Schoenberg have trampled them underfoot.
>
> His earlier compositions which, with happy fancy and considerable skill, exploit the possibilities of the diatonic system he has since abandoned, are regarded much as would be the Sunday-school certificates of an apostate to Satanism, the lisped prayers of one who has forgotten them to celebrate a Devil's mass. His gospel is black heresy, his dispensation a delusion and a snare!
>
> It is thus that the more rigid upholders of tradition, those who scorn taking the pains to master the idiom which serves to express his ideas, see him.
>
> (from *Leo Ornstein: The Man, His Ideas, His Work*. Frederick H. Martens, 1918.)

Of all the many fine piano teachers in New York City—one of the leading music centers of the world in 1925—Dene Denny chose to study with this colorful renegade.

Dene performed Ornstein's music in most of her own concerts. Despite his radical reputation, Ornstein's compositions were among the most conventional music on Dene's recital programs. His life story is an interesting and complex one: by the 1930s this brilliant pianist had withdrawn from the performing world entirely, moving instead into a life of composing and teaching. Leo Ornstein wrote his last work at age 90, and died in 2002 at the age of 108.

DENE DENNY Plays at The Golden Bough Friday Evening
Her Piano Will Be the
STEINWAY
The Instrument of the Immortals

MYRA HESS
renowned English pianist who was a recent visitor in Carmel says—"It is the exquisite singing tone which makes playing on a Steinway a pure joy.

RACHMANINOFF
whose concert piano is always the Steinway says— "I consider them to be perfect in every way".

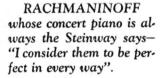

The Steinway alone is ade. quate to the subtile nuances of tone, the volume and sonority of modern music. It is a delight and an inspiration to have the Steinway as an assisting artist in a concert.
—DENE DENNY

Miss Denny not only demands the Steinway for her public concert work, but also possesses a Steinway concert grand, which completes her studio home.

Sherman, Clay & Co.
THE HOME OF THE STEINWAY PIANO
E. Phil Fuhrman, District Representative
Nearest Branch Office
464 MAIN STREET - - - WATSONVILLE, CALIF.

Dene Denny was an official Steinway Artist. Sherman, Clay and Company took out this full-page ad in the Cymbal a few days before Dene's debut recital in Carmel in June 1927.
Courtesy of the H. M. Williams Local History Department, Harrison Memorial Library

Dene and Hazel in the Denny-Watrous Studio in the late 1930s. Dene sits at one of her two Steinways, and Hazel stands in front of the enormous north-facing window. By the time this photo was taken, the Studio was no longer used for public events. *From the cover of the 1987 Carmel Bach Festival program book. Photo by Kaldor-Bates.*

The Denny-Watrous Studio

After returning to Carmel from the East Coast in March 1926, Hazel and Dene immediately set to work remodeling and expanding their cottage on North Dolores Street. As they had done in the Fisk House in San Francisco, they intended to use their home as a venue for concerts and other events. The expansion and upgrading of the cottage was the first step in their Carmel impresario career.

> Since their return [from NYC] they have begun their own Studio on their Dolores Street property, where they are making a very interesting combination of music room, shop, laboratory, and living quarters. (Pine Cone, March 20, 1926)

> Among the homes being erected by Denny and Watrous, who specialize mostly in unique little studios and homes of charm and color, is a little studio for Miss Clara M. Taft of Oakland, being erected at Monteverdi and 13th; a home for Miss Alberta Lindblad of Santa Cruz on Mission Street between Alta and Vista; and the completion of their own Studio on Dolores Street. (Pine Cone, May 29, 1926)

The cottage they built in 1922 bore all the trademarks of Hazel's style: wooden construction on a concrete foundation; board-and-batten exterior wall cladding; mixed roof styles including medium-pitched hip and cross gable roofs; and round-arched doors and windows. The interior consisted of a large central room plus the kitchen, bath, and bedroom.

By the time the remodel and expansion was completed in June 1926, the house had seven exterior doors to facilitate its use for public events. It still had a relatively small floor plan and the two-story height of the roof belied the structure's essential compactness.

The central architectural and artistic focus of the house was the dramatic central room, which the 1926 remodel now converted into the Denny-Watrous Studio. The walls were covered with a layer of sound board, a fibrous building material used to dampen excess echo in a large acoustic space (and perhaps also to lessen the volume of sound heard by neighbors). The north wall of the room was double-paned windows reaching almost from floor to ceiling, providing perfect light for creating or enjoying the visual arts.

An L-shaped viewing balcony wrapped halfway around the room, accessed by a tiny stairway and cleverly cantilevered so that it seemed to hang in the air with no supports beneath it to clutter the view or inhibit the movement of people on the main floor. (The photo on the opposite page was shot from the balcony.) For the next four years, their Dolores Street Studio would be an important venue for recitals, lectures and other artistic gatherings.

In 1924, when they registered to vote in Carmel, Dene was listed as "musician" and Hazel as "artist." In the 1926 Voter Registry, they are both listed as "builder." (Their 1924 Republican party affiliations also have changed: in 1926 Hazel is a Democrat, and Dene is a Socialist.)

As they were completing their own Studio in the spring of 1926, they were also taking part in a significant Carmel milestone: the opening of Carmel's first real art gallery.

The Carmel Art Gallery 1926

Introduction: all art and no gallery 1900–1924

Carmel-by-the-Sea is a town famous for its many art galleries, but it was not always so. During the first two decades of the twentieth century, as the number of part- and full-time resident artists grew, many of them displayed and sold their work in their own studios, and occasionally they also displayed each others' works. In 1912 artists Mary DeNeale Morgan and Ferdinand Burgdorff created calling cards inviting the public to their studios and stating the days and hours that their studios were open. They distributed these cards to Carmel's few stores and two hotels.

But potential art buyers—who very often were tourists—had difficulty finding their way around Carmel's tree-lined unpaved streets. The problems arose from a combination of factors that have been present since the town's creation and which help to preserve its character today.

First, although many houses in Carmel have nicknames, like Innesfree or Tuckaway, there are no house numbers. The address of a house is its actual location. For example, if a house on the east side of Lincoln Street is the third house north of the intersection of Lincoln and 11th Avenue, the address is "Lincoln, 3 NE of 11th." That is the proper address, and every Carmel resident and every UPS and FedEx driver would understand it. (The US Postal Service will not deliver to such an address and residents of Carmel-by-the-Sea must rent post office boxes.) This lack of house numbers is confusing enough today, and it must have been even more so in 1920 when Carmel had only 638 residents.

Carmel's main street is Ocean Avenue, stretching from Route One to the beach. Tourists and visitors to modern Carmel tend to spend much of their time in the central shopping zone—an area of 30 blocks extending for six blocks along Ocean Avenue and a few blocks to either side, where nearly all the art galleries, stores, and restaurants are located. After dark, the sidewalks for a few blocks along and near Ocean Avenue are illuminated modestly by a very few unobtrusive streetlights and by the light from the windows of the galleries and restaurants. Outside this commercial zone, the rest of Carmel has neither street lights nor sidewalks.

In modern times the factors above combine to preserve Carmel's charm in an age of commercialism. But in the 1920s—when there were no streetlights at all—issues were making it difficult for Carmel artists to earn a living in their own town, even though potential buyers were actively looking for them. Carmel, a community bursting with visual arts, needed a conveniently located gallery where local artists' works could be viewed daily by the general public.

Johan Hagemeyer's studio 1924

Johan Hagemeyer was born in Holland in 1884 and came to California to grow fruit trees. Trained as a horticulturist, he was also a serious photographer, and a single meeting in a New York gallery with American photography pioneer Alfred Stieglitz persuaded him to focus more on photography. He opened a studio in San Francisco in 1923, and in 1924 he bought a studio cottage near the Forest Theater (address: "Ocean, 3 SE of Junipero").

In the spring of 1924, in addition to showing his own photographs, Hagemeyer also hung at least four exhibits of works by other artists, and announced each event to the village via the newspaper. His first exhibit presented visiting Indiana artist George Wilstack in early March, followed in late March by Nellie Augusta Knopf, on sabbatical from her duties as Director of Art at the Illinois Women's College. During May, Hagemeyer displayed images by Berkeley-based photographer Louis A. Goetz, and in June he hung an exhibition of prints by Cézanne, Gauguin, Leger, Rousseau and others described as "modern masters."

During this time Hagemeyer met Carmel resident Edward Weston, who encouraged him to pursue his photography full time. And so, after his few months as a "curator" of his private gallery, Hagemeyer seems to have turned his focus fully to his own photographic work, and Carmel was once more without a display venue. In July 1924 Hagemeyer was among the guests at the party Dene and Hazel gave at their home for Henry Cowell, and he remained active in the Carmel community for two decades.

Hagemeyer's exhibits represent the first time in Carmel that someone had organized and publicly presented a series of exhibits of someone else's work, and for that reason a few historians have cited Hagemeyer's studio as the "first gallery" in Carmel. However technically correct that may be, the "gallery" phase of Hagemeyer's studio lasted less than twelve weeks, and it did not fulfill the deep need at the time for a full-time gallery showcasing local artists. The first real attempt to establish such a venue took place in 1926, and the project involved Dene and Hazel.

In mid March they returned from six months of study in New York. Filled with new ideas.

> The Misses Denny and Watrous, after several months' stay in the East, where they visited shops and made extended observations of the studios, tea rooms, and old homes of the New England states, are back at their work of designing, building, and decorating in Carmel. (Pine Cone, March 20, 1926)

"...a tea room and art gallery."

Nearly two years after Hagemeyer's gallery experiment, Harriet Stoddard and Fannie Yard (as Mrs. Sidney J. Yard) decided to give Carmel and its artists what they needed and deserved. (Both women were artists themselves, as was Mr. Yard, and Mrs. Yard had served as the Director of the summer school of the Arts and Crafts Club from 1910 to 1920.)

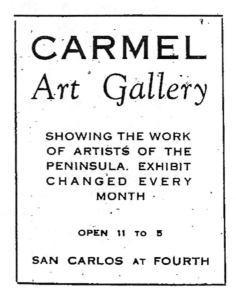

> "...the Misses Denny and Watrous are busy designing furniture and decorating houses in Pacific Grove and Carmel. One of the most interesting things they are doing is the work for Mrs. Harriet Stoddard on San Carlos, where the well-known old Hand residence is being converted into a tea room and art gallery." (Pine Cone, April 3, 1926)

Subsequent coverage in the local press chronicles the story of this "tea room and art gallery."

Carmel To Have Fine Art Gallery.

That which artists, both resident and visiting, have desired in Carmel for a long time is about to be realized. It has always been something of a wonder that Carmel, known all the world over as an art center, had no centrally situated, picturesquely located, open–at–all–times art gallery. However, we are now to have such an establishment.

The former Hand residence at San Carlos and Fourth, at the north easterly entrance into the residence and business section of Carmel, recently purchased by Mrs. Harriet Stoddard, has undergone numerous alterations under the direction of Watrous and Denny, until now a considerable portion of the house is especially well appointed for the display of pictures. Peninsula artists and others are now assured that they will have a permanent and attractive gallery for the display of their pictures, and the visiting public, who frequently come to Carmel to see pictures, will not be disappointed. (Pine Cone, April 3, 1926)

Carmel Now Has Fine Art Gallery.

It is no longer necessary for the curious visitor to wander up and down, seeking for the work of Carmel's artists. Instead of directing him to the many scattered studios we can now say: "You will find a representative collection at the Art Gallery on San Carlos above Fourth Street."

Mrs. H. G. Stoddard has done wonders in converting her home into a suitable place for the exhibition of pictures. It is surrounded by a lovely old garden, where honeysuckle and roses run riot, and all sorts of familiar flowers grow... It is hoped that the gallery will become widely known and that it will receive the appreciation it deserves

Tea is to be served on the wide porch and in the garden, and altogether we feel that the Carmel Art Gallery, with its home–like atmosphere, will soon become one of the favorite places in our town. It is something that we have always needed and we wish it every success. (Dora Hagemeyer in the Carmel Cymbal, May 18, 1926)

Carmel Art Gallery "Different" Just Like City Itself.

Like Carmel itself, and like the people who live here, its newly established Carmel Art Gallery is also "different." One arrives quite inconspicuously by a pathway winding its way through the trees and shrubbery. And then, quite unexpectedly, there is the tea garden, the portico with tables and chairs where tea is served outside during the sunny hours, and then the hospitality and warmth which greets the visitor as he or she enters to view the work of many of our Carmel and Peninsula artists.

The paintings used in the exhibition are changed about once a month, so the new artists and subjects are constantly being exhibited. The paintings are all priced and range from $100-$750. The Gallery, located at Fourth Avenue and San Carlos, is open daily from 11 AM to 5 PM, in all seasons and to all comers. (Pine Cone, May 22, 1926)

Studio Gossip By Daisy Brown

The Carmel Art Gallery on San Carlos at Fourth is attracting many of the summer visitors here, as well as the regular Carmel arts devotees. Fifteen paintings by Carmel artists have been hung during June. The pictures have been changed every month since the opening of the Gallery which was in May. Visitors are shown through the rooms by Mrs. Sydney Yard and Mrs. Harriet Stoddard, curators. (Pine Cone, June 25, 1926)

The following artists were mentioned in print as exhibitors in the Carmel Art Gallery between May 1926 and January 1927: M. de Neale Morgan, William Silva, Jessica Arms Botke, Cornelius Botke, C. Chapel Judson, Harold Knott, Alan G. Cram, Ferdinand Burgdorff, Edward Tristom, I. Maynard Curtis, Thomas Parkhurst, Sidney Yard, Myron Oliver, and Elizabeth Strong. Virtually all of the artworks specifically referenced in the press were oil paintings.

A few more small items appeared in the Pine Cone during the winter months. Ads for the Gallery continued to run in the Pine Cone until early spring of 1927.

According to their minutes, in 1928 the Carmel Music Society held one of their board meetings in the "Carmel Art Gallery," but no other details are given. This was probably the upstairs room in the Seven Arts Building which the newly-formed Carmel Art Association was renting as their gallery. (See below.) In any event, however long it was in business, it is fair to say that the first art gallery in Carmel was opened in 1926 on San Carlos above Fourth, and that "Denny and Watrous" were its designers and decorators.

Pine Cone ads courtesy of the H. M. Williams Local History Department, Harrison Memorial Library; and the Carmel Pine Cone.

Epilogue: The Carmel Art Association

In August 1927 at "Gray Gables," the home of Josephine Culbertson and Ida M. Johnson, a group of Carmel artists took matters into their own hands and formed the Carmel Art Association, with Pedro J. Lemos as the first president. For their first gallery space they rented the large upstairs room in the Court of the Seven Arts Building on the southwest corner of Ocean and Lincoln (both floors of the building are in use today as an upscale retail space). They installed a wood stove, covered the walls with burlap, and spent $80 on "suitable antique decorations." The gallery was open every afternoon from 2:00 to 5:00 and the first curator was Katherine Corrigan. The general public was invited to view members' exhibitions for a 10¢ admission fee.

Membership soared until October 1929, when the economy—and the finances of artists and art lovers—began to crumble. The Carmel Art Association could no longer afford to rent the space and pay the curator, and they vacated the Seven Arts Building. From 1930 through 1932, the CAA was without a home, and three times during this period they rented the Denny-Watrous Gallery on Dolores Street for exhibitions of members' works. The second of these shows, in July 1931, featured paintings by four distinguished Carmel artists, all members of the National Academy of Arts: Armin Hansen, Arthur Hill Gilbert, Paul Dougherty, and William Ritchel. Although the CAA netted only $9.53 from the show itself, the event at the Denny-Watrous Gallery generated a renewal of support for the Art Association.

In 1933 the Carmel Art Association acquired the Woodward/Remsen studio on the west side of Dolores St. between 5th and 6th Avenues. They have been at that location ever since, making it the oldest art gallery in Carmel, although not the first. The organization has a long and distinguished roster of current and former members, and is the second–oldest non–profit artist cooperative in the United States.

Visit their website: **www.carmelart.org**

Breaking the bonds of tonality 1926

3 measures from the first movement of Arnold Schoenberg's *Fünf Klavierstücke*, Op. 23.

By early July 1926, the remodel of the house on Dolores Street had been completed, Dene's Steinway was in place and tuned, and now in this new and acoustically splendid space Dene had work to do: Henry Cowell had invited her to solo in Los Angeles with his San Francisco New Music Ensemble. In late November she was to give the North American premiere of Fünf Klavierstücke (Five Pieces for Piano), Opus 23, by Arnold Schoenberg. This work had been written only three years before, and it marked an important milestone in 20th century music.

Readers who understand things like "12–tone serialism" and "retrograde of the tone row" will find the following dozen paragraphs elementary. But Schoenberg and what he represents were important to Dene Denny, and to the world of music. It is worth explaining why Opus 23 was so important to the 20th century.

For more than a thousand years, western music had been based on the three elements of Melody, Rhythm, and Harmony. A Melody is a series of tones, or pitches, one after another. Rhythm is the pattern of pulses or beats that place the tones into a time-based structure. Harmony is created when two or more tones occur at the same time. Every culture or society in the world uses these three basic elements of music and creates its own rules and traditions around them, and each new generation adds its own new perspectives and styles. There are many "musics" around the world, but this chapter is about the musical tradition that has its roots in southern Europe 1,000 years ago.

People raised within the Western European musical tradition understand the same basic principles without even knowing it. Most European "classical" music until the 20th century was based on an awareness of "tonality" or "key," and on the use of the diatonic scale ("Do Re Mi Fa…" etc.) or modes derived from it. This reliance upon accepted rules of harmony became increasingly important to musical aesthetics over the centuries. Josquin, Monteverdi, Bach, Mozart, Berlioz, Brahms, Debussy and Ravel all used the power of harmony in their attempt to reach the heart of the listener. By the end of the 19th century harmony could even challenge melody for supremacy: Puccini's opera Tosca welcomed the 20th century on January 14, 1900, with three chords that most lovers of Italian opera could identify, although there is no melody whatever.

For an easy direct experience of tonality, try this experiment: sing the song "Happy Birthday" all the way through but stop abruptly just before the very last note (that is, don't sing or make a sound on the final word: "you"). In that surprising empty space, one can almost feel the last word and hear the note, and those who have a good ear for music might even "hear" the final harmony in their imagination. Westerners who know this song expect that it will end on the last note, and some might actually find it somewhat disturbing when it does not. This has little to do with the missing word, it's because the next-to-the-last note was not able to "resolve."

The harmonic release we feel on the last two notes of Happy Birthday—"to you!"—is called, appropriately, a "resolution." In the key of C Major, the last two notes of the song are D resolving to C, and the last two chords are G Major resolving to C Major. The simple rules that govern this moment in the song are part of the rich and complex theoretical principles that make up the core of Western music. In the 19th century, composers felt increasingly free to stretch the rules, surprise listeners, and experiment with innovative effects, but the listener could reasonably assume that there would be some awareness of melody, harmony, and rhythm, no matter what dissonances and discords might also be present.

By the turn of the 20th century, certain musical explorers viewed this dependence on traditional concepts of harmony as outdated—a hindrance to musical creativity and progress. Perhaps, they thought, if musical tones could be released from the old harmonic structures and be allowed to relate to each other with total freedom, a new musical experience could be created. In short, the challenge was to escape the innate need for harmonic resolution by inventing a new way of writing music, in which the traditional concepts of "resolution," "tonality," "harmony," and "melody" no longer had any meaning.

Chief among these seekers was the Austrian composer Arnold Schoenberg (1874–1951). Coming of age in the 1890s, Schoenberg had of course heard and been influenced by the music of Brahms and Wagner, and in his early career his music was often lush and Wagnerian (e.g. his enormous cantata "Gurrelieder," which premiered in 1900). Beginning around 1908, Schoenberg began to explore paths beyond the musical aesthetics he had absorbed as a young man. He was not the only experimenter at that time, but in hindsight he was certainly the most influential. In his new compositions he attempted to eliminate tonal centers and the awareness of the traditional relationship and conflict between harmony and dissonance.

After much experimentation, Schoenberg realized that he could not rely only on his conscious mind to overcome his learned expectations. He began to explore new methods of composing that eliminated even the unconscious tendency to be influenced by the desire for tonality (he allegedly disliked the word "atonal").

By 1923 Schoenberg had developed a refined yet simple method that gave his music a clearer texture by enabling him to determine precisely how many times each tone appeared in a composition, thereby making sure that no tone was heard more frequently than any other. He described it as, "a method of composing with twelve tones that are related only with one another." The music was free of tonality, but it was not random.

The diatonic "Do Re Me..." scale referred to in the Happy Birthday explanation above is really made up 12 unique tones. This series of 12 tones is often called a semi-tone scale, because the notes are all 1/2 tone apart from their neighbors. For example, on the piano keyboard, start on any C and count all the keys to the B natural above it: C C# D D# E F F# G G# A A# B.

There are 7 white keys plus 5 black keys, producing 12 different notes with no duplicates. (1. This "7+5=12" is true from any starting note. 2. "Enharmonics," such as A-sharp and B-flat, are counted as one tone with two different "spellings.")

Schoenberg began with the twelve pitches of a semi-tone scale, and re-arranged them into a new sequence, thereby creating a 12-note series called a "tone row." All 12 notes are used, but they are in a different order as determined by the composer. This is a tone row: F A# D G# B E G F# C D# A C#.

The composer "builds" a musical composition with this 12-tone row by using it over and over in as many different and creative ways as possible. The tone row can be used forwards, backwards, or upside down forwards or backwards. One might even start and end in the middle of the tone row as long as all 12 tones are heard, and in the proper relation to each other. Here is same tone row starting on E: E G F# C D# A C# F A# D G# B. Any tone may be played in a different octave. All combinations, octaves and rhythms are possible as long as the composition is constructed from permutations of the original tone row.

With this method it is mathematically impossible for any particular tone to occur more frequently than any other note, and no tone could ever be favored or become more important than the others. Because the music was no longer based on the diatonic scale, all tones became equally important. Schoenberg and his twelve-tone method were an enormous influence on the course of music in the twentieth century. He himself was not rigid about his "method," and he varied his technique according to the particular composition. He was quoted as saying that he wanted his works to be seen not as 12-<u>tone</u> compositions but as 12-tone <u>compositions</u>.

The great pianist Eduard Steuermann was a life-long proponent of Schoenberg's music. In October 1923, he premiered Schoenberg's *Fünf Klavierstücke, Opus 23*, (Five Pieces for Piano) in Hamburg.

The fifth movement—"Walzer"—was the first published composition using Schoenberg's new twelve-tone technique.

Opus 23 surely must have been performed again after its premiere in 1923, at least in private or unpublicized events on both sides of the Atlantic, but there is no record of a performance of the work in the US until November 1926, when an eager audience would hear Dene Denny give the official US premiere of this radical and difficult music. But long before the Los Angeles concert, others were destined to hear Dene play Schoenberg.

Modern music at home

The Carmel Cymbal briefly mentions one of the first gatherings in the newly completed Dolores Street Studio: On Tuesday, July 13, 1926, Dene hosted "an evening of modern music" for 10 friends (including Hazel's sister Zanetta). Dene...

> "...gave a program which included numbers by Henry Cowell, Bela Bartok, and Schoenberg. She also played compositions by Bach and Chopin."

Dene may already have been acquainting herself with the Schoenberg Opus 23 in July, in preparation for the November 20th concert in Los Angeles, a high-visibility event that clearly was a major event both for her and for Cowell's San Francisco–based ensemble.

But for most of Dene's friends and admirers, her shift to this new and different music was puzzling, to say the least. Most classical music lovers in the 1920s had grown up listening to composers such as Schumann, Bach, Debussy, Liszt, Rachmaninoff and Chopin, and they were frankly dismayed by the new music of Schoenberg, Cowell, Ornstein, Honegger, Scriabin, Bartok, and the other composers whose music Dene was now playing.

And so perhaps on the night of July 13 she offered Bach and Chopin to her guests at the end of the "evening of modern music" as a gentle consoling nightcap of familiar 18th and 19th century melody and harmony.

A Season of Modernism 1926–1927

On a clear, starry evening on July 29, 1926, the Denny-Watrous Studio was host to the first of many lectures and non-musical presentations that would take place there until the opening of the Denny-Watrous Gallery downtown in 1930.

German artist Galka Scheyer was in the United States promoting the work of four avant-garde artists: German-American Lyonel Feininger, Russians Alexej von Jawlensky and Wassily Kandinsky, and the German-Swiss Paul Klee. All four were important expressionist painters, and Kandinsky is credited with painting the first purely abstract works. It was Scheyer who had nicknamed them the "Blue Four" (to reflect their much earlier association with the young Blue Rider expressionists in Munich). She had become their agent in 1924 and coordinated their first US exhibition in New York in 1925. While each member of the Blue Four did have some connection to the earlier group, the Blue Four was formed for promotional purposes after the four artists had each established his own reputation.

For the weekly Carmelite, Dora Hagemeyer wrote a long and detailed description of Galka Scheyer's lecture. Here are the first few paragraphs.

> Once in a while the gods seem to smile upon an event and arrange that everything shall be delightful. The new Denny-Watrous Studio was the scene last Thursday evening of Madame G. E. Scheyer's lecture on the Blue Four. The frankly modern atmosphere, the interested audience, the beautiful room, the starry night, and the magnetic personality of the speaker made a rare and very wonderful combination.
>
> Madame Scheyer had not spoken long before one began to realize that art as something static does not exist. It is a constant becoming. The vitality of the speaker, her understanding and her awareness gave one a sense of art as a living growing thing.
>
> "There is no stopping," she said, "and no standing still. One must move with the times." Yesterday there was Impressionism, today Cubism, tomorrow will bring us other "isms" and so on ad infinitum. The speaker took our breath away. She went beyond the sphere of the intellect and showed us arts as the flowering of the spirit. She spoke as one who burned with the things she wanted to impart and for this reason she was intensely convincing. (Carmel Cymbal, August 3, 1926)

Dene and Hazel seem to have relished being in a new community and working with other artists and creative thinkers, and they became trendy artistes themselves. In two press photographs taken in 1926 and 1927, Dene sports a razor haircut.

Imre Weisshaus, a French pianist who frequented Carmel in the late 1920s, met and admired fellow pianist Dene Denny (she performed several of his works in her concerts). In his memoirs, under his stage name Paul Arma, he remembers first meeting Dene's friend Hazel in November 1927:

> ...son amie, Hazel Watrous, est une femme excentrique, fumant la pipe, s'habillant d'une manière masculine, sympathique et accueillante.
>
> (...her friend, Hazel Watrous, is an eccentric woman, smokes a pipe, dresses like a man, [and is] likable and friendly.) (Paul Arma, unpublished memoirs.)

Henry Cowell returned to Carmel for a Concert at the Golden Bough in July and a series of concerts and lectures at the Denny–Watrous Studio. In Cowell's lectures, Dene played many of the examples of the music Cowell discussed. A writer from the Cymbal attended one of Cowell's lectures.

> After the lecture, Dene Denny played from Malpiero, Scriabin, John Ireland, Palmgren, and Eric Satie. Carmel is indebted to Miss Denny for a very unusual opportunity of hearing modern music well played. Music is the most difficult of the arts to come in touch with. Comparatively few play easily enough to follow the intricacies of the new music. The radio and the gramophone consider the popular taste only, and the concert program rarely goes beyond the classics.
>
> Henry Cowell is one of the outstanding figures in the musical world of today. His contribution is sincere and vital and to those who wish to understand modern music from the bones outward, and to hear it discussed scientifically and simply, should not miss these lectures. (Carmel Cymbal, October 6, 1926)

In early November the Peninsula Philharmonic Society of Monterey presented a concert by pianist Robert Schmitz at the Theatre of the Golden Bough, and the Carmel Cymbal reported on the after concert party:

> Miss Dene Denny and Miss Hazel Watrous entertained informally at their new Studio on Dolores Street. There were 30 or more of their friends gathered to meet Mr. Schmitz who gave the guests a delightful time by playing for them informally. Henry Cowell, also present, presented a "grand opera" as his contribution to the evening's entertainment. (Carmel Cymbal, November 17, 1926)

Five measures from Henry Cowell's *Voice of Lir,* from *3 Irish Legends* for solo piano. Yes, solo. It was written in 1920 and Dene played it on most of her recitals. The vertical lines are Cowell's "tone clusters." They indicate spans of notes to be played with the entire left forearm. Note also that the clusters are played one octave lower than written. *Downloaded from IMSLP.org. Public Domain.*

The Los Angeles concert, November 1926
"Los Angeles had never before heard a concert of completely contemporary music."

The Music Room of the Hotel Biltmore in Los Angeles was packed on Saturday, November 20, 1926. All the Los Angeles musical intelligentsia had come to hear Henry Cowell's New Music Ensemble give a concert of the very latest music, including several American premieres. Among the ten players were the eminent Persinger String Quartet and pianists Cowell, Dane Rudhyar, and Dene Denny. The lengthy evening included recent string quartets by Darius Milhaud, Alfredo Casella, Carl Ruggles, and Henry Cowell; solo piano compositions by Rudhyar and Cowell performed by the composers; and the American premiere of Schoenberg's *Fünf Klavierstücke, Opus 23*, played by Dene Denny.

> The five piano pieces by Schoenberg were a demonstration of remarkable musical memory on the part of Dene Denny, who played them. To the average ear they were a chaos of unreasoned acoustic accidents, but Miss Denny seemed to find sufficient continuity in them to retain them in her mind. (Patterson Green in the Los Angeles Examiner, November 20, 1926)

A writer for the Carmel Cymbal covered the Los Angeles concert:

> The first concert given by the New Music Society in Los Angeles caused more than a ripple of excitement. It excited something very like hysterics. As the angular and electric music of Varèse proceeded from the strings of the small ensemble playing in the Biltmore Hotel ballroom, the audience experienced emotional events it had never before known in a concert hall. So great became the tension that little puffs of laughter began to explode softly in the room—not the laughter of scorn or amusement, but simply the hysterical release of powerful and bewildering feeling. Los Angeles had never before heard a concert of completely contemporary music.
>
> At this concert the responsibility of bringing the music of Schoenberg to an audience for the first time—music which had caused extreme and violent excitement in Vienna and Berlin—devolved upon a young woman, Dene Denny. This pianist—unlike other feminine musicians, who rarely resist the temptation to confuse their musicianship with their wardrobe—appeared in the simplest and soberest of frocks, black, with a bit of a white collar, thus indicating that audience attention was to be directed to the composer, not to his interpreter. The simplicity and sincerity of Miss Denny's manner, the utter earnestness of her interpretation of Schoenberg's work, did much to convince an audience unaccustomed to the musical vocabulary of the moderns. It caught its breath; it entered into the music; it listened. (Carmel Cymbal, November 26, 1926)

Dene Denny wanted the audience to listen deeply to the music, and to that end her LA performance of Opus 23 bore two distinguishing characteristics of all her solo appearances: she performed the music from memory, and she played each piece twice.

First, when we memorize music, we learn it "by heart." We encounter the music more deeply as we work toward memorization because more is at stake. Once we've achieved memorization, we perform more freely and expressively when our eyes and visual cortex are not concerned with the printed page. Schoenberg's Opus 23 is an intensely cerebral and abstract work, and it is a supreme act of will and technique merely to learn it well enough to play it at all, much less memorize it. Dene studied and practiced the Schoenberg Opus 23 to the point where she could perform the work from memory, speak about it from the stage, and immediately perform it again with the same fire and engagement the second time. Several music critics remarked on the passion and emotion she demonstrated in her playing.

Second, Dene the teacher felt that it was really important to acquaint others with this new Ultra Modern music, and with the new theories and aesthetic principles that fueled it. But she knew it was difficult for many people to warm up even to the ideas of the composers, much less to the actual sounds of their music. So she played, and then spoke to the audience, and then gave the listeners a second chance by playing each work a second time.

Dene learned this technique of commentary and repetition from Henry Cowell: as a composer/pianist he was a pragmatist and knew full well that Ultra Modern music was challenging even (or especially) for sophisticated music lovers. Cowell taught Dene that when audience members listen to a new piece of music for the first time they experience an infinite variety of thoughts and feelings: they compare the music they are hearing to other music they remember; they try to figure out what on earth it all "means;" they wonder what everyone else is thinking about it right now; they puzzle over what the composer or the other people in the audience might expect them to be thinking; and they remain on edge by wondering what will happen next or perhaps simply by fearing that the music won't end soon enough.

This image was created by combining three microfilm images of a publicity photo taken in 1926 or 1927. *Original images courtesy of the H.M. Williams Local History Department, Harrison Memorial Library; and the Carmel Pine Cone.*

But if the performer plays the entire work, then turns to the audience and speaks a few words about the music, and then immediately plays the work a second time, the listener has a better idea of what to expect. He can relax a bit, give the work a second chance and, as Cowell said, begin really to "listen" to the music.

With perfect timing, the Carmel Cymbal printed this item just three days before Dene's Los Angeles concert.

Dene Denny is one of those rare pianists who play modern music exclusively, and play it well. Those of us who have enjoyed the enviable opportunity of becoming acquainted with the strange new dissonances of such composers as Schoenberg, Malipiero, Bartok, etc., feel that we have much to thank her for. All through the Henry Cowell lectures she has generously illustrated his references to the various composers. This has been done from a sincere belief in the value of modern music and the added enjoyment an understanding of it can bring to one's life experience, as well as to one's appreciation of music in general. Carmel is fortunate in having her as a permanent possession, for while one can read about modern music and talk about it, one can seldom hear it played. (Carmel Cymbal, November 17, 1926)

Dene truly believed in the importance of giving 20th century composers a hearing. As a musician, she served as the composer's advocate.

"The classics will never die," Miss Denny says, "but these men are entitled to the same respect as were Beethoven, Mozart or Bach in their day." (Berkeley Daily Gazette, January 29, 1929)

Berkeley, December 1926

For most classical players it's a painstaking process to memorize even the music of "mainstream" composers such as Beethoven, Mozart, Chopin and Debussy. But even as Dene had been memorizing the ten-minute Schoenberg Opus 23 for the November concert in Los Angeles, she also was preparing for the first of several major solo recitals, each featuring two dozen or more works by a dozen different living composers, and she intended to do it all from memory.

On Sunday, December 12, at the Berkeley League of Fine Arts at 2419 Haste Street, Dene unveiled a two-hour program of contemporary works for solo piano. She shared the evening with her friend Henry Cowell, who began the concert with a brief lecture on modern music. Then Dene played works by Ornstein (her recent New York piano teacher), Kodaly, Honegger, Scriabin, Malipiero, Goosens, Bartok and Schoenberg. At the close of this lengthy program, Cowell played several of his own compositions.

"The audience was enthusiastically appreciative and much interesting discussion followed." (Cymbal, December 17, 1926)

Berkeley, January 1927

Dene returned to Berkeley on January 27 for a concert in the charming and intimate venue of the Berkeley Piano Club, an event sponsored by the Alameda County Music Teachers' Association. Miriam Sellander, a vocalist, sang a few selections, and then Dene played works by Malipiero, Bartok, Scriabin, Cowell, Ornstein, and Schoenberg. The specific titles Dene performed in this and the previous Berkeley concert are not known.

The details of Dene's solo repertoire in these concerts are worth examining because a solo artist can in principle perform any repertoire she chooses. In her solo appearances Dene was unveiling the results of months of grueling work.

Dene at the piano in the Denny-Watrous Studio on north Dolores Street. Publicity photo taken in 1926 or 1927, printed in the Pine Cone. *Courtesy of the H.M. Williams Local History Department, Harrison Memorial Library; and the Carmel Pine Cone.*

The process of building a recital program begins with choosing the repertoire: no doubt starting with recommendations from Cowell, Ornstein, and other colleagues, she probably played through dozens of compositions and individual movements, trying things out, seeking the right pieces with which to build a recital program with shape and flow.

Then came the technical work with the compositions themselves, practicing the mechanics of the fingers on the keys.

And finally the Great Leap: putting the printed music aside and playing from memory.

Most of the composers represented in the two Berkeley concerts are included in almost every subsequent Dene Denny program, and it is these composers whose music and ideas Dene wanted the world to hear and understand.

Concert at home, February 1927

In early February, Dene gave an "informal evening" at home for 16 listeners. The 2/4/27 Pine Cone tells us she played a number of "modern pieces" but does not list the titles.

It is possible that she was testing and practicing works to be performed in her Carmel debut recital in June, on the stage of Edward Kuster's extraordinary Theatre of the Golden Bough.

Dene Denny's Carmel Debut 1927
"It was an unbelievably thrilling evening."

Private concerts and out-of-town engagements were excellent preparation for a very important event: Dene's debut in Carmel on June 3, 1927. In her advance publicity for the concert, Dene described it as an "all-modern piano recital with explanatory comments."

> An item of distinct interest is the announcement by Miss Denny that she will comment between the numbers on her program upon the new music and its place in the art-world. The resistance to the ultra-modern in music has worn down considerably in Europe as well as in New York City, largely by increased contact with it through recitals such as that to be given here by Miss Denny.

> Dene Denny is one of the best-equipped pianists in the country in the field she has adopted. At her recital Friday night ultra-modern works of German, Italian, Hungarian, French, English, Russian and American composers will be presented, with running comments and explanations bearing on the difference between the old-classic school and the new tone progressions and harmonies.

> Inasmuch as this is the first program of all–modern works for the piano to be given in the West, it is an event of considerable musical importance. Individual composers such as Henry Cowell and Rudhyar have given recitals devoted exclusively to their own works, and the New Music Society has given programs of orchestral works and piano works combined, but this is the first all modern program of composers for the piano to be given in the West, and one of the very few to be given in America. (Carmel Cymbal, June 1, 1927)

The concert took place in Kuster's Theatre of the Golden Bough on Ocean Avenue, with its first–rate acoustics, sophisticated lighting, and a seating capacity of 400. One of Dene's two Steinways had been moved from the Dolores Street Studio and was positioned in the center of the forestage.

Much of Dene's program was made up of excerpted movements taken from larger works—in this way music by a greater number of composers can be included in a single program.

Although the concert featured works by twelve composers, most of the individual movements were quite short—none lasted more than six minutes and most were less than three—and thus the entire concert contained only about 80 minutes of actual music, a relatively common benchmark for solo recitalists. Nonetheless the evening was a very long one: Dene commented on each composer's work and then performed it a second time.

For example, Dene began the concert by playing two brief pieces by Gian Francesco Malipiero. After playing them, Dene turned and spoke for a moment to the audience about the two pieces. Then she turned back to the keyboard and played both pieces again from the beginning. She performed everything on the concert this way. As always, she also managed to do this while playing all the music from memory.

(Please see the Appendix for a list of the repertoire played by Dene Denny in this and several other solo recitals.)

Theatre of The Golden Bough

FRIDAY EVENING

DENE DENNY

IN AN

ALL-MODERN
PIANO RECITAL
With Explanatory Comments

Admission $1 plus tax   Program at 8:30

Pine Cone, June 1, 1927. *Courtesy of the H.M. Williams Local History Department, Harrison Memorial Library; and the Carmel Pine Cone.*

The reviews were positive, but were as much about Dene as about the music.

> Dene Denny, pianiste infinitissimo [sic], accomplished a vitally interesting thing last Friday night at the Theatre of the Golden Bough with her program of modern music. She took a group of interesting people (with due apologies for egotism) into a realm they were not so very sanguine about entering, but who followed for the sheer joy of going in with her. By the power of her rare and exquisite personality she established herself, here in the wilderness of Carmel's pines, as the foremost disciple of modernity in the formation and rendition of beautiful sounds.
>
> It was an unbelievably thrilling evening. Most of us went almost reluctantly, many of us were there with a certain apprehension, all of us were principally motivated by curiosity. And then, onto a stage bare of all but a piano, walked Dean Denny. She sat on the bench and turned and talked and turned and played and turned and talked again and we found ourselves somewhere we had never expected to be, and we liked it immensely. I believe that most of us were sorry when Dean Denny released our hands and let us fall back out into Ocean Avenue. (Carmel Cymbal, June 8, 1927)

In the same issue of the Cymbal, another reviewer wrote:

> There can be no doubt of the individual triumph scored by Dene Denny in her program of modern music last Friday evening. The loveliness of her touch, the precision of her style and the ineffable distinction of rephrasing, and the most exacting of the new music, were a delight.

The program closed with Henry Cowell's "Harp of Life". New lovely sounds, made by tone clusters and concordances of close lying notes produced by the lower arm and side of the hand, and a haunting elusive melody, made "Harp of Life" one of the most notable selections of the evening. Miss Denny also played Cowell's "Voice of Lir" as an encore. Cowell is a modernist, he has brought something new to music but he brings something else to his compositions that comes gratefully to an audience in comparison with examples of music hot with modern condiments. (ibid.)

The Carmel Cymbal also printed comments heard in the lobby after the concert. They included:

"Miss Denny's workmanship was excellent, and she looked like a Greek goddess at the piano. She is to be congratulated on braving the trials of pioneering in music which is totally foreign to a California audience."

"I didn't know what it was all about, but the pianist made me wish that I did, and I want to hear more of it."

One week after the Carmel recital, on June 10, Dene repeated the same program in San Francisco at the San Francisco Women's Building.

Dene Denny's Modern Art:
Sincerity and Massive Technique, Backed by an Extraordinary Program,
Held Her Audience in Deep Interest

By Anna Cora Winchell

The recital given by Dene Denny, pianist, June 10 at the San Francisco Women's Building, was not an ordinary event. Miss Denny, who leans toward ultra-modernism in music and its expression, was able, through her sincerity and massive technique, to hold her audience in deep interest. And that is no slight achievement in the face of the fact that ultramodern music is not popular with the masses and has yet to make its way with many who are musically cultured.

The program alone was titanic...[lists composers]... and the technical requirements of these composers are sufficient to test the most facile performers.

Miss Denny was firm, composed, earnest, with a personality commanding respect for its intellectual grasp; the most bored or cynical could not doubt her determination to put forth new ideas in which she devoutly believes, without being aggressive.

Brief explanatory remarks aided in clarifying the listener's mind as he followed the tremendous dissonances and impoverished harmonies, and intelligent admiration was awarded Miss Denny for her task. Such a bill in its entirety has never before been undertaken in San Francisco by a single pianist on one program, whose material could have supplied three occasions.

How many converts were made to the cause of this type of music—which seems, as yet, disconcertingly chaotic—cannot be known without taking a census, but Miss Denny will long be remembered for the dignity of her renditions and for her quiet, though stable, convictions. (Pacific Coast Music Review, June 20, 1927)

After her June recitals, Dene apparently gave no more concerts for more than a year, but preparation for some major engagements in 1928 would bring her back to the piano.

Meanwhile, even before her June 3 Carmel debut, she and Hazel had begun planning their upcoming season of plays at the Theatre of the Golden Bough—a season filled with drama in every sense of the word.

The Theatre War 1927–1928

In 1928 and 1929, Academy Award winning producer and director Kenneth Macgowan traveled 14,000 miles throughout the United States making a survey of the current state of American theater. In the resulting book, *Footlights Across America*: Towards a National Theater, Macgowan suggested that the Little Theater Movement in the United States was in danger of overloading the market with plays. In the book, Macgowan describes a visit to Carmel in the summer of 1928. (The "open air stage" he refers to is the Forest Theater, and the "makeshift stage" is the Arts and Crafts Theater.)

> In the artist colony of Carmel-by-the-Sea in California, an open air theater, a most exceptionally modern Playhouse—the Theatre of the Golden Bough—and a makeshift stage have all been constructed; where nine plays were in rehearsal in one July; and where the population appears to include 2000 actors and no audience. It was at Carmel that a clergyman in one of the casts told the director that though his wife was desperately ill, he could promise to come to all the rehearsals but not the first performance.
> *(See End Notes for full reference to Macgowan's book.)*

Macgowan's statistics give only part of the Carmel picture that summer: in June, July and August 1928, there were 44 performances of 16 different plays on Carmel's three stages. But the tide of theater in Carmel had turned, and that busy summer would prove to be a bitter experience for the entire Carmel theater community. Dene Denny and Hazel Watrous found themselves at the center of the storm, and they in fact had helped to bring it on during the preceding 12 months.

By early 1927, there was almost too much theater in Carmel. Because of declining ticket sales the Arts and Crafts Club was having trouble keeping up with maintenance and operating costs of their theater, and were thinking of selling it. Edward Kuster was producing a wider variety of plays at the Golden Bough, including works frankly intended to appeal to a broader public, resulting in accusations of pandering and criticisms that Kuster's choice of repertoire was shallow and insignificant. He also began to capitalize on the dark nights at the Theatre by making it more available for lectures, films, and concerts such as Dene Denny's June 3 recital, described in the previous chapter.

In March 1927, Kuster solved some of his cash flow problems by selling the Golden Bough shops and all the property fronting Ocean Avenue, but he retained sole ownership of the Theatre itself, which fronted Monte Verde Street.

Although he had participated seriously in drama, dance, and concerts all his life, Edward Kuster had no significant professional training or experience as a director, and he decided to spend a year or two in Europe in order to connect with Max Reinhardt and other great theatrical innovators. (He indeed met Reinhardt, and later worked with him in Los Angeles.) Kuster put out word that the Theatre of the Golden Bough was available for lease beginning in September

1927. He also spread a rumor that a San Francisco-based movie theater operator was eyeing the Golden Bough with the idea of turning it into an ordinary movie theater.

The thought of a common movie house on Ocean Avenue was enough of an affront in itself, but that it should be the magnificent Theatre of the Golden Bough? The rumor riled the entire community, but it was Denny and Watrous who took Kuster's bait. In June they signed a lease and assumed full management of the Theatre of the Golden Bough for a period of 12 months beginning September 1, 1927, with an option to extend the lease for a second 12 month period should they choose to do so.

With no professional theatrical or managerial experience, Dene and Hazel were now the managing producers of an entire season of amateur and professional theater. The reaction in the press was positive. This unsigned article (which appeared two days before Dene Denny's June 3 Carmel debut) is given here in its entirety.

> Acquisition by Miss Dene Denny and Miss Hazel Watrous of the Theatre of the Golden Bough on a two-year lease is interesting and promising. Sharing in common with Edward Kuster, founder and managing director of the theater for the past four years, a fine intelligence in a broad human concept, Miss Denny and Miss Watrous will give us the benefit of a new viewpoint that should perpetuate the enviable record of the Golden Bough as a dramatic headlight [sic] of the West.

> Both women, while alive to the progress and possibilities of modern dramatic art, are particularly interested in music, and their management of the Golden Bough will undoubtedly result in many opportunities for Carmel to come in closer touch with the present development of music. And it is to be hoped that Miss Denny and Miss Watrous will continue the policy of Mr. Kuster in providing us with amateur theatricals.

> It is hoped that they can make some arrangements with the Carmel Players for the production of their plays with local casts at the Golden Bough. The Carmel Players suffer now and will especially suffer during the summer months, from the fact of the inaccessibility of the Arts and Crafts theater, and its location away from the business center of the city.

> The Cymbal extends to Miss Denny and Miss Watrous its heartiest congratulations and warmest wishes for their success, a success which it feels it can prophecy as well as wish. (Carmel Cymbal, June 1, 1927)

The Carmel Pine Cone added its own encouragement:

> The announcement of Denny and Watrous of their plans for the 1927–28 subscription season at the Theatre of the Golden Bough is both interesting and important, and promises much in dramatic education, sugarcoated with enjoyment.

> Beginning with the weekend of September 9, the two new lessees of the theater are planning a series of 12 plays, the first of which will be a serious dramatization of "Uncle Tom's Cabin" and the last to be an abstract production to the Nth degree. The plan is something new and original and should attract much attention beyond the centerline of Carpenter Street [i.e. beyond the actual city limit]. It is a plan that one might expect to find form in the minds of Dene Denny and Hazel Watrous. They are given to interesting creations. (Pine Cone, June 22, 1927)

There is no doubt that Dene and Hazel had stepped blithely into an already difficult theater environment in Carmel. Ticket sales and box office revenue were declining, and this would be problem enough for newcomers to theater management, but Dene and Hazel seem to have added to their own difficulties with an inexplicable blunder.

The Abalone League was a local amateur baseball and social club, and their primary involvement with "theater" was putting on an annual variety show called the Carmel Follies. Edward Kuster had given them free use of the Theatre of the Golden Bough for their 1925 and 1926 Follies and he had come to be on good terms with them.

In June, after it had been announced that Dene and Hazel would be the managers of the Golden Bough beginning on September 1, the Abalone League requested the use of the Theatre once again for their October Carmel Follies show. For reasons that are unclear, Dene and Hazel turned down the request, and the Abalone League responded angrily to this refusal by threatening to promote a boycott of all performances at the Golden Bough. This incident served as the final straw in the increasing resentment that had been building against Kuster and the Theatre of the Golden Bough since its opening in 1924. Dene and Hazel had not only stepped into the situation, they had made things worse.

Yet another wrinkle shows how complicated the local alliances were: the financially strapped Arts and Crafts Club had basically stopped using its theater on Monte Verde Street. Built in the same year as the Golden Bough, it had become dilapidated and rundown, and the Club had no money for repairs.

The Carmel Players—whose home had been in the Arts and Crafts Hall—reached an agreement with Dene and Hazel to perform at the Golden Bough. Dene and Hazel planned the repertoire and engaged George Ball as director, Rhoda Johnson to create the costumes and design the sets, and her husband Dick to manage the stage. The sets were built in the workshop of the Arts and Crafts Theater and carried several blocks to the Golden Bough for rehearsals and performances.

The Carmel Players were no mere gaggle of amateurs: though non-professional, they had a long tradition of high quality and consistently fine productions, and usually employed professional costume and scenery designers and stage directors. The Players had been leasing the run-down Arts and Crafts buildings, and they now looked forward to producing their shows in a newer and more professional venue. Opening the Denny-Watrous season with several Carmel Players productions obviously benefitted everyone involved.

But it did not. This announcement that the Carmel Players would actually collaborate with the Golden Bough vexed the old-timers, who were irritated that the Players had abandoned the comfy, down-home, good old days atmosphere of the Arts and Crafts Hall in favor of the glitzy, new-fangled and "professional" Golden Bough. To these veterans of Carmel's earliest theater days, the Carmel Players' change of venue seemed like the loss of a personal and precious tradition, and it was all the fault of Kuster, his "theatre," and Dene and Hazel.

By the end of June, Kuster was preparing to leave town and head for Germany. Nothing unpleasant had actually taken place yet, but animosity was continuing to grow and there was lots of talk. On June 22, the Carmel Cymbal described the word on the street:

> There are reports up and down Ocean Avenue of a dramatic war impending. It is to be a
> war, if it comes into being, that is based on silly sentiment, and will merely tend to carry

on the undesirable reputation Carmel has for a fostering of factions that mean nothing but murmur a great deal.

The impending war has for its human foundation the group of "old residents" who cherish the Arts and Crafts Theater and its wood shingles and electric fixtures. They want it to continue to function as a theater, as a dramatic center, because—well just because it was constructed for that purpose several years ago. Those who were prime movers in its construction—selecting a site, by the way, that was all but doomed at the start—would perpetuate the romance of its conception whether or not enough people can be led down a dark street to its doors to make it pay. [Note: the Arts and Crafts Theater, site of the present Golden Bough Playhouse on Monte Verde near 9th Avenue, was three dark blocks from Ocean Avenue.]

It was a bitter blow to these people when Edward Gerhard Kuster, with unquestioned beauty in his soul and stamina enough to crystallize it into a beautiful structure, created the Theatre of the Golden Bough. They refused at that time to weld their Arts and Crafts sentiment with the Golden Bough and share in the glory that came to Kuster as the founder and owner of the most unique little theater of the West. Silly sentiment held them back then and it is urging them on now to silly threats that they will fight the new managers of the Golden Bough.

The Carmel Players, who have been struggling, have been given an opportunity to appear at the Theatre of the Golden Bough and they have wisely accepted it. This is another bitter pill for the sentimentalists and it is their threat that they will set up opposition to the Carmel Players in their contract to produce six of the 12 plays [sic] in the Golden Bough subscription season. (Carmel Cymbal, June 22, 1927)

In the midst of this conflict, the community somehow came together for a crafts exhibit in the Arts and Crafts Hall in August. Contributions to the show included furniture created by the Denny-Watrous Studio, weavings by Edward Kuster's wife, and artwork and embroidery by Hazel's sister Zanetta, who was living on Dolores Street in her house across from Hazel and Dene. Zanetta had a studio at the Court of the Seven Arts where she created upholstery and drapes. At this time, Hazel and Dene were still running their ad in the Pine Cone for "Denny and Watrous: Designers, Builders, Decorators of homes."

The Denny-Watrous season at the Golden Bough opened on September 9 with the Carmel Players' production of *Uncle Tom's Cabin.*

If Negroes were still slaves and the traffic in human flesh had not yet been done away with, the reaction of the audiences to uncle Tom's cabin played at the Theatre of the Golden Bough last weekend could not have been any more real. After seeing it played, one understands why it has been produced more times than any other play in America. There were some familiar names in the cast, including Jadwiga Noskowiak, who played Ophelia in the Forest Theater's Hamlet and Juliet in the past season, as little Eva. (Pine Cone, September 16, 1927)

(* Noskowiak was a popular participant in Carmel theatricals. She married US Naval officer Stanton Babcock and their daughter, Barbara Babcock, became an Emmy Award-winning actress.)

The Carmel Players followed *Uncle Tom's Cabin* with Ibsen's *Hedda Gabler* and three more plays, all described in the press as excellent productions performed for small audiences. In November the Carmel Players ended their fall season with *The Admirable Crichton* by Sir James Barrie (the author of Peter Pan).

Nothing in the summer's gossip mill could have prepared Dene and Hazel for what actually happened as their season continued in September and October 1927. The Abalone League actually did engineer a boycott of Golden Bough performances, partly by negative word of mouth and partly by simply by scheduling parties and other events in direct competition with the Denny-Watrous schedule. Throughout the fall season, the Golden Bough productions played to almost empty houses. There were bills to be paid each month—the director, costumer, and stage manager; heat, electricity, janitor, maintenance; printing and ads; materials for building sets and costumes; and other operating costs. As lessees Dene and Hazel had to make up the shortfall out of their own pockets. Their optimistic dream of a thought-provoking season of drama was becoming a nightmare.

The increasingly rancorous gossip among the competing factions was destroying the congeniality of the theater community. By the end of 1927 the feud had become so bitter that old friends who belonged to different cliques refused to speak to each other on the street. Even as all this was taking place, Dene and Hazel were also involved in the creation of the Carmel Music Society, which presented its first concert in December 1927. CMS is discussed in the following chapter. In January 1928, the Monterey Herald weighed in.

> This somewhat of a row between the owner of the Theatre of the Golden Bough and the Arts and Crafts Club of Carmel is a temporary wash-out of the hopes that amateur dramatics might be placed on a firmer footing in Carmel.
>
> Were a better spirit of cooperation shown, with less high regard for personalities, Carmel dramatics could be programmed and budgeted with the same success in business planning that has made possible the unusual season of the Carmel Music Society. Carmel dramatics can be made a pre-guaranteed success. But not while its fate is over-influenced by the Prima Donna attitude. (Monterey Herald, January 10, 1928)

When word of this "row" reached Kuster in Europe at the beginning of the year, he realized that the Carmel situation was becoming unstable. Returning to California, he published a long statement in the Pine Cone from which these excerpts are taken:

> ... For the benefit of interested people who may not have accurate information on the subject I will say that some years ago I designed, financed and caused to be built the Theatre of the Golden Bough, first offering the Arts and Crafts Club the gratuitous use of the plant [the building] when erected.
>
> In the face of this offer the Club, led by Mr. Newberry, constructed its present theater adjacent to its old playhouse. I do not care to discuss the antagonism which the Theatre of the Golden Bough has had to weather during the first years of its existence. It was merely a normal and amusing expression of self-awareness of the backward-looking "old guard" of a fast-growing little town.

Last fall, certain affiliations having been accomplished, I felt that organized opposition was at an end. I undertook a two-year absence in Europe to study production methods and accumulate plays and other material to bring back to Carmel in the fall of 1929. The plant was leased to Miss Dene Denny and Miss Hazel Watrous in whose personal integrity, artistic vision, and business abilities I have complete confidence. They are obviously in entire sympathy with my aim that the Golden Bough shall be the finest thing of its kind in America. ...

It is not so gratifying, however, to learn that almost immediately after my departure the lessees of the theater were subjected by all sorts of people to various kinds and degrees of pressure subversive of the character of the theater and of the real interests of the community. I have no wish to inquire into the extent of the boycott which has been promised them if they do not do thus and so. The names of many of the people who have been promising to make the sledding rough for Miss Denny and Miss Watrous are familiar to me. They have never been so much actuated by community interests and love for the dramas as by a passion for the fussy excitements of personal politics and the wish to further the special interests of friends. (Pine Cone, Feb 15, 1928)

The Arts and Crafts Club, founded in 1905, had in fact established community theater in Carmel and was proud of that tradition. Now, some of its long-time members (Kuster's "backward-looking 'old guard'") felt that theater life in Carmel needed fixing and organizing, and that it obviously was up to them to do it, not Kuster. The old guard included community figures of stature who had played major roles (literally and figuratively) in the formative years of Carmel theater.

Knowing that Kuster would likely attempt to re-assert his influence in "their" theater world, the members of the Arts and Crafts Club published a bold statement of their decision to assume the role of theatrical leadership in Carmel "once again." According to their announcement, they would...

> ...take on in an active way the support, financial and otherwise, of the amateur drama here...The Arts and Crafts [Club] will give general supervision, attend to all financial matters, assist in the selection of plays and cast, advertise and give publicity, and in every way in their power advance the excellence of performances and their financial success. Opportunity will be given to other producers to put plays on during the year, and actors and actresses will be sought among the residents and visitors in Carmel. (Pine Cone, February 24, 1928)

The rest of the statement makes it quite clear: the leaders of the Arts and Crafts Club intended to assume sole management of all theater activity in Carmel, and to manage the finances, casting, promotion and production of all plays given at the Forest Theater, the Arts and Crafts Theater, and at the Theatre of the Golden Bough. They would pick the repertoire and choose the directors, although "opportunity will be given to other producers...."

When Dene, Hazel, and Kuster read this in the Pine Cone on Friday, they were surprised and furious. From comments made in the following weeks by Newberry and others, it's possible that a conversation was going on regarding some sort of community-wide organization of theatrical efforts. But it would seem that the Arts and Crafts Club overreached, without consulting all parties involved. The following day, this item appeared in the Carmelite.

Lessees of Golden Bough State Aims

A statement by Dene Denny and Hazel Watrous.

The recent articles in the Carmel and Monterey press regarding the amateur drama in Carmel force us as lessees of the Theatre of the Golden Bough to declare that certain statements contained in these articles are misleading and erroneous.

One such statement is in the first paragraph of the Carmel Pine Cone of February 24, reading, "The Carmel club of Arts and Crafts, will take on in an active way the support, financial and otherwise, of the amateur drama here." Whatever taking on the "support" of the amateur drama here "financial and otherwise" may mean, we, as theater lessees, feel forced to say that it has nothing whatsoever to do with the Theatre of the Golden Bough. Up-to-date of writing, no one representing the Arts and Crafts Club has called upon or conferred with us, the Theatre management. No plan or outline of "support financial and otherwise" has been presented to us by the Arts and Crafts. Under the lease which we as lessees of the Theatre hold with Edward Kuster, owner, it is the item that by June 1, 1928, the option which we hold on the management for the second year must be taken up or released. Whether or not we shall enter upon the second year depends entirely upon the support given to the theater productions, to our present policy, and the possibilities for the future.

To those who speak so easily of "the successful continuation of the amateur drama," we should like to say that we look upon the Theatre of the Golden Bough as a trust. We consider it as one of the few theaters in the world where there is an actual opportunity to bring together all the arts. Such a theater is too fine and rare a thing to be commercialized by the zeal of small town organization. We reverence the vision and generosity that inspired Edward Kuster to give the Theatre of the Golden Bough to the town of Carmel. For though he virtually offered it to Carmel and she rejected it, yet, in rearing it here on Ocean Avenue, and keeping it free from organized control, he has given it to all of us who go therein, and who delight in its quiet dignity.

We respect the high standard of Mr. Kuster's productions, and are completely in accord with his use of the Theatre. We undertook our present management with the purpose of building up to the finest in drama, always working toward the experimental, contemporary, modern idea. We looked to use the theater as a laboratory, where all creative local talent might find expression, and the best of the state's Little Theater Groups might find an audience. As lessees of the Theatre, together with Edward Kuster, owner, we invite the friends of drama to attend a meeting in the Theatre on Thursday evening next, March 1. (Carmelite, February 25, 1928)

The following editorial appeared in the same issue of the Carmelite, and the reference to "theatricals" in the second line is significant. The term "private theatrical" dates back at least to the eighteenth century and refers to a private, non-public, just-for-us theatrical event not intended to be seen by outsiders. More a theatrical happening than a "performance," this sort of presentation was part of the earliest Carmel theater experience. Mary Austin and George Sterling presented "private theatricals" for small groups of friends in the Arts and Crafts Hall soon after it was built in 1907.

In the excerpt below, the writer contrasts "private theatricals" with "drama." In this context, "drama" refers to a deeper and more refined theatrical creation intended for public consumption and evincing a level of skill, discipline and commitment that brings it into the realm of art.

Drama vs. Dollars [excerpt]
by a quiet observer

With absolutely no disparagement of the early delightful efforts in Carmel, we yet wonder how many of us are distinguishing between theatricals and drama, for with the development that is taking place here such a distinguishing process is necessary. It is nobody's fault that the town has grown, that its growth puts it in touch with bigger aspects than formerly, and that as a result many phases of our living, both practical and artistic, have been keeping pace with the growth.

Fully mindful of the history of theater activities here, and the developments from the parlor to the [Arts and Crafts] Club and on to the Forest Theater, we do not see why there should not be much greater unfoldment looked forward to and greeted heartily.

Contributing towards this progression in matters pertaining to the theater there is no doubt that the present management [Denny and Watrous] has the most forward outlook in our midst today. There is nothing exclusive about this; the outlook belongs to every one of us who cares to move forward, to everyone who is generous enough to cooperate in the theater aims. No one is to blame for having a vision, but he is to blame if he compromises that vision. It is the true artist who forgets all about playing safe where an ideal is involved.

And so it comes about that Carmel seems to be in the midst of a very amusing situation: making frantic efforts to do something that, if it had been awake, it would have known was done months ago. So far as we hear there is a rather busy endeavor underway to "save drama for Carmel." Now it so happens that the drama was saved for Carmel on the day that the Misses Denny and Watrous signed the lease for the Theatre of the Golden Bough. At that time we could not discover any club, society, group of players, producers, or just plain citizens, who were clamoring for the risk of this lease for the purpose of saving drama for Carmel, or any who were trying to find a way to establish themselves behind an anticipated deficit of $300 a month. We do happen to know that Denny and Watrous had the courage of their convictions, and unaided by so much as a "Go ahead, we will lend a hand," they waded in and saved drama for Carmel. Because of their earlier contacts they were approached by, and were able to approach, some big organizations. (Carmelite, February 25, 1928)

The March 1 meeting mentioned by Dene and Hazel in their published statement took place in the Theatre of the Golden Bough. The large and highly charged group of townspeople sat in Kuster's wicker chairs while Dene, Hazel and Kuster spoke from the forestage.

Dene began the meeting by stating on behalf of the three of them that the Club's recent published statement in the Pine Cone had come to them as an utter surprise. How, she asked, could Newberry and the others presume to speak for all Carmel theater enthusiasts, and how could they announce publicly their plan to produce plays at the Golden Bough without first discussing it with the owner and the lessees?

Then it was Kuster's turn. He had returned from Europe because of all this, and he felt very put upon by the entire situation. He had in fact paid for the Golden Bough entirely with his own money ($75,000 in 1924, well over a million dollars today), and had attempted therewith to raise the level of the theatrical experience in the Carmel community (although it apparently made no difference to him whether the community actually wanted it or not). Kuster believed (with good reason) that increasingly petty preservationists were sabotaging his work merely because he and his Golden Bough threatened to take away the small-town character of local theater that many of them had helped create.

And so Kuster stood onstage that evening with Dene and Hazel and told everyone in the audience exactly what he thought of them. He told the assembled Carmelites that he was sick of the infighting and pettiness. He had given them a theater that was becoming famous throughout America and abroad. He reminded them that he had offered them all a place in this theater at no cost to them and they had turned him down. Now their sabotage was helping to sink the Theatre altogether.

Apparently he saved his best zingers for Perry Newberry, who was sitting all alone in a row by himself. Newberry had been abandoned by his embarrassed friends at the start of the meeting, when they realized what was coming.

Newberry, quite well known for his loquacious eloquence, could muster nothing to say, although a few days later in the Pine Cone he played the incredulous victim, made light of it all, and tried to claim that he had discussed the Arts and Crafts plans with Dene and Hazel.

At the end of the meeting, Kuster made it clear that he was returning to Europe and planned to stay there for another year. In his absence, the Theatre of the Golden Bough was in the hands of Dene and Hazel, and he wanted everyone to get along or he would not hesitate to make good on his threat to turn it into a movie house. Kuster stayed in California for another six weeks, visiting San Francisco and Los Angeles, and then returned to Germany.

One week after the dramatic March 1 meeting, the theater enthusiasts in the Abalone [Baseball] League led by Charles Van Riper and Byington Ford jumped into the fray and announced their purchase of the Arts and Crafts Theater on Monte Verde. Since it was no longer being used by the Club, they thought they would have a go at theater themselves. The Abalones gave the rundown facility a complete renovation: the stage was enlarged, new seating was installed, and the interior was repainted in preparation for a May opening. The theater was officially renamed The Carmel Playhouse, but the building was often referred to at that time as the Abalone Theater.

And so Carmel entered the spring theater season, as emotions continued to crescendo. The former Arts and Crafts Theater was now owned by the Abalone League. The Carmel Players—formerly at the Arts and Crafts Club—were performing at the Theatre of the Golden Bough. A mix of Abalone and Arts and Crafts members were producing plays at the outdoor Forest Theater. Dene and Hazel carried on with their winter-spring season, giving each of the following plays two or three performances on consecutive nights:

January: Ferenc Molnár's 1909 play *Liliom*

February: The Pasadena Playhouse presented a comedy titled *Cake*. (Author unknown.)

March: Henrik Ibsen's *Ghosts* performed by a San Francisco troupe in modern dress with impressionist scenery.

April: The Carmel Players mounted their two final productions: Amelie Rines' *The Sea Woman's Cloak* and the 1925 Pulitzer winner, *Craig's Wife*, by George Kelly.

May: The Berkeley Playhouse presented the 1917 comedy *Lombardi Limited* by Frederic and Fanny Hatton and starring the popular film actor Leo Carillo, for whom the play had been written.

During this time concerts and other events also were taking place in the Theatre of the Golden Bough, some of which will be discussed in the following chapter.

The end of the Theater War in Carmel, June 1–August 31, 1928

For the summer Dene and Hazel engaged Morris Ankrum as director and actor. Ankrum (1896-1964) was a director and drama teacher at the Pasadena Playhouse at that time. In the 1930s he began a successful film and television career. In early May, Ankrum began rehearsals at the Golden Bough. He was scheduled to open the summer season on May 31, directing and starring in Eugene O'Neill's *The Emperor Jones*. O'Neill had been a rising star in the Greenwich Village experimental theater scene, but his plays had moved to Broadway in 1920 with *The Emperor Jones*. It was the first American play with a leading role written for an African-American, and the play is largely a one-man show: Jones, a deposed Caribbean island dictator, goes slowly crazy in the jungle while interacting with people and events that exist only in his imagination. The role was written for Charles Sidney Gilpin and was reprised with great acclaim in 1924 by Paul Robeson. It seems not to have been noteworthy at the time that a caucasian actor embodied the role of Rufus Jones in Carmel.

> Morris Ankrum took the part of Jones. If that is a sample of his acting, he is one of the finest ever seen in Carmel. He got all the humor and "Blues" of the Negro temperament. He managed his tall body with ease and expressiveness. He put into his climaxes animalistic terror, and left you cold with the horror of his fears. (Pine Cone, June 7, 1928)

At the beginning of May, the Abalone League had opened their refurbished "Carmel Playhouse" with *Seven Keys to Baldpate*, a melodrama by George M. Cohan, and followed it two weeks later with Maxwell Anderson's *Saturday's Children*. These performances did not conflict with the Golden Bough schedule. But the Abalones were just getting warmed up. They deliberately scheduled their production of the then-popular *Peg O 'My Heart* by Hartley Manners on the May 31 opening weekend of The Emperor Jones.

Two weeks before this intentional collision, Pauline Schindler wrote the following reflections in the Carmelite. Note that Dene and Hazel are no longer the newcomers. It is now the Abalone League who is the "second comer."

> Typical of a small town everywhere are the squabbles arising over issues which provoke the irony of the gods but break the hearts of their victims. Carmel is subject to the same psychology. There are now two theaters in a little community which barely supports the fine ardent efforts of one. This is so illogical that it must eventually provoke an unlovely and unwholesome competition. The Carmel Playhouse (the Abalone Theater) knows the valiance of the effort of the Theatre of the Golden Bough to present work of high quality, and the need for all the cooperation possible. We are sorry it offers instead a state of war and competition. Yet as a critic we respect all dramatic excellence, regardless of the personal virtues or villainies of the artist.

Nevertheless there remains one point so small, that it renders even its author almost invisible! The dramatic schedule of the Theatre of the Golden Bough was made public months before the Playhouse existed. This schedule was known to those who arranged the performance dates of the Playhouse. A perfectly amicable dovetailing of times and dates might have been arranged, so that even competition might have been a friendly thing. What a pity that the second comer did instead make a choice of less dignity, and no courtesy at all. Instead, he arranged his dates so that they conflicted with those of the Golden Bough, and so forced a state of mind in which it is almost impossible for either group of players to wish the other success.

This is scarcely the attitude of artists; it is much more like that of children playing at being cannibals. Certainly it is a state little likely to nourish the untrammeled production of works of art. Here is a tangle among people whose integrity and essential virtue one does not doubt. A much more gracious state would be one in which each group were free to wish success to the other. (Carmelite, May 16, 1928)

But in fact, at some point prior to the opening weekend of the Golden Bough's summer season, Dene and Hazel already had thrown in the towel. They sent a letter dated May 28 to Edward Kuster in Germany, typed on Theatre of the Golden Bough stationery.

The Theatre of the Golden Bough, May 28, 1928
Carmel-by-the-Sea, California

Dear Mr. Kuster,

We were glad to hear from you, though sorry to know that you have been ill.

No, things have not been going well. We have lost money on everything — (even on "Lombardi Ltd.") — Except for "The Garden of Allah," on which we made $20! People simply do not come. The Abalone League has taken all our dates, playing on the nights of our performances. The effort to kill the Theatre seems more organized than ever. We have heard it rumored that there is a definite intention of making it so impossible for us that we should be forced to give up, and then of making it so impossible for you that in desperation you will sell for a song to the opposition.

If one could weather the deficits and keep on with the right sort of thing, doubtless, in the end, the idea would win out. We are as appreciative as ever of what you have done, and as unfaltering in our concept of the function of the "Golden Bough" — but we can give you just one word on June 1, and that word we give you now: WE CANNOT TAKE UP OUR OPTION ON A SECOND YEAR'S LEASE. We have no more money to lose, and the overhead of the theater, together with the opposition, precludes even a possibility of coming out from a business point of view. We do not mind contributing time and some degree of experience, but we cannot lose any more money, and the sacrifice is too great for the result. It is a disappointment to withdraw before the point of accomplishment, but we can see no other way. As to what we owe you in rent, literally nothing has come in. When it does, we shall, of course, pay.

With kindest regards and best wishes, we are

Sincerely yours,

Dene Denny   Hazel Watrous

Dene and Hazel wrote this letter to Kuster during the rehearsals for The Emperor Jones, and the letter may have gone to the Post Office on May 29. Morris Ankrum's production of the O'Neil play opened on May 31, and even as Dene and Hazel managed the launch of their summer season they knew they were finished. At least the repertoire that summer was excellent, as it had been for their entire season. Following The Emperor Jones, they presented The Importance of Being Earnest by Oscar Wilde; Ten Nights in a Barroom by William Pratt; and To the Ladies by Kaufman and Connelly. These were followed by a new work selected by competition.

The preservationist theater clique in Carmel spent the summer of 1928 putting the Theatre of the Golden Bough out of business for good. After washing out the Golden Bough's opening weekend, the Abalones produced twenty performances of eight different plays during June, July and August to take the public's attention away from the Golden Bough and sink its ticket sales. They were abetted by Perry Newberry and the Forest Theater who also scheduled two of their productions to coincide with some of the Golden Bough's July performance dates.

During the final three months of the Denny-Watrous season at the Theatre of the Golden Bough, there were *44 performances of 16 different plays on the three stages in Carmel*. This was the summer Kenneth MacGowan described in *Footlights Across America*. (At the beginning of this chapter.)

Denny and Watrous with Morris Ankrum
Kuster's Theatre of the Golden Bough, Ocean Avenue

> *The Emperor Jones*, May 31, June 1, 2
>
> *The Importance of Being Earnest*, June 21, 22, 23
>
> *Ten Nights in a Barroom*, July 3, 4, 5
>
> *To the Ladies*, July 27, 28
>
> *Dark Haven*, Aug 25, 26 (winner of the Golden Bough playwright competition)

The Abalone League
Carmel Playhouse, Monte Verde Street

> *Peg O' My Heart*, May 31, June 1, 2
>
> *The Copperhead*, June 15, 16
>
> *The Whole Town's Talking*, June 28, 39, 30
>
> *The Barker*, July 19, 20, 21
>
> *The Thirteenth Chair*, Aug 2, 3, 4
>
> I*s That So*, August, 11, 13, 14, 18, 19
>
> *Tommy*, Aug 30, 31

The Outdoor Forest Theater

> *Taming of the Shrew* - Shakespeare, July 2, 3, 4, 5
>
> *Princess of Arabby* - Perry Newberry script, Thomas Cator music, July 13, 14
>
> *Young Herod*, July 27, 28
>
> *Inchling* - Rem Remsen, Aug 3, 4

By late June, Dene and Hazel had come up with a plan to finance the rest of their summer season. They called a town meeting at the Golden Bough, and together with Morris Ankrum they presented their proposal for a new organization called the Theatre Guild. According to the Pine Cone

> We are asked to join the theater Guild for the sum of one dollar, which will give us a voice in the organization's work and [allow us to] become a supporter of experimental drama in the village, which stands for development and progress in every line of art. (Pine Cone, June 8, 1928)

There was an implication of the "old Carmel" in this: "Let's get together and put on some theater." With membership fees and donations they managed to raise nearly $1,100, making it possible for them to cover the costs of the rest of their summer season. A few months later, the Pine Cone stated what must have been clear in hindsight by that point:

> The Theater Guild was organized last summer in order that the summer season of plays under the directorship of Morris Ankrum and under the Denny-Watrous regime, might be financed. (Pine Cone, October 12, 1928)

The most active members of the Theatre Guild were Hazel Watrous and Pauline Schindler, and even Herbert Heron took part. During the fall and winter months there were meetings, group readings of plays, a Christmas pageant, and other small-scale projects, but no actual stage productions. The group dissolved within twelve months.

In June, Denny-Watrous and the Golden Bough also announced a competition offering a $50 prize for the best play by a California author, known or unknown, to be handed in by August 1. The accepted play was to be directed by Morris Ankrum at the Golden Bough at the end of the month. (The time frame of this competition is incredible: the first announcement of the competition was sent out at the end of June; all entries were to be submitted by August 1; and the winning play—*Dark Haven* by Anne Murray Nichols—was produced on the Golden Bough stage on August 25 and 25.

On August 25 the curtain came down on the final performance of Dark Haven, and the Denny-Watrous season at the Golden Bough was over. Dene and Hazel were no longer theater managers.

Forced to take control of the Theatre himself once again, Edward Kuster returned to Carmel in August and began a valiant two-month attempt to generate enough advance ticket sales to support a 1928–1929 Golden Bough season. After failing to meet his financial goal, he returned the subscription money he had already received, and gave up. It was announced that Mr. Gerald Hardy of Fresno was the new lessee of the Theatre. Beginning in November it would be known as the "Carmel Theater" and would offer "two complete motion picture programs every night." The much smaller Manzanita Movie Theater, also managed by Mr. Hardy, would now be open only on a part–time basis.

Perry Newberry needed to have the final word in the Pine Cone: "*...this is the end of the story of Kuster's toy theater.*" This may have been an intended pun. Some in Carmel did indeed see the Golden Bough as Kuster's "toy," but the actual Toy Theater, founded in Boston in 1912, was one of the first community theaters in the US, and was at the forefront of the original Little Theater Movement that inspired Kuster.

"...the group production of a work of art."

One year later, an unsigned article in the Pine Cone recalled the Theater War:

> Plans for the summer of 1929 in Carmel present a sharp contrast with activities of last summer here. Remember the first days of the Carmel Playhouse? [The Abalone Theater] The copping of dates for production by the Golden Bough, the Carmel Playhouse, and the Forest Theater simultaneously? And how some people in Carmel went down Ocean Avenue on one side, while others walked on the other, in order to avoid speaking to one another?
>
> The three theaters represented respectively the high-brows, the low-brows, and the old-timers, irrespective of elevation. The Golden Bough under the magnificent direction of Hazel Watrous and Dene Denny as lessees produced works of art finely, and failed to make expenses. (Aha, too high-brow, crowed the low-brows.) The Carmel Playhouse produced witty comedies, and met equally hard times. (You see? Nodded the high-brows sagely.) The Forest Theater produced Shakespeare, and John Jordan [a local patron] reached his hand down deep in his pocket to make up the deficit. (Well naturally, shrugged the rest... If there is going to be a theater on every corner in Carmel...)
>
> So, Carmel learned its lesson, surrendered the Golden Bough to the purveyor of commercial amusement, and suffered starvation. Not only have we suffered the lack of fine plays; but we have missed also the activity of their production—the group production of a work of art. And we have missed coming together at the Golden Bough to see, hear, enjoy, and criticize. Only the Music Society has provided us this particular delight of reunion—one of the pleasantest things in the life of a small community. (Pine Cone, June 26, 1928)

For the rest of their lives, Dene and Hazel occasionally referred to their twelve months at the Golden Bough, always in a positive way. They mentioned the number, variety and modernity of the plays and the overall artistic success of the venture. In a 1949 interview, Dene recalled all that needed to be remembered:

> "In 1928 Edward Kuster went to Europe and we leased his beautiful little Theatre of the Golden Bough. That was our initial theatrical venture, and during the ensuing 12 months we presented 18 plays and more than a dozen concerts." (Dene Denny interviewed in the Carmel Spectator, June 30, 1949)

Understandably left unmentioned was the fact that during the 12 months of their lease they had averaged a net loss of about $300 per month, a total in 2014 dollars of at least $50,000. Most of this loss was covered by Dene and Hazel themselves. It would be nearly a decade before they would consider theater management again, and then it would be entirely on their own terms and not in Carmel.

On June 28, 1928, as the unpleasant Theater War summer was unfolding, journalist Lincoln Steffens' editorial in the Carmelite identified one of Carmel's problems.

Laugh, Carmel, Laugh

by Lincoln Steffens

There is something wrong in Carmel, very wrong, and I think I can put my finger on the root of the wrong because I'm a newcomer here.

Anyone that [sic] has lived long in Carmel must've become part of the wrong, and, therefore blind to it, and my fear is that if I stay here long I may become serious, too. I may cease to enjoy life and Carmel as I do now.

And that's what's the matter with Carmel: that it does not laugh enough. Not that it's arty; not that it groups; not even that it is cliquish. Every great city and every small town I have ever lived in, in any country, is all of these things. But Paris laughs at Paris, New York has humor for New Yorkers, and the Chinese of Peking smile at themselves. The Carmelites do not laugh at their neighbors: they would like to kill them, or their theatre, or their city plan, or their school, or their newspaper, or their false ideas of art. …

Lincoln Steffens in Carmel, 1926.
Library of Congress.

Just now for example, the conflict between the two local theater groups is coming to the breaking point, and the stronger theatre can and probably will kill the weaker. Too bad. Too ridiculous. To earnest by far. Two theaters are better than one, three better than two. To argue that Carmel is too small, or too—something—to make one theater success, is to miss the point—and the laugh. …

… all the idealists, whether in art or in politics, in marriage or in life, are going to split into factions and fight and kill off one another's theatres. And the faction that wins, being the only one, will split, passionately, into two groups, both of which are wrong or right. We shall have our two or three theaters all right. We shall have our waves of new and fresh, and our old and stale, idealists. Meanwhile, we shall have always—I believe and hope—a community in which we can let our children grow up aware, at least, that there is such a thing as art.

It is all right. Men don't run the universe, and the citizens of Carmel do not govern Carmel. Something else has its way in the end. But meanwhile, knowing this, we can, by reminding ourselves of it now and then—we can hate a little less, we can be not quite so ruthless and Ernest: we might even let the Golden Bough go on, and boost it, and the Abalones, too. Or, if that is beyond the capacity of our wit, we might use the occasion to learn to laugh at our own limitations.

(Carmelite, June 28, 1928)

The (double) demise of the Golden Bough

Under the direction of Edward Kuster, and Denny-Watrous, the Theatre of the Golden Bough on Ocean Avenue was in full-time operation as a live theater venue for 51 months, June 1924 through August 1928. It produced 52 plays under nineteen stage directors, and presented fifteen distinct theater ensembles—professional and amateur.

From November 1928 until May 1935, the Golden Bough operated as a movie house under the name "Carmel Theater." After the opening of the auditorium at the Sunset School in 1931, the Golden Bough was used only rarely for concerts or musical events.

Kuster returned to Carmel in 1929, and the Abalone League, beset by financial woes, sold him their entire complex—the original Arts and Crafts Hall and the 1925 theater, renovated in 1928. During the next few years Kuster was in and out of Carmel, and used that facility as a base for many projects. From 1932 to 1934 he also produced plays in San Francisco and directed the Fresno Players.

In 1935 Kuster tried to renegotiate his lease with the Golden Bough's current movie house tenant, so that he might produce live theater there one weekend each month. The manager was reluctant to disturb the ordered world of his movie house with actors and scenery, but he compromised and offered Kuster one initial weekend as a test. The play was "By Candlelight," a comedy by Siegfried Geyer, in Kuster's own English translation from the original German. Kuster had directed the play with success in Fresno, and hoped to repeat the experience in Carmel. A certain amount of publicity was generated by the fact that this was the first time in eight years that Edward Kuster had produced a play in his own Theatre of the Golden Bough. Opening night on May 17 was well attended—as was the second performance the following night—and it seemed like the production was a happy success.

At 8:00am on May 19, Mrs. Gussie Meyer of the Normandie Inn, a hotel across Monte Verde Street, saw smoke pouring from the open stage doors. Within a few hours, Kuster's spectacular and innovative Theatre of the Golden Bough was an ugly burned ruin. (The shops and ticket office were spared and are still standing today.) There were rumors of arson, and multiple anecdotes of a mysterious car or a suspicious late–night pedestrian and the like, but no specific suspect ever surfaced.

The Carmel Cymbal reported:

> The destruction of the Theatre of the Golden Bough means a complete loss to Edward G. Kuster who built it in 1924. The insurance on the structure and its contents totaled only about $8000 and this barely covers the cost of the antiques which had been borrowed as props for the play which was being produced. (Carmel Cymbal, May 22, 1935)

The "Notes and Comments" page in the same issue of the Cymbal eulogized the Theatre.

> Fire on Sunday morning wrote "tragedy" across Ted Kuster's dream, and the Theatre of the Golden Bough is gone. The fire also wrote tragedy across something that is, or was, the core of Carmel, and I wonder if the last vestige of the dream of those who first came here and settled in the pines is not gone with the going of the Golden Bough. It seemed to me, or it seems to me now, that what was embodied in Ted Kuster's hopes and aspirations was in actuality a symbol of what we who have known Carmel so long have been thinking we are losing with the waxing and widening of the current across the hill [i.e. from Monterey] and down into Ocean Avenue.

The fire Sunday morning really razed Carmel. There, behind those charred doors and in those charred ruins, lies the heart of things as we once ecstatically visualized them, and our last flank has been swept away by the grocery stores and the real estaters.

So, by the great unfillable [sic] gap it leaves, we can know the Golden Bough for what it was, a monument to the better things we had, and to our finer faith. (Carmel Cymbal, May 22, 1935)

After the Golden Bough

Kuster's magical Theatre of the Golden Bough was gone. He transferred the movie house operation to his Arts and Crafts/Carmel Playhouse on Monte Verde near 9th and gave it yet another new name: "The Filmarte." Then he left Carmel, managed a theater (called the "Golden Bough") in San Francisco briefly, and assisted the renowned German stage director Max Reinhardt in Los Angeles for several years, teaching classes and directing plays in Reinhardt's Theatre Workshop. In 1940 Kuster returned to Carmel, refurbished the Filmarte, renamed it the Golden Bough Playhouse, and presented plays, foreign films, and American art films.

In 1949 someone tempted fate by suggesting to Kuster that he give "By Candlelight" another try. He remounted the play, and several hours after the curtain came down on opening night the entire Golden Bough Playhouse was consumed by fire. As Kuster remembered it a few months later, "...in the early hours of the morning I heard, as in a dream, heavy knocking at our door and the barking of our dogs. In a few moments my wife roused me to announce that once more the Golden Bough had been destroyed."

Undaunted, Kuster rebuilt on the same site and in 1952 opened a new structure housing both a large theater and a small studio theater. This complex was the underlying basis of the Golden Bough Playhouse operated on that site today by Pacific Repertory Theater. Edward Gerhard Kuster died in Carmel in 1961.

As the town of Carmel continued to mature, so did its relationship to the performing arts. By 1928, theater had ceased to be an important and formative activity of Carmel residents. Theater would always be popular in Carmel, but the town was growing and becoming more complex. There were more "...grocery stores and real estaters." The community no longer needed the sort of theater activities which the early residents had used to create the actual character of the village

Even as theater was diminishing in importance, an audience for live music was on the rise in Carmel. So it was that back in the fall of 1927, while they were just beginning to deal with the offstage drama surrounding their season at the Golden Bough, Dene and Hazel also were involved in the startup of an unrelated and more harmonious creation: The Carmel Music Society.

Carmel Music Society 1927–1928
Bringing Concerts to Carmel: background

Although Dene and Hazel were not the originators of musical life in Carmel, it was they who spearheaded the creation of the Carmel Music Society and its annual concert series. As Dene and Hazel managed the Society's growth and leveraged its popularity during its first decade, they used the power of music to bring people together just as the Little Theater Movement had been doing on the theatrical stage.

A previous chapter entitled "Music in Carmel 1923-1924" includes a description of several attempts by local groups to direct some of Carmel's artistic energy towards community-made music—both choral and orchestral. Meanwhile others in Carmel and Monterey had been attempting to produce or sponsor concerts by local and occasionally out of town soloists or small ensembles.

The "Monterey Peninsula Philharmonic Society" had presented several professional musicians in concerts annually since its founding in 1922. It was, strictly speaking, a Monterey-based organization, although some of the leading figures lived in Carmel, including musicians David Alberto and Thomas Vincent Cator.

In July 1926 the Philharmonic Society published a brief fundraising plea in the Pine Cone, over the signature of the Society's President, Mrs. Edward A. Kluegel.

> In order to carry on the work of this organization, which is presenting artists of note in this community at a much lower admission charge than is asked in San Francisco, a wide and general interest must be taken by residents of this peninsula. (Pine Cone, July 29, 1926)

That August, the Philharmonic Society presented the Persinger String Quartet at the Golden Bough. The Pine Cone ran a preview article a week before the concert under the headline "Summer Music Festival May Result From Quartet Concert." David Alberto is quoted as saying that the Persinger Quartet might be persuaded to make Carmel its summer home or base of operations, however, that decision would be "based on the reception they received at the concert."

The Persinger Quartet is a good example of the high level of artistry that Carmel music lovers wanted to hear. American violinist Louis Persinger had been concertmaster of the San Francisco Symphony from 1915 to 1925, and was the teacher of Yehudi Menuhin (beginning when Yehudi was 6) as well as Ruggiero Ricci and Isaac Stern. About 1918 he organized the Persinger Quartet with three other San Francisco Symphony players: Louis Ford, second violin; Nathan Firestone, viola; and Walter Ferner, cello. One of the best-known string quartets at that time in the West and beyond, they had been part of the November 1926 concert in Los Angeles organized by Henry Cowell in which Dene had premiered Schoenberg's Opus 123.

Perhaps the Persinger String Quartet wanted to take it easy in Carmel, but the fact is that on August 26 they gave a concert consisting mostly of arrangements of works written by Mozart, Albéniz, Tchaikovsky and Grieg. There were no famous string quartets by Beethoven or Bartok or Debussy. The audience and the press were underwhelmed, the reception lukewarm, and no further talk was heard about a festival.

The statements issued by the Monterey Peninsula Philharmonic Society prior to the Persinger concert demonstrate one of the MPPS's weaknesses: marketing. Throughout its few years of activity, its marketing strategy seemed to be: 1. Announce a future concert. 2. Then announce that something else might develop from it. 3. Then tell everyone that if they don't buy tickets, #2 won't happen. Their approach to ticket sales did not generate excitement. To the contrary, the Society acted as if it were sufficient merely to mention the name of a great artist, and surely all educated, cultured individuals would feel compelled to attend.

In fact, David Alberto, composer and principal organizer of the Philharmonic Society, viewed his musical activities in much the same way that Edward Kuster had viewed his theater projects: the offerings we put forth to you the public are so self-evidently wonderful that no one would dare to not support them!

The Peninsula Philharmonic Society continued its booking activities for several more years before disbanding. Meanwhile Dene and Hazel realized what was missing, and set out to do something new.

An enduring organization

The Denny-Watrous theater season at the Golden Bough opened in September 1927 with Uncle Tom's Cabin, followed in October by three performances Henrik Ibsen's Ghosts. One week after the Ibsen production, Dene and Hazel invited a group of about 20 music lovers to their studio/home on north Dolores Street to talk about the future of music in Carmel. Below are the first five paragraphs of the many neatly typed pages of minutes documenting the proceedings of this group over the coming months.

> Thursday, October 20, 1927, Misses Denny and Watrous invited to their studio a group of interested people for the purpose of discussing Carmel's chances for music in the future.
>
> Miss Denny opened the talk by a statement of the condition of the music market, that is to say, the guarantees that high-class musicians demand. By reason of its seating capacity—about 400—the Golden Bough is unable to venture such guarantees without the backing of the community. There was strong response from those present as to their need to have good music at any price, and many ideas were advanced as to the best mode of assuring themselves of such.
>
> The fact was considered that the Peninsula abounds in individuals of leisure and wealth who would probably give abundantly to such an enterprise. Miss Rosenkranz, the delegate from the [Carmel] Woman's Club even declared that businessmen should be assigned to their quota of the support, as good business.
>
> It was finally determined that an organization would be necessary—and if an organization, then a strong one should be formed, <u>one that would endure</u>.
>
> Many schemes were talked over and a motion finally made that we find ourselves a name. Abandoning proposed names of Peninsula Musical Association and Carmel Music Club, the name Carmel Music Society was settled upon as best describing our ideal. Mrs. Clinton was appointed chairman pro tem, and Miss Corrigan, secretary, and Mrs. Blackman proceeded to take these notes. (CMS minutes) [emphasis added]

An organization takes shape

At the second planning meeting, on October 26, the organization made a very important decision: it was voted unanimously by those present that there be no professional musicians on the Music Society's Board of Directors. In the minutes it is specifically regretted that this rule will result in "...leaving out Messrs. Cator and Alberto, and Dene Denny."

Following that vote, board members were chosen and officers were elected. The first President of the Music Society was Mrs. Belle Marsh Kluegel (Mrs. Edward A.), who just the previous year had been President of the Monterey Peninsula Philharmonic Society. Other founding board members are listed as: "Mmes. Dickinson, Morrow, O'Shea, Blackman, Woodward, Willard, Serano (of Monterey), Anne Martin, and Messrs. Seideneck, Herron, Dickinson, and Watson."

The decision to exclude professional musicians from the board was not about professionals in general, and it clearly had nothing to do with excluding Dene. It seems to have been about David Alberto and Thomas Vincent Cator, musicians who tended to view the community as something that needed to be improved, and who believed that they had the skills and deep understanding of the musical arts to do it. Mrs. Kluegel had worked with both men for several years as President of the Philharmonic Society, and she may have been glad to be free of their influence while the new organization was taking form. The Music Society Board—most likely with Dene's understanding—had engineered a unanimous vote to make sure that the creation and shaping of the Music Society could not be dominated by strong-willed Carmel musical professionals who might be motivated by their own egos or private agendas.

Although Cator and Alberto were out of the Music Society picture, Dene was not, and the vote did not change her relationship with the Society at all (and the two men certainly knew that). She had been one of the original instigators of the Society, and at the first meeting in October it was she who explained to the 20 people present how such a thing might be possible. Now the organization she had helped create had given her the task of finding and booking the performers for the concert series.

The newly formed board of directors meanwhile created the organization itself: the constitution and by-laws were written and approved, and the Music Society was incorporated as a non-profit. Committees were formed from the dozen or more members and officers of the board (Membership, Publicity, Booking, Finance). No single person would run the Society: the board was a governing body that would manage its operations, finances and growth, and maintain the group's focus on a common vision.

The following is a statement of purpose in the Music Society's five-year report, published in June 1932:

> The Carmel Music Society was founded in 1927 for the stated purpose of bringing to Monterey Peninsula music that is represented by the most significant programs and artists the world is offering today. A second and correlated objective was the cultivation of interest in music in its educational and cultural aspects.

In the ensuing meetings the discussions included expenses and seat prices, groupings, children's attendance, potential board members, and much talk of the relative commercial value of various performing artists, a topic that was "discussed under Miss Denny's guidance."

They wasted no time and met every week or ten days for two months. They clearly were thinking in the long term and wanted carefully to create an organization that would "endure."

In mid November, as soon as they had secured the Hart House String Quartet for the Opening Night concert in December, the Society sent out a simple promo and fund-raising flyer. It was to be an actual Society, with levels of membership.

> The Carmel Music Society is enlisting your interest and support in an organization to stimulate and further, in and around this Peninsula, the presentation of high–class music. It is the aim of the Society to bring outside attractions of a high order, such as the Hart House String Quartet of Toronto, which has already been booked for December 9. Three other attractions of recognized excellence will follow, names and dates of which will be announced later.
>
> In order to carry on this work, the Society must have the financial co-operation of all those who love music, therefore we are asking that you assist by becoming a member of the Society. The different annual memberships are as follows:
>
> Patrons—$100.00 which includes two season tickets.
>
> Guarantors—$25.00 which includes one season ticket.
>
> Active membership—$2.00, which carries with it the privilege of being actively associated with a group whose sole function is to sponsor and assist in the bringing of good music to the Peninsula. The active member does his best by securing other active members and by promoting attendance at the various musical events. Active members will receive notices of concerts, and may secure their seats before the box–office is open to the public. (Full text of a promotional mailing from the Carmel Music Society in mid November 1927)

This mailing was signed (by hand) by the Music Society's president, Mrs. Edward A. Kluegel. Just one year before, as president of the Monterey Peninsula Philharmonic Society, she had signed that group's terse fund-raising plea published in the Monterey Herald, but the Carmel Music Society's mailer was different. It began with the usual fund–raising and promo language: it asks for "interest and support," and offers "high–class music," "recognized excellence," etc. It then gives an opportunity for moneyed patrons to make a donation over and above the cost of one or two tickets. (In 1927, such donations were not tax deductible—they were an outright gift to the organization.)

The new element that Dene and Hazel brought to the situation is embodied in the ideas and language of the final paragraph of the mailing. Of course, for $2, the "Active Member" received notices of concerts and could buy tickets before they went on sale to the public. Those perks are common today, and were not revolutionary. But the concepts in the rest of the paragraph are significant.

> "Active" membership "privilege" "actively" "associated" "group" "function" "sponsor and assist" "Peninsula."

It's not just Carmel, and the recipients are not merely potential audience members; they are being offered the opportunity, privilege and pleasure of belonging to a group of individuals who contribute toward a common goal of benefit to the entire Peninsula and beyond. In the mailer's three paragraphs, the word "active" appears five times. In other words, members of the

Carmel Music Society are involved. A sense of being part of something builds excitement, and excitement is contagious. As more Active Members joined at $2/year, the overall support and subscriber base grew, bringing the organization a stability that would enable it to survive the Great Depression.

The board of directors had a booking committee, and the minutes of its meetings describe several enthusiastic discussions of possible eminent artists. (The minutes mention that at one moment "a hush fell on the proceedings when the name Schumann-Heink became audible.") Nonetheless, that fall and for years to come it was Dene who led the booking process and proposed (for board approval) the artists to be presented each season. Dene contacted the agents, impresarios, and artists' managers by phone and by letter to determine 1.) Which artists might be on tour during the coming season; 2.) Which of them might already have engagements booked on the West Coast; 3.) What sort of fee they might ask for.

By all reports Dene Denny and Hazel Watrous were formidable people, women of imagination, intelligence and strong will. Producing in-house performances and events at the Fisk House in San Francisco had been a sort of dress rehearsal for what was to come now.

By the 1920s concerts were beginning to be financed in a new way. Through the first decade of the twentieth century, it was common for concert series, ensembles, and even orchestras to be financed or underwritten directly by a few extremely wealthy backers. But, with the changing economy, wealthy patrons were becoming less generous, and organizations like the Carmel Music Society were developing subscriber bases in order to raise money in smaller amounts from more people. But how could such a small organization (with a small concert hall) manage to engage world-class musicians and pay their high fees?

Carmel was not the only community asking that question, and during the 1920s, to supply the increasing demand for "culture" in communities all across the US, independent concert managers and artist representatives banded together into several cooperatives. Many of

Sol Hurok. Late 1920s press photo by Mishkin. *Courtesy of the author.*

these were absorbed into Arthur Judson's Columbia Concerts Corporation (later known as Columbia Artists Management), and by the end of the 1920s, Judson controlled two-thirds of all concert bookings in the United States. In addition to Judson, Dene also dealt with NBC, which had formed an agency like Judson's only smaller, and with independent agents, particularly the young Sol Hurok.

Later, in the 1930s, Judson's innovative "Community Concerts Service" packaged US concert tours of name performers and offered the packages to local concert societies who could not afford to book such major artists on their own. In the 1930s, Salinas and Monterey each had a Community Concert Association which booked and presented two to four concerts each season. The annual membership drive determined that season's budget, after which a committee member contacted Judson's agency to see whom they could afford. Only those who had joined the Association during the membership drive could actually attend the concerts: as an encouragement to annual membership, no single tickets were sold once membership was closed.

But Community Concerts Association did not yet exist when the Carmel Music Society was founded, and the Society was never affiliated with Community Concerts. One big difference is that Carmel Music Society concert attendance was not limited to annual subscribers only: single tickets were available to the general public (subscribers got a discount). The booking process, however, was much the same. The Music Society determined how much it thought it could spend. Dene determined which artists might be available and for how much. The booking committee made its choices, the board of directors voted, and the performers were booked. Because the performers' tour schedules were being coordinated by a central office in New York, an artist might—for example—appear in Carmel on the day before or after a concert in San Francisco, or on the way from San Francisco to Los Angeles. This made a reduced fee possible, a necessity for Carmel with its relatively small 400-seat theater.

The New York agencies enabled the Carmel Music Society in its earliest seasons to engage major international stars such as Mischa Elman, Jascha Heifetz, Gregor Piatigorsky, Joseph Szigeti, Vladimir Horowitz, the London String Quartet, and the Vienna Boys Choir. (For a roster of artists who have been presented by the Carmel Music Society since 1927, please see the Appendix.)

Meanwhile, Dene and Hazel continued to manage their ongoing theater season at the Golden Bough while also presenting concerts there by avant garde musicians such as Henry Cowell, Richard Buhlig, Imre Weisshaus, Anton Rovinsky and Luisa Espinel. In the 1927–1928 season, including the Music Society's concerts, Dene and Hazel produced at least 13 concerts at the Golden Bough and an equal number of events at their own Studio.

The Carmel Music Society's first artists

To open the debut season, the Carmel Music Society chose the Hart House String Quartet from Canada. The quartet had given its first concert in Toronto in 1924 with such success that the Massey Foundation offered to support the players by guaranteeing their salaries.

Because of this financial support, the individual players did not have to supplement their income with teaching or other performing. This underwriting not only enabled them to spend more time rehearsing and playing as a quartet, it also allowed them to accept more modest fees for concerts in places such as Carmel. After a period of further rehearsal, the Massey Foundation launched them on a coast-to-coast tour of Canada.

Their popularity soared, and for fifty years the Hart House Quartet was one of Canada's best-known chamber ensembles, although the four original players were three Europeans and one American: Geza de Kresz and Harry Adaskin, violinists, Milton Blackstone, violist, Boris Hambourg, cellist.

Several years after their first tour from Halifax, Nova Scotia, to Vancouver, British Columbia, violist Blackstone recalled the audiences:

> The Maritime towns seemed a little dazed by our music making; a little bewildered by it. We were not at all dismayed. We knew that a few more concerts would make many converts — as they have. The East — well, the East felt itself a little blasé. [i.e. Montreal, Ottawa, and Toronto] It was the home of Canada's culture and it knew all about string quartets — even if many of its residents had never heard one.

But the West! Here was a Canada which hungered for the pure tone of the string quartet. The Canada of British and European immigrants, people who knew what chamber music was and had longed for it. Time and again, when we came on the platform with our instruments, the applause was deafening. (Maclean's Magazine, March 1, 1931)

The passage above refers to audiences in western Canada, but the characterization also applies perfectly to the cities along the Pacific Coast from Seattle to Los Angeles. In the 1920s and 1930s there was a healthy demand for chamber music concerts.

The Hart House Quartet made its American debut in the fall of 1925 in New York's Aeolian Hall (a popular venue where Gershwin's "Rhapsody in Blue" premiered the year before). The repertoire was attention-getting: they began with one of Béla Bartók's string quartets, then the Debussy String Quartet, and finally Beethoven's String Quartet Opus 135 in F major.

Their next tour was to Europe, where the leading French musical journal, Monde Musicale, said: "They have immediately established themselves as one of the best quartets in the world." Their second tour of the United States brought the Hart House Quartet to Carmel on December 9, 1927, for the inaugural concert of the Carmel Music Society at the Theatre of the Golden Bough.

The Carmel Music Society's first concert

Less than a week before the Opening Night of their first season, the Carmel Music Society Board of Directors held its seventh meeting. (Dene was not on the Board of Directors, but the minutes indicate that she was in attendance at every meeting.) The treasurer reported that advance ticket sales were strong and that $1,146 had been taken in already. Future bookings were discussed, and Dene was authorized to engage pianist Walter Gieseking for the Society's second concert, on Monday, February 6.

The Carmel Pine Cone declared in advance of the Hart House Quartet concert,

> The opening concert of the Carmel Music Society promises to be a wonderful success. With such a list of patrons, guarantors and contributors, most of whom are season-ticket subscribers, and with such a splendid attraction, the evening cannot fail to be a beginning of something very big and very significant in Carmel. (Pine Cone, December 2, 1927)

To add to the excitement of the evening, parked outside the Theatre was chauffeur-driven car with California license number 1, the limousine of California Governor Clement C. Young.

To state that the Hart House concert was a success would be a ridiculous understatement. In researching this book, one of the author's great pleasures has been reading and transcribing the flowery prose of the Carmel journalists in the 1920s and 1930s. Composer Thomas Vincent Cator's concert review in the Pine Cone is a wonderful example:

Concert Presages Bright Future For Music In Carmel

> A wonderful audience, made up of the finest of Carmel's dwellers, came to the Theatre of the Golden Bough last Friday evening, to listen to the Hart House Quartet. Came to open the doors and windows of their souls, so that the choir invisible might for a few brief moments sing to them of things which their higher consciousness many times senses, but which they have seldom an opportunity to contact so intimately and so perfectly.

Yes, it was truly a feast for the Olympians which the Hart House gave us — Schubert's "Quartet in A Minor"; Wolf's "Italian Serenade," and Sir Edward Elgar's "Quartet in D minor."

The audience was without question held captive in the web of magic melody and harmony which of these artists wove about them, and, at the end, I believe everyone wanted to follow the players, as did the children the Pied Piper of Hamlin. This first concert of the newly formed Carmel Music Society was an auspicious beginning, and seems to presage much good for the future.

Gov. Young was there. The majority of Carmel's most important artists and artisans were present. Dene Denny gave us a brief but most appropriate foreword, in which she mentioned many good things to look forward to in the future. So there is every reason to feel elated and gratified and hopeful. (Pine Cone, December 16, 1927)

The more matter-of-fact writer for the Monterey Peninsula Daily Herald complimented the players but wrote mostly about the works being performed. Here are the first and last paragraphs from that review.

Peninsula Daily Herald

By John Terry

After the pelting hailstones of the Imre Weisshaus* concert, the Hart House String Quartet came to Carmel last night like a soft caressing rain. It was music that was a gentle benediction — exactly the sort of blessing that Carmel hoped for and gratefully received....

[...] But with reference to last night's success one group must be warmly complemented: namely, the Carmel Music Society. Their unflagging zeal during the past few weeks came to splendid fruition in the Hart House program. The Theatre of the Golden Bough was packed by an audience which will miss none of the future offerings of the Society. (Monterey Peninsula Daily Herald, December 15, 1927)

[* On November 20, just three weeks before the Hart House Quartet concert, Dene and Hazel presented French avant garde composer/pianist Imre Weisshaus at the Golden Bough. His odd—and loud—program included Vivaldi, Bartok, Kodaly, Pal Kadosa, and finally four pieces written by Weisshaus himself.

The second concert of the season was the great German pianist Walter Gieseking. 357 of the Golden Bough's 400 seats were filled. After Gieseking, the Society's season continued with the American contralto Kathryn Meisle in March, baritone Reinald Werrenrath in April, and American cellist Horace Britt in an extra, non-subscription concert in May.

Britt wanted to come to Carmel, and had offered to play a concert for the Society in return for a percentage of the ticket revenue, rather than a fixed fee. Britt's proposal was a very good bargain for the Music Society, and it also established the practice of presenting extra concerts following the regular subscription season. The development of these concerts over the next few years is at the core of this narrative.

On the verge of success

Back in the late winter, when cellist Horace Britt offered to come to Carmel in the spring for a lower fee (a 30/70 split of the ticket sales), the members of the board began to realize that one of their initial hopes had been confirmed: the Monterey Peninsula itself was a "draw" for performers who wanted to spend a bit of time, however short, in such a beautiful place.

> As Miss Denny reports, in her interviews with the booking offices there is a great sense of encouragement to our hope of one day being a true music center. The beauty of Point Lobos, the distinction of the Golden Bough, the quality of our audiences, impress the musical virtuosi to our great advantage. (CMS minutes, April 1928)

That is not to say that the early seasons were a financial success—fixed costs were significant, and had to be paid no matter how many tickets were actually sold. The fees of first-rate artists at that time averaged $400–$600. The Theatre of the Golden Bough rented for $75 per weeknight, or $100 on weekends (this included lights in the lobby and auditorium, heat, and janitor), plus $13 for a stage lighting operator, and if the concert featured piano, a mover and tuner would be necessary (the Golden Bough had no piano). And there were publicity fliers, posters, paid ads in the Carmel and Monterey newspapers, postage and printing, et al.

The Hart House Quartet in a 1928 press photo. *Courtesy of the author.*

For the first several seasons, until a solid subscriber and membership base could be developed, many of the Carmel Music Society's concerts resulted in a net loss. When necessary, as they did in their season at the Golden Bough as well as in the early seasons of the Carmel Bach Festival, Dene and Hazel made up the deficit out of their own pockets.

The season ends with modern music

The Denny-Watrous management continued to present events of its own, and in May Dene and Hazel produced an unusual month-long visit from their friend Dane Rudhyar, one of the "ultra-modernist" composers whose music Dene loved to play. At the November 1926 concert in Los Angeles at which Dene premiered Schoenberg, Rudhyar premiered several of his own compositions.

Rudhyar based much of his music on subtle metaphysical and non-musical concepts like color and vibrational energies. He is probably best known today not for his music but as the author of many classic books on astrology.

> Dane Rudhyar, composer-pianist, author, philosopher, returns to Carmel next week in response to the demand created by his recent brilliant lecture recital here. So strong a response to music as strikingly modern as Rudhyar's is due to at least two factors. One is of course the vitality and the high quality of the composer's work, together with the

unusual capacity of the artist to make his highly developed ideas clear to his audience.

But the important second factor of audience receptivity is most certainly due to the musical training which Carmel, by way of modern compositions and artists heard, has perhaps unconsciously received this year. Musical intelligence has been nourished in Carmel this year as never before, through programs of the Music Society, and the constant alertness on the part of the Misses Denny and Watrous to bring to us as much of the very best as they have dared. (Pine Cone, May 2, 1928)

Throughout the month, Rudhyar presented a series of lecture-recitals in five different Carmel homes, including the Denny-Watrous Studio. His five presentations were titled: *Living Tones versus Abstract Notes; The Dualism of Musical Substance; Tonality and the Principle of Musical Unity; Musical Evolution from 600 B. C. To 1900 A. D.;* and *The Trend of Contemporary Music in Europe and America.* Tickets for the series were $5.

Dene and the Carmel Music Society

The annual meeting of the Carmel Music Society's board and membership was held on May 23, 1928, and congratulations were extended all round. This meeting took place in what must have been a dreadful week or two for Dene and Hazel: while they had been engaged in the creation of the Music Society, they had also been struggling through their year of theater. Everybody knew that the Abalone League was planning to sink the opening weekend of the Golden Bough's summer season, and this deliberate scheduling sabotage had been reported and commented upon in the local press. There were still people in town who were not speaking to each other anymore because of the feud. Dene and Hazel may have already begun composing the May 28 letter (discussed previously) to Edward Kuster, wherein they gave notice that they would not renew their lease.

And yet, somehow, throughout this year of theatrical discontent, Dene and Hazel had also overseen the creation of one of Carmel's most distinguished musical organizations. The orderly, pleasant and productive startup of the Carmel Music Society had begun in late October 1927, and its first season had been an artistic success.

Irene Alexander, arts writer for the Monterey County Herald, wrote in 1952,

> ...the long-ago impulse to form the Carmel Music Society cannot be attributed to one single moment, nor to the inspired idea of any single individual.... The determination had already been fed by numerous well-springs.

This is true as far as it goes, but the whole truth is more pointed: in 1927 the "well-springs" of musical determination in Carmel were guided and focused by gifted leaders. It was Dene and Hazel who had convened the first gathering in October 1927, and it is clear that Dene was a prime mover—behind the scenes—throughout the first season.

Fritz Wurtzman, one of the early members of the Carmel Music Society Board, recalled in an interview decades later, "Dene Denny was the spark plug of the group in those first years."

In his memoirs, French composer Imre Weisshaus (under his stage name Paul Arma) describes Dene in 1927:

Elle est l'organisatrice de la vie musicale de Carmel et de sa région, avec un élan exceptionnel et un désintéressement sans faille.

"She is the organizer of the musical life in Carmel and its region, with exceptional energy and an utter selflessness."

At its founding the Society set out to create an organization "...that would endure" and ultimately outlive those who created it. Arma mentions Dene's "energy" and "selflessness," and these qualities led Dene to make choices that enabled the Carmel Music Society to manage the hot artistic temperaments of Carmel and also to survive the coming stock market crash and Great Depression.

July—December 1928

Dene's friend Henry Cowell returned to Carmel for a concert at the Theatre of the Golden Bough on July 18. Cowell and the piano were positioned on the forestage in front of the closed curtain, and dramatic lighting effects were used. Pauline Schindler's review in the weekly Carmelite is indicative of the community's willingness to tackle this difficult new music.

> ### Henry Cowell and the New Music of the Piano
> Slowly the lights of the Golden bough dimmed, the stage darkened, and Henry Cowell at the piano became a blue shadow against the curtain. He opened his program with "The Snows of Fujiyama," a composition whose cool and slender theme sparkles with an icy beauty. The tone clusters with which it glitters are of course Cowell's contribution to the music of his time.
>
> Henry Cowell plays with tones as the sculptor plays with clay, and lets the miracle of invention happen. Works like "The Banshee," whose music is particularly eerie, was performed by Cowell in an atmosphere of total darkness, a brilliantly creative tone-adventure.
>
> We venture to guess that if at the end of the program somebody had suddenly played a Waltz by Chopin, the audience would have burst into roars of laughter. From his audience, Henry Cowell evoked something of an inspired listening. Audience and composer entered the adventure together, and came out of it warm friends. (Carmelite, July 20, 1928)

One week after the Cowell concert, Aaron Copeland premiered his new piano concerto at the Hollywood Bowl in Los Angeles. His friend Henry Cowell was in the audience, and the two men stopped in Carmel on their way from LA to San Francisco. Late on a Sunday evening in July at the Denny-Watrous Studio, Copeland played his new concerto, with Cowell at the second piano playing the orchestra accompaniment, for "a puzzled audience."

Dene at the helm

By September 1928, the ill-fated Denny-Watrous season at the Golden Bough finally had ended. The Carmel Music Society was preparing for its second season, and the rancor that surrounded the Theatre throughout the summer months became a cause of concern: if the Golden Bough were to shut its doors to live events, where else in Carmel could the Music Society hold its concerts?

Suddenly the young organization was in need of a skilled leader. In the minutes of the September 12, 1928, board of directors meeting, it is noted that:

> ...Miss Denny was elected our president for the coming year, we deeming our instigator, booker and prime counsellor of the past year the proper one to see us safely through this second season.

Dene was also elected chair of the Booking Committee. David Alberto—one of the "professional musicians" excluded at the Society's founding—joined the board at this meeting, and was made the chair of the Publicity Committee. Perhaps he was still not a good fit for the Society; after his resignation in November the Society made Dene the chair of the Publicity Committee as well.

Because of artist availability, no Music Society concerts could be booked for the fall months, and the Music Society's second season was opened on February 12, 1929, by the distinguished London String Quartet.

Back to the Piano

In late September, free of their ties to the theater world after more than a year, Dene and Hazel left Carmel and motored to Yosemite National Park, where they spent a few days in the high Tuolumne Meadows area in the north of the Park. "There," wrote the weekly Carmelite on October 3, "from ten thousand-foot heights, they looked down upon earth, and having rested well, found it fair."

Soon after they returned home, the Carmelite learned that Dene was practicing some new piano repertoire.

> ### Return Of An Artist
> Dene Denny is again at her Steinway. This is good to hear, for a year of executive activity with the Theatre of the Golden Bough had very nearly silenced her instrument. Now, freed from the anguishes and anxieties of the artist struggling at the box office end of art, she becomes once again one of the few distinguished modernists of the piano on the Pacific coast. She is to open the Fortnightlies, the most modern of the season's concert series, in San Francisco next month. (Carmelite, October 10, 1928)

The Pine Cone praised Dene two days later.

> The Carmel Music Society, with Dene Denny presiding, is making plans for the coming concert season. An organization whose purpose it is to bring great artists to the community is privileged above the average in having for its president a well-known concert artist.
>
> Without quoting her directly, it is possible to indicate Miss Denny's attitude, which is one of breadth and scope. The field of art to which she is a contributor, the community of which she is a member, and the society of which she is the newly elected president, cannot but be enriched by the presence of an artist who is able to see and execute in broad terms.
>
> Miss Denny believes in modern expression—it is of today. It is here, and must be done. It may not—cannot remain as it is, but from it will emerge something supremely beautiful and fine. It is futile to compare the art of yesterday and that of today. The music given us by the masters is complete and can only be imitated. (Pine Cone, October 12, 1928)

Dene: San Francisco, November

Ida Gregory's Fortnightly Series had been presenting programs of modern music in San Francisco since 1923, and it was one of the city's trendiest concert series. Gregory, a San Francisco impresario, presented Dene in a solo recital on November 11, 1928, in the ballroom of the St. Francis Hotel. Although Dene played a few works from her 1927 Carmel recital, she was performing most of the repertoire in this program for the first time. (Details of Dene's piano repertoire may be found in the Appendix.)

In order to help promote Dene's performance of this same program one week later at the Golden Bough in Carmel, Ida Gregory herself wrote a "review" for the Pine Cone from which these paragraphs are taken. She begins by recalling the early seasons of the Fortnightly Series:

> How well I remember the reception that was given our earliest concerts. The attention they received was grudgingly given in the general atmosphere so bristling with antagonism that I was most uncomfortable for the artist.

> What a difference this morning! Miss Denny was enthusiastically recalled again and again [by applause at the end of the concert], and finally repeated the Prelude by Imre Weisshaus. As the patrons left they crowded around her to express their appreciation and ask questions about the music.

> It was one of the most successful programs we have ever given. My belief is that Dene Denny has a definite message in her interpretations of the music of our day and that every time she plays such a program she is leading those who wish to follow into a clearer understanding of the spiritual expression of our complex life today. (Pine Cone, November 16, 1928)

Dene: Carmel, November

When she performed her San Francisco program in Carmel on November 18, Dene made an even greater impression on her audience there than she had the year before. In advance of the concert the Carmelite wrote in great anticipation:

> ***Dene Denny Opens Concert Season In Carmel - Daringly modern program***
> In the last three years we have, even in remote Carmel, had opportunity to hear the music of our contemporaries. What was unintelligible to us then begins to have meaning now. We begin to understand the voices of our own times. We shall listen to this concert, not as we would listen to a recital in the familiar terms of Chopin, or even of the subtler Brahms. We shall need to seek—through the overtones and interpreting the elisions, accepting the fertility of dissonance, and with unprejudiced ears—the music of our own times, the utterance of our own selves.

> It is certainly worth suggesting, that children who are musical be brought to this recital... If the radio has not already debauched their ears they may be able to penetrate it much farther than we, the benighted grown-ups. (Carmelite, November 14, 1928)

The Pine Cone reviewed the actual event:

> Her gown was coal black nearly to the shoulders, where it abruptly broke into an equally frigid white. Severely plain and cut, it was without one frivolous tuck, frill or ornament.

Her hair shorter than a bob, was plastered to her head. This cool, intellectual presence for a moment made me feel that I've strayed into a Greek temple, and was about to pay obeisance-not to Venus-but to Minerva.

A few chords, a dozen measures, and my anxiety was surprisingly agreeably dispelled. Miss Denny may be expressing modern intellectuals, but she is expressing them emotionally. Her playing gave her away. There was a heart in her performance, heart that pulsated in the good old-fashioned way hearts have been in the habit of pulsating since Adam first saw Eve. Consequently her audience was charmed.

The ultra-modern whose work sees the light through Miss Denny's revealing fingers is lucky. Possessing all the qualities we take for granted in the public artist—such things as clean pedaling, technique, shading—Miss Denny goes farther. A personal quality, musical and poetic, into which mere technique never intrudes, arises from her playing. Her flexible touch is never hard, never blatantly harsh. No matter how modern the program became—and it had some pretty awfully modern moments—Miss Denny never failed to put a heartbeat into it. When played with feeling, the new intervals in modern music give a dreamy, wistful, atmospheric quality entirely out of keeping with modern business life. May we hear Miss Denny again and often, is the sincere wish of this reviewer. (Pine Cone, November 23, 1928)

The Carmelite acknowledges how far Dene has brought her listeners:

Few pianists are equipped to present as daringly modern a program as that which Dene Denny played at the Theatre of the Golden Bough on Sunday afternoon. And few audiences are prepared to hear such a program understandingly.

Dene Denny was fortunate in her audience, many of whom had gone through the preliminary stages of resistance to modern music. Last year's concerts here, the intense reactions and the discussion which they stimulated, did much to prepare this group for sympathetic listening. Miss Denny must've been happily aware throughout the afternoon of that intelligent and responsive undercurrent which gives a recital its glow, its warmth.

As an interpreter of music Dene Denny is like a window of crystal through which the composition somehow passes undimmed and undistorted. She is remarkably impersonal, projects herself restrainedly, studies the intention of the composer with an intense fidelity. (Carmelite, November 21, 1928)

Apparently Dene was a popular performer because of her personality, stage presence, integrity, musicianship and technique, but not primarily because of the music she actually played. In fact it is clear that many people came to her concerts to hear her play as opposed to hearing the music itself. It is an amazing achievement to be a popular performer in spite of your repertoire.

She plays well; her heart is in her work and she has such a vital earnestness that, whether you like her music or not, you are held to attention and sometimes won to admiration by the spirit of the performer. (Redfern Mason in the San Francisco Chronicle, December 1928, exact date unknown. Quoted in the Pine Cone, December 21, 1928)

New music and the San Francisco audiences

Of the ultra modern composers in America, it was Henry Cowell who had become San Francisco's own local celebrity: when he returned after one of his European trips, the San Francisco Call headline proclaimed: "Cowell Back, World Famed Composer." The article mentioned Cowell's international acclaim, and emphasized that his musical education had been "exclusively American." This theme of the All-American Artist became more important

Cowell publicity image, late 1920s. *Courtesy of the author.*

throughout the American music scene in the coming decade, and was in contrast to the fawning reception often given to European-trained musicians in the US in the first two decades of the 20th Century.

During the late 1920s in Carmel and the San Francisco Bay Area, Dene often served as pianist in Cowell's lecture/concerts. Cowell was a prolific and eloquent lecturer, and during his lectures on musical genres, eras, and styles, he played examples on the piano to illustrate his points. He was a highly accomplished pianist but in these lectures he wanted to focus on speaking, and so Dene accompanied him, performing examples of the music he discussed. His intention in the lectures was to stimulate, educate, and challenge his listeners, and to prepare them for actual concerts of Ultra-Modern music.

Henry Cowell's New Music Society ensemble presented 27 concerts in San Francisco between 1927 and 1936 in venues ranging from private homes and studios to auditoriums and concert halls. The entire atmosphere around these concerts was intense and adventurous and the venues were always jammed.

One such concert took place on December 3, 1928, at the California School of Fine Arts (located at 800 Chestnut and today known as the S.F. Art Institute). Cowell performed an entire concert of his own music, including works for solo piano and a new sonata for violin and piano. Several of Cowell's latest songs were premiered by mezzo-soprano Virginia Adams, the wife of photographer Ansel Adams. To help publicize the concert, Ansel wrote an advance item in the San Francisco Call, and had this to day about Cowell:

> Henry Cowell stands in the front rank of ultramodern composers. His music, while individual and idiom and inspiration, is based on most solid and correct harmonic grounds, and has been developed with a thorough knowledge of the physics of sound.
>
> Already among the foremost of the New Music, Mr. Cowell will enjoy a future of inevitable brilliance. This concert will mark an important epoch in his career. (San Francisco Call, November 29, 1928)

In her book, *Henry Cowell's New Music*, Rita Meade quotes critic Molly Merrick's description of the audience of a Cowell concert in San Francisco in 1928:

> ". . .a serious-minded audience with healthy curiosity. . . largely gray-haired individuals and youths. . .generous sprinkling of university people. . .faculty members of the University of California . . . one San Francisco composer-pianist and critics from all but one of the San Francisco daily papers."

The public loved the colorful individuals who wrote this music, their stimulating ideas and challenging theories, their new and innovative views of music, and their quirky personalities onstage and off. However, none of this personal excitement made the Ultra Modern music any easier to listen to. Fortunately, Cowell had allies in San Francisco. As Rita Meade writes,

> Celebrities, even those as radical as Cowell, were tolerated, indeed lionized, by San Francisco audiences, but new music was not. There were two groups, however, willing to support new ideas: some of the critics and the academic community. The critics suggested that the city was ripe for a change. (ibid.)

The San Francisco press led the charge: out with the old and in with the new. The academics, as always, loved a brainy twist to the arts, and this new music, with its emphasis on dissonance and complex structural concepts, was a refreshing change from what some saw as the prevailing sentimental attachment to "outmoded" musical aesthetics and the messy emotional world of 19th century music.

At the Denny-Watrous Studio

After their return from Yosemite in early October 1928, Dene and Hazel formally and legally established themselves as impresarios doing business as "Denny-Watrous Management." Over the next several decades as Denny-Watrous they presented concerts and events of all kinds in Carmel and in San José, and managed the Carmel Bach Festival from its inception in 1935 until the mid 1950s.

Two eminent Viennese architects had established a Los Angeles studio together: Richard Neutra and R. M. Schindler. Both men also had a presence in Carmel through their presentations at the Denny-Watrous Studio and later at the Denny-Watrous Gallery. On November 30, Neutra gave a lecture at the Studio on "The New Architecture."

Neutra's wife, Dione Neutra, also gave a program of her own at the Denny-Watrous Studio, singing folk songs of her native Switzerland while accompanying herself on the cello.

As 1928 came to a close, the Carmel Pine Cone reported on a holiday party at which Dene entertained:

> Mr. and Mrs. George Blackman of Carmel entertained a group of friends at tea on Saturday afternoon at their home on Carmelo Street. One of the delightful surprises of the afternoon was the playing by Dene Denny of several numbers from her recent recital here. (Pine Cone, January 4, 1929)

After a brief holiday, 1929 began with a recital by Dene in Berkeley, and the opening concert of the second season of the Carmel Music Society.

January–August 1929

Berkeley

After the holidays, Dene was back to work at the piano. On Sunday afternoon, January 27, 1929, in the Berkeley Piano Club once again, Dene performed the program from her November Carmel concert for her most sophisticated and discerning audience: the musical community in Berkeley. The Berkeley Daily Gazette was ecstatic:

San Francisco musicians joined a large audience of Berkeleyans Sunday afternoon to hear Dene Denny pianist at the Piano Club House, her program being a challenge to efficiency of technique combined with an almost uncanny insight into the meaning of composers. The latter were modern to the last moment of our present calendar and were explained by Ms. Denny as being entitled to stand alone as exemplars of musicianship.

<u>"The classics will never die," Miss Denny says, "but these men are entitled to the same respect as were Beethoven, Mozart, or Bach in their day."</u>

Miss Denny is marvelous technically, studiously and earnestly and is the only one of musicians hereabouts who has courage and ability to give us a 100% program of modern composition. (Berkeley Daily Gazette, January 29, 1929) [emphasis added]

Spring in Carmel

The performing arts situation in Carmel had changed greatly in only 12 months. The glut of productions on the town's three stages in 1928, and the rancor and ill-feelings that arose, had cast a pall over the theatrical activities in the town altogether. In place of theater, music was now assuming a greater importance. Dene and Hazel continued to do their best to liven things up.

"I am positive the piano should not be treated that way."

In early February, Denny-Watrous Management presented pianist and composer Imre Weisshaus once again at their Studio. (The recital referred to in the opening line took place on November 20, 1927, three weeks before the first concert of the Carmel Music Society.)

> A year and a half ago, there occurred in Carmel a piano recital which many of us have not forgotten. Imre Weisshaus, a young composer from Budapest, played in the Theatre of the Golden Bough to an audience which found itself reacting strongly. The next morning there were several who confessed to the same thing... They had been so much excited by the music that they had gone home to write about it—some were sleepless with excitement. The name Weisshaus stands with those of the vital younger composers and pianists who are most respected, from whom most is hoped, among the moderns. During his visit to Carmel, Weisshaus established friendships and loyalties, notably with Dene Denny and Hazel Watrous. And it is under their auspices that he plays, on Sunday evening next, at their Studio. The recital is public, with an admission charge of one dollar. (Carmelite, February 13, 1929)

Hal Garrott, who regularly wrote concert reviews for the Pine Cone, was not so enthusiastic about Weisshaus. He attempted, gently and with humor, to tell it as he saw it:

> No doubt Dene Denny is to be congratulated for presenting in the Denny-Watrous Studio, as in a laboratory, such ultramoderns as the pianist-composer Imre Weisshaus. Ultras, no matter what their line, deserve a hearing — from those who can listen to them.

> Who knows what music will be 10 years hence? Wagner was once hooted out of Paris. Yet, Wagner survived to touch the heart of the world... Likewise the ultras we are hooting today may write the music of tomorrow. How are we to know? Let us be patient and endure. Someday the light will be given us.

Meanwhile the sooner we learn to be honest with ourselves and others, the sooner the sheep will be separated from the goats—the sooner we shall know what the new music is to be. And as honesty begins at home, let me confess at once that the Weisshaus recital gave me no pleasure.

There were brilliant dreamy sprightly moments. There was stirring character to the opening Toccata. The pianist had his enjoyable spots, but they remain spots. What preceded and followed had put me in such a state, if Apollo himself had played a phrase, I would have hated it. Imre Weisshaus possesses technique, skill, and the usual tricks of the pianist's trade. Unfortunately, in all his fortissimo playing he permits himself to pound as one might hit with a meat ax. Even to express the most discordant of ultras, I am positive the piano should not be treated that way. It is not that kind of an instrument. Let the pianist take it out on the bass drum or stonewall but not the piano! (Pine Cone, February 15, 1929)

Just a few days later, the Carmel Music Society began its second season on a more mellow note, with a February 12 performance of the London String Quartet at the Golden Bough. At this point Dene had been president of the board for about six months, and was also Chair of the Booking, Publicity, and Ticket Committees.

The Oratorio

A few weeks after the London String Quartet concert, Fenton Foster announced that he would form an orchestra and chorus for a performance of Sir John Stainer's oratorio "The Crucifixion" on Good Friday in the Pacific Grove Methodist Episcopal Church and again the following evening in Carmel. Singers for the chorus were mostly from Pacific Grove but a few came from Carmel. The orchestra had only 16 members. This was the third conductor and third ensemble to perform this work on the Monterey Peninsula in a space of five years.

As was sometimes the case with community-based events in Carmel at that time, the actual performance did not take place on the advertised date. There was one performance, not two, on Thursday, March 28, the day before Good Friday. The Pine Cone review never actually mentions the location.

> Under the capable leadership of Fenton Foster, a peninsula chorus and orchestra presented Stainer's Crucifixion last Thursday night. The performance of singers and players was nicely synchronized, full toned and musically discriminating. Conductor Foster seemed the coolest person present, whether in the audience or on the stage, and impressed one as being sure of himself and of his hundred or more musicians. ...
>
> Now that we have a leader of Mr. Foster's fine personal and musical qualities, let our singers work up a chorus that will carry the fame of the Peninsula over the state and country. Such an achievement is possible. It has been done before by such towns as Bethlehem Pennsylvania, Dayton Ohio, and St. Olaf College in Minnesota. (Pine Cone, April 5, 1929)

The reviewer gave the singers and the orchestra encouragement and gentle praise:

The tone [of the chorus] was full, never weak, and never too loud. With sufficient practice working in the direction of virtuosity, this body might become outstanding. The orchestra surprised me. These instrumentalists should feel encouraged to meet frequently and practice diligently. The results would be well worthwhile. [ibid.]

For their second concert of their season, Carmel Music Society presented renowned pianist Alexander Brailowsky in March, replacing pianist Leo Ornstein, who had fractured his arm in an automobile accident. Ornstein was very near the end of his piano career, and this would have been his only public performance in Carmel. Brailowsky was an extremely lucky last-minute save, and it is impressive that Dene could get him on such short notice. He played an enormous program of Bach-Busoni, Scarlatti, Beethoven (the Appassionata Sonata), 8 pieces by Chopin, and works by Scriabine, Stravinsky, and Liszt.

In April the Music Society presented the Kedroff Quartet, a Russian vocal ensemble popular at the time, and in May violinist Albert Spalding performed. The Society produced two additional concerts after the subscription series: avant garde pianist Richard Buhlig and San Francisco tenor Fred Leedom Scott.

Dene Denny's next performance that spring was on April 10, when the Carmelite reports her taking the early morning train for a "dash up to San Francisco, where she played modern piano music at the Fairmont Hotel at the luncheon of University of California sorority alumnae." No further details are provided.

The Kedroff Quartet. Press photo late 1920s.
Courtesy of the author.

Dene and Hazel traveled together to Los Angeles in May, and Dene gave a recital in the studio of the eminent British-born pianist Winifred Hooke. The LA Times noted, "The studio was crowded and every one of note in the Los Angeles musical world was present." (The report gives no repertoire details.) Many members of the Pasadena Community Players were in the audience to show their support for the two women who had presented them in February 1928 at the Theatre of the Golden Bough. Although the 1927–1928 theater year had been an ordeal for Dene and Hazel, the Pasadena company's production of "Cake" had been an artistic pleasure for all involved.

Upon returning to Carmel, Dene and Hazel hosted a meeting of the Women's International League for Peace and Freedom. The WILPF was founded in 1915 as an organization through which women could claim their right and responsibility to participate in decision-making in all aspects of world peace and freedom. WILPF's first International President was Jane Addams. The weekly Carmelite printed a short piece under the headline "Labor and Peace"

One of the most interesting of the year's W. I. L. evenings occurred last Sunday at the Studio of Dene Denny and Hazel Watrous. Miss Denny spoke on "Labor and Peace." The new sophistication on the part of peoples regarding the actual motives behind wars was pointed out and illustrated by several recent cases in which the inclinations of the government to enter into war have been inhibited by its fear that the people would not tolerate it. The development of poison gases of super-destructive power has added to the deterrents of war.... (Carmelite, June 6, 1929)

At the end of the previous summer, Hazel and a dozen others had formed the Carmel Theatre Guild, "to foster and support fine drama" in Carmel. Their efforts were without success, and in May 1929 the Guild disbanded. The first golden age of theater in Carmel had ended. Although community theater continues in Carmel today, by 1929 it had lost its central place as a defining activity of the town. The Carmelite commented on this shift, with reference to what happened the year before:

> Dramatic activity, which was for years the chief organized occupation in Carmel of people of leisure and imagination, has not yet recuperated from the exhaustion of last summer due to overproduction....
>
> Or, has the poetic drama, the type of play apparently preferred by the Guild, less power to elicit response when produced under conditions of imperfect illusion, than 10 or 20 years ago, before the present period of high-powered, high-speed, contemporary plays set in. (Carmelite, June 20, 1929)

A summer of music

The Music Flourishes

> In the days of the Golden Bough, Carmel was known as a center of the drama. That is, the drama as distinguished from commercial amusement. From Maurice Browne and Edward Kuster to Morris Ankrum; from Shakespeare to Eugene O'Neill. The excellence of Bert Heron's Hamlet is still spoken of. The Emperor Jones still unforgotten.
>
> Now comes the shift
>
> The drama in Carmel—except for the light comedies and the mystery dramas of the Abalone League—lies in a state of coma. But you cannot keep an energetic community down. Carmel has become a music center. So we hear from out-of-town sources, and so, to our astonishment, we note as we survey its history of the last year or two. And not only a center of music, but a center of distinguished and significant music. Cowell, Rudhyar, Buhlig, Copeland… These are leaders in their generation.
>
> Ears, be ready. What a feasting we shall have… (Carmelite, July 17, 1929)

Thus began the glorious musical summer of 1929, with which Dene and Hazel, amazingly, had relatively little to do. But the list of concerts paints such a fine picture of the musical appetite of Carmel that it is worth describing briefly. Although most of these events took place in relatively small-scale or private locations, they all were public concerts performed for a subscription or ticket-buying audience.

The Monterey Peninsula Philharmonic Society had been presenting a few visiting artists in concert each season, but it no longer existed, making the summer of 1929 a presenter's free-for-all. On June 7 the summer season began with the avant-garde pianist Imre Weisshaus in a wild program performed at the home of Mrs. Henry Dickinson, one of the leading cultural patrons of Carmel.

Meanwhile, Mrs. Marie Gordon had organized a Wednesday Morning Musical Club at the Hotel La Ribera and presented pianists Henry Cowell, Imre Weisshaus again, Dane Rudhyar, and Harold Griffin; violinist Lea Luboschutz; tenor Laurence Strauss; and Russian basso Vasía Anikeef.

The Hotel La Ribera was Carmel's newest hotel. Located on the northeast corner of Lincoln Avenue and 7th Street, it was built in the spring of 1929 by Dr. Rudolf Kocher and one of Carmel's premier contractors, Hugh Comstock. When it opened, the local press hailed it as "one of the show places of the Monterey Peninsula." Renamed The Cypress Inn in the 1960s, the hotel is still one of Carmel's charming landmarks.

The Dickinson home, the home of architect Charles Sumner Greene, and the Denny-Watrous Studio were the venues for a three-concert series by pianist Richard Buhlig. Other summer events included a 2-piano recital at the Golden Bough and several other concerts at the Greene residence. It was a summer of music and harmony, with no conflict. In July, the San Francisco Examiner summed it up:

> Carmel has lost something of its old-time Bohemianism, but it has grown up charmingly, and I do not think that in the whole of America there is a more quaintly atmospheric street than Ocean Avenue. And today, when you speak of Carmel, you think of Monterey and Pacific Grove, Pebble Beach and the Carmel Highlands, for the locality has evolved as a unit. In the old days it was a retreat for writers; now the painters and musicians have discovered it. Carmel means to have music of its own, good music, as good as a wealthy community can command. (San Francisco Examiner article, reprinted in the Pine Cone, August 2, 1929)

Cover of Henry Cowell's New Music Quarterly (or "Quaterly" as misspelled here.) Hazel designed material for Cowell until 1936. *Courtesy of the author.*

Invitation to the Music Society's annual meeting, May 26, 1930. *Courtesy of the Carmel Music Society.*

Hazel Watrous 1929

Dene Denny was in the public eye because of her concerts, but since Hazel Watrous worked "behind the scenes" (literally and figuratively) and not in the spotlight there was much less written about her throughout her life. In the minutes and proceedings of the Carmel Music Society board meetings, and in the articles, reviews, and items in the press from 1927–1929, her name is mentioned rarely, and then nearly always in conjunction with Dene's name.

In two separate interviews Hazel averred that she knew nothing about music, but she and Dene formed a close partnership in life and work, and anyone who has been in such a relationship knows there are no secrets and that both partners are involved even if one is the "silent partner."

"My primary interest was applied design," Hazel stated in a 1949 interview, "although for a time I went in quite seriously for portraiture."

Only one portrait by Hazel Watrous has come to light (shown here), but we do have more than a decade of programs and posters for the Carmel Bach Festival, the Carmel Music Society, the Golden Bough Theatre, and Denny-Watrous productions.

Hazel also designed the covers for Henry Cowell's New Music publications in the 1930s. Although Hazel may not have been center stage, she was involved and busy. The mid-1920s housing boom in Carmel had served Hazel and Dene well and helped not only to bankroll them but also to establish them as contributors to and members of the community. By the time they had finished work on their home and Studio on north Dolores in 1926, Hazel had retired from her career as architect.

From then on, Hazel's work focussed on applied print and typography design. Advertisements, brochures, posters, and printed programs designed by Hazel were seen by countless theater and music lovers for more than two decades. The minutes of the Carmel Music Society board meeting in May 1929, acknowledge and thank Hazel.

Woodblock portrait of Henry Cowell by Hazel Watrous. Pine Cone, July 10, 1930. *Courtesy of the H.M. Williams Local History Department, Harrison Memorial Library; and the Carmel Pine Cone.*

"...in whom we have been notably fortunate. All posters, folders, programmes, bear the stamp of her originality and artistry."

The typeface with the lovely W (and g, e, and Y)

The typeface in the line above is based on "Kabel," released in 1927 by the great German calligrapher and typographic artist Rudolf Koch. That same year, Hazel Watrous began designing the printed material for the Carmel Music Society and the Theatre of the Golden Bough, and she began using the distinctive Kabel typeface in her designs only months after its first availability. She also used Kabel as the logo typeface for the Carmel Bach Festival for its first eight seasons. Inspired by Hazel's love of this typeface, Kabel is used throughout this book for chapter titles and section headings.

Hazel liked to "track" Kabel horizontally, giving it a greatly expanded appearance with lots of white space between the letters. For example:

BACH FESTIVAL   BACH FESTIVAL

In March Hazel joined the Seven Arts Press, located in the Court of the Seven Arts on the southwest corner of Lincoln Street and Ocean Avenue. Among other work, it printed the Carmelite, a weekly newspaper published from 1928 to 1932.

The Seven Arts Press has recently been clever enough, and fortunate enough, to acquire Hazel Watrous. This means a step forward (not to belittle the previous excellent work of that press, however) for typography on the peninsula.

Miss Watrous is an artist who can accomplish interesting and honest design in several media involving line, color and space. Together with Dene Denny she has for some time been practicing the profession of architectural design for small houses. One accomplishment of hers which has always seemed to the Carmelite as especially fine and significant service to the community, has been her design of the programs and posters used for the Theatre of the Golden Bough at times of plays and concerts. To compare the spacing, proportions, the dignity, of these with the other and usual sort of thing, is to become thankful for the existence of Miss Watrous.

The association of Hazel Watrous with Seven Arts Press adds art and true design to the fine workmanship of which it has always been proud. (Carmelite, March 20, 1929)

The Court of the Seven Arts at that time was a busy and interesting cluster of artists and studios, including the interior decorating shop of Hazel's sister Zanetta. According to Polk's *Monterey*

Pen and ink by Charlotte Morton for the Carmel Spectator. *Courtesy of the Carmel Pine Cone.*

County Directory of 1926, *"The Seven Arts Building was the original of Carmel's famous shops....*
the first devoted to things of beauty and utility instead of utility alone." The structures are
happily intact today, and well worth a visit.

The show goes on

One of the finest touring theater troupes in the western US at that time was the Moroni Olsen
Players. Olsen was a stage actor who went on to a career in Hollywood. Organized in 1923, the
ensemble was made up of ten to twelve professional actors of various ages and types. It was their
policy to present three new plays each season and tour them to a large number of Western cities
that otherwise did not see professional theater companies. The two young romantic leads in
the troupe in 1929 were Robert Young and Rosemary DeCamp, both at the beginning of their
careers.

In November, at the invitation of Edward Kuster, the Olsen troupe set themselves up at
the former Carmel Playhouse on Monte Verde, now operated by Kuster, and used the stage to
rehearse the new work on their upcoming tour: Karel Čapek's *The Makropolis Secret.* (Later
more commonly known in English as "The Makropolis Affair.") They engaged Hazel to design
the stage sets and costumes, and hired Emma Waldvogel, a Carmel seamstress and fabric
artist, to build the costumes. The play premiered in Prague in 1922, and had only recently been
translated into English. Nothing is known of Hazel's designs, and no written description of
them seems to exist, except for a fleeting mention by a theater critic in Boise Idaho:

> It is sufficient to say that the play was presented in the Olson manner — which is very
> nearly synonymous with perfection… The stage sets were after the modern trend, giving
> a feeling of distinct pleasure to play goers bored with conventional treatments.

Before Olsen and his players left Carmel to go on tour, they gave two performances of *The Twelve
Thousand*, by German playwright Bruno Frank, presented on the stage of the Theatre of the
Golden Bough. This was a momentous occasion: it was the first play presented on the Golden
Bough stage in fifteen months, and only the second production ever given at the Golden Bough
by a completely professional theater company having no volunteer or amateur participants. But
it was a sign of the times that the 400-seat theater sold only 241 tickets for the first performance
and a meagre 127 for the second.

> …the success of the theater depends on three factors—play, actors and audience. The
> theatrical performance without an audience is no performance at all—it is a rehearsal. It
> lacks vitality. It has no magic. This from the player's point of view.
> And what about the effect on an audience of its own meagerness. The answer is easy. It
> is deadly…. An audience, slim in numbers, with dozens of empty chairs separating the
> isolated spectators, lacks opportunity for the contagious enjoyment that is derived from
> sitting elbow to elbow in a well filled auditorium. It was a good show. It was the first in
> the Golden Bough in over a year. It is a pity that we have lost the trustful, hopeful play-
> going habit. (Carmelite, December 11, 1929) [emphasis added]

After the final rehearsal for these two performances, Hazel and Dene hosted the entire
company for a farewell party at their Studio. The Pine Cone relates that "There were music
and conversation and light refreshments and the Moroni Olsen Players carried away with them
another pleasant remembrance of Carmel Hospitality."

After creating her sets and costumes for "The Makropolis Secret" in November, Hazel apparently did no further stage design. She was busy co-designing the new Denny-Watrous Gallery, scheduled to open in the center of Carmel in less than eight weeks.

September-December 1929
"the seed of good taste"

The Music Society board met on September 20, and elected two new members: Edward Gerhard Kuster and Charles Sumner Greene. Kuster had returned from Europe and was leasing the old Carmel Playhouse/Abalone Theater on Monte Verde. Greene and his brother were well-known architects based in Los Angeles, but he had built a house in Carmel and was living there with his family. Other members of the board included Dene Denny, President; Hazel Watrous, Recording Secretary; Henry and Edith Dickinson (at whose home many early chamber concerts had been given), Mrs. Paul (Grace) Flanders, Katherine Corrigan, and others.

The minutes of the meeting show that a seed had been planted that is central to the Denny-Watrous narrative. A proposal is put forth in the meeting to present one or two additional after the regular subscription season. It was thought that it might be a good idea to offer these extra concerts "in the longer intervals between the regular series." The word "summer" is not mentioned. The minutes continue:

> These extra-series concerts would be planned primarily for their educational value and would be popular as to price, with special reductions for students of music. It is felt that the seed of good taste has been sown in the various school courses and orchestras and that it should be part of the community's task to assist by providing a fuller opportunity for an understanding of and an acquaintance with the best in music. (CMS minutes)

The preceding quote expresses values essential to the Denny-Watrous vision: the Carmel Music Society would present a few concerts outside its regular subscription series. These concerts should be educational and affordable, students should be encouraged to attend, and the community should assist in creating musical experiences.

Meanwhile, the first summer season presented by the Wednesday Morning Music Club had been an artistic success, and the organization wanted to establish itself in the community. Thomas Vincent Cator, one of the Club's supporters, wrote a long article in the Pine Cone on behalf of the Club with the headline "Wednesday Morning Music Club Made Permanent."

> ...This Club has not been created for the purpose in any way of opposing the Carmel Music Society. That Society, acting rather in the capacity of an impressario [sic], has brought fine artists and fine concerts to Carmel for which everyone is truly grateful. The Carmel Music Society plans to give only four big concerts of the winter season each year....
>
> The Wednesday Morning Music club intends to give a series of six concerts each summer, very likely at the Golden Bough...[or other venue]... where an audience of at least 150 can hear them.... This Club would not put on concerts during the winter months that would interfere in any way with the Carmel Music Society....
>
> ...The main purpose of the Club is to open up the way for a hearing of lesser artists — and especially our own artists, or artists staying in Carmel, whenever that is possible.... <u>In the</u>

future no complete program of ultramodern music will be given by the Wednesday Morning Music Club. This is by request of many of its most prominent members. They seem to feel that they can better appreciate this kind of music if it is administered to them in homeopathic doses. (Pine Cone September 29, 1929) [emphasis added]

Cator's reference above to "ultramodern music" was surely a reaction to Dene's friends Henry Cowell and Imre Weisshaus, each of whom had appeared in Marie Gordon's Wednesday Morning Series just weeks before. Dene's own resolve to promote ultramodern music did not falter: on October 15, she appeared as Guest Artist at the College of the Pacific in Stockton, where she played to an audience of more than 500 people. Although there is no documentation of the repertoire in this concert, it may have included works that she offered in San Francisco eight weeks later.

> Miss Denny has the sincerity and the background of musicianship that enables her to give direct clarity to her subject and its place in the realm of music for the layman as well as the musician. Her memory, in addition, is something to cause marvel. Great enthusiasm was evinced after the concert in the crowded reception room, and the following day Miss Denny was the guest of honor at a large luncheon of the Stockton club women given in a fashionable downtown apartment hotel. (The Stockton Daily Evening Record, October 18, 1929)

The head of the Conservatory at the College of the Pacific wrote in a letter to Dene that everyone admired her for her "technical proficiency and above all for the musical mentality which could master such a program and present it from memory."

On November 22, Henry Cowell performed his latest compositions in a well-publicized concert at the Denny-Watrous Studio, in which he also spoke of his experiences on tour in Russia the previous spring. The concert began at 8:15 and tickets cost $1.00.

Carmel Music Society Third Season

The weekly Carmelite printed a short item about the Carmel Music Society's upcoming 1929–1930 series that contained these lines about the young pianist who would open the season:

Vladimir Horowitz. 1931 press photo. *Courtesy of the author.*

> Two years ago the music Society presented Gieseking on his first Western tour. This year its season opens on December 14 with the young Russian pianist Vladimir Horowitz, likewise on his first concert tour of the West. He has been acclaimed "one of the greatest pianist of the rising generation"— a sweeping statement for which allowances may be necessary, but at least indicative of outstanding merit. That Carmel is to have the privilege of hearing this artist is due to the generosity of the patrons and contributors to the Music Society. (Carmelite, October 9, 1929)

Just six weeks after the great stock market crash of 1929, the 26-year-old Horowitz played to 387 listeners sitting in Kuster's wicker chairs at the Theatre of the Golden Bough. The Music Society season continued through the winter and spring with the Roth String Quartet, the John Smallman A Cappella Choir, and operatic soprano Claire Dux.

Dene in San Francisco, December 17

Henry Cowell and his New Music Society in San Francisco presented a series of three concerts at the Galerie Beaux-Arts at 166 Geary Street (Nov. 26, Dec. 5 and 17), and the lineup was typical of Cowell: a combination of thought and action, word and music, all of it new and avant-garde.

The series began with Arthur Hardcastle, a pianist who "...has developed, through his own scientific investigations, an entire gamut of new piano resonances..."

The second concert featured Imre Weisshaus, composer/pianist, Helen Engle Atkinson, violinist, and Dorothy Pasmore, cellist, performing music by European and American composers including Chavez, Kadosa, Webern, and Weisshaus.

The third concert presented Dene Denny in a solo evening. See the Appendix for the contents of this program. The San Francisco Morning Call wrote of Dene in advance of the concert:

> "Miss Denny is foremost among California musicians who specialize in playing modern works, and she brings forth to the Nth degree the wishes of the composer in her interpretations."

Impresarios again

By November 1929, Hazel and Dene had begun the redesign of the former offices of the Carmel Pine Cone on Dolores Street between Ocean and 7th, converting it into a full-fledged performance space to be known as the "Denny-Watrous Gallery." From now on, more of their time was taken up with the Denny-Watrous Management: running the Gallery on Dolores Street and producing concerts and events there and at the Golden Bough. Dene also continued to handle artist bookings and serve as president of the Carmel Music Society's board of directors.

Perhaps because of all this, Dene seems to have stepped away from the piano, at least in public. After the above-mentioned December concert in San Francisco at the Galerie Beaux-Arts, there is no further evidence of concerts by Dene as solo pianist. She would, however, make one more appearance at the piano, in a 1932 concert presented by the Carmel Music Society and described in Part IV.

The Denny-Watrous Gallery 1930

An item in the Carmel Pine Cone on December 4, 1929, titled "The Green Room" announces that Hazel and Dene have taken a lease on the space formerly occupied by the Pine Cone Press on Dolores Street south of Ocean Avenue.

> The front section of this space will be used for display and sales room of modern decorative arts, including the embroidery work of Emma Waldvogel and certain exhibits from the Bauhaus in Dessau. The large open space in the rear will be known as "The Green Room" to which will be transferred the activities of the Denny and Watrous Studio on [north] Dolores Street. Here will be seating capacity for small audiences and wall space for significant textile and decorative art exhibitions. (Pine Cone, December 4, 1929)

They scrubbed the interior, whitewashed and painted the walls and rafters, installed new lighting, and with the help of local realtor (and owner of the building) Ray DeYoe, they built a small stage. The "Green Room" name was soon dropped, and the "Denny-Watrous Gallery" quickly became a major hub of artistic activity in Carmel. At last Dene and Hazel had an ideal venue for all types of events. It was not merely an "art gallery." The space was large enough for nearly 200 people, it was centrally located with street-level access, and most important it was useable as gallery, lecture hall, or performance venue.

> The light was excellent. Artists liked to give concerts there, delightfully intimate ones, for the acoustics were good. There was a special flavor to the place, there were books to pick up and peruse, portfolios of etchings to mull over. (Carmel Cymbal, July 14, 1939)

Longtime Carmel residents may remember the "Studio Theatre and Restaurant," a dinner theater operating at that same location from 1957 to 1986. The author is honored to be married to a former member of that estimable troupe. Today the building is in use as an art gallery once again, and stands next to one of Carmel's landmark restaurants, the Tuck Box.

This Lewis Josselyn photo shows the new DeYoe Building, designed and constructed by M. J. Murphy for Ray DeYoe, soon after its completion in 1924. The Pine Cone Press occupied the building from 1924 through 1929, and it was the Denny-Watrous Gallery from January 1930 through October 1934. At the time of this photo, the Tuck Box to the right had not yet been built, and the building on the left is an early Carmel structure with a false front. Compare this image with the photo on the last page of Part Three, taken in 1928. *Courtesy of Pat Hathaway, CAViews.*

The first event in the Denny-Watrous Gallery was not a piano recital, or a watercolor exhibit, or a lecture. Dene and Hazel made sure to open their Gallery with something every community member could enjoy: the Ralph Chesse Puppet Theater from San Francisco.

A large and representative audience came to the new Denny-Watrous Gallery last Sunday night for the purpose of witnessing a most fascinating puppet show, as well as to look over the very attractive Gallery which is the town's latest and most-talked of feature. This Gallery is the old Pine Cone office miraculously metamorphosed, resurrected, transformed, transmuted, reborn and regenerated, and has become an abode of real beauty and artistic attractiveness under the careful guidance and ministrations of Miss Denny and Miss Watrous, who have used excellent taste and judgment in the matters of color scheme, wall decorations, hangings, etchings, paintings and the like. It was a real pleasure to sit in such a place and watch the show. (Pine Cone, January 14, 1930)

A basic list of Gallery presentations during the 1930 calendar year gives a rough idea of the number and types of events offered by Dene and Hazel. This chronicle was compiled from press clippings—ads, advance articles, and reviews—as well as other ephemera and brochures. The list is undoubtably incomplete.

The first year of the Denny-Watrous Gallery

January: (Official Opening) Ralph Chesse Puppet Theater from San Francisco
            Stanley Wood, watercolors
            The Southern Harmony Four ("colored vocalists")
            Francis Toor, lecture and exhibit of Mexican art
            Margaret Tilley, pianist
February: Five lectures by Ralph Johonnot on the use of color in home design and decoration
            Irving Pichel, reading Martin Flavin's "The Criminal Code"
            Ella Young ("Irish poetess")
March: Agnes Morely Cleaveland, lecturer on politics
            Edward Weston, photographs
            Jack Black, lecture on criminality
            Richard Buhlig, American pianist
            Amy Dewing Flemming, water colors
April: Ralph Chesse Puppets
            Photographs by Imogen Cunningham
            Embroidery by Emma Waldvogel
            Henrietta Shore, Canadian/American painter

"The Denny-Watrous Gallery is becoming a popular rendezvous Sunday nights, and we predict great success for these ladies. If the attendance grows much larger it will be necessary to raise the roof and install a balcony." *(Pine Cone May 15, 1930)*

May   Ernst Krenek's jazz opera "Jonny spielt auf" starring Rudolfine Radil
            Lecture and exhibit by architect R. M. Schindler
            Brett Weston, first one-man show (age 18)
            Robert Pollak, violinist
            Irving Pichel, dramatic readings
            Lajos Shuk, Hungarian cellist
            Orozco, art exhibit

June:	Fukushima, Japanese harmonicist, with
	Dominador Purugganan, Filipino tenor
	Winifred Hooke, British pianist
	Dane Rudhyar, composer and pianist
	Lucy Pierce, lithographs
	Merle Armitage, lecture:
	"Confessions of an impresario"
July:	Annual exhibit of the Carmel Art
	Association
	Halldiss Stabell, lecture and
	demonstration of good posture
	Henry Cowell, lectures,
	with Dene Denny, pianist
	Music of Russia; 20th Century European
	Music; Creative Music in America;
	Music Systems of India, China, Japan,
	Siam and Java
	Moroni Olsen, actor, reading "The Green Pastures" by Marc Connelly
	(1930 Pulitzer Prize play)

Pine Cone ads on this page and following page, courtesy of the H. M. Williams Local History Department, Harrison Memorial Library, and the Carmel Pine Cone.

"This charming little gallery is rapidly becoming a musical shrine." *(Pine Cone July 31, 1930)*

"May I add a brief appreciation of what Miss Denny and Miss Watrous are doing through their efforts in bringing to Carmel readings of unusual plays, rendering of modern music, and exhibitions of the various modern arts and crafts. They are keeping Carmel in touch to a remarkable degree with contemporary activity in the creative arts. They deserve our whole-hearted support." *(Carmelite, July 31, 1930)*

August:	Anna Mathea, Norwegian soprano
	Motoko Hino, Japanese dancer
	Dane Rudhyar, ultra-modern pianist and composer
September:	Dene and Hazel vacation in Yosemite and to Los Angeles
October:	Flori Gough and Lev Shore, cello and piano
	R. M. Schindler, lecture on modern architecture
	Ratan Devi, billed as a Kashmiri "singer of Hindoo ragas"
	Edward Weston, a duplicate of his current New York show
	Takane Nambu, Japanese singer
November:	Franz Marc, German impressionist
December:	Perry Dilly Puppet Company
	Noel Sullivan, baritone

After the Gallery's first year, it received less event-to-event coverage in the press. Nonetheless, through December 1935 the Denny-Watrous Gallery was one of the Carmel's primary artistic hubs.

The winter and spring months of 1930 in Carmel were musically quiet aside from Carmel Music Society and the performance schedule at the Denny-Watrous Gallery. At the end of the Music Society's third season, the Monterey Herald had to this to say:

> This is a place of many things, among them the contact with culture as well as with sports and industry. The Carmel Music Society, which has just announced the close of a "decidedly successful" music season, is one of the great contributors to the pleasure of living on the Monterey Peninsula.
>
> The people who make possible these concerts in the fall, winter and early spring of the year show a spirit that merits a public appreciation that they do not really expect to receive. They are people who came here to live and who wanted some of the things that this community has been too small to provide. Therefore to satisfy their cultural wants they banded together in a community enterprise of significant and rare value to all people who love music. (Monterey Herald, May 30, 1930)

Thrip'ny Opera

In June, Carmel was the scene of an American premiere that had nothing to do with Dene and Hazel, but it's well worth noting. In January 1929, in the middle of Edward Kuster's second year

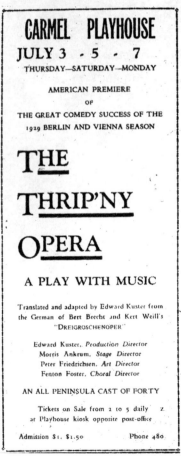

in Europe, he sent a letter to the Pine Cone. It is a very lengthy letter, typically so for Kuster. (A few months before, Kuster had sent a letter to the Carmel Music Society, and the minutes of the meeting note that Kuster's letter was "of the usual length.") In his letter to the Pine Cone, Kuster mentions in passing,

> "...I've translated a thoroughly good play that was one of the winter's hits."

The "thoroughly good play" was Die Dreigroschenoper, by Kurt Weil and Berthold Brecht. The most familiar English title is "The Three Penny Opera," but in Kuster's translation it was "The Thrip'ny Opera." The work had its premiere in Berlin in August 1928, and by the time Kuster left Germany in June 1929 it was playing to sold out houses in a dozen European theaters. Kuster translated the entire work into English, and obtained permission to produce it in Carmel.

Morris Ankrum, who had directed and starred in *The Emperor Jones* for Dene and Hazel in 1928, returned as stage director and to play the role of MacHeath. Kuster himself played Jonathan Peachum. The performances were July 3, 5, and 7, and it was poignant that this important production was seen not on the stage of Kuster's own Theatre of the Golden Bough (which was now being used as a movie house), but in the "Abalone Theater" now known as the Carmel Playhouse, on Monte Verde.

The reviewers loved the production, and the only complaint was the lack of good singing voices onstage. Thomas Vincent Cator voiced his critique with amazing eloquence:

And now I come to an important element in the presentation which I realize should be handled with gloves… Let us express the idea about as follows:—If it was the intention of the producers of the Thrip'ny Opera that the principals be extraordinarily well-fitted for their roles because of their lack of singing voices, then, upon this occasion they achieved a success that has hardly been paralleled in all of history. (Pine Cone, July 11, 1930)

This first North American performance of a major 20th century work has gone largely unmentioned in the history books, perhaps because—from the New York point of view—it took place in a little town on the California Coast without benefit of a New York professional cast. Nonetheless, Die Dreigroschenoper was given a full production onstage in Carmel nearly three years before its official premiere in New York City.

Summer Music

In May, Mrs. Marie Gordon announced in the Pine Cone the lineup of performers for her second season of the Wednesday Morning Music Club. All the performers were either local musicians or from the San Francisco area, with the exception of Olin Downes, the New York Times music critic, who lectured. The other five concerts featured harpist and contralto, tenor, pianist, cello and violin, and piano and dancer. The concerts took place on six Wednesday mornings from 11:00am to noon at Kuster's Carmel Playhouse on Monte Verde Street. One review refers to this as a "Summer Music Festival," but that phrase does not appear in the Music Club's own printed material until the following year.

On August 23, Denny-Watrous Management presented Henry Cowell's mystical opera "The Building of Bamba" at the outdoor Forest Theater. Cowell had recently produced the work in the open air at Halcyon, a spiritual community in Southern California, and he had brought the entire Halcyon cast to Carmel. The text of the opera was by J. O. Varian, Irish mystical poet, who gave a Druid interpretation prior to every scene. (It was several arias from this opera that Virginia Adams had sung with Cowell in a San Francisco concert several years before.) Unfortunately, the accompaniment was played on two pianos and organ and was unable to sustain the energy of the musical score (a group of instruments had been used in the Halcyon performance).

The fall and winter season

It was a four-concert season for the Carmel Music Society, beginning with the return of Walter Gieseking in November, and continuing in the winter and spring with the Aguilar Lute Quartet, Mina Hager, contralto, and the great cellist Gregor Piatigorsky. Four levels of Music Society membership were available "to those desiring to attend the concerts." Patrons, $100, Contributors, $25; Season Ticket Holders, $10; and Associates, $2.00. Each level provided its own ticket prices and perks, but single tickets at a slight premium were also available to the general public.

Edward Kuster also presented a handful of concerts at the Carmel Playhouse on Monte Verde, including several piano recitals, a dance presentation, and the "Russian Royal Chorus, a band of singers under the direction of Princess Mara Slavianski, who will appear in native costumes and using all native music." The group made their only US tour that season, and have since vanished into performing arts history.

A snapshot of Dolores Street

The image above of two Carmel cultural landmarks was captured in late 1927 or early 1928 (in the middle of the stormy Theater War described previously). The camera was looking northeast across Dolores Street from a spot just north of 7th Avenue. Shadows indicate that it is mid-morning.

On the left: The DeYoe Building, designed and constructed in 1924 by M.J. Murphy for Ray deYoe, a Carmel realtor. The Pine Cone Press occupied the premises from 1924 until 1930, when the entire building became the Denny-Watrous Gallery. The photo of the orchestra on the opposite page was taken in this building in 1932.

On the right: When it first opened, this tiny tea room was called Sally's, but since the 1940s it has been known as the Tuck Box. It was designed and built by Carmel architect Hugh Comstock in 1926–27 and was the only commercial structure he ever created. A garden hose hangs ready to water the newly-planted garden. In a few years, flowering bushes will tower over the stone gate.

Both buildings have been in continuous use since they were constructed in the 1920s.

The sign on the right advertises a film being shown a few blocks away at the Theatre of the Golden Bough, on the northeast corner of Ocean and Monte Verde. The poster shows Billie Love and Gilbert Roland in "The Love Mart," a 1927 silent film also starring Noah Beery. Dene and Hazel were leasing the Golden Bough at the time this photo was taken, and they were continuing Edward Kuster's practice of showing films in the Theatre during the dark periods between productions.

(On a side note, car aficionados mostly agree that the two–seater is a 1922 Buick 4-cylinder Roadster. It's showing some wear and tear, and is missing its spare tire.)

(Real photo postcard, c.1928, photographer unknown. Courtesy of the author.)

Part Four
The Monterey Peninsula Orchestra
1931–1934

The Monterey Peninsula Orchestra rehearsing in the Denny-Watrous Gallery, October 16, 1932.
Carol Weston, Associate Conductor. Mildred Sahlstrom-Wright, Concertmaster.

"This orchestra was definitely the beginning of the Carmel Bach Festival."
Carmel Pine Cone, July 19, 1946

"The Carmel Bach Festival holds its place today as an institution nationally accepted. But this has not just happened. It is not a matter of its having been non-existent in 1934 and existent in 1935.

Rather, it has been a gradual upbuilding from small beginnings. Every step on the road has been taken with forethought and fine understanding. There is a story back of it all, one in which the heroes are heroines, and the heroines, both of them, leading ladies.

The two who have led the way, guided the steps, and deviated not a jot from the goal, are Carmel's own Dene Denny and Hazel Watrous."

Ida Newberry, Carmel Pine Cone, July 1, 1938

AMATEUR ORCHESTRA

Try-outs for place in the orchestral concert of the Neah-Kah-Nie String Quartet on August ninth were held on Tuesday evening last. Representatives from Watsonville, Salinas, Pacific Grove, Monterey and Carmel were present, and enthusiasm ran high over the coming rehearsals under the direction of Michel Penha. Rehearsals will be held in the Denny-Watrous regularly on Monday and Thursday evenings at seven-thirty.

June 1932

A CAPPELIA CHORUS A REALITY

The first rehearsal of the A Capella Chorus, directed by Michel Penha, was held in the Denny-Watrous Gallery last Wednesday evening, at eight o'clock. The following were present: Sopranos: Frances Schreiman, Florence Thrift, Kathleen Murphy, Vera Hunter, Julia Keith, Mrs. Sund; Altos: Estelle Koch, Grace Knowles, Marjory Pegrim, Gertrude Bardarson; Tenors: Andrew Sessink, Dr. R. M. Hollingsworth, Lieutenant Sund; Basses: Jo Klegg, L. C. Fischer, Ray Faulkner, Everett Smith.

September 1933

"STABAT MATER" PRACTICES EVERY SUNDAY NIGHT

By March 29, when the Carmel Music Society present the Monterey Peninsula Orchestra, Michel Penha conductor, in a super-performance of Rossihi's "Stabat Mater," every school child and every adult should be able to hum the then familiar airs.

With the orchestra augmented to forty, patiently drilled by the indefatigable Mr. Penha, a chorus of seventy-five, prepared by Fenton Foster, and the four soloists, professionals from San Francisco, the production will be the biggest and most spectacular to date in the history of our Orchestra.

March 1934

January—July 1931

The Carmel Music Society opened the winter concert season in January 1931 with the Aguilar Lute Quartet. The four siblings—Ezekiel, Pepe, Paco and Eliza—had made their US debut only weeks before, and were at that time the only famous lutenists in the world. Great Spanish composers such as Manuel de Falla and Isaac Albéniz wrote music for them.

> With these four players the Spanish tradition is bred in the bone and nurtured by gifts that seem superior even for artists. The variety and tonal balance which they obtained is impressive — moments of acrid zest and revelation followed by moments of melting sensuousness. (Pine Cone, January 23, 1931)

On February 9 the board of directors of the Carmel Music Society met to consider an unusual and (at the time) confidential request.* Madame Ann Dare (the pen name of Mabel McMaster-Clarke, a San Francisco playwright) had sent a letter inviting the Music Society to present four concerts during the summer, underwritten financially by an anonymous benefactress who would guarantee to cover deficits that might arise. The concerts would take place in Carmel in July and would be given by the well-known Brosa String Quartet of London. It was the intention of the Brosa Quartet to rent a house in Carmel, give one concert per week for four weeks, and spend the remaining time rehearsing for their fall tour.

In its second, third, and fourth seasons, the Music Society had offered one or two "extra" concerts after the main subscription series. Their goal, as described in the minutes of several meetings that winter, was to enhance the educational potential of these post–season concerts in the future, with open rehearsals, special student ticket prices, and community involvement.

The Brosa Quartet proposal from Madame Dare did not meet this requirement. Also, the involvement of an anonymous benefactress, and the pre-designated ensemble, made it seem like an outsider was simply using the Music Society. After thorough discussion, the following motion was unanimously passed by the Music Society Board:

> That we as the Carmel Music Society state that we are heartily in favor of having the Brosa String Quartet brought to Carmel, but that we do not care to assume sole responsibility. However, if there is a group or groups who will unite to put it all in, we should be pleased to appoint a broad committee to cooperate with them in every way possible. (CMS minutes, February 9, 1931)

In their written reply to Ann Dare, the Music Society offered to be part of a community-wide effort by music lovers to manage the Brosa project, but their offer was declined. Only the Carmel Music Society board knew about this proposed Brosa project, and for a few weeks, the subject was forgotten in Carmel.

(The information in the preceding paragraphs is from a two-page letter sent by the Carmel Music Society to its membership more than a year after the fact, in June 1932. A copy is in the archives of the Carmel Music Society. Questions and misunderstandings had arisen regarding several decisions the board had made over a period of two years regarding requests from other concert presenters for collaboration and sponsorship. In the letter signed by President Edith (Mrs. Henry) Dickinson, the board sought to explain the rationale for their series of decisions.)

The two remaining concerts on the Carmel Music Society series were German contralto Minna Hager and the eminent cellist Gregor Piatigorsky. By the end of the decade, Piatigorsky and his family lived in Los Angeles, but in 1931 his home was in Paris. Piatigorsky's North American tour was was personally managed by Sol Hurok, who accompanied the cellist to Carmel.

Spring events at the Denny-Watrous Gallery included an Easter Sunday concert by the choir of the Russian Greek Church of San Francisco. Visual artists shown that spring included painter John O'Shea and photographer Edward Weston. Henry Cowell was back in May, lecturing on "Primitive Music," with recorded examples.

"...in utmost consonance and harmony..."

After Madame Ann Dare's offer of the Brosa Quartet was declined by the Carmel Music Society, she approached Mrs. Marie Gordon, who produced the Wednesday Morning Music Club summer concerts in 1929 and 1930. They reached an agreement in March, and Mrs. Gordon proudly announced the third season of her summer concerts, now to be known as the "Summer Festival of Music." Rather than presenting six varied programs as she had done previously, she announced that her 1931 Summer Festival of Music would consist of four Tuesday evening concerts by the famed London-based Brosa String Quartet.

In her original letter to the Carmel Music Society in February, Ann Dare had not divulged the name of the prime benefactress of the Brosa Quartet's appearance in Carmel. Now that the concerts were booked, it was announced in the Carmelite in May that Mrs. John B. Casserly, a well-known patron of the arts in San Francisco, had been enlisted as a guarantor for the four Carmel concerts and would thus cover any deficit resulting from the series (this was the "anonymous benefactress" mentioned in Ann Dare's letter to the Music Society in February).

It also could now be revealed that the Quartet's entire tour from England to the United States was being sponsored by Mrs. Elizabeth Sprague Coolidge. A pianist herself, and unrelated to the US president of the same last name, Mrs. Coolidge was a major and well-known benefactress of chamber music on both sides of the Atlantic. In 1918, for example, she founded the Berkshire Music Festival in Pittsfield, Massachusetts, out of which grew the Tanglewood Festival.

3rd
SEASON
Summer Festival of Music

Brosa String Quartette
of London

Sponsored by Mrs. J. B. Casserly
Brought to the coast by Mrs. Elizabeth Sprague Coolidge

INSTEAD OF WEDNESDAY MORNINGS AS HERETOFORE, THE RECITALS WILL BE HELD ON

**Tuesday Evenings June 16, 30
July 14, 28**

COURSE TICKETS — 4 CONCERTS $8
First two and last two rows
4 CONCERTS $6

Seats reserved at office of Hugh C. Comstock, opposite post office on Fridays and Saturdays 10 a.m. to 4 p.m.
Address mail orders to Marie Gordon
P. O. Box 132, Carmel

Courtesy of the H. M. Williams Local History Room, Harrison Memorial Library, and the Carmel Pine Cone.

A guarantor such as Mrs. Casserly allowed an individual concert presenter in a small community to move forward with concrete plans regardless of the amount of advance buy-in from local subscribers and ticket buyers. If for any reason the four concerts resulted in a financial loss, the deficit would be covered by Mrs. Casserly. Together with Mrs. Coolidge, Mrs. Casserly was making it possible for a famous string quartet to concertize in a small community that would not have been able to book the quartet directly. There would of course be local subscribers and ticket buyers for the Brosa concerts, but the ticket revenue in Carmel could not possibly cover the quartet's standard fee for four appearances. Without these two benefactresses—each of whom possessed both money and influence—at the center of things, the Brosa concerts in Carmel could not have happened.

The initial list of patrons for the visit of the Brosa Quartet to Carmel included Mrs. J. B. Casserly of San Francisco; Mrs. Elizabeth Sprague Coolidge of Boston; Mme. Olga Samaroff-Stokowski of New York, music critic of the NY Post and wife of conductor Leopold Stokowski; Mr. Nicolai Sokolov, the founding conductor of the Cleveland Orchestra; Dr. Aurelia Henry Reinehart, president of Mills College; Artur Rodziński, conductor of the Los Angeles Philharmonic; and about three dozen of Carmel's most recognizable names (not including Dene and Hazel). A local patron offered a large house in Carmel Highlands where the quartet could live and rehearse while in Carmel. On only a few days' notice, the brilliant San Francisco violist Nathan Firestone substituted for the Brosa Quartet's violist, who had broken his arm in an automobile accident, so upon their arrival in Carmel there was a lot of rehearsing to do.

Once again in the advance notices of their concerts, Marie Gordon and her colleagues were careful to state most delicately and explicitly that their summer concerts were not intended to interfere or compete with the Carmel Music Society's winter season. The article from which this excerpt is taken was written by cellist Preston W. Search.

> These musicals [sic], presented only in mid-summers, have come at a most refreshing time of the year, in utmost consonance and harmony with the eminent work of the Carmel Music Society's most exceptional artist's [sic] concerts given in winter months. The two undertakings are complemental; both represent and deserve the highest interests in Carmel. We bring this wonderful opportunity and distinguishing honor to the music lovers of Carmel and our summer visitors. The festival tickets are now ready. Eminent musicians from San Francisco, Berkeley, Oakland, Mills College, Palo Alto, San José, Los Angeles, Pasadena, and Fresno are coming for the event. (Pine Cone, May 8, 1931)

Ticket sales were so strong for the first of the four concerts that 40 extra chairs were squeezed into the Theatre of the Golden Bough. West Coast musical luminaries in the audience included Alfred Hertz, conductor of the San Francisco Symphony, and his Los Angeles colleague Artur Rodziński. However, despite the publicly stated hopes of the Club, neither Mrs. J. B. Casserly, Mrs. Elizabeth Sprague Coolidge, nor Mrs. Herbert Hoover were in attendance.

In their four Tuesday evenings, the Brosa Quartet played Purcell, Haydn, Mozart, Beethoven, Schubert, Debussy, Ravel, and more, but (as had been agreed by the Club two years before) no "ultramodern" music

The one bow to modernism was the inclusion of a work by the contemporary Dutch composer Bernard van Dieren. As usual, Hal Garrott finds a way to make his criticism amusing.

> An advance notice states that Brosa considered van Dieren too advanced for performances in New York, Washington, Philadelphia, Chicago, Los Angeles, but felt that, "...Carmel audiences would be interested in the extremely advanced and different writing of the modern genius of diverse accomplishments." I could wish that Carmel might have lived up to this high expectation, but have long suspected that the village (however much we like to think otherwise) is fully as dumb as New York—and almost as dumb as Chicago. If, as the program states, van Dieren is "the last word in quartet music," I much prefer the first. (Pine Cone, August 14, 1931)

The four-concert series was an artistic success, although concerts 2, 3, and 4 were not sold out and Mrs. Casserly of San Francisco did indeed have to cover a small financial deficit. In early August, the Brosa String Quartet left Carmel, never to return.

The new way

The summer of 1931 marks a turning point in the financing of concert presentations in Carmel. By devoting her entire "Summer Festival of Music" to four concerts by the Brosa Quartet, Marie Gordon was reverting to an older model: concerts of European music played by "name" European performers, with the bulk of the financial support for the events derived from a relatively small number of donors (some of whom had no personal connection with Carmel at all). Such generous, no-strings patronage might seem beneficial at first glance, but by relying primarily on only a few individual sponsors, an arts organization risks placing its financial health, not to mention its artistic direction, into those few hands, and the summer concerts in Carmel were a perfect example.

In this instance, Mrs. Coolidge and her Foundation in Washington, DC, had invited the famous Brosa Quartet to the US for a concert tour of major cities. During the tour, the Coolidge Foundation would cover the quartet's travel and living costs and guarantee them an agreed-upon fee regardless of expenses or the ups-and-downs of the actual ticket sales. Mrs. Coolidge had enlisted Mrs. Casserly's assistance in presenting the quartet in San Francisco. Mrs. Casserly in turn had contacted Carmel and offered to underwrite the quartet there for four concerts. To Marie Gordon this must have seemed like a fabulous deal: she did not have to book an array of different performers and then promote and manage six different concerts; she did not have to arrange for piano rental, moving, and tuning; it would be an exciting and glamorous "big name" event with guaranteed publicity and prestige; and there was no possibility of an out-of-pocket deficit for her.

However, this out-of-town financial support accomplished nothing beyond covering the quartet's fee for those four concerts no matter how many tickets were sold. The four Tuesday evenings produced this way had done nothing to build a continuing base of support for whatever Marie Gordon might choose to do the following summer, when Mrs. Coolidge and Mrs. Casserly might no longer be in the picture.

Further, other than those four Tuesday evenings, the quartet members had no presence in the community—no involvement or interaction with music lovers. They spent four weeks rehearsing in the Carmel Highlands house, but there is no report of anyone listening to the quartet rehearse, an experience many in the community would have enjoyed.

Although Marie Gordon called it a "Summer Music Festival" and hoped that it might add to Carmel's musical renown, it was still really a summer concert series, and one which had become less diverse and less connected to Carmel than in its previous two summers.

By contrast, the new paradigm of concert financing throughout the US in the 1920s and 1930s (as discussed in the earlier chapter, "Carmel Music Society ") was to create a broad base of local subscribers, with the goal of involving a larger portion of the community in supporting, listening to, and even making music. This approach tends to enhance organizational stability and longevity, and helps the community feel involved in the process.

Also, as demonstrated by the Little Theater Movement, 20th century artistic visionaries dreamed of using the Arts not only to entertain the mind but also to expand it. From Mary

Austin and George Sterling in Carmel's earliest days, to Maurice Brown and Edward Kuster at the Theatre of the Golden Bough, to Dene and Hazel and their Studio and Gallery, the goal was not only to put on a "performance" but to arrange an encounter in which the members of the audience were somehow changed.

Another shift in the early 1930s was an increasing interest in presenting American performers and American music. As classical music continued to flourish in America, many looked askance at the idea of paying premium prices for imported foreign musicians when North American musicians were closer at hand and sometimes offered more exciting, modern, and thought-provoking programs. This new way was the path Dene and Hazel would take in 1932.

Meanwhile at the Gallery

One way of describing the typical schedule of events at the Denny-Watrous Gallery is that Dene and Hazel liked to do different things, and they liked to do things differently. After a lecture in late June 1931, the Pine Cone praised the Gallery and its effect on the community:

> ### Denny-Watrous score again!
>
> Once more the entertainment at the Denny-Watrous Gallery was utterly different from anything I have experienced. How do these ladies manage each week to disprove the old saying, "There is nothing new under the sun?" This charming little Gallery is rapidly becoming a musical shrine. In it I have heard some of the greatest violin playing in a long concert-going career, much excellent piano playing, not to mention singing, dancing, readings and lectures....
>
> Everyone in the village, our merchants particularly, will do well to back such institutions as the Denny Watrous Gallery... Such an achievement would attract to our village not the riff-raff that litter California's beaches from border to border and drive desirable citizens away to seek other homes, but traveled cultivated families of means whose tastes will enrich our local life, supporting its art movement and contributing to its community spirit. They will flock to us as a refuge offering them an escape from the bane to cultivated American life: standardized commercialism. (Pine Cone, June 26, 1931)

Carmel felt itself in the public eye and was concerned with maintaining its appearances; the trendy Denny-Watrous Gallery was a feather in the town's cap. The community was weathering the Depression very well, and an item in the Carmelite in June stated, "Despite the Depression, shop locations in Carmel continue to be in demand. At present there are only three or four vacancies in the business district, and at least three new businesses in the immediate offing."

As with all towns that depend on the tourist industry, Carmel had a conflicted relationship with outsiders. As more visitors appeared, certain standards had to be maintained. In July the Pine Cone reported:

> "Sun-tan bathing suits which leave the upper extremities of the anatomy bare, will not be banned on Carmel's beach as long as they are 'within the bounds of decency.' " (Pine Cone, July 17, 1931)

A few miles south of Carmel is a beautiful, rocky, forested peninsula called Point Lobos. In 1603, Sebastian Vizcaíno had named it in honor of the barking sea lions on the rocks. Three centuries later, the State of California was considering adding this area to the state park system, but the Pine Cone reported that many Carmel citizens were opposed to the idea of a state park so near the town.

> The majority of Carmel artists and the civic leaders feel that by turning the Point Lobos [sic] into a state park and opening it to the general public, it will make the outskirts of the village the stopping place for auto campers and transient motorists of the type not desired here. (Pine Cone, August 7, 1931)

This is one instance when the early Carmel preservationists did not prevail.

The Denny-Watrous Gallery continued to present its forward-looking programs through the summer and fall. The Japanese dancer Motoko Hino returned to both dance and sing (two days before the first Brosa Quartet concert). The Southern Harmony Four "colored quartet" returned for their third performance in 18 months, and this time brought with them Thelma Brown, "...a singer of 'blues.'"

The brilliant Canadian violinist Kathleen Parlow gave two concerts at the Gallery that summer. Born in Calgary, Canada, in 1890, she had been a child prodigy and as an adult had earned the nickname "The lady of the golden bow." An anonymous item in the Pine Cone says:

> I could scarcely believe my eyes when I read that Kathleen Parlow is to appear July 18 and 25 in the Denny-Watrous Gallery in joint recital with the distinguished pianist, Margaret Tilly. If some of the leading eastern impresarios should hear about this, I feel certain they would faint from surprise. (Pine Cone, July 17, 1931)

The new string quartet

In August 1931, a group of music lovers gathered in a (sadly, undisclosed) Carmel home to hear a private concert by new string quartet from Oregon.

There was no mention of the event in the press at that time, but several articles in 1932 make reference to it. The four players apparently charmed all in attendance with their playing and their personalities, and they spent several weeks in Carmel relaxing, rehearsing, and attending events.

These musicians play a very important role in this narrative. The foursome had known one other for only a year, and within twenty-four months they would go their four separate ways. At the peak of their short and intense career as a quartet, they performed in Carmel on August 31 and met Dene Denny. That meeting is a pivotal moment in the core of this narrative.

From 1936 through 1947, this was the opening paragraph in the printed program of the Carmel Bach Festival:

> "The year 1932 marked the beginning of an inner musical life when Dene Denny and Hazel Watrous brought to Carmel the Neah-Kah-Nie String Quartet, with Michel Penha as its director and cellist. They presented the Quartet in five chamber concerts, admitting season ticket holders to weekly open rehearsals."

To place this string quartet and its members in context and understand their contribution to Carmel, we need to understand how the ensemble came to be.

Neah-Kah-Nie

The Quartet was the brainchild of a brilliant European–trained American violinist, whose name was Susie Fennell Pipes. She was born in Chicago in 1883, and moved with her family to Independence, Oregon in 1894. An early talent at the violin, she made her solo debut in Portland at the age of 12. When she was 16 she married 23-year-old lawyer John Pipes, who was devoted to Susie and encouraged her in her musical career. She studied in Chicago and in Berlin, where she met pianist Leopold Godowsky, violinist Eugène Ysaÿe, and studied briefly with the great Joseph Joachim, friend of Brahms and one of the greatest violinist of the 19th century. After returning to Oregon, Susie lived in Portland with her husband and children, taught at the University of Oregon, and performed as member of several chamber music ensembles.

Susie was a natural organizer, and she created the Portland Chamber Music Society and other such organizations in her travels in the Northwest in the 1920s. In 1929 she set out to realize her dream of playing first violin in a string quartet with members of her choosing. The group began to take shape in 1929, underwent several membership changes, and by the summer of 1930 Susie had found her three ideal colleagues and reached an unusual agreement with them.

In order to transform four individual players into a cohesive string quartet, they need to rehearse and perform without the interruptions of other playing and teaching obligations. But Susie and her hand–picked colleagues were all free-lance or orchestra musicians. How would they support themselves during the rehearsal months and the first year of concerts, when they could not yet command a substantial fee or fill large concert halls?

Susie Pipes had been persuasive enough to convince several important Portland music patrons to underwrite a string quartet that she had just formed— one that had not yet had rehearsal or given a concert. The underwriting that Susie had obtained paid a living wage to each of the four members of the quartet for the summer, during which they would rehearse full-time. After the initial rehearsal period, if the patrons approved of the result, the financial sponsorship would continue for a minimum of a year. The only requirement was that the four quartet members could accept no outside engagements so long as the agreement was in effect. The quartet's cellist played a major role in Carmel's musical life for most of the 1930s.

Michel Penha, press photo in New York, circa 1915. *Library of Congress.*

Michel Penha

Carmel owes a great debt to the Dutch cellist Michel Penha. Without his artistic leadership and collaboration, Dene and Hazel would have been unable to create the Carmel Bach Festival. The story of Michel Penha's work in Carmel has never been told before.

Michel Penha was born in Amsterdam in 1888 to a musical family. As a child he began his musical training on the piano but by age seven he was also playing the cello, following in the footsteps of his father and grandfather.

Penha was a pupil of several of Europe's finest cello teachers. He first studied with Isaac Mossel (1870-1923) at the Amsterdam Conservatory, where he graduated in 1905 at the age of sixteen. Mossel was principal cellist of Amsterdam's famous Concertgebouw Orchestra and was a very important teacher at that time. It was said that not all of Mossel's pupils became great cellists, but every great cellist had studied with Mossel.

In his late teens Penha studied with Hugo Becker (1864-1941), another of the most prominent cello teachers of the early 20th century, and he also spent time in Paris studying privately with French cellist Joseph Salmon (1864-1943). Penha made his solo debut in Amsterdam in 1907 at the age of nineteen, and then concertized in Europe for almost two years, with at least one trip to Central and South America.

Courtesy of the author.

In 1909 at the age of 22, Michel Penha immigrated to the US (he became a citizen in 1934). He lived first in New York City, where he taught at the precursor of the Juilliard School. There he met Carl Tollefson, Concertmaster of the New York Symphony, and his wife the pianist Augusta Schnabel. The three of them toured widely in the early 1910s as the Tollefson Trio. (There were two fine orchestras active in New York at that time, the "New York Symphony" and the "Philharmonic Orchestra Society." The two orchestras later merged and evolved into the modern-day New York Philharmonic.)

> The fluent easy manner of Penha's performance, which made the most difficult passages sound and appear easy, his temperament and thorough musicianship mark him as a cellist of rare ability. (Baltimore Sun, Sept 20, 1914)

In 1915 Penha left the Tollefson trio and made several lengthy tours with Chilean composer and pianist Alberto Guerrero (1886-1959) to Bolivia, Peru, Panama, Costa Rica, and Cuba. After returning to New York, Penha performed chamber music recitals throughout the northeast US, as soloist and also with his NYC-based Penha Trio. Another tour to South America in 1919 included appearances as conductor as well as cellist.

By mid 1920 Michel Penha had met Leopold Stokowski (1882-1977). The charismatic British conductor had come from the Cincinnati Symphony to the Philadelphia Orchestra in 1912, and during his 26-year tenure in Philadelphia he built the orchestra into one of North America's most important symphonies. Stokowski invited Penha to join the Philadelphia Orchestra as principal cellist. During his five seasons with Stokowski and the Philadelphia Orchestra, Penha's solo appearances included the Brahms Double Concerto and the Dvorak and Lalo Cello Concertos. This is a review of his first solo appearance with the orchestra, in September 1920.

Stokowski leads orchestra in fourth concert of series
Michel Penha demonstrates his artistry yet again

The Philadelphia Orchestra gave its fourth concert last evening at the Orpheum theater. Leopold Stokowski wielded the baton to the delight of the audience which greeted him with evident pleasure. Soloist of the evening was Michel Penha, first cellist of the orchestra, who chose the Concerto in A Minor by Schumann to demonstrate that the orchestra possesses an artist of full stature.

It was serious, almost pathologic music, seriously and affectingly played, this concerto, and with an accompaniment exquisite in its delicacy. We were made acquainted in the second movement with Mr. Penha's beautiful tone, his more than adequate technical equipment, which the last movement of the Concerto, with its interpolated cadenza, gave him full opportunity to display. We can heartily re-echo the statement that he is an unquestioned acquisition to the orchestra. (Philadelphia Inquirer, Sept 20, 1920)

By coincidence, French violist Romain Verney joined the Philadelphia Orchestra as Principal at the same time as Penha, and the two Europeans became friends. In 1925 after five seasons in Philadelphia they both moved west to accept first chair positions in the San Francisco Symphony. Verney played in the SF Symphony until his retirement in 1957, and also played in Carmel several times in the 1930s.

From September 1925 until May 1930, Michel Penha was an important part of the San Francisco Symphony. In addition to serving as Principal cellist, he was assistant conductor, which in those days meant that he conducted many of the rehearsals himself. Managing a productive rehearsal from the podium is a skill that not all conductors possess, but Penha was apparently very good at it. Penha also was an avid chamber musician and, as he had done in New York and Philadelphia, he formed or joined several string quartets and trios made up of the city's leading players.

Courtesy of the author.

The music director of the San Francisco Symphony 1915–1930 was the Frankfurt-born Alfred Hertz (1872–1942). Just after the turn of the century, Hertz had first made his name in America by conducting Wagner at the Metropolitan Opera. Bits of those performances in 1902 and 1903 were experimentally recorded by the Met's librarian Lionel Mapleson on wax cylinders known today as the Mapleson Cylinders. Hertz was also a frequent conductor on the Metropolitan Opera tours, and he was with the company in San Francisco during the great earthquake of April 1906. In 1915 he returned as music director of the city's four-year-old symphony orchestra.

During Michel Penha's five seasons as Principal cellist in San Francisco, Alfred Hertz led the Symphony in its first recording sessions. (These recordings, for the Victor Talking Machine Company, have been digitally remastered and released, as have the Mapleson Cylinders mentioned above.)

In June 1930, at the age of 42, Penha left the San Francisco Symphony and his position as head of the cello department of the San Francisco Conservatory. He had signed a contract with Susie Fennell Pipes to direct and play cello in a new string quartet in Oregon. His fee as leader of the quartet was well into five figures, enough to enable him to pay $13,000 later that year for a 1754 Guadagnini cello. (As of 2014, that priceless instrument is owned by Carter Brey, Principal Cellist of the New York Philharmonic.)

The Portland Oregonian said of Penha that summer: "He is single, plays a dangerous game of bridge, has traveled all over the world, and is something of a clever chef." Penha was also a snappy dresser and a real charmer, with coal black hair, brown eyes, and a resonant baritone voice.

Courtesy of the author.

A string quartet is born 1931

The four string players who gathered in Portland in June 1931 were Susie Pipes, first violin; Hubert Sorenson, second violin; Alexander Vdovin, viola; and Michel Penha, cello.

Each of the four players had met or worked with at least one of the others previously, so they were not total strangers, but the four of them had never played together as a quartet.

A fine string quartet is a team of soloists. All four must be in command of his or her instrument at the same high level of individual skill and artistry, and yet each must be exquisitely aware of what the other three are doing at all times. There is no conductor, and yet they perform music that requires a delicately and painstakingly worked out roadmap of tempo, loudness, shadings, color, subtlety, and nuance. A string quartet rehearsal is a delicate and complex hours-long process of give and take, experimentation, choices, disagreements, and compromises.

N-K-N photos this page courtesy of Dana Carlile.

All of this requires a significant amount of mutual understanding, empathy, and trust. Like great orchestras, most great string quartets have been playing together regularly, often, and for quite a while.

But in this case, time was at a premium. The four musicians were shaking hands for the first time at the end of June, and they were expected to give their debut concert in early fall for a discriminating Portland audience. The four musicians—two Americans, one Russian, and one Dutchman—had a lot of work to do in just eight or ten weeks, and in order to save

time Susie Pipes had wisely engaged Penha to be the director of the new quartet, to guide it in the interpretation of the repertoire they were preparing, not just in the preliminary rehearsals but throughout the concert season. All four players had studied with eminent European teachers, but Penha had by far the most impressive and extensive professional credentials and experience, both playing and conducting.

The unexpected gift that Michel Penha brings to this story is the manner in which he worked with other musicians. Unlike many great soloists, he was apparently not only a world class musical artist, he was also very adept in a directorial role. He had high standards but the people who worked with him—professional and amateur—enjoyed and respected him as a conductor. He knew how to make suggestions to musicians and what to say to get them to do what he wanted. The rehearsal process is part artistry and part psychology, and all the participants must view the leader with professional respect and personal trust. Every musician loves to work with and be challenged by a more experienced colleague from whom they can learn something. Michel Penha was one of those colleagues.

Pianist David Campbell, who worked with the Quartet in 1931, remembered Michel Penha not only as a "superb musician but as a kindly task master and brilliant wit."

On the beautiful Pacific coast of Oregon west of Portland is a sandy cove at the foot of a small mountain that the Tillamook Indians had named Neah-Kah-Nie (Said to mean "the place of the supreme deity," the place name is spelled Neahkahnie today). Near the beach were several cottages, an abandoned general store, and Sam

Courtesy of Dana Carlile.

Reed's Neah-Kah-Nie Tavern, where local musicians, sometimes including Susie Pipes and her colleagues, entertained the tavern guests on weekends. In late June the quartet arrived at this

Courtesy of the Carmel Music Society

beautiful and secluded spot on the Pacific Northwest coast. They made their home in the abandoned general store and had nothing to do until the end of August but rehearse every day under Penha's direction. Here they discussed, explored, chose, and rehearsed the repertoire for their first season of concerts. That summer, under the leadership of Michel Penha, the Neah-Kah-Nie String Quartet was born.

By early October 1930 they had returned to Portland, bringing the name of the quartet's birthplace with them. In October and November the Neah-Kah-Nie String Quartet gave a series of successful debut concerts in the homes of their principal patrons, fully satisfying their benefactors that the summer rehearsal time had been well spent and confirming the financial backing for their first season. They then headed south for their first tour of California, with concerts in Coronado, Pasadena, Redlands, Los Angeles, Santa Barbara, San Francisco, and elsewhere. Susie Pipes' dream was to perform chamber music in intimate settings such as private homes, the way it had been done in the 19th century, and many of the concerts given on this first tour took place in private homes. Such was their success that by the end of their first season the exclusive intimate concerts were phased out because of the quartet's increasing success in filling larger venues.

After a Portland radio broadcast in April 1931, they toured the Pacific Northwest for a month, and then said goodbye to violist Alexander Vdovin. American violist Abraham Weiss took his place, and the Neah-Kah-Nie String Quartet was in its final configuration.

In June 1931, the financial backing for their second season was confirmed, and after several weeks of rehearsals to accommodate their new violist the quartet headed south to California again. In August they stopped in Carmel and played a concert (unpublicized) in a private home. Dene Denny and Hazel Watrous were present that day and saw the potential in these four intense players. Before the Quartet returned to Portland, Dene booked them for a Carmel Music Society concert in the winter; the Quartet also signed a contract with Dene making her their booking agent and manager. With Dene's help, the Quartet secured more than 50 concert engagements during the coming season. The set out from Oregon in October 1931, and traveled thousands of miles up and down the West Coast in a Buick sedan. In February 1932, the Buick would bring them back to Carmel.

August–December 1931

The August 21 Pine Cone carried an announcement of "a musical event of importance" at the Denny-Watrous Gallery: a joint lecture by Henry Cowell and Nicolas Slonimsky (1894-1995), a Russian-born American conductor, composer, lecturer, scholar, and author. Slonimsky is best known today not for his musical compositions, but for his reference works, including the *Lexicon of Musical Invective* ("Critical Assaults on Composers since Beethoven's Time"), a hilarious collection of scathing insults directed at great musicians by the critics of their time. Slonimsky was also editor of the indispensable one-volume reference work, *Baker's Biographical Dictionary of Musicians*.

The Slonimsky-Cowell lecture at the Denny-Watrous Gallery took place on Saturday evening, August 29. The general impression from subsequent comments in the press is that the two men talked on and on while the audience kept hoping (in vain) for more actual music. The Pine Cone's Hal Garrott began his review with his usual tongue-in-cheek directness:

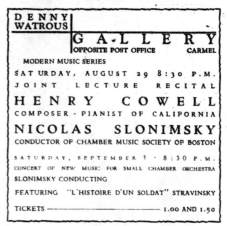

DENNY
WATROUS
GALLERY
OPPOSITE POST OFFICE   CARMEL
MODERN MUSIC SERIES
SATURDAY, AUGUST 29 8:30 P.M.
JOINT   LECTURE   RECITAL
HENRY   COWELL
COMPOSER - PIANIST OF CALIFORNIA
NICOLAS   SLONIMSKY
CONDUCTOR OF CHAMBER MUSIC SOCIETY OF BOSTON
SATURDAY, SEPTEMBER 5 · 8:30 P.M.
CONCERT OF NEW MUSIC FOR SMALL CHAMBER ORCHESTRA
SLONIMSKY CONDUCTING
FEATURING "L'HISTOIRE D'UN SOLDAT" STRAVINSKY
TICKETS ——————————— 1.00 AND 1.50

Courtesy of the H. M. Williams Local History Department, Harrison Memorial Library; and the Carmel Pine Cone.

> **Slonimsky And Cowell Talk While Audience Craves Music**
> The recital at the Denny-Watrous Gallery Saturday was a stimulating affair, arousing almost the entire gamut of emotions, running from desire to commit violence on the performer to the exquisite enjoyment of unusual sounds. Modern musicians play their compositions too little and explain too much. They seem to overlook the fact that the proof of the music is in the playing — as the proof of the pudding is in the tasting. What would you think of a cook who insisted on boring you to the verge of a nervous breakdown trying to demonstrate that if you are educated in a certain way from the age of six up, why, then certain combinations of soda, vanilla and cottage cheese ought to taste delightful. Spare your words, cook! Give us a taste. We'll tell you fast enough if we like the stuff. (Pine Cone, Sept. 3, 1931)

Slonimsky was based in Boston and had come to San Francisco to conduct the musicians of Henry Cowell's New Music Society in the West Coast premiere of Igor Stravinsky's *L'Histoire du Soldat* (The Soldier's Tale). Written in 1918, it is an intense work "to be read, played, and danced" ("lué, jouée et dansée") by three actors and a dancer, accompanied by a septet of violin, double bass, clarinet, bassoon, cornet or trumpet, trombone, and percussion. The libretto relates the parable of a soldier who trades his fiddle to the devil in return for unlimited economic gain. The actors portray the soldier, the devil, the narrator, and the minor characters. There is no mention in the reviews of vocalists or dancers, and it's clear (although disappointing) that only the music was performed in these concerts.

The day after their lecture, Slonimsky and Cowell returned to San Francisco to prepare for the concert on Sept 3 in the Theater of the San Francisco Community Playhouse. On Saturday evening, September 6, Slonimsky and the musicians repeated that concert at the Denny-Watrous Gallery before a diverse audience including Nea-Kah-Nie cellist Michel Penha, journalist Lincoln Steffens, and German-American soprano Elizabeth Rethberg. She was in California to sing with Ezio Pinza at the San Francisco Opera in Mozart's *Don Giovanni*, conducted by Fritz Reiner.

The concert began with several pieces by Anton Webern for clarinet and piano, followed by the Stravinsky "Soldier's Tale." The entire concert lasted less than one hour. After an intermission, Slonimsky and the players then performed the entire program a second time.

> Stravinsky's "The Story of a Soldier" performed at the Denny-Watrous Gallery Saturday night was the most successful representation of modern music I have heard in Carmel. The Misses Denny and Watrous showed great enterprise and courage in bringing nine musicians to Carmel, most of them members of the San Francisco Symphony Orchestra, under a distinguished leader, Nicolas Slonimsky, director of the Boston Chamber Music Orchestra.
>
> These musicians gave us a spirited performance — and then repeated the entire piece with an added mellowness and flow that put it over with many of the audience. Carol Weston, violinist, shared the burden of the production with the distinguished conductor, and negotiated the difficult rhythmic changes in startling phrases in a manner that gave significant meaning. (Pine Cone, September 13, 1931)

The solo violinist in the two Stravinsky performances was the concertmaster of Cowell's New Music Society, Carol Weston, a San José native living in San Francisco. Born in 1891, Weston was a popular San Francisco violin teacher until her death in 1969. In the fall of 1932 she would return to the Denny-Watrous Gallery to help train an orchestra soon to be formed.

The fall and winter season

The Denny-Watrous Gallery began its fall schedule with a September concert by Heiman Weinstine, a young Russian violinist. Meanwhile the Carmel Music Society was promoting its own upcoming season. Once again, the Society's concerts were held in the Carmel Theater on Ocean Avenue, the movie house formerly known as the Theatre of the Golden Bough. In late September, Marion Todd wrote in the weekly Carmelite:

The Music Society is now at the beginning of its fifth season. It was founded for the purpose of bringing great artists to the Peninsula and has never had reason to doubt that Carmel people appreciate the best and are glad to support the society on that basis. It is hoped that each year the number of season-ticket subscribers will be augmented until we automatically have a full house; until then we must count on the generosity of contributors and patrons whose co-operation so far has never failed us. (Pine Cone, October 9, 1931)

A few days later, the Pine Cone reported that the Music Society had incorporated something new into its series: dance.

The most brilliant and satisfying program [of concerts] of its history will be presented on the 1931–1932 series of the Carmel Music Society. A happy innovation is the booking of dancers on a series that has hitherto been restricted to straight music. The extraordinary response to the works of Kreutzberg, the German dancer, and significance of his contribution to the dance, together with its inseparable connection with music, have led to the society's placing Kreutzberg on its series. (Pine Cone, September 18, 1931)

On October 2 and 3, Dene and Hazel presented an unusual drama in their home on Dolores Street. The Pine Cone reviewer was amazed:

I saw the Bandbox Repertory Company of Pasadena at the residence of Misses Denny and Watrous, and I still tingle with the thrill of it. They play in an ordinary living room without curtain, scenery, and footlights. There is no make-up on their faces and their voices are not raised. For two acts I followed an intimate play, not greatly remarkable, with the absorption that attaches to one's private affairs. I have traveled hundreds of miles to attend famous productions that interested me less. In the bandbox's production the actors are all that count — they must be past masters of the technique of intimate characterization. The apparent simplicity and naturalness which seems so easy one is tempted to believe he could do it himself, really constitute the art which conceals art. (Pine Cone, October 9, 1931)

The Music Society season opened on October 23 with the Hungarian violinist Joseph Szigeti. A week before the concert, Pine Cone writer Hal Garrott praised the Music Society:

Szigeti is one of the greatest artists the Carmel Music Society have ever brought to the village. How they accomplished it I do not know. As yet, San Francisco has only succeeded in securing a date with this man to play with the Symphony Orchestra as a soloist. That means they are only to hear him in one piece, and no encores permitted. Thanks to our clever music society, Carmel is to hear Szigeti in a dozen different numbers, all in the intimacy of our charming little theater, where you can really hear what he is doing. It would cost you $25 at least to go to San Francisco to hear Szigeti play less than one 10th as much as he is to play here at a cost, to you, of some two dollars or less! The generous program Szigeti is to play here is made up of high-class favorites — a well selected group of pieces calculated to delight the average music lover. (Pine Cone, October 16, 1931)

The concert was sold out, but the sophisticated Carmel audience was lukewarm about Szigeti's performance. As Hal Garrott wrote in his Pine Cone review, the diminutive Szigeti was in fact "not a violinist of broad human appeal who stirs audiences profoundly," and so Garrott begins his review by praising the audience:

The eminent violinist, Szigeti, presented by the Carmel Music Society, played a recital in the Carmel Theater last Friday. He was enthusiastically greeted by the usual brilliant audience that opens the Carmel music season and attends every concert. Of course all seats were taken. (Pine Cone, October 30, 1931)

Sunset School auditorium wing, early 1930s. *Courtesy of the Carmel Bach Festival.*

There were two final newsworthy events in Carmel at the end of 1931. On November 13 a dedication ceremony was held for the newly completed addition to the Sunset School on San Carlos Street. Constructed at a cost of $75,000, the new wing contained five classrooms, an art room, a shop, a large gymnasium and a new auditorium with a proscenium stage.

> If there is luck in numbers, Sunset School should have it. The new assembly hall will seat just 777 persons, 166 in the balcony and 611 and the parquet. Architect Ryland solved a difficult problem and saved a goodly number of thousands by slanting the roof, instead of building up two walls and a roof across. The Gothic interior with its pointed arches is a thing of beauty and economy. The writer has lectured in 100 public school auditoriums throughout the United States, and never yet has he seen one to approach the beauty of Sunset's. (Pine Cone, October 2, 1931)

The auditorium's distinctive gothic arch motif is clearly shown in this photo from 1950. A larger version of this image may be seen on page 300. *Courtesy of the Monterey Public Library, California History Room Archives.*

The dedication ceremony consisted of music and speeches (strictly limited to three minutes each). The Pine Cone was careful to reassure its readers that the event was created by the school itself, and that, "*...it will snap through without hitches, and free of those long and boresome speeches which are apt to open places of learning.*" (Pine Cone, November 6, 1931)

In fact most of the program consisted of performances by students. The auditorium was crowded to the doors with pupils and parents and residents of Carmel who all were seeing the hall for the first time. The eighth grade girls' Verse Choir recited several poems. The dancing club performed Danish, Sicilian, and American folk dances. The Junior Glee Club sang three selections, and the orchestra played the *Dance of the Blessed Spirits* from Gluck's Orpheus and the first movement of Haydn's *Surprise Symphony*, and the Glee Club sang four selections.

The auditorium standing on this site today is completely new and was opened in July 2003. However, both the exterior and interior of the new auditorium incorporate important design elements from the 1931 original, including the pointed arches.

The other major year-end event was the first actual concert to be held in the new Sunset School assembly hall: a performance of Handel's *Messiah* on December 19, organized by the Carmel PTA.

The concert was repeated the following night in the Methodist Church in Pacific Grove. Fenton Foster conducted the volunteer chorus assembled specially for this concert, and a pianist performed the duties of the orchestra. Many of the arias and choruses were omitted, and the concert ended with the Hallelujah Chorus.

"...the ones who like bumps!"

The beauties of nature are important to Carmel residents, but opinions have always differed on the definition of the word. At the beginning of 1931, the Pine Cone reported that a City Council meeting had nearly been interrupted by an altercation:

The debate centered on the continued improving of Carmel's bumpy streets and sidewalks, and the occasional removal of trees. At that time a large tree stood in the middle of the intersection of Monte Verde Street and Ocean Avenue, forcing cars to drive around it. Similar trees growing in the Dolores Street intersection had recently been cut down, and that prompted the current furor. The preservationists and artists wanted to keep the tree growing in the center of the intersection, but the local merchants did not.

All Hooey, Says One Carmel Resident

Carmel's bumpy streets, its trees in the center of intersections, and its poetic atmosphere were termed as "hooey," last Thursday night by Harry Orcutt, one of the residents, who almost turned the usual conservative Council meeting of the art colony into a free-for-all fight. "I am dead against it as a property owner," Orcutt told the council. "Your artistic ideas have gone to your heads."

That set off the explosives. Mayor [Herbert] Heron, who had been leaning quietly in his chair, straightened up and prepared to jump to his feet.

"It is the bumps on the streets, the trees and the fact that Carmel is different, that has made it famous the world over," Heron cried. "The kind of people we want living in Carmel are the ones who like bumps!" (Pine Cone, January 23, 1931)

Herbert Heron's words sum up Carmel's quirky reputation as a town in which many residents wanted things to be just left alone—the sort of things that other growing communities back then would have considered necessary "village improvements." Whenever specific instances such as this arose and were debated, the community always worked its way back to the foundational idea of forever preserving as much of the residential (and tree-filled) character of the village as possible. That focus eventually became official and is today a defining part of the charter of Carmel-by-the-Sea.

As 1931 came to an end, Dene and Hazel had been living in their Studio and home on north Dolores Street for seven years. The streets in that "neighborhood" were still unpaved, and there were no streetlights anywhere in Carmel. In the center of town, concrete sidewalks were being built along both sides of Ocean Avenue for six blocks and for a block or so in either direction on some of the cross streets, particularly Lincoln, Dolores and San Carlos, and most stores and businesses were located in those few dozen blocks.

In November 1931, the Oakland Tribune commented on this reputation, under the headline "Carmel Battles On"

> Carmel annually gets national publicity by doing no more than discussing the subject of the advisability of having a Chamber of Commerce. As a place which enjoys a wide reputation because of its persistent efforts to ward off the manners and activities of the busy world, Carmel has grown from a cluster of cottages by the sea to a place of size and importance.

> While there are those cruel enough to say the fight against modernity is in reality the calculated method of genuine "live wires" to attract attention, those who know the community of art and culture are aware of the sincerity behind the campaign. It so happens Carmel is situated on the beautiful Monterey Peninsula, has blue waters, white sands, grotesque cypresses, and most interesting inhabitants. When it seeks to hide so many lights under a bushel, the resulting confusion only attracts added attention. Carmel may do without a Chamber of Commerce, but it cannot escape the facts and incidents which will turn footsteps in that direction. (Oakland Tribune, November 13, 1931)

January–May 1932

In early January 1932 in Portland, the Neah-Kah-Nie Quartet played a concerto concert with the Portland Symphony Orchestra under the direction of Willem van Hoogstraten. Susie Pipes and Theodore Sorenson performed the Bach D Minor Concerto for Two Violins, Michel Penha performed the Boccherini B-flat Major Cello Concerto, and Sorenson and Abraham Weiss played the Mozart *Concerto in E-flat Major for Violin and Viola*. It was satisfying repertoire, not too advanced for a local orchestra, but gratifying solo showpieces for the Quartet members.

One month later, on February 8, 1932, the Neah-Kah-Nie Quartet made their (public) Carmel debut, as the second event in the Carmel Music Society's season. On the forestage of the former Theatre of the Golden Bough on Ocean Avenue, the Quartet began with Beethoven's String Quartet Op. 18 No. 5, and then played four short pieces by Reinhold Glière and Ernest Bloch. After intermission they were joined by French pianist Robert Schmitz for César Franck's *Piano Quintet in F Minor*.

> For freshness of tone, warmth and vigor of climaxes, for friendly sparkling joyousness—I have not heard their equal in Carmel. They are sound in technique and ensemble, but they possess a quality that transcends finish and professionalism,... I can only describe it as a red-headed enthusiasm of tone that matches the hair of the first violin. (Pine Cone, February 11, 1932)

The Denny-Watrous Gallery was busy in March. There was a recital by Rose Florence, a West Coast singer who billed herself as a "mezzo-contralto." That month also saw one of the few theatrical productions presented in the Denny-Watrous Gallery.

John Galt Bell (1899–1949) was an actor and director who had family ties to Carmel. In his college days at Berkeley, Bell had taken part in a production of *The Drunkard*, a serious piece of temperance propaganda written in 1843 by W. H. Smith for P. T. Barnum. In late February at the Gallery, Bell directed and produced eleven performances of the play, and the production was a huge success. In July 1933, Bell and his friend Preston L. Shobe mounted a Los Angeles production of *The Drunkard* that ran there for thousands of performances over a period of twenty-six years.

DENNY
WATROUS
GALLERY
OPPOSITE POST OFFICE   CARMEL
PRESENTS
ROSE FLORENCE, MEZZO-CONTRALTO
TOMORROW SATURDAY NIGHT, FEBRUARY 13 AT 8:30
TICKETS $1.00 ———————————————— RESERVED $1.50

"THE DRUNKARD"
OLD MELODRAMA, 1846
GALT BELL   DIRECTING CARMEL CAST
FRIDAY, SATURDAY, SUNDAY NIGHTS, FEBRUARY 19, 20, 21 AT 8:30
ADMISSION $1.00 ———————————————— RESERVED CHAIRS $1.50

Courtesy of the H. M. Williams Local History Department, Harrison Memorial Library; and the Carmel Pine Cone.

In March the Gallery hosted a large exhibit of handcrafts from the Allied Arts Guild of California in Menlo Park. That was followed by a three-week show of photographs by Edward Weston, his third exhibit at the Denny-Watrous Gallery.

In March, the Carmel Music Society presented the great British pianist, Myra Hess. She was 42 and at the peak of her career. Then, as if as an April Fool's joke, the Society went from the famously sublime to the apparently ridiculous: the avant-garde dancer Harald Kreutzberg. An anonymous reviewer in the Carmelite went on at some length about what was lacking in the Kreutzberg own dancing, at least when compared to the marketing hype that had preceded him. The review ends with these words.

> "The redeeming feature of the program was the company of four dancers who owe their tutelage to Kreutzberg and who without pretension, without fanfare, are more than ordinary dancers. Sincerity shone through their work in such contrast to Kreutzberg, that I found myself wishing that he would remain offstage and

Harald Kreutzberg photo from a 1934 program book. *Courtesy of the author.*

> allow the girls to carry on the program. It reached the point where instead of seeing a consummate artist immersed in his art, I saw a strange little man chasing imaginary butterflies. It was reasonable to expect more—much more—of Kreutzberg, but his Carmel audiences did not get it. Anyway, I did not like him." (Carmelite, April 7, 1932)

"...a cultural and educational project..."

In March, Marie Gordon and the Wednesday Morning Music Club gave a peek at their 1932 Summer Festival of Music. The first concert would be the Pro Arte Quartet from Belgium, who were in residence that summer at Mills College, near San Francisco. The second concert was tentatively announced as a chamber opera such as Purcell's "Dido and Aeneas" presented by

Dr. Ian Alexander's ensemble from Berkeley. The third concert would feature a trio of local performers—tenor, cello, and piano. It was hinted that the fourth concert would be something important, but no details were offered.

Meanwhile, Dene Denny (no longer the Carmel Music Society's president) made a proposal to the Society that changed everything and ultimately made it necessary to write this book.

While the Neah-Kah-Nie Quartet was in Carmel for their February concert, Dene had proposed to them a summer residency during which they would play several concerts and hold open rehearsals. The quartet accepted, with the provision that the final concert of the series be a re-creation of the concerto program they had enjoyed playing in January in Portland. The three concertos required an orchestra, and Michel Penha promised to provide at least 20 players from the San Francisco Symphony, to be augmented by locals if needed.

On March 23, Dene met with the Music Society board and formally requested that the Society sponsor the summer music activities of the Neah-Kah-Nie String Quartet. As the manager of the Quartet, Dean presented a five-point proposal:

1. The Neah-Kah-Nie String Quartet would make Carmel its 1932 summer rehearsal headquarters;
2. The quartet would present four concerts, in one of which they would play concertos and be accompanied by an amateur orchestra to be formed locally;
3. The concerts would be presented at popular prices with special student ticket rates;
4. The quartet and the orchestra would have open rehearsal hours to which season-ticket holders would be admitted;
5. No financial or managerial responsibility would be assumed by the Carmel Music Society. The Music Society would be listed as a sponsor, but the "Denny-Watrous Gallery" would produce and manage the series of events and assume all financial liability.

The "amateur" orchestra mentioned in bullet point #2 above was an idea that occurred to Dene after the Quartet left town in February. She waited until her proposal to the Music Society had been approved by the Society's board before sending a telegram to Michel Penha that must have surprised him:

> *"Don't worry about the San Francisco musicians. Your orchestra is here. Dene Denny."*

This proposal, at last, was a project the Carmel Music Society could support. The following resolution was unanimously passed by the Board:

> Whereas there is a possibility that the Neah-Kah-Nie Quartet will make Carmel its summer rehearsal headquarters, the Carmel Music Society, recognizing this is a cultural and educational project, is glad to lend its name and sponsor the quartet's music activities as outlined. (CMS minutes)

The Carmel Music Society was moving forward in a steady and orderly way, because from the beginning it was the thoughtful effort of the members of a structured group. The Music Society board had thirty members at that time, with seven officers and six committees. An arts organization that is dependent on just a few people—administratively, artistically, financially—has little foundation on which to build its continuity and longevity. The "Wednesday Morning Music Club" was really not a club: Although she had boosters in the local press, it was Marie Gordon who did virtually all of the work to produce the series: securing the venues, selecting the schedule, booking the performers, creating the publicity, raising the money. It had been three years of valiant and resourceful work, and she had done it mostly by herself. Only after three seasons, just before her fourth summer, did she form what was described in the Pine Cone as a "tentative advisory board" of a half dozen Carmel residents. But it was too late—even after three seasons, the Wednesday Morning Music Club still had not established a foothold in the community.

Learning of the Neah-Kah-Nie plan for the summer, and perhaps seeing the writing on the wall, Marie Gordon met with the Music Society board on April 13 and gave it one more try. She asked the Music Society to "sponsor the merit and value of the Summer Festival of Music," stating that she had already booked the concerts, and no financial obligation was to be assumed by the Carmel Music Society. A quorum was not present and no decision was made, but a special meeting of the Directors was called on April 19, and "after careful consideration the following motion was passed and communicated to Mrs. Gordon":

> The Board of Directors of the Carmel Music Society recognizes the value and merit of the Summer Festival of Music but considers it unnecessary to sponsor an organization with a record of three years of successful achievement and a strong representative board of its own. (CMS minutes)

The Carmel Music Society Board had made a similar decision the year before in declining to partner with Marie Gordon for the Brosa String Quartet concerts. Because the Carmel Music Society was governed and run by its Board, and because at the very outset it had established organizational guidelines and a clearly stated vision, it had wisely turned down these earlier proposals, regardless of their short-term attractiveness.

By contrast, the Carmel Music Society's March 23 resolution to support the five-point Neah-Kah-Nie Quartet plan was the most important vote the Music Society had ever taken. By choosing to produce a summer experience that involved not only concerts, but open rehearsals and community involvement, the Board had put the elements in motion that would lead directly to the Carmel Bach Festival.

Marie Gordon and her supporters were understandably disappointed. She had continued to hope for some cooperation with the Carmel Music Society, but a partnership with the Music Society would benefit only her, there was no advantage in it for the Society. Marie Gordon's 1932 Summer 1932 Festival of Music did in fact happen, although it was somewhat different from the original plan. The chamber opera did not take place. The first concert was the local vocal-cello-piano trio, the second concert was listed as a "Carmel artists' concert" (there is no further coverage of it in the press), and the third concert was London's Pro Arte String Quartet.

Summer 1932

1932 and 1933 were the darkest years of the Great Depression. In 1929 there were 25,000 banks, and in 1932 there were 11,000. More than 25% of the workforce—12 million people—were out of work, and manufacturing output had dropped by more than 50%. Food riots broke out in Detroit and elsewhere. The Dust Bowl had begun, too, and destitute midwesterners were "migrating" to California. In this time of trouble and hardship, Dene Denny and Hazel Watrous brought joy into the community by creating an orchestra.

"Your orchestra is here"

Carmel-Bound

The Neah-Kah-Nie String Quartet, which is making Carmel its summer rehearsal headquarters and giving a series of four concerts in latter July and August, arrives next Wednesday. The Quartet goes immediately to Carmel Highlands where it has rented the Rowntree house for the summer.

Open rehearsal hours, to which season-ticket holders to the concerts will be admitted, will begin at an early date. Try-outs for the amateur orchestra concert will be held this month. First and second violins, violas, 'cellos, oboes, double bass, and French horn will be used.

Interested musicians should communicate with Dene Denny for a place in this event. Michel Penha will rehearse the players but Henry Eichheim is coming from the South to conduct. (Pine Cone, June 3, 1932)

There is no record of Michel Penha's reaction to Dene's telegram back in March informing him that, "Your orchestra is here," but he seems to have been an incredibly good sport about working with amateurs. He had been expecting to solo in a concerto accompanied by his reliable (and first-rate) colleagues from San Francisco, but suddenly he found himself in charge of auditioning and training a new orchestra of local non-professionals. Here was a brilliant musician, Stokowski's principal cellist, who found himself at the beginning of June sitting with Dene Denny in the Denny-Watrous Gallery listening to auditions by amateur musicians from Carmel, Monterey, Pebble Beach, Pacific Grove, Seaside, Salinas, and Watsonville.

While all this was happening in June, the Denny-Watrous Gallery hosted another series of concerts by American pianist and composer Richard Buhlig. The first evening was a concert of Bartok and Copland, the second was a lecture on J. S. Bach's abstract composition "The Art of the Fugue," and the final concert was a performance of that great work on two pianos played by Buhlig and Dene Denny. According to several scholarly chronicles, this was the first performance of The Art of the Fugue west of Chicago.

Another two-piano recital took place at the gallery later in June by the wonderfully named duo of Phillidda Ashley and Aileen Fealy.

On Sunday evening, June 24, 1932, the Neah-Kah-Nie Quartet held its first open rehearsal in the Denny-Watrous Gallery. They began work that evening on the Schumann Piano Quintet, for which they would be joined in the July 30 concert by the British pianist Harold Bauer. Until his arrival, the pianist for the rehearsals was Ralph Linsley of Pasadena. Linsley was a frequent chamber music colleague of Penha's and became a long-standing and important member of the Carmel Bach Festival.

The open rehearsals of the orchestra began the following night in the Gallery, and continued two evenings each week through August. Throughout the summer, the orchestra is given no official name.

This orchestra created an enormous community enthusiasm for music, and what made it a success from the very beginning was the open rehearsals. Season tickets ($4.25 and $3.00) included the four summer concerts and nearly thirty rehearsals at the Denny-Watrous Gallery that summer, twice weekly for the quartet and twice weekly for the orchestra. Folding wooden chairs were set up in the Gallery for an audience that often overflowed out into the street. Average attendance was 150, and people arrived an hour or more early to be assured of a seat. It is impossible to overstate the importance of the open rehearsal experience to the great success of all that happened at the Gallery between 1932 and 1935.

> How we used to pile into Denny-Watrous those summer nights! We'd come out blind and saturated with music and have to walk it off before attempting to go home to bed. (Marjorie Warren recalling in 1939 the first open rehearsals at the Gallery. Carmel Cymbal, July 14, 1939)

The following is most of an article written at the end of June, after the orchestra's second rehearsal.

"Musical America in the making"

> I wish everyone who cares for music as a real part of living could look in at the Denny-Watrous Gallery on a Monday or Thursday evening. From all parts of the Peninsula come men and women, young and old, to play their various instruments under the direction of Michel Penha. They realize what a privilege it is to work under such a fine musician as Penha, and those of us who look on know what fun they are having. Three great concerti they are rehearsing:—Bach, Mozart, and Boccherini, and at the final concert they will play under the baton of Henry Eichheim, for many years associated with the Boston Symphony and famous as a composer and conductor.
>
> It is thrilling to see the enthusiasm of this improvised orchestra and I happen to know that groups are practicing for hours daily,—for instance the earnest afternoon rehearsals in the Falkenberg home in Pacific Grove, made up of Beth and Marion Falkenberg, Billy Dickinson, Marion Knowles, Margaret Lial, and Molly Darling. The students are getting something from this ensemble that no amount of solo work could give them, and I feel that the community cannot adequately express its appreciation to Mr. Penha for his generosity in making this possible.
>
> This orchestra, which has grown out of the Neah-Kah-Nie Quartet's summering in Carmel, and is a feature of the second concert of the series, is one of the most significant things that has ever happened in Carmel, because it is the culmination of the work that is being done in our primary and secondary schools. The Civic Orchestra has become almost a national movement. Here is musical America in the making. Why talk of wonderful dreams for the future when we have this real opportunity here now. (Carmelite, June 30, 1932)

On July 1, an editorial in the Carmelite took one more opportunity to bemoan the "division of endeavor in musical activities" in Carmel between the Music Society and Marie Gordon's summer series. It regretted that the Music Society, heretofore active only from September through April or May, had now staked a claim to the summertime as well. The editorial portrayed the situation as a careless act of self-interest, with no regard for all the effort Marie Gordon had put into her summer series: the clear message was that the situation had been stable and cooperative, the relationship had been cordial, but then the Carmel Music Society had wrecked it.

But in fact it was not merely a conflict of schedules and dates, it was a conflict of ideals and vision. The Carmel Music Society did not wreck the concert situation in Carmel, they fixed it. Marie Gordon's Wednesday Morning Music Club, like the Monterey Peninsula Symphony Society before it, was based on the old model discussed above. They were run by just a few people, and they existed from season to season without a vision for the future. All they wanted to do was put on concerts.

But Dene and Hazel did not want simply to entertain their audiences in the summer of 1932, they wanted to change the community through music.

Redfern Mason, San Francisco music writer, visited Carmel and attended an orchestra rehearsal.

> Michel Penha is enjoying himself hugely and doing a good work in drilling the instrumentalists of the country for 20 miles around into an effective amateur orchestra. I attended a rehearsal and so did half the music-lovers of the community. The orchestra worked on two beautiful numbers, the Bach Double Concerto for violin and the little-known Double Concerto by Mozart for violin and viola. Penha is an excellent director and drill master. He knows just what he wants and his quiet humor helps him greatly in getting his own way. Of course, there will be a concert; but even if there were not, I think the joy of making beautiful music under the guidance of one who knows would repay the players a hundredfold for their labors. This orchestra would seemingly be an impossibility if it were not for the presence in the community of the Neah-Kah-Nie Quartet. (San Francisco Chronicle, August 2, 1932)

One analogy for a little startup orchestra of amateurs like this would be the so-called talking dog in the circus sideshow. The dog of course makes dog noises that sound like human words, and it's mildly amusing but meaningless. However, if such a dog actually were able to speak, the event would be so remarkable that it would be petty to find fault with the dog's grammar or syntax.

Many locals who heard the 1932 orchestra filtered their memories positively over the years, others did not. A few years later, one of the original orchestra members recalled the orchestra's sound in August 1932, as "...an unbelievable cacophony." Another listener remembered,

> ...those nights when the first rather febrile voices of the embryonic Monterey Peninsula Orchestra could be heard wailing up and down the avenue ... (Carmel Cymbal, July 14, 1938)

But the emotional effect of an orchestra of one's friends and neighbors, led by a charming and charismatic conductor, was such that listeners could easily overlook the shortcomings. As one of the author's teachers once said in a similar situation: "The orchestra did the best it could, and the audience imagined the rest."

The Summer Series opened on July 30 with the Neah-Kah-Nie String Quartet and British pianist Harold Bauer. The program began with a Mozart string quartet, then Bauer played solo works by Bach, Gluck, and Chopin, and a piece written for him by Ravel. Bauer, in his early 60s, was one of the senior concert pianists on the international scene, and it was an artistic coup to engage him for this opening concert. The program concluded with Schumann's *Piano Quintet Op. 44.*

The second concert of the Summer Series was the debut of the new orchestra, and Henry Eichheim had been invited from Santa Barbara to conduct. Born in Chicago in 1870, he had a distinguished career as composer, conductor, violinist, and ethnomusicologist. He was one of the first American composers to bring the sounds of Asian-Pacific instruments into Western orchestras. A traveling companion on one of his research trips to Fiji and Bali was his good friend Leopold Stokowski, who recorded Eichheim's "Japanese Nocturn" with the Philadelphia Orchestra in 1929. Eichheim also was an early advocate of contemporary French composers including Debussy, Ravel, and Fauré, in the United States. After 22 years as violinist with the Boston Symphony Orchestra, Eichheim settled in Santa Barbara, California, in 1922 and died there two decades later.

On August 9, with Eichheim on the podium, the Neah-Kah-Nie Quartet repeated the concerto program they had performed in Portland seven months before: Bach's D Minor Concerto for Two Violins; Boccherini's Cello Concerto in B Flat; and Mozart's Concerto in E Flat for Violin and Viola. The members of the quartet played in the orchestra when they were not soloing. The Pine Cone reserved its highest praise for Michel Penha's playing of the Boccherini Cello Concerto.

> It was great playing. The player became the cello itself. His own spirit spoke from its strings. The listener forgot his technique and became transported for a time beyond the music and into the fountain out of which it sprang. Only a true creator can thus transform himself and his instrument into the music itself so as to carry the spirit purely forth to the listeners. (Pine Cone, August 12, 1932)

As always with such community orchestral endeavors, especially in the startup phase, one gives praise and encouragement carefully, and the press was gentle with the orchestra by basically not alluding to how it actually sounded, except to mention that the musicians were all able to get louder and softer at more or less the same time. But the overwhelming message of all the press coverage was that—regardless of the playing—it was a very uplifting and inspiring event for everyone present. One week after the concert, Dora Hagemeyer wrote of...

> ...the spirit which has been born among the music lovers of Carmel. They have caught fire, and the Neah-Kah-Nie Quartet is the heart of that fire. (Pine Cone, August 19, 1932)

An anonymous "Appreciation" appeared in the same issue of the Pine Cone, ending with these words:

> In almost every amateur performance, a sensitive auditor sits on the edge of his chair, hoping against hope. This time there was such a sense of real power confined within its proper limits that one relaxed, and enjoyed, knowing intuitively that all was well. And the open rehearsals have been a marvelous means to this rapport between players and listeners. Perhaps we do not yet realize how significant they are. Thank you, Music Society; you are on the right track. (ibid.)

Allen Griffin included these words in a Monterey Peninsula Herald editorial:

> The development of this group of people, nearly all of them amateurs, from the struggle of note-playing together to the accomplishment of harmony in orchestration, marks one of the finest things ever done here, a really spectacular achievement when the time

element is considered. Penha was the magician; for last night's performance of the Monterey Peninsula Orchestra was a beautiful and magical thing. (Monterey Herald, August 10, 1932)

The Neah-Kah-Nie String Quartet presented the third concert of the Summer Series. They began with Bach—an arrangement for string quartet of five movements of one of J. S. Bach's orchestral suites. After three short works by living composers: Amilcare Zanella, Antonio Scontrino, and Roy Harrison, the concert concluded with Brahms' Piano Quartet, with pianist Ralph Linsley once again.

The fourth and final concert of the 1932 Summer Series, on August 23, was the most eclectic of all four. It began with 20th century Italian songs by Respighi and Pizzetti for soprano and string quartet, sung by Claire Upshaw. Michel Penha performed one of Bach's six suites for solo cello, but the printed programs give no clue which one. After intermission, Michel Penha and Dene Denny performed the *Sonata for Cello and Piano Opus 4* by the Hungarian composer Zoltán Kodály. It is a two-movement work lasting about 18 minutes, and a wonderful virtuoso showpiece for both players. The concert concluded with *String Quartet in D-flat* by Ernst von Dohnanyi.

Hal Garrott's review was published two days later, and in his long article he lauded the quartet, the concert series, and Dene Denny:

> After producing several times as many musical events as all other agencies put together, Dene Denny found time to appear on the farewell Neah-Kah-Nie program in the cello-piano sonata by Kodaly. Miss Denny has been working day and night, presenting one brilliant concert after another to record audiences. On top of all this she was able to perform the piano part of an exacting modern composition, with impeccable virtuosity and musical understanding.
>
> Perhaps it is just this musical understanding that enables Dene Denny to select performers and programs of such sound artistic value. Her ability to lure recognized virtuosi to play to the small audiences in the Denny-Watrous Gallery for the love of doing it, is a tribute to her standing with the profession. (Pine Cone, August 26, 1932)

For her performance with Michel Penha, the Carmelite also had special words for Dene:

> The last concert of the Neah-Kah-Nie String Quartet series brought to a close <u>one of the most valuable musical seasons Carmel has ever had</u>. The concert was assisted by two outstanding artists, Dene Denny and Claire Upshur. Dene Denny belongs to Carmel. She has kept alive the fire on the altar of progress in all forms of art. She refuses to cling to the past. She is always on tiptoe with her eyes on far horizons. If at times she seems to perceive a vision which to many seems more uncertain than the beauty of the past, we have learned to respect that vision.
>
> ...Dene Denny is a significant figure in the playing of modern music. In order to play the music of one's own age is necessary to be identified with such music. It is not often that the spirit of today find such a vital interpretation. There is power and virility in Dene Denny's playing. She does not seem to play the piano but rather to lift something vibrant with the meaning of this adventurous age. (Carmelite, August 26, 1932)

R. M. Hollingsworth caught the spirit of the summer in an article in the Monterey Peninsula Herald:

> It is one thing to enjoy the world's greatest artists for one brief performance and quite another to live, musically speaking, with an organization of the caliber of the Neah-Kah-Nie String Quartet for an entire summer... With modesty and simplicity they individually and collectively preached the musical gospel... with the result that we all became a great big musical family... thus combining a social feature with the tremendous educational advantages derived from frequent hearing of works to be performed. (Monterey Herald, September 2, 1932)

"this fervent band of amateurs, in tune with the infinite (if not always with each other)"

The experience of the orchestra rehearsals had been such a positive one that people did not want it to end, and Dene and Hazel apparently had been confident that this would happen. The contract with Michel Penha and the quartet kept them in Carmel through August and the beginning of September, but this fact had not been made public. Thus Dene and Hazel now could make the surprise announcement that Michel Penha would conduct one more "unscheduled concert" at the end of August, and the orchestra rehearsals would continue twice weekly. The repertoire for the concert was Mozart's *Jupiter Symphony* (probably one or two movements), an unnamed work by Greig, and a repeat of the Bach and Mozart concertos from the August 9 concert. (They could not perform the Boccherini cello concerto again, because Penha was conducting.)

The concert took place in the Denny-Watrous Gallery, and Dene and Hazel somehow managed to fit the orchestra and 200 listeners into that space. The Pine Cone's Hal Garrott described the Gallery on the evening of August 25:

> 200 happy sinners crowded into the Denny-Watrous Gallery for the final Neah-Kah-Nie farewell, and found salvation in a soul-stirring program. The local chamber orchestra under Michel Penha's wand worked miracles. This fervent band of amateurs, in tune with the infinite (if not always with each other), will continue to rehearse under a San Francisco conductor, whose name will be announced later. (Pine Cone, September 3, 1932)

This is the first mention in the press of the exciting news that the orchestra would not disband at the end of the summer. Michel Penha had agreed to serve as the orchestra's conductor for the coming twelve months, and had further agreed to select an associate to lead the rehearsals when he was on tour and unable to be there himself.

Although the Carmel Music Society had assumed no financial responsibility for the 1932 Summer Series, they now offered material support by providing funds to pay Michel Penha's fee as conductor. The summer events had generated the enthusiasm, and the Music Society had engaged the conductor. It was now only a matter of keeping the project alive. All other orchestras established on the Monterey Peninsula over the previous twenty years had played one or two concerts and then ceased to exist. The Carmel Music Society's financial support of Michel Penha at this point enabled the Monterey Peninsula Orchestra to survive and flourish. The community did the rest, as Dene and Hazel had hoped.

"The rehearsals did it."

Susan Porter wrote frequently for the Pine Cone in the 1930s, and her articles are both historically valuable and enjoyable because she usually attempted to write about the experience—for all present—rather than merely describe what happened "on stage." August 1932 marks a turning point in the history of classical music in Carmel. In early September, Porter recalled that summer of music, and her article is given here in its entirety. It is a wonderful description of the enthusiasm awakened by Dene and Hazel's first Summer Series, and also of the deep affection the community had developed for both of them.

A Musical Awakening

The quartet has left. The concerts are over. A lovely thing has ended. But we had it, that lovely thing, and we knew while we had it that it was lovely. And whether or not next summer brings it to us again, we know that we are different because of it, and so is Carmel. And so, for some of us, is music.

You who know music cannot guess the wistfulness of us others who hang about the walls of the temple watching the worshipers enter. And now we have been taken as far as the outer court of the temple and have begun to understand why you worship, and that is something.

The rehearsals did it. When we heard music repeated week after week, when we saw it as we might see a structure, built up before us, we began to wake and to become aware. A new thing quickened… And we flocked, all of us, to those rehearsals!

All ages came, and their faces in the softened light had the same look, and became quiet and beautiful as they listened, all touched with the same feeling. A new solidarity was revealed. And the young creatures went home in the darkness singing bits from Bach and Mozart instead of that awful hit song last summer, whatever it was…

A great deal has happened and will happen in that Denny-Watrous Gallery that we have grown to love so. Pictures and sculpture and talk, music and singing and dancing and talk, new ideas and old purposes and talk. In the old days we talked under the pine trees on Ocean Avenue and settled our destinies and planned our plans and fought our fights. The pine trees are too full of automobiles now, and we come — do we realize how naturally? — to the Gallery.

There is always someone there, animated and responsive. There is a quick bit of discussion, and eager bit of planning; something kindles and takes hold. Here is a new artist with a portfolio; here is Edith Dickinson talking Music Society plans; Henry Cowell comes in, looking as if the world had just been created and he had been there to see it; Lincoln Steffens saunters in and a remark seems to saunter out from his mouth so softly that one does not know one has been hit. Someone has a poem, someone wants only to sit still for a moment and watch and think. They are all at home in the Gallery and they are finding there, in a new guise, something they had loved in old Carmel, and that they had feared was lost for ever when old Carmel turned new. (Pine Cone, September 10, 1932) [Emphasis added.]

"The Carmel Plan"

The Neah-Kah-Nie String Quartet bid farewell to Carmel in mid September, but not before they had reached an agreement with the Carmel Music Society that placed the quartet at the center of the Society's 1933 winter and summer seasons. Their presence in Carmel was a perfect expression of the Music Society's vision of combining music and education to benefit the community.

The Music Society announced that the Neah-Kah-Nie Quartet would be based in Carmel for five months in 1933—February, March, June, July, and August. During February and March the quartet would not hold open rehearsals, but while they were in town the violinists and violist of the quartet would play in the orchestra. During the summer season, the quartet would play three concerts and would hold regular open rehearsals in the Gallery.

As a further part of this plan, Michel Penha would continue to conduct the Monterey Peninsula Orchestra (the new official name) in weekly rehearsals beginning in September, and an associate of his choice would rehearse the orchestra in his absence. Explicit in the plan was the intention of attracting musicians to Carmel from all directions.

Music Society Adopts The Carmel Plan

What will eventually become known as "The Carmel Plan" was adopted at the regular meeting of the Carmel Music Society Tuesday night. Undoubtedly this plan will be used by other communities. It is destined to make Carmel even more famous than it is, as well as more musical and more prosperous. Instead of paying out huge sums to over-night soloists at the rate of $1,000 a night, the society unanimously decided to spend the money in Carmel, where it will enrich our everyday life, as well as our merchants and property owners. There will be two other concerts in the winter season by outside soloists, for the benefit of those who feel that, to be a great virtuoso, an artist must hail from Paris, London, Budapest, or Timbuktu. (Pine Cone, September 17, 1932)

$6 **winter season**

CARMEL MUSIC SOCIETY
SIXTH ANNUAL SEASON - - 1932-1933

PROGRAM

WINTER SEASON:

1 January 14 _____ Vienna Boy Choir

2 February 4 _____ Michel Penha, 'Cellist

3 February 25 _____ Monterey Peninsula Orchestra

4 March 25 ____ _____ Austral, Mezzo-Soprano
with Amadio, Flautist

SUMMER SEASON:

5 June 16 _____ Pro Arte String Quartet

6 June 30 _____ Pro Arte String Quartet

7 July 15 _____ Neah-Kah-Nie String Quartet

8 July 29 _____ Monterey Peninsula Orchestra

9 August 5 _____ Neah-Kah-Nie String Quartet

10 August 19 _____ Neah-Kah-Nie String Quartet

11 August 26 _____ Monterey Peninsula Orchestra

All Concerts to be Given in the Sunset School Auditorium

summer season $6

Season Seats may be selected now from chart at Denny-Watrous Gallery, Carmel

Courtesy of the Carmel Music Society.

The Pine Cone's enthusiasm notwithstanding, there were a few members of the Music Society board who did, in fact, "...feel that, to be a great virtuoso, an artist must hail from Paris, etc." There were just a few, and their names are not referenced in the press, only a mention that several important individuals had withdrawn their financial support. It seems not to have mattered to the Society, and was never mentioned again.

The same Pine Cone article concluded:

I predict a brilliant future for The Carmel Plan, which offers tremendous value for every dollar the community spends on music. The Carmel Music Society has shown initiative and vision in adopting a revolutionary policy that promises so much. Carmel will gain a superbly trained orchestra composed of our own and neighboring musicians. The public will be admitted to rehearsals at least once a week — and it is at rehearsals that musical knowledge is gained. During five months of the year we will have for our neighbors the four splendid artists composing the Neah-Kah-Nie Quartet, and benefit by their influence.

We will have eleven major concerts during the year, seven of them by the same musicians who attracted the largest and most enthusiastic audiences in the history of the village at sunset auditorium this summer. Perhaps best of all, the series will be offered at popular prices. What more can one ask! (ibid.)

The concert season

The "1932-1933" Carmel Music Society season actually began in January 1933, and the Music Society leveraged this by offering an eleven-concert season, available in two parts: Winter Season, $6; Summer Season $6; or all eleven concerts (when purchased in advance) for $11. Single tickets were $1.75 and 50¢.

The following paragraph is from the Society's ticket brochure, released in October, 1932.

Entering upon its sixth year, the CARMEL MUSIC SOCIETY announces an enlargement of its scope, in keeping with its original intent. Retaining the outstanding characteristics of previous years, in which artists of the highest rank have been presented, the forthcoming season will include a series of chamber music concerts by visiting and resident quartets, three concerts by the Monterey Peninsula Orchestra and open rehearsals under the direction of Michel Penha. In embarking upon this program, the directors have been guided by the experience of the past summer, when it was shown that the membership of the society and the public at large desire not only to hear music, but to participate, in the broadest sense, in its making.

The open rehearsals in the Denny-Watrous Gallery continued to be a central part of the Music Society's plan. Only season ticket holders could attend the winter rehearsals, and even they had to pay an admission fee of 10¢ per rehearsal. From September 1932 through August 1933 there were thirty open rehearsals in the Gallery, and the Neah-Kah-Nie Quartet or its members were involved in nearly all of them. After viewing the ticket brochure, the ever-effusive Hal Garrott did the math:

Forty-one musical events at less than twenty-five cents (after deducting tax)—think of it! Forty-one Carmel nights—almost one each week for a year—not only rescued from boredom, but raised to Olympian heights of inspiration and joy! This is what the Carmel Music Society is offering for the coming season.

The Music Society is asking eleven dollars for eleven formal concerts by world celebrities and thirty rehearsals at which many of these celebrities will appear. The rehearsals are fully as enjoyable as the final concert and of greater musical value. Often one hears the artist go over a piece several times. He hears the critical comments of orchestra conductor and quartet leader. When he attends the final performance his enjoyment of the music is enhanced by familiarity with its content and an understanding of its beauty. Personally I prefer rehearsals to finished recitals, and great compositions cannot be heard too often.

At rehearsals one becomes acquainted with the stars, listens to their wit and wisdom, their keen musical criticism. One gathers their point of view and the composer's, senses what effects they are striving to attain. Even in practice a great artist's performance is a dazzling affair. Much of the greatest playing in the world occurs informally at rehearsals. (Pine Cone, October 3, 1932)

Carol Weston

The popular open rehearsals were about to begin once again, following the announcement of the new Associate Conductor, Carol Weston. She was born Carol Goebel in San José in 1891, but by 1900 her (American-born) father had de-Germanized the family name to Weston. Her mother, Ella Herbert Weston, was the western booking manager for the Ackerman and Harris vaudeville circuit and she promoted her child prodigy with great commitment. ("Legit" classical performers, especially young ones, appeared in vaudeville as edifying moments of culture amid the comedy and other entertainments.)

By age nine, "Carrie Weston, girl violinist," was making vaudeville appearances as far away as New York City. (In order to maximize the length of her girl violinist's career, Carrie's mother seems to have arranged for Carrie to be nine years old for three consecutive seasons.) She was 13 when she performed in one of San José's leading theaters and received this notice:

"The new vaudeville bill at the Victory Theater is proving entertaining to the patrons of the house.... Carrie Weston plays a violin solo, sings "Girl with a Baby Face," with a French accent, and dances. She does the latter the best. Her violin solo is marred by the accompanist. If she would ask the pianist not to play, her performance would be more effective. In fact if the pianist would not play at all during any of the acts it would improve the entire entertainment." (San José Evening News, June 22, 1904)

Carol Weston. *Courtesy of Bernard Chevalier.*

Carrie became Carol, who graduated from Notre Dame Academy in San José and the University of California at Berkeley, and then studied for a year in Europe with the great Leopold Auer, the teacher of Mischa Elman, Jascha Heifetz, and Efrem Zimbalist. Soon after returning to California she was hired as music director for Camp Curry, a popular tent and cabin summer resort in Yosemite Valley. She directed entertainment every night on the camp stage, with an eight-piece orchestra, vocalists, a comedian, and other performers. Back in San Francisco she led the orchestra of the Pantages Variety Theater for a season before heading to New York for more theater orchestra work. Such was the nature of the music business in those days, that in her early 20s—as an experienced, European-trained classical soloist and orchestra leader—she still made vaudeville appearances (playing classical music, with no singing or dancing) including New York's Hippodrome Theater, where she was no longer "Carol Weston, Girl Violinist." The name of her act was "Moments Musicales."

By the time Weston came to Carmel to conduct the new orchestra in 1932, she already had considerable experience leading San Francisco area orchestras, and was the principal violinist and leader of Henry Cowell's New Music ensemble, and violin soloist in Stravinsky's *L'Histoire du Soldat* at the Denny-Watrous Gallery in September 1931. There are several mentions in the press at that time referring to her as the only female "director" west of Chicago. (When referring to an individual who leads an orchestra—either with a baton or while playing the violin—"director" was a common synonym for "conductor" in the early 20th century.) She was president of the Berkeley Violin Club, a lecturer on music appreciation for the San Francisco Symphony, and the teacher of the violin instructors' class at Mills College.

Carol Weston. *Courtesy of the author.*

Carol Weston spent her life in San Francisco as violinist, conductor, and violin teacher. Her students remember her not so much as a rigorous teacher of technique, but as a passionate advocate of emotional expression in music. A few recall her dashing around the city in her Karman Ghia convertible, and what an ardent San Francisco Giants fan she was. Carol Weston died in Mill Valley, California in 1969 at the age of 78.

The rehearsals

Orchestra rehearsals began on September 18, 1932, with Michel Penha. Beginning October 2, Carol Weston took the train or drove to Carmel every weekend, rehearsed the orchestra in the Gallery for two or three hours on Sunday evening, and returned to San Francisco on Monday.

In addition to Weston, one other professional had been engaged: concertmaster Mildred Sahlstrom-Wright. She was born in Berlin and began her musical studies there. As a teenager she moved with her family to Minneapolis, and after graduating high school she returned to Europe and studied in Berlin and Prague. For the past several years she had been teaching at the University of California at Berkeley, and in 1930 she bought a house in Carmel. Sahlstrom-Wright was a teacher of violin technique and her guidance helped the string players live up to Carol Weston's desire for interpretive enthusiasm.

After only five rehearsals, the orchestra offered an evening of music at the Denny-Watrous Gallery on October 23. In a brief advance notice in the Pine Cone, the Music Society referred to the event as "the first special open rehearsal."

> Sunday evening sees the first special open rehearsal of the Monterey Peninsula Orchestra since the close of the summer season under Michel Penha. Noel Sullivan, bass, will sing two arias from Mozart's "Magic Flute," especially orchestrated. In addition the orchestra will play Mozart's "Kleine Nachtstucke" [sic] for strings, and the first movement of Schubert's "Unfinished Symphony." Carol Weston, associate director of the orchestra, will conduct. The Sunday evening program will be in no sense a formal concert. The

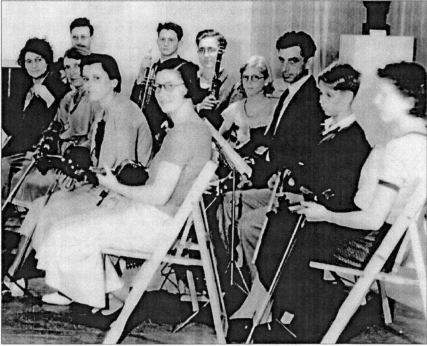

Courtesy of the H. M. Williams Local History Department, Harrison Memorial Library.

See first page of Part Four for the complete photo.

usual routine of rehearsals will continue, but the occasion will be somewhat special on account of Mr. Sullivan's contribution to the evening. Admission has been fixed on a nominal basis, the proceeds to be used in paying for music needed for the orchestra. (Pine Cone, October 21, 1932) [Note: tickets cost 10¢]

On the opposite page are three details of a photograph taken at a rehearsal on the evening of October 17, 1932, one week before the concert. Carol Weston stands in the center, and seated to her right is Mildred Sahlstrom-Wright of Monterey, the (paid) concertmaster. This was Weston's third Sunday evening rehearsal as the new associate conductor.

At this orchestra's first two concerts in August under Henry Eichheim and Michel Penha, the members of the Neah-Kah-Nie Quartet played in the orchestra when not soloing, and three or four other professional string players joined in as volunteers. But in this photograph, there are no professionals other than the concertmaster and the conductor, and everyone except the conductor is a local resident.

One of the two youngest players in the photo is cellist Beth "Ducky" Falkenberg (age ten), the dark-haired girl seated third from the left in the upper photo. The Schubert symphony movement begins with a lyrical passage for cellos alone, and Ducky played that beautiful melody in the concert, together with Doris Fee (seated to Ducky's left) and Max Hagemeyer, age ten (not visible). Fenton Foster is standing in the back with his double bass. As always in this orchestra's early years, a grand piano is in the very center of the group, to play the parts of instruments not present, and sometimes just to help keep things together.

This is a rare photo taken inside the Denny-Watrous Gallery on Dolores Street. Several prints are displayed on the wall, and at the far left is a stack of folding wooden chairs. Extension cords have been strung across the floor to power extra lights for the photographer and probably for the musicians.

The Pine Cone reviewed the event. Note the "Chamber Orchestra" reference.

Capacity Crowds Laud Concert of Local Orchestra

The Monterey Peninsula Chamber Orchestra and Noel Sullivan are popular attractions in Carmel. Sunday night every seat in the Denny-Watrous Gallery was taken long before the concert began. Additional chairs were rushed in and placed on the stage, and so close to the musicians that few dared to use their bow arms freely for fear of hitting a spectator.

At 8:30 the sign "Standing Room Only" went up — and still they came! To the regular concert faces were added the unusual physiognomies of the town's elite, and a strong representation from "Who's Who."

The orchestra more than lived up to the public's high expectation. Carol Weston, associate conductor in the absence of Michel Penha, is an inspiring leader. No pedantic time-beater of the German school, but a flaming spirit communicating liveliness with every gesture.

The program was difficult. The finely drawn melodic lines of the Mozart "Eine kleine Nachtmusik" are as transparent as glass. A daring feat for an amateur body of recent vintage to attempt so revealing a number!

Carol Weston. Press photo 1930. *Courtesy of the Carmel Music Society.*

Noel Sullivan's sonorous bass followed in two arias from Mozart's Magic Flute with string orchestra. Mr. Sullivan is the first vocalist to appear as soloist with the orchestra. Never before have I heard Mr. Sullivan to better advantage. Evidently the audience agreed.

By this time, one might consider the performers were had reached the high point—but no. During the intermission Dene Denny in a speech of congratulation to the musicians announced the final piece de résistance. Nothing less, if you please, than the first movement to Schubert's Unfinished Symphony! No mere chamber orchestra could play this great work and here is where our amateur body emerges from the chrysalis, spreading its wings as a <u>full-fledged symphony</u>. (Pine Cone, September 28, 1932) [Emphasis added.]

The success of the "Special Open Rehearsal" added even more momentum to the orchestra, and Carol Weston rehearsed the group every Sunday night through November, December, and January in preparation for concerts that she and Michel Penha would conduct in January and March.

Apparently no one in town had the energy for another big musical event before the end of the year, and there was no Messiah or Christmas concert at the school auditorium or the Golden Bough. The music lovers of Carmel were waiting for the Vienna Choir Boys to open the Carmel Music Society season in January, and the for return of the Neah-Kah-Nie Quartet in February.

1933

The first concert in the New Year was given by the Monterey Peninsula Orchestra on January 6 in the lounge of the San Carlos Hotel in Monterey. Under the direction of Carol Weston, and with no apparent coverage in the press, this was the orchestra's fourth public appearance:

I. Max Bruch: *Violin Concerto* - Marilyn Doty, age 10
   (perhaps one movement, or an arrangement)

II. J. S. Bach: Suite (unspecified)

III. Schubert: *Unfinished Symphony*, first movement

IV. Beethoven: *Egmont Overture*

The Carmel Music Society's Winter Season opened one week later with the Vienna Choir Boys (Die Wiener Sängerknaben). The varied program concluded with their famous performance of "Bastien und Bastienne," a tiny opera written by Mozart when he was only twelve. The Vienna Choir Boys returned to Carmel in 2004 on the Carmel Music Society Series.

On January 29, the Neah-Kah-Nie Quartet arrived in town for their two-month stay, and moved into a rented house just south of town in Carmel Highlands. Penha took over the orchestra rehearsals from Carol Weston, who had been leading the weekly rehearsals for five months. Michel Penha continued to rehearse the music by Mozart, Handel, and Beethoven that would be heard in the orchestra's upcoming Carmel Music Society concert. Quartet members Hubert Sorenson (second violin) and Abraham Weiss (viola) played in the orchestra. Mildred Sahlstrom-Wright continued as concertmaster. Susie Pipes was experiencing health problems and did not take part in the orchestra rehearsals.

On February 25 Michel Penha played a solo recital at the Sunset School auditorium, with pianist Ralph Linsley. The new auditorium was a little more than a year old, and already musicians and listeners were commenting on the hall's acoustical problems and dead spots. Penha had experimented with his setup for the recital, and decided to place his chair and music stand on some kind of low wooden box or packing crate, something that might act as a sympathetic resonator and reinforce the sound of the cello. By the time of the concert, a suitable wooden box had been custom-made for him by one of the most loyal supporters of music in Carmel at that time. The names of Henry Dickinson and his wife Edith appear often in the proceedings of music in Carmel throughout the 1920s and 30s. Henry played the flute in the Monterey Peninsula Orchestra. Both were founding members of the Music Society, and Edith was the third (and the current) President of the Society. The Carmel Pine Cone praised Henry Dickinson's ingenious construction:

> One of the evening's masterpieces, deserving of a place on the program, was Henry F. Dickinson's soundboard device which transformed sunset auditorium into an acoustically perfect concert hall. (Pine Cone March 3, 1933)

(For the next seven decades, Carmel audiences and performers coped with their "acoustically [im]perfect" auditorium.)

Penha Enthralls Large Audience With Cello Art

Michel Penha has voiced his desire to make the Monterey Peninsula his permanent home; to enter into its musical culture as one who would stimulate all youth to appreciation of music and encourage in every possible way those talented ones whose love of music finds its expression in playing.

Alice Sumner Greene
Courtesy of the author.

Scholarly director, sensitive ensemble artist, masterly virtuoso, Penha is indeed a bright meteor and fortunate in his landing field. One of the joys of hearing him is that the most difficult and spectacular passages are played with that swing of assurance which makes them appear easy. Penha and his cello pulsate in such harmony that the man, the music and the instrument seem inseparable. Certainly he is master of the technique of his medium, alert to the broadest comprehension of its literature, and alive with the warmth of musical emotion which results in rich tone. (Monterey Herald, February 27, 1933)

Penha's desire to live in Carmel was personal as well as professional. Architect Charles Sumner Greene and his family lived in Carmel in a beautiful home Greene had designed and built. In 1932 and 1933 there were musicales and rehearsals at the Greene home, and Michel Penha met and married one of Greene's daughters, Alice Sumner Greene. Known as "LaLa," she had two children by a previous marriage. It is amusing to consider that Penha's Carmel in-laws and friends had taken to calling Penha "Mickey." After a few years, LaLa, Mickey and the children moved to Pasadena, but until the end of the decade they maintained a residence in Carmel.

On March 11, as part of the Carmel Music Society Concert Series, Michel Penha led the

Monterey Peninsula Orchestra in its fifth and most ambitions concert, featuring two major concertos.

Monterey Peninsula Orchestra Concert #5

March 11, 1933, Sunset Auditorium, Michel Penha, conductor

I. Mozart: *Serenade for Strings* (4 movements)

II. Handel: *B Minor Concerto for Viola* – Abraham Weiss

III. Beethoven: C *Major Piano Concerto* – Ralph Linsley

IV. Beethoven: *Egmont Overture*

The orchestra was not a large ensemble, and had no trouble fitting onto the relatively modest stage of Sunset Auditorium. There were 28 players onstage (including all of the original 1932 members): 14 violinists, 4 violists, 3 cellists, 1 double bass, 1 flute, 1 clarinet, 2 trumpets, piano, and harmonium (a small pump organ powered by foot pedals). The piano and harmonium filled in for missing instruments. Ralph Linsley was the pianist (within the orchestra) throughout the concert and also the soloist in the Beethoven concerto. Likewise, Abraham Weiss soloed in the Handel viola concerto, and played in the viola section for the rest of the concert.

Michel Penha caricature. Pine Cone, March 7, 1933. Artist unknown. *Courtesy of the H. M. Williams Local History Room, Harrison Memorial Library, and the Carmel Pine Cone.*

Abraham Weiss, violist of the Neah-Kah-Nie Quartet, had fallen in love with Carmel and was planning to move there. The Carmel audiences in turn loved his tone and warmth of expression.

Pianist Ralph Linsley had been brought to Carmel by Penha in 1932. He was based in Pasadena, and was a highly respected accompanist, or in today's usage a "collaborative pianist." It's worth having a special term for it, because it is a specialty that many fine concert soloists never master. Linsley was one of the surprisingly few pianists who can play concertos and solo recitals and also play chamber music or accompany a vocal or instrumental soloist. Again and again, one reads of Ralph Linsley's gentle, self-effacing manner, from which emerged great moments of artistic fire onstage. He weaves his way through the rest of this book as a performer at the Carmel Bach Festival.

The March 11 concert lived up to its advance publicity. Here are some excerpts from a half-page review in the Monterey Herald.

"New Peninsula Orchestra Scores Another Triumph."

Laughter and tears came near mingling at Sunset School Saturday night when our new orchestra made its most recent public appearance. The large audience was thrilled by the "youngsters'" achievement, and deeply touched by the earnestness of effort.

Appreciation of the cultural value of the Monterey Peninsula Orchestra to its community was voiced on every side. Parents of young musicians felt unable to express their gratitude for such an organization in our midst. A mother wants to know in what other city, of any size, a lass or lad in their early teens could play in an orchestra with such artists as sat on the platform Saturday night, or under the direction of Penha?

Commendation of Penha's work was universal — his stirring leadership, the color and shading he achieved, fullness of effort with limitation of instruments, courageous choice of a difficult program — Mozart's Serenade could trick even old-timers. General rejoicing is felt over his promised return in June. (Monterey Herald, March 14, 1933)

The reviewer also noted listeners' comments in the lobby after the concert, including:

"The old-timers of Carmel inaugurated plays and then went to sleep. Meanwhile along came a new fledgling and sneaked up on them and suddenly, bang! Almost miraculously here is a Symphony Orchestra, right here amongst the pines of the seashore, playing Beethoven, and beautifully, too."

"Very well and solidly done. Of course there were many makeshifts in the way of instruments, the harmonium pinch hitting for the woodwinds. Considering the lack of physical material and the shifting personnel it was really an extraordinary concert."

"Perhaps the fullest enjoyment of the delightful program came to those who had witnessed, at the weekly rehearsals, gradual approach to the finish and brilliance of the final performance." (ibid.)

The Carmel Pine Cone praised Ralph Linsley:

Ralph Linsley's performance of the Beethoven C Major Concerto for Piano and Orchestra brought down the house. After four recalls the audience reluctantly permitted the program to proceed, though they would gladly have listened to Linsley all over again. This delightful pianist possesses a simple beauty of tone, a clear, immaculate technique, free from mannerism or any suggestion of ostentation.

After such playing many of us feared the orchestra was facing an anti-climax in its final number. But such was not the case. In a spirited performance of Beethoven's Egmont Overture, the Monterey Peninsula Orchestra rose to the high spot of the evening, making the concert incontestably its own. There was richness and the volume in the violins, colorful contrast between string and wind choir, effective shading, expertly built crescendos and diminuendos, and a dramatic interpretation that told the tragic story behind the music.

This concert scores a high mark in the musical history of Carmel and promises brilliant achievement for the coming season. Meanwhile the orchestra will gather in the Denny-Watrous Gallery a week from Sunday night to continue rehearsing under the baton of assistant conductor Carol Weston. (Pine Cone, March 14, 1933) [emphasis added]

The same writer had special words for Michel Penha:

> When Michel Penha appeared last year in Carmel, he was a distinguished visitor, a celebrity stopping with us for a limited season. Last night as he stepped forth to direct our orchestra we claimed him as our own — one of us. Some way must be found to keep this dynamic person on the peninsula even if we have to resort to prayer! What he has been able to accomplish for the community in so short a time is nothing less than amazing, and to whom is owed a greater depth than to him who brings our potentialities into their expression? Last night's program was beautiful — a musical triumph, offering in one evening the mushroom orchestra and two gifted young soloists. (ibid.)

Penha led one more orchestra rehearsal, and then he and the Neah-Kah-Nie Quartet departed from Carmel. They gave a two-week series of concerts at International House on the Berkeley campus, and then returned to Portland.

On March 25 the Music Society offered the fourth and last concert in its winter season: Florence Austral a noted Wagnerian soprano. Born Florence Mary Wilson in 1892, she had changed her last name to Austral in honor of her native Australia. In 1925 she married the Australian flautist John Amadio, and they toured widely together. Seven years later she would retire at age 48 after a long battle with multiple sclerosis.

Susie Pipes also was experiencing health problems and was becoming intermittently unable to play, and this—plus the end of their financial subsidy—forced the quartet to make a difficult decision. On April 23, 1933, the Portland Chamber Music Society presented a concert featuring the Opus 26 and 60 piano quartets of Brahms, both of which call for violin, viola, cello, and piano. Hubert Sorenson, Abraham Weiss, Michel Penha, and Ralph Linsley were the respective performers, and Susie Pipes did not play at all. At the end of the concert, Susie stepped forward, thanked the quartet's supporters and audience, and announced the end of the Neah-Kah-Nie String Quartet.

Susie Pipes continued to promote chamber music in Oregon, but she played less and less. By the early 1940s Susie had retired, and she died in 1950 at the age of 67. Hubert Sorenson eventually moved to San Francisco where he was active in chamber and orchestral music. He played in the Carmel Bach Festival Orchestra in 1936, and was a member of the San Francisco Symphony from 1955 to 1972. Abraham Weiss continued to be involved with Penha and Carmel for the next few years until he moved to Los Angeles for a freelance career. Although it existed for only about three years, the Neah-Kah-Nie String Quartet was a brightly burning artistic flame. Fortunately, it flourished at the perfect time to be an important part of the musical creativity in Carmel in 1932 and early 1933.

In June, publicity began to ramp up for the Carmel Music Society's 1933 Summer Series. The show would go on in Carmel, with largely the same cast of characters, but without the Neah-Kah-Nie Quartet. Instead, the concerts featured the Penha Piano Quartet: Nathan Abas, violin (former concertmaster of the San Francisco Symphony); Abraham Weiss, viola; Michel Penha, cello; and Ralph Linsley, piano. Concerts were in the Sunset School auditorium, and tickets were $1.50, $1.00, and 50¢. A season ticket cost $6, and included all seven concerts plus open rehearsal privileges. The open rehearsals continued to be a hot ticket.

Rehearsals of the quartet are open to ticket holders and take place on Monday evenings in the Denny-Watrous Gallery. Fans declare the rehearsals more fun than movies or baseball, and from the cars on Dolores Street on Monday nights and the throng in the little gallery, there are many who agree. (Pine Cone, June 20, 1933)

The Pro Arte String Quartet from Belgium was in residence at Mills College (near Oakland) once again, and they opened the summer series with two solid programs: on June 27 a conservative combination of Haydn and Beethoven, and on July 11 quartets by Mozart, Bartok and Ravel. The esteemed Pro Arte String Quartet was given a tastefully enthusiastic reception by the Carmel audiences. It was one of the great quartets in the world at that time, the official national quartet of Belgium, and had been playing together for 20 years. The Carmel reviews speak of "stately drama," "mature musicianship," and "seasoned approach." Nowhere in the reviews does one sense the kind of excitement that was being generated at the time by the "cacaphonous" local amateurs.

Finally, on July 25, came the third concert everyone was waiting for: the Monterey Peninsula Orchestra. In this concert Michel Penha left the familiar world of Mozart and Beethoven. He began with an early-18th century "concerto grosso" by Arcangelo Corelli, one of the so-called "Christmas Concertos." Corelli's concertos—for two groups of instruments rather than a single soloist and orchestra—are bright, harmonious, and playful, and great concert openers. The Corelli was followed by J. S. Bach's *Piano* [sic] *Concerto in D Minor*, with the distinguished English pianist Winifred Howe. After intermission, 11-year-old Miriam Sovoleff played the *Concerto No 4* by Henri Vieuxtemps (1820-1891). She omitted the third of the four movements; with its wild violin acrobatics it was out of reach of young Miriam. Penha concluded the concert with two movements of the *Caucasian Sketches* by Russian composer Mikhail Ippolitov-Ivanov (1859-1935). The "Procession of the Sardar" is a well-known concert favorite, with a rousing ending. Dr. R. M. Hollingsworth played the very prominent tambourine part and Roger Lee played the tympani.

In the fourth concert of the Summer Season, August 1, the Penha Piano Quartet made its Carmel debut, with Nathan Abas, violin; Abraham Weiss, viola; Michel Penha, cello; and Ralph Linsley, piano. They performed music by Beethoven, contemporary Czech composer Bohuslav Jirak, and Gabriel Fauré. Carmel was learning to love these musicians and what they brought to the community.

> Chamber music has been considered a gift of discrimination, but without question the reason its devotees have been limited in our land is due to lack of opportunity to really know the beauty of this music. Bringing chamber music to a community helps. Making chamber music IN the community stimulates the type of appreciation that follows musical education. Today this has become the larger aim of the Carmel Music Society and it is expressed in the Monterey Peninsula Orchestra and the Penha Piano Quartet. No visiting artists could have been greeted with greater enthusiasm then the audience at Sunset school last night bestowed the quartet, and we make no apology for that sentiment that responds with the added warmth to our own.

> Penha, Linsley and Weiss have lived with us and played with our amateurs and professionals until they are considered residents of the Peninsula. The concert was

one of the most enjoyable heard on a Music Society series and was so acclaimed by an audience that seemed of one mind in the matter. The triumph was not surprising since each member of the quartet as a musician of renown and distinction.

Abas [the violinist] has a full and vital tone which is at all times directed by a scholarly conception of the score. His technique is faultless. Weiss brings the viola to life as an instrument with a warm personality of its own and his work is as warmly received here. Linsley is a pianist whose tone and interpretation deserve increasing praise. His piano passages are clear as miniature bells and the fortes full of brilliance. Penha's cello talks as its master dictates, with a voice that speaks all shades of his emotional response to his music. The tone of his cello has a living vibrant quality. (Monterey Herald, August 2, 1933)

The Orchestra gave the fifth concert of the series on August 22, 1933.

I. Bloch: *Concerto Grosso*

II. Vivaldi: *Concerto for Violin in A Minor* – Mildred Sahlstrom

III. Beethoven: *Egmont Overture*

IV. Preston Search: *Cello Concerto* (premiere) played by the composer

V. Bizet: *Adagietto* and *Farandolo* from "L'Arlesiana"

> **Peninsula orchestra is playing an important part in the cultural life of the state**
>
> The final concert of the Monterey Peninsula orchestra was an overwhelming success — the crowded house was carried away with the feeling of pride and affection for the achievement of their own orchestra, and above all, for the leader, Michel Penha.
>
> At intermission, young David Hagemeyer [fifteen-year-old violinist] read a letter from the orchestra to Penha, after the conductor's second bow, pledging the support and affection of the members, and begging him to remain as their leader. Mrs. Henry Dickinson, president of the Carmel Music Society, spoke of the desire of the society to continue with the wonderful work of the orchestra, which in so short a time has developed so magnificently. She told of the heavy expense of carrying on with the work, and urged the support of the community. Miss Dene Denny asked for definite pledges of small sums to make the re-engagement of Penha possible, and several hundred dollars were pledged in the auditorium. Still more is coming in this week, and it looks as though the orchestra will be able to go on through another year. (Carmel Sun, August 24, 1933)

The Carmel Pine Cone acknowledged that a debt of gratitude was owed to the Carmel Music Society for its sponsorship. But, they added,

> ...to Miss Denny and her quiet but efficient coworker, Hazel Watrous, must go the full credit for the success of the Summer Series. It was they who assumed all the responsibility financially, did all the detail work which was a tremendous lot, and generously tendered the use of their Gallery for the rehearsals. The formation of the amateur orchestra was also their own idea and through their combined efforts the personnel of the orchestra was brought together and Mr. Penha was prevailed upon to coach them after the abandoning of his original plan to offer a symphonic concert with professional musicians from elsewhere.

If the perpetuation of this splendid nucleus is realized, this too must be accredited to the efforts of Misses Denny and Watrous and to the inestimable service of the dynamic and capable Penha by whose very personality a lot of immature players inexperienced in ensemble playing were welded into a most presentable chamber orchestra. Rehearsals of this body will continue every Friday night at the gallery under an associate of Mr. Penha, and he himself will when possible return to Carmel to review the progress of the orchestra, the outstanding purpose of which is to encourage and develop local talent whether in ensemble work or a soloist. (Pine Cone, September 1, 1933)

The Penha Piano Quartet closed the summer season on August 29 playing Brahms, Roussel, and Dvorak.

And so ended the second Summer Series of the Carmel Music Society. There was, however, one more concert of the Monterey Peninsula Orchestra, on September 23 in the Pacific Grove High School Auditorium. Billed as a "Pops Concert," it was made up of repertoire from previous programs: Mozart *Serenade*; Beethoven Piano Concerto with Linsley; Beethoven's *Egmont Overture*; excerpts from Bizet's "L'Arlesiana"; a piece by Spanish composer Granados; and Ivanov's boisterous *Caucasian Sketches*. This concert was the eighth public appearance by the Monterey Peninsula Orchestra since its debut in August 1932. After break, the Sunday night orchestra rehearsals began again in mid-October, once more under the baton of Carol Weston.

In early September 1933, Michel Penha announced the formation of a chorus in Carmel. He, Dene, and Hazel were beginning to plan a spring concert that would turn out to be a transformational experience for the entire Carmel community. Chorus auditions took place in the Gallery every day for a week, and the first rehearsal took place on September 13, with Michel Penha conducting and Alice Greene (LaLa Greene's sister) as piano accompanist. After Penha's departure, Fenton Foster led the weekly chorus rehearsals until early spring and continued to add to the chorus membership.

Fenton Foster was a Monterey businessman who had trained as a musician and played the double base. He had been involved in some of the early and fleeting orchestral experiments in Carmel, such the 1923 Arts and Crafts Club orchestra. In 1929 he conducted Sir John Stainer's oratorio *The Crucifixion* on Good Friday in Pacific Grove, and he led the performance of Handel's Messiah that opened the new Sunset School auditorium in December 1931. In the October 1932 photograph of the Monterey Peninsula Orchestra with Carol Weston, Foster is standing with his double bass by the rear wall.

Under Dene and Hazel's leadership, the activities of the six-year-old Carmel Music Society had clearly moved to a new level by September 1933. The Society had been founded in 1927 as a concert-presenting organization with educational and community enrichment goals as well. Six years later they were sponsoring an orchestra with year-round activities, and now they also had a chorus. Both ensembles were rehearsing weekly all winter under the direction of professional musicians who were paid by the Music Society (as was the orchestra concertmaster, Mildred Wright and the piano accompanist for the chorus). The weekly rehearsals were open to the general public for a 10¢ admission fee. Every Sunday at 8:00pm the sounds of the orchestra continued to spill out into Dolores Street, and now on Wednesday evenings the air would be filled with voices, too.

Penha's chorus—an ensemble of auditioned singers from throughout the region—occupies a very special place in Carmel: in 1935 this ensemble changed its name to the Carmel Bach

Festival Chorus, and as such today it continues to flourish as an all-volunteer group, just as it was originally conceived. This fine chorus of dedicated volunteers has been an important part of every Carmel Bach Festival season since the first opening night in 1935. This is the honor roll of the singers who were present on Sept 13, 1933 at the first rehearsal. (By March 1934, group had 75 members.)

> ### A Cappella Chorus A Reality
> The first rehearsal of the A Capella [sic] Chorus, directed by Michel Penha, was held in the Denny-Watrous Gallery last Wednesday evening, at eight o'clock. The following were present: Sopranos: Frances Schreiman, Florence Thrift, Kathleen Murphy, Vera Hunter, Julia Keith, Mrs. Sund; Altos: Estelle Koch, Grace Knowles, Marjory Pegrim, Gertrude Bardarson; Tenors: Andrew Sessink, Dr. R. M. Hollingsworth, Lieutenant Sund; Basses: Jo Klegg, L. C. Fischer, Ray Faulkner, Everett Smith. (Pine Cone, September 15, 1933)

In November, the Carmel Music Society opened its 1933-1934 season with the 42-year-old Russian violin virtuoso, Mischa Elman. He had become a naturalized American citizen ten years before, lived in New York City, and was one of the most celebrated violinists of his generation.

In mid-December, Fenton Foster led the chorus founded by Michel Penha in portions of Handel's Messiah at Sunset Auditorium, as he had done exactly two years before. Otherwise, December was a musically quiet month in Carmel, but 1934 would bring the town its most exciting musical event ever.

Carmel Winter–Spring 1934

In 1934 Hazel's mother, moved to Carmel. For the past twenty years Minnie had been living with her second husband, Elias Holden, in their house atop Russian Hill in San Francisco. Elias died in 1932, and Minnie—now nearly 76—could no longer live alone. Hazel and her sister, Zanetta Watrous Catlett, built a cottage on north Dolores Street in 1923 where Zanetta and her son lived for seven years before moving to San Francisco, but from the outset, the two sisters had intended the cottage to be a place where their mother might live in her old age. It was Minnie's home until 1940, when she moved across the street to live with Dene and Hazel for the final year of her life.

The Carmel Music Society opened its winter season with an evening of Spanish dance in January: Teresina and her troupe of dancers and guitarists.

A few weeks later, bass Noel Sullivan presented a solo recital at the Denny-Watrous Gallery, accompanied by pianist Elizabeth Alexander. He sang fourteen songs by Schumann, Brahms, Wolff, Mendelssohn, Gounod, and a half dozen American composers. Two of the songs were newly written by the 18-year-old Edward Harris, destined to become one of the most successful Hollywood and TV composers of all time. The poetry for those two songs was by Sullivan's friend, the African-American poet Langston Hughes.

Noel Sullivan and Roland Hayes at Sullivan's farm in Carmel Valley. *Courtesy of the H. M. Williams Local History Department, Harrison Memorial Library.*

In early March, the Music Society presented a solo recital by tenor Roland Hayes, one of the first successful African-American classical vocalists. Contemporary reports make it clear that Noel Sullivan sponsored the Hayes recital.

Sullivan was a vocal advocate of civil rights, and Hayes and poet Langston Hughes were among the many Afro-American artists who were guests at Sullivan's homes in Carmel Valley and San Francisco in the 1930s and 1940s.

The Stabat Mater

J. Fred Wolle, Director of the Music Department at the University of California at Berkeley, was the busiest conductor in the Bay Area between 1906 and 1909, with his professional University Orchestra and his huge "Bach Chorus." Dene Denny studied at Berkeley from 1903 until 1909, and lived in a sorority house adjacent to the campus for most of that time. She did not register for music classes at Berkeley, but the author enjoys imagining that Dene might have been in the chorus or the audience of Wolle's concerts between 1906 and 1909. (See "Bach in Berkeley 1906" in the Appendix for more about J. Fred Wolle and his activities at Berkeley.)

Among his many events was a special University concert with orchestra and chorus at the Hearst Greek Theater each April. For that annual concert, Wolle originally considered performing the same work every year: the *Stabat Mater* written by Italian opera composer Gioachino Rossini in 1831. Rossini's many great operas include the *Barber of Seville, Italian Girl in Algiers,* and *Cinderella*, and his *Stabat Mater* is written in the same operatic vein, filled with gorgeous melodies and dramatic color and expression. The work calls for orchestra, a chorus capable of singing well and in Latin, and four excellent vocal soloists (The soprano sings to high C, and the tenor to D.)

There are many compositions for orchestra and chorus that Michel Penha and Dene Denny— or vice versa—could have chosen for the Monterey Peninsula Orchestra's first choral concert. Good choices in English, Italian, German, French, or Latin were available: sacred works by Handel, Mozart, Haydn, or Schubert; Mendelssohn's *Elijah* or *St. Paul*; many Victorian English composers; et al.

For whatever reason, Rossini's *Stabat Mater* was the choice, and in January, the Music Society announced that performances would take place on March 29 in the Sunset School auditorium and the following night in the Pacific Grove High School auditorium.

> By March 29, when the Carmel Music Society presents the Monterey Peninsula Orchestra, Michel Penha conductor, in a super-performance of Rossini's *Stabat Mater*, every school child and every adult should be able to hum the then familiar airs.
>
> With the orchestra augmented to forty, patiently drilled by the indefatigable Mr. Penha, a chorus of seventy-five, prepared by Fenton Foster, and the four soloists, professionals from San Francisco, the production will be the biggest and most spectacular to date in the history of our Orchestra. (Pine Cone March 2, 1934)

How many performers took part? The actual printed program lists 32 in the orchestra, and 76 in the chorus. Also onstage were five or six uncredited professional string players from San Francisco and of course the four vocal soloists. This placed nearly 120 performers on the Sunset Auditorium stage, with the conductor's podium front and center.

Rossini's *Stabat Mater* calls for two soprano soloists, and in these concerts they were Marie Walman, a popular singer in the San Francisco area, and Calista Rogers, who had a busy West Coast career and was already known to Carmel audiences for her recitals at the Denny-Watrous Gallery. The tenor soloist was G. Marston Haddock, former Director of the Leeds College of Music in his native England, and currently an instructor at Stanford University in Palo Alto. Henri Shefoff, the bass, was a relatively new arrival on the music scene: a medical student in San Francisco, he and his voice had been discovered by several local opera companies. Gaetano Merola engaged him to sing a few roles at the San Francisco Opera in 1935, but he went on to become a physician and a member of the "California Rhythm Doctors," a group of musical M.D.s who performed in the 1940s to raise money for charity.

Robert Nagler (1893-1968) was the new concertmaster that spring, and he remained with the orchestra through summer 1937. Nagler was born in Montana to German immigrant parents, and returned to Germany to study violin at the Royal Conservatory in Leipzig. He arrived in California in 1923 and was active as a violinist and orchestra leader in theaters throughout the Pacific Northwest, including the Orpheum and Pantages vaudeville circuits. Vaudeville was fading, and by 1929 Nagler was living in Pacific Grove and playing with the Frederick Preston Search Trio at the Hotel Del Monte. Nagler later served on the faculties at Salinas Union High School and Washington Junior High School, and was a pioneer in bringing instrumental music into the rural schools.

As the concert approached, the entire town was buzzing.

> Oh Mum! The Stabat Mater is the 29th. And I refuse to miss that. If we left Ojai at four A. M. we could make it...
>
> (Letter from Valentine Porter to her mother, written from school about 300 miles south of Carmel. She was coming home for Easter vacation. In later years, Val Porter served as Carmel Bach Festival Administrator.)

The excitement is also evident in the Pine Cone's advance coverage of the concert, written like a Music Society press release. Two weeks before the concerts:

> Over teacups, bridge, and up and down the street, the talk is "Stabat Mater." City projects and school elections become of secondary importance as the date approaches of this most spectacular, eventful production of Rossini's "Stabat Mater" presented by the Carmel Music Society in the Sunset school auditorium on Thursday evening March 29 and in the Pacific Grove high school auditorium on Friday evening, March 30. (Pine Cone, March 16, 1934)

One week before the concerts:

> The high water mark in Carmel musical history will be reached Thursday night in Sunset Auditorium. I doubt whether San Francisco is capable of a finer presentation than the one to be presented in this village. In my experience I have encountered few orchestral leaders who surpass Michel Penha. As a drill master he is unsurpassed. The San Francisco Symphony was in better shape when Penha conducted its rehearsals than now.
>
> The thing this writer has been urging for years is about to take place — community participation in a musical event meeting the highest standards, conducted by a great leader, performed by recognized vocal artists and scores of thoroughly drilled resident musicians.

It lies within our power to start Carmel on its career as a music festival city. If you believe in building Carmel, advancing its prestige, attracting visitors and residents of the highest type, as well as profiting yourself by an inspiring evening, attend Thursday night accompanied by your family and friends. (Pine Cone, March 23, 1934)

As shown above, in the mid-1930s, the "Sunset School auditorium" was often referred to as "Sunset Auditorium," and this book will do so from now on. The mention of "festival city" in the last paragraph of the preceding Pine Cone excerpt is significant. After several false starts over nearly a decade, it seemed to many in Carmel that a music festival might finally be a possibility. This is made clear by the headline over the Pine Cone's review of the concert.

Stabat Mater Ushers In Carmel's First Great Annual Music Festival

With last night's performance of Rossini's Stabat Mater by more than 100 locally trained amateur musicians, Carmel stood upon the pinnacle of its musical history, a height hitherto undreamed of. Instead of contemplating the profound depths from which we have risen, our music lovers preferred to gaze upward to heights unscaled.

"Next year," announced Dene Denny, "Carmel will put on a Bach choral* with 250 voices and a full symphony orchestra. Tonight is only the first celebration of an annual festival destined to make our village as musically famous as Bethlehem, Pa. The outstanding Easter event on the Pacific coast will someday be the Carmel Music Festival." Dene Denny's predictions have a way of coming to pass, so we accept her words at face value.

The thrilling and colorful music electrified the great audience in Sunset auditorium. There was not a dull moment (though unavoidably a couple of hazardous ones) in Michel Penha's conducting. To keep 100 amateurs together is an achievement to tax the resourcefulness of any leader. To inspire such performers to rise above routine and produce music that lives, that touches the heart, that thrills, is the work of a great conductor.... (Pine Cone, March 30, 1934)

*(Dene's use here of the word "**choral**" refers to a chorus of singers, not to a musical composition. At that time, the term "choral" was used as a noun to denote a choir or chorus. Dene was familiar with this usage from her years in Berkeley and San Francisco. The "Berkeley Choral" was a large chorus formed in the 1880s which presented concerts for half a century. In its prime in the 1920s, it was a consortium of six adult choruses. Another example of the term comes from Lick-Wilmerding High School in the 1910s, where for several years Dene conducted the "L–W Choral," a mixed group (male and female) which sang at the school's musical, social and athletic events. In the quote above, Dene is imagining a 250–voice chorus, and it is joyous, enthusiastic, after–concert hyperbole.)*

But a "festival" lay at least a year in the future. There would be much planning and many changes until then. Meanwhile the Carmel Music Society continued the season with a return visit by the German pianist Walter Gieseking in April.

Abraham Weiss, violist of the Neah-Kah-Nie Quartet, opened his teaching studio in Carmel. He lived in Carmel for several years and played in the 1935 and 1936 Carmel Bach Festivals, before joining the Los Angeles Philharmonic and the Columbia Studios Orchestra in Hollywood.

The last notable concert of the spring season was a Denny-Watrous presentation at the gallery. On the evening of May 12, Michel Penha and pianist Ralph Linsley performed a program they had presented in Santa Cruz one week before. Penha played music by Frescobaldi, J. S. Bach, Saint-Saëns, Fauré, and Schumann. This was his final solo appearance in Carmel for two years.

> Celebrities as plentiful as raisins and a plum pudding made up the major part of the audience that crowded the Denny-Watrous Gallery last Saturday. The attraction was Michel Penha in a cello recital with Ralph Linsley at the piano. The program, like all of Penha's, possessed continuity and balance, and each selection was musically worthwhile. No other cellist equals Michel Penha in attracting Carmel audiences and holding them. (Pine Cone, May 18)

"...the women of Carmel..."

The concept of women of vision working together in partnership to bring joy and beauty into the world is a central theme of this book. In May 1934, at the end of the Carmel Music Society's seventh season, an unsigned item in the Pine Cone notes that the Society's achievements were originally conceived by, and continued to be managed by, women. The article is given here in its entirety.

> ### Great Artists Brought Here by Music Society
> In 1927 the music lovers of Carmel formed the Carmel Music Society and took a long step toward a goal that had been sought for years — the goal of bringing to town eminent artists in order that enjoyment and education might be had right at home. Carmel women have figured largely in this work.
>
> For the past seven winter seasons, an average of four important concerts have been heard each season, including some of the greatest living musicians, and results both cultural and financial have been far beyond the staunchest supporters' expectations. From just the booking of appearances [concerts], the Society has started fostering local music with its surplus funds, attention going particularly to the Monterey Peninsula orchestra which includes members from many communities.
>
> Meeting at first in the home of Dene Denny and Hazel Watrous, Mrs. Kluegel was elected president, to be succeeded by Dene Denny, who held office three years, Mrs. Henry Dickinson for two years, and the present head is Dr. R. A. Kocher [male]. Today the Denny-Watrous Gallery is the downtown headquarters for the Society, handling tickets, arranging programs and the like, and the two women are in direct managerial charge of both the Orchestra and the Penha Quartet. Intimate concerts are given in the Gallery, while the more ambitious evenings are held in the main auditorium of the Sunset School, and many times this roomy theater has been crowded to capacity.
>
> Three of the six officers of the Music Society are women, 22 of the 30 directors, and 162 out of 260 season members, thus showing that the women of Carmel have had important influence in organizing to secure music of the highest order, and in developing the already appreciative region into something unequaled for its size in the West. (Pine Cone, May 25, 1934)

Summer 1934

On May 18, the Carmel Music Society announced its Third Summer Series, and a special committee was formed to plan an aggressive door-to-door ticket drive.

> The Summer Season Committee of the Carmel Music Society met with fully 50 members present on Monday evening in the Denny-Watrous Gallery and mapped a sellout campaign for the series of concerts and other features of the coming months.
>
> The town will be divided into seven districts, each with its captain and lieutenants, and all persons contacted will be asked to become subscribers to this summer session. (Pine Cone, May 18, 1934)

The Summer Series included three concerts by the Penha Piano Quartet, one concert with the Monterey Peninsula Orchestra under the direction of Michel Penha, and one solo concert by an artist yet to be chosen.

In the press it's clear that the community knew that something very special was happening. This is Hal Garrott's lead editorial in the Pine Cone:

> ### A New Kind of Commerce Chamber
>
> If a prize were offered to the organization doing the most to foster the development of a fine art in a small community, it would not surprise me to see this prize awarded to the Carmel Music Society. Nor would it surprise music circles and centers big and little over the United States. The ones who would receive the surprise of their lives live here in Carmel, blissfully unaware of the magnificent achievement occurring right under their noses.
>
> In spite of numerous attempts, San Francisco has failed to support a first–class resident quartet. Carmel, with less than five one–thousandths of San Francisco's population, is supporting one. ... Enthusiastic reviews in the press, and numerous return engagements, prove the success of Carmel's resident quartet.
>
> Merchants who would ordinarily pay twenty–five to one hundred dollars annually for Chamber of Commerce service, would receive greater value by turning the money over to the Carmel Music Society.
>
> In scarcely three years time this Society has influenced enough big-time artists to live in Carmel to supply a season of concerts given exclusively by resident performers, concerts of such high quality they would pass muster in New York.
>
> Besides an outing in one of Nature's entrancing beauty spots, visitors to Carmel this summer will be offered musical entertainment and musical instruction unequaled except in a great metropolis. There will be three quartet concerts, a recital by an internationally known pianist who has toured most of the world and made a sensation in Chicago last year, and a program by the Monterey Peninsula Orchestra directed by Michel Penha who has had experience leading a great symphony orchestra.
>
> Besides these five major concerts, some 25 rehearsals of the quartet and orchestra will be open to holders of five dollar season tickets, one of the biggest five-dollars' worth ever offered.

Students will be admitted to play in the orchestra and receive instruction in ensemble playing for a small registration fee (those already in the orchestra excepted), and private instruction may be had in almost every branch of the art from literally scores of teachers.

The fame of Carmel as a music center has been carried to the corners of the earth by concert stars who have sojourned here. It is difficult to estimate what the movement fostered by the Carmel Music Society is doing for our city. Its benefits range from gains to businessmen for merchandise sold to a musical education for students attracted from all parts of the country. (Pine Cone, June 1, 1934)

A letter to the Pine Cone echoed those thoughts.

The Carmel Music Society has a great influence on the artistic and financial life of Carmel. The immediate plan of the Society will not only bring to Carmel artists of national renown, but it will rent our houses, buy our groceries and will contribute largely to the commercial prosperity of the village and its merchants. (Pine Cone, June 15, 1934)

After the great success of the *Stabat Mater* with Fenton Foster's augmented chorus of 75, thought had to be given to the next step for that group—maintaining such a large chorus was unfeasible and unnecessary. After a six week post-concert hiatus, word went out to the chorus members and to the community in May that once again auditions would be held at the Denny-Watrous Gallery during the first week of June. Not all of the chorus members returned, and Penha was able to choose the best of those who did. This established the precedent of holding annual auditions, an important process for any volunteer vocal ensemble.

In mid-June, the Carmel Music Society announced that Scottish pianist Winifred Christie would open its 1934 summer series, and it was no ordinary piano concert. In 1921, Christie's husband, Emmanuel Moor, had invented what was known as the Moor Double Keyboard Piano. Christie had performed on this instrument with major orchestras and conductors in Europe including Bruno Walther, and Wilhelm Mengelberg, and the previous season she had toured with the Boston Symphony Orchestra and given several recitals in Carnegie Hall. On the unusual and very large instrument she played Handel, Bach, Chopin and Debussy.

The second concert was the Penha Piano Quartet. When they had last played in Carmel, the violinist was Nathan Abas, former concertmaster of the San Francisco Symphony, and during the winter he had been replaced by the great Canadian violinist Kathleen Parlow. Just before the beginning of the summer Parlow was replaced by American violinist Theodore Norman, who had been working in Europe and had returned to make his home in Los Angeles. Once again the Pine Cone gets on board with advance publicity.

Brussels may have its Pro Arte String Quartet and London its London Quartet, but Carmel-by-the-Sea has its Penha Piano Quartet, now resident for the "Third Annual Summer Season," and we are satisfied that no visiting quartet, coming for an overnight concert, could possibly contribute what the Penha group is offering with its open rehearsals and annual chamber music series. Ralph Linsley, Theodore Norman, Abraham Weiss, and Michel Penha are in every sense summer Carmelites—they have all rented houses here and are an integral and vital part of our community life. (Pine Cone, June 29, 1934)

As always, the repertoire was a mixture of old and new: Beethoven, Saint-Saens, and several modern French works. After a hiatus of several years, Dora Hagemeyer had returned to the Pine Cone, and she reviewed the quartet's concert.

> The Penha Piano Quartet, in its first concert of the season, brought vividly to mind the fact that we have here among these pines the privileges of a great city without the noise and overcrowding. It seemed strangely clear that we in Carmel have something rare and fine in this quartet; something to be as sincerely grateful for as we are of our trees, our blue ocean and our hills. (Pine Cone, July 13, 1934)

In July, during the summer series but unconnected with it, soprano Calista Rogers returned to Carmel for three recitals at the Denny-Watrous Gallery accompanied by pianist Ralph Linsley. The first evening was Renaissance music, second evening Baroque, and the third was a program of German Lieder by Schubert, Schumann and Wolf.

Meanwhile the Music Society's Summer Series (or Season, or Session, depending on the writer) offered its third concert: the Penha Piano Quartet playing music by Schumann, Haydn and Brahms. Pianist Ralph Linsley played both the Summer Series concerts and the Calista Rogers recital series at the Denny-Watrous Gallery, and July was a busy month for him.

Hal Garrott had more to say about the audience than the performers.

> The remarkable thing about a Carmel Music Society concert is the audience. Other cities have distinguished resident artists, but, outside of university towns, I know of no audiences equal to Carmel's. The clever analyst credits the rise of ancient Athens to the intelligence of the average citizen. In this sense Carmel, too, is a sort of Athens. Backed by so remarkable a public, our village need set no limit to its artistic achievement....
> In three or four years Carmel's population has developed from a handful of summer concert-goers in the parlor of the Hotel La Ribera, to the largest audience I have ever seen anywhere to a chamber music recital, almost filling beautiful Sunset Auditorium. Our resident Penha Piano Quartet is worthy of this audience.... (Pine Cone, July 27, 1934)

Then began the run-up for the fourth concert of the Summer Series: the Monterey Peninsula Orchestra.

> When the Monterey Peninsula Orchestra gave its first concert three years ago, with no timpani, no French horn, no trumpets, no trombones, and a minimum of strings, it seemed an incredible achievement and so astounded and electrified the audience that the bravos and cheers could be heard a block away. On Tuesday evening the orchestra will give its annual summer concert and what Michel Penha has accomplished with weekly rehearsals three years ago can only be appreciated by hearing and judging for oneself. For the first time the orchestra will play a full symphony—the Italian Symphony of Mendelssohn. (Pine Cone July 27, 1934)

The orchestra had grown, and now included 16 violins, four violas, three cellos, double bass, two flutes, three clarinets, and pairs of French horns, trumpets and trombones. As always, a piano was in the orchestra to play along subtly and fill in for missing instruments. Theodore Norman, violinist of the Penha Piano Quartet, was concertmaster, Abraham Weiss was first viola, and Ralph Linsley was the orchestral pianist. Several professional wind and string players had been imported (as unpaid volunteers) from San Francisco, and as one journalist noted, the orchestra could no longer be considered amateur.

Memories of Rossini's *Stabat Mater* just four months ago were still fresh, and the excitement around the upcoming concert was enormous.

Let Us Crowd Sunset Auditorium to the Doors

The most important concert in Carmel's history will occur in Sunset Auditorium on Tuesday when the Monterey Peninsula Orchestra presents a program sufficiently popular to be enjoyed by anyone who has an atom of music in his makeup. By promoting this fine body the Carmel Music Society is doing more for the cultural and physical growth of our city than any Chamber of Commerce could. Musicians are flocking here from afar to attend our concerts, as well as for musical associations and contacts. Concert artists seek the prestige of a Carmel performance, and favor us at reduced fees to attain this advantage. Merchants profit financially, and all of us aesthetically, by this increase in our musical population. (Pine Cone, August 3, 1934)

The concert was another enormous success for the orchestra and the Carmel Music Society.

Miraculous performance of Monterey Peninsula Orchestra

The performance of the Monterey Peninsula Orchestra Tuesday night thrilled a large audience until it shouted bravo and recalled the players again and again. It is the closest this town has come to working a miracle. The miracle, really, was Michel Penha's conducting. When the baton is in his hand, there is not a dull moment. The players are vitalized and literally driven to dashing climaxes, or coaxed to lyric beauty of phrasing and colorful contrast. Michel Penha fairly tore his hair at times and pounded his stand, figuratively beating his players into a musical frenzy that moved the great audience to its depths. (Pine Cone, August 10, 1934)

The reviewer saved gentlest words for the chorus, which apparently was not yet performance-ready.

Carmel's new A Cappella Chorus was given a tryout before the intermission with four numbers, and one a hearty encore. The singers went on bravely and did their best. No doubt their performance was remarkable considering there were few rehearsals. The audience enjoyed it. But in my very humble opinion this group is not yet ready for a public appearance with so expert a body as the Monterey Peninsula Orchestra. (ibid.)

In actuality this brief summer appearance was just a carrot on a stick for the members of the chorus. Dene and Hazel understood that a music festival in 1935 would not be possible without core instrumental and choral ensembles already established and in place. The orchestra was on its way toward competence, and the chorus would have to catch up. By the summer of 1935, both ensembles needed to be capable of performing several entire concert programs within the space of a few days.

The 1934 Summer Series concluded with the Penha Quartet. They began with a Mozart Trio for violin, cello and piano, and then Abraham Weiss played a suite by Max Reger for viola alone. The quartet was joined by two additional violinists for the Ernest Chausson *Concerto for Piano, Violin, and String Quartet*.

After the final concert of the Summer Series, the Pine Cone took a moment to look back over the past several years.

In California there are many cities larger than Carmel. Yet I doubt whether any city in the state offers a finer season of concerts than in our little village by the sea. I know of nobody on the Pacific coast that equals our resident Penha Piano Quartet. To outdo it Elizabeth Sprague Coolidge is sending huge sums of money to Belgium to engage the Pro Arte String Quartet, under the mistaken notion that their playing in America will develop American music. But like everything else, music is developed by playing it ourselves, not by listening to others.

The efficient efforts of the Carmel Music Society, and the Misses Denny and Watrous, and the generous cooperation of our amateur and professional musicians, have made possible the brilliant season just ending. Plans for the future are, if anything, more ambitious than ever. If progress continues to equal that averaged in the last four years, Carmel will be as renowned for music as it has been in the past for great writers and painters. We need only recall several summers ago when Marie Gordon struggled to entice enough paid admissions into a hotel parlor to raise $10 for the soloist [at the Hotel La Ribera]. Two years later she was producing concerts in the [Arts and Crafts Club] Carmel Playhouse for audiences of 200, and then we graduated to the Golden Bough seating 400. Fortunately Sunset Auditorium was available to the 700 who sought admission when the Carmel Music Society took charge. (Pine Cone, August 24, 1934)

Post Script

For some, it may be hard to believe, but there were those in Carmel back then who protested and criticized the new auditorium in 1931 and 1932. They apparently wouldn't have minded a modest assembly hall, but believed that neither the town nor the school deserved such a large and grand auditorium. The Pine Cone review implies that the complainers are "ignorant" of the proliferation of concert events taking place in the school auditorium. It is a recurring problem: those who do not use a particular resource are unaware of its value to others in the community. The concert review excerpted above concludes with this line:

> So rapidly have local audiences grown, there are still Carmelites, ignorant of what has happened, who complain that Sunset Auditorium is too big for the town, and never should have been built. (ibid.)

Fall 1934

Dene Denny and Hazel Watrous had been in their Gallery on Dolores Street for nearly five years. It was a space formerly occupied by the Carmel Pine Cone, and now, in October 1934, the Newspaper and the Gallery were exchanging locations: the Pine Cone was returning to its former office space in the DeYoe Building on Dolores Street, and the Denny-Watrous Gallery was reopening in the larger Manzanita Building on San Carlos Street between Ocean and Seventh (the site of a Wells Fargo Bank today).

The Manzanita had been Carmel's first movie house. It was a wooden structure somewhat larger than their gallery on Dolores Street, with a larger stage, some theatrical lighting in place, multiple theater exits, more air and light, and more adjacent parking.

Dene and Hazel now had the potential to offer a wider variety of performing events. This move to a new location in no way diminished the importance of the Gallery to the community.

> A review of the history of the Denny-Watrous Gallery, since its foundation five years ago, shows it is a living Center for the musical and cultural life of Carmel. Its almost weekly attractions have made it possible for those living in the seclusion of a little town to share in such opportunities as are usually found only in a large city. (Pine Cone, September 21, 1934)

The article goes on to list a few of the events that took place at the gallery, all of which have been mentioned elsewhere in this book. Then the writer continues,

> ...It has been an adventure to follow these attractions, for every once in a while an entertainment quietly announced turns out to be something quite outstanding and remains in the mind as a memory of surprise and delight.
>
> But the most valuable thing the Denny-Watrous Gallery has done, from the point of view of Carmel, has been the founding of the Monterey Peninsula Orchestra, and the institution of open rehearsals of quartet and orchestra. So important did the activities of the orchestra and quartet seem, the Carmel Music Society offered to sponsor them, and the following year they brought them back themselves. [Note: "sponsor" means that the Music Society lent its name but gave no financial support in the first year.]
>
> For the Gallery there was endless work with little practical return— long hours and constant courage in the face of disappointments; faith and endurance without end. On the part of Mr. Penha, Mr. Linsley (who came a little later), Weiss and Sorensen and Norman, there was the great sacrifice entailed by the patient combining of their own superior art with a group of amateurs. The cooperation and friendliness with which the whole scheme was carried out was due mainly to the gallery and it is gratifying to hear that in the new place the work of the orchestra will go on.
>
> The new Gallery will open about the first week in October and on this occasion the many friends of Dene Denny and Hazel Watrous will take the opportunity of extending to them their sincere appreciation of all they have done for Carmel. (ibid.)

When Dene and Hazel opened their Dolores Street Gallery in January 1930, they had done so with an event for audiences of all ages—a puppet show. Now on October 7, 1934, for the opening of their new location, they chose something equally fun: a "Grand Show and Olio" by members of the cast of the *Drunkard* production that was currently enjoying a run at in San Francisco. An "Olio" is part of the wonderful tradition of the old American melodramas of the 19th century. After the play of the evening had concluded, the same performers then put on a show made up of songs, comedy and dance. The audience at the new Denny-Watrous Gallery heard all the best Olio acts from the San Francisco Troupe, including the 1890s bathing suit skit; a Bicycle Built for Two; and a comic pantomime of "Little Nell."

The show concluded with two silent films accompanied by music from the Gallery's old parlor organ: "East Lynne," and "The New York Hat" with Mary Pickford.

There were two shows that evening: to the tune of "Goodnight Ladies" the 7:00pm audience exited through the new large side doors, and the 9:00pm audience entered.

Just two days later, on October 9, an era ended with the death of a remarkable man. At the age of 78, J. Franklin Devendorf, the founder of Carmel, died at his home in Oakland. In 1902 he had filed the first real estate map of Carmel lots. The following year he entered into partnership with Frank Powers, acquired most of the land within the present city limits of Carmel, and formed the Carmel Development Company. It was Devendorf who first established the importance of trees in Carmel. In the early years he not only attempted to retain all possible existing trees, but he also had hundreds of new trees planted to beautify the town and help prevent erosion. Modern Carmel owes much of its beauty, personality and charm to the early vision of Frank Devendorf.

Following the raucous fun of the Olio on opening night, the Denny-Watrous Gallery presented the first concert of the winter musical season. Violinist Naoum Blinder, former concertmaster of the San Francisco Symphony, gave a recital with pianist Adele Marcus, who also played several solo works.

Marcus was a superb pianist who went on to a famous career as one of the greatest American piano teachers of the 20th century. Apparently, Pine Cone writer Thelma B. Miller thought that Marcus had played some solo pieces that were too physically strenuous for her. That can happen to a pianist of any gender. But Miller—herself a woman—suggests a solution that shows us how far the perception of female musicians has evolved since 1934.

> Miss Marcus stumbled into the common pitfall of women pianists; that of attempting numbers so big and so brilliant that the audience shares the tension aroused by performing an exhausting physical feat. There are some things which women pianists should never attempt; it is a small loss, since the literature is so rich with music in which the pensive feminine temperament finds full scope for expression. (Pine Cone, October 26, 1934)

Soon after the Blinder recital, the Carmel Music Society opened its eighth season with the famous Don Cossack Choir, one of the major ensembles that Dene Denny booked through Sol Hurok in New York. The rest of the 1934–1935 Music Society season featured world-renowned names: pianist Josef Hoffman, the Budapest String Quartet, and composer Igor Stravinsky playing a program of his own works.

The big news of the fall season locally was the departure of Michel Penha. He remains present in Carmel and in this story through the rest of the decade, but in September he announced that his touring schedule no longer left him time to direct the Monterey Peninsula Orchestra. Dene and Hazel needed to find a replacement, and Penha had someone in mind.

Ernst Bacon

Dene and Hazel made excellent choices in their professional colleagues. In the fall of 1934, as Dene later wrote, "Michel Penha's work called him away," and a new and inspiring leader was needed for the orchestra. Most of the music professionals brought to Carmel by Dene and Hazel to create and lead musical events between 1932 and 1938 were members of a community of first-rate musicians based in San Francisco. Penha, Eichheim, Weston, Bacon, and (soon to come) Usigli, all knew each other at least tangentially through the San Francisco musical scene. Ernst Bacon was well-known to all, and was a brilliant and logical choice as the conductor to succeed Michel Penha. After a two-month vacation, the Monterey Peninsula orchestra resumed rehearsals on November 2 with its new conductor on the podium.

A prolific, Pulitzer Prize winning composer, Ernst Bacon (1898–1991) wrote symphonies, an opera, works for piano, and more than 250 songs and instrumental works, and probably set more Emily Dickinson poems to music than any other composer. Bacon was born in Chicago, Illinois on May 26, 1898, one of four children. His father was obstetrician-gynecologist Charles S. Bacon. After receiving his medical degree, Charles Bacon traveled to Vienna to study with a distinguished Austrian obstetrician, and that doctor happened to have a beautiful daughter. That is how the former Marie Francisca Emile von Rosthorn, a descendent of the noble Esterhazy family of Austria, came to be living in Chicago with her American husband and four children. It was she who tutored her children in piano and made the entire family (including her husband) speak German every night at the dinner table. Anyone who spoke English was denied dessert. (Decades later, in 1935, native German speakers in Carmel commented on Bacon's pronounced Austrian accent when he coached the chorus in their German diction.)

While still an undergraduate at Northwestern University, Bacon wrote and published his first book, *Our Musical Idiom* (1917). Much later in his life he also published two notable essays in book form, *Words on Music* (1960) and *Notes on the Piano* (1963).

Bacon was a very gifted pianist, and after university and private training in Chicago he began his musical career in 1922 with solo appearances in Germany and the United States. In 1924, he moved to Vienna to study composition with Ernest Bloch and Karl Weigl and piano with Glenn Gunn and Malwine Bree. He also studied conducting with Eugene Goosens, who recognized Bacon's talent on the conductor's podium and at the piano and engaged him as assistant conductor of the Rochester Opera in 1923. While in Rochester Bacon also taught at the Eastman School of Music, the first teaching position in his long and distinguished academic career.

After a few years, Bacon headed west with his wife and two children and settled in San Francisco. An avid outdoorsman, Bacon joined the Sierra Club, where he met photographer

Ansel Adams, a trained musician who became a great admirer of Bacon's music. Bacon was best man at the wedding of Virginia Best and Ansel Adams, and he and Ansel remained lifelong friends and fellow mountaineers.

Adams later wrote to Bacon: *"You are like the clear dawn wind in the midst of the foul smogs of contemporary cultural decay."*

At the end of 1935, Bacon was named supervising conductor of the Federal Music Project in San Francisco. Because of his new time constraints, he resigned his Carmel musical obligations as of January 1936. Bacon worked with the Federal Music Project for several years, and then was named director of the School of Music at Converse College in Spartanburg, South Carolina. In 1945, he left Spartanburg and joined the faculty of Syracuse University, initially serving as director of the School of Music and then as "composer-in-residence" until his retirement in 1964. Ernst Bacon was married four times and had six children. He died at his home in Orinda, California, in 1990.

Ernst Bacon's sister Madi Bacon was also an important musical figure, and was particularly beloved in San Francisco. In 1948 she and Gaetano Merola founded the San Francisco Boy's Chorus, the first repertory children's chorus in the United States.

Although he plays a vital role, Ernst Bacon is part of this narrative only from November 1934 through December 1935. He had a long and distinguished career after that, and there is an enormous amount of information about him available online and in print, not to mention the many recordings of his music.

Ernst Bacon was such a prolific and multi-faceted composer, and his career so full and productive, that even a basic overview of his music is beyond the scope of this book. The author particularly recommends Bacon's wonderful songs for voice and piano, written in distinctively different styles as he moved through his long career.

The Ernst Bacon Society is a fine central resource for more information about this important figure in 20th century American music.

Visit their website: **www.ernstbacon.org**

Photos clockwise from opposite page: Library of Congress; Library of Congress; Carmel Bach Festival (Johann Hagemeyer).

CARMEL MUSIC SOCIETY PRESENTS ROSSINI'S

STABAT MATER

FOR ORCHESTRA CHORUS AND SOLOISTS
MICHEL PENHA————————CONDUCTING

THURSDAY SUNSET SCHOOL AUDITORIUM
MARCH 29 CARMEL————————AT 8:30
FRIDAY PACIFIC GROVE HIGH SCHOOL
MARCH 30 PACIFIC GROVE————————AT 8:00

1954

SOLOISTS: MARIE WALLMAN - - - SOPRANO
CALISTA ROGERS - - - SOPRANO
G. MARSTON HADDOCK - - TENOR
HENRI SCHEFOFF - - - - BASS

PROGRAM

GOOD FRIDAY SPELL FROM "PARSIFAL"————————WAGNER
STABAT MATER————————————————ROSSINI

I. Introduction, "Lord Most Holy"............... Chorus and Quartet
II. Aria, "Cujus Animam", Lord, Vouchsafe Thy Loving Kindness...Tenor
III. Duet, Power Eternal....................First and Second Soprano
IV. Aria, Through the Darkness .... Bass
V. Thou hast tried our Hearts.............. Bass Recitative and Chorus
VI. I Have Longed for Thy Salvation...................... Quartet
VII. Cavatina, I Will Sing of Thy Great Mercy .... Second Soprano
VIII. Aria, "Inflammatus", When Thou Comest .... First Soprano and Chorus
IX. Hear Us, Lord...................... Quartet, Unaccompanied
X. Fugue, To Him be Glory..................... Chorus and Quartet

---

MONTEREY PENINSULA ORCHESTRA

First violins: Robert Nagler, Salinas, concert master; Adele Bucklin, Leonard Cooper, Mafalda Guaraldi, Grace Knowles, Anne Mattsewez, Lyle Oje.

Second violins: Edna Lockwood, Leonie Arizala, Ernest Calley, Charles Frank, David Hagemeyer, Frances Maas, William Workman.

Violas: Abraham Weiss; Nancy Bragg, Geraldine O'Connell.

Cellos: Noel Marchant; Jean Crouch, Doris Fee   **Double Bass:** Fenton Foster

Flutes: Henry Dickinson, Dr. F. V. Randol   **Clarinet:** Arnold Chapman

Trumpets: Mrs. Jack O'Hanlon, Bud Todhammer, Gordon Bain

Trombones: H. Chandler Stewart, Percy Lee   **Bass Tuba:** Lynwood Dozier

Tympani: Roger Lee   **Harmonium:** Ralph Linsley

CHORUS————————————FENTON FOSTER DIRECTOR

Sopranos: Annie Anderson, Grace Bollinger, Alice Barnet, Grace K. Bazemore, Luella Clemens, Daisie Cowie, Ellen Eatwell, Emily Ferguson, Dorothy Green, Amelia Good, Marie Haley, Sophie Jean Hard, Baylor Hilton, Edith B. Hollman, Hannah Howard, Peggy Hunter, Barbara Ingham, Mabel Johnson, Alice Lee Keith, Verna D. Lillard, Mildred Lingscheid, Lois Martin, Grace Overly, Glenna Peck, Lucille Roberts, Frances Schreiman, Myrtle Stoddard, Margaret Swedberg, Esther Smith, Theda Shoemaker, May Sutliff, Pearl Thomas, Emma Winning.

Altos: Myrtle Arne, Betty Draper, Winifred France, Anne Greene, Emeline Hopkins, Mary B. Hurlbert, Estelle M. Koch, Louise Lovett, Constance Messenger, Edda M. Pappel, Sydney Robertson, Roberta Sutherland, Mary Wheldon, Maude Wentworth, Frances Wild, Grace Uhl.

Tenors: Leonard Abinante, Dr. Albert E. Clay, Paul M. Day, Charles M. Hall, Dr. R. M. Hollingsworth, Elgin C. Hurlbert, Howard Newbauer, Andrew Sissink, Walter Sutherland.

Basses: Noble Barter, Albert Campbell, John Draper, L. C. Fisher, Edward C. Hopkins, Charles T. Lillard, George Moser, Al Shoemaker, Chandler Stewart, Jr., Gordon Stewart, Everett Smith, Paul Taylor, Hollis Thomas, Paul Thomas, George H. Turner, Morris McK. Wild, Dr. W. B. Williams.

Acknowledgments: The Carmel Music Society expresses its deep appreciation of the courtesy and cooperation of the many friends of music who have helped to make this production possible, especially to O. W. Bardarson, Principal of the Sunset School, and the Sunset School Employees; Blue Bird Tea Room; Hugh W. Comstock; Curtis Candy Store; Home Food Shop; Homestead Cafe; Fenton Foster; G. A. Good Lumber Company; Charles M. Hall; Holman's Department Store; A. B. Ingham, Principal of Pacific Grove High School, and the Pacific Grove High School Employees; Misses C. and E. Kellogg; Hotel La Playa; Lial's Music Store; Charles T. Lillard; M. J. Murphy, Inc.; Old Cabin Inn; Clay Otto; Palace Music Company; Pine Inn; Rodgers and Dyke Pharmacy; Romylane Candy Store; Al Shoemaker; Carol Moore Turner; Chas. E. Watson, Florist; Whitney's Candy Store; Verne Williams, Village Sandwich Shop.

Photograph of Michel Penha (c.1937) and *Stabat Mater* program courtesy of the Carmel Music Society.

Part Five
Festival and Theater
1935–1938

Entrance to the Sunset School Auditorium. 1936 sketch by Charlotte Morton from the Carmel Cymbal.
Courtesy of the H. M. Williams Local History Room of the Harrison Memorial Library.

California's First Theater, c.1900, before its renovations.
Postcard, photographer unknown. Courtesy of the author.

"For this beautiful and spiritual experience, we thank the conductor, the visiting artists, the local artists, and Dene Denny and Hazel Watrous, who have never faltered in the face of discouragement, who have never lost their vision of their purpose, who have made this beautiful thing a reality for us and have built us up into an audience ready to receive it."

Carmel Pine Cone, July 17, 1942

"To those who live in Carmel and have a part in its valid artistic life, Miss Watrous and Miss Denny are Hazel and Dene. Both are beautiful women; both women of great charm. Their several distinguishments are so exactly complementary that the double light in which they have seen their ideal come to maturity has been a true and constant focus on the common vision. No stature to which the Carmel Bach Festival could grow in the world of noteworthy achievement could outdistance the recognition of the two women whose work it is."

Carmel Cymbal, July 14, 1938

Winter—Spring 1935

Scottish-American soprano Mary Garden (1874-1967) was a major star on the operatic stage in the early 20th century. Known as "the Sarah Bernhardt of opera," she was a gifted actress as well as a great singer. Garden gave a recital of songs by Claude Debussy at the Denny-Watrous Gallery on December 10, 1934.

Meanwhile, the Monterey Peninsula Orchestra was hard at work under the baton of Ernst Bacon in preparation for a February concert.

> The Peninsula orchestra managed a spirited volume of sound at its regular weekly rehearsal Sunday night at the Denny-Watrous Gallery. Is has become a pleasant custom for music lovers to attend the practice sessions....Ernst Bacon has a friendly and highly informal manner with his players, and infuses them with an enthusiasm which rises to moments of brilliant performance even in scores not yet perfectly mastered. The members of the orchestra and its friends have come to respect his indubitable musicianship and delight in his fascinating human qualities. (Pine Cone, December 21, 1934)

On January 21, 1935, Ernst Bacon introduced himself to the broader community with a solo piano recital at the Denny-Watrous Gallery. The first half of the program included music by Bach, Mozart, Schubert, Bartok, and several of Bacon's own works. After intermission he played three substantial works by Brahms. The German word "ernst" means "serious," and for this reason, Ernst Bacon's sister Madi said that it was a perfect name for her brother. The concert reviewer made a note of this aspect of Bacon's character.

> There were times in his playing when a brooding and poetical spirit came to the surface, and struggled as for escape against too conscious repression. The program began with Mozart. It is my theory that deep inner happiness and complete repose are necessary for complete communion with Mozart, and that Bacon lacks a little of this inner tranquility. (Pine Cone, January 25, 1935)

"...an occasion for glowing civic pride..."

In his 14 months in Carmel, Ernst Bacon won the hearts and the respect of all Carmel musicians and music lovers, and his next step on this path was the concert on February 17 by the Monterey Peninsula Orchestra.

> Many Carmelites have enjoyed the privilege of dropping in at the Denny-Watrous Gallery on Sunday evenings to hear Ernst Bacon conduct the orchestra. With an uneven group of players ranging from children to professionals, he has been able to surmount the difficulties confronting him, and produce really fine music. When the orchestra disbanded for a few months after the departure of Michel Penha, it was found to leave a strange void in the community's activities. Many had come to look upon the Monterey Peninsula Orchestra as a center which gave musical efforts some meaning. Without it music lovers were lost. With delight was received the news that the orchestra was to continue under the baton of Ernst Bacon. (Pine Cone, February 15, 1935)

The concert took place in the Denny-Watrous Gallery, and included the concerto for two violins by J. S. Bach, with violinists Mildred Sahlstrom-Wright of Monterey (former concertmaster) and

Opposite page: Hazel Watrous and Dene Denny. Photo by Johann Hagemeyer, early 1940s.
Courtesy of the Monterey Public Library, California History Room Archives

Anita Barrett of Palo Alto. The orchestra also performed the second movement of Beethoven's *Symphony No. 4*; *Spoon River* by Percy Grainger; and unnamed works by Byrd and Mussorgsky.

Initial Concert of Peninsula Orchestra Occasion for Civic Pride

The first concert of the Monterey Peninsula Orchestra under Ernst Bacon's leadership was an occasion for glowing civic pride Sunday evening but it was more than that. Mixed with the feeling of satisfaction at the accomplishments of this aggregation of professional students and capable amateurs was a feeling of envy. They are having such a gorgeous time, working together, and exploring new scores! Truly, the most significant function of music is being fulfilled here, in the banding together of a group of musicians, undaunted at the lack of a few instruments traditional to the symphonic aggregation, enjoying their weekly rehearsals and with no harrowing consciousness of definite and demanding engagements to be filled, or fear of a hypercritical public.

Mr. Bacon's personality and leadership have done something to this mixed aggregation of players. He conducts with a broad free sweep; he coaxes from his musicians something a little better than their best. His interpretations are sure and sensitive; he has understanding as well as leadership. We will not be surprised if this orchestra reaches heights beyond those expected by its community. (Pine Cone, February 22, 1935)

As if to keep the town on its toes, Dene and Hazel presented amazingly contrasting events just days before and after the orchestra concert. Two days before, they showcased a Japanese shakuhachi flute player at the Gallery, and Henry Cowell interspersed the program with an "entertaining discussion of Japanese music." Then, just after the orchestra concert, the Carmel Music Society presented one of the most widely performed and influential composers of the 20th century—Igor Stravinsky—in a recital of his music with violinist Samuel Dushkin. Their appearance on the stage of Sunset Auditorium was one of only twelve concerts on their North American tour.

Stravinsky and Dushkin Make Musical History for Carmelites

It was an historic occasion last Saturday night when Carmel heard Igor Stravinsky and Samuel Dushkin play.... Music lovers will date momentous happenings from the winter that Stravinsky and Dushkin toured together. Their like may never be seen again. (Pine Cone, February 22, 1935)

Just a few days after the Stravinsky concert, the Denny-Watrous Gallery presented the Latvian Singers from central Europe, in a program of Russian choral music that ended with a re-enactment of the Vesper Service of the Russian Orthodox Church. They came to the gallery with full altar settings, incense, clergy and choir, and used the entire gallery and stage for the ritual service.

The natural reverence and lack of theatricality with which the singers went through the Vesper service gave it a strong realism. It was a performance of moving beauty and dignity, the last touch of charm being the distribution of flowers to the audience. (Pine Cone, March 8, 1935)

Dene and Hazel had not lost their love for theater, despite their experience at the Golden Bough eight years before. They produced "plays" only a few times in their gallery between 1930 and 1935, but what few they presented were unusual and memorable. In April they engaged director Beverly Wright to produce *Six Characters in Search of an Author*, by Luigi Pirandello, with an all-Carmel cast. This mind-bendingly absurdist play premiered in Italy in 1921 and had been seen more than 100 times on Broadway in three different productions. The performance of such a play in Carmel was the sort of event the original pioneers of the Little Theater Movement had dreamed of: a new, important, and very thought-provoking play was presented by an amateur troupe in a community setting.

> Beverly Wright's production of "Six Characters," which opened last night at the Denny-Watrous Gallery is worthy of Carmel—the "real" Carmel—or what people have imagined the real Carmel to be. It is "real" Little Theater, if the little theater is what we dimly remember it was meant to be: experimental, courageous, and venturing into fields which neither the movies nor the commercial theater can explore. I expected the play to be arty, and flop. It is the most absorbing, dramatic thing I have seen for many a moon, beautifully smoothly done. (Pine Cone, April 12, 1935)

DENNY-WATROUS GALLERY
MARCH CALENDAR

SATURDAY MARCH 2	**Latavian Singers** *in Great Vespers of Russian Church preceded by a Carneval . . . Tickets $1.10 and 83 cents*
FRIDAY MARCH 8 *at 8:30 p. m.*	**Scottish Musical Players** ▸ *"Bonnie Prince Charlie"*
SATURDAY MARCH 9 *at 8:30 p. m.*	**"Cotter's Saturday Night"**
SATURDAY MATINEE *at 2:30 p. m.*	**"The Bonnie Brier Bush"** *Tickets 50 & 75 cents, $1.00 & $1.50 Children 25 cents at the Matinee*
SATURDAY MARCH 16 *8:30 and 2:30*	**Kingsland Marionettes**
SUNDAY MARCH 17	**Suemas MacManus** *Irish Writer and Speaker on Irish Literature*

Pirandello's "Six Characters in Search of an Author" is in Rehearsal and is being directed by Beverly Wright

The community agreed with the reviewer, and the play was repeated by popular demand the following weekend. Other performers at the Gallery that month included two artists with lovely and memorable names. Irish storyteller Seamus McManus delighted the audience with his traditional tales, and lyric soprano Marie Montana sang a mixed program of German, French, Italian and American songs, and a few arias. Montana returned to Carmel in July for the Bach Festival. In May, Dene and Hazel presented pianist Henry Cowell and dancer Tina Flade at the Gallery. In the words of the Pine Cone, Dene Denny and Hazel Watrous were "...continuing their undeviating standard of outstanding attractions..."

Although Michel Penha had been based in Los Angeles since 1934, and had not been involved in Denny-Watrous activities, he remained a member of the Carmel community and spent much time there. At the Eugene Marble ranch in Carmel Valley in early May he gave a public recital with pianist Ralph Linsley.

By April 1935, preparations were underway for the big musical events scheduled for July. The Monterey Peninsula Orchestra formed an advisory board that in turn created the Monterey Peninsula Orchestra Association. This membership organization was designed to raise money and generate support for the orchestra. They sent out an appeal:

> You are invited to become a member of the Monterey Peninsula Orchestra Association, which is being formed to ensure the continuance of one of our most cherished activities. The orchestra, with its center in Carmel, needs no introduction. It is making one of its few

appeals for funds since its inception three years ago. The organization, with its unlimited possibilities, has had the unique distinction of being an amateur group (including children and adults of all ages) directed only by professionals of widely recognized standing. Michel Penha, Henry Eichheim, Carol Weston, and now Ernst Bacon have all made altruistic and inspired contributions, and professional players have united their talents with the amateur group without fee. (Quoted in the Pine Cone, May 10, 1935)

Please note the words "without fee." A stipend of some sort was indeed paid to the conductors of this orchestra, however, the professional instrumentalists who played in the orchestra did so for free—their travel expenses were paid, they were given a dollar or two each day for food, and they were billeted in private homes, but they received no fee. This was the case for the Monterey Peninsula Orchestra and the Carmel Bach Festival Orchestra until the late 1950s. The Orchestra Association flyer continues:

The cultural value of community music-making cannot be estimated. Compensation for the director, musical scores, instruments, and the carrying costs can be met only by donations. The Carmel Music Society has sponsored the orchestra, and a few individuals have given generously; but if the project is to continue, the financial burden must be shared. (ibid.)

This fundraising effort was part of the run-up to the fourth Summer Series of the Carmel Music Society. The community did not yet have the full details of what was being planned for July, but it was clear to the planners that it was going to take money as well as artistic preparation, and to this end Dene and Hazel created a typically unusual event.

Colonel Joseph Stilwell, US Army, had built a house on Carmel Point in 1930 and lived there with his family. His daughter Winifred (known as "Doot") had been playing violin with the Monterey Peninsula Orchestra. Stilwell was a long-standing China specialist, and he and his wife and children spoke fluent Chinese. He had just been named military attaché of the US legation in Beijing ("Pekin" as the Pine Cone spelled it) and the family was getting ready to leave for China in June, but Dene and Hazel persuaded them to be the centerpiece of a Chinese-themed fundraiser at the Gallery on May 21.

The admission fee was 50¢ and the Stilwell family were apparently fun-loving and generous. Colonel Stilwell spoke about the life, language, and customs of China, and, according to the Pine Cone "...washed down his capsules of information about China with frequent drafts of entertainment." Stilwell's wife and daughters gave a comic skit in Chinese, and several Chinese items donated by the Stilwells were offered as door-prizes. The audience that evening also had the unique experience of watching "Vinegar Joe" Stilwell play small Chinese cymbals as his older daughter Nancy performed several pieces on her Chinese fiddle.

The Denny-Watrous Gallery is building a tradition as a social and cultural center of the village, and this atmosphere was vastly enhanced by Tuesday's Chinese evening for the benefit of the Peninsula orchestra. The Stilwell family proved themselves entertainers par excellence, and Carmel regrets not having discovered and used their individual and collective talents until just at the eve of their departure for China. Participants in the party, representative and gay, packed the Gallery to the doors. The orchestra will benefit to the extent of about $125.

Miss Nancy played her Chinese fiddle, accompanied by her father, whose performance on the cymbals suggested a noisy Saturday morning in the kitchen. (Pine Cone, May 24, 1935)

Postscript:

The members of the audience at the Chinese Party on Tuesday evening, May 21, 1935, would surely have seen and smelled the charred ruins of the Theatre of the Golden Bough—destroyed by fire just 48 hours before. One wonders how many at the Gallery had been in the audience at the Golden Bough on the preceding Friday or Saturday night.

Dene and Hazel's commitment to their gallery location on San Carlos Street is indicated by the new floor they installed in the gallery in early June. Seven rows of seats at the rear of the gallery were raised to provide better sight lines for everyone. A talent show was put on by local musicians to raise money for the new floor, and participants included baritone Steen Sconhoff, who was already "summering in Carmel" in anticipation of his involvement at the Bach Festival.

June 1935 The Bach Festival Prepares

In early June, performers started to arrive in Carmel. One important arrival was Philadelphia violinist Sascha Jacobinoff.

> ### Ernst Bacon Will Direct Series Of Events To Begin With Recital On June 25
>
> Many Carmel musicians and outstanding artists from California and elsewhere will participate in the first of an annual series of music festivals to be given here this summer. More than any previous event, the summer season in Carmel this year will serve to identify the village as a center of creative endeavors in music. Inspired by the 250th anniversary of the birth of Johann Sebastian Bach, the outstanding event will be a four-day Bach Festival, preceded and followed by a series of concerts of outstanding brilliance.
>
> Ernst Bacon, conductor of the Monterey Peninsula Orchestra, will be director of the festival, which is presented by the Denny-Watrous Gallery, sponsored by the Carmel Music Society and the Orchestra Association....
>
> Outstanding among the <u>dozen or more concert artists who are vacationing in Carmel</u> and will participate in the summer concert series of the Carmel Music Society or the Bach Festival, is Sascha Jacobinoff. (Pine Cone, June 7, 1935) [emphasis added]

"Philadelphia's Juvenile Virtuoso"

Sascha Jacobinoff was born in Philadelphia in 1896 as Samuel Jacobson. His parents, Nathan and Jennie Jacobson, came to the US from the Ukraine in the late 1880s as part of a large East European immigration to Philadelphia toward the end of the century. They named their son Samuel but called him Sascha (as an adult he changed his last name to Jacobinoff for professional reasons).

Sascha Jacobinoff was born in a three-room apartment over his father's butcher shop at 225 Fairmont Avenue, in a densely settled Jewish neighborhood called the Northern Liberties (an area defined then by 6th Street to the west, Girard Avenue on the north, Spring Garden

Street on the south, and the docks and harbor to the east). As a little boy Sascha was sent to the local violin teacher and quickly moved beyond that teacher's skill. His talent and potential enabled him to attend the Philadelphia Music Academy where he studied with Paul Meyer. In his early teens, Sascha began concertizing in the Philadelphia area and appeared on the regional vaudeville circuits. In August 1910 at age 14 he performed in the Keith Theater in New York:

> Sascha Jacobson, a violinist of undoubted talent, whose appearance yesterday was received with marked enthusiasm by the audience, made a decided hit. Mr. Jacobson had never been seen in vaudeville in this city before, and after hearing one or two of his selections hardly anyone would have denied him the title of "Philadelphia's juvenile virtuoso."
>
> (New York Sun, August 10, 1910)

That same summer he played a Mozart Concerto at Griffith Hall in Philadelphia and was heard by Mrs. F. B. Hurlburt of Germantown, a Philadelphia suburb. She and several fellow benefactors took young Sascha under their wing and made it financially possible for him to go to Europe to study.

On July 8, 1911, Sascha Jacobinoff and his mother Jennie departed New York City on the Graf Waldersee, a ship of the Hamburg American Line. After making sure that her son was well settled in Berlin, Jennie returned to Philadelphia. In Berlin, Sascha was a pupil of Carl Flesch, a famous violinist and pedagogue, whose pupils included Ida Haendel and Henryk Szeryng. Flesch's violin instruction books are highly regarded and still in use. During his nearly five uninterrupted years in Europe, Sascha also studied one summer with Leopold Auer and spent one winter in Italy studying with Arrigo Serato.

In 1913, Carl Flesch selected a violin for his student, a priceless 1779 Guadagnini. (Michel Penha's cello was built by Guadagnini 1754.) Erich Lachman was a German violin maker and a dealer who in 1912 had obtained the violin from Parisian dealer Paul Serdet. The instrument and its interior were structurally unaltered and just as the maker had left them.

Through the influence of Flesch, and the generosity of Sascha's American patrons, the 17-year-old violinist now had a superb world-class instrument. (Although Guadagnini came from the next generation after the golden age of Guarneri and Stradivari, his instruments are prized; at a New York auction in November 2013, a similar Guadagnini violin was sold for

$1.4 million.) Sascha played the Guadagnini until 1945, when he sold it back to Lachman, who had established his violin business in Los Angeles.

By 1915, Jennie Jacobson, concerned about the growing hostilities in Europe, had returned to Berlin to be with her son. A concert tour had been arranged for Sascha in Russia, France, England and Germany, but the sound of war was becoming louder than violins, and Jennie and Sascha fled Europe in March 1916, returning to Philadelphia via Denmark and Norway.

Sascha Jacobson had been born in the tiny apartment above his father's butcher shop in Philadelphia. Now he was twenty, he had studied with some of the greatest living violin teachers, he owned a superb 18th century Italian violin, and in his pocket he had letters of reference from the great Carl Flesch to all the major North American conductors.

Just before Sascha's return from Berlin, a young Russian-born violinist debuted in New York under the name "Sascha Jacobson." Because of this, Sascha Jacobson of Philadelphia officially became "Sascha Jacobinoff," and it is under this name that he performed for the rest of his life. The energy that had been put towards a European concert tour was now applied to creating Sascha's debut season in America. He signed with a Philadelphia booking agent and made his US recital debut in New York on January 22, 1917, in New York's Aeolian Hall.

Three images from Jacobinoff press material 1917–1919, courtesy of the author.

> Slight of frame, Jacobinoff showed genuine talent musically and an especial gift of beauty of tone, notably aided by a superb instrument on which he played. (New York Times, Jan 23, 1917)

By June 1917, Jacobinoff had given more than 40 solo recitals on the East Coast, some in larger venues and some for "Morning Musical Clubs" and organizations similar to the Carmel Music Society. The photograph shown here is taken from a publicity flyer printed in mid-1917.

"Plays with fire and fervency." (Philadelphia Evening Bulletin, November 14, 1917)

In November Sascha made his concerto soloist debut with the Philharmonic Society of New York. He soloed four times that season with Stokowski and the Philadelphia Orchestra and returned to New York for the Brahms Violin Concerto with the Philharmonic Society.

No doubt the name "Sascha Jacobinoff" had an appealingly evocative European air, especially for East Coast audiences, and whether or not his agent encouraged it, it was easy for local press and headline writers to assume Sascha was a European import. In March 1917, under the headline "Russian to Play Here at Concert," a Philadelphia Inquirer article made reference to Sascha's "first appearance in this country" the year before, without mentioning his actual Philadelphia birthplace. The New York Call in 1920 referred to "...the marvelous musical skill of Sascha Jacobinoff, the celebrated Russian violinist."

But a Red Scare was sweeping the US during and after WWI, and the words "Sascha Jacobinoff from Russia" sounded Bolshevist or worse. This sometimes made it necessary for his press releases to balance his Russian name with the reassuring fact of his "red-blooded" American birth, as in this advance notice for a 1919 concert in Indiana:

JACOBINOFF
VIOLINIST

Sasha Jacobinoff An Out And Out American Of The Red–Blooded Type—Born In Philadelphia

When Fort Wayne music lovers assemble at the Palace Theater tomorrow evening to hear Sascha Jacobinoff, the celebrated violinist, they will not only have the pleasure of hearing a real artist but an artist virile and strenuous—an artist of the true red-blooded American variety.
"What would you rather be than a violinist?" "Nothing—but next to a violinist I would rather be a baseball player than anything else." Sascha Jacobinoff, despite his name, is an out and out American of the good red-blooded variety, whose art is vitalized as much by a sturdy and healthy mental viewpoint as by the supreme facility of technique and interpretive ability, which those must have who seek to attain recognition and professional respect which this young American artist has already so abundantly achieved.
(Fort Wayne, Indiana, March 28, 1919)

Jacobinoff had a busy solo and chamber music career, and was a teacher in Philadelphia. He had made two trips to San Francisco years before, but this was his first visit to Carmel. He arrived on June 1935, accompanied by two of his best Philadelphia students, and jumped right into things.

> Mr. Jacobinoff arrived in Carmel over a week ago, and he is so much a part of the summer activity that he has already dropped in on two orchestra rehearsals and played in the ranks with both the "firsts" and the "seconds," sat on the sidelines in chorus rehearsals, and played chamber music with local music lovers. No happier choice could have been made than for Sascha Jacobinoff to open this 1935 summer season. (Pine Cone, June 21, 1935)

Dene and Hazel engaged Jacobinoff for three concerts during the 1935 Summer Series. He opened the entire Series with a solo recital on June 25. Three weeks later, in the Bach Festival's Opening Night concert, he played Bach's *Violin Concerto in E Major*. The next night he performed Bach's *B Minor Sonata for Violin and Keyboard*. (Bach wrote such works with harpsichord in mind, but for the first several seasons piano was the Festival's only keyboard instrument.)

Jacobinoff became very popular in Carmel that summer, and in the late winter Dene and Hazel invited him back to Carmel to conduct the 1936 Festival.

Festival rehearsals

The Carmel Music Society continued to flourish, and Dene and Hazel were still very much involved—they hosted the June 21 board meeting at their home as excitement was ramping up for the Summer Series. The newly elected president was Rudolf Kocher, builder and owner of the Hotel La Ribera. The 31-member board of directors included Dene and Hazel, and Dene continued as chair of the booking committee.

In 1932, 1933, and 1934 the Carmel Music Society presented their "Summer Series" as a part of the Society's subscription season.

Detail of 1934 program cover.
Courtesy of the Carmel Music Society.

Detail of 1935 program cover. *Courtesy of the H. M. Williams Local History Department, Harrison Memorial Library*

However, in 1935 the Carmel Music Society and the Monterey Peninsula Orchestra are listed as "sponsors" of the "Summer Series and Bach Festival." It is important to understand that the term "sponsor" meant that the two organizations formally lent their names to the endeavor but gave no actual financial or managerial support. In fact, the eight–concert series in July and August 1935 was not part of the Carmel Music Society's subscription series at all. The entire series of eight events was conceived, booked, publicized, produced, and managed by "Denny-Watrous Gallery," and Dene and Hazel assumed all responsibility, including the financial risks.

The costs of the eight-concert series were covered in part by ticket revenue and by donations from individual subscribers such as Noel Sullivan, a major financial angel of the Festival in its early years. The inevitable deficits in the early years were covered by Dene Denny and Hazel Watrous personally.

The 1935 Summer Series and Bach Festival was "Presented by the Denny-Watrous Gallery." From 1936 through 1957, Dene and Hazel listed themselves as "Producing Managers." An "Advisory Committee" was created in 1936, but Denny-Watrous Management was the sole proprietor until 1958, when a governing board was created, with Dene as President and General Manager.

In later years Dene is quoted as referring to the Summer Series of 1932, 1933, and 1934 as the "Chamber Series." In July and August 1935, there was once again a "Summer Series" of chamber concerts: 1.) Sascha Jacobinoff, violin; 2.) the Abas String Quartet; 3.) Danish pianist Gunnar Johansen; and 4.) Waldeen, billed as an "American creative dancer."

By previous "Summer Series" standards, this was a great lineup of four events. But between the second and third concerts, Dene and Hazel placed a brand new four-day event on a scale never seen before in Carmel. They intended those four days to mark the beginning of an annual summer music festival.

Why Bach?

For more than a century Johann Sebastian Bach has lent his name to music festivals: there are by far more "Bach Festivals" around the world than festivals devoted to any other composer. John Frederick Wolle founded his Bach Choir of Bethlehem, Pennsylvania, in 1898 and they held their first Bach Festival in 1900. Albert Riemenschneider founded a Bach Festival at Baldwin-Wallace College near Cleveland in 1932. Both of these professional-level Festivals continue to flourish today, as does the Bach Festival of Winter Park Florida, founded in 1935.

On March 30, 1934, the Pine Cone quoted Dene's dream of a Bach chorus and an "Easter event" in 1935, but one of the most surprising discoveries in the course of writing this book was that the original intention of the founders was not to hold an annual "Bach Festival." Bach was a natural choice as the theme for the first festival because 1935 happened to be his 250th birthday and celebrations were happening all around the world. (It was also the 250th birthday of George Frideric Handel and Domenico Scarlatti, but Bach was better known and easier to sell to the general public.)

Comments and quotes in the press by from September 1934 through late January 1936 make it clear that the plan of Ernst Bacon and Denny-Watrous intended to produce a "...Mozart Festival in Carmel" that summer. The decision to make the event an annual "Carmel Bach Festival" was not publicly announced until April, 1936.

In early June, Dene and Hazel mailed a brochure to the local community and beyond, inviting the recipients to "Spend Your Vacation in Carmel-by-the-Sea. Include the Carmel Bach Festival in your vacation schedule." It was surprising to some that famously reclusive Carmel seemed to be advertising itself to the world. The Pine Cone was quick to clarify and assuage the fears of the Carmelites.

> A good deal of confusion exists about what Carmel's attitude is on community publicity. No one would say seriously, even in Carmel, that advertising a Bach Festival would menace Carmel's traditional exclusiveness. If any are lured to Carmel by the bait of a Bach Festival, which sounds pretty heavy, we say that they are brave souls, the right kind of people, and we will welcome them with open arms.
>
> We think that this is good community advertising, and the sort we are proud to have go forth. We are proud of the ambitious program for the summer, and of Dene Denny and Hazel Watrous, who are presenting a series of concerts and the Bach Festival, one of Carmel's most ambitious musical undertakings to date.
>
> The music of Bach is beautiful as well as "high-brow." Carmel will have entertainment of impeccable taste to offer its visitors this summer; truly representative of the community at its best. The orchestra and chorus, made up principally of local people, will show what

amateurs can do in the way of making good music under capable direction. The visiting artists are entering into the spirit of community life, and are our own for a little while. We could do with much more of this type of "advertising," and if Carmel is wise it will give every possible support and encouragement to the orchestra, the Music Society, Ernst Bacon, the conductor, and the impresarios of the Denny-Watrous Gallery. (Pine Cone, June 21, 1935)

Excitement around the summer concerts grew as the out-of-town performers began to arrive in June. The orchestra was roughly 50% local residents—including a few professionals—and the rest came from near and far, amateur and professional, and all of the players were unpaid.

There were twenty-six violinists in the orchestra, making the violin section that summer larger than the entire Monterey Peninsula Orchestra had been back in July 1932. A half dozen professional violinists volunteered from Berkeley and San Francisco. Jacobinoff brought two students with him from Philadelphia. A music teacher from Fresno spent the summer in Carmel in order to play in the orchestra. A grad student at Berkeley gave up summer courses to play in Carmel and study with Jacobinoff. Bacon invited a doctor friend from Berkeley who was a fine violinist.

Dene Denny had been rehearsing the chorus since late winter, first practicing Bach four-part chorales scheduled for two of the festival concerts. These chorales had been good tools for voice building and ensemble training, after which Dene began rehearsing some of the more complicated festival repertoire.

In the world of volunteer choirs, there is one unvarying law: "There Are Never Enough Tenors." As of late June they were still searching:

> The Bach Festival chorus of Carmel singers held its first rehearsal with the community orchestra Sunday night at Denny-Watrous Gallery. Many auditors [listeners] were present, and heard the magnificent Bach chorales begin to take on form and substance under the baton of Ernst Bacon.
>
> The chorus is exceptionally well organized except in the tenor section. This is still not large enough, and all chorus members were instructed at the Monday evening rehearsal to go over lists of their friends in search of good tenors. Ability to read music and carry a tune are the only requisites; it is not necessary to have a voice of solo quality.
>
> If there are any tenors on the Peninsula who have not been approached with a personal invitation, they will be received practically with open arms if they will show up voluntarily next Monday evening at 7:45 PM at Denny-Watrous Gallery. (Pine Cone, June 28. 1935)

Ernst Bacon

The unsigned article below appeared on the front page of the Carmel Pine Cone just six days before the opening of the 1935 Summer Series and Bach Festival, and is given here in its entirety. The opening paragraph is comic rhetoric: Bacon did receive a fee, although apparently not much, hence the joke. The woodblock portrait by Perry Newberry accompanied the article.

Several months ago Dene Denny went to San Francisco and said to Ernst Bacon, "How would you like to come down to Carmel and conduct an amateur orchestra—for nothing?" And Ernst Bacon said, "Why, I'd be delighted!" That, at least, is the story that is told, and from that nonchalant conversation has arisen an impetus to musical affairs which promises to make history in Carmel.

Mr. Bacon commuted from San Francisco for a while, rehearsing the orchestra on Sunday evenings. Early in the summer he and Mrs. Bacon and their two children took a cottage here and work began in earnest toward the Bach Festival. His closer contact with musicians under his guidance has resulted in a sort of guild feeling. Bacon is musical to the core, and his idea of an evening's relaxation, after teaching and conducting reversals all day, is to gather some of the more serious students together for chamber music until the small hours of the morning.

Rehearsals of the orchestra have a certain resemblance to a master class in music. Auditors [listeners] as well as players are adding to their knowledge and understanding of music from the conductor's scholarly comments and analysis of the Bach Festival music. Of more consequence than their mastery of the scores is the inner spiritual development which is resulting from associating with a man of unquestioned musicianship, high-souled devotion to music, and the type of leadership which draws young people to him. A man young in years, Bacon seems to those who are associated with him to have that quality which metaphysicians call an "old soul."

Editorial, Carmel Pine Cone, July 12, 1935. Woodblock by Perry Newberry after a photo by Sybyl Anikeef.
Courtesy of the H. M. Williams Local History Department, Harrison Memorial Library; and the Carmel Pine Cone.

1935 Summer Series and Bach Festival

The Summer Series began on June 25 with a solo recital by Sascha Jacobinoff, accompanied by Carmel pianist Alice Austin. They played Bach, Handel, Sarasate, Debussy, Schubert, and Schumann.

> Carmel's outstanding season of summer music had an auspicious beginning Tuesday evening in the concert of Sascha Jacobinoff. The virtuoso achieved a magnificent variety of total quality and color, characterized by crispness of attack, and a gratifying smooth brilliance. (Pine Cone, June 28, 1935)

This was followed a week later by the Abas String Quartet. Dutch violinist Nathan Abas was former concertmaster of the San Francisco Symphony and had appeared in Carmel the previous summer as violinist in the Penha Piano Quartet. The second violinist was Theodore "Ted" Norman, the violist, already beloved to Carmel audiences, was Abraham Weiss; and the cellist was newcomer Fritz Gailliard. Norman and Weiss both played in the string section of the orchestra for the Bach Festival concerts.

Ernst Bacon and his wife and children had been living in Carmel since late May. Bacon's parents, Dr. and Mrs. Charles Bacon, arrived from Chicago at the end of June. They attended all the rehearsals, and Mrs. Bacon was quoted as saying that she was her musical children's "severest critic."

At a City Council meeting on July 9, a motion was made to appropriate $100 to help defray the cost of the Bach Festival. The finance committee left the room and deliberated privately, after which they returned to the meeting and gave the proposal a thumbs down. At the end of the meeting, the city attorney rose and proposed the creation of a committee of twenty, each of whom was responsible for raising $5. He put his money on the table, as did the mayor, the chair of the finance committee, and several others present, including the Pine Cone reporter who was covering the meeting. Within several days, the $100 had been raised.

The excitement was growing in town not only because of the number of musicians arriving in Carmel, but also because they were going to be staying in town for a week or two.

> Around the nucleus of amateur and professional musicians of Carmel comprising the Festival chorus and orchestra has sprung up an impressive aggregation. Lured by the extensive preparations, more than a score of able musicians have either come here for the entire summer or are expected here for the festival week as members of the orchestra, chorus, or as soloists. (Pine Cone, July 12, 1935)

"...nothing to repel the untrained lover of music..."

There was, however, concern that the name "Bach" might be off-putting to those who feared his music might be "highbrow." Reassurances were given:

> The festival will take the form of four evening concerts devoted entirely to the music of Bach, which under the baton of Ernst Bacon, conductor three of the four concerts, emerges as fresh, vital, eternally youthful and significant. While of magnificent quality, there is nothing "highbrow," nothing to repel the untrained lover of music, about the music of Bach. The most naïve listener will be thrilled by the full swelling harmonies, the lyric sweetness, the high spiritual content of this ageless music. It will be a true feast of beauty, for both participants and listeners. (Pine Cone, July 12, 1935)

From its very beginning, the Carmel Bach Festival has always offered lectures in addition to the concerts. In 1935, Beatrice Colton, a graduate of UC Berkeley who studied in Paris and then returned to join the Berkeley music faculty, lectured at the Denny-Watrous Gallery at 11:00am on the four concert days. Her presentations were: "Bach as a Musical Personality," "Bach as Master of Form and Design," "Bach's Use of Harpsichord and Clavichord," and "The Painter in Sound." These lectures were free to Festival ticket holders, or 40¢ for the general public.

The Denny-Watrous Gallery was a very busy place that summer, as was the Pine Cone writer who created this two–sentence paragraph:

> The busiest place in Carmel, and the most exciting, this week, has been the Denny-Watrous Gallery. In fact, it might be called a mad-house, if it were not for the extraordinary and happy self-possession of Dene Denny and Hazel Watrous, who have continued to care for the innumerable details of preparation for the Bach Festival while cordially receiving the flood of incoming musicians for all of whom the gallery is headquarters and other home, making schedules for final rehearsals, and carrying on all this work to the accompaniment of instruments being tuned—which after all, does not sound so much different from some modern music. (Pine Cone, July 19, 1935)

The open rehearsals continued to inspire. Six years later, Susan Porter recalled,

> That was an exciting first summer. The town was small then and of course more close-knit than now. We met Ernst Bacon and came regularly to the rehearsals in the Denny-Watrous Gallery. We saw our children sitting there, chins on the wooden rails, eyes intent on the musicians, and we knew they would go to bed humming not the jazz songs of the month before but scraps of Bach. (Susan Porter reminiscing in 1941 about the first Carmel Bach Festival in 1935. Carmel Cymbal, July 11, 1941)

At this moment, a dynamic Italian conductor literally enters the scene. Gastone Usigli was born in Venice and had lived in the United States for about eight years. He was full of drama and energy, becoming well-known as a conductor in California, and his reputation had preceded him to Carmel. At the Denny-Watrous Gallery, a Pine Cone writer was chatting with soprano soloist Marie Montana when...

> ...just as we finished talking with Miss Montana, a murmur ran among the musicians — "Usigli is here!" and sure enough, there was Gastone Usigli, the guest conductor for Saturday evening, that moment arrived in town and bee-lining it for the place where all the music was in the air. (Pine Cone, July 19, 1935)

Ernst Bacon and Gastone Usigli were both based in San Francisco, and they had developed a cordial professional relationship there. Bacon had invited his friend, wisely, to share the conducting duties at the 1935 Festival. There were three concerts in Sunset Auditorium on Thursday, Friday, and Saturday, and a final concert on Sunday in the historic Carmel Mission. Usigli was the conductor of the Saturday concert only, after which he would next return to the Festival in 1938. More details about Usigli's life enter into the narrative at that point.

Bach Festival Opening Night
Thursday , July 19, Sunset School Auditorium

The program for the Bach Festival's opening night concert lists 10 soloists: a quartet of singers, three violinists, a cellist, a flutist, and Ernst Bacon himself at the piano. The concert began with a four–part Bach chorale, *Was Gott thut, das ist wohl gethan* ("Whatever God does, is rightly done"), accompanied by the orchestra.

The chorale was followed by a concerto for two violins, cello and orchestra by Antonio Vivaldi as arranged by Bach. After this, the chorus and vocal soloists returned for Cantata BWV 79, *Gott der Herr ist Sonn und Schild*, a brief work mostly for chorus, with alto and bass solos, sung in German.

After intermission, flutist Grace Thomas played Bach's *Sonata in B minor* BWV 1030, with Ernst Bacon at the piano. Then the fine American soprano Marie Montana sang two Bach arias. First, "Jauchtzet Gott" from the soprano solo cantata of the same title, BWV 51; followed by "Seuftzer, Thränen" from Cantata BWV 21.

Marie Montana's arias are examples of two practices common to many of the early Bach Festival concerts: short excerpts from longer works were performed, and sometimes the players (pragmatically) used instruments quite unintended by Bach.

First, until the early 1950s, the Festival regularly performed brief excerpts of larger works, such as Marie Montana's two arias. In defense of this (now outdated) practice, it should be kept in mind that many audience members in 1935 were hearing all these compositions for the first time. Although the specific choice of the two arias may have been simply a programing decision based on what Marie Montana wanted to sing, by performing excerpts from multiple works in its concerts, the Festival was educating its listeners by acquainting them with an array of Bach's greatest hits.

Second, in the performance of Montana's two arias, the "obbligato" instruments specified by Bach were not used. In the music of the Baroque era, the Italian word obbligato (or obligato) refers in this context to a prominent instrumental solo line in a vocal aria that is essential and is played on a specified (obligatory) instrument. In his vocal arias, Bach commonly wrote obbligato solos for violin, viola, cello, flute, oboe, or trumpet, and sometimes he used two or even three obbligato instruments at once. The obbligato of an aria is of equal importance to the vocal line, and a Bach aria is often a duet between the instrument and the voice, rather than a vocal aria with instrumental accompaniment.

The obligato instrument in Marie Montana's first aria is a fanfare-like trumpet, and in the second aria it is a mournful oboe. However, no trumpet player is credited among the soloists on the printed program; the two trumpet players in the orchestra were local residents and could never have tackled Bach's difficult and often stratospheric trumpet writing; and no oboist was listed in the Festival Orchestra that summer at all.

Marie Montana's two arias were listed in the printed program exactly as shown below (spelling and punctuation of the original have been retained):

Aria, "Jauchtzet Gott in Allen Landen." From Cantata No. 51.
Aria, "Seufzer, Thraenen, Kummer, Noth," from Cantata, "Ich hatte viel Bekuemmernis".
Marie Montana
Violin obligato, Winifried Connolly

According to the conventions of printed programs for classical music, this would seem to indicate that the violinist played the obbligato for at least the second aria. In that case Ms. Connolly would have played an oboe solo on the violin. This is not hard to imagine, and the nature of the melody would lend itself to violin. However, it's not clear if she also played the martial trumpet obbligato in the first aria, something that is difficult to imagine. Some entirely different solution to the lack of trumpet, including involvement of piano or an all-orchestral arrangement, may also have been found. (Bacon and Usigli were facile composers, and in his years as Festival Conductor, Usigli often used his own re-orchestrations and arrangements of Bach's major works.)

Pragmatic instrumental changes such this were not uncommon in the Festival's first two decades, and actually were a non-issue in the general concert world at that time. In many cases, the instruments Bach called for—and players who knew what to do with them—simply did not yet exist in California. More examples will be given in later chapters.

> The first fruits of many months of intensive preparation for the greatest musical effort in Carmel's history were triumphantly harvested last evening with the first concert of the four-day Bach Festival. From the first strains of the magnificently combined Festival Orchestra and Chorus, to the commanding closing chords of the Concerto in A Major, with Sascha Jacobinoff's violin dominating in the role of soloist, the evening was calculated to rouse to high pitch enthusiasm for the ensuing programs.
>
> The opening chorales serve to show what can be accomplished by a gifted conductor in the way of inspiring amateur singers to surpassingly fine performance. The work had shading and color, dynamic fervor, sweetness as well as power. The community orchestra, augmented and rounded by more than a dozen assisting artists from the San Francisco Bay region, gave the finest performance of its career. (Pine Cone, July 19, 1935)

The second concert was mostly instrumental. Danish pianist Gunnar Johansen played the Chromatic Fantasy and Fugue, and then baritone Noel Sullivan sang three sacred songs by Bach, accompanied by piano. Noel Sullivan was beloved in Carmel for many reasons, one of which was his engaging singing. He performed a set of songs or arias such as this at each of the Festivals for the next decade. After intermission Sascha Jacobinoff played the Sonata No. 1 in B Minor for "violin and piano," with Marjorie Legge Wurzmann.

There was no harpsichord at the 1935 Bach Festival, and the official piano for all concerts that summer was Baldwin, supplied by Palace Music Store in Monterey.

Gastone Usigli led the third concert, on Saturday evening, and began with the *Suite in D Major* for orchestra. Then baritone Steen Sconhoft sang a recitative and aria from the *St. Matthew Passion* ("Mache dich, mein Herze, rein"). For this aria, Bach's original accompaniment is written for full orchestra, with no obbligato solo at all, but the 1935 Festival program mysteriously lists "Claudio Silva, cello obligato" for this aria. The *Concerto in C minor for Two Keyboards and Orchestra* followed next. Bach wrote the concerto for two harpsichords, and it was played in this concert on two Baldwin grand pianos by Winifred Howe and Alice Austin.

Italian pianist and composer Ferruccio Busoni composed challenging arrangements of Bach's music that transform it and transport it into the colorful world of the piano. The Chaconne from Bach's *Partita for Solo Violin in D Minor* is a 15-minute workout for unaccompanied violin, and Busoni transformed it into a virtuosic piano fantasy. It was played in this concert by Ernst Bacon. The concert ended with the *Concerto in D Minor for Two Violins and Orchestra*, with soloists Doris Ballard and Rita Lorraine.

DENNY-WATROUS GALLERY Presents

1935 SUMMER SERIES
AND BACH FESTIVAL

SPONSORED by THE CARMEL MUSIC SOCIETY and
MONTEREY PENINSULA ORCHESTRA ASSOCIATION

BACH
FESTIVAL

CARMEL, CALIFORNIA
July 18, 19, 20, 21, 1935

PROGRAM————————THURSDAY, JULY 18
SUNSET SCHOOL AUDITORIUM

ERNST BACON, Conductor

SASCHA JACOBINOFF, violinist. MARIE MONTANA, soprano. EVELINA SILVA, contralto. ROBLEY LAWSON, tenor. STEEN SCONHOFF, baritone. RIFKA IVENTOSCH,
violinist. ROBERT NAGLER, violinist. CESARE CLAUDIO, cellist. GRACE THOMAS,
flute. ERNST BACON, pianist.

Choral, "Was Gott thut, das ist wohl gethan."

Vivaldi-Bach—Concerto grosso for two solo violins, cello and orchestra.
    Allegro—Largo—Allegro
                    Rifka Iventosch, Robert Nagler, Cesare Claudio

Cantata, "Gott der Herr ist Sonn und Schild"
    I. Chorus, "Gott der Herr." II. Aria, alto. III. Choral. IV. Recitative, bass.
    V. Duet with Choral Response. VI. Choral, "Erhalt uns in der Wahrheit."

INTERMISSION

Sonata in B minor for flute and piano.
    Andante—Largo e dolce—Presto. Allegro.
               Grace Thomas - Ernst Bacon

Aria, "Jauchzet Gott in Allen Landen." From Cantata No. 51.
Aria, "Seufzer, Thraenen, Kummer, Noth," from Cantata, "Ich hatte viel Bekuemmernis".
                Marie Montana
           Violin obligato, Winifred Connolly

Concerto, E major, for violin and orchestra.
    Allegro—Adagio—Allegro assai
              Sascha Jacobinoff

The piano is the Baldwin, the official piano of the Summer Series and the BACH FESTIVAL.
Courtesy of Palace Music Store, Monterey

LECTURE ON BACH
By BEATRICE COLTON

DAILY AT 11 A. M., DENNY-WATROUS GALLERY. THESE LECTURES
ARE FREE TO ALL SEASON TICKET HOLDERS.

The opening night concert of the 1935 Carmel Bach Festival
Courtesy of the H. M. Williams Local History Room, Harrison Memorial Library

Carmel Mission by Moonlight—A Sonnet
by Herbert Heron

The moon is cold; the ocean air is chill.
Alone with lonely owls the Mission stands,
The staring belfry towering on the sands
That hold in Serra's grave the ever still
Repose of mighty labors—love and will—
In rest profound, where once the brooding bands
Of dark-souled beings lifted up their hands

To God, and heard the angel voices thrill.
Mute are the bells that called the nights of old:
Forever lost the chanted melody,
That mingled with the sounding of the sea.
The lofty moon, through clouds of windy cold,
Mocks in her silver faith their vanished gold:
The altar-lights of warmth and mystery.

(First published in Art and Progress Magazine, May 1911)

Herbert Heron was an important early Carmel resident. An actor and playwright, he co-founded the Forest Theater in 1910, constructed the Seven Arts Building on Ocean Avenue in 1925, and was mayor of Carmel in the 1930s when Hazel Watrous was on the City Council.

By 1911, the year this poem was written, the Mission was somewhat restored and was no longer abandoned.

In later years, the poem was quoted elsewhere with two changes: chanted to rapturous, and mocks to mourns. The poem above is the original 1911 version.

The Mission Concert 1935

Junípero Serra's mission was restored and in use once again by the time Daisy Bostick wrote this description in 1925.

> The old Mission, recently restored, stands in austere beauty, though many of the adobe walls of the stockade which surrounded it in the old days have crumbled into fine dust. It nestles serenely on the lower slopes of the wide meadow extending to the sea. Now, as then, the waves drone their responses to the Padre's call to prayer; the trees still whisper their secrets of love, beauty and romance; wild things,—raccoons, foxes, coyotes,—play hide-and-seek in the moonlight; the sand on the beach glistens just as white, the cliffs that border it rise just as gaunt, as in the days when Serra loved it. Indeed, so greatly to the love and appreciate the beauties of the country round about it he described it often as "The Garden of God." (Bostick/Castelhun, 1925)

In 1931, Monsignor Philip Scher, pastor of the Presidio Chapel in Monterey, engaged Harry Downie to supervise the restoration of the Carmel Mission. In 1933, now a Bishop, Scher elevated the Mission to an independent parish, transferring the chapel from the Franciscan Order to the local diocese. Dene and Hazel arranged for the final concert of the 1935 Bach Festival to be held in this 18th century space. It very possibly was the first time that the 150–year–old Carmel Mission was used as the venue for a public ticketed concert.

The evening began with a four-part chorale, Erhalt uns in der Wahrheit, accompanied by orchestra. Then the soprano and baritone reprised their duet from the Opening Night concert. Concertmaster Doris Ballard played the Sonata in G Minor for solo violin. Soprano Marie Montana sang two arias from the St. Matthew Passion (with proper obbligato this time). The concert continued without intermission, and the alto, tenor, and bass soloists joined the chorus for Bach's Cantata 12, *Weinen, klagen* a brief cantata, mostly for the soloists, and ending with the same words (in a different musical setting) that were heard at the opening of the Bach Festival four days before: *Was Gott thut, das ist wohl gethan*—"Whatever God does, is rightly done."

With those words the first Carmel Bach Festival came to a close. (The Festival ended with music, followed by silence—applause was not permitted in the Mission.)

After all this, there were still two remaining concerts in Dene and Hazel's Summer Series. Pity poor pianist Gunnar Johansen, who had to follow the euphoric excitement of the Bach Festival. His concert on July 30 was politely reviewed and attended. On August 6, the final event in the series was Waldeen Falkenstein, one of the great precursors of modern Mexican dance. Even she could not match the level of excitement that had been generated by four days of non–stop Bach.

Carmel's first major music festival had been an artistic success, but because it was essentially a privately produced venture we do not know how it did financially. Regardless of the bottom line, great positive momentum had been generated not only locally but far beyond the borders of Monterey County. Now it was up to Dene and Hazel to build upon this initial success and turn the Festival into a tradition.

Facing page: Carmel Mission, c.1900. *Postcard, courtesy of the author.*

"With mingled dread and curiosity..."

Five days after the Carmel Mission concert, the following editorial appeared in the Carmel Pine Cone. It begins by allaying fears and then goes on to describe a hopeful future.

A New Tradition

Last week Carmel experienced one of the greatest events of its history, which was also in a sense the planting of the signboard on the path of its possible future. Without attempting to pass judgment on the musical quality of the Bach Festival, although many whose judgment we trust assure that it was excellent, there can be no question of the effect it had upon its participants and the hundreds of people who attended the four Bach concerts. No one could mingle in the happy throngs in the foyer at Sunset school, or with the rapt and reverent audience at Carmel Mission Sunday evening without sharing the authentic festival mood conjured up by the music.

With mingled dread and curiosity, we realize that Carmel faces the loss of her traditional isolation. During Bach Festival week we saw a possible saving grace in the situation. If we can guide our destinies so that the people to be drawn here can be just such people as those who came to attend the Bach Festival, we need not fear for the future. It was a pleasure and a privilege to mingle with such visitors. Many distinguished people were here, and those not famous in their own right were obviously of fine high character and cultured background.

Carmel must act, quickly and strongly, to clinch the advantages of the situation. From the impetus of the festival this year, it is evident that an annual summer festival of music is feasible. There can be no question of its desirability. Along with the many other fine traditions of Carmel's past, here is another eminently worthy to be established. No such crystallization of musical interest has before been witnessed here. That fine feeling must not be allowed to die away without having its ultimate and far-reaching effects.

Music is almost never self-supporting. Usually the protégé of cultured and wealthy people, it is also sometimes given a strong foundation by civic support. We believe that the true music enthusiasts should not, in this case, be required to carry the whole burden. The whole village has, and will in future, benefit actively by the enterprises of the musical people. If a civic subsidy is necessary, let us plan for it, and demand that it be granted.

In Ernst Bacon, Carmel has a conductor of whom it may well be proud; not only for his outstanding musical ability, but for the quality of man he is. It would be well for us if he could be retained here permanently. The influence which he exerts on the young people in and around the orchestra group is fine and wholesome; better acquaintance through the Bach Festival has caused the whole community to respect and love him.

The little tads now sawing on their violins and learning the rhythms of music at the Sunset School orchestra will graduate naturally into the community orchestra as they grow older. They and their playmates are being grounded in an appreciation of music. Their interest in the orchestra and in music generally will be natural and spontaneous. It is fine for the children; it is fine for all of us to learn that music is a natural, integral part of life. A community steeped in music is protected from many less desirable influences. Let us have more of it, and let us encourage it as part of our civic program. (Pine Cone, July 26, 1935)

Fall 1935

The Orchestra's Final Concert

The locals were excited, the orchestra players were eager, and after a break of four weeks orchestra rehearsals began again under Ernst Bacon. Discussion had already begun about a December concert with orchestra and chorus.

> After a month's rest, the community orchestra and chorus will be called together again the last week in August to begin work on Christmas music, the nature of which has not yet been definitely determined. Mr. Bacon will come down from San Francisco every second week-end, as he did last fall and winter. (Pine Cone, August 2, 1935)

The first orchestra rehearsal was set for August 26, and an announcement appeared in the Pine Cone a few days before. The out-of-town volunteers and professionals from the summer were gone now, and more locals were needed.

> Ernst Bacon will be through Sunday evening for the first autumn rehearsal of the community orchestra. They will meet on Sunday evening at 8 o'clock at the Denny-Watrous Gallery, to consider possible new scores, and particularly Christmas music, which will probably be the orchestra's next public appearance.
>
> Many of the players who augmented the orchestra for the Bach Festival have now left for their homes elsewhere, and a general invitation is being set out for old and new resident players to meet with the conductor Sunday evening to carry on the fine standards set by previous seasons.
>
> On Monday evening at the gallery, Mr. Bacon will begin the reorganization of the community chorus which assisted with the Bach Festival. It is not necessary to have a voice of solo quality; just to be interested in good music, to carry a tune, and a fair ability to read music. No one need be scared out if they are not rapid readers of new music, members of the chorus help each other, and after a few rehearsals even such difficult music as was given during the Bach Festival acquires familiarity and loses its terrors. (Pine Cone, August 23, 1935)

Meanwhile plans were firming up for the Monterey Peninsula Orchestra's winter concert. By the end of September, as unlikely as the choice might seem, it looked like the Christmas concert would feature the choral movements from Brahms' beautiful "German Requiem."

The Gallery's final months

The Denny-Watrous Gallery was presenting at least several events each month, and they opened the fall musical season in Carmel with Marya Ostrova in a program of Czech, Slovakian, and Russian songs with piano. On October 11 and 12, modern dancer Myra Kinch performed at the Gallery, assisted by several other dancers and composer-pianist Manuel Galea. A few days later, baritone Steen Sconhoft gave a song recital accompanied by Ernst Bacon at the piano. The program included several of Bacon's own songs. California pianist William Fleming, recently returned from Europe, gave a recital of 20th century music. The Gallery also offered a six week course in Improving the Speaking Voice, with two two-hour sessions per week.

To raise funds for the Monterey Peninsula Orchestra, the advisory board held a cooked food sale on November 23, just before Thanksgiving.

Carmel's Best Cooks to Contribute to Orchestra Food Sale Tomorrow

About 50 persons, among them Carmel's best cooks, have promised donations for the orchestra benefit cooked food sale which will be held all day tomorrow on Ocean Avenue. Late today the offerings were to arrive at the Denny-Watrous Gallery, with additional contributions to be delivered tomorrow at the scene of the sale. A veritable bazaar of Thanksgiving goodies will be the result. Everyone is helping with the village's pet project, the community orchestra, which fosters the talents of so many musicians, but is hampered by a slim treasury. (Pine Cone, November 22, 1935)

It was a successful event.

Success beyond the brightest hopes attended the cooked food sale of the community Orchestra Association last Saturday. Every crumb was sold, and a total of $170.43 was realized. (Pine Cone, November 29, 1935)

Ernst Bacon had been commuting to Carmel every other weekend for two months to rehearse the orchestra and chorus on Sunday and Monday evenings, respectively. In the off weeks, the chorus rehearsals were led by pianist Winifred Howe and the orchestra rehearsals by Joseph Czikowsky, District Supervisor of the San José Federal Music Project.

At the beginning of December the Christmas concert was publicly announced. We know the program contents but not the program order, except that the evening began with Christmas carols accompanied by the orchestra. Chorus and orchestra performed movements #1, 2, 4, and 7 from the *German Requiem* by Johannes Brahms. Tenor Andrew Sessink sang a group of Brahms songs with piano, and the orchestra played several unspecified selections of its own. When the music was over, the folding wooden chairs were stacked and the floor was cleared so that all present could enjoy dancing and refreshments.

During the Bach Festival in the summer, the orchestra had been augmented by nearly 20 players who were either professional or at least very adept. But the orchestra that played in this December concert was very much like the original Monterey Peninsula Orchestra in 1932. Some years later, a retrospective article quotes a member of the early orchestra who recalled the sound of the locals-only group as "an unbelievable cacophony." But the community loved this orchestra and the people in it, and, just as love is blind, love can also be deaf. Once again, the orchestra did the best it could, and the audience imagined the rest.

"...the magic of making music together, because you love it..."

For this concert on December 21, the orchestra numbered 26, including piano and harmonium, both of which played along with the orchestra to fill in the missing instruments and help keep things together. There were 34 singers in the chorus: 9 sopranos, 12 altos, 4 tenors, and 9 basses. (As always, there was a shortage of tenors.) Thelma Miller, a frequent contributor to the Pine Cone, was singing in the chorus and wrote her review from that perspective.

The presence of an audience and of Ernst Bacon, who, as a conductor, has a way of drawing from music-makers something a bit better than they knew they possessed, made of the program something better than the performers had expected, to be honest with you. The rehearsal schedule had been a bit broken up, and a good many people in both the orchestra and chorus had to miss practice periods. The music was difficult, but the amateur musicians were there because they love music, and for no other reason. The result was that some of the listeners, who also love the music itself more than they do a flawless performance, were genuinely moved by its emotional content. For some, that miracle of the Bach Festival was repeated on a small scale; the spiritual exaltation transcending anything that any individual musician there could have evoked. It is the magic of making music together, because you love it.

...After the concert a small group remained for dancing. Laura Dierssen and Cesare Claudio played, and later Mr. Bacon, and "a good time was had by all."

P. S.—I forgot to mention the Christmas carols. The orchestra played them and the chorus sang them, and to our surprise some of the listeners said they had never heard these old favorites more beautifully sung. This is a really difficult way in which to write a review, if you know what I mean. (Pine Cone, December 27, 1935)

*Laura Dierssen was a violinist in the Bach Festival Orchestra and Cesare Claudio was the Principal Cellist. His father was concertmaster of the San Francisco Symphony.

This was the last independent concert of the Monterey Peninsula Orchestra. It served as the orchestra of the Carmel Bach Festival through 1946, but was listed in the Festival programs as the "Monterey Peninsula Orchestra." Not until 1947 would the name of the orchestra be changed to the "Bach Festival Orchestra."

The chorus, on the other hand, was listed in the 1935 Festival programs as the "Bach Festival Chorus." After the December 1935 concert (as the "Community Chorus"), it, too, continued to perform only as the Bach Festival Chorus and gave no further independent concerts outside of the Festival.

"...the beginning of a new phase..."

Dene Denny and Hazel Watrous began their impresario partnership in 1923 in the third-floor ballroom of the Fisk House in San Francisco. After moving to Carmel, they presented concerts and events in their home on North Dolores Street until they opened the Denny-Watrous Gallery in January 1930.

This 1935 Christmas concert—with the enormity of the Brahms Requiem and the crowd that was no doubt overflowing into the street—was the final event in the Denny-Watrous Gallery. Dene and Hazel were giving up their Gallery, but they were also giving up the responsibility of maintaining (at their expense, year-round) one performing venue in which all their events had to take place. They were done with upkeep, maintenance costs, tax, rent, janitor, and utility bills.

Denny-Watrous Gallery To Close Doors This Week-End

With the closing at the end of this week of the present Denny-Watrous Gallery on San Carlos Street, comes the beginning of a new phase in the career of Dene Denny and Hazel Watrous, Carmel's leading impresarios for the past seven years. Rather than maintaining their own theater, they will conduct their activities in the manner of impresarios in the larger cities: booking attractions and placing them in the most advantageous quarters, depending upon the type of offering. Intimate quarters will be used for essentially intimate programs, and larger quarters for concerts of greater scope. They will maintain a ticket and business office in a down-town location not yet announced. They will continue to bring to Carmel outstanding and significant attractions in music and the dance, adding to the brilliant and impressive list of distinguished and out-of-the-ordinary attractions which they have sponsored in the past....

For the past year and a half on San Carlos, and before that on Dolores, "The Gallery" has been one of Carmel's real creative arts centers. Relying not on "big names" alone, though there have been plenty of those, but giving an opportunity for new, experimental music and musicians to be heard, Carmel's intimate concert hall has consistently kept step with the best metropolitan offerings. There are impresarios and impresarios; Dene Denny and Hazel Watrous have made their mark by a singularly whole-souled and selfless devotion to music and the allied arts. The new arrangement, they feel confident, will make it possible for them to do more effectively what they have always done well. (Pine Cone, December 27, 1935)

Winter–Spring 1936

The winter concert season began with the first event presented by Dene and Hazel after closing their gallery. An audience in the assembly room of the Pine Inn on January 18 heard the Byzantine Vocal Ensemble, a five-voice male a cappella group.

The Carmel Music Society season began with the Hart House String Quartet. In December 1927 at the Theatre of the Golden Bough they opened the Carmel Music Society's first season, and now after nine years they were back again in Carmel. The audience in Sunset Auditorium gave them a rousing welcome. Barely three weeks later, Jascha Heifetz, the 35-year-old superstar violinist, gave the Music Society's  second concert. The enthusiastic audience forced him to repeat one of the selections during the concert, and brought him back for three encores.

Meanwhile, at the Pine Inn once again, Denny-Watrous presented Lota, a singer and dancer who played an ancient instrument called the Cithara. The assembly room at the Pine Inn was a perfect venue for more intimate musical events presented by Denny-Watrous over the next few years.

The third concert of the Carmel Music Society series was the great Martha Graham and her dance company.

She is a phenomenon. It is indeed rare to find an artist so at one with the spirit of her own time, and so aflame with her own conviction. She is extraordinarily sincere, and sure of herself; there is nothing tentative in what she expresses, and she dances with her whole organism. Any individual who has that triumphant sureness of purpose, in whatever field of expression, deserves and receives respect and belief. (Pine Cone, April 3, 1936)

Jascha Heifetz, 1938. Martha Graham, 1936. Press photos courtesy of the author.

Graham was to be followed in April by the distinguished English pianist Myra Hess, who cancelled at the last minute. A substitute for Myra Hess was found in the dashing Nino Martini, a tenor "Endowed with youth and beauty, as well as one of the loveliest tenor voices on the stage today." Martini, nicknamed "The Cavalier of Song," was well known for his national radio broadcasts. He had just completed a series of performances at the Metropolitan Opera (*La Boheme, Rigoletto*), and was on his way to Hollywood to make two new films. Neither the Hart House Quartet, Martha Graham, nor even Heifetz could match the turnout for Martini's concert. The Sunset Auditorium was completely sold out, extra chairs were placed at the front, and additional audience chairs were placed on the stage. This provided the opportunity for yet another Carmel reviewer to talk about the audience.

> Carmel audiences are exceptionally responsive, as anyone will agree who has been part of regulation audiences in regulation communities, who believe in taking their enjoyment more or less secretly, not sure that it is quite the "right thing" to express approval, to say nothing of enthusiasm. When Carmel likes an artist, it manifests that liking not only by thunderous applause but by a tangible exciting electromagnetic current, which catches up audience and entertainer in a unity of response and purpose which makes active participants of the hearers, and gives the artist a sense of belonging intimately to the group. (Pine Cone, April 24, 1936)

At the end of its ninth season, the Carmel Music Society was in solid financial shape.

> The organization found many reasons to rejoice over its accomplishments this year. Having assumed the heaviest financial obligation of any season in its nine years, it had also the largest box office receipts in its history, the greatest number of people attending concerts, and end of the year with a small surplus. (Pine Cone, May 29, 1936)

The 30-member board of directors at that time included major, long-time supporters of music in Carmel such as Dene Denny, Hazel Watrous, Mr. and Mrs. Henry Dickinson, Mr. and Mrs. Paul Flanders, Dora Hagemeyer, Mr. and Mrs. Fritz Wurzman, Mrs. William Sloan Coffin, Mr. and Mrs. Rudolf Kocher (owners of the Hotel La Ribera) and Madeline Curry (a local music teacher who rehearsed the Bach Festival Chorus in the spring in the late 1930s).

In late 1935, Ernst Bacon accepted an invitation to administer the San Francisco District of the Federal Music Project. Because of this new full-time commitment, in the late winter he withdrew from participation in the 1936 Festival in Carmel. The Federal Music Project is a largely unknown and unappreciated part of President Roosevelt's "New Deal." Bacon and Usigli were both involved in the FMP, and so were Dene and Hazel, on a smaller scale. The FMP did wonderful things in the 1930s, and it deserves to be better known.

The Federal Music Project

Even before the Crash of 1929, musicians' lives already were being affected by advances in media technology. Radio occupied a central place in the home, just as TV and the Internet do now, and by 1925, more than 40 million American homes had a radio. Wind-up talking machines and their 78-rpm records were becoming more available and affordable. Both of these developments were reducing the demand for live music at parties, celebrations, and other events. With the end of the silent film era in 1928, the days of the pit orchestra were over. In-house hotel orchestras also were becoming a thing of the past, and even larger symphonies were forced to reduce their membership. (The San Francisco Symphony suspended its 1934–1935 season when its parent organization went bankrupt. At the same time, the S.F. Opera cut its season in half, and was kept alive by large donations from patrons.)

By 1934, while the US unemployment rate overall neared 25%, approximately 70% of formerly fully employed American musicians were out of work. (A.F.M. statistics)

After taking office in 1933, President Franklin D. Roosevelt proposed an array of government sponsored projects in order to raise employment, and he understood that the arts were important to American culture—promoting the "common welfare" included cultural enrichment, especially at that time. In 1935 the US Government established a program called Federal One, the first instance of the United States government giving money to the arts. Federal One was made up of four divisions: the Federal Art Project, the Federal Writer's Project, the Federal Theater Project, and the Federal Music Project (FMP). The FMP is today the least known of the four divisions, partly because it escaped the political issues and controversies that afflicted the other three. At the time, the work of the FMP was lauded by both political parties and by politicians around the world. Federal One was based on the assumption that professionals in the arts are as deserving of government assistance as any other workers. By supporting arts professionals from 1935 until 1942, America was enriched during those hard years, and the entire arts community was able to survive the Great Depression and be part of the thriving US growth in the 1940s and 1950s.

The primary goal of the FMP was work relief; a secondary goal was to democratize music by providing accessible performances and by bringing music to the schools; the third goal was to educate the public in the appreciation and expression of music. The first National Director of the Federal Music Project was Dr. Nikolai Sokoloff, the founding conductor of the Cleveland Orchestra. Sokoloff and his administrators believed that "good" music had an edifying effect on society, something to be desired in the social and economic upheaval of the 1930s. By "good music" they meant works written in the general European classical music tradition, including works by living composers. Jazz and folk music were not part of the FMP yet, but eventually a fifth division would be added, tasked with documenting American music.

More than half of the FMP budget went to the five principal areas of musician unemployment: New York, Boston, Chicago, Los Angeles, and San Francisco. The remainder of the budget was spent in the other forty-four states.

In late 1935, Ernst Bacon became the Supervisor of the San Francisco District (this full time commitment was the reason he left the Carmel Bach Festival). The FMP also asked him to oversee activities in East Bay, including Oakland and Berkeley, but Bacon believed the region was too large to be administered by one person. At Bacon's suggestion, Gastone Usigli was named Supervisor of the East Bay district in mid 1936, just after becoming a naturalized US citizen.

Nationwide, the FMP was very busy in its first two years.

WPA Project Record

Although it almost passes belief, 35,413,314 persons attended the events of the Federal Music Project throughout this country since October, 1935. And what did they hear? No less than 39,219 programs by Project symphony and concert orchestras; 24,414 band concerts by WPA bands and 369 performances of operas and operettas, according to a report submitted to Ellen S. Woodward, Assistant Administrator of the Works Progress Administration, by Dr. Nikolai Sokoloff, the Project's national director.

Furthermore, 11,940 recitals were given before and aggregate audience of 6,150,610 persons by students of the Project's teaching classes in twenty-six states. (New York Times, November 14, 1937, page 187)

The FMP engaged music teachers and musicians to lead choruses, bands, and orchestras. Ensembles of all sizes and levels performed in community centers, schools, hospitals, parks and rented venues.

As conductor of the San Francisco Federal Orchestra, Ernst Bacon led an ensemble of professionals in concerts of a wide array of repertoire, but avoided opera or staged musical works. Because of the demographics and needs of the Bay Area, Bacon felt that staged operas or operettas would deplete the resources elsewhere in the district.

Los Angeles was another matter. LA was well-acquainted with shows and spectacles of all kinds. Gastone Usigli became the Los Angeles FMP Supervisor in late 1936, and during his three years in LA he not only conducted the Los Angeles Federal Orchestra, he also led staged productions of everything from Gilbert and Sullivan to Verdi and Wagner. Furthermore, Usigli not only conducted, he was also the stage director, and he must have maintained a frantic pace. For example: *Aida* is one of the grandest of operas, and difficult to present, yet just one week later, on October 5, Usigli staged and conducted a performance of another blockbuster, Wagner's *Lohengrin*.

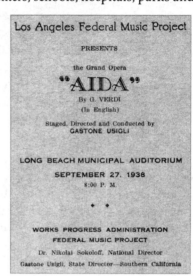

Los Angeles Federal Music Project

PRESENTS

the Grand Opera

"AIDA"

By G. VERDI

(In English)

Staged, Directed and Conducted by
GASTONE USIGLI

LONG BEACH MUNICIPAL AUDITORIUM

SEPTEMBER 27, 1938

8:00 P. M.

· ·

WORKS PROGRESS ADMINISTRATION
FEDERAL MUSIC PROJECT

Dr. Nikolai Sokoloff, National Director

Gastone Usigli, State Director—Southern California

Detail from the printed program of the FMP production of *Aida* on September 27, 1938, "Staged, Directed, and Conducted by Gastone Usigli." *Courtesy of the author.*

The passes of the Los Angeles (commuter) Railway featured a different advertisement each week, and in October 1937 it featured Gastone Usigli in his role as conductor of the Los Angeles Federal Orchestra.

Dene Denny was the Monterey District Supervisor of the FMP for about a year, beginning in late 1935, and led daily rehearsals of a local chorus and band. On the Monterey Peninsula, the effects of the FMP and the need for it were not as profound as they were in the major metropolitan areas. By the end of 1936 Dene resigned the position in order to spend more time in San José managing the new Denny-Watrous Concert Series.

Los Angeles Railway Weekly Pass, October 1937. *Courtesy of the author*

Legacy of the FMP

The Federal Music Project kept professional musicians working so that they could be ready for jobs in the private sector when times got better. American composers and their new music were showcased and promoted. And during intensely hard times the government had the great good sense to provide the American people with access to uplifting live entertainment, when few people had the resources to put on a live show and even fewer had money to buy a ticket.

More than 50 orchestras were created by the Federal Music Project in the 1930s. Some of these "federal orchestras" changed their names in the 1940s and are still performing today, including the Utah Symphony, Oklahoma City Philharmonic, Hartford Symphony, Portland Symphony, Syracuse Symphony, and the San Diego Symphony. The Buffalo Philharmonic began as a federal orchestra, and performed for decades in Kleinhans Hall, funded by the New Deal in 1939.

Carmel Bach Festival 1936

> The Carmel Bach Festival is established. It is the intention of Dene Denny and Hazel Watrous to make it an annual event, bringing for its direction each year a conductor of eminence, and for its concerts, soloists of national standing, at the same time developing and maintaining a permanent local orchestra and chorus, whose devotion to the music of Bach will build toward that tradition which comes along through generations of native music-making. (From the introduction in the 1936 Carmel Bach Festival program book.)

As late as January the 1936 Festival was still being referred to in the Carmel and San Francisco press as a Mozart festival). There is no record of what discussions took place after Ernst Bacon's departure in the winter, but by the end of April Dene and Hazel had discarded the Mozart idea. The previous summer, they had presented "a" Bach Festival, and now in 1936 they made a commitment. On April 24, Denny-Watrous announced in the Pine Cone that violinist Sascha Jacobinoff would return to conduct the "1936 Carmel Bach Festival." This marks the first official use of the Festival's full name.

Once again Jacobinoff drove from Philadelphia to Carmel, departing on May 10 and this time accompanied by four students who would play in the orchestra during the summer. In the months before Jacobinoff's arrival, Bernard Callery conducted the weekly orchestra and chorus rehearsals in the "lunch room" of the Sunset School, known today as Carpenter Hall. Jacobinoff arrived in Carmel on June 1, and led the rehearsals from then until the opening night on July 20.

Theater life in Carmel was stagnant, and the Forest Theater had fallen on hard times. Theater lovers were morose. A month before the first Bach Festival concert, the Pine Cone ran an editorial.

> ### The Bach Festival
>
> If the prospect of summer dramatics seems slim, music comes into its heyday in Carmel this summer. Last year's Bach Festival was an experience never to be forgotten by those who participated in it, either as performers or as listeners. The festival this year will be all that it was last year, and more. The music will be all new;—so vast is the Bach repertoire that we can have many annual festivals without ever repeating ourselves—the soloists are of a high caliber; the highest of musical ideals are activating the entire enterprise. The festival is attracting attention all over the state; eventually it will be one of the nationally important summer festivals of music.
>
> The importance of such a venture to the community can scarcely be overstated. While the spiritual values are the important ones, and we contend that no community can be the center of such a project and not undergo a process of spiritual regeneration, there is

SECOND ANNUAL
CARMEL
BACH
FESTIVAL

MONDAY - TUESDAY - THURSDAY - SATURDAY - SUNDAY

JULY - 20 to 26 ————————— 1936

Details from 1936 ticket brochure and program booklet. On the cover: Chandler Stewart and his sons, the debut of the Heralding Trombones at the Carmel Bach Festival..
Courtesy of the Carmel Bach Festival.

CARMEL
BACH FESTIVAL

JULY 20 to 26, 1936

MONDAY — TUESDAY — THURSDAY — SATURDAY — SUNDAY
EVENINGS AT 8:30 ————————

CONDUCTOR OF THE FESTIVAL

S A S C H A   J A C O B I N O F F

MEMBERS OF THE ADVISORY BOARD
CARMEL BACH FESTIVAL ASSOCIATION

O. W. Bardarson	Mrs. Thelma Miller
Mrs. John Bathen	Mrs. James S. Parker
Mrs. F. M. Blanchard	Mrs. Caroline Pickit
John Catlin	Everett Smith
Mrs. William S. Coffin	Mrs. Gwendolyn Stearns
E. W. Ewig	Noel Sullivan
Mrs. Katherine MacF. Howe	James Thoburn
Conrad Imelman	Miss Emma Wahdvogel
John Jordan	Willard W. Wheeler
Miss Ella Kellogg	Miss Helen Willard
Dr. R. A. Kocher	Mrs. W. B. Williams
Milton Latham	Dr. Mast Wolfson
Mrs. Eugene Marble	Judge George Wood

——— D E N N Y - W A T R O U S   M A N A G E M E N T ———

CARMEL
BACH FESTIVAL

PRESENTED BY DENNY-WATROUS MANAGEMENT

JULY - 20 to 26, 1936

SASCHA JACOBINOFF, Director

MONDAY, JULY 20
8:30 p. m.

Sunset School Auditorium. — Sascha Jacobinoff, conducting
Three Chorals .... Festival Chorus
Overture, C major .... Orchestra
Concerto for Piano and Orchestra, D minor, TAMARA MORGEN, soloist
Cantata, "Jesu, Priceless Treasure," Festival Chorus with Orchestral accompaniment.
Soloists:
RUDOLPHINE RADIL, soprano, RADIANA PAZMOR, contralto, LAWRENCE STRAUSS, tenor, JOHN FERRY, bass.

TUESDAY, JULY 21
8:30 p. m.

Sunset School Auditorium — Sascha Jacobinoff, conducting
Brandenburg Concerto V for Flute, Violin, Piano and Strings
Soloists:
MARION MOULIN, FRANK COSTANZA, RALPH LINSLEY
Cantata, "Jauchzett in Allen Landen" for soprano voice, trumpet and strings
Soloist: RUDOLPHINE RADIL
Pastorale - - - - - - - - - - - - - - Strings
Air from Bach Suite - - - - - - - - - - - Strings
Concerto D minor for two violins and orchestra
Soloists: FRANK COSTANZA, ABRAM KAROL

WEDNESDAY, JULY 22—No Concert

THURSDAY, JULY 23
Program of Piano Works

Chorale G major, Fantasie and Fugue A minor, arranged for two pianos
Soloists: CREIGHTON PASMORE, VICTOR TRERICE
Concerto C major for three pianos
OLGA STEEB, CREIGTON PASMORE, VICTOR TRERICE
Works for solo piano: Prelude in E flat minor, Prelude and Fugue in C sharp minor, Sarabande and Passapied, Caprice in C minor, Chromatic Fantasie and Fugue
OLGA STEEB

FRIDAY, JULY 24—No Concert

SATURDAY, JULY 25
8:30 p. m.—Sunset School Auditorium

Quintet from Brandenburg II for string quartet and piano.
Soloists:
SASCHA JACOBINOFF, HUBERT SORENSON, ABRAHAM WEISS
DORETHA ULSH, RALPH LINSLEY
Aria, "Only Be Still," from Cantata 93, for tenor voice
LAWRENCE STRAUSS
Prelude and Fugue in D major from Organ Prelude - - Strings
Sonata for flute and piano
MARION MOULIN, DOUGLAS THOMPSON
Three sacred songs, self-accompanied
RADIANA PAZMOR
Concerto E major for solo violin and orchestra
Soloist: SASCHA JACOBINOFF.   BERNARD CALLERY conducting

SUNDAY, JULY 26
8:30 p. m.—Carmel Mission
Sascha Jacobinoff, conducting

Sanctus, from B minor Mass - - - - - - Festival Chorus
"Agnus Dei" from B minor Mass
RADIANA PAZMOR
"Arioso" - - - - - - - - - - - - - - Strings
Three Sacred Songs for bass voice
NOEL SULLIVAN
Cantata, "A Stronghold Sure" - Festival Chorus, Orchestral Accompaniment
Soloists:
RUDOLPHINE RADIL, RADIANA PAZMOR, LAWRENCE STRAUSS, JOHN FERRY

Tickets on Sale, DENNY-WATROUS OFFICE at Thoburns—Ocean Ave.
Season seats: 7.70, 5.50, incl. tax. Single seats: 1.75, 1.50, 1.00, 50c—plus tax

Daily Lecture on BACH at Pine Inn by MYRA PALACHE. Admission 40c

an economic side not to be overlooked. The summer music maintains the high standards of Carmel. It helps to emphasize the quality of the village as a place devoted to the arts. It brings people here, and people of the finest type only. It is the best possible antidote for the raffish resort atmosphere which would be fatal to all that Carmel holds dear.

There can be no question as to the worthiness of the Bach Festival to receive community support, the stamp of community approval; from the business people, the noncommercial residents, the city fathers. No divided allegiance will appear here; Carmel is solidly behind the Bach Festival, and again this year it will be a great experience. (Pine Cone, June 12, 1936)

A long article in the Pine Cone included the same reassurance that had appeared the previous summer.

… Though the music of Bach has been much associated with a cloistered, reverent, "high brow" atmosphere, increased familiarity with the Bach repertoire discloses such infinite beauty, variety and definiteness of tunc and rhythm, but even people who have no formal musical training can enjoy and appreciate it. In addition such music as a community chorus and orchestra are now learning for their contribution to the festival, has a majesty and sonority that carries the spirits of both performers and listeners to the heights. (Pine Cone, June 19, 1936)

At the beginning of July a meeting was held to form a Carmel Bach Festival Association.

The idea of the Bach Festival was originated last year by Miss Dene Denny and Miss Hazel Watrous, who assumed both the financial risk and the hard work connected with the two festivals. It is possible that the advisory board which is at present working with Miss Denny and Miss Watrous in an informal capacity may organize at the end of the summer as the permanent community sponsors of what is felt will become a valuable annual event. (Pine Cone, July 3, 1936)

In 1936 there were 26 members on the advisory committee. The Bach Festival did not have a governing board of directors until 1958, and the advisory board offered support and advice to Dene and Hazel until then.

In early July, excitement began to build once again as professional musicians arrived in Carmel from San Francisco, Los Angeles, Fresno, Sacramento, and a half-dozen cities outside California. The 1936 Festival was five concerts over a period of seven days: Monday, Tuesday, Thursday, Saturday, and Sunday. The 1935 festival had come as a surprise for much of the community, and those not directly involved in the advance preparations had not really known what to expect. In 1936, on the other hand, expectations and hopes were very high.

For the second time, beginning next Monday evening, Carmel will have the memorable experience of being steeped in the music of Johann Sebastian Bach for an entire week. For 100 resident musicians, the immersion process has been going on for a number of weeks. By today, practically all the guests artists will have arrived for final intensive rehearsals with the orchestra and chorus today tomorrow and Sunday. In no other California city does an equally fine aggregation of musicians gather together for community music making, a chorus of 50, orchestra of some 40, and a score of soloists of national fame.

There is no other summer festival of music of this significance on the entire Pacific coast. Famed Carmel has added to its stature all over the nation because of the scope of the second annual Bach Festival as arranged by Dene Denny and Hazel Watrous, Carmel's own impresarios. (Pine Cone, July 17, 1936)

Through the vision and untiring efforts of Dene Denny and Hazel Watrous, Carmel at last has hit upon the ideal civic enterprise, one of which we may be keenly proud, and which unites us all in the sense of a task eminently worth performing. (Pine Cone, July 24, 1936) [emphasis added]

Once again lectures were given at 11:00am on the five concert days. This year the lectures took place at the Pine Inn and were free to ticket holders. The general public paid 40¢.

Another advance article praised the conductor, Sascha Jacobinoff.

In marked fashion, a Festival of music mirrors the personality of its director, both as to the selection of works and in their interpretation. Sascha Jacobinoff as a violinist is noted for the rich and colorful quality of his tone. It will be noted that color and brilliance are keynotes of this year's Bach Festival, to emphasize a frequently overlooked side of the master composer. In Jacobinoff, the Carmel Festival has a director with a happy blend of qualities: the background of well-rounded professional experience, innate artistry, gifts which command the respect of artists, and a knack with amateurs which wins their loyalty and inspires them to work their hardest and discover unexpected reserves within themselves. (Pine Cone, July 17, 1936)

Shown here is the main entrance to the old Sunset School auditorium as it appeared from 1931 until 2000. From the courtyard, the audience entered the lobby through two large Gothic-arched doorways. During the construction of the new Sunset Center Theater in 2002 and 2003, the entire facade was preserved intact, moved about 50 feet from the construction site, and then installed inside the foyer of the new auditorium. With this happy stroke of architectural imagination, modern audiences enter the new auditorium through the two original arched doorways.

Above the two arched doors is a small window overlooking the courtyard. On the opening night of the festival, as audience members were arriving and the performers backstage in the auditorium were preparing for the 8:30 concert, the windows above the arched doors were opened and the bells of four trombones appeared,

Entrance facade of the Sunset School auditorium, early 1930s. *Courtesy of the Carmel Bach Festival.*

establishing in that moment an important Carmel Bach Festival tradition.

Since its founding in 1900, the Bethlehem Bach Festival in Pennsylvania (drawing from its Moravian roots) featured a trombone quartet playing Bach chorales outside the concert hall just prior to their performances. Perhaps someone in Carmel was inspired by this example, but for whatever reason, the Bach Festival now had its own Heralding Trombones: in 1936 they were Monterey grocer Chandler Stewart and three of his sons.

Thelma Miller of the Pine Cone was entranced by this new experience.

> A moment of enchanted beauty opened the festival on Monday evening. From the balcony window just over the entrance of Sunset Auditorium came the finely blended tones of four trombones playing a slow and solemn chorale. Early arrivals paused and looked up, and the members of the orchestra and chorus, already assembled backstage, poured out into the courtyard. Little knots of people gathered, conversation instinctively hushed. Automatically the men bared their heads. To the eye was presented a composition worthy of the attention of a Rembrandt; the Gothic arches of the school building were a substantial and peculiarly appropriate background for the listeners in attitudes of reverence, and the twinkling lights were diffused by the streamers of fog drifting down through the dark pines. In that moment, if not before, the spirit of the Festival was born, gripping the hearts of those who shared it. (Pine Cone, July 24, 1936)

The Heralding Trombones were such a hit that for the next seasons they performed from their window during intermissions as well as prior to the concerts. Until 1942, they also played from the tower of the Carmel Mission before Festival concerts, and were nicknamed Tower Music.

FOURTH ANNUAL CARMEL
BACH FESTIVAL
JULY 18 to 24 1938

Today the Tower Music pre-concert serenades are a popular and cherished Festival tradition.

The opening concert of the 1936 Bach Festival began with three chorales, including a repeat of a favorite from the previous summer. This was followed by the *Overture in C Major for Orchestra,* with clarinets playing the oboe parts. This particular instrumental switch (clarinets for oboes) happened in six of the first fourteen Bach Festivals, based on the availability of oboists capable of playing Bach's challenging solos; the Bach Festival's last documented use of clarinets instead of oboes in Bach's music was in the *Mass in B Minor* in 1950.

After intermission, Tamara Morgan played the *D Minor Harpsichord Concerto* (on piano) and the entire concert concluded with Bach's Motet *Jesu, Priceless Treasure,* BWV 227, sung in English by the Chorus and accompanied by orchestra. (The program mistakenly called the motet a "cantata.") The entire 1936 Festival schedule is shown in the facsimile of the ticket brochure on page 241.

Sascha Jacobinoff was officially the "Conductor of the Festival." The title "Musical Director" [sic] first appeared at the Bach Festival in 1952. Jacobinoff was a lithe, nimble and exacting conductor, and the audience and musicians loved him.

Tradition in the making in Carmel as second Bach Festival stirs music lovers

...Sascha Jacobinoff was the leavening agent of the festival this year. The effects of his firm and electrifying hands on the reins are everywhere perceptible, and when his name is mentioned, words of praise follow. He is given credit for raising the orchestra to a new point of excellence, and for whipping the chorus into an instrument which has made beautiful and thrilling music this week.

Jacobinoff's conducting was as delightful as his violin playing. With his right hand he thrust with his baton like a lance as if to dig out the melody from the vein of harmony, and meanwhile his left hand was outspread with prehensile digits which projected to prompt the various instruments he wished to respond. (Pine Cone, July 24, 1936)

On the Saturday concert, Jacobinoff played the *E Major Violin Concerto*, as he had done on opening night of the festival the previous summer. His concerto performance was conducted by Bernard Callery, who served as assistant conductor for the next few festival seasons. Callery was born in 1913 in Santa Clara of Irish immigrant parents. A life-long music educator, he taught in schools in San José, Sacramento, and Auburn, where he retired.

The Bach Festival's effect on the community in 1936 was even greater than it had been the year before. This editorial appeared in the Pine Cone five days after the final concert.

CAUSE FOR PRIDE

The second annual Bach Festival is over, and it is been a success of a sort to cause civic entrepreneurs all over the West to sit up and take notice. The sight of Sunset auditorium filled almost to capacity for four nights in one week, the audiences increasing each night to a sell-out on Saturday evening, and Carmel Mission on Sunday night with every seat occupied, is an eye-opener for skeptics. This is an enterprise which has captured the imagination of a larger public than Carmel alone can offer. Dene Denny and Hazel Watrous have had a large and inspired vision, and the practical ability to bring it brilliantly into realization. Carmel is fortunate in having them; very rarely is the finest musical taste combined with executive ability sufficient to operate such a tremendous enterprise smoothly.

Through all the busy weeks leading up to the festival, and last week with its myriad details and long hours of most difficult work, the serenity, good nature, and confident knowledge of what they were about that has been displayed by these two women has been remarkable. Big projects of this sort have gone on the rocks and disintegrated just through fatigue and frazzled nerves on the part of the promoters. Efficiency has played as large a part in the success of the Bach Festival as artistic understanding.

Carmel has a peculiar attitude toward its only industry:—ministering to the traveling public. Behind the largely assumed indifference to "outsiders" is a more realistic recognition that the life of the community very largely depends upon a steady flow of visitors. Even many retired people who come here for peace and quiet are not above owning a few rental homes from which they hope to profit during the summer months. Whatever the attitude, it is a foregone conclusion that Carmel has, and will increasingly continue to have, a very definite attraction for vacationers and world travelers. The sort of people who come here, whether they make themselves a nuisance or a civic asset, depends very largely on what we offer them. It is undesirable from every standpoint that Carmel should have a reputation as a place to "let down" and indulge in conduct of which the visitors would not be guilty in their own hometowns.

Our own best protection is to fill the village to the saturation point with the sort of visitors who share the ideals of the best of the resident population. The people who come to Carmel because it is a Bach Festival town represent the cream. Many of them will, in time, remain longer than the week of the festival. Their very presence contributes to an atmosphere which undesirable people do not find congenial. The festival audiences last week were largely made up of interesting, intelligent-looking people, the sort one is proud to see in Carmel.

It is safe to say that Carmel has never sponsored a finer enterprise than the annual Bach Festival, nor one more worthy of continued support and encouragement. (Pine Cone, July 31, 1936)

The fall season was quiet, as the Great Depression maintained its hold on America. There was no Christmas concert that year in Carmel, but considerable cheer was generated by the December 11 announcement that the 1937 Carmel Bach Festival would be led by the very man who had originally helped to create the orchestra and chorus: cellist Michel Penha. He had been living and working in Los Angeles for the past two years and would be coming to Carmel in mid December to hold two rehearsals each with the orchestra and the chorus. Apparently, membership discipline in the orchestra was being increased, and the December 2011 announcement included the following lines:

> After the rehearsals with Penha have begun, no inexperienced players will be accepted into the orchestra, so that the orchestra rehearsal of next Sunday night will be the last opportunity for beginners to join. (Pine Cone, December 11, 1936)

With those last rehearsals led by Michel Penha, the orchestra and chorus bid farewell to 1936 and began to think about the 1937 Bach Festival.

Ralph Linsley

When the Neah-Kah-Nie String Quartet came to Carmel in the summer of 1932, pianist Ralph Linsley came with them. He was rehearsal pianist for their first concert until the actual pianist arrived in town, and he performed with the Quartet in Brahms chamber music later that summer. Linsley also played in Carmel several times in 1933 and 1934 but he did not participate in the first Carmel Bach Festival in 1935. He was back in 1936, however, and established a relationship with the Bach Festival that endured until his retirement in 1973. The Bach Festival program that year featured an article about Ralph Linsley written by Joy Belden, excerpted below.

"Mr. Bach Festival"

"Ralph Linsley, continuo."—familiar words! They have appeared in every Carmel Bach Festival program since 1936, and they aptly describe Ralph Linsley's part in both orchestra and Festival. The continuo underlies the counterpoint, holding the various voices together, providing support on which the whole harmonic structure rests. Similarly, Ralph's work in the festival underlay all other activities. He arranged auditions, scheduled rehearsals, planned the moving and tuning schedule for the keyboard instruments—and played the continuo. He carried in his amazing memory a vast amount of information and detail, and acted as a consultant in everything.... He graduated from Yale University in 1927, Phi Beta Kappa. He moved with his parents to California and was invited to join a group that met at the California Institute of Technology to sing Bach. The weekly sessions grew into the Bach Society of Pasadena, a chorus of 50 voices conducted at first by Michel Penha, later by Richard Lert, always with Ralph Linsley as accompanist....

"At the outbreak of World War II, Ralph, like many others, answered a draft call in September 1942, and was given an assignment as chaplain's assistant, based in North Africa. With his portable organ he visited the Gold Coast, Nigeria, the Anglo Egyptian Sudan, the Holy Land and Arabia.

"When Staff Sgt. Linsley was separated from the Army in 1945, he resumed his concert work, accompanying over the years such artists as soprano Nan Merriman, tenor Tito Schipa, soprano Dorothy Kirsten, and too many others to mention. In the intervals of travel he was drawn irresistibly to explore the Baroque period. He studied first with Alice Ehlers, then entered the school of music at the University of Southern California where he majored in harpsichord. He took his degree as master of music in 1954" *(from Joy Belden's article in the 1973 Carmel Bach Festival program book.)*

In the 1963 Bach Festival program book, there is a mention of Ralph Linsley's 25th anniversary with the Bach Festival. The article concludes with these lines:

First contact with the festival for most participants over the years has been with Linsley. He is, more than any other person, "Mr. Bach Festival" and all who have heard the festival performed in it owe him an immeasurable gratitude. (1963 Carmel Bach Festival program.)

In his oral history, Sandor Salgo, Conductor and Musical Director of the Festival 1956–1991, used that same nickname when recalling how important Linsley had been to him and to the Festival.

Ralph Linsley with the Bach Festival Chorus, c.1950. *Photos these two pages courtesy of the Carmel Bach Festival.*

...in 1936, Ralph Linsley, a pianist and harpsichordist from Los Angeles, joined Mr. Penha to form a piano quartet. Ralph Linsley joined the Festival at that point, and he became the general coordinator and organizer of the Festival. I have to add in the warmest possible terms that he was my right hand during my years in Carmel, and tireless in helping out wherever he was needed, whether it was smoothing the ruffled feathers of the players or poring over the program proofs late at night. Whatever needed to be done, he was there to do it, even coaching singers and playing for rehearsals. Some people called him "Mr. Bach Festival." (Salgo Oral History, UC Berkeley)

Carmel and San José 1937

The Carmel Music Society presented a four-concert series beginning in January 1937. The opening concert was Harold Bauer, the distinguished English pianist who had appeared with the Neah-Kah-Nie String Quartet in the opening concert of the 1932 Summer Series.

Richard Crooks, the popular Metropolitan Opera tenor, became ill on the day of his concert and had to be bundled up and driven to his throat doctor in Los Angeles. It was an enormous disappointment. There must be something about tenors: as with Nino Martini, not only was the Crooks concert sold out, with ticket buyers coming from King City, Salinas, and Santa Cruz, but the fire company had once again agreed that 75 additional chairs could be put in Sunset Auditorium, including 40 on the stage. Crooks returned two weeks later and sang for the expected more–than–full house.

The final concerts of the Music Society spring season were Nathan Milstein, violinist, and Trudi Schoop, a Swiss dancer with a comedy dance troupe.

In late 1936, Dene and Hazel assumed management of a San José concert and performing arts series that had been operating for two years at the San José Civic Auditorium. They booked the performers and publicized the events, just as they were already doing in Carmel, but with two big differences.

First, it was an entirely commercial artistic enterprise. They were impresarios whose intention was to produce events and make money. Second: they had a much bigger venue. The Civic Auditorium—with 3,378 seats—had nearly five times the seating capacity of Sunset Auditorium. Even after their additional expenses in San José (apartment and office rental, travel, publicity, actual costs of renting and staffing the enormous auditorium for the performances, etc.) their potential net revenue per event was considerable. This increase in ticket revenue, together with a larger stage, meant that there was no practical limitation to the size of the ensembles or the scope of the events. Thus, in addition to great soloists such as Yehudi Menuhin and Marian Anderson, they presented major North American orchestras on tour as well as touring opera companies from the US and Europe, Broadway shows, stage plays with major stars, and ballet productions with orchestra.

For example, on February 1, Denny-Watrous Management presented the Ballet Russe de Monte Carlo at the Civic Auditorium. The world-famous company was led by dancer and ballet master Léonide Massine, at that time the greatest of all Russian dancers. The entire touring company totaled more than 130 and included a full orchestra.

The third advantage was location: the city of San José is in an area that was (and is) much more densely populated than the Monterey Peninsula; with their knack for clever booking, Dene and Hazel had no trouble attracting audiences to fill the enormous venue. Their San José performances drew sell-out crowds, and the series there was by far the most lucrative of all their impresario activities together. They presented a dozen or more concerts, plays, ballets, and opera performances each season in San José; they entertained countless thousands of people; they generated a dependable income for themselves for two decades; and, most important to this story, they were able to use their San José income to help cover deficits in their projects in Carmel, including the early Bach Festival seasons and the new theater company they were about to create.

California's First Theater

"Many a miner passed through this door,
Who swore he would never come in anymore.
'Twas here they eased him of nuggets of gold,
This was the place where booze was sold.
One drink was enough to make him want more,
And pretty damn soon he was flat on the floor.
On sobering up he would always swear off,
Then come in the next day for a drink for his cough."

A placard with these words is said to have been displayed by the door of the house built in Monterey in 1844 by John Alfred "Jack" Swan, a Scotsman, itinerant sailor, and ship's cook. In 1844 he sailed into Monterey Bay aboard the Mexican schooner California, captained by John B.R. Cooper, an early Monterey pioneer. Swan had been to Monterey before, and he liked it, so he either quit, jumped ship, or was fired (depending on who is retelling the story).

Swan salvaged lumber from an old shipwreck and built a timber house on the southwest corner of Pacific and Scott Streets in Monterey. By the mid 1840s, even before the discovery of

gold, East Coast Yankees were coming to California. The predominant cuisine in Monterey at that time was Mexican, and the Easterners missed their old familiar foods, so Swan cooked and sold food they knew: fruit pies and other baked goods, roasted vegetables, and pasties. The pasty (pronounced "pass-tea") has its roots in the British Isles, and is a pastry dough filled with meat or vegetables and baked. It forms a complete meal that can be wrapped and carried easily and eaten without utensils.

The food business was a success and so Swan added an informal tavern to the setup inside the cabin. With his profits he built a large adobe addition as a lodging house for itinerant sailors. At the end of the Mexican War in early 1848, Colonel John D. Stevenson's 1st New York Volunteer Regiment had been stationed in Monterey for months with nothing to do, and they occasionally put on small skits and shows to amuse themselves. Their paychecks stopped after the war ended, and they persuaded Jack Swan to allow them to convert the adobe building into a theater for the production of melodramas—as a purely short-term profit-making venture.

Upper right: a modern photo of the exterior of Swan's cabin. *Courtesy Library of Congress.* Lower left: First Theater in the mid 1930s. *Courtesy of the author. Other First Theater material public domain or courtesy of the author.*

They built a small stage, and benches were made from planks set across old nail and gunpowder kegs. Swan brought in whale oil lamps, built footlights with candles, and hung curtains and backdrops made from blue and red blankets.

In the mid to late 19th century, the "melodrama" was a popular type of theatrical presentation. Melodramas are intended to appeal to the emotions, there is no subtlety or nuance: morality is polarized, good battles with evil. With their sensational story lines and unlikely "deus ex machina" plot twists, melodramas were the soap operas of their day.

The first play presented on Swan's stage was Nathaniel Bannister's "Putnam, the Iron Son of '76," a new patriotic melodrama and among the most successful stage plays of the 1840s. All the actors were men, and those playing female characters wore bandanas around their heads. Tickets cost a staggering $5, a sign of the hunger for amusement in the outposts of the New World, and the opening night proceeds totaled more than $500.

That performance on June 3, 1848, is the first documented theatrical performance in California presented for a paying audience, earning Jack Swan's adobe the official title "California's First Theater."

Later that summer the soldiers departed for home with their theater earnings, and Swan partitioned the adobe once again and used it for a few more years as a lodging house for sailors. From 1860 to 1890 Swan spent much of his time in British Columbia, and the building fell into

disrepair. It was abandoned after Swan's death in 1896, and acquired by the California Historic Landmarks League in 1906 and donated to the state of California as a historic landmark. Over a period of three decades, a gradual restoration took place, and during that time the building was used as a tea room, book store, and curio shop. By 1935, it was a "museum" housing a dusty and eclectic accumulation of 19th century artifacts and furniture. A 1935 article describes the contents of the museum:

> "...a bamboo gun used by Filipino insurgents against the Spaniards; a baby octopus; a hand-made bed; typical Spanish fireplaces; a chair made from the Vizcaino-Serra Oak; an old oak table; billboards from 1847; Grecian and Persian pottery; a table used by Gen. Castro at the customs house in 1846; an old spinning wheel brought from Massachusetts in an oxcart; a half bushel measure sent in 1852 from Washington to the customhouse; one of the four pianos Gen. Vallejo brought around the horn in 1847; relics of the Donner party. These are only a few of the exhibits that contributed much of the flavor of old Spain to the observer." (Pine Cone, July 23, 1935)

After closing the Denny-Watrous Gallery in December 1935, Dene and Hazel were surveying other performing venues on the Peninsula. When they saw Swan's dusty old structure they

understood its historic and artistic potential as a venue for 19th century melodramas such as *The Drunkard*. They leased the building from the state of California with the stipulation that all plays performed must have been written prior to 1900. A new stage and new wooden benches were built, and the interior of Swan's original timber cabin was refurbished and converted to a foyer and bar. Once they had leased the theater, Dene and Hazel founded their theater company: The Troupers of the Gold Coast. All Troupers were volunteers, and the only paid members of the company were the costume designer, stage manager, set designer, and (sometimes) the stage director. Rhoda Johnson had done the costumes in 1927 for several plays in the Denny-Watrous season at the Theatre of the Golden Bough, and Hazel invited her to the First Theater, where she was a core element of the troupe for decades. Her husband Dick served as stage manager, as he also had done in Carmel.

Tatters, the Pet of Squatter's Gulch, written in 1840 by Levin C. Tees, was the Theater's first production. Dene and Hazel brilliantly chose the date of June 3 for their opening night, the 89th anniversary of the first performance on that same stage back in 1848. As with every production by the Troupers of the Gold Coast over the decades, the drama of the evening was followed by an aftershow entertainment called the "Olio," in which the cast of the play performed a rollicking vaudeville pastiche of singing, dancing, skits, and broad comedy.

The play was directed by Galt Bell, who had directed "The Drunkard," the big success in 1932 at the Denny-Watrous Gallery. Charles "Blackie" O'Neal came up from LA to play a leading role and serve as MC for the Olio. O'Neal was an actor who became a successful Hollywood screenwriter, and was the father of actor Ryan O'Neal. He is typical of the professionals who joined the Troupers of the Gold Coast from time to time to be part of the fun. Opening night tickets were $2.50, and for the rest of the run they sold for $1.10 and 50¢. "Tatters" was a phenomenal success, and was brought back for a second run in July and again in August.

Theatrical history was made in a historic setting last evening, when a museum piece of the theater which may rival "The Drunkard" in popularity came to the tiny stage of Monterey's quaint First Theater. The man at the helm of "Tatters, the Pet of Squatter's Gulch," was also the man who launched "The Drunkard" on its incredible career: Galt Bell, a producer who has become a specialist in the revival of 19th-century melodrama.

The privilege of attending a performance in the quaint little theater is alone worth the trip over the hill [from Carmel]. The settings by Phil Nesbitt are worth at least half the price of admission, and the show itself is a large bonus. On the tiny stage the figures of hero and villain loom in heroic mould. The Nesbitt backdrops are drawn into the action by representing actual objects and persons on the stage, like a naïve effort to make the stage appear larger than it is. And the way the hard-working cast "doubles" in entr'actes and the after show olio, perfects the illusion of a ragbag touring "rep" show doing its best to please the yokels of some hinterland 50 years ago. (Pine Cone, June 4, 1937)

Although it is easy to lampoon these melodramas as shallow, silly and absurd, it is important to understand that the Troupers of the Gold Coast presented them (more or less) "straight," without goofing around on the stage or reacting self-consciously to the sometimes ridiculous script. In a 20th century revival of 19th century melodrama, the comedy derives from the modern audience's reaction to a straight presentation of the over-the-edge dialogue and plot. If the actors simply deliver their lines sincerely and as written, the results are inevitably hilarious, especially with the vocal participation of the audience. For example, this is a monologue delivered in the first act of "Tatters" by one of the leads.

"They would select me as the tool for their bloody crime, but they make a great mistake. Haven't they already embittered my life with their hatred, scorn, and neglect, both of me and my mother—mother—alas! I have no mother. The curse of blight and desolation that has fallen on my life never inflicted a more bitter pang than when it robbed me of her.

"Ever since I was a little boy, I have had to toil in the mill to support my poor bed-ridden mother. I used to roll her little cot-bed out on the porch under the shadow of the big maple trees that stood by the door—so that she could amuse herself listening to the whisper of the leaves and the sweet song of the birds (they were her only companions from morn till night accept our faithful dog). Three days ago I left my work without a thought or fear of the dreadful blow was so soon to overtake me. I bore good news, too—my employer that very day had promised to promote me.

"As I walked gayly up the pathway—calling to let my mother know of my approach—the strange and solemn stillness was all the answer, broken as I neared the gate by the wild wailing of the faithful dog. A sudden terror seized me, my limbs almost refused to obey my will. The few steps intervening between me and the porch seemed endless. But last I stood face to face with the bitter truth. I was alone. There on the cot lay my mother peacefully smiling in the embrace of death!"

The author had the great good fortune of attending performances at the First Theater during the 1990s, but for those who have not experienced a melodrama, this review gives a glimpse of the boisterous atmosphere.

> "Tatters, the Pet of Squatter's Gulch" closed its second five-night run Monday night, and went down in history as one of those phenomenal successes which indicate that the public's fickle fancy has been exactly suited. It played to capacity houses every night, and some enthusiasts saw it three or four times.
>
> The performance was never exactly the same twice, it was too spontaneous for that. You never could tell how the audience would react, and the audience was really half the show. After they got really warmed up to the situation they did not stop with just hissing the villain, but they yelled frantic warnings at the heroine when the dastardly villain was about to abduct her, answered rhetorical questions from the stage, and responded politely to all asides addressed to the audience.
>
> This may become one of those historical occasions, from which Carmel events are dated... Galt Bell found the script, staged the show, and wrote a good deal of it as he went along. Norman McNeil played accordion music for the play and accompanied part of the Olio. The settings and curtains were by Phil Nesbitt, and Dene Denny and Hazel Watrous were the impresarios. (Pine Cone, July 9, 1937)

Once more, Dene and Hazel had come up with a good idea, and once again it involved the community on both sides of the footlights. The First Theater was within blocks of downtown Monterey, it offered a fun and utterly unique theatrical experience, and it became popular with tourists and beloved among the locals. The Troupers performed year-round, and when a play reached the end of its run it closed on Saturday and a new play opened the following Friday. From 1937 until her death in 1954, Hazel was a familiar figure to First Theater audiences, and she attended nearly every performance.

> Hazel, in particular, loves her work with this little theater. She watches the tiny stage and the actors appearing before their exaggerated sets and she has a strange feeling that they haven't yet begun to touch the possibilities that await them. The plays should take on the feeling of a miniature, she feels, and that there is more of true theater here, than on the conventional stage. Much of her work is with the costumes, and you all know how much of our delight comes from those. (Carmel Cymbal, July 14, 1939)

Virtually all the plays produced at the First Theater were mid to late 19th century melodramas, but on just a few occasions they explored other repertoire. In 1939 the Troupers experimented with Henrik Ibsen's play *A Doll's House*, and Gilbert and Sullivan's *HMS Pinafore* was produced in 1941. Aside from those exceptions, however, the Troupers of the Gold Coast performed only American (and, often but discretely, British) plays written between 1850 and 1900, and did so with great success until 2000.

Bach Festival 1937

By the third Bach Festival, the community was getting into the swing of things and a bit of the initial novelty was wearing off. No longer did the local press breathlessly cover every detail of the preparation and rehearsal process. The best news was that the beloved Michel Penha was coming back to conduct. Even better, the ebullient Sascha Jacobinoff would be back too, as violin soloist.

The 1937 Carmel Bach Festival featured five main concerts, just as in 1936: Monday, Tuesday, Thursday, Saturday, and Sunday, all at 8:30pm. The first four were in Sunset Auditorium, and the final concert was in Carmel Mission.

For the first time, organ recitals were scheduled for 4:00pm on Wednesday and Friday at All Saints Church, about two blocks from Sunset Auditorium. E. Richard Weissmueller played two different all-Bach programs, bringing the total number of Festival concerts to seven, in seven days. Lectures were given at the Pine Inn at 11:00am on the five main concert days, free to ticket holders and 40¢ for the general public.

The 1937 festival was richly described by Thelma Miller in the Pine Cone, and her excitement is understandable. In 1935 and 1936 she wrote reviews of the festival but from the point of view of a Chorus member. This year she chose to sit in the audience for the entire week.

> Broadly speaking, this is the first year that I have "heard" the Festival chorus, as I reluctantly abandoned my place in the alto section in favor of this seat in the audience. I am glad now that I did, for otherwise I never would have realized the full impact of the festival; the picture of massed men and women on the stage, as a living background for the soloists....
>
> The brilliant conductor Michel Penha, succeeded admirably in making each aggregation a foil for the other. Penha is a dynamic conductor; his baton cuts the air with a whiplike swish. He leaves nothing to chance: with flexible wrist he guided his musicians through certain rather intricate passages and kept them, cleanly, exactly, on the beat. (Pine Cone, July 24, 1937)

The 1937 Festival opening-night program was: three Bach chorales for chorus and orchestra; the *Overture in D Major for Orchestra*; the *D Major Keyboard Concerto* played on the Baldwin grand piano by Lillian Strieber; and Cantata BWV 30, *Freue dich, erlöste Schar*, for vocal soloists, chorus and orchestra.

The second concert began with the *Brandenburg Concerto III*, followed by several sacred solos by Noel Sullivan. Then Sascha Jacobinoff and his longtime colleague Olga Steeb performed the Sonata in G major for Piano and Violin. Michel Penha brought down the house with the *Suite in G Major for Cello*, and the concert ended with the *Concerto in C major for Two Harpsichords and Orchestra*, performed on Baldwin grand pianos by Ann Greene and Winifred Howe.

> The cumulative effect of the festival is calculated to impress vividly what one understands theoretically: the enormous range of Bach's music, the amazing versatility with which he composed for all instruments and combinations of instruments known in his day. And nowhere was this better illustrated than in the Suite in G Major for Cello accompanied, played by Michel Penha, long Carmel's favorite cellist, and conductor of the festival. Masterly execution made this a personal triumph for Penha, and the thunder of applause

was a token not only of admiration for an amazing performance but of personal affection. Hitherto undreamed of possibilities of the cello were revealed, and even more so in the first movement of the C major cello suite which he played as an encore. (Pine Cone, July 23, 1937)

In the second concert, Miller witnessed a timeless problem for concert producers.

Tuesday night the auditorium was packed. The soloists that night were all local or had appeared in previous festivals, and their combined popularity was a strong drawing card. There was considerable hubbub of people running up and down the aisles during the playing of the first number, the Third Brandenburg Concerto. The ushers did their best to cope with the situation, and did not seat a large coterie of 8 o'clock diners until the end of the number, but the situation was not conducive to a good hearing of the concerto. (Pine Cone, July 30, 1937)

By mid-Festival, Miller has seen what the audience sees, and writes beautifully about what is happening.

Pausing midway of the Bach Festival to evaluate that which has already been heard and to prepare for that which is to come, one realizes that in this third year the festival has attained its majority. Two years ago it was community music-making which someway acquired a soul. It surpassed the expectations of those associated with it and turned out something better than the sum total of individual efforts and abilities. If the festival has lost something of that first fine rapture, as inevitably happens when an enterprise grows beyond the intimate, spontaneous quality of its origin, it has gained in quality. The music of Bach is being better performed this year than it was during the first two festivals.(Pine Cone, July 23, 1937)

The Thursday concert was devoted entirely to the piano. Wanda Krasoff began the concert with three major works by Bach, played on the Moor Double Keyboard Piano. The rest of that concert, and considerable excitement, was provided by pianist Eduard Steuermann, who performed a mixture of J. S. Bach's original compositions and arrangements of Bach by Ferruccio Busoni. (Steuermann was a student of Arnold Schoenberg and a proponent of his music. In 1923 in Hamburg, Steuermann gave the world premiere of Schoenberg's *Fünf Klavierstücke*, Opus 23, the same work Dene Denny played in 1926 in Los Angeles.

The Saturday audience heard the *Overture in B Minor* for strings and flute; the *Concerto in A Minor* for violin; and one of Bach's very few lighthearted works, the *Coffee Cantata*.

The Sunday concert was once again in Carmel Mission. Soloists, Chorus, and Orchestra performed the sacred cantata *Gottes Zeit ist die allerbeste Zeit* (sung in English, as "God's time is the best time"). A flute sonata followed, and the concert concluded with a repeat of the opening night cantata (sung in German), *Freue dich, erlöste Schar*. The beginning of the Mission concert was particularly exciting: the opening cantata was broadcast on AM radio coast to coast by the NBC Blue Network. The post-Festival editorial in the Pine Cone is given below in its entirety, in three segments.

A WORTHY ENTERPRISE

Another Bach Festival has gone down in history, and there is something of a letdown in the village this week. This year, more decisively than the two previous years, consciousness of the festival deeply pervaded the whole community. This week of music has become the annual event which it seems the fashion for every town to have, not only for the good of trade, but for the sharing of a common interest, the welding process which makes a community out of a lot of individualists.

The strangers who came to the village to hear the music were interesting-looking people. The Bach Festival is an important element in our first-line defenses against a Coney Island crowd. As we have remarked other years, only the finest sort of people, the kind we are honored to entertain, are attracted to a festival of music. The sort of tasteless ballyhoo used to draw crowds to lesser enterprises cannot be used to advertise a Bach Festival. Publicity has to be on a dignified plane; not that Dene Denny and Hazel Watrous would ever stoop to advertising in bad taste. (Pine Cone Editorial, July 30, 1937)

Once again, to counter the common idea that Bach's music was "highbrow," the Festival ran a few articles in the Pine Cone and the Monterey Herald showing actual Festival participants as the "ordinary people" they really were—storekeeper, grocer, garage mechanic, schoolteacher, etc. The Pine Cone editorial continued,

One element in the publicity, however, which seems of rather doubtful wisdom has been a little tendency this year to play up the humble station of some members of the chorus and orchestra. It is scarcely newsworthy. The rich and great are not apt to go in for cooperative community enterprise, but rather people who have more of a habit of relying on their own resources for amusement. We would not be in favor of emphasizing this aspect of the situation to the point of making people self-conscious who have participated in the festival just for the fun of it. (ibid.)

The Pine Cone editorial concluded with praise for Dene and Hazel.

In the Bach Festival, Dene Denny and Hazel Watrous have found an enterprise worthy of their particular blend of talents, and it is gratifying to see them reaping the success they so well deserved. This is the crest and climax of their endeavors in Carmel, and it has achieved impressive stature. In three years the festival has built slowly and securely on a foundation of community interest that guarantees its survival.

We have learned that Bach is neither formidable, boring or monotonous, but rather a source of an infinite variety of beautiful music.

As well as goodwill, the Bach Festival has the advantage of good experienced management. Many have seen visions in Carmel, but all too few have had the patience for hard, plugging work, and executive ability to give their inspiration concrete form. Miss Denny and Miss Watrous have the artistic background from which the vision arises. Either by native endowment or by the experience they have gained here, they have become extraordinarily efficient in choosing people to work with and for them; in managing enterprises involving large numbers of people, the public on one side, musicians on the other.

With imperturbable good nature, the Denny-Watrous Management takes the music-makers in hand, temperaments at all, from the major stars to the local amateurs, and welds them into a unit all working together for the greater glory of music. (ibid.)

Fall 1937

Compared to the performance activity eight or nine years before, the fall months of 1937 were quiet in Carmel. Dene and Hazel continued to manage the Troupers of the Gold Coast and were also spending a considerable amount of time in San José, where they had leased an apartment and office. As Denny-Watrous Management, they did not produce another event in Carmel until May 14, 1938.

In October the Carmel Music Society announced its upcoming season. The series began in December with the "brilliant young pianist" Rudolf Serkin. Still a European resident at that time, he had made his US orchestral debut the previous year at Carnegie Hall with the New York Philharmonic and Arturo Toscanini, and was currently a very hot item on the concert circuit. Three more events in the series took place in the winter and spring months of 1938: a Hindu dance company; a return of violinist Nathan Milstein; and the Budapest String Quartet.

Rudolf Serkin booking as in Musical America Magazine, 1937. *Courtesy of the author.*

Hail to Music!

It is warming to the cockles of our editorial heart to contemplate the Carmel Music Society as it enters the 11th season of highly successful operation. This is one Carmel organization that has had a better than average record. It has not only managed to live on, it has constantly grown, both in members and in scope. [Note: "members" refers to season subscribers and contributors, not to members of the board of directors.]

And it has hung up a record of another kind: its board has been, since the first, one of the most harmonious organizations in Carmel's history. That fundamental harmony is of course one of the secrets of the Music Society's success. There is nothing like an interested organization to make a project successful. In Carmel it is the "thing to do" to belong to the Music Society. And that is in no snobbish sense. The organization reaches into every cranny in the town, everyone knows about it and is interested, even if not musically wise. There is a certain holiday spirit in the air... on the day of a concert, with everybody asking his neighbor "are you going tonight?" (Pine Cone, November 19, 1937)

Spring 1938

In late January it was announced that the 1938 Carmel Bach Festival would be led by the 41-year-old Italian conductor, Gastone Usigli. Many in Carmel remembered him as the guest conductor at the 1935 Bach Festival. Usigli was based in San Francisco and Los Angeles, and would travel to Carmel on weekends for rehearsals beginning late in the spring. Meanwhile, bi-weekly rehearsals of chorus and orchestra resumed on Sunday February 6 at the Sunset School under assistant conductor Bernard Callery. It was announced that:

The chorus on Sunday will begin its rehearsals of that greatest of all works of music, and the greatest of all of Bach's works, the Mass in B Minor, which Mr. Usigli desires to present (with cuts, of course) for the final concert of the festival. (Pine Cone, February 4, 1938)

Courtesy of the author.

The second event on the Carmel Music Society subscription series was a performance on February 19 by Shankar and his Hindu Ballet. Born in Uday-pur, India, and trained there and in Paris, Shankar and his dancers presented what the New York Times called "one of the strangest and most exotic spectacles in the experience of sophisticated New Yorkers." Shankar had just finished a successful 28 performance run in New York City and the company was now on tour across the United States before returning to India. The troupe included two dozen Indian musicians, and the advance publicity pulled out all the stops, including the information that the two leading female dancers are "Hindu princesses who come from a renowned maharaja's family." The Music Society brought Shankar and his dancers back to Carmel again in 1952. According to the reviewer, the Carmel audience was almost too sophisticated for its own good.

> Although it was a capacity audience, with extra chairs at the front of the auditorium and standing room at the back, I thought that I felt the shade of restraint in the applause the other night. They were enjoying it, oh yes; but there was a bit of puzzlement, as if it were not quite right to let down and applaud with real abandon until they were quite sure that they "understood" what the dancers were trying to "say." The program was a sensuous ride of gorgeous color, extraordinarily beautiful movement, and exotic music. (Pine Cone, February 25, 1938)

Image above and facing page, courtesy of the H. M. Williams Local History Department, Harrison Memorial Library

Just a few weeks later the Music Society featured violinist Nathan Milstein. The Pine Cone said that Milstein "has an amazing technical proficiency, temperament of force and fire, a kind of thunderous beauty which gives to his playing an elemental, emotional richness." The Society season ended with the eminent Budapest String Quartet playing Beethoven, Sibelius, and Mozart.

On May 14, 1938, Dene and Hazel produced their first Carmel event since the end of the previous summer. Viola Morris and Victoria Anderson were English singers who toured as a vocal duo, singing with piano and unaccompanied. For an audience at the Pine Inn the two women performed four centuries of music. In eight weeks they would be among the soloists at the fourth Bach Festival.

A few subtle changes were made in the rehearsal process leading up to the 1938 Festival. Preliminary rehearsals had been taking place since February, and only those who had become part of the orchestra in those preliminary rehearsals could now continue with Usigli. Once Usigli began to rehearse in mid May, no new members would be accepted into the orchestra (this was done to raise the bar and also to avoid last-minute local drop-ins).

Intensive weekly rehearsals for orchestra and chorus began in May, led by Gastone Usigli and Bernard Callery. Under Usigli, the entire Festival became both more challenging and more fulfilling for performer and listener. Ernst Bacon (composer/pianist), Sascha Jacobinoff (violinist), and Michel Penha (cellist) were superb musicians and well-liked in Carmel, but Gastone Usigli was the first actual "conductor" to lead the Orchestra or the Festival. Not only that, based on every eyewitness description of his rehearsals, he was of the old school of Italian conductors who guided, cajoled, and inspired their ensembles through a sometimes unpredictable combination of deep musical understanding, psychological persuasion, assertion of authority, Italian charm, and frequent outbursts of fiery theatrics.

> Mr. Usigli is putting his people through the hard school that makes a finished performance, and there is a splendid standing up to it. Depth and range are, in everything, matters of a struggling extension of our powers, and the participants in the music festival are fortunate in having a conductor with the vision to see that they have it in them, even if they sometimes doubt it themselves. (Carmel Cymbal, June 3, 1938)

With the arrival of Gastone Usigli in Carmel, "The early years" of the Bach Festival, as Dene Denny later called them, were coming to an end.

Gastone Usigli

Great truths win universal recognition slowly and laboriously, and among the worthiest conquests today is the fact that the supreme greatness of Bach's art is unanimously acclaimed.

The understanding of Bach's music, and in particular his vocal music, stimulates the highest intellectual delight; it derives from the realization that his great industry and supreme skill as craftsman inspired him to serve the noblest and most vital principles of life: his music fills men with "triumphant joy" because it makes them dream and hope for those things that are denied by the realities of life.

There is not only a psychological need for Bach's music (for it is truly a breviary of our inner life and an inexhaustible treasure of religious inspiration) but also a physiological reason why his music should provide comfort and nourishment in an era of unrestrained sensationalism, of confusion of values and standards, of hectic and cruel strife. His music seems to restore the inner balance that life is liable to disrupt, satisfy the longing for harmonious order, and provide emotional rest. Truly it fortifies the weak and rewards the good.

Does not Bach's Magnificat reflect the eternal rhythm of the universe, with its vivid, exultant, relentless animation, as if maintaining the steady pulsation of the cosmos? Yes, it does, and both voices and instruments carry a hymn of humanity, gratefully acknowledging this truth.

~ Gastone Usigli, written for the Carmel Cymbal, July 17, 1941

Photo this page courtesy of the H. M. Williams Local History Department, Harrison Memorial Library

Gastone Usigli was born in 1897 in Venice, Italy. His father was a lawyer, his mother was a gifted amateur musician, and both parents were cultured lovers of the arts. There was always music in the Usigli home, and Gastone and his three siblings each received musical mentoring from an early age. As an adult Usigli fondly recalled his excitement when, at the age of five, he was first able to span an octave on the piano keyboard with his thumb and little finger. (Dene Denny recalled a similar childhood memory.) By the age of seven he was the "conductor" of the Usigli family orchestra when they made music together at home.

At nine he began to write musical scores; at 14 he made his debut as fifth assistant conductor for Wagner's opera Parsifal in Venice. By his late teens he had become an accomplished pianist and was competent on a half dozen other instruments. Usigli's father insisted that his son complete a university degree, but Usigli pursued a musical education as a parallel activity. He enrolled as a Philosophy and Letters student at Turin University but continued to maintain his independent musical activities (he was already working professionally as a piano accompanist for opera classes in Venice.)

Usigli served in the Italian army in World War I, and it did not go well for him. Between 1915 and the end of hostilities in 1918, 615,000 Italian soldiers were killed in action or died of wounds sustained in combat. As always, some of the injured survivors were wounded physically, and others psychologically, by what they had experienced in the Great War.

When first interviewed in Carmel in 1935, Usigli told of his "wartime neurosis" and his nervous breakdown at the war's end. The ensuing period of recovery led him to a life-changing decision: although he had completed his Philosophy and Letters Degree in Turin, he turned away from the intellectual rigors of academia and shifted his life's focus to music, another rigorous discipline but one with which he could, as he put it, "heal the psychic wounds of war." (Pine Cone, July 19, 1935)

Usigli studied piano, composition and conducting at the Conservatory in Bologna and graduated in 1924. He continued his studies at the Berlin Conservatory, where he was a piano pupil of the great teacher, pianist and composer Ferruccio Busoni. Returning to the University of Turin, he earned a Doctor of Music degree.

Usigli's early European experience was impressive. During his student years in Bologna in the 1920s, and in several return visits to Italy after settling in San Francisco, Usigli was guest conductor at the Venice Opera ("La Fenice") for five seasons. There he worked with Edoardo Mascheroni, a friend and colleague of Verdi and conductor of the premiere of *Falstaff.*

At the age of 24 he conducted Wagner's epic 5-hour opera Die Meistersinger in Venice, and the city awarded him an inscribed medallion. (Legend of course has it that he conducted the performance from memory.) He also led the orchestras of Milan, Rome, Treviso, and Berlin, and was one of the youngest conductors at Milan's La Scala Opera House. Opera was always part of his repertoire, and after coming to the United States he appeared as opera conductor in San Francisco, Philadelphia, Chicago, and Los Angeles.

"Usigli proves himself among the ace-conductors… For parallel interpretations one thought of Monteux and Stokowski." (San Francisco Chronicle, 1932)

In 1926 Usigli sailed through the Panama Canal and up the Pacific Coast to visit his sister, Eveline, in Vancouver, British Columbia. While on his way back to Italy, Usigli's ship made a stop in San Francisco, where he lingered happily until his tourist visa expired. He later said that

as his ship first passed through the Golden Gate (there was no bridge yet) and into San Francisco Bay he was so struck by the beauty of the city that he uttered the old-fashioned Italian exclamation "Per Baccho!" (by Bacchus) and in that moment knew that he would make San Francisco his home.

Usigli returned to Italy for the winter, and then sailed once again for California in the spring, arriving in San Francisco via the Panama Canal in April 1927, but this time he came as an immigrant who intended to stay. Although he made several trips back to Italy in the coming decades, Gastone Usigli became a US citizen in 1936 and made his home in San Francisco until his death in 1956.

Usigli was a notable champion of contemporary music, and between 1933-1941 he conducted more than 250 works by American composers, more than any other conductor in the United States at that time. The list includes several operas, most notably Morris Rugers grand opera "Gettysburg," which had its Hollywood Bowl premiere just weeks after the 1935 Bach Festival.

In 1932 Usigli founded the San Francisco Chamber Symphony, with which he presented young soloists performing works by American composers. With that orchestra alone he presented more than 100 American orchestral works, two American operas, and featured more than 150 young American soloists.

Gastone Usigli was also a distinguished composer. In 1924, while he was still in the midst of his studies at the Conservatory in Bologna, his orchestral tone poem "Don Quixote" won the annual competition founded by Italian publisher Giulio Ricordi. The Ricordi Prize is the Italian equivalent of America's Pulitzer Prize in Music, and one of the judges that year was Arturo Toscanini. Usigli's repertoire as a composer includes over 500 orchestral works, 35 operas, and 100 choral works. A list of Usigli's compositions performed in California may be viewed in the Appendix. Usigli's archive is in the collection of the Bancroft Library at the University of California at Berkeley.

In the 1930s Gastone Usigli married Elizabeth Etienne, known by her friends as "Betsy." She was a biological chemist at Stanford Medical Center and a passionate music lover. Later, after her husband's death, Betsy served as a member of the board of directors of the Carmel Bach Festival.

Photos on these two pages courtesy of the Carmel Bach Fesival

Bach Festival 1938

"Our greatest desire," says Dene Denny, "is to preserve amateur music making, augmented by outside professional help, and to be under the direction of conductors of the first rank. Only in this way can the highest standards of musical excellence be maintained. And there must be no slightest deviation from that high standard of excellence." (Pine Cone, July 1, 1938)

"The unusualness of our festival," says Hazel Watrous, "is of course its nucleus of home talent. It would be impossible fully to estimate the inspiration that the Bach Festival has created and the possibility it gives for local participation in it. This is of untold value and of ever-increasing wonder to those on the outside who are watching its development." (ibid.)

Dene Denny, Hazel Watrous, Betsy Usigli, Gastone Usigli. c.1940. Courtesy of the Carmel Bach Festival.

"Do not laugh at your mistakes. Take them seriously. A mistake is a sacred event. It will be followed by a moment of exultation. Only by our mistakes do we grow—but not if we take them lightly." (Gastone Usigli quoted in the Pine Cone, July 14, 1938)

In the first grade classroom of the Sunset School, at 2:00pm on Sunday, May 15, Gastone Usigli stood before the orchestra of the Carmel Bach Festival for the first time. It was not yet the entire orchestra, only about 20 players. Nearly 20 others, all professionals, would show up less than a week before the first concert. The locals had been rehearsing bi-weekly since early February, and they were ready to be propelled to the next level of musicianship by the arrival of the professional players in July. The 1938 orchestra included several students from San José State College who drove to Carmel and back each Sunday—for their convenience the orchestra rehearsed in the afternoon and the chorus in the evening. Lynda Sargent attended the rehearsals that day, and shared her recollections thirteen years later:

> I was present when Usigli conducted his first chorus rehearsal in a bare room in the Sunset School. It was a memorable day for Carmel. I saw him raise his baton, I saw him downbeat, I heard the scratched tentative voices of the few local songsters fumble for the notes and thin out along the blackboards of the school room. I saw the master lay down his baton on the table and saw the look that came into his eyes, a look almost of despair. And then I saw miracle happen. Every fiber in the man was transmuted. All the will and passion and purpose of a man composed of will and passion and purpose leapt up and glorified him. "Now," he said, sternly and commanding, "open your mouths and sing!" (Pine Cone, January 20, 1951.)

Maestro Gastone Usigli was a conductor of stature, skill, and experience. He had conducted in the great opera houses of Italy, and at the Hollywood Bowl, and now he was standing in a first grade classroom in a small town in California in front of a group of local amateurs who were supposed to be his orchestra and chorus.

Images on this and the opposite page courtesy of the Carmel Bach Festival.

Perhaps in his whole career of distinguished achievements—as conductor, composer, performer—no project has challenged his patience, his integrity, his endurance more than the Carmel Bach Festival. Accustomed to a large and professional group of musicians, he has here taken the local material in hand, working furiously and demandingly with eager amateurs and frightened beginners. And miraculously, with these he has bent his genius to accomplish an almost mystical bond; a bond that is warm with human understanding and cold with the will to bring out in his chorus and orchestra a great deal more than they knew they had; indeed perhaps more than they had. If you have been privileged, as we, to attend rehearsals, you have seen a magnetic force at work. (Carmel Cymbal, July 14, 1938)

By the end of May, the local press had begun once again to generate excited anticipation of the festival.

Carmel's fourth annual Bach Festival is a musical event whose magnitude is making Carmel the summer music center of the West. No other music Festival has such an impressive program, covering a week of time. Even Eastern festivals are looking with great respect on Carmel's achievement. (Pine Cone, May 20, 1938)

It was clear to everyone that Dene and Hazel had accomplished something that benefitted the Carmel community and enhanced its reputation nationally. Despite the Great Depression, the Carmel City Council understood the Festival's promotional value (in contrast to their doubts in 1935). "The annual Bach Festival is one of the few bright spots we have left," a city councilman is quoted as saying. Dene Denny had made a written request for support, stating that "this most important event in Carmel's year, although having arrived at a point of national consequence, yet continues to fail to meet its costs." The City Council quickly and unanimously appropriated the requested sum of $100 to aid in the promotion and advertising of the Festival.

This feeling of civic gratitude toward Dene and Hazel intensified at the end of June, when it was announced that the NBC Blue Network had asked to broadcast the Festival's final concert—selections from the *Mass in B Minor* at Carmel Mission.

FOURTH ANNUAL
C A R M E L
BACH FESTIVAL
JULY 18 to 24, 1938

GASTONE USIGLI
CONDUCTOR OF THE FESTIVAL

DENE DENNY   HAZEL WATROUS   Producing Managers

This announcement gives an idea of the importance these events have become [sic] in the musical world. A national broadcast by request of one of the greatest radio stations, lasting an hour, is an honor of the first class. In all parts of America, men and women will listen to Carmel's instrumentalists and vocalists at the Mission San Carlos…. That a town of 3000 inhabitants could put on so significant a presentation as has been shown in previous years, is a thing to arouse the world's interest and wonder. It has been commented upon in musical circles everywhere, has been told in newspapers and magazines, has aroused other larger cities to emulation….

The credit due to the Misses Dene Denny and Hazel Watrous for the unfolding of success since their original conception of the Bach Festival in 1935 should not be overlooked, or ever be forgotten. The two names, bound in a long partnership, stand for the best in musicianship in Carmel. Our town is proud to have honest claim to them as residents, although their influence and activities of covered a large field in central California. In the Carmel Music Society, in amateur dramatics, and in the Bach Festival, in over a decade of musical and theatrical advancement, these two women have been an inspiration to others, and a hard-working couple by themselves. (Pine Cone, June 17, 1938)

The following paragraphs are taken from an article by Lynda Sargent in the Cymbal.

The days walk along toward July 18, toward midsummer and the Bach Festival. For all those connected with the festival they are busy days indeed, with one thing after another pushing in to be done. With Dene, concentrated and lovely, hurrying up Dolores Street and Hazel's smile as constant as time....

Usigli is hard, hard at rehearsal. He is an unsparing man, and he lifts his fingers and says, "Kick this high!" There is the un-finite [sic] good taste in him of the man who has little lack of knowledge on which to peg his judgment. Throughout the years of conducting orchestra, chorus and opera in his own land, Italy, he watched and listened. Now he watches, but has earned authority of speech....

With the coming and going of the Daylight Limited [train] faithfully backwards and forwards to and from San Francisco and Los Angeles, the eminent performers and guests of the Carmel Bach Festival will make their annual pilgrimage here this week....

Rehearsals are now open to those who have already secured their season tickets. These rehearsals are solemn quiet affairs, held Saturday and Sunday evenings and with grave earnestness. You are welcome if your wish is to see the way music is built into its ultimate structure.

When we went into rehearsal room the other night, [the chorus] was struggling passionately with the unfamiliar words and strangely difficult music [of the Mass in B Minor]. Music that passed their understanding and for the grasp of which they had to lean heavily on the conductor. "Incarnatus est" they were all singing. "No! No! Make that 'est' short, short—Now—Good—Now again—" And the chorus looked earnestly at Mr. Usigli and sang "Incarnatus est" full and sweet—as they had no idea it could be sung. By this time we [listeners] had learned, now we knew how to listen to each shading. To each small but vital increase in the truth of the matter. We knew, too, that finally the masterful voice would shout: "Now, all together!" (Carmel Cymbal, July 1, 1938)

Even during the rehearsals, it was clear that Gastone Usigli was transforming the Bach Festival.

With the authority and force behind which live twenty-five years of eminence at the podium both in this country and his native Italy, Gastone Usigli has gone ahead with the materials at hand here for chorus and orchestra and molded a festival of music. Unsparing, uncompromising as to his goal, completely at home in the vocabulary of the baton, he has succeeded in infusing into his musicians not only a real grasp of the technical problems involved but an understanding of the spirit of the man who composed the music. (Carmel Cymbal, July 15, 1938)

Another writer in the Cymbal caught the spirit and praised Dene and Hazel.

> There is no doubt whatever that the orchestra and chorus have gained tremendously—decisively—in maturity of technique, and what is so much more vital than anything else, in understanding of the language Bach spoke. There is an almost bitter intensity in their efforts; a conviction which carries convincingness. In large part, Miss Denny and Miss Watrous are also responsible for this. One conductor can do it. But they have had various conductors, all working, to be sure, to the same good end. But it is, rather, what is expected of them by the women who are sponsoring them, that animates all the performers throughout the year to prepare for the event.
>
> To those who live in Carmel and have a part in its valid artistic life, Miss Watrous and Miss Denny are Hazel and Dene. Both are beautiful women; both women of great charm. Their several distinguishments are so exactly complementary that the double light in which they have seen their ideal come to maturity has been a true and constant focus on the common vision. No stature to which the Carmel Bach Festival could grow in the world of noteworthy achievement could outdistance the recognition of the two women whose work it is. (Carmel Cymbal, July 14, 1938)

The following news item appeared in the Pine Cone just three days before opening night of the Bach Festival.

> ### Village is Pleased with Council's Appointment
> *New Member Represents Active Artistic Element*
> The Carmel City Council, sitting for more than the usual three weeks upon the egg, finally hatched out the new council member Wednesday evening. Miss Hazel Watrous was duly sworn in to take the place of Gordon Campbell, who resigned to become US Marshal to China. The swearing-in took place after police chief Robert Norton had made a little sortie to Monterey, where he found Miss Watrous rehearsing her Troupers of the Gold Coast. While the council was appointing its new commissioner of public health and safety (whose name had been a closely held secret), Miss Watrous' band of troupers went on with their rehearsal, completely mystified as to why she had been taken into custody by Chief Norton.
>
> Councilman Watrous...represents ably the active artistic element in Carmel, as she has been for many years, with her partner, Miss Dene Denny, active as an impresario of musical and art efforts and at present is in the throes of producing the fourth Bach Festival.
>
> "If you want to get a job done, go to a busy man" is the proverb. The Council did exactly this. The immediate public reaction to the Council's appointment has been most favorable. (Pine Cone, July 15, 1938)

In the minutes of the Council meeting that night, Mayor Herbert Heron expressed perfectly what Carmel new about Hazel.

> I am sure that the selection of Miss Watrous will meet with the approval of the great majority of the people of Carmel. She is an outstanding representative of what Carmel is known and loved for. (Carmel Cymbal, July 14, 1938)

The Fourth Bach Festival

The schedule for the 1938 Bach Festival was the same as 1937. Four Sunset Auditorium concerts were held on Monday, Tuesday, Thursday, and Saturday at 8:30pm. The fifth concert was on Sunday at Carmel Mission at the same time. John MacDonald Lyon played 60-minute organ recitals at 4:00pm on Wednesday and Friday in All Saints Church.

Sascha Jacobinoff was Guest Conductor of the Thursday evening concert. He rented a house in Pacific Grove, and was one of the leaders of the Pacific Grove Summer School of Music. His presence attracted some advanced violin students who were admitted to the Bach Festival Orchestra.

Usigli designed the opening-night concert with a flair for drama. It began with the majestic *Overture in D Major for Orchestra,* followed by the florid and exciting soprano solo cantata *Jauchtzet Gott in allen Landen* (The first of the three arias from this cantata had been performed on opening night of the first festival).

After the cantata, four Baldwin grand pianos on loan from Holman's Department Store in Monterey were rolled onto the small and now very crowded stage for the *Concerto in A Minor for Four Keyboards and Orchestra.* One or more of these pianos may well already have been in place; there was absolutely no room to store them backstage.

The Carmel audiences loved the Bach concertos for two, three, and four keyboards, and at least one of them was performed every summer until after World War II.

After a stage-clearing intermission, the concert ended with Bach's *Magnificat in D Major* for orchestra, chorus, and soloists. Like other major works in the early decades of the Festival, this last work was not performed in its entirety. The three large choral movements within the work were omitted and only the opening and closing choruses were sung, with all the vocal solos (in order) in between.

The Clarinet

The Bach solo cantata for soprano, *Jauchtzet Gott,* BWV 51, consists of three soprano arias with trumpet obbligato solo in arias #1 and #3. There was no trumpet player at all in the orchestra that summer, however, and none is listed on the program page for this concert. Another puzzle is the lack of oboist credit among the evening's soloists: there were three oboists listed in the orchestra roster that summer. In the *Magnificat* a vocal trio includes a prominent oboe solo; one soprano aria relies utterly on the oboe obbligato and would sound ridiculous if that solo were omitted. Here are the soloists as listed in the printed program that evening:

Note the final soloist on the list. All of the music on this concert was written by J. S. Bach and none of it even remotely calls for clarinet (the modern clarinet as we know it did not exist in Bach's lifetime). The clarinetist in this concert, however, did indeed play the oboe obbligato in the *Magnificat* aria "Quia respexit" and received a compliment in the Pine Cone: *"The clarinet solo which accompanied [the soprano] had a remarkable blend of tone quality with her voice."* This sort of pragmatic substitution—especially involving clarinets—continued at the Bach Festival for more than a decade.

Alice Mock, *soprano*
Anne Greene, *pianist*
Adoph Teichers, *pianist*
Mary Walker, *pianist*
Ralph Linsley, *pianist*
Viola Morris, *soprano*
Victoria Anderson, *contralto*
Edith Anderson, *soprano*
Andrew Sessink, *tenor*
Allan Watson, *bass*
Alfred Regeth, *clarinet*

According to the San Francisco Chronicle music critic (see p. 269) such instrumental substitutions were merely "Some of the dodges and subterfuges..." common at the time.

Once again, with no apparent trumpet, it remains unclear what sort of accompaniment was used for "Jauchzet Gott." There are three reviews of the concert, and all three praise the solo soprano, yet none mentions a solo instrument; it seems likely that the solo cantata was performed with string orchestra alone. Usigli was a facile composer, and during his 15 Bach Festival seasons he often put his skill to use by subtly "revising" (i.e. rewriting) Bach's music to suit the limitations of his ensemble in Carmel.

The rest of the 1938 festival resembled the previous year's format. On Tuesday, Assistant Conductor Bernard Callery led *Brandenburg Concerto VI*, and solo pianist Homer Simmons filled the rest of the evening with Bach. Thursday evening included the *Sonata in A Major for Flute and Piano*; before and after it Sascha Jacobinoff conducted the *Overture in C for Orchestra*, the *Brandenburg Concerto III*, and the *D Minor Concerto for Two Violins*.

> It is a lifetime job to begin even a superficial acquaintance with the great musical master, Johann Sebastian Bach. (Gastone Usigli in the Carmel Cymbal, July 10, 1938)

The Saturday concert offered the *Overture in B Minor for Orchestra*; *Brandenburg Concerto IV*; *Concerto in G Minor for Keyboard* (piano); and the (shortened) *Magnificat* once again, for orchestra, chorus, and soloists.

Sunday was the Grand Finale of Gastone Usigli's first festival season: an abbreviated version of the *Mass in B Minor* in the Carmel Mission, broadcast coast to coast live at 8:00pm Pacific Time. Less than half of the entire work was performed: eleven of the twenty-six movements were omitted, including a third of the Gloria, half of the Credo, the entire Sanctus, and the final three movements. This condensed version fit the one-hour time limit of the live radio broadcast.

Courtesy of the Carmel Bach Festival.

But another issue, unrelated to broadcast time limitations, was the vocal difficulty of Bach's great *Mass*. Singers who have encountered it know that the choral parts of the *Mass in B Minor* are very often more challenging than the solo arias. By omitting the most difficult choruses, it was easier (i.e. possible) for the chorus to sing the Mass at all. (They had programed the Sanctus in 1936 but canceled it at the last minute, and they still were not ready to perform it in 1938.) To give the chorus an additional break, the soloists sang certain difficult choral passages. The Festival performed the *Mass in B Minor* every other year or so, adding one or two movements each time, until 1959, when Sandor Salgo conducted a complete performance of the work for the first time in Carmel.

Here is what the four radio stations in Seattle, Washington, were broadcasting on July 24, 1938, at 8:00pm. KRJ–970 was the NBC Blue Network affiliate broadcasting the Festival concert. Bach was competing against "I Want a Divorce," Frank Dailey and his Orchestra, and Dr. Charles Fuller's "Old Fashioned Revival Hour." (Seattle is in the same time zone as Carmel; on the East Coast the concert was heard at 11:00pm.)

"...one of California's most important musical phenomena."

SUNDAY

A.M.	KOMO—920 KC	KJR—970 KC	KIRO—710 KC	KOL—1270 KC	A.M.
		Evening Programs			
6:00	*Carefree Carnival ...	*Horace Heidt and ...	" Conducted by	*The Marines Tell ...	6:00
6:15	" (Beryl Carew) ...	" (His Brigadiers) ...	" Massino Freccia) ..	" (It to You)	6:15
6:30	*Win Your Lady	*Cheerio: Music	*Headlines and	*Good Will Hour	6:30
6:45	" (Jim Ameche) ...	" (and Talks)	" (Bylines)	" (J. J. Anthony) ...	6:45
7:00	*Column Quizz	Music Graphs	*Vincent Lopez Orch...	News Flashes	7:00
7:15	*Irene Rich: Drama ..	*Reggie Childs Orch. ..	" (Dance Music) ..	Twilight Tunes.....	7:15
7:30	*Hobby Lobby	*Lou Breese Orch.....	*Leighton Noble Orch..	*Old-Fashioned Revival!	7:30
7:45	" (Dave Elman) ..	" (Dance Orch.).....	" (Popular Music) ..	" (Hour Featuring ..	7:45
8:00	*I Want a Divorce ...	*Fourth Annual	*Frank Dailey and ...	" Dr. Charles	8:00
8:15	Let's Celebrate	" (Bach Festival ...	" (His Orchestra) ..	" E. Fuller)....	8:15
8:30	*One Man's Family ...	" Broadcast from ..	*Henry King Orch. ...	Salon Concert	8:30
8:45	" (Domestic Drama)	" Carmel, Calif.) ...	" (Popular Music) ...	*Sons of the Pioneers.	8:45
9:00	*Hal Burdick, Nite Ed.	*Jan Garber Orch.	Gems of Melody	*Newscast	9:00
9:15	*Dance Orchestra	" (Popular Music) ..	*Dick Jurgens Orch...	*Mitchell Ayers' Orch..	9:15

Bach Cantata To Be Played From Carmel

From California's historic Carmel mission, built in 1770, the KEX audience will hear a performance of Johann Sebastian Bach's cantata, "Gottes Zeit," tonight between 8:30 and 9, when a portion of the final program in the third annual Bach festival at Carmel is broadcast.

Soloists include Alice Mock, soprano, formerly of Oakland, Cal., and for several years with the Chicago Civic Opera company; Evelyn Snow, contralto; John Daggett Howell, bass-baritone; Andrew Sessink, tenor, and Noel Sullivan, basso.

Mishel Penha, distinguished cellist and conductor, will direct the 40-piece orchestra and the festival chorus of 50 voices.

The Bach festival, conducted by Penha, is being held in the little village of Carmel, famed artists' colony on the shores of the Pacific, whose many natural beauties attract visitors from all parts of the world.

Announcement of the broadcast on KEZ (Portland).

The local press coverage was not as colorful or personal as it had been in previous years, because the two Carmel newspapers decided to get more "professional." The Pine Cone invited a young music writer from the East Coast to cover the instrumental performances, which he did in an intelligent and perceptive way. They also brought in a young pianist/composer to cover the vocal music, and she, too, focused on the musical details, as a good critic is expected to do. But because they had no context in which to put these concerts—that is, they had no knowledge of where and how the Festival had originated, and what the achievement represented for the community—their reviews lack the sense of wonder and joy so evident in previous years. The writer for the Cymbal, on the other hand, was new to concert reviewing and had insufficient vocabulary and experience to write pictorially and engagingly about the events.

These three writers had intelligent and reasonable things to say about notes, style, balance, clarity, tempo, timbre, and all the other factors trained musicians are taught to discern, evaluate, and enjoy. All said the concerts were lovely, well-intentioned, and this and that, and they hoped that everything might be better next year. For example, one of the Pine Cone reviewers wrote this about the Mission concert on Sunday:

"Although by no means an outstanding performance, Maestro Usigli did wonders with the material at his disposal..."

Fortunately someone had been in Carmel all month who was able to comprehend and write about the artistic experience of the week-long Festival.

The most beautifully written review of the 1938 Carmel Bach Festival appeared in the San Francisco Chronicle on July 31, over the byline of Alfred Frankenstein, the Chronicle's highly respected music critic. He had been in Carmel since mid June, and had presented the five morning lectures at the Festival. His half-page San Francisco review began by describing the Carmel Mission concert from a wiser and radically different point of view.

BACH MAGNIFICENTLY SERVED IN CARMEL FESTIVAL

When the last notes of the Osanna in Bach's *Mass in B Minor* died away last week at Carmel Mission, and the fourth annual Carmel Bach Festival was suddenly a thing of the past, the more mystically minded in the audience might have had reason for holding that we had seen and heard a Descent of the Spirit. A more prosaic analysis might have revealed earthlier reasons for the tremendously moving performance but, whatever the cause, it is certain that one hour of music was in itself sufficient to have put the Carmel Festival on the map as one of California's most important musical phenomena....

The fantastically perfect optical setting of the ancient church, and its rich emotional associations, helped also to the total effect as did the tension of the participants, who were singing and playing not only for Carmel mission but also for NBC's endless millions. Finally, there was Gastone Usigli at the conductor's podium.

All these things conspired to create an interpretation of the Mass in B Minor, or rather, about a third of it, that will remain for long memorable in the minds and hearts of those who were privileged to experience it, as one of the most dramatic, exalted, and satisfying of a lifetime.

And this despite, or perhaps because of, the fact that the presentation was technically very far from perfect. <u>Some of the dodges and subterfuges adopted to make up for inadequacies—such as the substitution of clarinets for oboes—were altogether unexceptionable.</u> Another—the frequent substitution of solo vocal quartets and quintets for choral movements the chorus had not had time to learn—indicates the chief direction in which the festival will progress. [Emphasis added.]

The most important fact about the seven days of music making is not that many works of Bach were represented in performances that ranged from the mediocre to the miraculous, but that it was both a California festival and a success. Without benefit of star names, with orchestral forces made up almost exclusively of students and amateurs, a chorus composed practically entirely of lay townspeople, and conductors and soloists who have never had any build-up in Time Magazine, Bach was magnificently served. This went on for an entire week, and the audience ate it up. This is the sort of thing we are perennially told cannot be done and is not worth attempting. But it has been done for four consecutive summers in Carmel, and will continue.

A more heterogeneous group of music makers can scarcely be imagined. The butcher, the baker, and the real estate operator took a hand or a voice... The picture of the whole was of an inspired community effort on behalf of music, involving participants of the most miscellaneous proficiency, age, and condition of servitude, all directed toward a common end. That in itself would not have amounted to much, however, had it not met with a reception equal to its intentions. It is all very well to extol the value and importance and desirability of such activities. People have been preaching down that rain barrel for years, and all they usually get for it is a hollow echo. Carmel has shown how to make it work. The festival has been rewarded for its community effort with ever-increasing audiences during the last four years, and those audiences, no doubt, will continue to grow....

Behind any phenomenon such as this there is always the persistence, the patience, the skill and the taste of an organizer or two. In this case the responsible personalities are Dene Denny and Hazel Watrous, who organized the festival in the beginning, and have guided it with passing good sense. One evidence of their good sense is the engagement this year of Gastone Usigli as musical director. The three of them deserve endless credit for some beautiful concerts of Bach, but still greater credit for proving that, glory be, it can happen here. (Alfred Frankenstein, San Francisco Chronicle, July 31, 1938)

Denny-Watrous followed the Bach Festival with an August 6 concert at Sunset Auditorium in which French pianist Daniel Ericourt played Beethoven, Chopin, Ravel, and Debussy.

The Fall season was musically quiet in Carmel. The Carmel Music Society opened its season on December 3 with the as yet relatively unknown Danish soprano Povla Frijsh. In the New Year the Society presented dancer Angna Enters; French pianist Robert Casadesus, and the Pasquier Trio. Noel Sullivan was now the president of the Carmel Music Society and chair of the booking committee.

It is clear from the absence of Denny-Watrous Management activity in Carmel that Hazel and Dene were fully involved in the management of the concert series in San José. They rented an office not far from the Civic Auditorium, and from that location they sold tickets and handled publicity. Whenever tickets were on sale, at least one of them was in San José five days per week, and preceding major events they both were there. Their office address is also listed as their San José residence in several documents of record.

On November 5 their concert season in San José opened with Lincoln Kirstein's "American Ballet Caravan," followed in January by Jascha Heifetz; Marian Anderson in February; and the Pasquier Trio in March.

Backstage at the 1941 Carmel Bach Festival. Gastone Usigli and Hal Garrott, writer for the Carmel Pine Cone. *Courtesy of the H. M. Williams Local History Department, Harrison Memorial Library*

The Early Years of Denny-Watrous Management were over, and Dene and Hazel were moving on and up to bigger things.

Gastone Usigli's first Mission Concert. A special moment in Carmel Bach Festival history was captured in this spectacular photograph, taken from the organ loft in the Carmel Mission on the evening of Sunday, July 24, 1938. The photo shows Gastone Usigli leading Bach's *Mass in B Minor* (abbreviated) on the final day of the 1938 Carmel Bach Festival. The one-hour concert was broadcast live nationwide on the NBC Blue Network. The four seated soloists in the photo are soprano and alto Viola Morris and Victoria Anderson, a vocal duo from England; tenor Andrew Sessink, from Monterey (left); and bass Allan Watson from San Francisco (right).   *Courtesy of the H. M. Williams Local History Department, Harrison Memorial Library.*

Tuesday July 18, 1950. The Carmel Bach Festival's new concertmaster, Ervin Mautner, plays Bach's *Violin Concerto in E Major*. Gastone Usigli conducts. *Courtesy of the Carmel Bach Festival.*

Part Six
Establishing Traditions
1939–1950

Gastone Usigli conducting the 1941 Carmel Bach Festival ensemble on the stage of the Sunset School Auditorium.
Courtesy of the Carmel Bach Festival.

Gastone Usigli conducting the 1942 Carmel Bach Festival ensemble in Sunset Auditorium.
Courtesy of the Carmel Bach Festival.

Introduction to Part VI

"1938 marked the end of the early period." (Foreword to the 1953 Bach Festival Program.)

Time begins to move faster now in this story. Dene and Hazel have become true impresarios, working with performers at every level of artistic experience—from the most renowned international stars to absolute amateur beginners. Parts III, IV, and V described in some detail how Dene and Hazel learned to do all this, and how they brought the Carmel community together in the midst of the Great Depression by using the community's own energy to create the excitement for their performance events. By the beginning of 1939, all their labors since the early 1920s were beginning to pay off.

The Denny-Watrous Management Concert Series in San José was a perfect situation for them. It demanded a lot of work and time, but the series was profitable, and the San José revenue helped cover the deficits of the Carmel Bach Festival in its early years.

The Carmel Music Society was doing well, and staying mostly in the black. Dene and Hazel assisted with the booking of artists, Hazel designed the printed matter, and both continued to serve on the board of directors.

The Troupers of the Gold Coast at California's First Theater was a great success. The First Theater received overall supervision from Dene and Hazel. Hazel in particular was frequently present for rehearsals and performances, and she worked closely with Rhoda Johnson, the seamstress and costume builder, in choosing the fabrics for new costumes.

The Bach Festival—after only four seasons—was already considered a "tradition" by the local community, but the organization, the sense of purpose, the people, and the artistic spirit were not frozen in time or form: the Festival continued to grow and evolve through the coming decades. By giving the conductor's baton to Gastone Usigli, Dene and Hazel had committed their festival to the challenging, exhilarating, and never ending quest for excellence that is part of the package with a fine conductor, but that is not to say that Usigli called all the shots. Dene and Hazel worked closely with him in choosing the repertoire for the main concerts, but Dene and Hazel remained "Producing Managers" until 1958. They developed, financed, publicized and managed the entire event, and nothing happened without their OK.

Their lives as impresarios were very full.

Trombones on the cover of the 1939 Carmel Bach Festival program book.

Courtesy of the Carmel Bach Festival.

Spring 1939
Four months with Dene and Hazel

The following dozen paragraphs recount documented Denny-Watrous professional activities during the first eighteen weeks of 1939. The life of a successful impresario can be very busy in any case, but Dene and Hazel had the added factor of managing performances simultaneously in Carmel, Monterey, and San José.

1939 actually began for Dene and Hazel in late December, 1938, when tickets went on sale in San José for the January 15 concert by Jascha Heifetz. The illustrious violinist drew an audience of more than 2,500 to the San José Civic Auditorium. Monterey was well represented in the audience that night, because Dene and Hazel had invited the Troupers of the Gold Coast to be their guests at the concert.

On February 3 they traveled to Los Angeles, where they celebrated their birthdays; Dene turned 54 and Hazel 55. They met with Gastone Usigli and secured a contract with him to lead the 1939 Carmel Bach Festival. While they were in LA, impresario Sol Hurok invited Dene and Hazel to be his guests to hear Arthur Rubinstein play Tchaikovsky's *B-flat Minor Piano Concerto* with the Los Angeles Symphony under Otto Klemperer. The already-famous pianist was one of Hurok's artists, and Dene and Hazel engaged Rubinstein for the following season in San José. After a week in Los Angeles, Dene and Hazel traveled north and stopped in Carmel long enough to manage the start of the Bach Festival Chorus pre-season rehearsals. Madeline Curry prepared the local Chorus members during March, April, and May in the music room of the Sunset School. In those days the Chorus grew from week to week, and qualified new members were admitted until early June (especially those rare tenors).

After a few days in Carmel, Dene and Hazel headed north to San José to manage the February 28 solo recital by the African-American contralto, Marian Anderson, around whom a tempest had been building in Washington, DC for more than a year. Sol Hurok was Anderson's agent, and he had been trying to arrange a solo concert by Anderson in Constitution Hall, an auditorium owned by the Daughters of the American Revolution. It had opened in 1929 and had a seating capacity of more than 3,700, making it the largest concert hall in the District of Columbia.

For Hurok and Anderson, it was a non-negotiable stipulation that the audience be racially integrated, but the DAR at that time was white-only, and so was their auditorium. After months of negotiations and proposals, the DAR issued their final decision at the end of February. Although a limited number of seats could be sold to African-Americans, they would be required to sit in a separate area and there would be no racially-mixed seating.

On the morning of Marian Anderson's San José concert, in a dramatic and famous act of conscience, the First Lady of the United States,

Sol Hurok and Marian Anderson, February, 1939. *Courtesy of the author.*

Eleanor Roosevelt, announced in her nationwide newspaper column that she was resigning from the Daughters of the American Revolution because of her "complete disagreement with the attitude taken in refusing Constitution Hall to a great artist." (She was only one of thousands who resigned from the DAR over this issue.) That evening, Anderson's concert in the San José Civic Auditorium was far beyond sold out, filled to overflowing with standees, and with additional seating onstage. The official capacity of the auditorium was 3,378, but Denny-Watrous Management sold more than four thousand tickets. The energy and emotions of the evening must have been unforgettable.

> Miss Anderson's voice is one that appears only once in a century; a voice which ranges from pure, rich, cello tones to the high, sweet notes of the flute.... Besides being endowed with perhaps the greatest voice of our time, and the intelligence and understanding to use it, Marian Anderson also possesses a beautiful and gracious stage presence; in short, she is a great artist in every way. In response to overwhelming applause, she generously gave five encores. (San José Mercury, March 10, 1939)

Following the DAR debacle, the Department of the Interior was persuaded to sponsor a Marian Anderson concert in Washington, and on Easter Sunday, April 9, 1939, she stood by a grand piano on a stage in front of the Lincoln Memorial in Washington and sang for a crowd of more than 75,000 people. The entire incident put Marian Anderson and the issue of racial discrimination in the national spotlight. Anderson returned to San José in 1940 and 1941 for appearances in the Denny-Watrous series. (The DAR eventually reversed their racial policy and invited Marian Anderson to perform in their auditorium in 1943. When she made her farewell tour in 1964, she chose Constitution Hall as the venue for her first concert.)

At the beginning of March Dene and Hazel returned to Carmel where they oversaw the opening of a new production at the First Theater. Then it was back to San José to promote the concert of Belgium's Pasquier Trio on March 23—the final event of their spring season there. They returned briefly to Carmel at the end of March, and then traveled again to Los Angeles, where they met with Gastone Usigli and pianist Ralph Linsley. The main repertoire had been chosen, and in LA they made final plans for the summer. Usigli and Linsley had been rehearsing for several months with the vocal soloists who were based in Los Angeles.

While in Los Angeles Dene and Hazel also met with Michel Penha and invited him to perform in the Tuesday evening concert at the Festival. On May 2 they arrived back in Carmel and remained there for the rest of the summer. After their return, they

Dene Denny and Hazel Watrous, winter 1938. *Courtesy of the H. M. Williams Local History Department, Harrison Memorial Library; and the Carmel Pine Cone.*

issued an announcement of their 1939–1940 San José concerts: a stellar lineup of violinist Yehudi Menuhin; soprano Lily Pons; pianist Arthur Rubinstein; and Marian Anderson.

1939 Bach Festival

Bach Festival Week for Dene makes her feel as though Carmel were surrounded by a group of high mountains which eventually we expect to scale. This year, more than any preceding festival year, she senses something unfolding that is big enough for both the audience and the participants to feel. It's a transcending thing, and we all share in it. It is an inner communion which approximates, perhaps, what music was meant to say. Music like Bach's, ...is absorbed like Life itself in all good time. We cannot hurry the process. Each year we're nearer to complete understanding. Each year we feel it more. (Carmel Cymbal, July 14, 1939)

The harpsichord appears

1939 marked the first serious, high-profile presence of the harpsichord in the Carmel Bach Festival. Usigli had experimented with the instrument the previous summer, but it had not been highly visible in the repertoire. The harpsichord plays two roles in early 18th century music. In nearly every orchestral work it is part of the "continuo" section; playing with cello and sometimes double bass, the harpsichord adds to the harmony and overall texture of the ensemble sound. The other role, something new for which Bach is partly responsible, is that of soloist in a concerto. Bach wrote a wonderful series of keyboard (harpsichord) concertos, and they were performed regularly—on grand pianos—during the Festival's early decades; the "Concerto for Three Pianos" was the concluding work on the Saturday concert in 1939.

The Brandenburg Concerto V has a prominent solo harpsichord part generally thought to have been written by Bach to display his own virtuosity; it requires a harpsichordist with technique, artistry, and flair. Alice Ehlers, born in Vienna, was a pupil of the harpsichord pioneer Wanda Landowska. One of the very few renowned harpsichord soloists of the day, she traveled the world with her own custom-built instrument, appearing in solo recitals, Baroque chamber music, and concertos with major orchestras. In her North American tours in the late 1930s, most of the people in her audiences had never heard the harpsichord before, but for those associated with the Bach Festival it was an eagerly-awaited addition.

It is too difficult to say just what ways, what vital spots, this year's program has been lifted above all the foregoing ones. The eminence of Madame Alice Ehlers, with her incomparable interpretations of Bach's music on an instrument with which he himself was familiar — on which, indeed, he composed much of his music — perhaps makes a combination that takes precedence over any single solo undertaking yet achieved by the festival management. (Carmel Cymbal, June 30, 1939)

In the opening night of the 1939 Carmel Bach Festival Ehlers played in the *Brandenburg Concerto V* and also performed Bach's *Italian Concerto* (a work for harpsichord solo).

On May 12, a brochure was mailed to Festival subscribers and to newspapers and other media across the country. Once again the Festival offered five evening concerts, on Monday, Tuesday, Thursday, Saturday and Sunday; the first four were held at Sunset Auditorium and the fifth at Carmel Mission. Organ recitals were given at 4:00pm on Wednesdays and Fridays. Repertoire included ten assorted concertos (from one violin to three pianos), Cantatas 11 and 201 (in English) and numerous instrumental and vocal solos. In the final concert at the

Mission, they gave another shot at the *Mass in B Minor*: they were able to perform sixteen of the 24 movements, one more than the previous year. In 1939 the Festival caused a comment in the press by departing for the first time from the all-Bach tradition.

> Tuesday night's concert will be of unusual interest, departing as it does, for the first time in the Festival's now hoary life, from the music of Johann Sebastian Bach. All of Tuesday's works will be by the sons of Bach. (Carmel Cymbal, June 30, 1939)

"...the Bethlehem of the West."

Dr. and Mrs. Albert Riemenschneider and their son Paul were in the audience of the 1939 Bach Festival. Riemenschneider was the director of the Conservatory of Music at Baldwin-Wallace College, near Cleveland. Inspired by a 1931 visit to the Bethlehem Bach Festival, Riemenschneider founded a Bach festival at Baldwin-Wallace College in 1932. There is only one second-hand report of his impression of the Carmel Bach Festival: John McDonald Lyon, who played the two organ recitals in the Festival, wrote a letter to Dene Denny after returning to his home in Seattle. "Bethlehem" refers to the Bethlehem (Pennsylvania) Bach Festival, founded in 1900.

> Dear Miss Denny,
>
> I thought the 1938 Festival was good, and I was glad to have had a part in it. But I thought the 1939 Festival was fine beyond all my expectations or hopes....
>
> This year's festival was, for me, the high spot of all the Bach I have heard. My use of the superlative occurs after spending the whole afternoon of the last day of the festival with Albert Riemenschneider, undoubtedly the greatest authority on the music of Bach in this country. I got the impression that he came to Carmel just a little bit dubious, and went away pleasantly surprised. And I know he was surprised on Sunday night with the great performance of the *Mass in B Minor*. I talked to him about it on his way out of the Mission, and I can assure you he was delighted. ...
>
> The program-building for the concerts in Sunset auditorium was masterly. There was perfect balance, and entirely satisfying amount of variety, and a nicety of planning that was unusual....All with whom I talked seem to agree that this year's festival reached a new standard of excellence. I want to add my words to the sincere congratulations you and Miss Watrous are receiving. I send you my best wishes, my appreciations, and the hope that the Carmel Bach Festival may continue permanently as the Bethlehem of the West. (Open letter in the Carmel Cymbal, August 17, 1939)

Something spectacular happened in the summers of 1938 and 1939: under Gastone Usigli's direction, the festival first showed its true potential to become a nationally significant event. In 1939, at least 50% of the members of the orchestra were professional musicians from orchestras including San Francisco, Cincinnati, St. Louis, Seattle, New Orleans, and Los Angeles. The Chorus was still local amateurs, augmented by a few visiting singers and college students. The vocal soloists continued the Festival practice of singing as member of the Chorus when they were not actually soloing. All of the out-of-town instrumental and vocal professionals received a travel reimbursement and meal allowance, and stayed in private homes. (It was becoming socially prestigious to host one of the visiting musicians.)

However, not everyone in Carmel was thrilled with the idea that the event seemed to be taking on a more professional character.

> Not since the first year or two of the festival, when the boys and girls in the village gathered in the little gallery on Dolores Street and held open rehearsals for the town to hear, has local excitement run so high. There has been, in the past several years, feeling among some, that, with the talent available here on the Peninsula, the festival ought to remain essentially a community enterprise. It was never meant that way. The dream that Miss Denny and Miss Watrous have constantly held throughout was of an event national in scope....

> So it is a most heartening thing that this year the doubters have vanished away, and it is the implacable dream itself that has done this. And yet, in a most vital way, it will always belong to Carmel. All about us, we see the men and women who stuck through its most uphill years; who have rehearsed long hours after the day's work; Dene and Hazel who put superhuman devotion and labor into it; Usigli who unravels the tangled threads of vision and makes it come true in our sight. The beauty of our town and the hospitality of our townspeople, the support of the grocer in the restauranteur, and the happy concord of effort and faith. (Carmel Cymbal, July 19, 1939)

As if to clean Bach out of the ears of the community, Denny-Watrous management followed the Bach Festival with a performance on August 16 by Devi-Dja and her Bali-Java Dancers, complete with costumes and clangorous Balinese instruments.

Carmel Fall Season 1939

After the Festival, Dene and Hazel split their time between San José and Carmel, making sure that at least one of them was in San José at all times during the concert season. Yehudi Menuhin played to a sold-out house at the Civic Auditorium on October 6, and Metropolitan Opera soprano Lily Pons filled the house in November.

The Carmel Music Society began its season on October 6 with Lincoln Kirstein's young avant garde ensemble, "The American Ballet Caravan," dancing to music by Bach, Copland, and Eliot Carter. This production had opened in May at the Martin Beck Theatre in New York and was now on tour with a full company of dancers, a small orchestra, and their own stage lighting. A few days later they appeared in San José on the Denny-Watrous series there. Noel Sullivan, Carmel Music Society president, hosted a reception for Lincoln Kirstein and the members of the Ballet Caravan at the Carmel Art Association on Dolores Street on the day after the performance. Later that month rehearsals began for a production of Henrik Ibsen's play A Doll's House at the First Theater in Monterey. The Pine Cone tells us that Hazel was "down this week from San José to see how the Troupers of the Gold Coast are getting along."

In one final note for the year, on December 15, the Carmel City Council established an ordinance which continues to be debated in Carmel to this day.

> By a unanimous vote of four members, Councilman Hazel Watrous being absent, the City Council Wednesday night gave first reading to an ordinance prohibiting the playing of musical instruments in any place in Carmel where liquor is sold to the public. An urgency clause was inserted in the ordinance which puts it into effect immediately on final passage which will be at the next meeting of the Council this coming Monday afternoon. The ordinance does not include radios in its ban, but does prohibit the playing of phonograph records. (Carmel Cymbal, December 15, 1939)

The War Years 1940–1945

As this narrative continues through the 1940s, the story is no longer about the individual inspirations and hands-on work of Dene and Hazel, and more about the management and growth of what they have established.

Now that Gastone Usigli had led two successful Festivals, everyone expected that he would return in 1940, and the public announcement had been made at the end of December. On January 7, Madeline Curry once again began to prepare the local Chorus for the summer Festival, meeting bi-weekly in a classroom at the Sunset School.

Hazel's mother, Minnie, had been living in her cottage across Dolores Street since 1934. Now nearing 82, she was no longer able to live alone, and in the spring Dene and Hazel added a room to the front of their house so that Minnie would be able to live with them. Minnie Jefferds Watrous Holden spent the last 14 months of her life in that house.

Woodblock portrait of Gastone Usigli by Mary Burr for the Carmel Pine Cone, 1941. *Courtesy of the Carmel Bach Festival and the Carmel Pine Cone.*

The Carmel Music Society continued its season with a popular San Francisco tenor and chamber ensemble. One month later, audiences in both Carmel and San José benefitted from Dene Denny's connection with Sol Hurok, when Arthur Rubinstein, one of the century's great pianists, played to full houses in Sunset Auditorium (for the Music Society) and two days later in the San José Civic Auditorium (for Denny-Watrous). The Music Society concluded its season with Robert Virovai, violinist.

Dene and Hazel also brought Marian Anderson back to San José for a concert on February 28, 1940, exactly one year after her triumphant 1939 concert. Anderson returned to San José in 1941, once again on February 28.

Cowell in Prison

1940 was a turning point in a story of disgraceful tragedy and injustice. Henry Cowell was arrested and convicted in 1936 on a morals charge involving consensual oral sex with a 17-year-old, one of a group of neighbors whom Cowell had allowed to build a swimming pool in his back yard. Although Cowell did not consider himself a homosexual, there is a common misunderstanding that the charges involved homosexuality, but that was not so. Homosexuality was not mentioned in the charge ultimately brought against him. Cowell was charged with one count of violating section 288a of the California penal code, which prohibited "non-traditional" sex, in this case oral sex. Although this "crime" was his only offense, the case was blown out of proportion by the general hysteria in the press about sex, sex criminals, and homosexuals. It is shocking today to consider that Henry Cowell was given the maximum sentence of fifteen years in prison, and sent to San Quentin State Prison, north of San Francisco. Section 288a of the penal code stipulates that both parties shall be charged, but the young man was not arrested.

Cowell's musical output hardly diminished. He directed the prison band, taught classes for thousands of inmates, and composed nearly sixty compositions. Cowell's appalling imprisonment was protested by leading figures in the arts, including Dene Denny and Hazel

Watrous, who must have been deeply pained by the imprisonment of their friend. During his time in San Quentin, Cowell received more than 200 visitors, including his friend Percy Grainger, dancer Martha Graham, and Dene and Hazel. With steadfast support from Cowell's friends across the country, those in power were able to persuade the governor to parole Cowell in 1940, and he received a full pardon in 1942.

The sweet voice of peace. . .

World War II was well underway, and wartime fears and anxieties affected even the residents of Carmel-by-the-Sea.

Sweet Voice of Peace in Our Coming Bach Festival

I write this on the morning of Wednesday, May 22, 1940. The Germans are today about 100 miles from London and within sight, almost, of Paris. In the interval between now and Friday morning when the Cymbal goes onto the street, something of grave importance to you and me is bound to happen in the world. In the seven weeks between now and the opening of the Bach Festival of Carmel on July 15, it seems practically a certainty that we in America shall have been shaken to our deepest depths by world events....

1940 Carmel Pine Cone front cover, with caricatures of Bach and Hitler. Courtesy of the Carmel Bach Festival and the Carmel Pine Cone.

In a way it is difficult to approach the Bach Festival this year, so much is going on that seems so urgent. But this very circumstance makes 1940 the most stirring, the most needed, the most phenomenal of all the five foregoing years of music....

I judge it [the Carmel Festival] to be the first among the undertakings of this town. Measured by the size and artistic significance it has attained, by the willingness and even eagerness of well-known professional musicians to give up part of their busy time to it, and by the promise of what it may become, there is no other enterprise within a good many miles of here that will anywhere near compare. In a community where there is a tradition of artistic endeavor of one kind or another, and great pretensions to such things, we should take no small pride in the Carmel Bach Festival. (Carmel Cymbal, May 24, 1940)

The 1940 Bach Festival schedule was once again Monday, Tuesday, Thursday, and Saturday in Sunset Auditorium, and Sunday at Carmel Mission. The series of five morning lectures and the organ recitals on Wednesday and Friday continued as well, and the organist in the recitals this year was Frank Asper, organist of the Mormon Tabernacle in Salt Lake City.

The Monday concert included Bach chorales, an overture for orchestra, a harpsichord concerto, and the first half of the *Christmas Oratorio* sung in English. Tuesday was Handel, Scarlatti, Vivaldi, and other Italian instrumental music. Thursday and Saturday were a mix of cantatas (*Peasant Cantata; Phoebus and Pan*), concertos, and excerpts for solo piano and solo voice.

The Sunday concert was again an abbreviated, 1-hour version of the *Mass in B Minor*. The demand for Festival tickets had been growing, especially for the Mission concert, but that venue had only about half the seating capacity of Sunset Auditorium. The solution was to present the entire Sunday concert twice, at 4:00pm and 8:00pm—a tiring day for the entire ensemble, especially at the end of a week of concerts and rehearsals. (On top of that, the 8:00pm performance was once again broadcast live nationwide on the NBC Blue Network.) From 1940 through 1957, the Bach Festival often ended with a grueling double-concert day. Usigli continued to be a beacon of inspiration.

> There is a saying to the effect that no one is irreplaceable. I think we may take complete issue with this. I think we are safe in saying that whatever the Carmel Festival has achieved of authority and musical performance is due to Gastone Usigli; when he came here two years ago the one thing the Festival needed was the impassioned and implacable will to perfection that has been his unique and personal contribution to the success of the enterprise.
>
> An intensely human and lovable man, Usigli comes to Carmel as a representative of a world we see too little of, the great world of real sophistication, of simple and impeccable tastes, of the love for his fellow beings which takes itself out in so behaving that, by sternness and often harshness, he makes them aware of their littlenesses and so aware of something potentially big.
>
> "I like raw meat and raw fruits," he writes to us, "and that is probably the cavemen in me. I like Bach and Wagner above all composers because they, infinitely better than any others, have expressed what is noble and lofty in human nature and have consequently sung humility and kindness—that is the highly evolved animal in me."
>
> It is possible that no other living man could have so suited the peculiar ideals upon which our Festival takes its sustenance. As long as we can keep him here, we have in him a guarantee of musical soundness, of integrity of spirit, of a jealous reading of this music which exacts exclusive devotion to the inherent godliness of man. (Carmel Cymbal, July 12, 1940)

In October, Dene and Hazel once again turned their attention to their San José events series, now in its fifth year; all winter at least one of them was in San José Monday through Friday. Their 1940–1941 season included Bidu Sayou, Brazilian soprano; Serge Rachmaninoff, pianist; Misha Elman, violinist; and John Charles Thomas, baritone. In addition to their concert series, Denny-Watrous Management presented touring plays, orchestras, dance companies, and Broadway shows.

The pre-season chorus rehearsals for the 1941 Festival were led by Charles Fulkerson, a young pianist and composer who had been involved with the festival for several years. In 1941 he played in one of the keyboard concertos at the Festival and served as Usigli's assistant. The principal cellist in the 1941 Bach Festival orchestra was Jean Crouch, 25. She was a charter member of the original 1932 orchestra and had played nearly every season since then. In 1940, Jean and Charles had been married, and they both taught music at Monterey Union High School. This was the first of many times that romance would blossom at the Carmel Bach Festival.

FESTIVAL OF FAITH
Dedicated to Gastone Usigli

Here where the green tranquility of pines
Enfolds the westward landflow to the sea,
The faith of Bach finds voice again, and shines
Unshaken by the world's catastrophe.

From every little line of running flame
That multiplies itself into a fire,
The full creation echoes with acclaim
To God alone; and earth becomes acquired.

Point if you must across the tragic waves
Where wreck and havoc ride the midnight air
And right itself is ceded to the wrong—
Truth is not mocked. Once more the spirit braves
The chaos of negation to declare
Eternal order and undying song!

— Dora Hagemeyer   July, 1941

On July 17, 1941, the Carmel Cymbal featured this poem by Dora Hagemeyer, and the portrait of Gastone Usigli by Johann Hagemeyer, Dora's brother-in-law. Next to the poem was the essay by Usigli shown on page 259.

Gastone Usigli was a charismatic leader and a demanding conductor. He challenged the Bach Festival singers and players to accomplish more than they thought they could, and the result was uplifting and fulfilling for the participants and those close to them. Dora's son played cello in the orchestra, and she understood the positive effects of Usigli, Bach, and music itself.

"Across the tragic waves" refers to the war that had been raging in Europe since 1939. The US entry into that war was only five months away.

Photo courtesy of the Carmel Bach Festival.
Poem courtesy of the Carmel Pine Cone.

"...a living participation in the music of Bach."

> *"It has been our aim to advance the standard of performance each year. That we have been able to do so as definitely as we have, the last four years, is due to our conductor, Gastone Usigli.*
>
> *His genius for conducting, his musical integrity with its inexorable standard of perfection, his wide experience with both chorus and orchestra, and his consecrated devotion to music have transcended the difficulties of irregular and incomplete rehearsals, elevating the singers and players to a living participation in the music of Bach."*
>
> (Dene Denny quoted in the Carmel Cymbal, July 17, 1941)

The saga of H.M.S. Pinafore

In August 1941, Dene and Hazel announced something new: the Bach Festival Chorus and Orchestra would continue with weekly rehearsals in the fall, in preparation for Gilbert and Sullivan's *H.M.S. Pinafore*, conducted by Gastone Usigli and directed by Ronald Telfer. Tryouts began in early September, with Usigli and Telfer present, and rehearsals began on September 15.

Dene and Hazel brought two very different kinds of dance to Sunset Auditorium that fall. In September, they presented Veloz and Yolanda, who were touring the country performing onstage as ballroom dancers. In October they presented Katherine Dunham, known as the "Marion Anderson of Dance," with her dance company.

Meanwhile, there was a change in plans for *H.M.S. Pinafore*. It is not clear if Usigli was forced to withdraw because of other commitments, or if he and Telfer were unable to find soloists equal to Gilbert and Sullivan's operetta, a work that demands vocalists of excellent quality. For whatever reason, instead of a fully staged production in Sunset Auditorium conducted by Usigli, *H.M.S. Pinafore* would be performed at the First Theater by the Troupers of the Gold Coast, with Dene Denny at the piano.

The operetta was given during the Christmas season in a greatly shortened version, and, as with every other performance at the First Theater, it was followed by the usual olio vaudeville show. A big hit, *Pinafore* was extended into January 1942.

The Troupers attempted to perform the operetta in a semi-legitimate fashion, but because of the limitations of some of the singers and the overall circumstances, it was more First Theater than Savoy Theater. The reviewer, accustomed to melodramas, got into the act and covered the event as he would any First Theater production.

> Into the fat, succulent part of the Right Hon. Sir Joseph Porter, Edward Hopkins sank his thespian teeth, with the result that the juice of excellence oozed over the edge of the stage, and over the ever cooperative audience which dutifully migrates to each new Gold Coast production. In other words, brother, he was good. The hero was portrayed by that real trouper, Eddie George, despite the fact that he sometimes forgot that Pinafore was operetta, not melodrama, and overlooking the truth that he was forced to reach for notes beyond his range. (Pine Cone, December 26, 1941)

Scenes from the 1941 Carmel Bach Festival. Dene Denny chats with baritone soloist Sten Englund in the Sunset Auditorium balcony. Chorus members waiting in the small stage left area in the Sunset School auditorium. Below, one of many parties hosted by Noel Sullivan at his farm in Carmel Valley. *Courtesy of the Carmel Bach Festival.*

Carmel Music Society and the San José Concert Series

From this point on, the narrative will not include every performance presented by the Carmel Music Society or by Denny-Watrous unless the event was unusual or it generated press worth reading. It has not been possible to reconstruct the list of concerts, performances, and other events presented by Dene and Hazel in San José. However, a complete history of performances presented by the Carmel Music Society is included in the Appendix of this book.

In February 1942, a small item appeared in the Pine Cone:

> **The Bach Festival WILL be Held This Summer.**
> In spite of you know what and regardless of all you may have thought, the Carmel Bach Festival will be held this summer and Dene Denny announces that the affair will be even more brilliant than ever. (Pine Cone, February 13, 1942)

In June 1942, the Troupers of the Gold Coast celebrated their fifth anniversary.

> Dramatic history was written on the Monterey Peninsula that night five years ago. All the playgroups which have brought fame to the Peninsula, luring summer visitors to Carmel and its environs, the Troupers of the Gold Coast under the Denny-Watrous Management, represent the only group which has ever operated continuously over a period of five years. During that time some 286 performances have been given, with never a flop, and the first theater has gained a state-wide reputation as a center of entertainment and hilarious amusement. (Pine Cone, June 12, 1942)

The eighth Bach Festival

The Carmel Pine Cone noticed that the Bach Festival was "broadening" its focus. Two of the five main concerts featured no Bach at all: Tuesday was a montage, and Thursday was all Mozart.

> Tuesday night Bach Festival program contained not a note of Bach but was given over to miscellaneous composers. Such an evening has become a tradition of the festival. It serves as a relief to those who can take just so much Bach, and helps to point and emphasize his greatness for those to whom he is undoubtedly "The Master." (Pinc Cone, July 24, 1942)

Just prior to the opening concert, the Pine Cone offered its support.

> Carmel will have its eighth annual Bach Festival this summer because two women, Dene Denny and Hazel Watrous, were possessed of a dream and were willing to give and to keep giving all they have, year after year, to its realization. Their zeal is unflagging, their courage dauntless, and their ability keen.
> Everyone knows that Bach Festival week is the best week of the year in Carmel. The whole villages creative alive, quickened by the enthusiasm of artists from far and near and stirred up to deeper appreciation of all the good things we have here. The summer of 1942 gives the festival peculiar significance. It will go on in spite of the war, blackouts, and rubber shortage. This determination to carry on the usual pattern of our life whenever possible is the best civilian defense we can have. It strengthens our own morale and serves as a candle in the dark for those less fortunate. The music of the Masters refreshes and recreates all listeners.

> For this beautiful and spiritual experience, we thank the conductor, the visiting artists, the local artists, and Dene Denny and Hazel Watrous, who have never faltered in the face of discouragement, who have never lost their vision of their purpose, who have made this beautiful thing a reality for us and have built us up into an audience ready to receive it. (Pine Cone, July 17, 1942)

The 1942 Bach Festival presented five main concerts, plus two organ recitals (played by Clarence Mader, organist of Immanuel Presbyterian Church, Los Angeles). Monday and Saturday evenings were as usual mostly Bach; Tuesday was a potpourri of music from the Renaissance to Beethoven; and Thursday was all Mozart. As in 1941, the Festival offered two performances of an almost-complete version of the *Mass in B Minor* at Carmel Mission on Sunday.

In late July, the Pine Cone asked, "The Bach Festival is over, and the question being asked the Denny-Watrous management is 'What's next in the way of entertainment that is unusual and exciting?' " As they had done in the past few summers, Dene and Hazel brought in a completely different sort of performance in August. That summer it was Jose Cancino's Spanish dance troupe, whom they had presented in Carmel a few years before.

By the spring of 1943, the preparatory rehearsals for the 1943 Festival had already begun, and hopes were high that it would continue despite the War. In May a disappointing announcement appeared in the Pine Cone over the signatures of Dene Denny and Hazel Watrous.

> An announcement that will sober and disappoint hundreds of music lovers on the West Coast is reluctantly given out by Dene Denny and Hazel Watrous. The ninth annual Carmel Bach Festival will not be held as planned, but will have to be deferred until July, 1944, or to such date as victory sets.
>
> The Denny-Watrous management had gone far in their plans for this year's festival, had engaged soloists and made arrangements for a week-long program that would equal in excellence the beauty of last year. However, difficulties of maintaining a high standard of the Festival steadily mounted. Depletion of the ensemble and uncertainties of many orchestra and choral participants due to poor conditions; and problems of transportation, food and housing for outside participants during their stay in Carmel have presented steadily growing problems which have reached insoluble proportion.
>
> The fact that the Carmel Bach Festival is not only a musical but a spiritual experience, enriching and exalting to those who participate and share in it, whether as performers or audience, has made its producing managers and the Festival committee feel that it must go on. But its postponement will come as an acute disappointment not only for Carmel but for the conductor, Gastone Usigli, for Ruth Terry, ... and the other vocal soloists. (Pine Cone, May 14, 1943)

Denny-Watrous activities continued full steam, despite the War. Their 1943–1944 San José season was spectacular: Marian Anderson; Nelson Eddy; Lawrence Tibbett; Arthur Rubinstein; and the touring opera company of the great basso Salvatore Baccaloni. They also presented eight touring ballet and theatrical productions including Ethel Barrymore in "The Corn is Green."

While the Bach Festival was on hiatus, Gastone Usigli and his wife occasionally came to Carmel for pleasure rather than work. The Usiglis had developed a friendship with Noel

Noel Sullivan with Elizabeth and Gastone Usigli at Sullian's farm in Carmel Valley. *Courtesy of the Carmel Bach Festival.*

Sullivan and they also enjoyed the dachshunds that greeted them when they visited Sullivan's farm in Carmel Valley; in 1945 Sullivan gave a puppy ("Brenda") to his friends Gastone and Betsy. Usigli's only professional appearance in Carmel during this time was a recital in April 1945 with soprano Dorothy Warenskjold. She was then at the beginning of an important career that would lead to the Metropolitan Opera. Noel Sullivan's review praised the two performers and bemoaned the very small audience.

History briefly attempted to repeat itself in 1945, when a new group was formed to sponsor (non-Bach) concerts in the summer months. Under the imposing name of Monterey Peninsula Music and Arts Foundation, the group announced the incredible lineup of violinist Joseph Szigeti on July 13, soprano Lotte Lehmann on July 27, and pianist Arthur Rubinstein on August 10. (Claudio Arrau actually performed, instead of Rubinstein.) Szigeti was a lucky catch: during the past few years he had often visited Carmel with his family. The MPMAF sponsored concerts irregularly for a few years, but did not endure.

Bach returns

The summer of 1945 brought rejoicing at the end of the War, and at the announcement that preparations were beginning in October for the resumption of the Carmel Bach Festival in 1946.

NINTH ANNUAL
CARMEL BACH FESTIVAL
JULY 22 to JULY 28, 1946
PROGRAM FOR THE WEEK

GASTONE USIGLI............CONDUCTOR

DENE DENNY AND HAZEL WATROUS   PRODUCING MANAGERS

After the War 1946–1950

SOLI DEO GLORIA

All things eternal speak to God alone.
Time cannot reach them with the ills of change.
They stand forever lifted past the range
Of small concerns, a towering overtone.
They draw the listener from the petty round
Of self-inflicted duties, till he stands
Above the stress, above the small demands,
In that high place where unity is found.

So these great fugues of Bach, sublime of form,
Rise from a world discordant and distressed
Into immortal motion and repose.
The many come and go; the sun, the storm
Beat on the tides of ages without rest;
But here through time undying music flows.

[Note: Bach often wrote S.D.G at the end of his compositions.
It stands for Soli Deo Gloria, "Only for the Glory of God."]

THE SOIL OF PLENITUDE

Bach was the earth of song—the merest seed
That fell by chance into that fertile ground
Became a tree of music, branched and freed,
Lyric with leaves and rising flower-crowned.
Bach was the wide dark soil of plenitude;
In him unfolded utterance, strong and warm.
The simplest theme he nurtured was imbued
With natural growth, development and form.

Oh vast and fruitful spirit! would that we,
The least of us to whom one gift is given,
Could live with such devotion as to be
The unremitting servitors of heaven!
Creation has its own inherent power;
It seeks the soil in which to root and flower.

CHORALE PRELUDE

What golden water bubbling from its source
Into the open acres of the sun
Ever came tumbling brighter on its course
Then this clear music rippling on the run.
In outline shining as a Grecian frieze,
Or like a life-length clip from some great whole
It comes forth singing with delight and ease
The unconditioned music of the soul.

There seems no marked beginning, growth and end.
It is already at the highest place
When poured full-voiced and perfect at the start;
And when the rhythmic lines of cadence lend
A draught of silence for a little space
The song goes on forever in the heart.

These poems by Dora Hagemeyer appeared in the Carmel Pine Cone on July 17, 1946. Hagemeyer began writing for the Pine Cone in the early 1920s and is the author of many of the most enjoyable articles and reviews excerpted in this book. She was the sister-in-law of photographer Johann Hagemeyer. In 1932, her son Max (age ten) joined the Monterey Peninsula Orchestra. Now, at the age of twenty-two, Max was once again taking his place in the cello section under the leadership of the beloved maestro, Gastone Usigli.

The tireless, flaming zeal of Gastone Usigli, united in perfect harmony with the vision, high purpose, judgment and brilliant executive abilities of Dene Denny and Hazel Watrous, have brought the Carmel Bach Festival to its present nationally recognized place among The Music Festivals of the Nation. (Pine Cone, July 19, 1946)

Susan Porter, another long-time Pine Cone contributor, wrote of the return to Carmel of this major event after a hiatus of three years.

A newcomer to Carmel, if he be sensitive, is aware just now of something stirring in the village. He is growing used to passing little groups of people who stand talking earnestly together. But now the scraps of talk that drift to him seem different:—"At rehearsal last night..." "Yes, they will give the Magnificat twice..." "The new Hungarian basso..." "Wait till Usigli comes down [from San Francisco]." And if he should stroll past Sunset School at night he might hear how music floats out from the windows, and how Bach is hummed and whistled in the darkness as the performers go home. I hope someone has told him by now how the Bach Festival began, with what high vision and quiet purpose, and how it quickened and grew strong. During the war-years the festival remained a reality in our thoughts. We waited, knowing it would return, as surely as we knew the war would be won. Its continuity remained unbroken. It is an entity, an organic thing, and we believe that it has grown stronger in its silence. And perhaps we, as listeners, have grown also. (Pine Cone, July 19, 1946)

In this San Francisco Chronicle cartoon by Sotomayor, Usigli conducts while three angels hover around Bach: Dene Denny, Hazel Watrous, and Noel Sullivan. *San Francisco Chronicle, June 24, 1946. Courtesy of the Carmel Bach Festival.*

As it had before the war, the Festival gave five evening concerts, but now all five took place in Sunset Auditorium. (The Diocese had decided that the Mission was not a concert venue. The Bach Festival did not perform in the Carmel Mission again until 1962.)

Most of the music was favorite repertoire from previous summers. The Magnificat—with all the internal choral movements still omitted—appeared on the first and fourth concerts. The Festival featured four Bach cantatas, several concerti, and other smaller Bach works. Tuesday night once again explored non-Bach music. The first half was Italian Baroque, followed by four Italian and English Renaissance madrigals with orchestral accompaniments written by Usigli. The concert ended with a Mozart piano concerto. On Sunday, twenty (of the twenty-six) movements of the *Mass in B Minor* were performed, and only one performance was given that day.

The 1947 Bach Festival continued in the same format as 1946, and also gave a second performance of the nearly complete *Mass in B Minor* on the final day. The Wednesday and Friday organ recitals were each given twice, at 3:00 and 4:00pm at All Saints Church.

...if they make love the way they sing...

Immediately after the Festival, Time Magazine readers from coast to coast read Usigli's wry comments about his amateur Festival Chorus.

> *TIME Magazine, Monday, August 4, 1947*
> *MUSIC: BACH BY THE SEA*
>
> In 13 years the well-to-do resort town of Carmel, Calif, has become a kind of Bayreuth of Bach. Last week Carmel again paid its tribute to the master with a full week of his music. A good many Carmelites frankly preferred the Shriners' circus in nearby Salinas. But those who gave Bach a try got preludes and fugues on the organ, cantatas, all the Brandenburg concertos and a few works by other 18th Century composers. The big event was two performances of the great *Mass in B Minor*. It rated a B minus for Bach —the strings were uneven and the chorus occasionally mushy—but it deserved an A for effort.
>
> The festival was started by two women, Dene Denny and Hazel Watrous, who went to Carmel for a vacation 24 years ago, and have been there ever since. They have sometimes lost money on the Bach festival, but make it up on a San José theatrical booking agency and a Monterey theater that they run.
>
> The only paid festival performer among the chorus of 69 and the orchestra of 43 was Conductor Gastone Usigli. The chorus, mostly townspeople, had rehearsed weekly since September, but not until just before the festival did Usigli gather, orchestra and chorus together for an exhausting rehearsal.
>
> Says he: "Community singing is fine, but it is best for Christmas carols. A local chorus can do Gilbert & Sullivan, but the *Mass in B Minor*—ah! that is another matter. I have to extract something from these young people that they never knew they had. Sometimes I think that if they make love the way they sing, it must be horrible." [Emphasis added.]

The 1948 Bach Festival offered the same schedule , including two performances of a more-nearly-complete *Mass in B Minor* on the final Sunday. Two choral movements were still omitted entirely: Cum Sancto Spiritu and Credo in unum Deum; the Crucifixus (written for chorus) was performed by the soloists. Usigli also omitted sections within movements for reasons of concert length or vocal difficulty, and when necessary he rewrote the connecting measures to hide the internal omissions. (This is mentioned by Sandor Salgo in his Oral History.) The violin, flute, and horn obbligato solos were performed on proper instruments. The two oboes were again replaced by clarinets.

The Carmel Pine Cone ran a profile of Dene and Hazel, excerpted below.

Tell me, who is Denny-Watrous?

This hyphenated word resolves itself into two remarkably blended yet clearly defined personalities—the Bach Festival is a culminated expression of the very rich art capacities of Dene Denny and Hazel Watrous. Many persons associate them with music only. They have entered into—and with distinguished success—practically all the arts during the time they have lived in Carmel. They have integrated art into the community life; brought it out of the cold air of the priest-craft which too often surrounds it, in which the initiates talks down to the layman; and they have done it with never a concession to mediocrity.

Open rehearsals for Bach chorus are one example of their nearness to community living. This is the key to the pattern they have woven with the years, in Carmel and far beyond its environs, bringing fine art warmly, closely, to the least informed and those most informed. Tall, clear, sure Dene Denny; reposeful, purposeful, piquant Hazel Watrous. That is how they looked twenty-five years ago when they first came to Carmel. That is how they look now. Two charming unruffled, poised women; they never seem hurried, never seem to have forgotten anything; there is always time for the graciousness of living.

Yet right now they direct [i.e. produce] impresario concerts and New York stage plays in San José, direct first theater productions in Monterey, and this Bach Festival with its multiplicity of detail, flowing magnificently, apparently effortlessly, all the way through its weeklong unfoldment....

These two brilliant women have progressed with a fine creative sureness through individual expression in music, painting, design, architecture, to an equally creative combined expression in drama, concert management, and Bach Festival—living arts in a community of artists. We hail with affection and respect Dene Denny and Hazel Watrous—Denny-Watrous are people, and of a rare quality. (Pine Cone, July 16, 1948)

Soloists in the Concerto for Four Pianos at the 1949 Carmel Bach Festival: l. to r.: Randolph Hokanson, Charles Fulkerson, Maxim Shapiro, and Ralph Linsley. *Courtesy of the Carmel Bach Festival.*

One week later, the Carmel Spectator chimed in:

> Carmel's two leading ladies are one, in the merging of their great talents, their ambitions, and their indefatigable energies. Two nationally known artists, two renowned impresarios, two successful business administrators, two highly individual and charming women. Carmel's two leading ladies are one, in the merging of their great talents, their ambitions, and their indefatigable energies. It is to this unique "team" that Carmel owes much of its cultural development, the story of which has crossed the nation; its architectural individuality; its leadership in the theatrical world; and its material prosperity.
>
> Through the verdant garden where an impromptu fountain sprayed sunlit rainbows we strolled into their studio [on N. Dolores Street]. What a beautiful room it is, with its two concert pianos forming the central pattern of polished ebony, the great double height panoramic window, many paned, the fireplace with its deep purple chimney, the "Little Person with a Cello" painted by Maxine Albro especially for the studio, the emerald green velvet cushioned Victorian chairs. A blend of the old and the new perfectly balanced, rarely accomplished. Down a step, off the studio, is the intimate "sitting room," a triumph in its modern functional, albeit comfortable, furnishings, its gay colors, books that made one long to linger, a rare and beautiful picture of Johann Sebastian Bach. (Carmel Spectator, July 23, 1948)
>
> (The subject of the painting was Jean Crouch Fulkerson, cellist in the orchestra.)

In 1949 the Carmel Bach Festival added a sixth main concert: the new schedule was Monday, Tuesday, Thursday, Friday, Saturday, Sunday—with two performances of the *Mass* on Sunday (including a portion of the Credo). Usigli featured a keyboard concerto on every concert, including both Bach and Mozart concertos on Tuesday. The Friday concert concluded with the *Concerto in A Minor for Four Pianos*, a work Usigli had conducted in his first summer in 1938.

The Last Chord has Sounded

The last majestic chord has sounded, the last pure note of the anthem has been sung. The beloved maestro bows and bows, he smiles at his soloists, his orchestra and his choristers as they stand in acknowledgment of the salvos of applause from a grateful audience. And many hearts filled to overflowing are just a little saddened. Carmel's Twelfth Bach Festival comes to a close as friends linked by their love of great and sacred music leave the auditorium....

Backstage, violins, flutes, cellos—all the delicately contrived instruments with their burden of beauty—are carefully, lovingly placed in their cases. The choristers doff their surplices—there are good-byes in the air, there are hand clasps and murmurs of "Til next year," and all the while, two well-beloved ladies stand by—not in idleness, but with that amazing calm that is part of their fame, smoothing every difficulty, anticipating every detail of the closing moments of a great week of great music—Carmel's Twelfth Bach Festival comes to a close, and not only Carmel, but hundreds of lovers of great music once again thank Dene Denny and Hazel Watrous for their unique imagination, their magnificent powers of organization and their long unceasing hours, days and weeks and years of work—for their creation—the festival. (The Carmelite, July 28, 1949)

During the Festival, Dene and Hazel entertained at their Studio, and Noel Sullivan put on huge parties for the Bach Festival ensemble.

> Of the many parties that graced the festival week, gala was the Denny-Watrous affair, when, crowding the spacious Studio, musicians entertained musicians. Lavish and fun the luncheon at Noel Sullivan's beautiful Hollow Hills. The lively chatter of more than 200 guests, the fun in the cerulean blue pool, the flowers, the meadows, the gentle deer. And inside the house, magnificence that only a great connoisseur of old world art treasures could achieve. It was all a memory to be long-held in one's heart. The 12th Festival in Carmel has come to a close, the music in our hearts will live, always. (Carmel Spectator, July 30, 1949)

The Bach Festival Chorus was still mostly amateur—except for the vocal soloists who were expected to sing along. "Amateur" included students from San José and volunteers from Los Angeles who boosted the size of the chorus to nearly 60. Angie Machado, a Monterey music teacher and singer, was the Festival's Assistant Choral Director from 1946 through 1954.

> Since Christmas, Angie Machado has been coaching the chorus in the infinite complexities of the simple phrases that make up a chorale, a full Mass in B Minor chorus, and all the incidental things the chorus must do. It was obvious tonight that she has done a genuinely invaluable and top drawer job; obvious, too, that she has been fine and unassuming and left to the conductor his special function of interpretation. She sat modestly in the far back seat, while Maestro Usigli wrung out of her pupils the last delicate modulation of tone and tempo, but at the end of an hour on the two Greek words [Kyrie eleison*] there came at last that incredibly profound white perfectitude of sanctified song, as it came from the deeply religious and compassionate heart of the composer. (Pine Cone, July 14, 1950)

(The Greek words "Kyrie eleison" [Lord, have mercy] appear at the beginning of the Latin Mass. The first and third movements of the Mass in B Minor total about 12 minutes in length, and the entire text for each movement is "Kyrie eleison.")

The Festival Chorus was a central pillar of the Festival—the element that most connected the Festival to the community.

> The chorus is the oldest Carmel contribution to the festival.... More than any other single factor, the chorus is to the festival the spirit in which it began and which, it is devoutly hoped, will never die in our or any time; the spirit that sets the Carmel Festival apart from all the others; the spirit of Carmel.... Along the way, as the festival has grown, it is been necessary to abandon much of the purely local talent and substitute a more professional cast. But still, on a July night when the fog fingers down through the trees, men and women that are our own gather throughout the year to rehearse the music of Bach, as they have gathered so for all the years of the growth of this wonderful event. (ibid.)

In anticipation of the 1950 Bach Festival, the greatest praise, as always, was reserved for Dene and Hazel.

But It Can Be Done

"It cannot be done. It simply can't be done." With just those words on people's tongues and just that judgment in their hearts, Dene Denny and Hazel Watrous set off on their flight to interstellar space, ignorant of the meaning of such words, clear in their direction, sure their goal, to make out of a little whistling among the trees the resounding and glorious achievement that the 13th Carmel Bach Festival will be. The difficult, they agree with someone who once said it, immediately: the impossible may take a little time....

And little by little, or big by big, these gentle and beautiful women, each with her own charming smile, each with her individual gift, became here the synonym for the best that Carmel had to offer. Never deviating from an excellence of judgment and taste that has remained throughout the years, they built with their singular constancy up to their vision. The vision of a Festival of Music, dedicated to the greatest master of sacred song would ever lived.

They have done what people said could not be done. They have made the Carmel Bach Festival one of the truly great and truly unique music events in the world. After all, for women like Dene and Hazel, the impossible takes a little time. (Pine Cone, July 14, 1950)

In a one-time-only experiment, in 1950 the Bach Festival opened on a Sunday with the *Mass in B Minor* and ended on the following Sunday with the Festival's first performance of Bach's dramatic oratorio The *St. John Passion* (in English and in Usigli's shortened version).

Usigli was of the generation of musicians who were just beginning to understand the interpretive beauties of the Baroque repertoire, and he tended to disregard the repeated sections in arias and choruses. For example, a "da capo" aria ("from the beginning") has three sections: A, followed by B, followed by a repeat of A. Usigli, however, sometimes chose to perform only the first A section. An alternative is to perform A and B and then end with just the orchestral introduction to A. In Usigli's view, the repeats were "mere reiteration."

> Both musical and dramatic considerations often should mitigate against repeating the second section of an aria or of a concerted episode, when these amount to mere reiteration... There is no more reason to include such episodes than to perform in most cases the long repeats of older symphonies; in both cases, the considerations of form that originally had prompted those devices have ceased to exist. (Music an Dance in California and the West, 1948.)

Tenor James Schwabacher made his Bach Festival debut in the role of the Evangelist (narrator) in the *St. John Passion*. Schwabacher was an important San Francisco singer, teacher, patron, and administrator. He became a great friend of the Bach Festival, and performed and lectured at the Festival for more than three decades.

In 1950, more daytime recitals were added to the schedule. Pianist Maxim Shapiro played both volumes of the "Well-Tempered Clavier" in three morning concerts at the Carmel Woman's Club, just across the street from Sunset Auditorium. On Tuesday, Ludwig Altman played Bach and Telemann on the organ at All Saints Church at 3:00 and 4:00pm. On Thursday there were two more afternoon recitals at All Saints in which Altman was joined by Usigli and several instrumentalists for mixed program of organ solos and chamber music.

A noteworthy feature of the 1950 Carmel Bach Festival was the performance of Bach's *The Art of the Fugue* arranged for orchestra by Gastone Usigli. His orchestration included flutes, oboes, bassoon, clarinets, full string orchestra, and two pianos.

Meanwhile, Denny-Watrous Management was busy as usual.

Presented by
DENNY-WATROUS MANAGEMENT
WED. EVE., NOVEMBER 18th at 8:00 Sharp
Opening Concert   SAN JOSE CONCERT SERIES
CIVIC AUDITORIUM, SAN JOSE

KREISLER

DIRECTION
C. J. FOLEY
BOSTON

Tour Direction: NBC Artists Service

1954–1955 Season

Denny-Watrous Attractions

IN MONTEREY

California's First Theatre, State Monument
Corner of Pacific and Scott Streets, Monterey
The Troupers of the Gold Coast in an evening of incomparable entertainment
"THE FATAL WEDDING"
DIRECTED BY RHEA DIVELEY
Followed by 12 hilarious Variety Acts
Every Friday, Saturday and Sunday nights, at 8:15, throughout July and August
Tickets $1.50, incl. tax, at Staniford's Drug, Carmel, and at First Theatre

IN CARMEL

FRI. AUG. 13: JULIAN KARLOYI
The distinguished Hungarian Pianist will be heard in a solo recital of works of Caesar
Franck, Chopin, Schumann, Listz, Ravel, Debussy, Saint-Saens.
Tickets $3.30, $2.75, $2.20, $1.65. On Sale at Graham Music Company,
Carmel. At Abinante's Music Store, Monterey.
Coming: PAUL DRAPER, Tap Dancer Supreme.

IN SAN JOSE

OCT. 11: YMA SUMAC and Company of Dancers, Andean
Drummers, Musicians
NOV. 1, 2: "THE SEVEN YEAR ITCH" with EDDIE BRACKEN
NOV. 4: MARGE and GOWER CHAMPION with Company
DEC. 3: GINA BACHAUER, Pianist
DEC. 6: THE LONDON FESTIVAL BALLET
S. Hurok presents this extraordinary attraction under the patronage of H. H. Princess
Marie Louise, direct from the Royal Festival Hall London.
TAMARA TOUMANOVA, Guest Artist. ANTON DOLIN,
Artistic Director.
Featured Dancers include the two famous Russian-trained Hungarian Nora Kovach
and Istvan Rabotsky who escaped last spring from behind the Iron Curtain.
JAN 25: SAN FRANCISCO SYMPHONY ORCHESTRA
Enrique Jorda, Conductor. Ruth Slenczynska, Piano Soloist
FEB. 12: BALLET RUSSE DE MONTE CARLO
Reorganized, brilliant Company of 125. MARIA TALLCHIEF,
Prima Ballerina. Frederic Franklin and many stars.
FEB. 18: ISAAC STERN, Violinist
MAR. 21: FIRST PIANO QUARTET
MAR. 25: JOSE GRECO SPANISH DANCERS
Mail orders for San Jose attractions should be addressed to:
DENNY-WATROUS MANAGEMENT, Civic Auditorium, San Jose

DENNY-WATROUS ATTRACTIONS
California's First Theatre, State Monument
Pacific and Scott Streets, Monterey
Since opening June 3, 1937
Number of performances . . . 1,120
62 Plays — 452 Troupers

Currently running, the hilarious farce-comedy
"THE UNKISSED BRIDE"
DIRECTED BY RHEA DIVELY
Every Friday, Saturday, Sunday Night, at 8:15
Tickets $1.50, $1.20 incl. tax. On sale at First Theatre, Monterey 5-4916
and at Staniford's Drug Store, Carmel

See the dramatic hit of a decade in SAN JOSE
THOMAS MITCHELL in
Elia Kazan's production
"DEATH OF A SALESMAN"
with
JUNE WALKER   **PAUL LANGTON**
Thursday Evening, September 21, at 8:30
Civic Auditorium, San Jose
"A monumental play has come to town. An evening of greatness in the theatre." John
Hobart, San Francisco Chronicle.
"A superbly written play . . This is theatre—theatre you dream about." Hortense Morton,
San Francisco Examiner.
"Thomas Mitchell is magnificent." Fred Johnson, Call-Bulletin.
Tickets $3.60, $3.00, $2.40, $1.80, $1.20 incl. tax. Address Denny-Watrous Management,
Civic Auditorium, San Jose, after August 15. CY 3-6252.

15th ANNUAL SAN JOSE CONCERT SERIES
LILY PONS, Oct. 26 . . . RUBINSTEIN, BALLET RUSSE DE MONTE CARLO, VIENNA
CHOIR BOYS, BARBER OF SEVILLE, SPIVAKOVSKY, SAN FRANCISCO SYMPHONY
ORCHESTRA, Pierre Monteux, Conductor. Piano Soloist.

Season Tickets $14.40, $12.00, $9.60 incl. tax.
Single Tickets $3.60, $3.00, $2.40, $1.80, $1.20 incl. tax.

Address Denny-Watrous Management, Civic Auditorium, San Jose. CY 3-6252.

1950–1951 Season

DENNY-WATROUS MANAGEMENT
PRESENTS
SAN FRANCISCO SYMPHONY ORCHESTRA

PIERRE MONTEUX, Conductor

DANIEL ERICOURT, Pianist,
Guest Artist

PROGRAM

Overture to "Benvenuto Cellini"	Cellini
Symphony No. 5	Beethoven
Concerto for Piano, E flat Major	Liszt
Daniel Ericourt	
Two Nocturnes	Debussy
Clouds	
Festivals	
Overture to "Tannhauser"	Wagner

San Jose Civic Auditorium **FEB. 18**
FRIDAY EVE. - 8:30 P.M.

RESERVED SEATS NOW ON SALE
Civic Auditorium Box Office - Telephone BAllard 1441

Posters courtesy of the Carmel Bach Festival.
Display ads are from 1949 and 1954 Carmel
Bach Festival programs.

1940 Carmel Bach Festival backstage. From left to right: Julian Lieban, tenor; Noel Sullivan, bass; Terry Koechig, contralto; Ross Worsley, bass; June Steens, alto, Gastone Usigli; Marcella Haward, soprano; Russell Horton, tenor; John Burr, Bass. *Courtesy of the Carmel Bach Festival.*

1947 Carmel Bach Festival backstage. From left to right: Hazel Watrous, Maxim Shapiro, Gastone Usigli, Elizabeth Usigli; Noel Sullivan, and Dene Denny. *Courtesy of the Carmel Bach Festival.*

Gastone Usigli holds court at one of Noel Sullivan's garden parties. *Courtesy of the Harrison Memorial Library.*

A pre-concert photo onstage, Saturday, July 24, 1948. The concert included Bach's Overture in D, the Mozart Concerto for Three Pianos, and Bach's secular cantata, "Phoebus and Pan." Everyone in the photo participated in the concert except Elizabeth Usigli, Hazel, Dene, Spencer Barefoot, and Noel Sullivan. **From left to right**: Willard Culley (horn), [unknown female], Alan Robinson (horn), Elizabeth Usigli, Hazel Watrous, Dene Denny, William Harvey (cello), Spencer Barefoot (SF critic), Peter Roberts (bass), Nannette Levi (concertmaster), Maxim Shapiro (piano), Gabriel Bartold (trumpet), Phyllis Moffet (soprano), Floyd Stancleff (flute), Gastone Usigli, Janice Moudrey (alto), Jolen May (flute), Ralph Isbell (bass), Ruth Terry (alto), Noel Sullivan (bass), Julian Lieban (tenor). *Courtesy of the Carmel Bach Festival.*

Judging from the orchestra personnel, this photograph was taken in 1950 or 1951, but it is unclear what is taking place, considering Usigli's white trousers. Below left, he consults with a soloist. Below right, Usigli conducts a concerto with three pianos while the resident Sunset Auditorium bat flies overhead. It was nicknamed "Johann Sebastian Bat." *Photo above courtesy of the H. M. Williams Local History Department, Harrison Memorial Library . Images below courtesy of the Carmel Bach Festival.*

Gastone Usigli conducts the Brandenburg Concerto III at the 1950 Carmel Bach Festival in Sunset Auditorium. (The chandeliers were restored and re-installed in the newly-built Sunset Center in 2003.)

Courtesy of the Carmel Bach Festival.

Part Seven
Entering the Modern Age
1951–1959

Gastone Usigli rehearses the orchestra stage right in Sunset Auditorium. Irwin Mautner is concertmaster and Ralph Linsley is the pianist. The photo may have been taken in 1950, Mautner's first year in the orchestra. *Courtesy of the Carmel Bach Festival.*

SIXTEENTH ANNUAL CARMEL
**BACH
FESTIVAL**
JULY 20 to 26, 1953

Dene Denny and Hazel Watrous. Clockwise from top left: At the Merienda Festival in Monterey in 1951, photographer unknown. Photo by Kaldor-Bates. 1953 Carmel Bach Festival program cover. Photo by Johann Hagemeyer. *Courtesy of the Carmel Bach Festival.*

1951–1954

The Carmel Bach Festival returned to a six concert schedule in 1951: Monday, Tuesday, Thursday, Friday, Saturday, and Sunday. The final concert was the St. John Passion, abbreviated and in English. Approximately one third of the 1951 main concert repertoire was non-Bach, including three Mozart concertos, two Beethoven concertos, and other works by French and German composers who lived in the century before Bach. There were three keyboard recitals in the afternoons.

> In striving to bring outstanding performances in the field of music, the stage, and art to Carmel, Dene Denny and Hazel Watrous have contributed much to the cultural life in the locality. The development of their careers is interwoven with the advancement of music and the stage in San José, Monterey and Carmel, and most notably with the progress of the annual Bach Festival.... As managers they are constantly challenged by the problems involved in keeping the Bach Festival going so smoothly that for everyone else there are no problems and difficulties but a triumphant performance of fine music. (Pine Cone, July 14, 1951)

At the 1952 Bach Festival, Gastone Usigli and his ensemble finally were able to perform every movement of the *Mass in B Minor,* although 1.) the entire Crucifixus movement was sung by the four vocal soloists, 2.) Usigli actually shortened a few of the other chorus movements, and 3.) sections of the Mass that the chorus had simply been unable to master were sung by the soloists, who were singing along in the chorus during the entire concert anyway.

Ticket demand was great enough to compel the Festival once again to offer two performances on the final Sunday, at 3:00 and 8:30pm. During the week there were two organ recitals and four chamber music recitals.

The 1953 Carmel Bach Festival featured the first Festival performance of the *St. Matthew Passion*, a crown jewel in the music of Johann Sebastian Bach. Written in 1727 in Leipzig, it tells the Easter story as recounted in the Gospel of Matthew. It is unique among Bach's major works— and fiercely difficult to perform—for several reasons. First, it requires two separate orchestras on stage—strings, flutes, oboes, and keyboard. The orchestras face each other and sometimes play separately and sometimes together. Second, two independent choruses are needed as well, and each much be capable of performing by itself. Third, six vocal soloists are required: soprano, alto, two tenors, and two basses. Bach also calls for several early instruments such as viola da gamba, recorder, and organ. (Harpsichord was commonly used until the middle of the 20th century when it became more widely understood that the organ was more appropriate for performances of Bach's church music.) It was for only one of these reasons that Usigli had not yet attempted the *St. Matthew Passion* in Carmel. At the expense of artistic quality, there are certain workarounds for some of the orchestral and vocal solo issues, but for the biggest problem—the two equal and independent choruses—there was no solution in Carmel. The existing Bach Festival Chorus could not be divided into two halves that each would be capable of performing Bach's difficult music.

The Chorale is born

Gastone Usigli spent much of his time in Los Angeles as the conductor of the Los Angeles Federal Music Project Orchestra in the 1930s (where he led fully staged operas such as *Aida, Lohengrin,* and *Carmen*). In the 1940s he continued to maintain a presence in LA as vocal coach and voice teacher. For the 1947 Festival, Usigli had invited six singers from Los Angeles to join the Bach Festival Chorus: he rehearsed them a bit in LA and they arrived in Carmel just two weeks before opening night. In the music business, such additions are called "ringers" and serve to strengthen the ensemble sound; they were not soloists. (The Bach Festival Orchestra had been using ringers since its first season.) Often the moniker implies that the ringers are paid while the others are not, but that was not true in Carmel. At the 1952 Bach Festival, the out of town orchestra members, the chorus singers from LA, and the vocal soloists received a $7 round-trip travel reimbursement and $3 per day for food while in Carmel. They were housed as guests in private homes. In effect, they were volunteers almost like the locals.

Some of the LA chorus ringers were would-be professionals, and others were serious amateurs who took part in Los Angeles music-making as soloists or in the choruses of the Pasadena Symphony, Los Angeles Philharmonic, Hollywood Bowl, and other area organizations. From 1947 through 1952, this contingent of LA singers was a group of individuals singing in the Chorus, and not yet an "ensemble" in and of itself. That shift was sparked by a chance conversation during the 1952 Festival, as recalled many years later by one of the LA singers (who was by profession a physicist and acoustician).

> I had been after him [Usigli] gently always to perform the St. Matthew Passion. It had always been my favorite. And always he would say, "You know that we do not have the chorus for it." And then, finally, one day in 1952 I met him as we walked along to a rehearsal, and he was more jovial than usual; so, I mustered up all my courage and ventured, "Maestro, when are we going to tackle the St. Matthew?" And again came the sad reminder, "You know...." But at least he walked a little slower and seemed to sigh a little harder. So I tried again. "How about a deal? Would you tackle it if I agreed to bring you a small chorus trained for the first chorus parts?" He stopped dead in his tracks and looked through my eyes. Then he blurted, "that's a deal!" Then, a few more steps and he stopped again and looked at me. "How do you propose to do this?" "We will," said I.
>
> And so it was, that in the following spring of 1953 we started scouting the church and school choirs [in Los Angeles], raided the Roger Wagner Chorale, and gathered a little band of singers. (Excerpt from an article written for the Bach Festival by Paul Veneklasen in 1963)

In July 1953, with the help of that little band of (pre-rehearsed) singers from LA, Gastone Usigli and the Carmel Bach Festival did indeed perform the *St. Matthew Passion* for the first time. The names of the LA singers and the locals are listed together alphabetically in the roster of the Chorus: 21 sopranos, 15 altos, 11 tenors, and 11 basses. There is no indication as to how the 58 singers were divided into Chorus I and Chorus II. The Passion was sung in English, and at least 45 minutes of the music was omitted (the complete work is at least three hours long). As always, the Festival ended on a Sunday, and they performed this great oratorio twice—at 2:00 and 8:00pm.

It became known in LA that a pleasant summer or two in Carmel might be a stepping stone for promising professionals; some of the LA singers in the 1950s went on to solo careers, including Thomas Paul, Cora Lauridsen, and Paul Mayo. From 1953 through 1957, the LA singers served as the professional-level core group of the Festival Chorus, and their names continued to be listed together with the locals, in alphabetical order.

Usigli's successor, Sandor Salgo, officially separated the two groups in 1958, returning the Festival Chorus to its fully amateur status and forming a new, 28-voice paid ensemble called the "Festival Chorale." This new Chorale retained a significant core of Los Angeles singers until the early 2000s; currently its members come from all across the continent. Today the Chorale and Chorus perform certain concerts together at the Carmel Bach Festival as they did in the 1950s, and the Chorale also presents concerts of its own. This mix of professionals and amateurs represents one of the defining characteristics of the Carmel Bach Festival.

The 1954 Carmel Bach Festival Opening Night featured two of Gastone Usigli's Festival trademarks: 1. excerpts from a larger work, and 2. some of the Baroque works were performed in Usigli's own arrangements. The Chorus and Orchestra began the concert with the opening and closing choruses from Bach's *Magnificat*. In fact, Usigli included a chorus or two from the Magnificat or the Mass in B Minor at almost every Festival. In Usigli's typical programing at the Bach Festival, for example, two soprano arias from the *St. Matthew Passion* might be nestled between a Brandenburg Concerto and a Violin Concerto, or a pianist might play a Toccata and Fugue between an Orchestral Overture and a Cantata.

The musical arrangement by Usigli on Opening Night was his orchestration of *The Seven Words of Christ on the Cross* by Heinrich Schütz, a composer who pre-dated Bach by 100 years. This was not an "edition" in today's musicological sense—one that called for the instruments that would have been used by Schütz in the 1600s. Usigli's orchestrations of 17th and 18th century music were for a modern orchestra, with flutes, oboes, bassoons, strings, and piano. The Thursday concert included another Usigli arrangement: Bach's *A Musical Offering*, for full orchestra and two pianos. Usigli's orchestration of Bach's *Art of the Fugue* also was performed in several seasons at the Festival, as were his full orchestra accompaniments for English and Italian renaissance madrigals. He was a prolific composer, and a partial list of his compositions is in the Appendix.

Hazel Watrous 1884–1954

The decade of the 1950s was a time of artistic growth and financial prosperity, but was also a time of farewells.

The first sadness to befall Carmel was the death of Hazel Watrous on October 2, 1954. She had been in San José for two weeks, and died unexpectedly on a Saturday morning. That evening the Troupers of the Gold Coast were on stage as usual, and Dene Denny waited until after the final curtain before breaking the news to the players that their beloved theater shepherdess had died. A memorial service was held the following weekend in San José, and Hazel Watrous was buried in the Monterey City Cemetery on Fremont Street.

Dene Denny was devastated by Hazel's death, and the poignant evidence is visible in photographs taken in the summer of 1955. By March of that year she knew that she could no longer manage the San José concert business alone, and on May 1 she sold her interests in the San José concert series to Wendell Watkins, who had been an assistant in their San José operations for seven years.

The 1955 Carmel Bach Festival schedule was in the established six-concert format, with a main concert every evening except Wednesday, when the dress rehearsal for the Sunday concert took place. A few organ and chamber music recitals were given during the mornings and

In June, 1955, Gastone Usigli and a few San Francisco-based orchestra players arrive at the Monterey Bus station. Usigli stands on the left. Others unidentified. *Photos on these two pages courtesy of the Carmel Bach Festival.*

afternoons. Festivals such as this tend to find the particular schedule that works for their personnel, their venues, and their repertoire, and this was just such a schedule. Once again, on the final day, the ensemble gave two performances of Usigli's (shortened) version of the *Mass in B Minor,* at 2:30 and 8:30pm. The entire Festival was dedicated to Hazel Watrous.

Usigli had announced his intention of performing Cantata 147 by J. S. Bach at the 1956 Festival. To honor their friend Hazel Watrous, the entire 1955 ensemble chipped in to purchase the vocal scores and orchestral parts needed for the performance the following year. This note appeared in the 1956 Bach Festival program on the evening when that cantata was performed.

"As a memorial to Hazel Watrous, co-founder of the Carmel Bach Festival, the music of Cantata No. 147 was purchased by the Soloists, Chorus and Orchestra of the 1955 Festival to be a permanent addition to the Festival library."

In July 1955, as Carmel and the attendees of the Bach Festival honored the memory of Hazel Watrous, no one knew that the closing in Carmel Mission was Gastone Usigli's last appearance on the Bach Festival podium.

This poignant photo was taken during the 1955 Carmel Bach Festival. Dene Denny and Gastone Usigli are with Angie Machado, chorus master and Usigli's assistant at the Festival. Hazel Watrous died the previous October, and after more than 30 years of "Denny-Watrous," Dene is now alone. Compare this with the photo on page 262.

Courtesy of the H. M. Williams Local History Department, Harrison Memorial Library.

Addio Usigli 1897–1956

In March 1956, the Italian community of the entire San Francisco Bay Area was celebrating the first visit to America of Giovanni Gronchi, the newly-elected President of Italy. Among the

festivities were many sparkling musical events throughout the city, spanning several weeks.

On March 8, San Francisco's musical and political glitterati gathered for a cocktail party at the home of Kurt Herbert Adler, General Director of the San Francisco Opera. Gastone Usigli was by now at the height of his career, esteemed as conductor, composer, and teacher, and of course he and Elizabeth were among the party guests. After the cocktail party, the Usiglis were driven to the Italian Consulate, where Gastone had been given the honor of conducting a special concert of Italian music for the visiting President and other distinguished guests. The entire evening was a great success, and after midnight Gastone and Betsy returned happily to their home at 2240 Larkin Street. While reading in bed, and surely still aglow from the happy and successful musical evening, Gastone suddenly

Portrait by Johann Hagemeyer, late 1930s.

complained of feeling ill. The family doctor was summoned, but within minutes Gastone suffered a massive heart attack and died with Betsy at his side.

San Francisco writer Alexander Fried knew Gastone Usigli and eulogized him in the San Francisco Chronicle:

> In a shockingly sudden, tragic aftermath to a happy Italian–American ceremonial occasion, California music suffered a grievous loss early yesterday in the death of Gastone Usigli, distinguished conductor, composer, and teacher....
>
> His death leaves more than one breach in the music of Northern California. He was already preparing for his annual task is director of the Carmel Bach Festival. And as head of the Marin Symphony, he conducted a regular concert only a week ago. Aside from his
>
> loss to music, he will be missed in a rare and exceptional way by his many friends, of both the general cultural community and the community of Italian origin. He had a breadth of intellect and understanding that few specialized musicians attain. He was a man of books, of thought and universal spirit. He was vivacious and original in his ideas. He was articulate not only in Italian and English, but also in other languages, notably German.... In this summer's Bach Festival, he was to have done something unusual by directing an opening performance of Mozart's Requiem in honor of the Mozart Bicentennial. The *Requiem* will be not merely Mozart's, not merely Bach's. It will be Gastone Usigli's own.
>
> (San Francisco Chronicle, March 11, 1956)

Italy, 1920s.

Just before the 1956 Bach Festival, Dene Denny wrote her own remembrance of Usigli.

Gastone Usigli

by Dene Denny

For fifteen years he went in and out among us: few realized the greatness of his stature, the nobility of his purpose. But none who came to know him in the orchestra or chorus, or in just a casual conversation, could ever forget the impact of his presence.

When Gastone Usigli first directed the Carmel Bach Festival in 1938, the local chorus often registered no more than 15 in number for rehearsals, with no tenors, and every section frighteningly incomplete. The orchestra was largely amateur, and inexperienced. With selfless devotion, he fashioned our first performance of the monumental Mass in B Minor, elevating the orchestra and chorus beyond their accepted capacities to a transcendent glory of sound.

It was of this performance, which was really not a performance but spiritual experience, that Alfred Frankenstein wrote in the San Francisco Chronicle, July 31, 1938: "… An interpretation of the *Mass in B Minor* that will remain for a long memorable in the minds and hearts of those were privileged to experience it as one of the most dramatic, exalted, and satisfying of a lifetime… The more mystically minded in the audience might have had reason for holding that we had seen and heard a Descent of the Spirit…"

Year after year our beloved maestro shared his vast knowledge, his outpouring of inspiration, his unflagging energy, his vision, each year with more impressive results, until, when he stepped from the podium for the last time in 1955, the Bach Festival had attained a standard of excellence that placed it among the major music festivals in the country.

Our unceasing gratitude and perpetual acknowledgement of his influence live on, each one of us measurably richer for having known him. A poignant memory grips us as we relive the exaltation that startled us as we glimpsed the sublime heights of the "Et resurrexit," the "Confiteor," and the "Benedictus," the music swelling to the Gothic arches of the auditorium and softening into a splendor of serenity, as Gastone Usigli conducted the final pages of the *Mass in B Minor*. (Pine Cone, July 12, 1956)

Sandor Salgo 1956

Only a few days before Gastone Usigli's sudden death on March 8, Dene Denny had attended a performance of the San Francisco Symphony led by a young Hungarian-born American conductor named Sandor Salgo. He had come to the US in the late 1930s as a violinist, and was a very popular professor at Stanford University. When Dene received news of Usigli's death, she immediately was compelled—in the midst of mourning—to take care of the Carmel Bach Festival, with opening night just over four months away. She phoned James Schwabacher, a San Franciscan who had become a valued and admired tenor soloist at the Festival. She discussed Sandor Salgo with Schwabacher, and asked him to phone Salgo and warn him that Dene would be calling. Soon after, she made the call and invited Sandor Salgo to conduct the 1956 Carmel Bach Festival.

Sandor Salgo was born on March 10, 1909, in Budapest, Hungary, to Jewish parents Morris and Rose Sálgo. He attended the Franz Liszt Academy of Music in Budapest where he studied violin and his professors included Zoltán Kodály and Béla Bartók. After graduating in 1928, he studied with conductor Fritz Busch in Berlin and with the great violin teacher Carl Flesch in Dresden (Sascha Jacobinoff was also a pupil of Carl Flesch). Salgo began his professional career as a chamber musician with the Roth String Quartet and also played in several European orchestras. As concertmaster of the Budapest Opera, he played under conductors such as Richard Strauss, Eric Kleiber, Hans Knappertsbusch, and Bruno Walter, and in the orchestra of the Bayreuth Festival he played under Wilhelm Furtwängler and Arturo Toscanini.

In 1937, Sandor Salgo was part of a string quartet that serenaded the bed-ridden wife of the US Ambassador to Budapest. Later that year, the grateful Ambassador helped Salgo obtain his first American visa to come to the United States on short notice to substitute for the second violinist with the Roth Quartet on an American tour. Soon after, concerned with the continued rise of anti-Semitism in Europe, he wrote to Princeton University, a place where the Roth quartet had been warmly welcomed, and in 1939 he received an invitation to teach violin and music theory in Princeton at Westminster Choir College. During his decade in Princeton, Salgo became an American citizen (1946) and played chamber music with Albert Einstein. He served almost three years in the US Army as conductor in an orchestra formed in New York to make soundtracks for training films, and as the cymbal player in an Army band. In Princeton he met and married (1944) Priscilla Patterson, a gifted choral conductor. As Priscilla Salgo, she was Director of the Festival Chorale from 1960 through 1991.

In 1947, Stanford University in Palo Alto, California, established a music department and in 1949 Sandor Salgo was invited to join the faculty, where the brilliance of his musicianship, the depth of his intellect, and his irresistible charm and wit made him a highly popular professor. For example, his introductory course to the music of Ludwig van Beethoven—taught for non-musicians—was the second most popular class at Stanford University for more than a decade. (The most popular class in those years was a course in human sexuality, a fact that Salgo found amusing and loved to relate.)

Photos courtesy of the H. M. Williams Local History Department, Harrison Memorial Library

In 1949 he was named the Director of Opera and Orchestras at Stanford, and the breadth of the repertoire he brought to the Stanford orchestra over the years, and the quantity of major 20th century compositions, is breathtaking. In 1951 (only four years after his arrival in California) Salgo was named conductor of both the San José Symphony and the Modesto Symphony. The Marin Symphony had been led by Gastone Usigli until his death, and Salgo immediately was invited to lead that orchestra as well. He was music director of the orchestras in San José and Modesto until 1970, and in Marin until 1989.

Salgo also guest conducted orchestras in the US and Europe, including the East Berlin Staatsoper. Although Salgo traveled to Europe many times in his life, he never returned to Hungary—and never spoke Hungarian—because of the painful memories of the anti-Semitism he had witnessed and personally experienced there in his youth.

As the Bach Festival drew near, a Carmel Pine Cone editorial acknowledged Dene Denny's role in the Festival, and her courage in keeping on despite the loss of her two friends, Hazel Watrous and Gastone Usigli.

With courage and vision

Sometimes the right combinations of circumstances occur together and something extraordinary comes to birth. It may be a cathedral, a painting, a school or simply a day when things are right, but behind each of these creations is usually to be found some extraordinary human being. It is true of the Bach Festival as it is true of all fine things except mountains and trees and beaches. The spirit moves a human being in the right time in the right place and something is made which gives a large part of humanity reassurance.

Dene Denny, with her ideal of what might be accomplished clearly before her, has made the Bach Festival. For years she and Hazel Watrous and Gastone Usigli have worked at many activities but their most precious work was the Bach Festival. After a stint of teaching music and art, Dene Denny and Hazel Watrous came to Carmel to enter one of the most hazardous professions in the world—that of producing-managers for the theater. For anyone to make a successful career in this field is remarkable but they did it. The San José concert series they managed for years. The first theater in Monterey has been their work from the beginning, but most remarkable of all has been this music festival in Carmel.

There was a man in Carmel some years ago who said, "Bach Festival? Who wants to hear his music? Nobody goes to that anymore!" He was wrong. The audiences have been drawn from all over the United States to hear the week of music which Dene Denny's insight, tenacity, knowledge and love of music have made possible. The problems and difficulties have been terrific. To find over 100 capable musicians, to see that chorus and orchestra are trained, to house all Festival personnel, to arrange programs, to find places for visitors to stay, these are only a few of the manifold problems involved. They are not important. When the Bach Festival is in full tide, smoothly moving only, no one wonders about the difficulties. Everyone simply takes for granted that this is a beautiful thing. Of course it will be good.

Dene Denny was a pianist herself. After graduating from the University of California and earning her master's degree in music with a membership in Phi Beta Kappa, she opened her music studio in San Francisco and gave the first exclusively contemporary recitals on the West Coast. That she is a musician herself is evident in the planning of the festival. A respect for the music itself is paramount. Nowhere else in America is such a festival exist. Particularly in the production of John [sic] Sebastian Bach's great choral works has the Bach Festival in Carmel been remarkable.

It is her wish that the festival this year be a memorial to the two people who shared her vision and the work which brought the vision to sensible reality. The festival is an occasion for joy. The audiences, the feeling of Thanksgiving that again they may listen to living music and this year when the Bach Cantata No. 147 is sung on opening night for Hazel Watrous, and when the Mozart *Requiem* is sung on Sunday, July 22, for Gastone Usigli, audiences and performers alike will rejoice in this great music. (Pine Cone, July 12, 1956)

Gastone Usigli had planned to open the 1956 Carmel Bach Festival with Mozart's *Requiem in D* Minor in honor of the Mozart bicentennial. Now, with Usigli's death, a requiem at the Bach Festival took on new and more somber significance, and so it was moved to the closing spot on the final concert on Sunday. The Requiem—and the entire 1956 Bach Festival—were dedicated to the memory of Gastone Usigli.

The 1956 Festival was in the established seven-day format. Concerts took place Monday through Sunday (with only a single concert on Sunday). Most of the repertoire in the 1956 Festival had already been chosen by Usigli, but for the Festival opener, instead of the Requiem, Salgo chose one of Bach's most joyous works, the *Magnificat in D*, well known to be a favorite of Usigli's. Since Salgo's entry into the Carmel scene had been rather sudden and he had a lot to manage—he already was conductor of three orchestras and had a full-time teaching position—Richard Lert, conductor of the Pasadena Symphony, was invited to help out by conducting the all-Mozart concert on Thursday.

Courtesy of the Carmel Bach Festival.

By the end of the Festival it was clear that Sandor Salgo had achieved a stunning success. The Festival concluded with the Mozart *Requiem*, and James Schwabacher, the tenor soloist in the concert, later recalled a backstage encounter with Dene Denny during the applause that evening:

I remember Dene Denny, who was one of the founders of the Festival, saying to me after Sandor's Mozart Requiem—as we were taking our bows—she said, "Well, Jimmie, you know this is the man who's obviously going to be our new conductor," because of the enthusiasm he evoked from the orchestra and from the audience. And so that's how Sandor got his job, basically. (Schwabacher Oral History, UC Berkeley)

Postscript

Sandor Salgo was Conductor and Musical Director of the Carmel Bach Festival for 36 seasons. He had an old world style and charm that was gracious and persuasive at the same time.

> Sandor Salgo was perfectly suited in musical gifts, training and experience for the role he was to play. Although this was paramount, another key factor was his temperament and style or, to sum it up, his personality. The contrast with Usigli was striking. For one thing, Usigli—who had shaped the San Jose Symphony from a casual community into a more disciplined and serious orchestra, founded the Marin Symphony, and set the concept and began the tradition at the Carmel Bach Festival—was a strict, emotional and temperamental maestro of the old school. He was demanding but not always easy. Salgo, on the other hand, brought all of the musicianly qualities to the table without that emotional baggage. (Robert Commanday, Introduction to Salgo Oral History)

Salgo often said that his aim was to connect performers and listeners with what he often referred to as "the spirituality of the music."

> What I tried to do—and the Bach Festival was my life's work—was to focus on the spiritual message of the music. The spirituality with which these great works were written expresses the essence of Bach's art—the aura of reverence and the profundity of feeling they expressed was what I tried to communicate. (Salgo Oral History)

Mark Volkert, Salgo's final Bach Festival Concertmaster, described Salgo's professional style: "No one captures the drama of the piece like Mr. Salgo. He is always scholarly, never mannered, and he captures the emotions just precisely. It was a romantic style."

The Marin Symphony Executive Director at the time of Salgo's death in 2007 recalled how Salgo's personality and charm added to his work: "He had a European graciousness that inspired people on both sides of the stage and brought them to new heights of musical understanding."

Salgo won worldwide recognition for his contributions to music; he was the recipient of the German Order of Merit First Class for furthering German music (1972); the Dinkelspiel Award for Outstanding Service to Undergraduate Education from Stanford's President, Richard Lyman (1974); and the Chevalier des Arts et Lettres from the French government for furthering French music (1981). His contribution to music in the San Francisco area is immeasurable, and in 2007 Robert Commanday in the San Francisco Chronicle described Salgo's career as "the longest, strongest, most far-reaching career of any conductor in the Bay Area."

Gastone Usigli, in his fifteen seasons with the Carmel Bach Festival, had laid the foundation for the modern Bach Festival by leading the development of the enthusiastic but rag-tag group that he inherited in 1938 into the semi-professional (but still unpaid) ensemble he conducted in 1955. Now, under the leadership of Sandor Salgo, the Carmel Bach Festival would rise to a new level of artistry, professionalism, and international reputation.

Sandor Salgo knew that he was speaking to posterity when he added these words to the final interview of his oral history.

> In closing, I would like to recall the words of that great musician, Franz Joseph Haydn, who at the end of his career collected his friends and the members of his household, and said to them: "Before God and man, I did my duty joyfully and cheerfully. May others do the same."

The 190–page transcript of Sandor Salgo's oral history is freely available online, and is filled with insights and fascinating details about his entire life and career. (See End Notes.)

Noel Sullivan 1890–1956

Courtesy of the Carmel Music Society.

In September 1956, a special friend of the Bach Festival died, and must here be honored. He has appeared from time to time in this narrative since 1930, however, in this book as in real life, he has not spent much time in the spotlight. Reginald Noel Sullivan, a native San Franciscan (born in 1890) with a second home in Carmel, was educated, musically trained, cultured, and deeply heartfelt in all he did. A cultivated man who used the first name Noel, he served at one time or another on the board of every arts organization on the Monterey Peninsula, and was president of several, including the Carmel Music Society. A European-trained pianist and baritone, he played the organ at the Carmel Mission, sang solos, and led the Mission choir. He also gave solo recitals of diverse repertoire at the Denny-Watrous Gallery and in other local and San Francisco venues, as well as at popular musicales in his homes in Carmel and San Francisco. At each of the first thirteen Carmel Bach Festivals, Sullivan made a cameo appearance in one concert, singing two or three sacred songs or arias. By all accounts he did not have a strong voice, but those present when he sang recall that he more than made up for any deficiency in vocal gift with his musical intelligence and the emotional power of his delivery.

Noel Sullivan had three sisters, two of whom had married. He and his third sister, Ada, were the heirs to the fortune of their mother's brother, James Duval Phelan, a banker and politician (Mayor of San Francisco, US Senator, etc.). Phelan's home was a palatial villa on 175 acres west of San José, known then and now as "Villa Montalvo." At the time of his death in 1930, Phelan's finances were a mess, and the value of the actual inheritance was drastically less than it should have been. Villa Montalvo by that time had become priceless real estate, but Phelan's will bequeathed it to the public as an arts center, diminishing the value of the inheritance further. Noel Sullivan used his still-considerable inheritance to bring beauty and harmony into the world. Ada had become a Carmelite nun, and so it was up to her brother to spend their uncle's money, something he did wisely and compassionately.

It is certain that Noel Sullivan contributed financially to the Carmel Music Society and Carmel Bach Festival in their early seasons (that is, outright donations over and above the ordinary membership or subscription fees), but the actual size of his aid is impossible to know. Sullivan was also one of several generous local patrons who occasionally underwrote the appearance of a particularly expensive artist on the Carmel Music Society series. As Casserly and Coolidge had done in the summer of 1931, these local patrons promised to cover any deficit and/or to make up the difference between the Music Society's modest budget and the high fee of some particularly desirable performer. In the first few Music Society seasons, the appearance of major artists such as Gieseking, Horowitz, Piatigorsky, and Szigeti required local financial sponsors to assume part of the cost.

Noel Sullivan was deeply involved in cultural activities in the Monterey Peninsula, and hosted large musical gatherings at his Carmel Valley home, Hollow Hills (now the site of Carmel Valley Manor). Sullivan's housekeeper later recalled,

"In those days, 45 guests for dinner was not at all uncommon, or 75 for a picnic lunch at the farm. Mr. Sullivan could not live without lots of people coming out, and everyone more or less expected that he would entertain them in a grand style." (Sullivan's housekeeper, as quoted in Rampersad. *The Life of Langston Hughes*. 2001.)

Sullivan was an early advocate and supporter of humanist causes. He was chairman of the California Committee of the American League to Abolish Capital Punishment, and he also supported the civil rights movement. Until World War II, African-Americans performing in San Francisco were excluded from good restaurants and hotels. Sullivan's San Francisco home was a luxurious mansion on Hyde Street, and he extended the hospitality of his home to many visiting performers, but especially to African-American artists such as contralto Marian Anderson, tenor Roland Hayes and baritone Paul Robeson. Several contemporaries mentioned that Sullivan was instrumental in bringing Roland Hayes to Carmel for the Bach Festival and a solo recital. A notable example was his friendship with Langston Hughes, the African-

Courtesy of the H. M. Williams Local History Department, Harrison Memorial Library

American poet. At the Denny-Watrous Gallery in 1930, Sullivan performed a recital that included settings of several of Hughes' poems by John Alden Carpenter, and he was well aware of the poet's literary reputation. In 1932, when Hughes came to Berkeley to give a reading, Sullivan—although they had never met—invited Hughes to be a guest at his San Francisco home. Hughes spent several months living there in a suite of rooms with a staff of housekeepers to wait on him.

Sullivan subsequently offered Hughes the use of his Carmel cottage ("Innesfree" at 13th Avenue and Carmelo Street) for one year; Sullivan provided a cook and groceries and also paid the utility bills. Later, during a dark and troubled part of Hughes' life, Sullivan built a small one-room mexican-style house for Hughes on his Carmel Valley estate, Hollow Hills. In that cottage Hughes began to refine the notes he had begun in Chicago for his autobiography, *I Wonder as I Wander*, in which he wrote, "To Noel Sullivan I am indebted for the first long period of my life when I was able, unworried and unhurried, to stay quietly in one place and devote myself to writing."

Sullivan was also a devout Irish Catholic, and even built a small chapel on his Carmel Valley farm. His sister Ada was a member of the Santa Clara Carmelite Monastery near San José, where she later became the Prioress, Mother Agnes of Jesus. ("Monastery" in this sense refers to a cloistered, contemplative, and prayerful community of women who do not interact with the outer world.) Sister Agnes Sullivan had been instrumental in bringing the Carmelites to Northern California, and Noel Sullivan was deeply devoted to his sister and to the Carmelite order. In 1925, the Vatican approved the founding of a new Carmelite Monastery in Carmel. Five nuns from the Santa Clara monastery (not including Sister Agnes) established the Carmel Monastery in a new frame house, where they lived for five years. In 1931, on a hill overlooking the Pacific Ocean, a beautiful monastery and chapel were constructed—a gift to the Carmelites from Noel Sullivan. In accordance with his wishes, Sullivan was buried in the chapel cemetery. Jerry Smith was a Sullivan family friend, and he reminisced in 1992.

Noel Sullivan was a great friend of our family since he and my mother's mother Helen met as teenagers. A pacifist Irish Catholic, dramatic, passionate, generous, wealthy and socially prominent, Noel bought a fleet of ambulances, and maintained and operated it on the front in Europe during World War I (I remember being told that Hemingway based the character of his ambulance-driver protagonist in *A Farewell to Arms*, though not the story, on Noel), built the Carmelite Monastery in Carmel, California (and is interred on the premises), performed as an accomplished concert singer and instrumentalist, patronized and supported numerous writers and other artists, and provided a home for scores of injured animals in Carmel Valley at his Hollow Hills Farm, a place I recall as one of peace, joy, and beauty. Noel died in 1956, but I remember him well and fondly and with a sense of

Courtesy of the Carmel Bach Festival.

kinship which has grown with the years. My mother repeatedly affirmed that he was the most saintly person she had ever known; on the back of a framed photo of him, she wrote: "A living example of love, compassion, and care, for all God's creatures, both human and animal ... he cried and he laughed—he had beauty in his soul!!" (Immortalist Magazine, December 1992)

These lines are from the review of Noel Sullivan's 1930 recital at the Denny-Watrous Gallery.

> It is seldom that a singer reaches the heart of his entire audience as Noel Sullivan did.... Those who were privileged to hear him felt that they had been somehow fed and sustained. It seemed as if this earnest voice sang from the heart of the singer to the hearts of the listeners; as if it sang of the sorrows and joys of life compassionately because it knew them well, tenderly because it felt them, sympathetically because it understood them. In listening to Noel Sullivan it is more than listening to music. It is as if a voice came from the heart of the world, a cry from the innermost life. (Carmelite, December 11, 1930)

Sandor Salgo's "experimental approach" 1957–1959

When Sandor Salgo began making his own Bach Festival programing decisions in 1957, the repertoire quickly became more diverse and the concerts more cohesive. Both Usigli and Salgo were clearly first rate musicians, deeply intelligent and perceptive, and they both were dedicated to contemporary music as well as the music of past centuries. Salgo, however, had a broader and more nuanced knowledge of pre-19th century repertoire, and this can be seen in the 1957 Festival, the first Festival programed by Sandor Salgo and Dene Denny.

It is important to keep in mind that nothing at the Festival happened without Dene Denny's approval. Although she did not choose the repertoire, it had to receive her OK, and she had definite ideas about how the music should be presented.

In 1992, Salgo recalled his discussion with Dene about the future of the Bach Festival:

> I talked with Dene [in 1957] about the direction of the Festival, and what the Festival's aims were, and we agreed that it should be devoted to the performance of Johann Sebastian's music. But in a larger sense I wanted to explore his roots and that meant of course the Italians—mainly Vivaldi and Albinoni, his favorite Italians—and German Baroque composers such as Buxtehude, who was his teacher, and Schütz, and others.
>
> It was my aim to explore the roots of Bach's music and then try to show the tremendous influence Bach had and continues to have on our age. That meant looking at the latter 18th century and even at the 19th and 20th centuries. There is hardly a composer who has not been touched by the Leipzig Cantor....
>
> I discussed my programming approach with Dene, and she gave me her blessing. She said, "These are new ideas, but I think they are interesting, so go ahead with them." ... She saw that there had to be progress and encouraged me. I also had great support from Alfred Frankenstein, the music critic from the San Francisco Chronicle. He always came to the performances and applauded the novelties, and he encouraged me to maintain an experimental approach. (Salgo Oral History, UC Berkeley)

Sandor Salgo believed he could maintain the heart and spirit of the organization while raising the musical standards.

> As we progressed and reached higher performance standards, we required a more professional organization and fortunately, my presidents and board members recognized this need and we started to pay the artists. Of course the beauty of the music, combined with the beauty of Carmel, was a powerful inducement for fine artists to come and to perform with the Bach Festival!
>
> As I told you, the chorus was started by Dene. It was a very enthusiastic and hard-working community group, but for some important pieces I had to import at least twenty or twenty-five professional singers [most from LA, some from Stanford] and I needed someone to prepare them. So after two years, in 1958, I asked Priscilla to train the chorale. The Carmel chorus was prepared by local music teachers Angie Machado and finally Ken Ahrens, who was also a fine organist and our librarian. I went down periodically during the winter, from February on, to take some of the chorus rehearsals, because the *Mass in B Minor*, for instance, requires a long preparation period. (ibid.)

Salgo also quickly changed the way the Festival presented large-scale works. Gastone Usigli had conducted the *Magnificat*, the two *Passions*, the *Mass in B Minor*, and even some of the larger cantatas, in his own shortened versions. In addition, while the *Magnificat* and the *Mass* had been sung in the original Latin, the German text of the *Passions* was sung in an English translation. Salgo believed, correctly, that in order to be taken seriously the Festival must perform all its repertoire complete and in the original language and instrumentation.

At first, Dene expressed doubts about how the audience might react to the *St. Matthew Passion* (3+ hrs.) or the *St. John Passion* (2.5 hrs.) performed complete and in German. She also was concerned about the pace of the changes.

> Dene didn't want me to go too fast with those, and she asked for the *St. Matthew Passion* to begin with in the cut English version, and the *Mass* [in B Minor] with the cuts which

Maestro Usigli had introduced. So I did that for one year [*St. Matthew Passion* in 1957] and then I rebelled—it is such a musical mutilation! I thought we could do them uncut in the original language, without losing the audience. And we did it.... We developed a three-year cycle: the *Mass in B Minor* and the *Passions according to St. Matthew* and *St. John*... (ibid.)

Salgo also began including much more music by composers other than Bach. The main concerts of the 1957 Bach Festival under his direction featured the music of J. S. Bach, his son Carl Philipp Emanuel Bach, Claudio Monteverdi, Franz Joseph Haydn, Telemann and Graupner (contemporaries of Bach), Mozart, Lully, Purcell, Tartini, Orlando di Lasso, Benedetto Marcello, and Thomas Arne. On the final Sunday, two performances were given of the *St. Matthew Passion*, at 2:30 and 8:30pm. The work was performed as it had been under Usigli's baton: in English, and in Usigli's shortened version that omitted nearly a dozen arias and choruses. Another innovation in the 1957 printed program was the inclusion of brief program annotations written by Edward Colby, Music Librarian at Stanford University.

Sandor Salgo established the important tradition of expanding the Festival's repertoire forward:

He believed that the spirit of the Bach Festival was also stimulated by the inclusion of music by Bach's musical descendants as far down the line as Stravinsky. If there was originally some resistance or criticism to this from the Festival's early and loyal patrons, as I had always heard, Salgo coasted over this. (Robert Commanday, Introduction to Salgo Oral History, UC Berkeley)

There were two major additions to the Bach Festival in 1958. Sandor Salgo invited Rosemary McNamee Waller to be the Festival's Concertmaster, a position she held for three decades. And a new ensemble appeared on the roster: the Festival Chorale. This 26–voice group of LA singers had its roots in the 1952 conversation with Usigli described previously. In 1958, they officially became the Festival Chorale, and in the printed program their names now were listed separately from the Chorus. They were however still considered members of the Chorus, and the term "Chorus" in the printed program always included everyone: local singers and Chorale members.

Salgo's new professional Festival Chorale opened the 1958 Bach Festival with the cantata *Christ lag in Todesbanden* performed by the Chorale, Orchestra, and Soloists. That was followed by the *D Minor Harpsichord Concerto*. After intermission, the same ensemble plus the full Chorus performed Bach's *Magnificat* in its first complete presentation at the Festival. (For the opening of the 1956 concert two years before, Salgo conducted Usigli's shortened version.)

Death visited the Bach Festival stage that summer. Maxim Shapiro, a favorite piano soloist at the Festival for nearly two decades, had arrived from an extensive European concert tour barely in time for the final rehearsals in Carmel, and he was exhausted. During the Saturday evening concert as he was playing Mozart's *Piano Concerto No. 26*, the "Coronation Concerto," he suddenly gave a signal to Sandor Salgo to stop the music. Shapiro, obviously ill, was helped from the stage, and an intermission was announced. The remainder of the concert was performed, after which news arrived that Shapiro had died of a heart attack in the ambulance on the way to the hospital.

The 1958 Festival concluded with the *St. John Passion*—complete, as Salgo wanted, but still in the English translation that had been used by Usigli.

The Bach Festival in Carmel is one of the important musical events of our country. To it come people from all over the world. Lasting an entire week, it presents the finest musicians and artists available. As we listened to the magnificent performances, breathed in the fragrance of the pines, walked the quaint streets, strolled on the snowy white sandy beaches, we made up our minds this paradise was for us! It is really a thrilling experience to be part of the excitement of it all during that week in July. Crowds pour from everywhere; the little town bulges at the seams, wondering where to put them all.

Small groups on every corner and at the post office discuss the big event. "How can I get a ticket?" "Are they really sold out?" "Should we have only Bach?" "Why not more Mozart?" "What do you mean, I cannot get a ticket—I live here."

There is a tingle in the air, and when, on the first night, all the ticket holders stand mutely in the courtyard of the Sunset School while four trumpeters* from the belfry of the tower sound out the call to the great Bach Festival, one's breath comes in little gulps....

The Carmel Bach Festival owes its life and permanence to one indefatigable worker, Miss Dene Denny. She and her friend, Miss Hazel Watrous dreamed this dream 21 years ago. From a very small beginning it has become an institution of world fame. (Long Beach Independent-Press-Telegram, Sunday, August 3, 1958)

(After WW II, the pre-concert Tower Music became a mixed brass ensemble, able to play more varied repertoire. In 1958, Tower Music was: two trumpets, one French horn, and two trombones.)

In the 1958 Bach Festival program book, Sandor Salgo's brilliantly talented wife Priscilla (Patterson) Salgo is listed as one of the three assistant choral directors. In 1961 she became the Director of the Festival Chorale and would serve in that capacity through 1991.

Priscilla Patterson Salgo and Sandor Salgo.

The 1959 Festival program is pure Sandor Salgo, and is engaging on both artistic and historical levels. According to the program book, the concerts endeavor "to re-create the historical and musical environment of Johann Sebastian Bach and the leading composers of his time."

Monday: Handel's English-language oratorio Samson

Tuesday: Music of his own that Bach might have played at the Court of Frederick the Great.

Thursday: Bach's musical relation to the Italian masters of St. Mark's Cathedral in Venice (music by Bach, Monteverdi, Gabrieli, etc)

Friday: The music of London in Handel's time (music by Handel, Johann Christian Bach, Stanley, Purcell, and Orlando Gibbons)

Saturday: "An eighteenth-century 'pop' concert" featuring one of Bach's secular cantatas written to be performed in a coffee house, followed by the humorous "Farewell Symphony" by Haydn.

On Sunday, Salgo led the Festival Soloists, Chorus, Chorale and Orchestra in a milestone event for Carmel-by-the-Sea: Bach's *Mass in B Minor* was performed in its entirety. No music was omitted, the full Chorus sang all the choral movements with no help from the soloists, and every note was as Bach—not Usigli—had written it. With admirable stamina, the Festival gave two performances of the entire work, at 2:30 and 8:30pm.

Photo above courtesy of the H. M. Williams Local History Department, Harrison Memorial Library

Following the second performance, during the applause, Sandor Salgo brought Dene Denny out onto the stage of Sunset Auditorium, where she received a standing ovation. The photograph shown here, taken eight weeks before her death, captures the poignant moment of Dene's last public appearance, in the late evening of July 26, 1959.

Dene Denny 1885–1959

After Hazel's death in 1954, Dene had begun taking steps to make sure that their organizations would remain in good hands after her own death. Her first step, in 1955, was to sell her interest in the San José concert series to her assistant there.

Her health continued to deteriorate, and in 1957 she was diagnosed with a "terminal illness" (according to Salgo). Early in 1958, Dene brought about the incorporation of the Carmel Bach Festival as a non-profit performing arts organization, and she oversaw the election of a governing board of directors, of

July 26, 1959. Dene Denny and Sandor Salgo on stage at the end of the final concert of the 1959 Carmel Bach Festival. This was Dene's last public appearance. *Courtesy of the Carmel Bach Festival.*

which she was president. She is listed in the 1958 Festival program as "President and General Manager." The long-standing Advisory board continued to serve as an overall connection to the community. The attorney for the incorporation was Dene's own lawyer, longtime Festival patron Peter Ferrante, who would later serve as Bach Festival board president himself.

There was just one more thing to take care of: the precious little adobe theater that she and Hazel had lovingly managed since 1937. For 22 years the Troupers of the Gold Coast had given weekend performances almost year-round, seamlessly moving from one production to the next. By 1959 the Troupers had produced more than 100 plays and given more than 1,500 performances. On September 22, 1959, this item appeared in the Monterey Herald.

Dene Denny, 1958, Courtesy of the Carmel Bach Festival.

> California's First Theater will get a new manager as a result of the State Parks Commission meeting yesterday at Asilomar. Miss Dene Denny, holder of the state concession to produce theatrical events in the First Theater, requested that Charles Thomas, as her manager, be allowed to operate the theater on the state concession until January 1. At that time, Miss Denny said, she desired the concession to be awarded to Thomas and to be in force from then on. Miss Denny gave illness as a reason for her request. Miss Denny's request was unanimously approved, and the commissions ruling marked the end of Miss Denny's 22–year career as producer-manager of California's first theater. (Monterey Peninsula Herald, September 22, 1959)

On September 24, just two days later, Dene Denny died in the Carmel home that she and Hazel had built with their own hands more than thirty-five years before.

The following is an excerpt from the obituary in the Monterey Herald that appeared on the afternoon of Dene's death.

> Dene Denny, the beautiful and gracious lady who has been one of the greatest single contributors to the cultural life of the Peninsula for well over 30 years, died this morning at her Carmel home on Dolores Street near 1st Avenue. Death came at 6:00am after a long period during which she carried on valiantly in spite of failing health.
>
> Miss Denny's appearance last July at the Carmel Bach Festival [photo], which she founded in 1935 with her associate the late Hazel Watrous, and fostered tirelessly through the years, called forth a resounding ovation from the audience and the musicians. The public tribute paid to her at that time by a member of the Bach Festival Board of Trustees [Directors], expressed the sentiments of an entire community among which she had lived and worked for so long.
>
>> "We wish to salute you, Dene Denny for your great contributions to society; for your fortitude, judgment, inspiration and leadership in music. Among many accomplishments is this unique, important yearly Bach Festival, famous throughout the musical world. We congratulate you on all your achievements and place your name with love and high honors in our own Hall of Fame." ...
>
> There is scarcely a phase of Carmel's cultural life which has not felt the beneficent impact of Dene Denny's unique personality and gifts.... The stimulus of her spirit and the charm of her gentle, dignified manner will be treasured as they are missed. (Obituary, Monterey Herald, September 24, 1959)

This short unsigned item appeared in the Herald on the following day.

> In the death of Miss Dene Denny, the Monterey Peninsula has lost more than one of its beloved citizens. It has lost an influence, a standard, a defense of good taste and artistic merit. It has lost one who always stood firmly against cheapness, was not satisfied with the mediocre, who abhorred the tawdry.
>
> With the late Hazel Watrous, Miss Denny set a pace in the early cultural and musical development of the Peninsula which has since become one of its most valuable characteristics and assets.
>
> Her death comes at a time when the Peninsula is in the course of change and great growth. Her life work offers a model of how we should strive to channel this change in gross. Dene Denny will be missed. The people of the Peninsula can pay no greater tribute to her than by insisting that the Monterey Peninsula of the future be on high standards that she represented. (Monterey Herald, September 25, 1959)

"...she was its artistic heart and soul."

The final word about Dene comes from her friend and colleague Alfred Frankenstein, music critic of the San Francisco Chronicle. He was the author of the uplifting review of the Mission Concert at the end of Usigli's first Festival in 1938; as a friend and insider since the Festival's beginning, he knew that, although Hazel had been deeply involved, Dene had been the musical organization's guiding force.

San Francisco Chronicle, September 27, 1959
By Alfred Frankenstein, Music Critic

Last July Carmel played host to its 22nd annual Bach Festival. It consisted of 12 programs. The repertoire covered practically the whole history of Music from 1600 to 1800, including many esoteric and extraordinary compositions one would not otherwise hear in a lifetime.

There was not a seat to be had, and, just as music lovers from all parts of the country stood in line for tickets, so singers and instrumentalists from everywhere were knocking on the door for the privilege of participating.

The Carmel Bach Festival, in short, has attained a status comparable to that of the summer music festivals for which people make the grand tour of Europe. For this we may thank its founder and managing director, Dene Denny, who died last week after a long illness.

Miss Denny kept in the background, gave credit to the festival's musical directors, and pretended, as so far as the public was concerned, merely to be its business head. Actually she was its artistic heart and soul. A musician herself, she knew exactly what the musical directors were up to, encouraged them to experiment, take chances, and explore. This was in keeping with her point of view throughout her life.

The Bach Festival was not her only field of activity but it, and its vivid spirit and tradition, are her major monument. It will continue under the direction of the society she founded for that purpose. But we shall miss her sorely.

On February 6, 1960, friends of Dene Denny gathered at All Saints Church in Carmel for a "Quiet Hour" in Dene's memory. Rudolf Schafer, organist, and a group of local musicians performed a Vivaldi violin concerto; the Concerto for Violin and Oboe by J. S. Bach; a string quartet by Haydn; and an organ concerto by Handel.

The Author's Conclusion to This Story

The three performing arts organizations created by Dene Denny and Hazel Watrous on the Monterey Peninsula between 1927 and 1937 endured long after the two founders were gone, a testament to their planning and artistic vision. Many others tried to do similar things on the Peninsula in the early 20th century—concert series, orchestras, choruses, and the like—but nothing lasted longer than two or three years, if that.

Dene and Hazel succeeded in their work not by doing something "to" the community, but by partnering *with* it. The Carmel Music Society and the Carmel Bach Festival are their living monuments, and the two organizations are perfect examples of the Denny-Watrous approach. Dene and Hazel envisioned something that they believed would bring joy to the community, they figured out a way to do it, and—this is what made the difference—they got people so excited about their vision that everyone worked together to help them make it a success. The key word here is "together."

Dene Denny more or less wrote the motto for this book in the moment in 1932 when she decided against a professional orchestra and sent a telegram to Michel Penha, informing him, *"Your orchestra is here."* In the midst of the darkest years of the Great Depression, Dene and Hazel—with the support of the Carmel Music Society—inspired and guided the local community in the creation of the Monterey Peninsula Orchestra and Chorus.

After three years of grooming and hard work, those ensembles became the Carmel Bach Festival in 1935.

During those early developmental years in the 1930s, Dene and Hazel chose brilliant and unique conductors: Michel Penha, Henry Eichheim, Carol Weston, Bernard Callery, Ernst Bacon, Sascha Jacobinoff, and Gastone Usigli. But there would have been nothing to conduct in Carmel back in those days, were it not for Dene and Hazel. It was they who figured out how to bring everyone together.

Courtesy of the Carmel Bach Festival.

Another essential aspect of the Denny-Watrous philosophy was the importance of education and discovery. In their first year together in 1923, they presented music, art, puppet theater, lectures, and salons in the rooftop ballroom of the Fisk House in San Francisco. They continued in Carmel, where they flourished as impresarios of all the arts, and brought together a diverse array of people and ideas in all manner of artistically and intellectually stimulating situations.

Dene and Hazel were life-long teachers who sought to deepen people's love of the arts and understanding of each other, and they often accomplished this by offering the community a real sense of engagement in the creative process. For three decades, they partnered with each other, with their colleagues, and with their neighbors. Their story shows us that there is strength in partnership; that it's good for people to connect on many levels with each other; and that we can evolve as individuals, organizations, communities, and societies if we find ways to work together toward common, uplifting goals. Dene and Hazel did their work in the arts, but the same principles apply to all of life, and are the true meaning of "evolution." It's not a matter of "survival" or "winning." Evolution is about partnering: creating an integrative relationship from which something new emerges, something enduring that we never could have accomplished alone.

A final postscript

John Steinbeck was awarded the Nobel Prize in Literature "for his realistic and imaginative writings, combining as they do sympathetic humour and keen social perception."

In early 1960, Steinbeck set out to cure a case of writer's block by taking a road trip around the United States with his dog Charley. The resulting book, Travels With Charley, was published in 1962, and reached #1 on the New York Times Non-Fiction Best Seller list within months.

While on his road trip with Charley, Steinbeck visited the old haunts he remembered well from his childhood and youth in Salinas and Monterey, and he had this to say about the Carmel he saw in 1960:

> *"Carmel, begun by starveling writers and unwanted painters, is now a community of the well-to-do and the retired. If Carmel's founders should return, they could not afford to live there, but it wouldn't go that far. They would be instantly picked up as suspicious characters and deported over the city line."*
>
> John Steinbeck, *Travels with Charley*

Appendix

The Carmel Music Society opened the winter concert season in January 1931 with the Aguilar Lute Quartet. The four siblings—Ezekiel, Pepe, Paco and Eliza—had made their US debut only weeks before, and were at that time the only famous lutenists in the world. Great Spanish composers such as Manuel de Falla and Isaac Albéniz wrote music for them. *Courtesy of the author.*

After the Impresarios

California's First Theater 1937–2000

In 1952, LaVerne Seeman joined the Troupers of the Gold Coast as an actress, and eventually moved into a leadership role as well. Hazel Watrous, the shepherd of the Troupers, died in 1954, and in 1958 Dene Denny relinquished management of the Theater. Ms. Seeman remained with the Troupers and ultimately became the manager of the thriving company. In 2000, the state of California asked the Troupers to vacate their theater temporarily so that some repairs might be made to the old adobe building. The Troupers gave a final show on New Year's Eve, December 31, 2000, and then put their costumes and props into what they believed was temporary storage.

After a full inspection, however, the State Parks administration realized that a structural upgrade and earthquake retrofit would cost more than $1 million. Plans for the renovation were called off, the theater was permanently closed to the public, and the Troupers of the Gold Coast were exiled from the wonderful venue in which they had flourished for more than 60 years. At the time of the theater's closing in 2000, the Troupers had an archive of 2,400 American and British plays from the 19th century.

The First Theater was in full operation from mid-1937 through 2000, and during that time more than 2,000 actors performed with the Troupers of the Gold Coast. They produced hundreds of different plays in a total of more than 5,000 performances—every one of which concluded with an Olio. Each of those Troupers had the unique experience of performing on the stage of California's First Theater, thanks to Dene and Hazel.

The Carmel Music Society 1927–present

www.carmelmusic.org

The Carmel Music Society's distinguished performance history speaks for itself, and a complete list of artists presented by the Society is included in this Appendix. The list includes many of the greatest musicians of the 20th century.

Today the Music Society still operates as it was originally created: board officers and committees run the organization and handle the booking and (in Hazel's absence) a designer is paid to create the programs and other printed matter. In 1977 the Music Society established an annual competition for young musicians. Winners' names are included in the above-mentioned list. As the Carmel Music Society nears the end of its ninth decade, it owes its longevity to the countless volunteers who have served on its Board, and to the unique community that has supported the Society's efforts.

The Carmel Bach Festival 1935–present

www.bachfestival.org

Dene Denny's youngest sister and last surviving sibling, Sylvia Denny Landon (1902-1992), was interviewed by the Carmel Bach Festival Administrator, Nana Faridany, in the early 1980s. Ms. Landon remembered her sister's estimation of Sandor Salgo.

> Dene was devoted to Sandor, and I think she felt that her Bach Festival would be safe in his hands.... Sandor said to me that of all the things he had done the Festival was dearest to his heart. (Carmel Bach Festival program book, 1984)

During Sandor Salgo's 36-year tenure on the Bach Festival podium, he made many changes and instituted new customs which became traditions. In 1962 Salgo persuaded the Diocese to allow the Festival once again to present a concert in Carmel Mission (the Festival had not performed there since 1942). On Wednesday, July 19, at the stroke of Midnight, Salgo led the Festival Chorale, Orchestra and Soloists in a program of 16th and 17th music by Heinrich Isaac, Giovanni Gabrielli, and Marc-Antoine Charpentier. This was just the first of three dozen imaginative concert programs Salgo created for his candlelight concerts in the Carmel Mission each summer.

Salgo also brilliantly and compassionately managed the inevitable transformation of the Orchestra and Chorale into fully professional ensembles, and under his leadership the Festival Orchestra, Chorale and vocal soloists for the first time received a fee. As Sylvia Denny Landon later said,

> I feel that the Carmel Bach Festival will become an institution; under his direction and his able vision it has gone steadily forward. Sandor did more choral works and was able to do this because he brought in a host of singers... and with the solid background of experienced singers he was able to have marvelous choral works.... Usigli worked with local talent, and it was exciting to have the community all involved, but when you are trying to make it more professional, you have to bring people in. (ibid.)

In 1959 Salgo began a decade-long series of Handel oratorios, and throughout his tenure Handel's music was frequently heard at the Bach Festival. As discussed above, Salgo firmly established that all major works on Festival concerts be performed complete and in their original language and orchestration (the orchestra would no longer play Usigli's shortened arrangements of Bach's music). Salgo also introduced opera to the Festival, including Mozart (Marriage of Figaro, Cosi fan tutte, Magic Flute, et al.); Beethoven's Fidelio (with the young Jess Thomas, a Salgo discovery, as Florestan); Monteverdi's Orfeo; and works by Handel, Lully, Purcell, Haydn, and others. These operas were fully staged productions, and extremely difficult to produce in an auditorium with a small stage, no wing space, and no orchestra pit, but they were hugely popular.

Responding to an expanding economy and a solid classical music market, Salgo lengthened the Festival, first to ten days (1961); then two weeks (1973); and finally three weeks (1981). Sandor Salgo's final concert at the Carmel Bach Festival was the St. Matthew Passion on August 4, 1991. The author sang the Evangelist in that performance, and recalls the moment when the final chord died away into silence and, after a long stillness, Maestro Salgo lowered his hands and closed the score on his music stand. It was the final concert of his conducting career. After retiring, Salgo remained intellectually very active; UC Berkeley recorded and transcribed his extensive oral history, and he also wrote an engaging and scholarly book about the musical life of Thomas Jefferson. (See End Notes) Sandor Salgo died in 2007 at the age of 97; everyone who ever knew him remembers him with respect and affection.

In 1992, German conductor Bruno Weil was named Music Director of the Carmel Bach Festival. That summer, the Festival opened as usual on Monday night and ended on Sunday afternoon three weeks later. Weil immediately instituted a schedule change, and in 1993 the Festival opened on Saturday night, as it has done ever since. That year also marked the Bach Festival debut of the dynamic Australian-British violinist Elizabeth Wallfisch as concertmaster.

Sandor Salgo did many things to enhance, refine and expand the Carmel Bach Festival, and Weil and Wallfisch continued to lead this process of artistic growth and evolution. Salgo's Baroque style was "middle of the road" in the 1960s, but by the early 1990s his approach was being eclipsed by a younger generation with new ideas, more historically informed interpretation, and more frequent use of historic instruments. Elizabeth Wallfisch is a consummate artist on both the modern violin—in 1993 the standard at the Festival—and on the Baroque or "historic" violin. The technique of playing in the 18th century style is different for both hands. A chin rest is routinely not used, the bow is held and applied differently, and there are many other subtle factors which can open the door to different interpretive choices: that is what Weil and Wallfisch wanted.

Over the next few years, the Bach Festival attracted many new players to the orchestra, most of whom had a special interest in music of the 18th century. Most of the concerts in the 1990s were still being played on modern string instruments, but more and more of the players were using a Baroque-informed technique even when playing on modern instruments, and the sound of the orchestra began to change. In the late 1990s, the Festival began featuring period string instruments in a few of its Main Concerts. As a result of all this, the sound of the Festival ensemble became more transparent, and Weil was able to interpret the music with more agility and, sometimes, more speed. Although Weil's interpretation of Baroque music at that time was not radical in any way, it seemed so at first, in 1992 and 1993, to Carmelites accustomed to Salgo's slow tempi and richer, more 19th century orchestral sonorities. Weil's so-called "fast" conducting became such a topic of local conversation during his first few seasons that the City of Carmel-by-the-Sea presented him with a framed speeding ticket for conducting too fast.

Bruno Weil served as Music Director through the 2010 Bach Festival, and he and Elizabeth Wallfisch brought the Festival to a new level of excellence and international prestige. Bruno Weil was also a central and influential figure in the movement to create a new Sunset Auditorium. Planning began in the summer of 1993, one year after his arrival; ten years later, in July 2003, Bruno Weil and the Carmel Bach Festival inaugurated the newly built concert hall. Andrew Megill joined the Festival in 2007 as Associate Conductor and Director of the Chorale, and brought the choral ensemble (the Festival Chorus and the 28-voice Festival Chorale) to the same high artistic level as Weil's Festival Orchestra.

Paul Goodwin, the Bach Festival's fourth Music Director, made his Carmel debut in 2011. The British conductor (and former oboist) continued the Festival's integration of period and modern instruments throughout its performance schedule, and also introduced historic woodwind and brass instruments into the orchestra.

Carmel Bach Festival Growth 1935–2014

Since its inception, the Carmel Bach Festival has adjusted the number of its concerts in response to trends in ticket demand.

"Main concerts" listed below are onstage in Sunset Auditorium or the Carmel Mission, usually with conductor.

The Festival also presents chamber music recitals featuring a single musician or small ensemble. For the first several decades, these Festival recitals and chamber concerts took place in the morning or afternoon at All Saints Church, Church of the Wayfarer, or the Carmel Woman's Club.

By the late 1980s, the chamber music concerts were taking place only on stage in the 700-seat Sunset Auditorium. Although the same type of music was still being performed, the intimacy of the venue had been lost from the chamber music series.

In 1991, Sandor Salgo and Bach Festival Administrator Nana Faridany asked the author to present three vocal recitals with pianist Timothy Bach in historic locations in Monterey: La Mirada (part of the Monterey Museum of Art), Casa Serano adobe, and Colton Hall (where the California constitution was written in 1850). The Wednesday twilight vocal series was continued for three more summers at Casa Serano with a few additional performers, and its success led to the establishment in 1995 of the Festival's Twilight Series at the Robert Louis Stevenson School. The success of these early evening concerts led to the exploration of other Festival venues on the Monterey Peninsula.

Today, the Carmel Bach Festival produces concerts in Sunset Center, Carmel Mission, and more than a dozen other venues in Carmel, Monterey, Pacific Grove, Pebble Beach, Seaside, and Salinas. The following comparison makes this clear.

1991 Festival: 21 days, 21 main concerts, 20 chamber music recitals

2014 Festival: 15 days, 15 main concerts, 36 chamber music recitals

Sandor Salgo conducts Bach's *St. John Passion* at the 1983 Carmel Bach Festival. To the left, the author in his Festival debut as Evangelist. The aria soloists were Nancy Gustafson, Alyce Rogers, Gregory Wait, and Herbert Eckhoff. Douglas Lawrence sang the role of Jesus.

Michel Penha   1888–1982

Ernst Bacon   1898–1990

The conductors who created the Carmel Bach Festival 1931–1939

MPO=Monterey Peninsula Orchestra   CBF=Carmel Bach Festival   NKN=Neah-Kah-Nie Quartet

	Michel Penha	Ernst Bacon	Sascha Jacobinoff	Gastone Usigli
1931	Played private concert with NKN			
1932	Solo recital; NKN; MPO Conductor			
1933	NKN Concerts; MPO Conductor			
1934	Penha Quartet; MPO Conductor	MPO Conductor		
1935	Solo Recital	CBF Conductor; MPO Conductor	Solo Recital at CBF; Solo twice at CBF	CBF Guest Conductor
1936			CBF Conductor; Solo at CBF	
1937	CBF Conductor; Solo at CBF			
1938	Solo recital		CBF Guest Conductor	CBF Conductor
1939	Solo at CBF			CBF Conductor

Sascha Jacobinoff   1896–1960

Gastone Usigli   1897–1956

Carmel Bach Festival Performance Schedule

From four concerts in four days to fifty-one concerts in fifteen days

1935: Ernst Bacon and Gastone Usigli, conductors. Four main concerts, Thu, Fri, Sat, Sun.

1936: Sascha Jacobinoff, conductor. Five main concerts, Mon, Tue, Thu, Sat, Sun.

1937: Michel Penha, conductor. Same as 1936, plus two organ recitals at All Saints Church.

1938–1942, 1946–1948: Gastone Usigli, conductor. Same as 1936, plus 2–4 organ or chamber music recitals.

Through 1957, the Sunday main concert is often performed twice on the same day.

The number of chamber music recitals varies from year to year.

1949–1955: Usigli adds Friday concert. The schedule is Mon, Tue, Thu, Fri, Sat, Sun (two-performance day) plus 2–4 organ or chamber music recitals.

1956: Sandor Salgo's first year. Same schedule as 1949–1955. 6 chamber music recitals. 1 concert on Sunday.

1957: The last occurrence of a double performance of the final Sunday.

1958–1960: Same as 1957. Single concert on Sunday.

1961–1972: 10 days (Fri–Sun)

1962: The Carmel Mission concert is re-established, at 11:00pm on Wednesday evenings.

1973–1980: Two weeks (Mon–Sun)

1981–1992: Three weeks (Mon–Sun)

1991: Salgo's final season. 21 days, 21 main concerts, 20 chamber music recitals

1992: Bruno Weil's first year. Same schedule as 1991.

1993–2007: 22 days, Saturday to Saturday. 22 main concerts. Increasing number of chamber concerts.

2008: The final 3-week Festival: 22 days, 22 concerts, 41 chamber music recitals

In 2009, in a proactive response to the general economic climate, the Bach Festival reduced the length of its performance schedule by one full week.

2009: 15 days, 15 main concerts, 30+ chamber music recitals

2010: Paul Goodwin becomes Music Director. The schedule continues as in 2009.

2014: 15 days, 15 main concerts, 36 chamber music recitals

Carmel Music Society Performance History

A "season" typically begins no earlier than late September and concludes the following April or May. In a four–concert season, the first concert often took place in January. Summer Series in 1932, 1933, and 1934 were sold by separate subscription. Beginning in 1977, an *asterisk after an artist's name indicates the winner of the most recent Carmel Music Society Competition.

From December 1927 through May 1932, CMS performances are held at the original Theatre of the Golden Bough on the Southeast corner of Ocean Avenue and Monte Verde Street. Seating capacity 400. The performers are placed in front of the proscenium on the large forestage.

1927–28

Hart House String Quartet (12/9/27)
Walter Gieseking, pianist
Kathryn Meisle, contralto
Reinald Werrenrath, baritone

Extra–Series Concert:
Horace Britt, cellist

1928–29

London String Quartet
Alexander Brailowsky, pianist
Kedroff Vocal Quartet
Albert Spalding, violinist

Extra–Series Concerts:
Richard Buhlig, pianist
Fred Leedom Scott, tenor

1929–30

Vladimir Horowitz, pianist
Roth String Quartet
Smallman A Cappella Choir
Claire Dux, soprano

1930–31

Walter Gieseking, pianist
Aguilar Lute Quartet
Mina Hager, contralto
Gregor Piatigorsky, cellist

1931–32

Joseph Szigeti, violinist
Neah-Kah-Nie String Quartet
 and E. Robert Schmitz, pianist
Myra Hess, pianist
Harold Kreutzberg, dancer

Beginning July 1932, performances are held in the Sunset School auditorium, San Carlos Street at Ninth Avenue. Seating capacity 700+. Conventional proscenium stage. CMS concerts are also occasionally held in All Saints Church.

1932 Summer Season

Neah-Kah-Nie String Quartet
 and Harold Bauer, pianist
Monterey Peninsula Orchestra debut
Neah-Kah-Nie String Quartet
 and Ralph Linsley, pianist
Neah-Kah-Nie String Quartet
 with Dene Denny, pianist
 and Claire Upshaw, soprano

1932–33

Vienna Boys Choir
Michel Penha, cellist
Monterey Peninsula Orchestra
Florence Austral, soprano,
 with John Amadio, flutist

1933 Summer Season

Pro Arte String Quartet (2 concerts)
Penha Piano Quartet
 (violin, viola, cello, piano (3 concerts)
Monterey Peninsula Orchestra
 (2 concerts)

1933–34

Mischa Elman, violinist
Teresina, Spanish dancer
Roland Hayes, tenor
Walter Gieseking, pianist

1934 Summer Season

Winifred Christie, pianist
 (Moor double keyboard piano)
Penha Piano Quartet (3 concerts
Monterey Peninsula Orchestra
 & Chorus

1934–35

Don Cossack Chorus
Joseph Hoffman, pianist
Igor Stravinsky, pianist
 with Samuel Dushkin, violinist
Budapest String Quartet

1935

Summer Season and Bach Festival
Sascha Jacobinoff, violinist
Abas String Quartet
Bach Festival: four concerts
Gunnar Johansen, pianist
Waldeen Falkenstein, dancer

1935–36

Hart House String Quartet
Jascha Heifetz, violinist
Martha Graham, dancer
Nino Martini, tenor

1936–37

Harold Bauer, pianist
Richard Crooks, tenor
Nathan Milstein, violinist
Trudi Schoop Comic Ballet

1937–38
Rudolf Serkin, pianist
Shankar with Hindu Ballet
Nathan Milstein, violinist
Budapest String Quartet

1938–39
Povla Frijsh, soprano
Angna Enters, dancer
Pasquier String Trio
   (violin, viola, cello)
Robert Casadesus, pianist

1939–40
American Ballet Caravan
   (Lincoln Kirstein, dir.)
San Francisco Trio (violin, cello, piano)
   with Lawrence Strauss, tenor
Arthur Rubinstein, pianist
Robert Virovai, violinist

1940–41
Argentinita with Spanish Dance
   Ensemble
Sylvia Lent, violinist
Dorothy Maynor, soprano
Vronsky & Babin, duo-pianists

1941–42
Lotte Lehmann, soprano
Germaine Leroux, pianist
The Trapp Family Singers
Gregor Piatigorsky, cellist
Ross Worsley, bass baritone

1942–43
Carmen Amaya & Gypsy Ensemble
Witold Malcuzynski, pianist
Roland Hayes, tenor
Belgian Piano Quartet

1943–44
Paul Draper, dancer,
  with Larry Adler, harmonicist
Alexander Brailowsky, pianist
Horace Britt Trio (flute, harp, cello)
Ezio Pinza, bass

1944–45
Robert Casadesus, pianist
Roth String Quartet
Anne Brown, soprano
Erica Morini, violinist

1945–46
Jan Peerce, tenor
San Francisco Opera Ballet
Adolf Baller, pianist
Alexander Schneider, violinist
  and Ralph Kirkpatrick, harpsichordist
Andres Segovia, guitarist

1946–47
Jussi Bjoerling, tenor
Guiomar Novaes, pianist
Maggie Teyte, soprano
Trudi Schoop, comic ballet
Rudolph Firkusny, pianist
The Alma Trio (violin, cello, piano)

1947–48
Markova and Dobin, ballet
Jacques Thibaud, violinist
Marion Anderson, contralto
Benno Moiseiwitsch, pianist
Martial Singher, baritone

1948–49
Harald Kreutzberg, dancer
Jennie Tourel, mezzo-soprano
Joseph Schuster, cellist
Rudolf Firkusny, pianist
Nathan Milstein, violinist

1949–50
Pierre Bernac, baritone
  with Francis Poulenc, pianist
Pro Musica Antiqua
Dorothy Warenskjold, soprano
Maryla Jonas, pianist
Griller String Quartet

1950–51
Tropicana Ballet
Intimate Opera Company
Gregor Piatigorsky, cellist
Erica Morini, violinist
Lili Kraus, pianist
Bidu Sayao, soprano

1951–52
Yi-Kwei-Sze, bass–baritone
Yehudi Menuhin, violinist
Shan-Kar with Hindu Ballet
Blanche Thebom, mezzo-soprano
Arthur Rubinstein, pianist

1952–53
Gina Bachauer, pianist
Ballet Russe de Monte Carlo
Victoria de los Angeles, soprano
Leonard Warren, baritone
Zino Francescatti, violinist
The Griller String Quartet
The Alma Trio
  (violin, cello, piano)

1953–54
Leonard Warren, baritone
Salzburg Marionette Theatre
Joseph Szigeti, violinist
Pierre Fournier, cellist
Leonard Pennario, pianist
Helen Traubel, soprano

1954–55
Cesare Siepi, bass–baritone
Societa Corelli Chamber
Orchestra
Clifford Curzon, pianist
Isaac Stern, violinist
Mattilda Dobbs, soprano

1955–56
Elisabeth Schwarzkopf, soprano
Dance Theatre Berlin
Grant Johannesen, pianist
William Primrose, violinist
George London, baritone

1956–57
Zinka Milanov, soprano
Joseph Schuster, cellist
Festival String Quartet
Frank Guarrera, baritone
Luboschutz and Nemenoff,
   duo–pianists

1957–58
Nan Merriman, mezzo–soprano
Les Ballets Jarúne Charrat de France
Festival String Quartet
Isaac Stern, violinist
Guiomar Novaes, pianist

1958–59
Eileen Farrell, soprano
Dietrich Fischer–Dieskau, baritone
I Musici Chamber Orchestra
Jose Greco & Company, Spanish
   dancers
Louis Kentner, pianist

1959–60
Nan Merriman, mezzo–soprano
Ballet Español Roberto Iglesias
Jorge Bolet, pianist
Quartetto di Roma (string quartet)
Roger Wagner Chorale

1960–61
Societa Corelli Chamber
Orchestra
Leon Fleischer, pianist
Janos Starker, cellist
Theodor Uppman, baritone
Leontyne Price, soprano

1961–62
Goya and Matteo, dancers
Orchestra San Pietro of Naples
Russell Oberlin, countertenor
Seymour Lipkin, pianist
Anna Moffo, soprano
Jaime Laredo, violinist

1962–63
I Solisti di Zagreb, Chamber
   Orchestra
Victoria de los Angeles, soprano
Rosalyn Tureck, pianist
Goldowsky Grand Opera: "Rigoletto"
George London, baritone

1963–64
Paris Chamber Orchestra
Grace Bumbry, soprano
Ruggiero Ricci, violinist
John Browning, pianist
Richard Tucker, tenor

1964–65
Brian Sullivan, tenor
Societa Corelli, Chamber Orchestra
Byron Janis, pianist
Teresa Berganza, mezzo–soprano
Zara Nelsova, cellist

The Sunset School Auditorium
becomes the Sunset Center,
a city-run performing arts
complex.

1965–66
Igor Oistrakh, violinist
Ezio Flagello, basso
Moura Lympany, pianist
Goldowsky Opera: "La Boheme"
Solisti Veneti Chamber Orchestra

1966–67
Regine Crespin, soprano
John Browning, pianist
Bach Aria Group
Stuttgart Chamber Orchestra
Henryk Szeryng, violinist

1967–68
Vladimir Ashkenazy, pianist
Western Opera: "Barber of Seville"
Thomas Paul, bass–baritone
Austin Reller, violinist
Gary Graffman, pianist
Chamber Orchestra of Philadelphia

1968–69
Oakland Chamber Orchestra
Roy Bogas, pianist
Benjamin Britten's "Curlew River"
Young Uck Kim, violinist
Rosalind Elias, mezzo–soprano
Raymond Lewenthal, pianist

1969–70
Brussels Chamber Orchestra
Gerard Souzay, baritone
Western Opera Theater:
"The Medium" (Menotti) "Gianni
   Schicchi" (Puccini)
Wiliam Masselos, pianist
Zara Nelsova, cellist & Grant
   Johannesen, pianist

1970–71
Alicia de Larrocha, pianist
Mary Costa, soprano
Martha Graham dancers
Itzhak Perlman, violinist
Hamburg Chamber Orchestra

1971–72
Garrick Ohlsson, pianist
James McCracken, tenor
 with Sandra Warfield, mezzo–
   soprano
I Solisti di Zagreb Chamber
   Orchestra
Julian Bream, Guitarist
Western Opera: "Cenerentola"
   (Rossini)

1972–73
Ah Ahk–Performing Arts of Korea
Garrick Ohlsson, pianist
Marilyn Horne, soprano
Czech Nonet
Lilit Gampel, violinist

1973–74
Los Angeles Chamber
Orchestra with Neville
Marriner, Conductor
 with Christoph Eschenbach, pianist
Douglas Lawrence, bass–baritone
Valentina Oumansky
Dramatic Dance Ensemble
Gary Graffman, pianist
 with Leonard Rose, cellist

1974–75
John and Richard Contiguglia,
    duo–pianists
Aman Folk Ensemble
Jean–Pierre Rampal, flutist
 with Robert Veyron–Lacroix, pianist
Glenn Dicterow, violinist
    & James Field, pianist
Frederica von Stade, soprano

1975–76
Igor Oistrakh, violinist
Misha Dichter, pianist
Jeannine Altmeyer, soprano
Netherlands Chamber Orchestra
Jose Carreras, tenor

1976–77
Ronald Turini, pianist
Eleana Obraztsova, mezzo–soprano
Yugoslav Folk dancers
Storck duo, Harp & Cello
Nina Bodnar–Horton, violinist

1977–78
Pinchas Zukerman, violinist
Sherrill Milnes, baritone
Ronald Turini, pianist
San Francisco Chamber Orchestra
Dave Abel, Violin
 with Paul Hersh, pianist
Craig Nies, pianist *

1978–79
Kyung–Wha Chung, violinist
Pittsburgh Chamber Orchestra
Barry Tuckwell, french hornist
 & Andre Michel–Schub, pianist
Jean–Philippe Collard, pianist
Leona Mitchell, soprano
Neil Rutman, pianist *

1979–80
Grigory Sokolov, pianist
Donald Gramm, bass–baritone
Toulouse Chamber Orchestra
Stephanie Chase, violinist
Ruth Golden, soprano *

1980–81
Shlomo Mintz, violinist
Hermann Prey, baritone
Southwest German Chamber
    Orchestra
Murray Perahia, pianist
Judy Lin, pianist *

1981–82
Jean–Philippe Collard, pianist
Ransom Wilson, Flautist
Swiss Chamber Orchestra
Elly Ameling, soprano
Diane Hidy, pianist *

1982–83
Annie Fischer, pianist
Scottish Chamber Orchestra
 with Jaime Laredo,
    violinist & conductor
Nathaniel Rosen, cellist
New York Vocal Arts Ensemble
Ann Gresham, soprano *

1983–84
Evelyn Lear, soprano
 with Thomas Stewart, baritone
I Solisti di Zagreb
    Chamber Orchestra
Uto Ughi, violinist
David Wehr, pianist *

1984–85
Richard Stoltzman, clarinetist
Empire Brass Ensemble
Håkan Hagegård, baritone
Babette Hierholzer, pianist
Mia Kim, violinist *

1985–86
Uto Ughi, violinist
Victoria de los Angeles, soprano
Music from Marlboro
Jean–Bernard Pommier, pianist
Robert Swensen, tenor *

1986–87
Leontyne Price, soprano
Misha & Cipa Dichter, duo–pianists
Hermannn Prey, baritone
Carter Brey, cellist
John Sutherland Earle, pianist *

1987–88
Jeffrey Kahane, pianist
James Morris, bass
Cleveland & Meliora String Quartets
Annie Fischer, pianist
Julius Baker, Flautist
 with Norma Jean Hodges, soprano
Marvis Martin, soprano
Lisa Smith, guitarist *

1988–89
Jean–Yves Thibaudet, pianist
Budapest Chamber Orchestra
Anne–Sophie Mutter, violinist
Yo–Yo Ma, cellist & Emanuel Ax,
    pianist
Neil Rutman, pianist
Derek Anthony, bass *

1989–90
Hambro Quartet of Pianos
Eugenia Zukerman, Flautist
Jean–Yves Thibaudet, pianist
Thomas Allen, baritone
William Kanengiser, guitarist
Quink Vocal Ensemble
Bryan Verhoye, pianist *

1990–91
Santiago Rodriguez, pianist
Dawn Upshaw, soprano
Camerata Musica of Berlin
Alicia De Larrocha, pianist
Nadja Salerno–Sonnenberg,
    violinist
 with Cecile Licad, pianist
Qi–Xin Pu, violinist *

1991–92
Grant Johannesen, pianist
Beaux Arts Trio
Itzhak Perlman, violinist
Jorma Hynninen, baritone
Empire Brass
Earle Patriarco, baritone *

1992–93
Anne Akiko Meyers, violinist
Lynn Harrell, cellist
Frederica von Stade, mezzo–
    soprano
Guildhall String Ensemble
 with Richard Stoltzman, clarinetist
Yefim Bronfman, pianist
Mark Anderson, pianist *

1993–94
Paula Robison, Flautist & Ruth
    Laredo, pianist
Ilana Vered, pianist
Pinchas Zukerman, violinist &
    violist
 with Marc Neikrug, pianist
I Solisti di Zagreb Chamber
    Orchestra
Thomas Hampson, baritone
Thorsten Encke, cellist *

1994–95
Marilyn Horne, mezzo–soprano
Franz Liszt Chamber Orchestra
Radu Lupu, pianist
Leonidas Kavakos, violinist
Krystian Zimerman, pianist
Cynthia Clayton, soprano *

1995–96
Midori, violinist
Sergei Leiferkus, baritone
Emanuel Ax, pianist
Canadian Brass
Trio Fontenay (violin, cello, piano)
Yongmei Hu, pianist *

1996–97
Kalichstein–Laredo–Robinson Trio
    (violin, cello, piano)
Misha & Cipa Dichter, duo pianists
Denyce Graves, mezzo–soprano
Joshua Bell, violinist
 with Jean–Yves Thibaudet, pianist
Abbey Simon, pianist
Andrea Plesnarski, oboist *

1997–98
Gil Shaham, violinist
Budapest Strings
Ben Heppner, tenor
Matt Haimovitz, cellist
András Schiff, pianist
Lanya Chianakas, mezzo–soprano *

1998–99
Sergei Nakariakov, trumpeter
Beaux Arts Trio
    (violin, cello, piano)
Vladimir Feltsman, pianist
Cho–Liang Lin, violinist
Ruth Ann Swenson, soprano
Heidi Hau, pianist *

1999–2000
Florence Quivar, mezzo–soprano
Hilary Hahn, violinist
Jean–Yves Thibaudet, pianist
Moscow Chamber Orchestra
 with Justin Blasdale, pianist
Empire Brass
Felix Fan, cellist *

2000–2001
Bo Skovhus, baritone
Arcadi Volodos, pianist
St Petersburg String Quartet
Munich Chamber Orchestra
Gil Shaham, violinist
 with Orli Shaham, pianist
Kenneth Goodson, baritone *

From early 2001 through June
2003, Sunset Auditorium is under
construction. Carmel Music society
concerts are held at All Saints
Church in Carmel.

2001–2002
Moscow Chamber Orchestra
Louis Lortie, pianist
Denyce Graves, mezzo–soprano
Italian Saxophone Quartet
Dale Tsang–Hall, pianist *

2002–2003
Stewart Goodyear, pianist
Sharon Isbin, Guitarist
Burning River Brass
Ruth Waterman, violinist/lecturer
Emanuel Ax, pianist
Caroline Campbell, violinist *

As of 2003, concerts are held in
the new Sunset Center Theater
and occasionally in All Saints
Church.

2003–2004
Prague Chamber Orchestra
Christopher O'Riley
 with Fred Hersch, duo–pianists
Arnaldo Cohen, pianist
Nadja Salerno-Sonnenberg, violinist
 with The Assad Brothers, guitarists
Andre-Michel Schub, pianist
 with David Shifrin, clarinetist
Sonia Gariaeff, soprano *

2004–2005
Mark Delavan, baritone
David Finkel, cellist & Wu Han,
    pianist
I Solisti di Venezia
Frederic Chiu, pianist
Vienna Choir Boys
Beaux Arts Trio (violin, cello, piano)
Judy Huang, pianist *

2005–2006
Andrâs Schiff, pianist
Alon Goldstein, pianist
    & Amit Peled, cellist;
with Alexander Fiterstein,
    clarinetist
Corey Cerovsek, violinist
with Julien Quentin, pianist
Salzburg Chamber Soloists
Olga Kern, pianist
Katie Kadarauch, violist *

Carmel Music Society assumes
management of the concert series
produced by the California Mozart
Society, and incorporates those
concerts into its own series.

2006–2007
Academy of St. Martin in the Fields
    Chamber Ensemble
Lynn Harrell, cellist
    & Gavin Martin, pianist
Arnaldo Cohen, pianist
Janaki String Trio (violin, viola,
    cello)
John Williams
    & John Etheridge, guitarists
St. Paul Chamber Orchestra
    Ensemble
with Reiko Aizawa, pianist
Brian Thorsett, tenor *

2007–2008
Frederica von Stade, mezzo-
    soprano
    with Jake Heggie, pianist
Philharmonia Baroque Orchestra
Alexander String Quartet
Gil Shaham, violinist
    with Akira Eguchi, pianist
Michael Roll, pianist
Ivan Zenaty, violinist
    & Paul Hersh, pianist
American Brass Quintet
Altenberg Piano Trio
    (violin, cello, piano)
Elizabeth Schumann, pianist *

2008–2009
The Romeros Guitar Quartet
Adaskin Trio (violin, viola, cello)
    and Tom Gallant, oboist
Takâcs String Quartet
Hans Boepple, pianist
Voices of London (6-voice a
    cappella)
Bennewitz String Quartet
Triple Helix Piano Trio (violin,
    cello, piano) &Paul Hersh, violist
Yefim Bronfman, pianist
Dana Booher, Saxophonist *

2009–2010
Academy of Saint Martin in the
    Fields Chamber Ensemble
Alexander Quartet
    & Eli Eban, clarinetist
Susan Graham, mezzo–soprano
    with Malcolm Martineau, pianist
Menachem Pressler, pianist
    with American String Quartet
Gustavo Romero, pianist
Albers String Trio (violin, cello,
    piano)
Timothy Fain, violinist
    & Cory Smythe, pianist
Rossetti String Quartet
Devon Guthrie, soprano *

2010–2011
Angel Romero, guitarist
    with Nefretiri Romero, mezzo-
    soprano
The Gryphon Trio (violin, cello,
    piano)
Misha & Cipa Dichter, duo–pianists
Soloists from Opera San José
Lynn Harrell, cellist
    with Jon Kimura Parker, pianist
Janina Fialkowska, pianist
    & The Chamber Players of
    Canada
Bennewitz String Quartet
Allan Vogel, oboist
    with The Wind Soloists of New
    York
Tanya Gabrielian, pianist *
Irene Kim, pianist *

2011–2012
Nobuyuki Tsujii, pianist
The Gryphon Trio (violin, cello,
    piano)
Astrid Schween, cellist
    with Gary Hammond, pianist
Frederica von Stade, mezzo-
    soprano
    with Kristin Pankonin, pianist
Israeli Chamber Project
Garrick Ohlsson, pianist
Nadja Salerno–Sonnenberg,
    violinist
    with Anne-Marie McDermott,
    pianist
Pavel Haas Quartet
Jae-in Shin, violinist *

2012–2013

Lynn Harrell, cellist
and Jon Kimura Parker, pianist
Jeffrey Kahane pianist
Los Angeles Piano Quartet
Philharmonia Baroque Orchestra
 With Elizabeth Blumenstock, violinist
 with Nicholas McGegan, conductor
Hans Boepple, pianist
Opera San José
Takâcs String Quartet
Lydian String Quartet
Clarissa Lyons, soprano*

2013–2014

Vadym Kholodenko, pianist:
 Winner, 2013 Cliburn Competition
Brentano String Quartet
Opera San José
Elizabeth Wallfisch, violinist
      & David Breitman, fortepianist
      (two concerts)
The Gryphon Trio (violin, cello, piano
      with James Campbell, clarinettist
Musica Pacifica Baroque Ensemble
Louis Lortie, pianist
David Finckel, cellist
      & Wu Han, pianist
Michael Noble, pianist*

2014–2015

The Romero Guitar Quartet
Hagen String Quartet
Philharmonia Baroque Orchestra
  with Elizabeth Blumenstock, violin
Opera San José
Jon Kimura Parker
      & Jamie Parker, pianists

In April, 1944, Ezio Pinza performed for the Carmel Music Society and at the San José Civic Auditorium for the Denny-Watrous Management. *Courtesy of the author.*

Dancer Myra Kinch (above) and violinist Mischa Elman (below), early Carmel Music Society artists. *Courtesy of the author.*

The Monterey Peninsula Orchestra 1932–1946

Occasionally in the press and even in its own printed matter, this orchestra was also called the Monterey Peninsula Chamber Orchestra and the Community Orchestra.

1931

Neah-Kah-Nie Quartet plays private informal concert in Carmel in August.
Dene Denny becomes their agent and handles their concert bookings.
During the 1931-1932 season the quartet performs more than 40 concerts in cities on the Pacific Coast.

1932

Neah-Kah-Nie Quartet appears on the Carmel Music Society Subscription Series in February.
June, July, August 1932
The Quartet lives in Carmel for eight weeks and is the focus of the first Carmel Music Society Summer Series.
An orchestra of local musicians is created, and it accompanies a concerto concert.
Quartet and orchestra rehearsals are open to the general public twice weekly.

MPO Concert #1

(Part of the 1932 Carmel Music Society Summer Season)
Henry Eichheim, conductor
Aug 9, 1932, Sunset School Auditorium
Concerto Concert featuring members of the Neah-Kah-Nie Quartet.
   I.   Bach: *Double Concerto in D Minor* - Susie Pipes and Hubert Sorenson
   II. Mozart: Concerto for Violin and Viola in E-flat Major - Hubert Sorenson and Abraham Weiss
   III. Boccherini: *Cello Concerto in B-flat* - Michel Penha

The printed program includes the line: "Quartet and Orchestra Management, Dene Denny"

MPO Concert #2

(An ad hoc bonus concert of the 1932 Carmel Music Society Summer Season)
Michel Penha, conductor
August 25, 1932, Denny Watrous Gallery
Two concerti are repeated from the August 9 concert with the same soloists.
   I.   The concert begins with short works by Grieg and Granados
   II. Bach: *Concerto for Two Violins* with Susie Pipes and Hubert Sorenson
   III. Mozart: *Concerto for Violin and Viola* with Abraham Weiss and Hubert Sorenson
   IV. Special appearance by Miriam Soloveff, 10 years old, Pupil of Carol Weston

   The Boccherini is omitted, because Penha is conducting.

Penha leaves Carmel to go on tour with his quartet.

Carol Weston is engaged to rehearse the orchestra weekly during his absence.
Mildred Sahlstrom-Wright is engaged as concertmaster and begins on Sept 25.
In September, the name "Monterey Peninsula Orchestra" is first used.

MPO Concert #3

("Special Open Rehearsal." An admission fee is charged.)
Carol Weston, conductor
October 1932, Denny-Watrous Gallery
  I.   Mozart: *Eine kleine Nachtmusik*
  II. Mozart: 2 Sarastro arias from Mozart's *Magic Flute* – Noel Sullivan, baritone
  III. Schubert: first movement of *"Unfinished"* symphony

After the popularity of the 1932 summer events, the Music Society decides to invest its efforts more directly into the community by bringing the Quartet back to Carmel as a resident ensemble and using its presence to educate, entertain and enlighten the community. The Neah-Kah-Nie Quartet is engaged by the Music Society for a total of five months in 1933: February, March, June, July, and August.

1933

MPO Concert #4

Carol Weston, conductor
January 7, 1933, Ballroom of San Carlos Hotel, Monterey
  I.   Max Bruch: Violin Concerto - Marilyn Doty, age 10 (perhaps one movement, or an arrangement)
  II. J. S. Bach: Suite (unspecified)
  III. Schubert: *Unfinished Symphony*, first movement
  IV. Beethoven: *Egmont Overture*

This concert is mentioned in the Pine Cone Jan 6, 1933. It is not found in the Society's material.

MPO Concert #5

(Part of the 1933 Carmel Music Society Subscription Series)
Michel Penha, conductor
March 11, 1933, Sunset Auditorium
  I.   Mozart: *Serenade for Strings* (4 movements)
  II. Handel: *B Minor concerto for viola* – Abraham Weiss
  III. Beethoven: *C Major Piano Concerto* – Ralph Linsley
  IV. Beethoven: *Egmont Overture*

MPO Concert #6

(Part of the 1933 Carmel Music Society Summer Subscription Series)
Michel Penha, conductor
July 25, 1933, Sunset Auditorium
  I.   Corelli: *Concerto Grosso*
  II. Bach: *Piano Concerto in D Minor*
  III. Vieuxtemps: *Violin Concerto Nr. 4* (Mvmnts 1, 2, 4)
  IV. Ippolitov-Ivanov: *Caucasian Sketches* (2 mvmnts.)

MPO Concert #7

(Part of the 1933 Carmel Music Society Summer Subscription Series)
Michel Penha, conductor
August 22, 1933, Sunset Auditorium
  I.   Bloch: *Concerto Grosso*
  II.   Vivaldi: *Concerto for violin in A Minor* – Mildred Sahlstrom
  III. Beethoven: *Egmont Overture*
  IV.   Preston Search: *Cello Concerto* (premiere) played by the composer
  V.   Bizet: *Adagietto* and *Farandolo* from "L'Arlesiana"

After Penha's second bow, David Hagemeyer (member of the second violins) reads a letter from the orchestra pledging their support and commitment and affection, and "begging him to remain as their leader."

MPO Concert #8

Michel Penha, conductor
September 23, 1933, Pacific Grove High School auditorium
"Pops Concert"
  I.   Mozart: *Serenade*
  II.   Beethoven: *Concerto No.1 in C Major* - Ralph Linsley
  III. Beethoven: *Egmont Overture*
  IV.   Bizet: two movements from *"L'Arlesienne"*
  V.   Granados: *Intermezzo* from the opera *"Goyescas"*
  VI.   Ivanov: *Caucasian Sketches*

1934

MPO Concert #9

Michel Penha, conductor
March 29, 1934, Sunset Auditorium
March 30, 1934, Pacific Grove High School auditorium
Orchestra of 40, Chorus of 75 (prepared by Fenton Foster)
  Rossini: *Stabat Mater*

MPO Concert #10

(Part of the 1934 Carmel Music Society Summer Series)
Michel Penha, conductor
August 7, 1934, Sunset Auditorium
Theodore Norman, violin and Abraham Weiss, viola
Orchestra is 7, 7, 4, 4, 1; flute, clar, horn, 2 trmpts, 2 tromb, harmonium, piano, tymp, tuba.
Includes 6 pro players from SF
  I.   Mendelssohn: *Italian Symphony*
  II.   A Cappella Chorus: Bach, Pearsall, Gretchaninoff, Czech folk song
        (The press said bless their hearts but they were not ready.)
  III. Mozart: *Concerto K364 for Violin and Viola* – Norman and Weiss
  IV.   Massenet: Overture to *Phédre*

In October, Ernst Bacon is named conductor of the orchestra and immediately begins rehearsing Beethoven's Symphony #4 for the January concert

MPO Concert #11

Ernst Bacon, conductor
Sunday, February 17, 1935, Denny Watrous Gallery
  I.   Beethoven: Symphony #4, second movement
  II. Bach: *Double Concerto in D Minor* – local violinists
  III. Percy Grainger: *Spoon River*
  IV. Byrd: *Pavana*
  V.   Mussorgsky: *Gopak*

1935

Carmel Bach Festival, July 18, 19, 20, and 21: the orchestra plays in all four concerts, but retains its own name.

MPO Concert #12

Ernst Bacon, conductor
Saturday, Dec 22, 1935, Denny Watrous Gallery
(New location: former Manzanita Theater on San Carlos Street)
"Christmas Concert"
  Bach Orchestral Suite
  Choral movements (1, 2, 4, 7) of Brahms *German Requiem*
  Christmas Carols

Beyond 1935

The concert on December 22, 1935, was the final independent performance given by the Monterey Peninsula Orchestra. Beginning in 1936, the orchestra appeared only as the orchestra of the Carmel Bach Festival each summer. In 1946, the orchestra was still listed in the Carmel Bach Festival program as the "Monterey Peninsula Orchestra." In 1947 the name of the orchestra was officially changed to the "Bach Festival Orchestra."

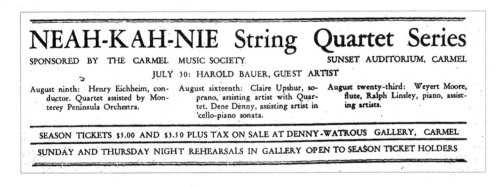

The Monterey Symphony

For decades on the Monterey Peninsula, music lovers who remembered the names Denny and Watrous shared an assumption that Dene, Hazel, and the Carmel Music Society had been somehow involved in the creation of the present-day Monterey Symphony. The generally accepted story seemed relatively obvious at first glance:

    A.) In 1932 Dene, Hazel, and the Carmel Music Society formed the Monterey Peninsula Orchestra. It played nearly forty concerts between July 1932 and July 1946, twelve on its own and the remainder as the orchestra for the Carmel Bach Festival.

    B.) In 1942, several modest attempts were made to create an orchestra. Among the names tossed around was "Monterey County Symphony."

    C.) The Monterey Peninsula Orchestra apparently ceased to exist after 1946.

    D.) In 1947, the "Monterey County Symphony" made its debut.

The writers of several published articles over the years saw this string of events in different ways, and made the assumptions that Point A led ultimately to Point D, and that Dene and Hazel somehow had a hand in it.

Points A and B are true but unrelated. Point C is false: the orchestra's name was changed, but the membership and activity continued. Point D is true, but it does not seem to be connected directly to A, B, or C.

The Monterey Symphony presents its history clearly on its website and in its printed material. Nonetheless, as recently as 2003, in a description of the 1932 orchestra at the Denny Watrous Gallery, a local historian wrote: "Thus, the Monterey County Symphony was formed, under the sponsorship of the Carmel Music Society." More recently, during the research for this book, dozens of local residents mentioned that Dene and Hazel had "founded the Carmel Music Society, the Bach Festival, and the Symphony."

The source material

The Local History Room of the Harrison Memorial Library in Carmel has a concise collection of primary source material documenting the creation of the Monterey County Symphony in 1946 and 1947, including a detailed typewritten account of the orchestra's first eighteen months; a comprehensive collection of press clippings from that period; and printed programs of the first several concerts. This material is a contemporary written record of: the names of the original organizers; the proceedings of the preliminary brainstorming discussions and multiple town hall meetings in Carmel and Salinas in 1946; a description of the rehearsals in early 1947; the roster of the players; the date of incorporation and the names of the board of directors and officers; the pre and post coverage of the debut concert in May 1947; and details of several subsequent concerts into 1948.

By combining all this information with additional press coverage from microfilms, the story can be recounted. All of the following events are documented in the public record.

    1. In the summer of 1932 the Monterey Peninsula Orchestra was formed by Dene Denny and Michel Penha, with the endorsement of the Carmel Music Society. The orchestra rehearsed and performed in the Denny-Watrous Gallery on Dolores Street in central Carmel, and the players were almost all local amateurs; the only professionals were the

violinists and violist from Penha's Neah-Kah-Nie String Quartet. Later concerts usually included a handful of (unpaid) regional professionals who played with the orchestra in the concerts and the last few rehearsals.

2. Between August 1932 and December 1935, this orchestra rehearsed (intermittently) year-round in the Denny-Watrous Gallery in Carmel and performed twelve concerts in Carmel, Pacific Grove, and Monterey. The conductors of the orchestra during those years were Michel Penha, Henry Eichheim, Carol Weston, Bernard Callery, and Ernst Bacon. During this time the orchestra was small—15 to 25 players—and always included a piano in order to fill in for instruments that were to be missing. This orchestra performed symphonies, concertos, and other orchestral repertoire, as well as the Rossini Stabat Mater (1934) and the choral movements of the Brahms Requiem (1935).

3. In July 1935, the Monterey Peninsula Orchestra became the core ensemble of the first Carmel Bach Festival. In December 1935, it gave one more concert of its own, and from then on, its only appearances were as the orchestra of the Bach Festival. From 1935 through 1946, it was listed every summer in the Bach Festival Program as the Monterey Peninsula Orchestra.

4. Just before and after the Second World War, a group of local music educators attempted to form an orchestra under the auspices of the Carmel and Monterey Adult Schools. The members of the orchestra were local music teachers, local adult amateurs, Salinas Junior College students, and a few high school students. This orchestra received several names in the press: Peninsula Orchestra Society, Peninsula Concert Orchestra, Monterey Peninsula Symphony Orchestra, and Monterey County Symphony Orchestra. Clifford Anderson, former concertmaster of the Santa Rosa Symphony, had recently moved to Monterey to teach at Monterey High School, and he was one of the ringleaders who got the various music teachers to team together. The orchestra played two informal concerts before the War, and two more shortly afterwards. The concerts were conducted by multiple music teachers, each leading a separate piece on the program. There is no indication in the public records and press that this orchestra was connected with the Carmel Bach Festival Orchestra or with the new orchestra described in point 6 below.

5. At the 1946 Carmel Bach Festival (July 22–28), only a dozen of the forty players in the Monterey Peninsula Orchestra were local amateur musicians. They were joined by a few university students from Stanford, San José, and Southern California, who played for room and board. 60% of the orchestra members were first-rate professionals from around the country, most of whom had a penchant for Bach and the Baroque. The 1946 orchestra at the Bach Festival included flutist Doriot Anthony of the National Symphony (later known as Doriot Anthony Dwyer); Jules Salkin, principal violist of the Indianapolis Symphony; cellist William Harry and violinist Doris Ballard, both from the New Orleans Symphony; oboist George Houle of Stanford; clarinetist Franklin Sabin of the Pasadena Symphony; and French hornist Wendell Hoss, a virtuoso who was famous for playing and recording Bach's Six Cello Suites on the French horn.

1946 was the last summer that the "Monterey Peninsula Orchestra" would be listed in the Bach Festival program under that name.

6. In early September 1946, six weeks after the Bach Festival, a group of music lovers, patrons, amateur musicians, and music educators met to discuss the creation a new year-round regional orchestra. Their goal was to establish a "Monterey County" orchestra made up of local residents, and with no professionals from outside the area. The organizational framework took shape in meetings throughout the fall, culminating in a county-wide gathering on December 15 at Carmel High School at which a representative of the Oakland Symphony gave advice and answered questions. Of the organizers of the orchestra described in point #4 just above, only Clifford Anderson (Monterey High School) and Lorell McCann (Salinas Community College) were also members of this new group.

7. After the big December 15 meeting, the organizers put out an open invitation to all interested instrumentalists, and, on the evening of January 6, 1947, about sixty musicians showed up at Carmel High School. Chairs and music stands were arranged based on the numbers of instruments present, music was handed out, and the assembled players read through Johann Strauss' *Tales of the Vienna Woods* and overture to *Die Fledermaus*; Chabrier's *Espana Rhapsody*; the slow movement from an unnamed Beethoven symphony; and a few other works. Conductor for the evening was Dr. Leon Minear, music teacher and assistant principal at Carmel High School. While all the musicians were professional trained, very few of the players were, or had ever been, anywhere near being "professionals," and it's possible that a few of the instruments had been taken out of their dusty cases only weeks before. The group cannot have sounded very coherent, at least by modern standards, but everyone present had a great time and the evening of music–making lit a spark.

8. Weekly rehearsals began immediately and culminated in the orchestra's first public appearance in early May, when it gave a free concert for the soldiers at Fort Ord, a military base just north of Monterey. Immediately after that event, the orchestra was incorporated as the Monterey County Symphony, and Mrs. Henry McGowan was elected President of the Monterey County Symphony Association.

9. On May 28, 1947, at the Sunset School Auditorium in Carmel, the Monterey County Symphony gave its first concert. There were 11 players from Monterey, 15 from Salinas, 23 from Carmel, 11 from Pacific Grove, 3 from Fort Ord and 1 from Seaside. (See details of the program below.)

10. For the 1947, Carmel Bach Festival six weeks later, no doubt as a courtesy to the newly-formed organization and even moreso to clarify its own identity, the Monterey Peninsula Orchestra changed its name to the "Bach Festival Orchestra." This was a long-overdue renaming, as the orchestra had performed no concerts of its own for nearly twelve years. Only the name of the orchestra was changed, not the personnel: the Bach Festival orchestra in 1947 was virtually the same as the years before and after, especially the local players.

11. In the written accounts and press coverage of the creation and first 18 months of the Monterey County Symphony, neither the Carmel Bach Festival nor the Monterey Peninsula Orchestra nor the names Denny and Watrous are ever mentioned. There is

no hint of their presence and not a single reference is made to them. Given the local prominence that Dene and Hazel had achieved, it seems unlikely that they could—or would—have participated materially in the startup of such a high profile organization and yet still have remained unmentioned and anonymous in press coverage and printed material. Of course they were well acquainted with many of the new orchestra's founding board members, including Noel Sullivan, Peter Ferrante, Eben Whittlesey, Fritz Wurtzman, and Hal Garrott, but those names were familiar to the entire Monterey Peninsula and such individuals participated in many local arts organizations.

12. According to their own printed rosters, there was no overlap of membership between these two orchestras at precisely the time one would most expect to see it: in the new county orchestra's first concerts. There were no musicians from the 1946, 1947, or 1948 Carmel Bach Festival Orchestra who also played in the concerts of the Monterey County Symphony in 1947 and 1948. The The Monterey County Symphony started from scratch with a completely different roster of players, none of whom were playing at that time in the "Denny-Watrous" orchestra.

How it happened:

1.) The Monterey Peninsula Orchestra was created in 1932 by Denny-Watrous as a community music-making experience, but once it joined the Bach Festival in 1935, it played only in the summer and took in more and more imported professionals. By 1946, the original year-round community orchestra had become the semi-pro Bach Festival orchestra, and most of its players were not even residents of California. This was good for the Bach Festival, but disappointing to lovers of orchestral music in Monterey County.

2.) The Monterey County Symphony was not an offshoot of the Monterey Peninsula Orchestra, at least not in the sense some came to imagine. On the contrary, the Monterey County Symphony was created in 1946 partly in reaction to the large percentage of non-local musicians who played in the Bach Festival. The organizers wanted to return to the concept of a year-round orchestra for regional musicians. It is explicitly clear throughout the discussions and proceedings in 1946 and early 1947 that the intention was to create a new orchestra consisting of musicians residing in Monterey County, including the cities of Salinas and King City.

3.) The founding board members included patrons who had also helped the Music Society and the Bach Festival to grow, but the Monterey County Symphony was created from scratch with no direct help from Denny-Watrous or the Carmel Music Society. It was founded by the music teachers, musicians, generous patrons, and music lovers of Monterey County.

4.) Dene and Hazel may not have been directly involved in the creation of the Monterey Symphony (as it is now known), but the organization emerged from the same community energy that Dene and Hazel tapped for their organizations. The orchestra was a new and fresh expression of Monterey County's deep love of music and the performing arts. Founded by music teachers and other members of the regional community, the Monterey Symphony has grown in artistic stature, and its members today are superb musicians from Central California.

Monterey County Symphony Debut Concert, May 28, 1947

The official public debut of the Monterey County Symphony took place at Sunset Auditorium. Lorell McCann, Leon Minear, and Clifford Anderson shared the conducting duties, and each played in the violin section when not on the podium. The program was:

Friedman: *Slavonic Rhapsody No.2* (McCann)

Johann Strauss: *Overture to Die Fledermaus* (McCann)

Beethoven: *Piano Concerto No. 3*, final movement: *allegro* (Minear)

Sibelius: *Finlandia* (Anderson)

Bizet: *L'Arlesienne Suite* (Anderson)

Beethoven: *Symphony No. 1*, first and last movements (Minear)

Eben Whittlesey was a former Carmel mayor and a founding member of the board of directors of the Monterey County Symphony. He wrote a review of the concert:

Symphony Concert Makes Musical History

Musical history for this region was made Wednesday night with the first concert on the Peninsula of the Monterey County Symphony Orchestra, playing at Sunset Auditorium. Two things were very apparent to the large and enthusiastic audience: first, that we have in our midst, after only five months of weekly rehearsals, an orchestra whose performance can give pleasure to the most critical listeners, and secondly, that we do not have a proper auditorium in which to present its concerts....

The arrangement of the players on the small stage had been the subject of much prayerful consideration by the conductors, and limitation of space compelled the placing of the piano at one side, where it was not heard to best advantage. [Beethoven Piano Concerto] All of these factors should give impetus to efforts to launch the auditorium project which has been the subject of considerable discussion in the past year....

The 60 piece orchestra surprised all of its hearers by the finished quality of its performance, by smooth and sensitive interpretation of the music, by the good coordination of ensemble playing, and by the good execution of all solo passages. (Pine Cone, May 30, 1947)

Sources for this chapter:

Local History Room, Harrison Memorial Library, Carmel
Carmel Music Society archive
Carmel Bach Festival programs 1935-1950
Microfilm: Carmel Pine Cone, Monterey Herald, San Francisco Chronicle.

Visit the Monterey Symphony website: www.montereysymphony.org

Dene Denny, pianist 1920-1932

Dene Denny's professional career as solo pianist was brief, but in the span of only 37 months she performed an amazing variety of music, and all from memory. This is a list of repertoire Dene is known to have played in public, and is not a complete list of her solo performances.

The Wager Swayne studio recitals are listed for background. It was typical repertoire at that time for serious piano students, and there is no indication that she performed such repertoire after 1924.

Studio recitals by students of Wager Swayne

San Francisco, c. 1919-1923
Various locations in San Francisco and Berkeley
(Some pieces were listed without opus numbers, etc.)

May 28, 1920 (age 35)

> Schnittke: *Sur les steppes*; Anton Rubinstein: *Barcarolle* (opus unknown)
> Raff: Suite No. 204, Movement 3 "Rigaudon"

March 26, 1921

> Chopin: *Berceuse* in D-Flat Major: Liszt - 6 Etudes, No. 3. *La Campanella*
> Mozkowski: *Caprice Espagnol*

April 5, 1922

> Chopin: *Berceuse* in D-Flat Major and *Polonaise* in A flat major

October 7, 1922

> Chopin: *Waltz* (opus unknown); Debussy: *Arabesque* (No 1 or 2)
> Rachmaninoff: *Prelude* in G Minor, Opus 23 No 5

May 5, 1923

> Chopin: Étude and *Ballade* (opus unknown)
> Liszt: *Rhapsody* (opus unknown)

Professional debut

November 20, 1926
Music Room of the Hotel Biltmore, Los Angeles
New Music Ensemble of San Francisco,
Henry Cowell, director and pianist
with the Persinger Quartet and Dane Rudhyar, pianist

> Schoenberg's *Fünf Klavierstücke*, Opus 23. Dene Denny, pianist
> (North American premiere)

Carmel Debut

June 3, 1927

Theatre of the Golden Bough, Carmel, Presented by Denny and Watrous

June 10, 1927 (same program

San Francisco Women's Building, San Francisco

Presented by the Fortnightly Series and Ida Scott Gregory Management

In her first solo recital in Carmel, Dene performed music by twelve composers, all written within her lifetime. Most of the 32 individual movements listed below are only one or two minutes long, but it would be wrong to assume that it was a short evening: the actual performance was more than twice as long at it looks on these pages. For example, after opening the concert with "Dittico" and "I partenti" by G. F. Malipiero, Dene turned to the audience and spoke about the music, and then turned back to the keyboard and played both pieces again. Next on the program was "Sept Pieces Breves," a seven-movement work by Arthur Honegger. Dene played the entire work, commented on the music, and then played all seven movements again.

She performed everything on the concert this way, and she managed to do it while playing all the music from memory, as she did in all her concerts, at least from 1926 onward.

Although the Roman numerals below give a clue, "excerpts" indicates that Dene played one or more movements taken from the larger named work. Spellings used in the source material (such as "Scriabine" and "Schönberg") are retained.

G. Francesco Malipiero:	*Poemi Asolani* excerpts
	II. Dittico; III. I partenti
Arthur Honegger:	*Sept Pieces Breves*
	I. Supplement; II. Vif; III. Tres lent; IV. Legerement
	V. Lent; VI. Rythmique; VIII. Violent
Leo Ornstein:	Fourth Sonata
	I. Moderato con moto; II. Semplice; III. Lento; IV. Vivo II.
Eugene Goosens:	*Hommage à Debussy*
Zoltan Kodaly:	*Neuf Pieces Pour Le Piano* excerpts
	V. Furioso; VI. *Moderato*; V. *Triste*
Bela Bartok :	*Bagatelles*, Opus 6 excerpts
	III. Andante; VII. Allegretto molto capriccioso
Dane Rudhyar:	*Moments*: VI. *Tenderness*
Francis Poulenc:	*Trois Mouvements Perpetuels*
	I. Balance-Modere; II. Tres Modere; III. Alerte
Alexandre Tcherepnine:	*Eight Preludes* excerpts
	II. Lent; VI. Agitato; VII. Rubato
Alexander Scriabine :	*Deux Poemes*: II. *Etrangeté*
Arnold Schönberg:	*Funf Klavierstücke*, Opus 23
	I. Sehr langsam; II. Sehr rasch; III. Langsam
	IV. Schwungvoll; V. Walzer
Henry Cowell:	*The Harp of Life*
Encore: Cowell:	*The Voice of Lir*

Solo Recital

November 11, 1928
Grand Ballroom, St. Francis Hotel
San Francisco
Presented by the Fortnightly Series
and Ida Scott Gregory Management

November 18, 1928
Theatre of the Golden Bough,
Carmel
Presented by Denny-Watrous Management

Ernest Bloch:	*Five Sketches in Sepia*
G. Francesco Malipiero:	*Poemi Asolani* II. Dittico; III. I partenti
Francis Poulenc:	*Mouvements Perpetuels* I. Balance-Modere; II. Tres Modere; III. Alerte
Zoltan Kodaly:	*Neuf Pieces pour le Piano* V. Furioso; VI. Moderato; V. Triste
Bela Bartok:	from Opus 261 [sic]
F. Mompou:	*Canco I Dansa*
Arthur Honegger:	*Sept Pieces Breves* I. Supplement; II. Vif; III. Tres lent; IV. Legerement V. Lent; VI. Rythmique; VIII. Violent
Arnold Schönberg:	from Opus II [sic]
Imre Weisshaus:	*Prelude*
Leo Ornstein:	Fourth Sonata
Igor Stravinsky:	*Chez Petrouchka*
Henry Cowell:	*The Harp of Life*

Dene Denny, 1927 PR photos, recovered from microfilms. Courtesy of the Carmel Pine Cone and the H. M. Williams Local History Room of the Harrison Memorial Library.

Dene's last documented solo appearance

December 17, 1929
Gallerie Beaux-Arts, Whittel Building, 166 Geary, San Francisco
Presented by Henry Cowell's New Music Society

The program is given here exactly as listed in the San Francisco press.

Arnold Schönberg: Opus 23, *Fünf Klavierstücke*

Samuel Feinberg: Opus 8, No. 2, *Prelude*

A. Weprik: Opus 13b, *Drei Volkstänze* Allegro–Lento–Allegro

Bela Bartok: Opus 6, No. 7, No. 11

Zoltan Kodaly: Opus 3, No. 5, *Furioso*

A Mossolow: Opus 11, Quartieme Sonate

Nicholas Roslavetz: from *Cinq Preludes*

A Scriabine: Opus 63, No. 2, *Entrangeté*; Opus 68, No. 9

Carmel Music Society Summer Concert Series

August 23, 1932
Kodaly: *Cello Sonata*
with Michel Penha, cellist

Presented by Denny-Watrous and the Carmel Music Society, this was one of four concerts in the first Carmel Music Society Summer Series with the Neah-Kah-Nie String Quartet.

This is the final documented public performance by Dene Denny as pianist.

Orchestral compositions by Gastone Usigli performed in California

1897
Gastone Usigli born in Venice

1927
Usigli immigrates to the US and settles in San Francisco.

1930
Symphonic Scherzo: Don Quixote
(Awarded the Ricordi Prize in Composition, 1924.)
US Premiere: San Francisco Symphony Orchestra, Gastone Usigli, guest conductor.
Curran Theatre, San Francisco, January 24 and 26, 1930.
San Francisco Symphony Orchestra, July 6 and 8, 1930, Bernardino Molinari, conductor.

1931
Tone Poem: Song of a River in a Night of War
(*Canto del fiume in una notte de guerra*).
Sketches, 1917; finished, 1920; re-orchestrated 1921.
Premiere: San Francisco Symphony Orchestra, Gastone Usigli, guest conductor.
Tivoli Opera House, San Francisco, December 11 and 13, 1931.
Other performances: III Festival Internazionale di Musica, La Fenice Opera House, Venice, September 8, 1934. Gastone Usigli, conductor.

1934
Tone Poem: Flight
Premiere: San Francisco Chamber Orchestra, Gastone Usigli, conductor.
Veterans' Auditorium, San Francisco, March 27, 1934.

Prelude for String Orchestra
Premiere: String Orchestra of the San Francisco Conservatory of Music, Gastone Usigli, conductor.
Gold Ballroom of the Palace Hotel, San Francisco, May 20, 1934.
"Written expressly for his students at the San Francisco Conservatory of music."

1935
String Serenade
Premiere: State Emergency Relief Administration of California [S.E.R.A.] Chamber Orchestra of San Francisco, Gastone Usigli, guest conductor.
Veteran's Auditorium, San Francisco, April 4, 1935.

1936

Tone Poem: Humanitas
Premiere: W.P.A. Federal Symphony Orchestra of Oakland,
Gastone Usigli, conductor.
Oakland Auditorium, Oakland, October 11, 1936.
Other performances:
San Francisco, December 14, 1936;
Los Angeles, March 3 and April 22, 1937;
Santa Barbara, August 1, 1937;
Marin, February 14, 1954.

1942

Symphonic Poem: Prometheus Unbound
Premiere: San Francisco Symphony Orchestra, Gastone Usigli, guest conductor.
Civic Auditorium, San Francisco, January 13, 1942.

1950

Passacaglia and Fugue
Premiere: San Francisco Symphony Orchestra, Gastone Usigli, guest conductor.
Opera House, San Francisco, February 2, 3, and 4, 1950.

1956

Rondeau Serenade
Premiere: Symphony Guild Orchestra of Marin, Gastone Usigli, conductor.
Angelico Hall, Dominican College, San Rafael, February 29, 1956
(eight days before Usigli's death on March 8, 1956).

Source:

Jean Gray Hargrove Music Library, Berkeley, California 94720-6000
http://www.lib.berkeley.edu/MUSI/

"Gastone Usigli Memorabilia and Musical Compositions 1932–1956"
Collection number: ARCHIVES USIGLI 1

Finding aid and inventory:
http://www.oac.cdlib.org/findaid/ark:/13030/tf2j49n6fj/

Photo courtesy of the Carmel Bach Festival.

Bach in Berkeley

In September 1903, at the age of 18, Dene Denny entered the freshman class at the University of California at Berkeley. In 1907 she graduated with a Bachelor of Letters in English and Philosophy, and remained in Berkeley, living at the Chi Omega sorority house, until June 1909, when she received the Master of Letters.

In the fall of 1905, at the beginning of Dene's third year, the University of California at Berkeley became one of the few North American universities with a music department. To create and head the new department, the University engaged John Frederick Wolle (pronounced "Wally"), an American conductor and brilliant organist who received his training in the US and Germany. Wolle (known as J. Fred) came to Berkeley from his home town of Bethlehem, Pennsylvania, where he was organist and choir director of the Central Moravian Church and had recently founded the Bach Choir of Bethlehem (1898) and the Bethlehem Bach Festival (1900), today the oldest Bach festival in North America.

Wolle was a musician of great skill and depth with wide-ranging musical tastes, but in Bethlehem for decades he had demonstrated a particular devotion to the music of Johann Sebastian Bach. Wolle led the American premiere of the St. John Passion in Bethlehem in 1888, followed by the American premieres of Bach's Mass in B Minor and Christmas Oratorio, and Joseph Haydn's The Creation. His Bethlehem performance of the St. Matthew Passion was among the very first in North America.

It was Wolle's Bach connection that made him especially attractive to the Berkeley administrators: cultivating the arts, they believed, was a means of developing and maintaining

an orderly and refined society, and the most powerful musical tool for this social agenda—many believed—was the music of the great J. S. Bach. In an interview in the North American Sunday, Wolle himself said he hoped that his presence in Berkeley would encourage "an awakening of the Bach cult."

Soon after his arrival on campus in the fall of 1905 (Dene's junior year), Wolle set out to establish a "great Pacific Coast Bach Chorus" of students, faculty, and local residents. He also received financial underwriting to create a professional University Orchestra. (This was several years before the creation of the San Francisco Symphony.)

With these two ensembles he performed Handel's *Messiah* in the Greek Theater at 3:00pm on Tuesday, November 27, 1906. A University announcement said the concert would feature "the University Chorus of 230 voices, assisted by the University Orchestra and trained soloists." Tickets were $1 and 75¢

Beginning with the 1906-1907 academic year, Wolle offered university classes in harmony and counterpoint, and also helped establish a series of free performances held in the Greek Theater on Sunday afternoons. (Dene performed in that series in 1919, ten years after her graduation.) With his University Orchestra, Wolle led an astounding number of instrumental concerts in a wide array of music, making him at the end of that decade one of the busiest conductors in America. He also found time to serve as organist of Berkeley's First Congregational Church.

The Great Bach Festival

During his six years at UC Berkeley, Wolle produced and conducted California's first Bach festival: in April 1909, he led a performance of the Mass in B Minor in the Greek Theater; some estimates put the attendance at 10,000, with more than 1,000 turned away.

A second "California Bach Festival" was held in May 1910, and featured the St. Matthew Passion on Saturday and the Mass in B Minor on Sunday. On the morning of the St. Matthew Passion performance, the following item appeared in the Pacific Coast Music Review.

> This afternoon is the great day. The Greek theater will be crowded with a festive throng that is eager to celebrate the advent of the second California Bach Festival under the distinguished leadership of Dr. J. Fred Wolle, the only musician in America who possesses sufficient patience and tenacity to insist upon the recognition of the matchless works of Johann Sebastian Bach.
>
> This afternoon will also settle once and for all the question of the feasibility of annual California music festivals. We sincerely believe that the people of California are eager to support events of this kind. A double chorus, a double orchestra, a children's choir of 500 schoolchildren from Oakland and Berkeley, a big pipe organ, a concert grand piano and nine efficient soloists will interpret Bach's wonderful passion music according to St. Matthew.
>
> An entire year has been devoted to the study of this work and every artistic point has been well thought out. A genuine musician cannot afford to miss this work.
>
> (Pacific Coast Music Review, May 31, 1910)

The Great
Bach Festival

Spring, 1910

St. Matthew's Passion and B Minor Mass

Under the Direction of

Dr. J. Fred Wolle,
Founder of the Bach Festival in America

An Orchestra of Sixty
A Chorus of Two Hundred and Fifty
A Children's Choir of Five Hundred
Soloists of the Highest Standing

Associate Member Five Dollars a Year,
Including Two Tickets for Each Concert
Active Members No Dues and No Initiation Fee : : : :

NOTICE TO SINGERS

Rehearsals for the great Bach Festival are taking place every Monday evening at Christian Church, Corner Dana Street and Bancroft Way, in Berkeley, and anyone sufficiently interested in the works of Johann Sebastian Bach to study the same thoroughly and participate in an Annual Festival, given in his honor, and for the purpose of permanently establishing the worth of his great Music in California, are invited to become members of the Bach Choir. Address Miss Lillian D. Clark, Secretary of the Bach Choir, 1522 Spruce Street, Berkeley, Cal. Phone Berkeley 3294.

IF THERE ARE SUFFICIENT APPLICATIONS FOR MEMBERSHIP FROM OAKLAND AND SAN FRANCISCO, REHEARSALS WILL BE HELD IN BOTH CITIES EVERY WEEK.

By the time of the second Festival in May 1910, however, the fast-growing Bay Area music world was becoming saturated with orchestras. Attendance at Wolle's concerts was falling, and the subsidies which had underwritten the startup of his professional University Orchestra had come to an end. In addition, Wolle himself was contending with sometimes vicious gossip and factionalism in the Bay Area musical world. Because he had been the most active conductor in the region for several years, he was a target for attacks in the press and backbiting in the musical community. In 1909 Ralph Metzger and the Pacific Coast Music Review had come to Wolle's defense, describing his rivals and attackers as "a number of vultures, who seek to rob the successful conqueror of the trophies which he has earned by the sweat of his brow." (PCMR, March 15, 1909)

Wolle became discouraged by the artistic jealousy and mud-slinging, and by the apparent lack of support from the University administration, and he also was concerned about the failing health of his mother in Pennsylvania. The final enticement to leave Berkeley was an invitation and offer of financial support from Charles Schwab, President of Bethlehem Steel, who wanted

Wolle to return to Bethlehem and take up his baton there once more. (There had been no Bach Festivals in Bethlehem during his absence.)

There would be no Third California Bach Festival in 1911. Instead, Wolle and his family left Berkeley in June and returned to Bethlehem, where his father and grandfather had been musicians before him. There once again he conducted the Bach Choir of Bethlehem in its annual Bach Festivals each May. Wolle died in Bethlehem on his seventieth birthday, April 4, 1933.

Epilogue in Carmel

Exactly one year later, on the central California coast where Wolle's name was known to only a few, Bethlehem was a topic of conversation. On March 29 and 30, 1934, the Carmel Music Society presented Michel Penha and the Monterey Peninsula Orchestra, Chorus, and soloists, in two rousing performances of Rossini's *Stabat Mater* in Carmel and Pacific Grove.

In the afterglow of the concert's success, Dene Denny said in an interview: "*Tonight is only the first celebration of an annual festival, destined to make our village as musically famous as Bethlehem, Pennsylvania. The outstanding Easter event on the Pacific Coast will some day be the Carmel Music Festival*" (Carmel Pine Cone, April 2, 1934). The Carmel "Music" Festival did become a reality the following year, with four days of Bach in July 1935.

Food For Thought

J. Fred. Wolle founded and chaired the UC Berkeley Music Department from 1905 to 1911, and Dene Denny attended UC Berkeley and lived adjacent to the campus from 1903 to 1909. Given Dene's love of music, the question arises: did they meet? Although their times on campus overlapped by four years, no evidence has emerged to document a meeting of the two, either in musical ensembles or in the classroom.

If this were a book of historical fiction, one might place Dene Denny—in her final spring at Berkeley—in the audience of Wolle's performance of the Mass in B Minor in 1909 in the Greek Theater, and imagine her thrill at hearing that work for the first time. Or we could imagine Dene in her junior year, among the 230 singers in the University Chorus who performed Handel's Messiah at the Greek Theater in December 1906, less than eight months after the Great Earthquake. But that would be fiction: despite all attempts the author has found no hint of any intersection in Berkeley of the lives of the founders of two of America's oldest and most distinguished Bach Festivals.

Further Reading

For more information about J. Fred. Wolle (and about the early history of the Bach Choir of Bethlehem), a splendid source is Paul J. Larson's wonderful and comprehensive book listed below. Dr. Larson is Professor emeritus, Moravian College, in Bethlehem, Pennsylvania, and serves as official historian of the Bach Choir of Bethlehem. I am grateful to have been able to draw on his thoughtful research. The book is out of print but not difficult to obtain.

The Bach Choir of Bethlehem is America's oldest Bach Choir and continues to flourish today under the leadership of Music Director Greg Funfgeld. To learn more about the Bach Choir of Bethlehem and the Bethlehem Bach Festival, you may visit their website: **www.bach.org**.

References:

Paul J. Larson. *An American Musical Dynasty: A Biography of the Wolle Family of Bethlehem, Pennsylvania.*
Bethlehem: Lehigh University Press, 2002.

Leta E. Miller. *Music and Politics in San Francisco.*
Berkeley: University of California Press 2012.

Sources accessed online:

Pacific Coast Music Review 1905-1910; *San Francisco Call.*

Images

"Music Across the Bay" graphic: Pacific Coast Music Review, 1910.

Ethel Adele Denny: UC Berkeley 1907 Senior Record.

Photograph of J. Fred Wolle: *The Outlook* (periodical), August 1, 1903

Greek Theater, Berkeley: 1907 Postcard. Performers unknown.

Advertisement for Wolle's 1910 Bach Festival at the Greek Theater: Pacific Coast Music Review, 1910.

(All images courtesy of the author.)

Concert at the Greek Theater, 1907. Performers unknown.
Courtesy of the author.

3-Minute History of Photography

Early attempts at light-sensitive material

In 1825, French inventor Nicéphore Niépce (1765-1833) captured a landscape scene which is today the oldest existing photograph produced by a camera. The "film" used was a polished pewter plate, and it required an exposure of at least an entire day and possibly several days.

In 1835, the oldest existing photographic negative was made by Englishman William Fox Talbot (1800-1877). He treated paper with silver chloride to produce durable camera negatives from which he then made contact prints, thus becoming the first to use the two-step negative-positive process which has been central to most (non-digital) photography ever since.

Positive image created directly on a metal sheet

Louis Daguerre (1787-1851), a colleague of Niépce, publicly introduced his own Daguerreotype in 1839. This process produced highly detailed permanent images on silver-plated sheets of copper. At first, an image required several minutes of exposure time, causing the subjects to sit in awkward stiffness. Chemical and optical improvements helped reduce the exposure time to a few seconds. With Daguerreotypes, photography suddenly entered the public awareness and Daguerre's process was used worldwide within a few years. By the 1850s, millions of Daguerreotypes were made in the United States each year. Daguerre gave his patented process free to the world in return for a lifetime pension from the French government.

Wet emulsion glass negatives

Frederick Scott Archer, an English sculptor, invented the "wet plate" process in 1851. It was used for making glass negatives as well as positives such as ambrotypes and tintypes, and because it was glass (rather than Talbot's paper) it was a more physically stable medium, facilitating great detail. However, after capturing the image the photographer had to develop the wet glass negative quickly before the emulsion dried. The wet plate process involved many specific, precise, and timely steps:

1. The tripod was positioned, the camera focused, and all was readied for the photograph to be taken.

2. A clean glass plate was evenly coated with a viscous solution of collodion (a flammable, syrupy solution). Then in a light-proof box or darkroom, the coated plate was immersed in a silver nitrate solution and the silver nitrate particles became suspended in the collodion, sensitizing it to light. After being removed from the silver nitrate solution, the wet glass plate was placed in a flat, light-tight plate holder and then the holder was inserted into the waiting camera.

3. One side of the plate holder was a "dark slide". Once the entire holder was inserted in the camera, the dark slide was pulled out of the camera, and at the same time the lens cap was removed, allowing light through the lens to expose the still-wet plate. After the appropriate number of seconds, the lens cap replaced, the "dark slide" was re-inserted, and the plate holder was removed from the camera. From that point, time was of the essence, and the glass negative had to be developed before the collodion solution dried.

4. In the darkroom, the glass plate negative was removed from the plate holder, developed, washed in clear water, and treated with fixer so that the image would not fade. Then it was washed again and dried. Photographers working in remote locations (such as Matthew Brady and his Civil War photos in the 1860s) traveled with some sort of portable darkroom, and developed the negatives as they took them.

5. After developing, the photographs were printed on paper.

French photographer André-Adolphe-Eugène Disdéri (1819-1889) is credited with being the first to use photography to make a carte de visite (visiting card or calling card) in 1854. A "wet plate" camera with multiple lenses captured eight different poses on one large negative. A positive was printed on albumen paper, and the images were cut apart and attached to small mounts. The fact that these photos could be reproduced at low cost and in great quantity helped bring about the decline of the daguerreotype for portraits.

Dry glass negatives

A dry emulsion for glass negatives was first developed in 1871 by Richard Maddox and refined over the next two decades. It enabled photographers to apply a gelatin emulsion to a glass plate and allow it to dry. Although still fragile, "dry plates" could be stored temporarily before and after their use in the camera. Gone was the need to rush to the darkroom to develop the wet glass negative quickly before the emulsion dried.

Stephen West Watrous, the father of Hazel Watrous, began his photography career in the 1860s with wet emulsion, but, according to Hazel, he was an early experimenter with dry emulsion in the 1870s.

Film

A clear flexible celluloid negative base was introduced in 1887, making the manufacture of roll film and movies possible.

A portrait taken by Stephen Watrous in his Visalia studio in the 1880s, using a dry glass negative. *Courtesy of the author.*

Camera

Within two years, the Kodak #1 box camera appeared. It was the first easy-to-use camera, and Kodak's slogan was: "You press the button, we do the rest." For the first time, photography was available to everyone.

New Kodak Cameras.
"*You press the button, we do the rest.*"
Seven New Styles and Sizes
ALL LOADED WITH
Transparent Films.
For Sale by all Photo. Stock Dealers.   Send for Catalogue.
THE EASTMAN COMPANY, Rochester, N. Y.

The California School of Arts and Crafts

A nuanced explanation of the Arts and Crafts Movement is far beyond the scope or intension of this book, but Hazel Watrous incorporated Arts and Crafts ideals into her print and architectural design, and she was an instructor at the summer sessions of the School of Arts and Crafts, so it is worthy of a brief mention.

An organization called the Guild of Arts and Crafts of San Francisco was founded in 1894; it was the first Arts and Crafts Society in the United States. The Arts and Crafts movement had begun a decade earlier in England, inspired by the Victorian writers John Ruskin and William Morris, who decried the mass-production of cheaply made decorative arts and architecture. Instead, they sought to raise artisans to the status of artists, to create affordable, hand-made art, and to level the hierarchy of artistic genres and mediums. While the movement flourished internationally, the Guild of Arts and Crafts of San Francisco had dissolved only a few years after its creation, the victim of internal disagreements among its members. In 1903 a new and lasting organization had replaced it, the California Guild of Arts and Crafts.

Beginning in the 1890s, high level art education in San Francisco had been centered around the California School of Design (also known as the Hopkins Institute), which, despite its name, was a school of Fine Arts. A few area colleges offered courses and degrees in the fine arts (painting, sculpture, etc.), but no Northern California institution offered courses in applied and decorative arts (design, jewelry, furniture, architecture, etc.).

German cabinetmaker Frederick Wilhelm Henry Meyer studied art in Berlin and then came to San Francisco, where he held a variety of jobs as an artist. In 1902 he left his position as Art Supervisor for the Stockton Public Schools and taught at the University of California at Berkeley and at the California School of Design in San Francisco.

In 1906 Meyer was President of the California Guild of Arts and Crafts, and at a Guild dinner a few months after the earthquake he gave a short lecture about his vision of a school that would not only teach figure and landscape painting, sculpture, etc., but also teach practical and applied design, mechanical drawing, commercial art, and all the crafts, as well as train teachers to teach these art forms. Unknown to him, a reporter was present, and an account of his talk appeared prominently in the press. To his surprise an immediate enthusiasm grew for such a school.

The California School of Arts and Crafts (today known as the California College of the Arts) held its first classes on the fifth floor of the Studio Building at Shattuck Avenue and Addison Street in Berkeley. In the first year there were three classrooms and three teachers: Meyer himself, ceramicist Rosa Taussig, and artist Perham W. Nahl. Meyer's wife, Laetitia, was the school secretary, and talented designer Isabelle Percy West joined the faculty that fall.

Frederick Meyer's goal was to give his students the sort of training that would enable them to earn a living with their art. In this he was committed to the idea that theory and practice must go hand in hand, that the artist must be an artisan and vice versa.

The Arts and Crafts Movement was a major artistic force in the early decades of the 20th century, and its influence can be seen in the work of many designers of the time, including Hazel Watrous and other Carmel architects.

References

This is a select, annotated list of principal resources on which Carmel Impresarios is based. It is by no means a complete list of all sources consulted in the writing of this book; only the most important are included here. The intention is to point the interested reader/researcher toward accessible and productive sources of information.

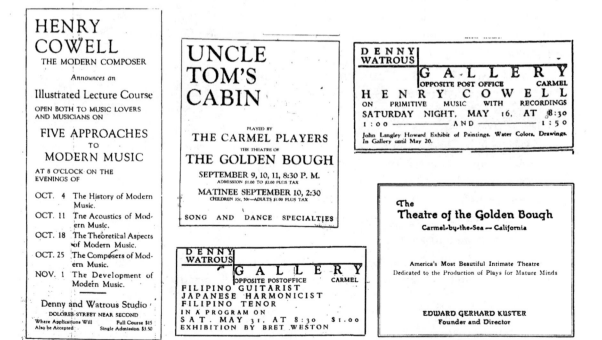

General Sources

The Six Carmel Newspapers:

Microfilms in the archives of the Henry Meade Williams Local History Roomof the Harrison Memorial Library, Carmel

The Carmel Pine Cone: 1915–present
The Carmel Cymbal: 1926–1941
The Carmelite: 1928–1932
The Carmel Spectator: 1949–1955
The Californian: Late 1930s (An unrelated Californian is published in Salinas today.)
The Carmel Sun: appeared briefly in the 1930s

Other Newspapers

Most of these newspapers were accessed online (see below).
San José Mercury, San Francisco Call, San Francisco Chronicle, San Francisco Daily News, Los Angeles Times, Monterey Herald, New York Times, Santa Cruz Sentinel, the Yreka Journal, and many others

Books

The *Images of America* Series
Arcadia Publishing, Charlestown, South Carolina www.arcadiapublishing.com
This is a well-known and wonderful series of photo-centered books, and a great way to get a feel for the history of a place. Volumes in this series which are relevant to the subject matter of "Carmel Impresarios" include: *Carmel-by-the-Sea; Carmel–a History in Architecture; Hotel Del Monte; Pacific Grove; Monterey; Seaside; Capitola; Carmel Valley; Santa Clara; Timbuctoo and Smartsville;* and *Visalia.*

Bostick, Daisy, and Dorothea Castelhun. *Carmel at Work and Play.*
Carmel, CA: Seven Arts, 1925. Republished in the 1970s. Out of print.

Online Resources

The internet is a wonderful source of information, and offers access—mostly through genealogy websites—to an ever-increasing array of public records and databases. The best services are not free; the author subscribes to Ancestry.com, but is not affiliated with it. Fee-based websites such as Ancestry.com give access to online research tools useful for all historians:

Federal, state and local databases such as Federal Census records; Voter Registration; Birth, Marriage and Death Records; etc.

Annual City Directories: (the "phone book" before the telephone): San Francisco, Oakland, Alameda, Monterey County, and others were used extensively for this book.

North American digitized newspapers:

www.newspapers.com
www.genealogybank.com
California Digital Newspaper Collection www.cdnc.ucr.edu

Other online archives of primary source information:

The Internet Archive www.archive.org
Online Archive of California www.oac.cdlib.org
California Genealogical Society www.californiaancestors.org
Library of Congress www.loc.gov

San Francisco Earthquake

Virtual Museum of the City of San Francisco
www.sfmuseum.org/1906/06.html

The website of the National Archives of the United States
www.archives.gov/exhibits/sf-earthquake-and-fire/

The permanent online earthquake exhibit from the Bancroft Library of UC Berkeley:
www.bancroft.berkeley.edu/collections/earthquakeandfire/index2.html

Everett, Marshall, ed. *Complete Story of the San Francisco Earthquake*
Henry Neal, Chicago, 1906
This is one of many books hastily published in the summer of 1906. It is a compilation of essays, eye witness descriptions, first person accounts, and often lurid lithographs and illustrations. The author has several such books, but this is his favorite. The subtitle is typical of the overwrought language used to sell books like this:

"Embracing a Full Account in Pictures and Story of the Awful Disaster that Befell the City of San Francisco and all the other Towns and Cities shocked by the fatal Earthquake, and illustrated with a Vast Gallery of Startling Pictures."

Public transportation in San Francisco before the bridges

Until the mid 1930s there were no bridges across San Francisco Bay, and the available public transportation for commuters was one of the most extensive systems in the world. The information available on this subject online and in print is limitless, and the cable cars, trolleys, and ferries still operating in San Francisco serve as a living museum.

For lots of details and good photos, one excellent online source is:

The Cable Car Guy Website (Trolleys, Cable Cars, and Ferries)
www.cable-car-guy.com

Charles F. Heath. *Bridging The Bay With Our Ferries: The Development of the World's Largest Ferry System.*
This comprehensive article about the ferries was written in 1921 by the Southern Pacific Railroad Superintendent, and is available on the Cable Car Guy website.
San Francisco-Southern Pacific Bulletin, March 1921.
Online at www.cable-car-guy.com/ferry/html/sp_bridging.html
(accessed December 18, 2013)

Determining birthdates

Written records disagree about Dene and Hazel's birth years. Most modern sources say they both were born in 1888, but research for this book shows that to be an impossibility. The error first appears in the April 1930 Federal Census, which asked for age at last birthday. Dene and Hazel gave their ages as "42," making their birth year 1888 or posibly 1887. But at the time of the 1930 census, Hazel actually was 46 and Dene was 45. Early census records (1900, 1910) and other documents make it clear that Dene was born on February 11, 1885. Nonetheless, "1888" appears on the headstone Dene shares with Hazel in the Monterey City Cemetery.

The 1930 census error mentioned above also applied to Hazel. The 1900 Federal Census asked for the month and year of birth as well as the "age at last birthday," and "Feb 1884" and "age 16" are given for Hazel. The 1910 and 1920 census data agree. In the Federal Census in April 1930, Hazel gave her age as "42," which would make her birth year 1888. If true, then she would have enrolled in teacher's college at age 12, hardly a possibility. As with Dene, Hazel's new birth year of 1888 seems to have agreed with her, and it is found in the California and federal databases as well as in Edan Milton Hughes' 1989 book, "Artists in California, 1786–1940." Her headstone in the Monterey City Cemetery gives her birth year incorrectly as 1888.

Dene Denny

Early influence of music as a child in Siskiyou.

Henry Cowell recalling a conversation with Alan Lomax, who had spoken with Dene

Piano Performances 1909-1932

Berkeley Daily Gazette, Carmel Carmelite, Carmel Cymbal, Carmel Pine Cone, Carmel Spectator, Los Angeles Times, Monterey Herald, Pacific Coast Music Review, San José Mercury, San Francisco Call, Stockton Daily Evening Record, Yreka Journal

Wager Swayne student recital info 1920-1923

Pacific Coast Music Review; San Francisco Call
Patterson's American Education, Volume 2, by Homer L. Patterson

"Kohler and Chase Building at 26 O'Farrell Street"

Pacific Coast Music Review (The building is still standing today.)

The nickname "Dene"

Where did Ethel Adele Denny get the nickname Dene? The following is pure speculation.

In the English language, the word "dene" is an archaic traditional word for "valley," especially a wooded valley. In this sense it is frequently found as a component of English place-names, such as Rottingdean and Ovingdean. A "hazeldene" is a valley filled with hazel bushes. The Druids believed hazel nuts conferred wisdom and a hazeldene was looked upon as a special place.

In England there is a town called Hazeldene, and there are countless Hazeldene Streets, Roads, Alleys, Courts, Drives, and Lanes, in various versions and spellings: Hazeldene, Hazel Dene, Hazelden, Hazlingden, Hazeltine, Heseltine, Hazelton, et al. There are English businesses and organizations that use the name Hazeldene, including a Hazeldene lettuce distributor, Hazeldene school, and multiple Hazeldene Parks. There also are three towns named Hazeldene in Australia, and one in South Africa.

During the 19th and well into the 20th century census records show that "Hazel Dene" was widely used as a first–middle name combination for women in the UK and the United States: Hazel Dene Rogers, Hazel Dene Smith, Hazel Dene Purvis, etc. ("Dene" also appears in many other first/middle name combinations, but the frequency of "Hazel Dene" is noticeable.)

A second clue: Dene's actual name was Ethel Adele Denny, but for more than a decade during her college and early professional years, she added an accent over the third letter in her middle name: Adèle. This diacritical accent does not exist in the English language and surely didn't come from Siskiyou County. Dene was "dressing up" her name, as if "Ethel Adele" was too plain. If she was bored with her given names, she might have been receptive to a nickname.

(1915 Lick-Wilmerding High School yearbook. Courtesy of the author.)

Perhaps someone, somewhere, saw Hazel and Ethel together in the mid 1920s and made a witty mental association; perhaps a silly joke was made at a party; perhaps in New York in 1926 an English friend gave Ethel a new nickname; perhaps Ethel thought it up herself; or perhaps it was an chance incident so oddly simple, complex, or random, that one would never think of it. In any event, 90 years later, we have only a weak etymology-based hypothesis, but that doesn't mean it's not worth thinking about.

Gastone Usigli

There is no single source of information about Gastone Usigli, and his depiction in this book is drawn from dozens of places. He is mentioned in three superb books listed elsewhere in these End Notes: *The Dream Endures*, by Kevin Starr; *Music and Politics in San Francisco*, by Leta E. Miller; and *All This Music Belongs to the Nation*, by Kenneth Bindas.

Usigli is mentioned in scores of articles in the local Carmel press 1935-1956, most of which are either advance notices of upcoming concerts or reviews of those concerts. This material offers excellent but brief profiles, interviews, and articles based on interviews, all of which combine to paint a picture of Usigli professionally and personally. *The following are among the most helpful profiles of Usigli.*

Carmel Pine Cone, July 19, 1935 and July 17, 1942

Carmel Cymbal July 17, 1941. and 1938–1942 in general.

San Francisco Chronicle, March 9, 1956 (obituary)

Gastone Usigli's extensive professional archives are in the Bancroft Library at UC Berkeley. A finding aid is available online:

www.oac.cdlib.org/findaid/ark:/13030/tf2j49n6fj/admin/

Sandor Salgo

The best way to learn about Maestro Salgo's life is to read it in his own words.

Sandor Salgo. *Teaching Music at Stanford, 1949–1974, Directing the Carmel Bach Festival and the Marin Symphony, 1956–1991*

Oral history transcript, with an introduction by Robert P. Commanday.

Interviews conducted by Caroline C. Crawford in 1994–1996.

Regional Oral History Office, The Bancroft Library, University of California, Berkeley, 1999.

Full text available online: www.archive.org/details/teachingmusic00salgrich

Sandor Salgo wrote this elegant book when he was in his 90s:

Sandor Salgo. *Thomas Jefferson: Musician and Violinist.*
Chapel Hill: The University of North Carolina Press, 2001.

Michel Penha

After leaving the narrative in this book in 1939, Michel Penha lived a long life and was an active chamber and orchestral musician well into his 70s. In the following decades he was a member of eminent West Coast ensembles including the Abas Quartet; the California Quartet; the San Francisco String Quartet; the Roussel Trio with Doriot Anthony, flutist, and Harry Rumpler viola; the Los Angeles Bach Ensemble; the California Trio; and the Penstamur Trio. He also organized and directed several series of Bach concerts in Pasadena and had a long career as a studio musician MGM Studio in Hollywood. How the West Was Won, Ben Hur, and An American in Paris are among Penha's many film soundtrack credits. Michel Penha died in Los Angeles in 1982 at the age of 93.

Dana Carlile's book about the Neah-Kah-Nie Quartet contains valuable information about Michel Penha's career, especially in the 1930s.

The website www.stokowski.org has complete rosters of seven major US orchestras, including Philadelphia and San Francisco. Both have bios of Penha.

Internet genealogy and newspaper research provided the rest.

Noel Sullivan

Virginia W. Stone. *The Master of Hollow Hills*
Noticias del Puerto de Monterey: A Quarterly Bulletin of Historic Monterey
Monterey History and Art Association, June 1986.

Langston Hughes friendship
http://users.rcn.com/jazzinfo/v09n01May99/LangstonHughes.html

Langston Hughes. *I Wonder as I Wander: An Autobiographical Journey*
Hill & Wang, 1993

"Forty five guests for dinner..." and other Hollow Hills details
Arnold Rampersad. *The Life of Langston Hughes*, Vol 1

Carmelite Monastery, Carmel, California
www.carmelitesistersbythesea.net
Noel Sullivan paid for the construction of the monastery in 1931, and is interred there.

Music in California 1900–1950

Books

Kevin Starr. The Dream Endures: California Enters the 1940s
Oxford University Press, 2002

Leta E. Miller. *Music and Politics in San Francisco: From the 1906 Quake to the Second World War*
University of California Press, 2011.

"Music Comes to Main Street"
From: *Music as a Social Force in America & The Science of Practice*
Robert Haven Schauffler and Sigmund Spaeth. New York, The Caxton Institute, 1927.

Kenneth Bindas. *All This Music Belongs to the Nation: The WPA's Federal Music Project and American Society*
Univ of Tennessee Press, 2003.

Dana Carlile. *Susie Fennell Pipes and the Neah-Kah-Nie String Quartet*
Privately published, 2011. Out-of-print.
Fine depiction of the typical life of a professional musician on the West Coast in the late 19th and early 20th centuries.

Online

Music and Dance in California and the West
(Originally published by the Bureau of Musical Research, Los Angeles, 1948)
Musical America Magazine online archives
Pacific Coast Musical Review, 1907-1930

Craig H. Roell, "Federal Music Project"
Handbook of Texas Online
http://www.tshaonline.org/handbook/online/articles/xmf01
Published by the Texas State Historical Association. Accessed January 31, 2014.

Regional Oral History Office
Bancroft Library, University of California, Berkeley.
www.bancroft.berkeley.edu/collections/roho.html
    Johann Hagemeyer (Photographer, lived in early Carmel)
    Elsie Whitaker Martinez (Knew many SF writers and theater people)
    Sandor Salgo (Music Director, Carmel Bach Festival 1956–1991)
    James Schwabacher (Tenor soloist at many Carmel Bach Festivals)
    Madi Bacon (Ernst Bacon's sister, founder of the SF Boy's Choir)

The Little Theater Movement

Dorothy Chansky. *Composing Ourselves: The Little Theatre Movement and the American Audience*
Carbondale: Southern Illinois University Press, 2005.
A wonderful volume in a great series of books.

Kenneth Macgowan. *Footlights Across America: Towards a National Theater*
New York: Harcourt Brace & Company, 1929

Academy Award winning producer, director. In 1928 and 1929 he traveled 14,000 miles to make a survey of the current state of theater in America. Great descriptions of current events, and many photos, floor plans and schematics of theaters. 1930s originals or digitized copies of this book are easy to locate by searching online for the title.

Bill Bryson. *One Summer: America, 1927.*
New York: Doubleday, 2013
One of Bryson's finest books, this is a vivid and detailed wide-angle snapshot of a fascinating time.

Theater in Carmel

Morgan Evans Stock. *The Carmel Theater from 1910–1935*
Dept. Of Speech and Drama, Stanford University: Unpublished master's thesis, 1952,
Courtesy of the Henry Meade Williams Local History Room of the Harrison Memorial Library.

Morgan Stock's unpublished thesis is the only comprehensive study of the history of theater in Carmel-by-the-Sea. It includes a list of every play produced on the stages of Carmel between 1907 and 1950. Stock also interviewed several people who participated in productions at the original Theatre of the Golden Bough, including Edward Kuster. The thesis contains a few minor errors of dates and chronology which in no way diminish its great value and usefulness as a source of information and insight.

The Theatre of the Golden Bough

Edward G. Kuster's scrapbooks and theater ephemera are in the archives of the Henry Meade Williams Local History Room of the Harrison Memorial Library in Carmel. The author made many wonderful discoveries in Kuster's memorabilia, especially:

Photos of the exterior and interior of the Theatre of the Golden Bough.

San Francisco Chronicle article by Redfern Mason about the Theatre and its first production.

The original letter sent by Hazel Watrous and Dene Denny to Edward Kuster, May 28, 1928.

Susan Porter. "The Theatre of the Golden Bough."
Theatre Arts Magazine, Feb 25, 1925, p96
Porter was well acquainted with Carmel theater, and her articles and reviews appeared in the Pine Cone in the 1920s and 1930s.

The town meeting at the Theatre of the Golden Bough, March 1, 1928

Perry Newberry published a detailed account in the Pine Cone as seen from his point of view, including the fact that his friends left him sitting alone. Two other contemporary accounts, in the Pine Cone and the Carmelite, describe the arrangement of the participants in the auditorium, the agenda and order of discussion, and the mood and tone of voice. In addition to these contemporary accounts, this stormy meeting was referenced several times in the local press over the next few months and once again in June 1929.

The Ultra-Moderns

Arma, Edmée; Arma, Paul (Imre Weisshaus). *Mémoirs a deux voix*
Unpublished, 1945. Accessible online, various sources.

Michael Broyles. *Mavericks and Other Traditions in American Music*
New Haven, Conn, and London: Yale University Press 2004.

Michael Broyles and Denise Von Glahn. *Leo Ornstein: Modernist Dilemmas, Personal Choices.*
Indiana University Press 2007.

Frederick H. Martens. *Leo Ornstein, the man, his ideas, his work*
Published in 1918. Available online or as digital reprint.

Rita H. Mead. *Henry Cowell's New Music, 1925–1936*
UMI Research Press, Ann Arbor Michigan, 1981, 1978.

Leta E. Miller. *Music and Politics in San Francisco: From the 1906 Quake to the Second World War*
University of California Press, 2011.

Deborah Rifkin. *Making it Modern: Chromaticism and Phrase Structure in Twentieth-Century*

Tonal Music.
Theory and Practice, Vol. 31, (2006), pp. 133-158.
Published by: Music Theory Society of New York State
JSTOR stable URL: http://www.jstor.org/stable/41054376
Accessed October 2013.

Nicolas Slonimsky, Laura Diane Kuhn, ed. *Baker's Biographical Dictionary of Musicians*
Ninth edition, Schirmer Books (2001)
OCLC 44972043; ISBN 0-02-865525-7; ISBN 9780028655253
Ninth edition, eBook (copyright 2001; eBook released 2007)
 ISBN 978-0-02-866091-2; ISBN 0028660919

Leo Treitler, ed. *Source Readings in Music History*
Oliver Strunk. Sixth Edition. New York: W W Norton & Company, 1998.

"Henry Cowell's Imprisonment"
Oxford University Press Blog post by Joel Sachs Tues Sept 25, 2012
www.blog.oup.com/2012/09/henry-cowells-imprisonment/

Schönberg/Schoenberg spelling.
During the Nazi regime, Arnold Schönberg's music was among the works labeled by the Nazis as "Degenerate Art." He fled Germany in 1934, and after arriving in the United States he altered the spelling of his surname to Schoenberg and became a US citizen. That spelling is used in this book.

Monterey Peninsula and Carmel

Natural history

The elevation of the Monterey Peninsula ranges from 0 to 825 feet (250 meters), and the climate is a cool Mediterranean type, strongly influenced by the prevailing winds from the West. The winds are cooled when they pass over the Pacific Coast's Alaska currents and the cold water welling up from the submarine canyons just off Monterey Bay. The weather on the Peninsula is noted for its cool, humid summers, frequently bathed by sea fog. The variety of natural habitats offers a wide array of flora, including a notably high number of shrubs and trees known only on the Peninsula.

Cupressus macrocarpa
(Monterey Cypress, Macrocarpa)

Willis Linn Jepson, co-founder of the Sierra Club with John Muir and Warren Olney, was professor of biology at UC Berkeley for four decades. In the early 1900s he realized the importance of the diverse and unusual tree and flora population on the Monterey Peninsula. He encouraged Samuel F. B. Morse of the Del Monte Properties Company to explore the possibilities of preserving the wooded environment. Today it is known as the Del Monte Forest, and most of it is included in a private community known as Pebble Beach.

Cupressus macrocarpa (Monterey Cypress, Macrocarpa) is a species of cypress confined to two small protected groves in the Del Monte Forest, and in Point Lobos Reserve and Carmel Highlands just to the south. (The famous and often-photographed "Lone Pine" on the 17–Mile–Drive is not a pine at all. It is really a Monterey cypress.)

The pine forest habitat on the peninsula is dominated by the actual Monterey pine (Pinus radiatus). Curiously, this species is also native only to the Monterey Peninsula. Two small stands grow 50 miles north of Monterey and 100 miles south, and stands also grow on two remote islands off the coast of Mexico.

Other Del Monte Forest flora include the Knobcone Pine and Bishop Pine, the rare Monterey manzanita, and the endangered Hickman's potentilla and Yadon's piperia. Rare plants in the Monterey Peninsula chaparral habitat are Hickman's onion, Sandmat manzanita, Hutchinson's larkspur, Tidestrom lupine; Gardner's yampah and Monterey Knotweed.

Willis Linn Jepson co-founded the Sierra Club with John Muir and Warren Olney, and was professor of biology at UC Berkeley for four decades. In the early 1900s he became convinced of the importance of preserving the unusually diverse tree and flora population on the Monterey Peninsula. He encouraged Samuel F. B. Morse of the Del Monte Properties Company to explore the possibilities of preserving the distinctive wooded environment.

Today the forests of the Monterey Peninsula are known as the Del Monte Forest, and most of it is included in a private community known as Pebble Beach.

Junípero Serra and the Carmel Mission

Online

Mission San Carlos Borroméo del río Carmelo
Official website: www.carmelmission.org

Collection of old photographs in the Calisphere online archive
www.calisphere.universityofcalifornia.edu/
(From their homepage, search for Carmel Mission)

SFMuseum: the Virtual Museum of the City of San Francisco
http://www.sfmuseum.net/bio/jserra.html
(From the SFMuseum home page, a search for Serra produces a list of other related information on that site.)

In Print

Carmel-by-the-Sea; Carmel: a history in architecture; Carmel Valley.
Images of America Series, Arcadia Publishing.

San Carlo Borromeo

Carlo Borromeo (1538–1584) was born in a castle near Milan into one of the most wealthy and ancient families in Northern Italy. Martin Luther had written his famous Ninety-Five Theses just 21 years before, and Protestantism was already making inroads on the primacy of the Catholic church. At the age of 26 Borromeo was appointed Archbishop of Milan by his uncle Pope Pius IV, and he went on to become a leading reformer of the Catholic church in response to the rise of Protestantism. Following his death, popular devotion to Borromeo grew quickly and support began gathering for his sainthood. On November 1, 1610, Carlo Borromeo was canonized by Pope Paul V.

19th and early 20th century Carmel

Libraries

The Henry Meade Williams Local History Room of the Harrison Memorial Library
Sixth Avenue and Mission Street, Carmel
Website: www.hm-lib.org
Carmel-by-the-Sea has a very fine library, staffed by people who apparently love what they do.

Bancroft Library, University of California, Berkeley.
Regional Oral History Office www.bancroft.berkeley.edu/ROHO/
Interview with Johan Hagemeyer, Madi Bacon, James Schwabacher, Sandor Salgo, and others.

Books

Carmel; Carmel Valley; Monterey; Monterey's Hotel del Monte.
Images of America Series, Arcadia Publishing.

Ray A. March. *River in Ruin: the story of the Carmel River*
Bison Books, 2012.
A fabulous history of the Monterey Peninsula told from the point of view of water usage. Also available as eBook.

Monterey Peninsula
Compiled by Northern California Writers' Project of the WPA
Part of the American Guide Series, 1946 (available in modern reprints)

John Steinbeck. *Cannery Row.*

Jack London. *Valley of the Moon.*

Stephen Allen Reynolds. *Carmel–its poets and peasants* [out of print]
Bohemian Press, 1925

James Karman (Editor). *The Collected Letters of Robinson Jeffers, with Selected Letters of Una Jeffers: Volume One, 1890-1930*
Stanford University Press, 2009
Jeffers attended the Carmel Bach Festival and was a friend of Noel Sullivan.

Online

Southern California Architectural History
www.so-cal-arch-history.com
A wealth of early twentieth century Carmel history is discussed in these fine essays by John Crosse. Accessed December 2013.

Carmel Valley Association
www.carmelvalleyassociation.org
Carmel River History (pdf) available for download:
www.carmelvalleyassociation.org/assetts/docs/CV_Voices/Carmel_River_History.pdf
Accessed October 2013

The First Art Gallery in Carmel

The art gallery designed by Denny-Watrous in 1926 is described in a dozen Pine Cone articles and as many display advertisements over a period of nine months.

Information about the history of the Carmel Art Association came from Carmel Pine Cone archives and from the CAA's publications and website: **www.carmelart.org**

Carmel Bach Festival Sources

Most of the Carmel Bach Festival's 1930 and 1940 archival material is in the H. M. Williams Local History Room of the Harrison Memorial Library in Carmel. Those holdings include programs, ephemera, press clippings, and dozens of important photos, many of which are shown in these pages.

The Carmel Bach Festival's own archive provided about two dozen photos, a few of its earliest programs, and other bits of ephemera. Most of the Bach Festival's archival collection is from the late 1950s onward, and consists of countless photos, slides, press clippings, and program books.

The official Carmel Bach Festival website: **www.bachfestival.org**

Carmel Music Society Sources

The Carmel Music Society's scrapbooks and files contain a wealth of primary source material including decades of printed programs and other artist marketing material, photographs, press clippings, ephemera, and the minutes of the Society's first several years of operation. Those two dozen typewritten pages contain a fascinating and detailed week-by-week account of the Society's creation and early operation.

A smaller but valuable archive of similar material (with few duplicates) is held in the H. M. Williams Local History Room of the Harrison Memorial Library in Carmel.

An insightful article in Gallery Magazine, March 16, 1997, by Barbara Rose Shuler also contained some new details that inspired productive research for this book.

The official Carmel Music Society website: **www.carmelmusic.org**

19th century general research

Albert Hendrickson Denny and Siskiyou County

Several detailed accounts of A. H. Denny's life, including his journey on the Oregon Trail, were written during his lifetime and are a goldmine of information about this impressive fellow. Albert deserves his own book.

Gardner Landon. *Albert Hendrickson Denny, a research project*
(Landon was the husband of A. H. Denny's youngest daughter Sylvia)
Unpublished 40-page footnoted manuscript (1990) provided by the Siskiyou Historical Society, Yreka.

Harry L. Wells. *History of Siskiyou County, California* (1881)
A large work which includes detailed biographies of prominent citizens. It was published in 1881, one year after A. H. Denny's first wife died, and one year before he met and married the future mother of Dene Denny.

The Siskiyou Pioneer
The annual publication for members of the Siskiyou County Historical Society.
Numerous editions 1956-2013 provided a wealth of information including several articles by sons and daughters of A. H. Denny.
Siskiyou County Historical Society
www.siskiyoucountyhistoricalsociety.org
910 S. Main Street, Yreka, CA 96097 (530) 842-3836

Books:

Gail L. Fiorini-Jenner and Monica Jae Hall. *Western Siskiyou County: Gold and Dreams*
Arcadia Publishing. ISBN-13: 978-0738523972
A wonderful account of Siskiyou and Scott Valley history, this is one of the books that inspired "Carmel Impresarios."

Joaquin Miller. *Life Amongst the Modocs.*
Semi-autobiographical novel (pub. 1873) based on Miller's years in the mining towns and Indian camps of northern California during the 1850s. The text is public domain and available online.
Free eBook: www.archive.org/details/amongstthemodocs00millrich
Paperback: ISBN: 978-0930588793, Heyday Press, 1996

The Jefferds and Watrous Families

Tulare County Historical Society
PO Box 295, Visalia 93279
559.635.4896
www.tularecountyhistoricalsociety.org

"Autobiography of Forrest Gooch Jefferds,
as dictated to his daughter Minnie Watrous"
(ca 1895)
Bulletin of the SCCHGS (April and July, 1978 issues)
Other information is available online:
Santa Clara County History and Genealogical Society
www.scchgs.org

Capitola Historical Museum
410 Capitola Avenue Capitola, CA 95010
http://www.capitolamuseum.org

Early ad for the trans-isthmus railroad.
Courtesy of the author.

Walking to California in the 1850s

The so-called "Oregon Trail" was at first just a string of rivers and natural landmarks that (with luck) could be followed for 2,000 miles from Missouri to Oregon. The overland travelers— known as "Emigrants"— began trailblazing to the Pacific Coast around 1840 with the rise of "Oregon Fever," a craze for homesteading in Oregon created by (wildly) optimistic descriptions of the region. In 1847 the Mormon Exodus began, following the Oregon Trail until it reached Western Wyoming, where the Mormon Trail forked southwest to the Salt Lake Valley. By 1848, 5,000 emigrants had followed the trails to Salt Lake, 10,000 to Oregon, and 2,000 to California.

But those numbers are meagre in comparison to what happened after gold was discovered in California in 1848: suddenly it was as if the whole continent had tilted westward and the population began sliding toward the Pacific Ocean.

From 1848 until 1870 more than 500,000 people journeyed west on the Oregon Trail to California, the Pacific Northwest, and Utah. The heaviest travel took place in 1852, when Albert and Edgar Denny were among the 70,000 emigrants who followed the trail across Wyoming's South Pass on their way west.

But even as the number of travelers increased there still was no easy way to get to California, and emigrants always faced hardship and risked death. Estimates vary, but as many as 1 in 10 emigrants died during the trip. The leading cause of death was being run over by a wagon wheel. Accidental firearm injury was the second leading cause, the third leading cause was stampeding livestock. Cholera was the most terrifying ailment on the trail, especially 1849-1853, when it killed at least 7,000 travelers. The primary threat from Indians, especially in Wyoming and Nebraska, was theft of possessions and livestock. Only a very small number of emigrants actually died as a result of encounters with Native Americans.

Some emigrants, like Albert and Edgar Denny, started from their homes with their oxen, wagon, and most of their supplies. But others traveled light to one of the river towns of Independence and St. Joseph on the Missouri, or St. Louis and other towns further north of it along the Mississippi.

In these places families and smaller groups congregated and prepared for the four-to-six month trek. They acquired the rest of their supplies, and some needed a week or two to train their new oxen. For many emigrants, the jumping off town was the last "city" they would see not only on their journey but for the rest of their lives.

In the early spring, wagon trains were forced to wait in these towns until the scouts came back with the report that the grass was high enough to support the livestock on the way. At that point, usually mid-May, the first wagons headed west and slowly the others followed, at about 2 miles per hour all the way to Oregon.

The 1840s emigrant Francis Parkman describes the typical jumping-off town.

> "A multitude of shops had sprung up to furnish emigrants with necessaries for the journey. The streets were thronged with men, horses and mules. There was an incessant hammering and banging from a dozen blacksmiths' sheds, where the heavy wagons were being repaired, and the horses and oxen shod. While I was in the town, a train of emigrant wagons from Illinois passed through--a multitude of healthy children's faces were peeking out from under the covers of the wagons."

> (Francis Parkman, The Oregon Trail: Sketches of Prairie and Rocky-Mountain Life (also published as The California & Oregon Trail). Accessed online.

The length of the trip varied greatly due to weather, illness, and accident, but from the jumping-off town to Oregon or California the average journey took around 5 months. About 1 out of every 250 travelers kept a written diary, so there is a wealth of information about the trails in bookstores, libraries, and online.

Annual travel on the Oregon Trail

1812-1848: 5,000 to Salt Lake; 10,000 to Oregon; 2,000 to California.

1849: Perhaps as many as 40,000.

1850: 65,000. The most disastrous of the migration years with nearly 5,000 deaths from cholera.

1851: Fewer than 10,000.

1852: Close to 70,000.

1853: About 35,000.

1854: Some 20,000, with over half going to California and the rest to Utah.

1855: The majority of an estimated 7,000 went to Utah.

1856: An estimated 12,000; two-thirds went to California.

1857: Not more than 6,000, with two-thirds again going to California.

1858: An estimated 7,500.

1859: 20,000 to California/Oregon/Utah; 60,000 to Colorado after discovery of gold there.

1860: Around 20,000. Harder to compute; more of an estimate other years.

1861: Fewer than 10,000.

1862: About 20,000. The increase was caused by discovery of silver and gold in Montana and eastern Oregon.

1863: About 20,000.

1864: About 40,000; most to Montana.

1865: Did not exceed 20,000; most traveled to Colorado and Utah.

1866: 25,000

[Source: Merrill Mattes, Platte River Narratives, pp. 2-5]

Days on the trail

Average length of the journey from Independence, Missouri to California or to Oregon:

1841-1848: California: 157 days; Oregon: 169 days

1849: California: 131; Oregon: 129

1850: California: 107; Oregon: 125

1850-60: California: 112; Oregon: 128

1841-1860: California: 121; Oregon: 139

[Source: John Unruh, Jr. The Plains Across: The Overland Emigrants and the Trans-Mississippi West, 1840-60, p. 403]

[Note: In 1852, Albert and Edgar Denny originated their trip in Milwaukee, thus adding another 70+ days to the numbers above. They actually took around 210 days to journey from Milwaukee, Wisconsin to Yreka, California.]

National Historic Trails Information

Armchair travelers and actual explorers can find a huge amount of information online. Of particular interests are the organizations that retrace the routes and post photos on their websites (see below).

In some cases, the best route in 1850 is still the best route today, and some stretches of the National Historic Trails are paralleled today by interstate and state highways, and other portions are near main roads and are easily accessible by car or on foot. The websites below offer information about the trails, and detailed guides for following the general route of the various trails by car.

National Park Service

www.nps.gov/
From the main nps.gov home page, use the Search feature to find the wealth of information here on the Overland Trails. Accessed December, 2013.

Oregon-California Trails Association

http://www.octa-trails.org
The nation's largest and most influential organization dedicated to the preservation and protection of overland emigrant trails and the emigrant experience. Wonderful source of information. Accessed December, 2013.

Trails West

http://emigranttrailswest.org
Founded in 1970, Trails West, Inc. is a non-profit organization of emigrant trail enthusiasts who research, locate and mark emigrant trails, and then publish guides to interpret them. Like the O-C Trails website above, this website is filled with fine resources and links. Accessed December, 2013.

Books about the Trails

There are so many fine modern books about the Oregon Trail that it is pointless to begin listing them here. Readers wishing to learn more about the trails may choose from a staggering array of first-hand accounts, historic studies, and historical fiction. Nonetheless, here is fine current book about the entire trail system, and two early 20th century volumes.

Arthur King Peters. Seven Trails West
Abbeville Press (1996) ISBN: 978-1558597822
A comprehensive and beautifully written book about all the overland trails.

W. J. Ghent. The Road to Oregon
Tudor Publishing Co; New York, 1934
Comprehensive early-20th century book on the Oregon Trail, but prejudiced against Native Americans.

Hiram Martin Chittenden. *The American Fur Trade of the Far West*
R.R. Wilson, Inc, New York, 1936
An excellent early 20th century book, with flavor and first-hand reports. Subsequent research has shown the book to contain small errors in both text and notes.

Sailing to California in the 1850s

Especially in the late 1840s and 1850s, at least half of the those who traveled to California from the East Coast traveled by sea. In the mid-19th century, a voyage from New York around the tip of South America and then north to San Francisco could last five to eight months and cover nearly 20,000 miles.

An alternative was to sail from New York to the mouth of the Chagres River on the Atlantic side of the Isthmus of Panama (7–10 days). Then a week would be spent in canoes, pole boats and on mules traveling up the river and across the isthmus, through a jungle infested with alligators, mosquitos and sand flies. Finally the travelers could "lay up" in Panama City on the Pacific side, recuperate from the jungle trek, and wait for a ship heading for San Francisco. This New York–Panama–San Francisco journey took four to five weeks, but it was shortened by at least a week when the Panama Rail Road opened in 1855.

Passenger manifests and ship information

www.sfgenealogy.com
A special niche website for genealogy and history in the greater San Francisco region. Their "California Bound" page has links to databases of travelers arriving in San Francisco by ship. Also has description and details of the Isthmus crossings.

www.maritimeheritage.org
The Maritime Heritage Project is an archive of information about travelers and ships sailing from world seaports into San Francisco Bay during the 1800s. A marvelous resource of data about people and vessels.

Voyages mentioned in this book

Forrest Gooch Jefferds
September-October 1851, NY to San Francisco

1. From New York to Chagres, ship unknown

2. Across the isthmus by canoe and on foot

3. From Panama City to San Francisco on the Republic
Launched in 1849; wooden hull; steam engine; twin side paddles and a propeller.
This journey is described in detail in the autobiography Jefferds dictated to his daughter, Minnie.

Amasa and Sally Ann Denny and 12 family members
May-June 1857, NY to San Francisco

1. From NY to Chagres, ship unknown

2. Across the isthmus by canoe and on foot.

3. From Panama City to San Francisco on the Brother Jonathan *(see image on next page)*
Launched in New York in 1850, operated by the California Steam Navigation Company. 1181 tons, 221 feet long, propelled by twin side paddles as well as sails on two masts. Her hull was made of white oak, live oak, locust and cedar. She had two decks, two masts, round stern, and a sharp bow. Her main salon was 70 feet long with 12 staterooms on each side, and she had berths for 365 passengers.

Albert and Eliza Denny
May 1865, NY to San Francisco

1. From New York to Chagres on the Ocean Queen

Launched in 1857 as Queen of the Pacific. 2,801 gross ton ship, with a length of 327 feet and a beam measuring 42 feet. It had a straight stern, two stacks, and two masts. Her hull was wood, with twin side-paddle, and a speed of 12 knots. There were staterooms and berths for a total of 350 1st & 2nd class passengers.

2. Panama Railroad from Chagres to Panama City

3. From Panama City to San Francisco on the Constitution

Launched New York in 1850, it had twin side paddles and two masts for sails. It operated up and down the West Coast by the Pacific Mail Steamship Company.

The S.S. Brother Jonathan. Courtesy of the author.

Postscript: The tragedy of the Brother Jonathan

When Amasa and Sally Ann Denny and 12 relatives traveled to California via Panama in 1857 (previous page) they sailed the final leg from Panama City to San Francisco on this beautiful ship. A few years later, her name was briefly changed to "Commodore." The company soon restored the ship's original name, but the re-christening apparently did not erase the bad fortune that is said to befall a ship whose name has been changed. In 1865, caught in a gale while heading from Portland to San Francisco, the Brother Jonathan struck an uncharted reef about four miles off the coast near Crescent City. The ship sank in 45 minutes, and only about 30 of the 235 passengers and crew were saved. It was one of the worst accidents in California maritime history.

Dennis M. Powers. Treasure Ship: the legend and legacy of the S. S. Brother Jonathan. Citadel Press, 2007

Acknowledgments

Over a period of more than two years, many people have contributed to this book, some in essential and major ways, and some with a small tip or suggestion.

Nothing could have been done without the help of my wife Ginna BB Gordon, who gave intellectual, artistic, and emotional support in every possible way, and was enthusiastic about this project non-stop for more than two years. She conceived the book cover, and we designed it together; she proofread an early manuscript; and gave artistic and editorial input during the entire journey. Ginna also took part in all sorts of research and trips to interesting places, including Dene and Hazel's former homes. During the writing of this book, I have consumed at least one thousand of her lattés. Thank you, Ginna, for everything you did to make this book possible.

Richard Flower, of Carmel, was a catalyst. In September 2011, I set out to research the history of the Carmel Bach Festival for a special Festival concert in 2012—an overview of 75 years of history, not Dene and Hazel in particular. In the first stage of research, Richard hunted through the Pine Cone microfilms and came up with a rich collection of targeted press clippings from the 1930s, '50s, and '90s. That material piqued my interest, and ultimately led to this book. He continued to provide occasional intriguing pointers during my research, read through the 500–page manuscript, offered historical corrections, and made valuable suggestions about chronology and cross–reference. Dick is a man of letters and I am grateful for his friendship and help.

Richard is also one of the few people I know today who actually interacted with Dene and Hazel. During his college years in San José in the 1940s, Dick and some friends became a tad boisterous way down in the front row of the San José Civic Auditorium during a performance by Carmen Amaya's flamenco dance troupe. Their verbal interaction with the dancers onstage would have been appropriate in a tavern in Seville, but it was not acceptable to Denny-Watrous Management. Dene and Hazel personally came into the auditorium and firmly told the young men to be quiet

The Henry Meade Williams Local History Room of the Harrison Memorial Library in Carmel was an utterly essential resource, and provided a wealth of information and surprises. The Local History collection is fabulous, and History Librarian Ashlee Wright was a delightful colleague, advisor, mentor, and guide. Meeting Ashlee and working with her was one of the best things that happened during this project. Carmel-by-the-Sea is fortunate to have such a fine library.

Carmel Impresarios could not have been written without the Carmel Pine Cone. This weekly publication has been Carmel's paper of record since 1915, and its back issues are an eyewitness chronicle of the evolution of Carmel-by-the-Sea. Without the Pine Cone archives, no book about Dene Denny, Hazel Watrous, or Carmel would be possible. The Pine Cone's Publisher, Paul Miller, graciously and generously gave permission for the reproduction in this book of images and extended excerpts from the Pine Cone and the Cymbal. I am deeply grateful to be able to access these archival treasures and share them with the world.

Over the past decade, I have developed a familiarity with the photographs in the archive of the Carmel Bach Festival, and some of them bring back personal memories. (Photos in recent decades sometimes include me, but fortunately I am not old enough to be included in the narrative of this book.) The Carmel Bach Festival is an important part of my heart, and has always been much more than just a musical engagement. I came for the music and stayed for the people. My thanks go to Betsy Pearson, Board President; Debbie Chinn, Executive Director; Music Directors Sandor Salgo, Bruno Weil, and Paul Goodwin; and the hundreds of performers, staff, board members, and volunteers I've worked with over the years. We all are part of Dene and Hazel's legacy together.

Anne Thorp and Peter Thorp, Co-Presidents of Carmel Music Society, made the Society's archives available for research. It is a significant collection of photos and printed matter—particularly from the Society's first several decades. The archival riches include a detailed account of the Society's creation in 1927, minutes of the first several seasons, and several enormous old-fashioned scrapbooks of photos and clippings that have been viewed only rarely in past decades. The Carmel Music Society's archives are a gold mine of information and ephemera, and the very experience of going through these scrapbooks was a thrill comparable to paging through the scrapbooks Edward Kuster maintained for the Theater of the Golden Bough. Thank you, Anne and Peter, for making the material available to our white–gloved hands.

The Carmel Journalists

This book contains eyewitness reports and concert reviews from six Carmel newspapers. Each wordsmith had a different ability with the pen, and each had a unique point of view and style. For one in particular, every sentence, no matter how simple, or, perhaps, complex, could be, that is, at least somewhat, improved by adding, if you will, more commas. Another orotund essayist enrobed his rhetorical flourishes in a fulsome aura of obfuscatory verbiage. A particularly successful local concert might be described as 1.) the best the writer has ever heard, 2.) a historic Carmel milestone, or 3.) a deeply personal experience that's hard to write about. The Carmel journalists could be dry, fawning, pompous, academic, humorously scornful, gently evaluative, boosterish, or just mediocre, but they all tried to praise and criticize honestly and positively. After all, Carmelites had been writing reviews of each other onstage for decades.

The following authors are quoted in this book. Most were active at some time between 1922 and 1950.

> David Alberto, W. K. Bassett, Thomas Vincent Cator, Doris Cook, Hal Garrott, Betty Patchin Greene, Dora Hagemeyer, Dr. R. M. Hollingsworth, Una Jeffers, Elayne Lavrana, Francis L. Lloyd, Michel Maskiewitz, Redfern Mason, Thelma B. Miller, Jane Millis, Nelly Montague, Rachel Morton, Ida Newberry, Susan Porter, Lynda Sargent, Pauline Schindler, Lincoln Steffens, and Marjorie Warren.

An extra word of admiration goes to Thelma B. Miller, who distinguished herself not only by her frequent contributions to the Pine Cone in the 1930s, but by her demonstrated fondness for the word "aggregation." This is most evident in an article on February 22, 1935 (included in this book), in which she uses the word three times in two paragraphs. Within my area of focus and research, I came across the word "aggregation" twenty-one times in eighteen Pine Cone articles written by Thelma Miller. Only six of these occurrences appear in this book.

Archives

Dennis Copeland, Museums, Cultural Arts, & Archives Manager of the Monterey Public Library, helped locate two wonderful photos. The Customs House Museum in Monterey (part of the California State Parks System) made available their collection of printed programs and other ephemera of the First Theater and the Troupers of the Gold Coast.

Important research material for this book was also provided by many institutions outside Monterey County. The Bancroft and Hargrove Libraries of the University of California at Berkeley provided valuable resources for several eras in this narrative. The registrars and administrations of UC Berkeley, California College of the Arts, and the San Francisco Art Institute were helpful in tracking down clues or pointing me in the right direction.

Pat Hathaway of CAViews in Monterey provided several key photos from his phenomenal archive. The Special Collections staff of the Library of George Mason University in Virginia provided the original audio recording of Ernst Bacon's oral history 1935–1938. The San Francisco Performing Arts Museum, Pasadena Community Theater, and Capitola Museum/Historical Society all provided friendly and helpful guidance and information.

The people at the Siskiyou County Historical Society in Yreka, California, were cordial and helpful in many exchanges of mail and email, so much so that the author has been a member since 2011. The Society's online resources are helpful, and they located several wonderful photos and illustrations for this book. Back issues of their annual journal, *The Siskiyou Pioneer*, provided valuable information about the Denny family.

Individuals

The copy editor, eagle-eyed and wise, was Gail Lindus. It was she who noticed that I had misspelled Dene's name in three different ways in the manuscript. Her ability to read a 500–page (illustration–free) manuscript while entering so many delicate and important corrections, is epic. If there are misplaced commas in this book, I put them there after Gail was finished.

Thomas Eller, great-grandson of Albert Hendrickson Denny, kindly provided the wonderful 1893 photo of the Denny family on the porch at Oak Farm, as well as other rare photos from Siskiyou in the 1800s.

In 2011, Jack and Jane Buffington of Lincoln, California, gave to the author a 1949 newspaper that contained the first clue that oboes replaced clarinets in early Carmel Bach Festival orchestras. That opened a Pandora's box of fascinating research.

Dana Carlile of Portland, Oregon, is a grand-nephew of violinist Hubert Sorenson, a member of the Neah-Kah-Nie String Quartet. Dana's excellent book about Susie Pipes and the quartet was invaluable, as were his photos of the quartet. Many thanks go to Dana for writing the stories of those fascinating people.

Bernard Chevalier and his sister Denise Chevalier shared anecdotes and impressions of their violin teacher, Carol Weston, and provided a wonderful photograph of her.

Ginna and I visited two extraordinary homes where Dene and Hazel lived and worked. Gail Baugh and Jim Warshell are the owners and residents of the Fisk House in San Francisco, where Dene and Hazel lived from 1922 until 1924. We are grateful for their generous and warm hospitality, and for the memorable experience of climbing the red-carpeted stairway to the third floor ballroom, roof deck, and conservatory.

In Carmel, the house on Dolores Street that Dene and Hazel began in 1922 and completed in 1926 is today owned and beautifully occupied by Carol and Don Hilburn. Carol and Don love and honor the Denny-Watrous legacy with dedication and enthusiasm, and there could be no more perfect residents at Harmony House.

Virginia Stone of Carmel shares my admiration for Noel Sullivan, and I am grateful for her research and her thoughtful suggestions. When I needed a bit advice about economic statistics and the cost of living, I was lucky enough to be able to turn to a Nobel Laureate, my friend and neighbor William Sharpe. If the math is wrong, it's my fault. Thanks go to Carmel Bach Festival volunteers, especially Geri Fleischer, Suzanne Dorrance, and John Castagna, for their early work in organizing the Bach Festival's eight decades of photos.

And finally a deep bow of gratitude to those dear Carmel friends no longer with us, who shared their stories over the years—Nancy Lofton Morrow, Nana Faridany, Emile Norman, Bill Stewart, Ken Ahrens, Arnold Manor, and Virginia Adams. Thank you all.

A Carmel Bach Festival audience in Sunset Auditorium in the early 1960s.
Courtesy Carmel Bach Festival.

Index

The 17–Mile Drive through the Del Monte Forest, as it looked just after the turn of the 20th century. A horsedrawn carriage is approaching. *Postcard, postmarked 1911. Courtesy of the author.*

About the Author

David Gordon, known as "one of the world's great Bach tenors," has appeared with virtually every major North American symphony, and with other prestigious orchestras and music festivals on four continents. He came to Carmel in 1983 to perform at the Carmel Bach Festival and, like Dene and Hazel, he never left.

David's work with young professional singers expanded the Virginia Best Adams Master Class into one of the Bach Festival's most delightful events, and his lectures and concert narrations create enthusiastic audiences. David lives in Carmel Valley with his wife, Ginna BB Gordon. To learn more about him, visit www.luckyvalleypress.com.

The lobby of Sunset Auditorium, 1960s. Looking west toward the two main entrance doors. The auditorium is through the doors to the left. *Courtesy of the Carmel Bach Festival.*

The publisher welcomes comments,
suggestions, and corrections.

Please contact Lucky Valley Press by email:
info@luckyvalleypress.com
or
PO Box 5474   Carmel CA 93921
www.luckyvalleypress.com

TEXT
Minion 10.5/12.8
DISPLAY
Kabel

CPSIA information can be obtained at www.ICGtesting.com
Printed in the USA
BVOW01s0229200614

356917BV00002B/5/P